British Colonisation of Northern Nigeria,

1897–1914

WITHDRAWN
University of
Illinois Library
at Urbana-Champaign

D1593266

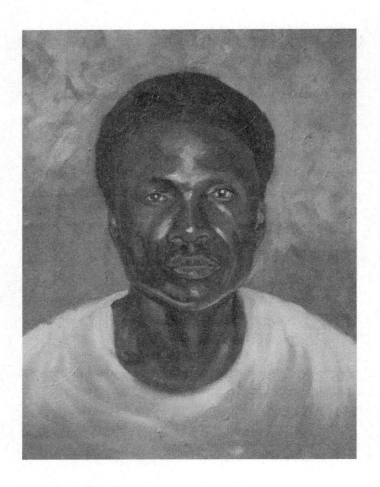

About the Author

Mahmud Modibbo Tukur (1944–1988) was a distinguished scholar and inspiring teacher of history. He was head of the Department of History and Dean of the Faculty of Arts and Social Sciences, Ahmadu Bello University, Zaria, Nigeria. A leading activist and trade unionist who, as National President of the Academic Staff Union of Universities in Nigeria, was at the forefront of struggles for academic freedom and improved infrastructure in the nation's institutions of higher learning. He fought tirelessly in upholding the rights of the people and instilling democratic values in the country's larger polity.

BRITISH COLONISATION
OF NORTHERN NIGERIA,
1897–1914

A Reinterpretation of Colonial Sources

Mahmud Modibbo Tukur

With an Introduction
by Michael J. Watts

Published by Amalion Publishing & the Academic Staff Union of Universities (ASUU) 2016

Amalion Publishing
BP 5637 Dakar-Fann
Dakar CP 00004
Senegal
www.amalion.net

Academic Staff Union of Universities
c/o ASUU National Secretariat
University of Abuja, Main Campus
Giri, Nigeria

Copyright © Mahmud Modibbo Tukur Educational Endowment Foundation 2016

ISBN 978-2-35926-046-5 HB

ISBN 978-2-35926-047-2 PB

ISBN 978-2-35926-048-9 ebook

Cover designed by Anke Rosenlöcher

Printed and bound in the United Kingdom by CPI Group (UK), Ltd., Croydon, CR0 4YY

All rights reserved. No part of this publication may be reproduced, transmitted, or stored in a retrieval system, in any form or by any means, without permission in writing from Amalion Publishing, nor be otherwise circulated in any form of binding or cover than that in which it is published.

Contents

Tables   x

Maps   x

Illustrations   xi

Preface   xiii

Foreword   xvii

Acknowledgements   xx

Abstract   xxiii

Abbreviations   xxv

A Glossary of Non-English Words   xxvi

Introduction: Laying the Foundations of the Colonial State
     in Northern Nigeria – Mahmud Modibbo Tukur's
     Contribution to Nigerian Historiography   xxxv
     Michael J. Watts

1. Resistance and Surrender to British Invasion, 1897–1903   1
    Introduction   1
    Conditions in Bida, Ilorin, Agaye, Lapai and Kontagora
    Emirates at the Time of British Invasion, 1895–1901   2
    The Impact of the British Defeat of Bida   3
    Resistance and Surrender by Ilorin, 1897   4
    Resistance by Yola   5
    Non-Resistance by Muri, Bauchi, Gombe and Zaria, September
    1901–April 1902   8
    Resistance in Kano and Sokoto, and the Surrender
    of Gwandu and Katsina, February–March 1903   17

An Exceptional Situation in Borno   32
Conclusion   39

2. The Nature of the British Occupation
    and Its Immediate Impact   41
    Introduction   41
    The Conquest of Bida and Ilorin   42
    The Occupation of Agaye and Lapai   43
    The Occupation of Kontagora and Bida   45
    The Occupation of Yola   47
    The Pursuit of the Sarkin Musulmi and the Battle of Bormi   49
    The Occupation of Bauchi   53
    British Violence against Non-Muslim Communities   56
    "Unofficial" Violence by Mercenaries   62
    Criminals Come to Their Own   64
    Attitudes Towards the Sarkin Musulmi's Hijra   67
    The Wholesale Deposition of Emirs and Chiefs   70
    Disarming the Emirs   73
    The Territorial Implications of British Conquest   74
    Abolition of the Office of Sarkin Musulmi   80
    Erection of Tariff Barriers Between the Emirates   90
    Conclusion   91

3. Relations Between the New Emirs and the British   95
    Introduction   95
    Abuja, Bauchi, Keffi, Ilorin and Nassarawa   96
    Borno   100
    Gwandu, Kano, Katsina, Yola and Zaria   105
    Attitudes Towards the British-Appointed Emirs   119
    Popular Hostility Towards the British   124
    Conclusion   129

4. The Extension of British Administrative Control
    to the Small Towns and Villages of the Emirates   131
    Introduction   131
    Precolonial Local Government Versus British Aims   131
    The Formation of Homologous Districts   134

	Resident District Heads	141
	Duties of District Heads and Basis for Assessing Them	143
	Qualification for District Headship	144
	Grounds and Non-Grounds for Deposing District Heads	145
	Relations Between the District Heads and the Residents	148
	The Cost of District "Administration"	150
	Conclusion	153
5.	The Impact of District Reorganization	155
	Introduction	155
	The Creation of Redundancy	156
	Relations Between Emirs and the New District Heads	161
	Conciliatory Methods of Control	169
	Popular Hostility Towards the Reorganization	171
	Conclusion	172
6.	The Establishment of the Native and Provincial Court System	173
	Introduction	173
	The Precolonial Judicial System of the Emirates	174
	The Establishment of Native Courts	176
	The Structure of Native Courts	178
	The Role, Functions and Powers of the Native Courts	180
	Relations Between the British and the Native Courts	185
	The Methods, Forms and Degree of British Control	187
	The Role of Emirs in the Native Judicial System	198
	Clashes Between Emirs and Qadis	200
	The Role of District Heads	202
	Conclusion	204
7.	The Imposition of British Taxes	205
	Introduction	205
	The Kurdin Kasa and the Jangali	206
	The Kurdin Kasa: Basis of Assessment	219
	The Fate of the Zakka	225
	Other British Taxes	227
	Forced Labour	236

Conclusion   246

8. The Attitudes of the Various Classes
    Towards British Taxation   247
    Introduction   247
    Grounds for Resistance to British Taxation   248
    The Emirs and District Heads vis-à-vis the Kurdin Kasa
      and the Jangali (1903–1914)   251
    The Response of the Common People to the Imposition
      of the Kurdin Kasa and the Jangali   259
    Conclusion   276

9. Disbursement of Revenues   277
    Introduction   277
    The Proceeds of the Taxes   278
    Allocation of Collected Revenues   280
    The Native Authorities and the Allocation
      of Their Share of Revenues   281
    The Establishment, Management and Control of Treasuries   283
    Control of the Native Treasuries   284
    Role and Attitude of Emirs   285
    Directions of Expenditure   287
    Creation and Disposal of Surplus   293
    Conclusion   295

10. Changes in the Economy of the Emirates
    and the Influx of European Firms   297
    Introduction   297
    The Introduction of British Currency   298
    Ousting the Maria Theresa Dollar, the German Mark
      and the Cowrie   300
    The Subordination of the Old Economy   304
    The Precolonial Economy of the Emirates   305
    The Influx of European Firms   313
    Increase in European Population
      and Expansion of Export Trade   314
    The Business Methods of the Firms   317
    The Example of the Niger Company in Yola   317

Relations Between the Colonial Regime and the Firms   324
Impact of the Establishment of the Firms
on the Emirates' Economy   325
Conclusion   325

11. The Nature, Extent and Essence
of British Social Policy in the Emirates   327
Introduction   327
The "Abolition" of Slavery   328
The Introduction of Western Education   332
Police, Prisons, etc.   340
The Cost of the Introduction of Western Education   343
The Attitude of the People of the Emirates Towards Western
Education   344
The Fate of Islamic Education   348
Health and Welfare   352
Widespread Famine   353
Medical Facilities   355
Population Decline   356
Inter-communal Relations   358
Conclusion   365

General Conclusion   367

A Note on Sources   371

Notes   397

Bibliography   497

Index   517

Tables

Table 6.1. Cases Handled by Courts by Province, 1907 to 1915   185

Table 9.1. British Share of Taxes from Yola Emirate by Years   279

Table 9.2. Zaria Emirate, Revenue for Ten Years, 1904–1913   279

Table 9.3a. Kano Native Treasury Expenditure, 1909–1910   288

Table 9.3b. Kano Native Treasury Extraordinary Expenditure   289

Table 9.4. Sokoto Native Treasury Monthly Expenditure, 1911   290

Table 9.5. Katsina Native Treasury Expenditure, 1909–1910   291

Table 9.6. Native Treasury Revenue and Expenditure, 1909–1914   293

Table 10.1. Price Differences in the Canteen and Native Market   323

Table 11.1. Register of births and deaths, Kano 1912 and 1913   356

Table 11.2. Estimated deaths from famine   357

Maps

Map 1. Sokoto Caliphate and neighbouring states   xxx

Map 2. European advances into parts of West Africa   xxxi

Map 3. Nigeria at the turn of the 20th century   xxxiv

Map 4. The end of an era in Bormi, 1903   xlvi

Map 5. Northern Nigeria and its Provinces   154

Illustrations

1. Sultan Attahiru I, the Sultan of Sokoto   xxxii

2. Sir George Dashwood Taubman Goldie   xxxiii

3. Sir, later Lord, Frederick Lugard   xxxiii

4. Shehu of Borno, Abubakar Garbai El-Kanemi (1902–1922)   40

5. Abdullahi Bayero, eldest son of Emir Muhammadu Abbas   71

6. British troops and the infamous Maxim guns   92

7. Lieutenant-Colonel, later General, T.N.L. Morland   93

8. Mr. W.P. Hewby   94

9. Shehu Abubakar Garbai of Borno.   94

10. Emir Aliyu Babba of Kano (1894–1903)   130

11. Sir William Frederick Gowers, Resident Yola Province   245

12. Sir Richmond Palmer, Resident, Kano Province (1915–1916)   245

13. H.W.S. Goldsmith, Resident, Zaria Province by 1914   245

14. Sir Ralph Moor, Consul-General of Niger Coast Protectorate   245

15. Sir E.P.C. Girouard   246

16. Workers on the Gwari section of the Baro–Kano railway   296

17. Workers on the Gwari section of the Baro–Kano railway   296

18. The opening of Jebba Bridge in 1916 by Lord Lugard, Governor-General of Nigeria   324

19. Soldiers of the 3rd Nigerian Frontier Regiment of the Royal West African Force aboard the SS Accra   326

20. Adverts calling on investors to profit from cotton   366

Photo credits

Nos. 1, 4, 5, 6, 10, 11, 12, 13, 14, 16, 17, and 19 National Archives Kaduna (NAK), Nigeria; 2. Painting by Sir Hubert von Herkomer, National Portrait Gallery; No. 3. "An earnest African", Caricature by Leslie Ward, Men of the Day No.0639: *Vanity Fair* 1895; 7. *Generals of the British Army Portraits in Colour with Introductory and Biographical Notes* by Francis Dodd, The Project Gutenberg EBook of Generals of the British Army, 1917; 8, 9, 18, *Up against it in Nigeria* by Langa Langa, London, Allen and Unwin, 1922; 15. *The Times History of the War in South Africa, 1899–1902*, Edited by L.S Amery, London: S. Low, Marston and company, Ltd., 1909; 20. British Cotton Growing Association caravonica cotton trees-introduction of into N. Nigeria, 1905, Secretariat Northern Province Collection (1900-1924), National Archives Kaduna, Nigeria.

Preface

This book is an edited version of the doctoral dissertation entitled *The Imposition of British Colonial Domination on the Sokoto Caliphate, Borno and Neighbouring Areas, 1897–1914: A Reinterpretation of the Colonial Sources* by Mahmud Modibbo Tukur (1944–1988) submitted for the award of a Doctor of Philosophy degree in the Department of History, Ahmadu Bello University (ABU), Zaria, Nigeria in 1979. The study was jointly supervised by Professor Abdullahi Smith (1920–1984) and Dr. Yusufu Bala Usman (1945–2005), who were among the finest historians in Nigeria at the time. Professor Smith was the founder of the Department of History in ABU who laid the foundations of painstaking empirical research, while Dr. Bala Usman was at the forefront of scholars who gave a theoretical and ideological direction to historical research in the Department. It is not surprising that the study by Mahmud Modibbo Tukur turned out to be a work of rich empirical data and adequate theoretical framework, while at the same time demonstrating the scholar's ideological leanings.

At the initial stage of his research, Mahmud Tukur registered for an MA (History) degree and proposed to write a dissertation on "The Role of Emirs in Twentieth Century Northern Nigerian Societies," as suggested by Professor Smith. However, in the course of the research, a number of factors influenced the author to change his focus from a study of the role of emirs to that of the role of emirates. Among these factors was a range of compelling historiographical issues that confronted him while reviewing the primary and secondary literature on his subject of study. Those issues related to the prevalent misrepresentation of the nature of the societies and polities in Northern Nigeria before British colonisation, and the consequent justification/rationalization of British colonial conquest as contained in studies by Margery Perham, Robert Heussler, S.J. Hogben, A.H.M. Kirk-Greene, H.S. Hogendorn and other writers.

Perhaps, more than any other study, Abel O. Anjorin's doctoral dissertation entitled *The British Occupation and the Development of Northern Nigeria,*

1897–1914, submitted to the University of London in 1965, was a catalyst in the decision by Mahmud Tukur to change the topic and focus of his research. The study by Anjorin claimed that slave raids were common in Hausaland before the British colonisation and were abolished after colonisation for humanitarian and closely related reasons. For Anjorin, British colonisation was not external aggression but a righteous intervention necessary for the elimination of injustice, and the establishment of an honest and compassionate administration for the benefit of the colonised. These, according to him, crystallized along with other factors, into the social and economic 'development' of Northern Nigeria under the British.

Mahmud Tukur disagreed with this thesis and decided to write what amounts to be a counter-thesis by adopting a topic and a scope of study similar to Anjorin's. As the research progressed, a panel of examiners that was constituted upon the recommendation of his Supervisors found the study by Mahmud Tukur to be of an outstanding quality, and approved that the draft thesis should be upgraded from an MA to a PhD. The thrust of Tukur's argument is that a correct reinterpretation of the British colonial sources would demonstrate that the theses and arguments offered by Anjorin and other scholars with similar views on the nature and process of British colonisation of the emirates were untenable. He set out to do this through an intensive and extensive archival research that few historians in Nigeria had accomplished then. The result is a brilliant counter-thesis that demonstrated the violent and exploitative character of British colonialism in Northern Nigeria in the period 1897–1914. Such brilliance, exhibited with so much depth and clarity, has made Mahmud's doctoral dissertation a model for dissertation writing in ABU's Department of History since then. The renowned Dr. Yusufu Bala Usman once stated that the study by Mahmud Tukur was "the best PhD thesis written by anyone, anywhere in the world, on any aspect of Nigerian history since 1960."

In preparing the manuscript for publication, we restricted editorial changes to the barest minimum in order to enable readers gain first-hand insights into the arguments of the author as they were in the original dissertation. However, we shortened the title by changing it to *British Colonisation of Northern Nigeria, 1897–1914: A Re-interpretation of Colonial Sources*, which does not in any way affect or undermine the focus of the author on the Sokoto Caliphate and its neighbours. Part of our justification for effecting the change derives from the fact that the Sokoto Caliphate and the neighbouring areas examined by the author constituted over three quarters of the Northern Nigeria area in both population and landmass.

Furthermore, apart from the Introduction by Prof. Michael Watts, we wrote the introduction to Chapters Two, Three, Five, Six, Seven, Eight, Nine, Ten and Eleven and the conclusion to Chapter Four. However, other changes that we made in the book are mainly restricted to the correction of typographical errors, incomplete documentation, inappropriate capitalisation of words, and spelling of names of persons or places. Similarly, in addition to correcting a few non-English words, phrases and titles, we also inserted, deleted or transferred punctuations in some places, in order to facilitate easier reading and comprehension. While we have ensured that consistency in the use of terms and categories is maintained throughout the book, readers may note that we have retained the use of the terms 'Borno' and 'Bornu' by the author. The former was used by the Borno populace since precolonial times to refer to the polity, while the latter was used by the British during colonisation, for referring to Bornu Province and Bornu Emirate. Both terms were in use in the Province during and after the period of the study by Tukur.

In addition, we have revised and updated the Glossary to include a few non-English words and phrases contained in the manuscript, and abbreviations that were not captured under the Glossary at the beginning of the study have been written in full in the main body of the work. Mahmud Tukur was known for writing long sentences and citing long quotations from other writers. In such cases, we left many of the sentences untouched, except in few cases where we have had to break a sentence into two or more in order to make its meaning clearer. Similarly, some quotations of more than three lines have been indented. In addition, in the Notes on Sources, we have written the dates individual informants were interviewed in full; similar changes have been done in limited cases in the literature in some of the chapters.

In proposing these and other editorial changes, we feel confident that the substance, meaning and style of Mahmud Tukur's writing remain unchanged. The outcome is a book as close as possible to the original thesis and whose content would not have been significantly different were Tukur himself to edit it. Nonetheless, it is pertinent for readers to note that our editorial task was not easy because of the voluminous nature of the work, extensive quotations contained therein and the density of its documentation. However, the task was equally exciting and intellectually rewarding because of the originality of the study and the profundity of the arguments of the author.

This publication is a project of the Academic Staff Union of Universities (ASUU), of which Mahmud Tukur was the President from 1982 to 1986. In preparing the manuscript for publication, we acknowledge with gratitude the funding and other support provided by the Dr. Mahmud Modibbo Tukur

Educational Endowment Fund (MTEEF), a committee of ASUU. This book is the result of the collective effort of the following members of the Mahmud Tukur Publications Committee: Dr. Oladipo Fashina, Prof. Biodun Ogunyemi, Dr. Usman Ladan, Prof Abubakar Momoh, Prof. Abdullahi Sule-Kano, Prof. Segun Ajiboye, Prof. Mahmud Lawan, Dr. Adelaja Odukoya and Dr. Victor Igbum. Special mention must be made of Dr. Usman Ladan, the historian in the committee, whose commitment and depth of understanding of the subject made possible special insights into the substance of this editorial work. The support and cooperation provided by the family of Mahmud Tukur, especially his immediate elder brother, Alhaji Bashiru Tukur, and his eldest daughter, Hauwa Tukur, who is also a member of the Board of Trustees of the MTEEF, have been of inestimable value. Finally, we wish to thank Professors Alkasum Abba and Bawuro Barkindo for their editorial advice.

Dipo Fashina, PhD & Usman Ladan, PhD,
Ahmadu Bello University,
Zaria, Nigeria.
10 November 2015

Foreword

This is one of the most important books published in recent times on the history of British colonisation of Northern Nigeria. It is important because of the contemporary relevance of its subject matter and the extraordinary competence with which the author handles his exposition. Before we proceed any further, a few words on the author are therefore necessary. Mahmud Modibbo Tukur was President of the Academic Staff Union of Universities (ASUU) from 1982 to 1986. Apart from being a committed unionist, he was also a brilliant scholar, a competent administrator and a great humanist. Although he lived a relatively short life of 44 years, he left behind an immortal legacy of honesty, hard work, patriotism and total commitment to the emancipation of the oppressed classes. When Mahmud Tukur became President of ASUU, he selflessly devoted his time and energy into strengthening the union, promoting its unity and cohesion, inculcating discipline among its members, and giving it a clear and potent ideological direction. While engaged in his academic pursuit, trade union struggles and political activism, Mahmud became a household name in Nigeria, equally admired by the oppressed classes and despised by the corrupt and reactionary ruling class. Nearly three decades after his death, his fond memory is still fresh in the minds of his countless admirers all over the country.

Mahmud Tukur devoted over half of his lifetime to pursuing a career in scholarship at Ahmadu Bello University, Zaria, where he became a prominent historian. The present book is the outcome of his research for a doctoral degree conducted in the Department of History of the University. This book is a testament to Mahmud Tukur's quest and respect for knowledge, commitment to rigorous empirical research, proclivity for theorising empirical data and insistence on the production of socially relevant knowledge. In other words, he was not a proponent of seeking knowledge for its sake but an advocate for using knowledge to understand and transform social reality. This was a major factor influencing his choice of topic of the present book. At the time Mahmud Tukur commenced his research on the subject matter of this book in the early 1970s, a majority of African countries have achieved independence from European colonialism. Although colonialism was receding, and other forms of imperialism were facing mounting resistance, there were still a number of scholars idealizing colonialism within and outside Nigeria.

The most reactionary among such scholars argued that precolonial African societies were static tribal entities engaged in constant warfare, slave raids, extortion and maladministration. Therefore, they added, European colonisation was a blessing because it halted tribal wars, abolished slavery, curtailed over-taxation, restored law and order, and established a good government presided over by compassionate colonial administrators. Such scholars denied the violent character of colonialism, insisting that the wars of colonisation, like in the specific case of the Sokoto Caliphate and its neighbours, were forced upon the British by "stubborn" emirs, who wrongly perceived all white men as "intruders", and hence, resorted to intrigues and other forms of "intolerant behaviours." They asserted that, even when confronted by such "intransigence," the British were reluctant to resort to wars because they "deplored bloodshed." Hence, British colonialism was portrayed in good light, with attention to its self-assumed liberating mission, denial of its exploitative character and projecting the sum total of what occurred under colonialism as development facilitated through indirect rule. Although such simplistic conception of colonialism is now rarely peddled, the failure of the postcolonial state in Nigeria and other parts of Africa, has allowed a modified form of it to resonate among certain quarters even in the present day.

Mahmud Tukur was outraged by such an apologetic conception of colonialism, profoundly disagreeing with it in this book. He argues that precolonial African societies were not made up of warring tribal units staging constant slave raids; and that, the people in Northern Nigeria never welcomed the British and bitterly resisted colonisation. The British suppressed the resistance with unprecedented violence, mass deposition of Emirs and the appointment of new ones as replacement. Dr. Tukur further argues that the British did not abolish slavery after colonisation, dismissing the British Anti-Slavery Proclamation as a mere legislation against vagrancy. Similarly, the author shows that the inherited precolonial taxes were not significantly reduced or eliminated; rather, the British introduced new and heavier taxes after colonisation, which they collected with ruthless efficiency. The book convincingly disputes the existence of indirect rule in Northern Nigeria by showing that British colonial officials were directly in charge of taxation, Native Treasuries, courts, prisons and general administration. The author contrasts the hasty establishment of the instruments of state repression by the British with the slow provision of education, health-care and other social amenities desired by the people. Dr. Tukur concludes by demonstrating that pre-existing industries, agriculture and commerce were undermined by the enforced use of British currency, colonial taxation, forced labour and the import-export trade operated by European trading companies. Finally, he characterises what happened under British colonialism in Northern Nigeria as state sponsored violence, paving the way for domination, exploitation and underdevelopment.

This book by Mahmud Modibbo Tukur has succeeded in exposing the true nature and consequences of British colonialism from the point of view of the colonised. It is not difficult for anyone who reads it carefully and logically to discern that the violent and exploitative nature of British colonisation laid the foundations of the colonial state, which in turn, shaped the character of the post-colonial state now influencing our lives on a daily basis. This fact, among others, poses a number of compelling questions of contemporary relevance to all of us. One of such questions we need to pose here is: if Britain was directly responsible for our violent colonisation, exploitation and consequent under-development, can we rely on it and its so-called western allies in our current search for a path to development? Nigerian students, scholars, workers, peasants and their allies, have a patriotic duty to read this book so that we can collectively reflect on the best way for liberating our country from the shackles of imperialism.

Nasir F. Isa, PhD
President,
Academic Staff Union of Universities (ASUU),
Abuja, Nigeria.
16 November 2015.

Acknowledgements

In the course of my research and writing, I did incur a lot of gratitude to a very large number of people, some of whom I shall mention in a list of informants at the end of the study. Among these are Professor Abdullahi Smith, the Director of Arewa House, Kaduna and Dr. Yusufu Bala Usman, the Head of the Department of History, Ahmadu Bello University, Zaria. The former, apart from teaching me Nigerian history at the undergraduate level, was responsible for my employment as an Assistant Research Fellow and deployment to the Northern History Research Project, later Arewa House. This posting afforded me not only the opportunity to participate in the establishment of a new institution but also the time to gather material both at the Archives and in the field, and to write much of the first draft. He also suggested my original topic, namely "The Role of the Emirs in Twentieth Century Northern Nigerian Society," supervised the writing of the first draft and permitted both the change in topic and the extension of the period of registration that this necessitated. Dr. Usman, for his part, not only gave me an all round support and encouragement, but also took over the supervision of the thesis after my return to the History Department to teach.

I owe a special gratitude to the staff of the Search Room at the National Archives, Kaduna and of Arewa House in the period 1973–75 when I worked very intensively at the Archives and wrote much of the first draft. Worthy of special mention in this regard are Alexander Yohanna, Musa Garga, Usman G. Kutigi and Zakari Ya'u at the National Archives, and Hassan Muhammadu, Inusa Mamman, Theresa Olubiyo and Alfred O. Omoniyi at the Arewa House, the latter four for typing the first draft of the thesis. In Ibadan, I would like to thank Professor J.F. Ade Ajayi, Dr. Arif and Dr. Adeleye, the first two for providing me with accommodation for one month in November 1972, and Dr. Adeleye for making me always welcome at his office where we held a number of very useful discussions. So also do I thank the staff of the Search Room at the National Archives, Ibadan, and of the Africana Section in the Library of the University of Ibadan.

At Kano, I would like to thank Professor S.A. Galadanci, now Vice-Chancellor, Sokoto University, who in 1974 gave me a letter of introduction to the Emir of Kano whom, along with the Madaki, I am grateful to, for each granting me an audience and approving of my conducting interviews in Kano. Similarly, I thank Alhaji Salihi Bayero for putting himself at my disposal throughout my one month stay in Kano, suggesting informants and often providing transport and escorts to convey and introduce me to such informants; and Alhaji Mai Sangon Dan Rimi for being my chief informant as well as taking a keen interest in my research and welfare while I was in Kano, and for being ever friendly, jovial and accommodating. So also do I thank Professor M.A. Al-Hajj, formerly of the History Department, Khartoum University in the Sudan, for his constant encouragement. In the same way, I thank Mr. John Lovers, Dr. Muhammed Nur Alkali, and M. Isa Abba Alkali, all of the History Department in Bayero University Kano, for exchanging views and, in the case of Isa, even notes with me.

At Sokoto, I owe a special gratitude to Waziri Junaidu, the late Alhaji Umaru Gwandu, Alkalin Alkalai Bello Mai Wurno, now of the History Bureau, Alhaji Ibrahim Tambawal, and Alhaji Abdurrahman Gara, now in the Niger State Civil Service and M. Abdullahi Magaji, both of whom, while working in the State Miltary Governor's (SMG) office at different periods in 1973 and 1974, were detailed to run the History Bureau, and in that capacity facilitated my stay and research in Sokoto. Elsewhere outside Zaria, I would like to thank Alhaji Liman Ciroma and Alhaji Adamu Fika of the Federal Civil Service for their support of the Northern History Research Scheme (NHRS) project in general, and of my research in particular.

Back at Ahmadu Bello University, Zaria I would like to thank my academic colleagues in the History Department for their criticisms and views which I gathered both in private discussions and at the Postgraduate Seminars, at some of which I presented sections of this research for discussion. I would like to make a particular mention of Modibbo Ahmad and Alkasum Abba, who helped me with proof reading and the footnotes. My thanks are also due to my students during the 1975/76 to 1978/79 sessions for the inspiration I got from them during lectures and tutorials. So also do I thank Professor O.S.A. Isma'il, now of the History Department, Khartoum University, Dr. Izzeddin Musa and M. Ahmed Kani, and other staff of the Northern History Research Scheme, as well as the staff of the Departmental Library, for permitting me to borrow theses and books from the Postgraduate Room and the Library. I also thank the entire staff of the Departmental Office, especially Christopher Ugwoke, who typed the second draft of the thesis, and also Messrs Moses Ikom, Aliyu Gambo and Joseph Titus who cyclostyled the last draft of the thesis. I also extend my thanks to Dr. Patrick Wilmot of the Sociology Department and Dr. Michael Mason, formerly of the History Department, for reading some of the chapters and making useful suggestions. Elsewhere in the University, I thank Dr. Mahdi Adamu of the Centre for Nigerian Cultural Studies, M. Kyari Tijjani of the Centre for Research and Consultancy, and Mr. Akin Fadahunsi of the Centre for Economic and Social Research, for their support and encouragement. I also highly appreciate the assistance of Dr P.K. Tibenderana of the Center for Nigerian Cultural Studies (CNCS) for passing on to me his archival notes on the slavery issue, Dr. Khalil Mahmud and the staff of the Media Unit and Africana Section of Kashim Ibrahim Library (KIL) for facilitating my work at the library, Mr. Barka Mshelthlila of the Faculty of Agriculture for typing the final draft of the thesis and making an excellent job of it; Messrs Ado Jos of the CNCS and Hyacinth Amedu of the Geography Department for reproducing the maps that accompany the thesis, and the staff of the Bindery Unit of the KIL for providing the thesis with covers.

Among my relatives, I would like to thank Professor Iya Abubakar, the for-mer Vice-Chancellor of ABU and M. Bashiru Tukur of the Vice-Chancellor's Office, for the encouragement and moral as well as material support which they gave me ever since my Elementary School days. So also do I thank my father and all my other relations back in Adamawa for their understanding and tolerance, especially with regard to my neglecting to take a leave and come home ever since January 1977. Finally, I am very grateful to my wife Fadimatu Zahra'u and our kids, Inna Keso, Dada Mallum and Usumanu Modegel – my wife for patiently bearing with my preoccupation with my writing and teach-ing during the course of which I converted our dining table into a writing table and littered the house with all manner of paper that I insisted should never be shifted except by me; our children for not bothering me when I did not want to be bothered, and for learning not to touch any paper in the sitting room until they had specifically requested and obtained my permission to do so; and both she and they, as well as Ummu and Joseph, for providing our house with the warmth and gaiety that helped to make it a home, fit for living and working in. To each one of the individuals and groups mentioned above and to other friends too numerous to mention by name, but who facilitated my work in diverse ways, I once again offer my profound gratitude.

Abstract

This book is concerned with British occupation of the Sokoto Caliphate, the perfecting of the instruments of British domination over the conquered emirates, and the political, economic and social consequences of this domination in the period up to 1914. Chapter One of the study examines the political and military conditions in the Sokoto Caliphate at the end of the nineteenth century and how these conditions shaped the response of the Caliphate to the subsequent British invasion. Among the factors highlighted are the presence and the political and military activities of European trading companies, especially the British Royal Niger Company (RNC), which had been part of the political and military situation in the Caliphate for three decades by the end of the nineteenth century.

The study then goes on, in Chapter Two, to highlight the violence, bloodshed, looting and arson that generally characterized British occupation and "pacification" of the emirates, as well as the dire political and social consequences of that occupation. In Chapter Three, the political situation resulting from the occupation is depicted and shown to have been characterized by the depositions of British-appointed Emirs, generally unfriendly relations between the British and these Emirs, contempt by the generality of the population towards the Emirs, and hostility by the population towards the occupiers.

Chapters Four, Five and Six explore the extension of British administrative and judicial control, through the creation and manipulation of Resident District Heads and District Alkalis and the smaller towns and villages of the emirates. The consequences of that extension for the people of these towns and villages, as well as for the political structure of the emirates are also explained. Chapters Seven to Ten discuss the imposition of British taxation, the manner of collecting the taxes, their yields, the disbursement of the revenues collected, including the establishment and control of the Native Treasuries, and the impact of this new system of taxation on the economy of the emirates. Also discussed are the creation of a new political economy through the new system of taxation, the introduction of British currency and the influx of European, mainly British, commercial firms. Chapter Eleven discusses the form, content and impact of British social policy. This includes a discussion of British attitude towards serfdom, their introduction of western education, their attitude towards the general health of the people, especially their handling of the epidemics and famines which were endemic in the emirates throughout the period under study. A General Conclusion and Notes on Sources complete the study.

Abbreviations

AHAK	Arewa House Archives, Kaduna
BSOAS	Bulletin of the School of Oriental and African Studies
CO	Colonial Office
CSO	Colonial Secretary's Office
JAH	*Journal of African History*
JAS	*Journal of the African Society*
JHSN	*Journal of the Historical Society of Nigeria*
NHRS	Northern History Research Scheme
NAK	National Archives, Kaduna
NAI	National Archives, Ibadan
ONAREST	Office Nationale des Recherches Scientifique et Technique, Yaounde, Cameroon.
RECAD	Research Bulletin, Centre for Arabic Documentation, Ibadan
SNP	Secretary, Northern Provinces

A Glossary of Non-English Words

Some of those words whose meanings are obvious from the context have been left out.

A = Arabic, F = Fulfulde, H = Hausa, K = Kanuri, N = Nupe, Y =Yoruba.

Ajele (Y) — a royal messenger from the ruler of Oyo to the districts of the alafinate; later adopted by Oyo's successor states, apparently including the Ilorin Emirate.

Ajia (K; H) — treasurer; also the title by which District Heads have been generally referred to in Borno since the imposition of British colonialism.

Al'adu (A;H) — a precolonial industrial tax in the emirates.

Alkali (A;H;F;K) — a judge.

Amir al jaish (A) — Commander of the faithful; the formal title of the head of the Sokoto Caliphate who was also referred to by the Hausa and Fulfulde equivalents of this title viz: *Sarkin Musulmi* and *Lamido Julbe*, respectively.

Ardo (F) — a clan or lineage head; now mainly used to refer to a District Head or a village Head in Adamawa and Sokoto.

Balogun (Y) — a high ranking military commander in Oyo and its successor states.

Barde (H) — the title of an important military commander in the emirates.

Bulama (K) — Village Head in Borno.

Chima (H) — an official who mediated between the government of Borno and any one of its districts, towns and ethnic groups.

Chiroma (H) — a royal title in some of the emirates often given to the prince most favoured to succeed the Emir.

Dambo (F) — the title of the chief of the town (later district) of Ingawa in Katsina Emirate.

Danburam (H) — the title of a state official in Kano Emirate.

Dangaladima (H) — the title of the most senior prince in Gwandu Emirate and often in Sokoto.

Dan Kogi (H) — the title of a town chief in Sokoto.

Dan Sarki (H) – a male member of the ruling dynasty in an Emirate.

Digma (K) – the title of a high ranking state official in Katsina.

Fito (H) – a precolonial toll collected at the borders between the Sokoto Caliphate and the states neighbouring it.

Galadima (K) – the title of a very important provincial governor in Borno, later adopted in Hausaland and the emirates generally.

Hosere (F) – mountain.

Hijra (A) – c.f. Fulfulde "perol" – flight from oppression.

Iyalema (K) – the group of middle rank officials in Borno from whom representatives of the Shehu were chosen for accompanying British officers on tour.

Jakada, pl. *jakadu* (H) – a state messenger usually serving as a link between Emirate officials resident in the capital and town and village chiefs living outside the capital.

Jangali (K;N) – a precolonial tax on cattle in the emirates preserved and transformed by the British.

Jizya (A) – a tax paid to an Islamic government by non-Muslims living inside a Caliphate, as an acknowledgement of the government's authority and in return for being allowed to live in accordance with their own laws and customs.

Kaigama (K) – the title of the most important military commander in Borno; later adopted by some of the emirates, especially Fombina.

Karofi (H) – a precolonial agricultural tax in a number of the emirates.

Katuka (H) – the title of a state official in Zaria.

Kaura (H) – the title of an important state official in Katsina.

Kofa (H) – the official in Sokoto Town through whom the Caliph had dealings with a given Emirate.

Kurdin Kasa (H) – a poll-tax imposed by the British in the emirates and in Borno.

Lamdo Adar (F) – the title of an emirate official in Yola in the nineteenth century.

Lamdo Kabi (F) – -ditto –

Lamdo Katsina (F) – ditto –

Liman (A;F;H;K) – the leader of congregational prayers.

Limamin Juma'a – the title of one of the two imams in Zaria Town.

Limamin Kona – ditto –

Ma'aji (H) – treasurer in the emirates.

Madaki (H) – the title of an important military commander in the emirates.

Magaji (H) – the ruler of a single town or cluster of villages.

Magajin Gari (H) – the title of a high ranking state official in Sokoto, Kano and Katsina.

Magira (K) – the official Mother of the ruler of Borno.

Makun (N) – the title of the most senior prince in Bida and other Nupe emirates.

Mallam (H) – a learned man.

Mallama (H) – a learned woman.

Mallum (F) – a learned person below the rank of Modibbo.

Marafa (H) – the title of the most powerful (but not the highest ranking) military commander in Sokoto in the last decade of the nineteenth century.

Maslaha (A) – the general interest of the Islamic community.

mayo (F) – river.

Modibbo (F) – a learned person.

mudu (A; H) – a measure of grain.

Qadi (A) – a judge.

Qadiriyya – one of the two religious orders in Northern Nigeria; predated the Sokoto Jihad and served as the basis of discipline among the followers of Shehu Uthman dan Fodio.

Ribat (A) – a military settlement at the edge of a Muslim territory, a type of settlement actively encouraged by the leadership of the Sokoto Caliphate in the nineteenth century.

Sa'i (A) – title of the state official in charge of collecting and allocating the zakat in Sokoto.

Sallama (H) – the title of a palace official in Kano.

Sarakuna – paramount chiefs, plural of Sarki

Sardauna (H) – the title of a state official, usually of royal blood in Sokoto and Adamawa.

Sarki (H) – king, ruler.

Sarkin Baura (H) – the title of a military commander in Sokoto.

Sarkin Dawaki Maituta (H) – the title of a military commander in Kano.

Sarkin Sudan (H) – the title of two important members of the Sokoto Caliphal dynasty, based at Wurno and Kontagora.

Sarkin Yaki (H) – the title of the most important military commander in Sokoto and a number of the emirates.

Sarki Turawa (H) – the title of the leader of the Arab community in Yola in the nineteenth and early twentieth centuries.

Shahada (A) – martyrdom.

Shari'a (A) – the corpus of Islamic law.

talaka, talakawa (H) – the commoner classes in the emirates.

Taqiyya (A) – dissimulation; false "cooperation" with an enemy of Muslims.

Tariqa (A) – Islamic religious order, of which there are in fact several.

Tijaniyya (A) – one of the two main Islamic religious orders in Northern Nigeria; introduced into the Caliphate by Al-Hajj Umar al-Futi in the 1820s.

Ubandoma (H) – the title of an important state official in Sokoto.

Ulama, ulema (A) sing. Alim – the learned.

Waziri (A) – the most important state counselor in the Sokoto Caliphate and in Borno.

Yaron Sarki (H) – a middle rank representative of the Emir designated to go on tour with a British officer.

Yerima (K) – the title of an important state official in Borno; the title of the prince most favoured to succeed the Emir in Adamawa.

Zakat, zakka (A) – an Islamic tax on wealth assessed at about 1/10th of the wealth per annum.

Map 1. Sokoto Caliphate and neighbouring states

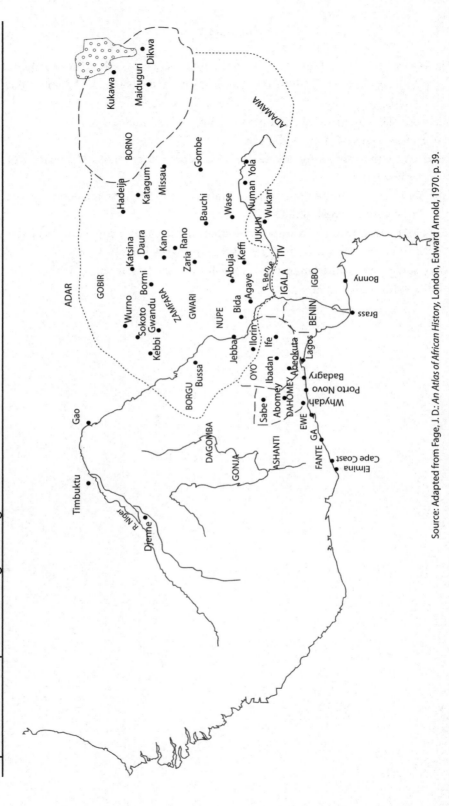

Source: Adapted from Fage, J. D.: *An Atlas of African History*, London, Edward Arnold, 1970, p. 39.

Map 2. European advances into parts of West Africa, c. 1800–1900

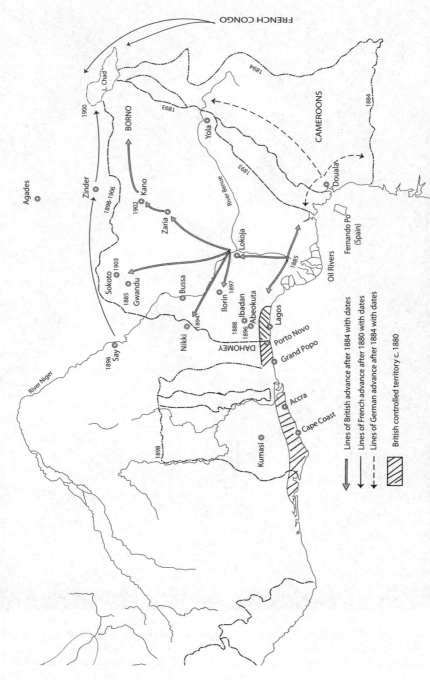

Source: Adapted from Fage, J. D.: *An Atlas of African History*, London, Edward Arnold, 1970. p. 41.

1. Sultan Attahiru I, the Sultan of Sokoto, who refused to surrender to the British, was pursued to Bormi where he was killed on 27 July 1903 along with over 600 of his followers.

2. Sir George Dashwood Taubman Goldie of the Royal Niger Company (RNC)

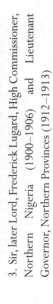

3. Sir, later Lord, Frederick Lugard, High Commissioner, Northern Nigeria (1900–1906) and Lieutenant Governor, Northern Provinces (1912–1913)

Map 3. Nigeria at the turn of the 20th century

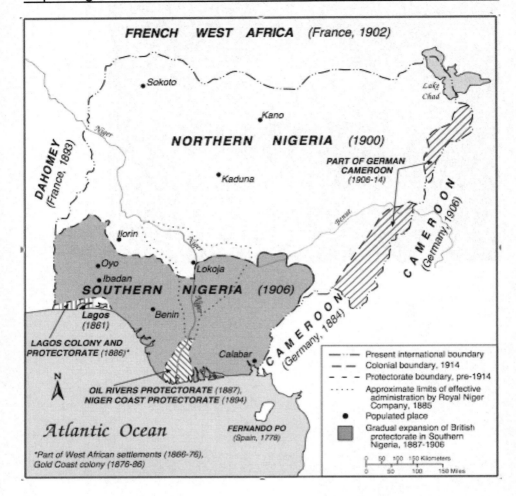

FRENCH WEST AFRICA (France, 1902)

Sokoto

Lake Chad

Kano

DAHOMEY (France, 1893)

Niger

NORTHERN NIGERIA (1900)

Kaduna

PART OF GERMAN CAMEROON (1906-14)

CAMEROON (Germany, 1906)

Ilorin

Niger

Benue

Oyo

Lokoja

Ibadan

SOUTHERN NIGERIA (1906)

Niger

CAMEROON (Germany, 1884)

Lagos (1861)

Benin

LAGOS COLONY AND PROTECTORATE (1886)*

Calabar

N

OIL RIVERS PROTECTORATE (1887),
NIGER COAST PROTECTORATE (1894)

Atlantic Ocean

FERNANDO PO (Spain, 1778)

*Part of West African settlements (1866-76),
Gold Coast colony (1876-86)

— · — · — Present international boundary
— — Colonial boundary, 1914
- - - Protectorate boundary, pre-1914
· · · · · Approximate limits of effective administration by Royal Niger Company, 1885
● Populated place
▦ Gradual expansion of British protectorate in Southern Nigeria, 1887-1906

0 50 100 150 Kilometers
0 50 100 150 Miles

Introduction:
Laying the Foundations of the Colonial State in Northern Nigeria – Mahmud Modibbo Tukur's Contribution to Nigerian Historiography

Michael J. Watts

Hegel remarks somewhere that all great world-historic facts and personages appear, so to speak, twice. He forgot to add: the first time as tragedy, the second time as farce….Men make their own history, but they do not make it as they please; they do not make it under self-selected circumstances, but under circumstances existing already, given and transmitted from the past. The tradition of all dead generations weighs like a nightmare on the brains of the living. And just as they seem to be occupied with revolutionizing themselves and things, creating something that did not exist before, precisely in such epochs of revolutionary crisis they anxiously conjure up the spirits of the past to their service, borrowing from them names, battle slogans, and costumes in order to present this new scene in world history in time-honored disguise and borrowed language. – Karl Marx, *The Eighteenth Brumaire of Louis Napoleon*, 1852.

The historical record [in the Nigerian National Museum in Lagos]…is syco-phantic, inaccurate, uncritical and desperately outdated, as if each dictator was sent a form to fill in with his 'achievements' and it was left at that.….History which elsewhere is a bone of contention has yet to enter the Nigerian pub-lic consciousness, at least judging by institutions like the museum…..What, I wonder, are the social consequences of life in a country that has no use for history? – Teju Cole, *Every Day Is for the Thief*, 2014, p.79.

It is a salutary experience to read Mahmud Tukur's pathbreaking book from the vantage point of the current historical moment in Nigeria's post-colonial history. *British Colonisation of Northern Nigeria, 1897–1914*, originally submitted as his PhD dissertation to Ahmadu Bello University (ABU) in 1979, was drafted during the 1970s, a period of bristling Third World nationalism in the wake of the Biafran War and in a period in which Nigeria was being radically reshaped by the impact of oil. In the years between the oil boom in 1973 and the oil bust of the early 1980s, the ABU campus was a crucible of intense political debate and it was history, and the history and political economy of the North in particular – what sort of history, whose history, and what was the nature of historical legacy – that stood at the centre of this vibrancy. It was a period and a debate in which many participated (one thinks of Patrick Wilmot, Bjorn Beckman, Sule Bello, Abdullahi Mahadi and many others) but it was without question presided over by two towering intellectual figures: Yusufu Bala Usman and Ibrahim Tahir. Mahmud Tukur was in a profound sense forged in this crucible.

But the 1970s world of *Kasar Hausa* – of northern political hegemony and of a growing and dynamic commercialized economy – has changed profoundly. In contrast to that period, Nigeria is now a 'mature' oil-state, driven by two cardinal principles: how to capture oil rents and how to sow the oil revenues? Over the last four decades and more, oil has seeped deeply and indelibly into the political, economic and social lifeblood of Nigeria. In 2013 over 87 percent of government revenues, 90 percent of foreign exchange earnings, 96 percent of export revenues and almost half of Gross Domestic Product (GDP) are accounted for by just one commodity: oil.

Yet to compile an inventory of the achievements of Nigerian oil-based development is a dismal exercise. Between the period when Tukur was working on his dissertation and 2000, the number of people subsisting on less than one dollar a day in Nigeria grew from 36 percent to more than 70 percent, from 19 million to a staggering 90 million. The total poverty head count rose from 27.2 percent in 1980 to 65.6 percent in 1996, an annual average increase of 8.83 percent in the 16-year period[1]. Between 1996 and 2004, the poverty head count actually declined to 54.4 percent except that over the same period, the percentage of population in the core poor category rose from 6.2 to 29.3 percent before declining to 22.0 per cent in 2004. The inequality-adjusted HDI index places Nigeria below Ethiopia (ranked 174th on the Human Development Index). The most recent Millennium Development Goals[2] reveals some good news. Maternal mortality fell by 32 percent, from 800 deaths per 100,000 live births in 2003 (one of the highest maternal mortality rates in the world, at the time) to 545 in 2008. Under-five mortality has fallen by over one-fifth in five years, from 201 deaths per 1,000 live births in 2003 to 157 in 2008, though this level remains high by global standards. In a major step forward, 88.8 percent of children are now enrolled in school.[3] Yet the details of net primary and secondary school enrollment reveal that massive swaths of the country are in a dire position. By 2007, the midpoint for implementation of the relevant MDG programs in Nigeria, the percentage of the population living in extreme poverty should have fallen to 28.8 percent, if the MDG target was to be met.[4] In fact, the poverty headcount ratio at the national poverty line is 54.1 percent. These figures signify only that after a half century of oil wealth, Nigeria stands in the 156th position out of 187 countries, slightly below the sub-Saharan Africa average and roughly on par with Haiti. What is on offer in the name of oil-development is the catastrophic failure of secular nationalist development.

Nowhere is this failure more visible than the North, the region that so concerned Mahmud Tukur, where there was an especially precipitous decline in human security, concurrent with the crumbling of both remains of the old emirate system and the failure of local government. All human security indexes are astoundingly low. The North-Western and North-Eastern geopolitical zones recorded the highest regional poverty rates at 70.4 percent and 69.1 percent, respectively. According to the Oxford University Poverty and Human Development Initiative, the multidimensional poverty index (measuring ten health, education, and living standard variables) is 0.51 in the North-Eastern zone, reflecting a greater extent of deprivation than the score of 0.15 in the South-South.[5] Life expectancy in some of the northern states is a full five years shorter at 45 than the national average of 50 for men and women. Across the Shari'a states: malnutrition is almost twice the national average in the Shari'a states; the human poverty index is 45.88 compared to 27.8 in the non-Shari'a states; female literacy in the north is 17 percent compared to 69 percent in the south; the percentage of married women using contraception is 3.4 percent in the Shari'a states compared to 14 percent nationally; and not least total fertility rates in the north are over 7 per woman making for a massive youth bulge (the comparable figure in the Niger Delta, for example, is 4.7). Overall the picture is one of economic descent and declining per capita income coupled with radically diminished health and education standards, but also of a crisis of legitimacy for the institutions of secular national development, and for northern ruling classes facing growing hostility from millions of *talakawa* (commoners). As Murray Last (2007) puts it, northern youth have come to occupy a world of material, political and spiritual insecurity.

In the Muslim north, rising inequality, material deprivation, and poor governance has nurtured a popular Islamist insurrectionary movement, labeled Boko Haram which is the Hausa nickname for the group officially known in Arabic as Jama'atu Ahlis Sunna Lidda'awati Wal-Jihad (the People Committed

to the Propagation of the Prophet's Teachings and Jihad). Salafist in orientation, Boko Haram, by drawing on historical traditions of popular justice, has
since 2003 become more brazen, better organized, and more technically profi-
cient in launching assaults against security forces. Assassinations carried out by
motorcycle riders target representatives of the state they believe have cheated
or failed them: politicians, officials, rival religious scholars and especially representatives of the dreaded police and security forces who routinely engage
in extra-judicial killings, according to international human rights groups. Paul
Lubeck's brilliant analysis[6] shows how Boko Haram's carefully executed jail
breaks or calls for imposing Shari'a law throughout Nigeria gather most of the
media attention, but the movements greatest power arises from energy generated by the demographic time bomb ticking within the region, coupled with
social and economic collapse, a low adult literacy rate, and the implosion of
the textile sector (once the region's largest industrial employer). Impoverished
and uneducated, the rural poor flee to the northern cities, often assuming the
guise of Quranic students who share a common urban religious spaces with
unemployed secondary and university graduates. This convergence, according
to Paul Lubeck, is critical because school leavers have learned to use the digi-
tal tools of Islamist insurrectionary tactics now downloadable from accessible
global media sources[7]. Between 2009 and 2012, Boko Haram has killed almost 1000 people across the North including a devastating attack on a United
Nations compound in the capital city of Abuja. On Friday January 20, 2012,
following the afternoon prayers, twenty coordinated bomb attacks on policy
and security installations were launched in Kano: close to 200 persons were
reported dead. Other reports indicated that at least five of the detonations
were perpetrated by suicide bombers and many other undetonated bombs have
been discovered around the city. In 2013, over 1000 people were killed in three
northern states[8]. In April 2014, Boko Haram abducted more than 200 girls
from a school in Chibok, Borno State. Northern Nigeria, in short, is in a fully-
fledged state of emergency.[9]

Boko Haram must be placed on the larger landscape of the adoption of
Shari'a law in the twelve northern states of Nigeria and the complex social and
political fragmentation of Islam in Northern Nigeria. The weakening of the Sufi
brotherhoods and the rise of neo-Salafist reform movements are closely bound
to the corrupt oil oligarchies and the moral decay of the state from which the
deep and longstanding strains of Muslim populism draw strength. The more
militant and radical groups like Boko Haram oppose what they see as partial
restoration of Shari'a law at the state level, the more they insist that Nigeria
should become transformed into a true Islamic state with full adoption and

implementation of Shari'a. More critically, these developments can only be grasped historically, and one of these historical reference points is precisely the terrain of Tukur's hugely significant book, namely the laying of the foundations of the colonial state.

*****

When I met Modibbo in the mid-1970s on the ABU campus, it was a hot-bed of theorizing, informed in particular (but not exclusively) by the Marxist tradition and by student radicalism of various stripes. Tukur makes this clear in his own genealogy cited in the Sources section of this book, drawing upon not only Marx but Lenin, Mao, Cabral, Nkrumah and especially Walter Rodney. His PhD supervisor, Bala Usman had, in his own dissertation, submitted to ABU in 1974, focused on the precolonial history of Katsina[10]. It was clearly influenced by radical political economy (though he was criticized by some ABU students for a lack of fidelity to Marx!), but mostly through the work of Frantz Fanon. Tukur's goal was to provide a political economy of the *founding* of the British colonial state, and in doing so to provide a radical counterpoint to the Whig history of the same period written by Abel Anjorin in his book *The British Occupation and Development of Northern Nigeria 1897–1914* published in 1965. In the Department of Sociology at ABU, Ibrahim Tahir had submitted a dissertation at Cambridge University in 1975 in which, influenced by the work of Max Weber and Ernest Gellner[11], he analysed the success story, as he saw it, of the colonial growth and transformation of Kano. His brief was a century of commercial de-velopment in Kano – a bourgeois revolution no less – from the end of the nine-teenth century and the dynamic commercial alliance between the *sarauta* class and the extended patrimonial merchant households ('corporations'). Needless to say, Tahir's political and theoretical dispositions were quite unlike those of Usman and Tukur. Into this mix was inserted a posse of clever and committed post-graduate students and a number of Left-leaning expatriate faculty (Gunilla Andrae and Bjorn Beckman who wrote on labour, Bill Freund on the history of the Nigerian tin industry, and especially Robert Shenton who later developed and extended Tukur's work on early colonial political economy[12]). It was an extraordinary group who were in different ways challenging the orthodox ac-counts of Northern Nigerian history (the so-called vent-for-surplus model and related anodyne accounts of the impact of European mercantile activity and colonial state practice) using, broadly speaking, the tools of Marxian political economy.

One part of this revisionist history was a rethinking of the agrarian question in Northern Nigeria and how merchant capital and the Nigerian colonial state transformed the relations of production associated with the late Sokoto Caliphate. This is, of course, central to Tukur's book. Agriculture had a particular salience because ABU was home to one of the most distinguished schools of agricultural economics (and agricultural science) on the continent (the Institute for Agricultural Research [IAR]), and had – with considerable support from the US land grant colleges and USAID – generated a mountain of survey data on farming systems and provided a large body of neoclassical analysis of the northern agrarian systems, emphasizing market efficiency and smallholder productivity. There were other foundations too. Jamaican anthropologist M.G. Smith, an influential figure on the ABU campus, had provided a provocative interpretation of the Hausa states and of rural livelihoods in *Kasar Hausa*[13]; and not least the brilliant economic anthropologist Polly Hill of Cambridge University[14] – niece of John Maynard Keynes – had offered a detailed and compelling account of a rural Hausa community near Katsina, and subsequently in the intensely settled zone of peri-urban Kano, with much historical detail to boot. It was the combination of Hill's foundational work – deploying the ideas of Russian populist Alexander Chayanov in which she downplayed structural rural inequality and emphasized the adaptability and resourcefulness of Hausa farmers – and IAR's extensive, if often uncritical, survey work which provided a touchstone for Tukur's and others' revisionist account of Nigeria's political economy. At the center of much of this historical research – a whole generation of Nigerian historians were mining the Kaduna and Ibadan archives at this time – was a re-reading of the historical dynamics of capitalist development in Northern Nigeria from 1900, through careful village and household-based ethnographies and fieldwork, and a sort of methodological engagement with basic questions of political economy (how might exploitation or 'surplus' be quantified, how could money-lending and seasonal crop loans be accurately documented, how could landholding and landed inequality be measured and so on).

What, then, does Tukur's work represent, and what did it challenge when it appeared in 1979? First of all it represented one part of what Bala Usman called a "new African historiography". While one key object of critique was Anjorin's largely Panglossian account of the imposition of British rule, Tukur's dissertation represented a sort of program of research by attempting, as it were, to invoke James Scott,[15] "seeing like a (colonial) state". In this sense, a part of Tukur's project was epistemological. He recognized the usefulness of the British colonial archive (and related other private and non official records) and while acknowledging that there were always silences and outright deceit and deception in these records, there was also a sort of ideological and practical clarity in what was at stake in the colonial project. The colonial state was in the business of securing the foundations for colonial political economy: securing order or stability, securing an administrative structure, providing self-finance (and revenue) and acquiring the resources and profits required of empire for the Workshop of the World.

In this task, Tukur's program of research recognized a number of indispensable foundations: that indirect rule obfuscated the enormity of the transformation of the structures of the Caliphates and the emirate system; that laying the foundations of the colonial state was violent and oppressive (here is a resonance with Fanon); that Northern Nigeria resisted and collaborated in complex ways which varied among and within the emirates (Tukur in other words laid the framework for a fine grained and discriminating analysis of local conditions and dynamics); that the colonial state was a contradictory and unstable enterprise balancing, for example, the desire to raise revenue against the permanent threat of resistance or instability on the one hand, and famine and starvation on the other; that the relations among colonial administrators, and indeed between the colonial governors and the colonial office, were contested and contentious; that what passed as colonial policy (for example the abolition of slavery, or education and health) required a radically new, and much less benign, analysis; and finally, and not least, that the reshaping the North under early colonial rule (what I called "laying the foundations of the colonial state") had enduring and important legacies for not just the colonial period *tout court,* but also for the post-colonial era as well. On this final point Tukur was fully aware that these legacies entailed Islam and the powers of the *ulema*, the class prerogatives of the *sarauta*, the influence of emerging merchant capitalists, or the armies of the *talakawa*.

One of the most compelling aspects of Tukur's book is his brilliant account of emirate dynamics in the early colonial period and its sensitivity to the contradictory forces at work. On the one hand, the British disposed of emirs, ignored the powers and traditions within the Sultanate, and made emirate authority directly regulated by the Residents and Governor. At the same time, colonial rule had many paradoxical effects some of which were grounded in the limits to its power and authority. As Lubeck (2010) argues,[16] with so few British officers serving without cultural support from evangelical Christian missionaries, their impact on northern societies was limited in the face of widespread Muslim cultural and political resistance. Colonialism extended the infrastructural power of the state over Muslim rulers and colonial subjects, mostly due to improvements like rail and road transport, radio and telegraph communications, and superior weaponry, to the same degree it centralized the power of emirs over their subjects by eliminating traditional checks on arbitrary rule. As Lubeck notes, within the northern provinces, where at least a third of the population were non-Muslims, the British not only extended the territorial range of Muslim rule over non-Muslims but they introduced a colonialized version of Shari'a law into the increasingly Christian, non-Muslim areas.

Of course, many of the questions laid out in Tukur's book were taken up in more detail by subsequent scholars working through similar sources. My own work[17] addresses for example the relations between Chapters 7 and 11, that is to say between revenue collection, commercialization of the peasantry and subsistence crisis. The colonial state, I argued in keeping with Tukur's analysis, was engaged in a biopolitical balancing act. On the one hand, the old indigenous anti-scarcity system – the moral economy of subsistence – was eroding, often quickly and under force; while on the other hand, the effects of commercialization and states' exactions vastly expanded the likelihood of famine, which raised the possibility of millions perishing. British imperialists reluctantly and ineffectively institutionalized a minimalist anti-famine policy (colonial welfare) for the indigent and invoked, with varying degrees of commitment, the "will to improve" colonial subjects who suffered from various indigenous deficits (recalcitrance, foot dragging, economic irrationality) and incompetencies. Another issue raised by Tukur was slavery, both its putative abolition and the extent of slave-labour in the Caliphate. Mohammed Salau's important book on a late nineteenth century slave plantation near Kano city, provided evidence that slave-based production was not only extensive but was key to the so-called groundnut revolution of the early twentieth century[18]. In another vein, Stephen Pierce, using the work of Michel Foucault, provided an innovative re-reading of land tenure in colonial (and post-colonial) Kano turning on the colonial state's misreading and simultaneous fetishization of land tenure which is installed at the heart of government[19]. And not surprisingly a group of young Nigerian scholars deepened our understanding of rural accumulation and agrarian dynamics, focusing in particular on the relation between polygamous farming households, economic mobility and accumulation, the organization of the grains trade, new centers of state-sponsored irrigated production, and the impact of neo-liberal reforms on the rural poor[20].

Islam is another issue not fully developed in Tukur's book[21], though of course in Chapters 6 and 11 he addresses Islamic education and the so-called "Native Courts". The larger question of colonialism and the refiguration of Islam and especially the Sufi brotherhoods is addressed explicitly by Muhammed Umar[22]. He seeks to undermine the consensus position that British rule strengthened and expanded the position of Islam in colonial Africa and in Northern Nigeria in particular, using Arabic texts that disclose a counter narrative that shows how emirs, judges and the *ulema* resisted British efforts to gradually "modernize" Shari'a. British efforts to modernize Shari'a distorted the integrity and true practice of Shari'a law by subverting rules of evidence and legal procedures, by appointing emirs unqualified in Shari'a law who presided over truly qualified Muslim judges, by introducing "Anglo-Mohammedan" law from the British empire, and not least, with the judicial reforms of 1933, made the decisions of Shari'a courts subordinate to British courts of appeal. All these had reverberations for the ways, especially after Independence, the British allowed the northern Muslims to control the largest region in exchange for eliminating Shari'a criminal law.

*****

The colonies, and Northern Nigeria is no exception, were always much more than a canvas on which Europe painted a modern picture of itself. As Tukur's book shows, the colonial project in northern Nigeria entailed imperial compromises in what they could achieve in political and economic terms but also in acknowledging that the colonies were centers of experimentation and agency. As Helen Tilley notes in her important book *Africa as a Living Laboratory*, the colonies actually became the laboratories of modernity, they provided the bricks and mortar of disciplines, theories, and institutions[23]. Formal colonial rule brought forth armies of scientists, research centers, commissions, and field expeditions and at the same time had the effect of Africanizing science – that is to say, converted Africa, in key domains, into an object of scientific scrutiny, on the one hand, and drew Africans and African knowledge into a constitutive process of what Tilley calls "vernacular science," on the other. Africa's laboratories were many and multifaceted[24] and were achieved through institutions, networks, and the circulation of ideas – and importantly an interplay between field and laboratory sciences – that were often at the heart of imperial government broadly construed. The disciplines of ecology, geography, and anthropology were central to the vernacularization of scientific knowledge. In other words, the localization of scientific knowledge had a way of entering into the archive of global science even if Africans themselves were rarely at the helm of decision-making.[25] Northern Nigeria proved to be an African laboratory too: of smallholder agriculture, of conservation and afforestation, and of rights to subsistence. The market, new crops and new farming practices, the role of colonial scientific practitioners, and an array of African actors collectively constituted the mix within which both ecological and conservation ideas and practices were debated as part of the wider challenges of colonial rule. These sorts of experiments and the agency exercised by Africans are gestured to in Tukur's book and are entirely consistent with the sort of historiography he sought to promote.

*****

Northern Nigeria is a different place from the 1970s landscape in which Tukur's book was hatched. It resembles now what Nigerian scholar Ike Okonta has described as a 'boiling cauldron'. The challenges facing the North, indeed the country as a whole, are truly daunting. Nigeria is held up as the worst exemplar of virtually every species of developmental failure: rampant official corruption, corporate bribery, decaying social and physical infrastructure, military indiscipline, ethnic and religious insurgencies, to say little of the country's criminal economy, its industrial and agricultural decay, and deplorable health indicators and its demonstrated failure to effectively revive its manufacturing sector – the textile sector, historically the backbone of the North's manufacturing economy, has almost disappeared. The failure to produce electric power is devastating: the seventh most populous country in the world has roughly as much grid power as Stockton, California.

Perhaps more than any other change, the new political sociology of Islam stands as a sharp contrast even to the late 1980s when Mahmud Tukur tragically died. Many northern Muslims, while certainly not endorsing the violence of Boko Haram, nevertheless echo the conclusion reached by Tijjani Naniya, a Kano historian, who makes the point that against the backdrop of forty years of corruption and military rule the return to civilian rule in 1999 was seen as a great opportunity. While the solutions proposed range from redefinition of Nigeria federation, to regional autonomy and resource control, some Northern Nigeria states, he noted, are opting for a return to the Shari'a: "To these states, the strategies for social transformation and economic development induced by the West have failed. The alternative for them is for a return to their religio-cultural heritage represented by the Shari'a"[26]. Paul Lubeck makes the point powerfully: "Today, there are quotes from the Qur'an in English and Arabic posted on road signs throughout Kano City as well as billboards exhorting the ummah to realize a "republic of virtue" by fulfilling the ideals of dar al-Islam. … the Shari'a movement has introduced a new form of citizenship, that of the ummah, one which is both regional and global, to complement Nigerian citizenship"[27]. All of this would have been front and central to Mahmud Tukur's field of vision were he alive today. He would have brought a historian's eye to the current crisis of course but a political vision too. Modibbo was a man of the Left and a university trade union activist (He rose to the position of President of the Academic Staff Union of Universities (ASUU) from 1982–1986). His commitment to the powers of civil society, to the need to build robust organizations capable of defending and advancing the interests of the excluded, and to a state capable of providing public goods, is needed more than ever.

*****

Michael J. Watts is a Class of 1963 Professor Chair and Director of African Studies at the University of California, Berkeley, USA. He has published widely on political economy and political ecology, energy and the environment; famine; risk and vulnerability; and violence and dispossession. He was awarded a Guggenheim Fellowship in 2001 for his work on oil in Nigeria.

Map 4. The end of an era in Bormi, 1903

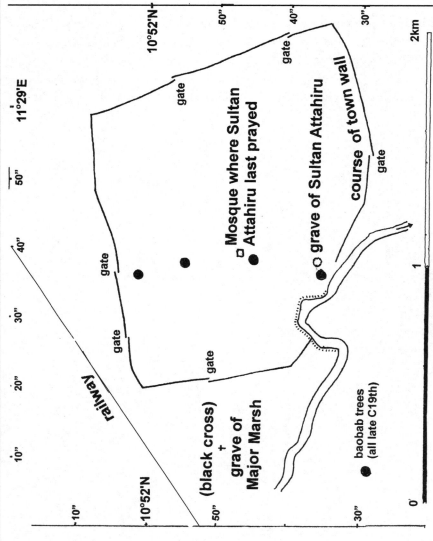

Source: P.J. Darling (2007)

1

Resistance and Surrender to British Invasion, 1897–1903

Introduction

When the British launched their invasion of the emirates of the Sokoto Caliphate in 1897, they met with a stiff physical resistance. This resistance was not maintained right up to the last emirate to be invaded.[1] The progressive weakening of resistance has exceptions to it, and was in fact a reflection of the cumulative hopelessness that repeated British victories over successive emirates created in the minds of the rulers of the Sokoto Caliphate. If one is to suggest a turning point in the attitude of the emirates towards British conquest, the point at which their attitude changed from that of a determination to resist to one of marked fatalism, one would suggest the last quarter of the year 1902. In this regard it should be pointed out right away that whereas the Sarkin Musulmi, Abdurrahman, until his death on 10 October 1902, was still resolved to resist the British by force, his successor, Attahiru b. Ahmadu who was selected on 13 October 1902, started with an ambivalent attitude, amidst divided counsel, and ended up with a stoic, indeed heroic, fatalism, but fatalism nonetheless.[2]

Thus, the emirates where the British met with stiff, though mostly short-lived physical resistance, were Bida, Muri and Ilorin in 1897, Agaye and Lapai, both in 1900, then Bida again, Kontagora and Yola in 1901, Keffi and Abuja[3] in 1902, and Kano and Sokoto in 1903.[4] On the other hand, the emirates where the British met with little or no physical resistance mainly included Ilorin in 1900, Bauchi, Gombe, Zaria and Gwandu in 1902, and Katsina, Hadeija and Katagum in 1903. Looking at this list, it is clear that Ilorin and Muri in 1900 were exceptions for the period 1897 to 1901 while Kano and Sokoto were exceptions for the period 1902 to 1903.

Conditions in Bida, Ilorin, Agaye, Lapai and Kontagora Emirates at the Time of British Invasion, 1895–1901

Ideally, to understand the factors that conditioned the response of the government of each emirate to British invasion, a brief account is necessary of the internal and external circumstances that surrounded the encounter of each government with the British. We shall here attempt to give such an account to the extent that it is possible to do so at the present stage of our knowledge of the nineteenth century histories of the various emirates. To illustrate the arguments advanced above about the progressive weakening of the resistance of the governments of the emirates, I shall try to take the emirates in the chronological order in which they fell to the British.

The first emirate ever to taste defeat in the hands of the British did so in the hands of the Royal Niger Company in 1897. This was Bida,[5] whose "pioneership" in that direction resulted from the fact that she was one of the most southerly riverain emirates, the headquarters of the Company itself being located at Lokoja in her territory.[6] This first defeat of the Emir of Bida took place in 1897, at a time when the Emir did not have the experience of any other Emir to go by. Besides, the Emir was still working on the premise that the Company was a group of *musta'mins* that was trying to grow overmighty.[7] Hence when the Company attempted an unprovoked aggression, it did not occur to the Emir of Bida to do anything than to resist the military aggression of the Company with force.[8] This, the Emir did and was worsted with very heavy casualty in the encounter.[9] Indeed it should be emphasized that the encounter between Bida and the Company in January 1897 was not the first one between them. It was simply the most serious one, conclusively revealing to the Emirate both the change in the balance of power between her and these foreign traders, and the intention of these traders to become the rulers of the Emirate. Earlier, on several occasions: 1887, 1889–90 and 1891, the Emir of Bida, Maliki, the immediate predecessor of Abubakar, had come very close to attacking the Company, which by now had declared Lokoja to be independent, established a garrison there, appropriated to itself the right to collect duties from foreign traders, in order to exclude some of these traders from operating in the Emirate, to try the Emir's own subjects and to encourage them to revolt against the Emir.[10]

On all these occasions, the Emir fell short of attacking the Company, because the latter, as yet unsure of its military superiority, hurried and made amends in one form or another to the Emir, and got some of his chiefs to intercede with him on its behalf. In fact on one occasion, namely, December 1891, the Company sent out a conciliatory delegation made of no less personages than Goldie and the Earl of Scarborough, with a letter from Queen Victoria to the Emir, Maliki.[11] Then early in 1896 the Emir, this time Abubakar, correctly reading the import of an Anglo-French rivalry in Borgu, made no secret of his willingness to preempt Royal Niger Company designs on his territory.[12] This time too, it was the deceptive conciliatory attitude of the Company that averted hostilities between it and Bida. That is to say the company which, for its own imperialist interests opposed the establishment of a French military post at Bajibo, made it seem that it was out of sympathy with the Emir and his people that it opposed the establishment of the post. This pretence was, how-ever, utterly exposed when, on the withdrawal of the French from Bajibo, the Company established its own post there as well as at Leaba and Jebba.[13] When the scales were once again lifted from the Emir's eyes, he did not hesitate to take measures to force the Company to close these posts. Thus, he ordered Bida canoemen not to take provisions to Leaba and Bajibo. It was only when the Company this time showed itself quite willing to fight that the Emir, who was still trying to work out an alliance against the Company with Bussa and Ilorin, temporarily suspended the blockade, pending the outcome of his efforts to form that alliance.[14] As soon as it became clear that Bussa would not join the alliance while Ilorin was undecided, the Emir went ahead to order Bida pilots to leave the Company's services and at the same time captured a detachment of Company forces together with their arms. From then on the battle had been joined, and it was logistic and tactical problems rather than a lack of will on either side that postponed the main showdown till January 1897.[15]

The Impact of the British Defeat of Bida

The news of the heavy defeat of Bida, of the power and the violence of the British, the temporary ouster of Abubakar, and the appointment of a puppet Emir by the Company, spread in the Caliphate. Externally, this had the effect of warning the other Emirs and the Caliph at Sokoto that the foreign traders who had hitherto enjoyed their welcome and protection were no longer will-ing, or militarily bound, to remain subordinate to them. Internally, the de-feat strengthened the predisposition towards capitulation of defeatist elements among the Emir of Bida's chiefs and lent their arguments an added weight.

Indeed, lest the patriotism that the Emir displayed in standing up to the Company be taken lightly, it should be pointed out that he had among his own chiefs those who were at least vacillators if not downright traitors, chief among them the Makun, whom the Company appointed "Emir" after it had ousted

Emir Abubakar.[16] The existence of this unpatriotic element in that Emirate at this point in time merits pointing out for another reason, namely that some of the arguments of those who favoured surrender in later episodes during the British conquest of the Caliphate, while not to be entirely dismissed in the light of the sorrowful experience of the earlier emirates, should at the same time not be taken at face value. That is to say that the decision of these elements was much more deliberate than the explanation given by Waziri Buhari in his letter would allow.[17]

Yet again when the British once more invaded her in February 1901, Bida, whose redoubtable Emir, Abubakar, had triumphantly returned to his capital after the British had ousted him in 1897,[18] the Emir, mainly because he had lost much of his territory and income to the British,[19] but also as a result of the realization that there was a limit beyond which he could count on the continued support of at least some of his leading chiefs and princes, was first predisposed to accept British protection.[20] But British hostility towards him and the people of his emirate generally, especially as exemplified by the activities of the British garrison at Wushishi,[21] steeled the will of the Emir once more to resist the British, with consequences which we shall see below. It remains to add that the fence sitting and vacillation that had marked the conduct of the Makun and others of his ilk in 1897 became accentuated in 1901.[22]

Resistance and Surrender by Ilorin, 1897

The next Emirate to be invaded by the Royal Niger Company in February 1897 was Ilorin. This invasion occurred only one month after the Company's first invasion of Bida Emirate. However, while this was the first time the British actually invaded the Emirate of Ilorin, it was not the first time they threatened her. For, in 1893 the British colonial regime in Lagos, during the war that had been going on between Ilorin and Ibadan, adopted a very hostile and aggressive attitude towards Ilorin.[23] In the peace treaty which that regime imposed on the two belligerents that year, Ilorin was made to cede some territory to the Protectorate of Southern Nigeria to which Ibadan had been already incorporated. Then in 1895 the Lagos colonial regime organized the expulsion of Ilorin's *ajeles* from some other Ilorin towns which the regime encouraged to throw off their allegiance to Ilorin.[24] At this point the then Emir of Ilorin, Muhammadu, was overthrown in a coup organized by his Baloguns, who were angered by his inability to stand up to the British colonialist regime in Lagos. In his place the Baloguns appointed Suleiman whom they reduced to their puppet.[25] Next, on March 31, 1896, Ilorin, now effectively under the Baloguns, moved to repulse the aggression of the Lagos regime by attacking its troops stationed at Odo Otin,[26] which seems to have been within Ilorin's territory before the establishment of the station.[27] The British defeated this effort with a heavy casualty by killing fifty men of the Ilorin army.[28] Yet on April 2 Ilorin made another move to dislodge the British from that post, only to be yet again frustrated by the superior fire power of the British.[29]

In the light of the foregoing and of the fact that in January 1897 the British inflicted a heavy casualty and destruction on Bida, Ilorin's acceptance of battle in February 1897 when the Royal Niger Company invaded her must be counted an act of great courage and patriotism on the part of the Baloguns and the people of Ilorin. However, the fact that in the encounter with the Company, Ilorin suffered much heavier casualties[30] than it had suffered in the hands of the forces of the British regime in Lagos ten months earlier, and the fact that this time, in addition to the loss of life, Ilorin town itself suffered damage as well as being captured by the invaders, all went to strengthen the hands of the Emir, Suleiman, who was inclined towards accepting British colonialism.[31] So also did the fact that after forcing out the Emir and the Baloguns from Ilorin town, Goldie did try to identify the family of Afonja and reinstate it.[32] Hence, though after the surrender of the Emir and the Baloguns, the Company, as in Bida, withdrew without leaving either a garrison or a Resident, when Lugard's "Proclamation" arrived in 1900, the Emir had absolutely no inclination to reject it. Far from resisting the proclamation he hastened to send not one but two letters couched in very abject language to Lugard, accepting the protectorate.[33] Not that there were lacking in Ilorin those who, in spite of all that they had seen and experienced of British might, were still willing to stand up to Lugard. Indeed all the four leading Baloguns were for war and were to remain openly or passively defiant of the British until two of them, Balogun Akinjogbin and the Mogaji, and one other chief, Ajia Ogidiolu, were arrested and exiled to Yola after an anti-British demonstration in the town early in 1907.[34] But the Emir's attitude neutralized their predisposition and Ilorin did not offer physical resistance when the British Resident arrived to take charge of the Emirate later in 1900.[35]

Resistance by Yola

In Yola[36] those who stood for resistance ultimately prevailed over those who favoured surrender without a fight, in spite of the experiences of the earlier emirates. The triumph of the party was largely due to the fact that the Emir, Zubairu himself, was among them. However, there was a party, led by the Qadi

Hamman Joda, and apparently including both the Emir's younger brother, Bobbo Ahmadu, and the Emir's nephew, Yerima Iyabano. By now the emirates of Bida, Ilorin, Agaye, Lapai, and Kontagora had already fallen and Yola was aware of these developments. Besides, within the Emirate of Fombina itself the Germans had already occupied the sub-emirate of Tibati, inflicting heavy casualties on the sub-emirate's troops, and were by 1901 already advancing on the sub-emirates of Bamnyo and Ngaundere.[37]

Thus, it was not ignorance of the might and predisposition of the British[38] that led the Emir of Yola into offering resistance to them. Rather it was a strong hatred for the Europeans who had already agreed to divide his Emirate and an equally strong attachment to the ideal of a caliphate, in particular the Sokoto Caliphate, whose capital had not yet fallen,[39] that made the Emir determined to resist the British, whatever the consequences. In addition to his strong hatred for the Europeans and attachment to the Sokoto Caliphate, there was also a determination on his part, from the time he acceded to office, that at the time of his death he would leave intact to his successors all the territories conquered by his father, Modibbo Adama, and his senior brother, Lamido Lawwal. To this end he spent all the eleven years of his rule reasserting Yola's authority over all those sub-emirates that had taken advantage of his immediate predecessor, Lamido Sanda's preoccupation with the consolidation of the civilian institutions of the Emirate's government to assert a very large measure of independence for themselves.[40] So much was Lamido Zubairu preoccupied with preserving the territorial unity and integrity of his emirates that it has been said that throughout the eleven years he was Emir he never spent one full month in Yola.[41] This claim may be an exaggeration, but it is sufficiently indicative of the great seriousness with which Zubairu took his responsibilities as an Emir.

But the party that was predisposed towards an accommodation with the British was not an insubstantial one either, including as it did some few princes and the capital's leading *ulema*.[42] The predisposition of this party towards accommodation was partly the result of the illusion that the British would not interfere with Islam — an illusion that the leading *ulema* of the Caliphate generally shared, and partly the result of events in other emirates and in Yola itself in the previous five years or so.[43] Concerning these events, it should be pointed out that in his efforts to preserve the territorial integrity of his Emirate, Lamido Zubairu had to contend not only with the Germans' and the Royal Niger Company's aggressions and assaults, but also with threats posed first by Hayat b. Said and then by Rabeh b. Fadl Allah.[44] Given Hayat's antecedent as a great-grandson of Shehu Uthman dan Fodio the *ulema*, on the whole, and a number of chiefs and princes as well,[45] found it difficult if not impossible, to endorse the Emir's declaration of war on him, and when he did, some of them became alienated from the Emir.

One mallam at least, Modibbo Sufiyanu, is said to have pushed his sympathies with Hayat's cause to an extent that his behaviour constituted a threat to the emirate's integrity even after Hayat's dislodgement from Balda, his headquarters. Thus, apart from giving Hayat two of his own sons as lieutenants while the latter was sojourning in Yola,[46] Modibbo Sufiyanu seems to have continued contact with M. Hayat while the latter was acting as Imam to Rabeh at Dikwa.[47] On discovering this alleged contact, the Emir took against the Modibbo measures which, even taking into consideration the seriousness of the latter's conduct, were extreme. Thus, the Emir at first thought of executing the Modibbo but gave it up on the intervention of other *ulema*, especially Modibbo Usumanu b. Raji.[48] But he banished the Modibbo from the Emirate, and insisted that the Modibbo must leave with all his children, including those daughters of his that were married to people who were not implicated in the Modibbo's anti-Emirate activities.[49] All those who were married to the Modibbo's daughters had to divorce them and the Modibbo, with the whole of his family, was escorted to the border with the Emirate of Muri from where he continued to Jalingo and settled.[50]

This action further antagonized the *ulema* as a group. This antagonism, in addition to the awareness of British power and illusions about British post-conquest intentions, made the *ulema* by and large fence-sitters. It should also be added that at least one of the *ulema*, the man who played a leading role in the negotiations that led to Yola's surrender after the battle of September 2, 1901, and the withdrawal of the Emir from the town, the Qadi Hamman Joda, had spent over ten years in the Middle East beginning from the early 1870s. He had witnessed British domination in Egypt and the extension of British domination over the Sudan, though, in all probability, he had no direct experience of the Mahdia.[51] This experience predisposed him towards both correctly appraising British power and feeling that the British would not interfere with Islam.[52]

In the light of preceding British activities within the Sokoto Caliphate and of the existence of an influential and articulate party of accommodation in Yola, Lamido Zubairu's ability to rally his forces to resist British aggression was very remarkable. This was more so if it is also remembered that he demonstrated this capacity several times over in the "German" sector of Fombina where, in town after town, he rallied large forces to resist, and lost with heavy casualties, the German conquest of his Emirate.[53]

Non-Resistance by Muri, Bauchi, Gombe and Zaria, September 1901–April 1902

From the point of view both of the validity of the thesis of resistance to British occupation and of actual resistance offered to it, the encounter between Yola and the British marked a turning point. In terms of effectiveness, the futility of resisting the British with force had by now been exposed by so many repeated failures. In point of fact, henceforth non-resistance became the rule and resistance the exception among the emirates.

Muri

The Emirate of Muri was occupied "a few weeks" after the occupation of Yola[54] and the British met with no resistance there. The Emir, Hassan, submitting peacefully.[55] Perhaps the peaceful submission of Muri is easier to explain than the submission of any other emirate. Throughout the period from the death of the founder, Hammaruwa, in c.1833 until 1880, Muri had been extremely disunited.[56] Indeed, at certain points in that period the Emirate did not even have the semblance of unity. Some of her subordinate districts, such as Gassol and Wurio, asserted their independence under dissident princes of the central dynasty.[57] It was only in c.1880 that her seventh Emir, Abubakar Nya, was able to impose a rather tenuous central government authority throughout the Emirate.[58]

Then, from the inception of the Emirate in c.1817 until 1892, she was engaged in a continual and inconclusive war against the Jukun chiefdoms on whose territory she was established, especially Kona. It was only in the latter year that Abubakar Nya, with the aid of a French expedition under Lieutenant Mizon, was able to subdue Kona. But the tenuous unity and peace that Nya was able to establish did not hold for very long. For on the eve of his death in c.1896, four years after the effective suppression of Kona, an accomplishment which had been achieved with the aid of an external force, Gassol and Wurio once again raised the standard of revolt against him.[59] In addition, the two dissident districts, under members of Muri's ruling dynasty, heavily defeated the Emirate's army, commanded by Hassan, the man who was soon to become Emir.[60] A year later, the Wurio and Gassol rebels were joined by a younger brother of the new Emir, one Muhammadu Mapindi, who had his own quarrel with the new Emir, whom he felt was not catering for their numerous younger brothers and sisters.[61] At last the Emir was able to regroup his forces and repulse the rebels who were moving towards Jalingo, the Emirate's capital, with the aim of ousting the Emir and installing an appointee of their own.[62]

Then there is the fact that Muri was no stranger to the power and ambition of the Europeans, the British in particular. On the contrary, the Royal Niger Company had been established at Ibi within the Emirate since c.1883 and in 1884, 1888 and 1891 did sack and burn the Muri town of Jibu.[63] For once, an Emirate, and a comparatively weak one at that, was able to apply military sanction successfully against the Company when, in 1889 Abubakar Nya sacked the company's posts at Kunini and Lau.[64] But the intervention of the Sarkin Musulmi, on the Company's appeal to him, secured the return of the Company's property to it.[65] Then the Emirate once again witnessed European military power in action when Lieutenant Mizon aided the Company to subdue Kona in 1892. Furthermore, the Royal Niger Company sacked the Muri towns of Wurio and Suntai in 1897 and 1899.[66] In Suntai, resistance was stiff and casualties very heavy for the defenders. Then there were the sack of Wase in Bauchi Emirate by the Company in 1898, the Company's defeat of the emirates of Nupe and Ilorin in 1897, the British occupation of the two emirates in early 1901, and especially the defeat and occupation of neighbouring Yola later that year. Hence, by the time the British arrived at Jalingo later in 1901, and, significantly, in the company of the dissident Muhammadu Mapindi, who had taken refuge in Yola since the RNC sack of Wurio in 1897, the attitude of the Emirate Government in Jalingo was already in favour of non-resistance.

Bauchi

In the case of Bauchi, its decision not to offer physical resistance to the invading British must be understood against the background of British successes against the more southerly emirates from Bida in January 1897 to Yola in September 1901, against the history of relations between Bauchi Emirate itself and the British prior to 1902, as well as against the internal history of the Emirate in the previous two decades.

Concerning this internal history, the most important point is that in 1881 Bauchi experienced a very bitter civil war which was precipitated by the decision of the second Emir, Ibrahim b. Yakub to ensure succession to his son, Usman, by abdicating in his favour, a move that was understandably resented by all the other sons of Yakub as well as very large segments of Bauchi's population.[67]

War broke out when the Emir of neighbouring Missau, Salih, marched in the face of stiff resistance from the rural population to reinforce Usman in the capital, where the balance of internal forces seemed to have already tipped in favour of Halilu b. Yaqub, a rival claimant to the office.[68] In the battle that followed, all the sons of Yaqub except the ex-Emir Ibrahim and one Aliyu Garga were killed, Halilu himself being executed after capture.[69] So were large numbers of the town's inhabitants including her leading *mallamai* who on the whole had supported Halilu's candidature on account of his learning.[70] In addition, the Missau forces of intervention engaged in wanton destruction of life and property as well as capturing and enslaving large numbers of the residents of the town, both slave and free.[71] Still other residents fled the city for neighbouring emirates such as Muri and Gombe.[72]

Needless to state, the brutality with which Usman's opponents were treated both deepened the hatred that survivors among them had for him and alienated many other people who had either initially supported him or had remained neutral. Also, since support for Usman and Halilu had cut across family boundaries, the bitterness and shock that followed the civil war was very much widespread, was generally directed against Usman as its cause, and continued into the mid–1880s.[73] In the meantime the Sarkin Musulmi, Muadh b. Bello, who had sanctioned Ibrahim's abdication and the appointment of Usman, had died in 1881 and been succeeded by Umaru b. Ali b. Bello, whose prestige was not tied down to supporting Usman's cause. Hence, following repeated complaints from leading figures in Bauchi, the Sarkin Musulmi summoned Usman to Sokoto and formally deposed and detained him there.[74]

In Usman's place the Sarkin Musulmi appointed Umaru b. Salmana b. Yaqub and charged him with healing the political and psychological wounds that the civil war had inflicted on the Emirate ruling class.[75] Umaru, who had rather shrewdly maintained a neutral posture during the civil war,[76] performed this task admirably well. Thus, he rehabilitated the sons and brothers of those who suffered a loss of position or property, recalled from exile those who had fled the Emirate, secured the liberation of those who had been enslaved by the Missau forces, and at the same time compensated the brothers of the deposed Emir, Usman, by appointing his younger brother, Muallayidi, to the important office of Chiroma or heir apparent.[77]

Next, Umaru moved to assert his control over the districts, most of which had, during the period of Usman's Emirship, assumed a large measure of independence for themselves. This, too, Umaru was able to do, in some cases through the actual use of force, but in most cases as a result of the fear which the use of force against the earlier districts aroused in the others. Umaru also took measures to contain Ningi's raids into Bauchi, raids which had increased in frequency and destructiveness during the period of civil war in the Emirate.

Naturally, Umaru's policy of centralization aroused opposition on the side of the erstwhile district chiefs. In such cases he very often deposed the resistant chiefs. However, when, in 1900 he called in the chief of Gwaram, Muhammad Lawal, with the obvious intention of detaining him in Bauchi and appointing another person in his stead, the latter refused to answer the summons.[78] Nor did Umaru choose a plausible ground for calling the chief in, his ground being that the chief had refused to hand over to him for enslavement a group of families which had immigrated to Gwaram from Fali District when they were still not Muslims, but who had since their immigration embraced Islam, intermarried with the people of Gwaram and thereby became legally immune from enslavement.[79] Then, Umaru went on to commit another blunder, namely, to declare Muhammad Lawal a rebel and to set out against him at the head of an expedition.[80]

Naturally Umaru failed to get support from his chiefs.[81] Hence, in spite of a seven-month siege against Gwaram, he failed to break its will mainly because most of his troops merely pretended to fight.[82] More dangerously, the Emir of Missau, this time Muhammadu Manga, like his predecessor during the civil war, was apparently threatening to intervene on behalf of Muhammad Lawal, and to buy him off Umaru promised Manga that when Gwaram fell he, Manga, was free to take "all the wealth in Gwaram."[83] At this point the Emir of Jama'are, a father-in-law of Muhammad Lawal, persuaded him to surrender on the understanding that the worst that could happen to him was deposition and the loss of his property.[84] On this understanding Muhammad Lawal surrendered and was treacherously executed by Umaru even though Umaru had already received an order from the Sarkin Musulmi to withdraw from Gwaram and pardon the chief.[85] Upon the execution of Muhammad Lawal, the Emir of Missau was permitted to enter Gwaram, capture all those he could, as many as nine thousand, and burn down the town.[86] The only people not enslaved were those who managed to escape and hide in other districts. Manga sent some of his booty to Umaru and yet gave yet some to the Emir of Jama'are. To avert the Sarkin Musulmi's anger, Umaru sent him some of the captives, but these were promptly freed by the Sarkin Musulmi, who also sent a circular to Bauchi, Kano and Missau ordering the immediate release of other Gwaram captives.[87] This way Umaru had almost fallen into the same position in which Usman had earlier on found himself after succeeding his father and precipitating a civil war. Umaru had horrified and alienated large segments of the people of Bauchi, including his chiefs, and incurred the anger of the Sarkin Musulmi.

The events of 1880–1900 not only helped create paralyzing contradictions within the Bauchi ruling class, they also so preoccupied the attention and energies of the Emirate's rulers that the latter remained all but oblivious to the British danger growing on the Benue immediately to the southwest of the Emirate, until it was too late to do anything against that danger. Thus while Bauchi was so engrossed in its own internal problems, the RNC had established "trading stations" nearby at Ibi and Loko in 1883, and in 1889, the Company had come to blows with the Emirate of Muri over the Company's raids against Jibu and Muri town.[88] But it was not until July 1898 that the Company tried to establish a formal contact with Bauchi. This was during the sully into the emir-ate by Lieutenant H. Bryan of the West African Frontier Force (WAFF) on a recruitment expedition.[89] He carried a letter from W.P. Hewby, the Company's agent at Ibi, to the Emir in which Hewby cheekily solicited the Emir's assistance in the recruitment of troops.[90]

The Emir, who must have heard of the clashes between Muri, Bida, Ilorin, Lapai and Agaye with the Company, even though he might not have had the opportunity to ponder over the significance of those clashes, rather than out-rightly chasing the Lieutenant out of his Emirate or collaborating with him out-right, decided to do nothing definite. Instead he told the Lieutenant that while he would not give him assistance, the Lieutenant could go ahead and do the recruiting, provided that he recruited no slaves.[91] However, he warned Hewby in his reply that no more white men should come to his emirate, an indication that he fully knew what to expect from the British.[92]

Meanwhile, on September 9 of the same year, on the pretext of avenging the chief of Amar, whose town the sub-Emir of Wase had attacked on account of the chief's friendly attitude towards the Company, Hewby personally led a force of 90 non-commissioned officers and men in an attack on this sub-emir-ate of Bauchi.[93] Though Wase put up a very determined resistance, the town was captured, its people killed or dispersed, and the town burnt down.[94] The chief, Kobri, was fatally wounded and later on died at Zongo.[95] The British refused to withdraw until the people of Wase had returned and surrendered. Then they were made to choose a new chief, the Ubandoma Muhammadu, whom Hewby gave a letter to take to Bauchi so that the Emir would confirm his appointment, and the Emir did;[96] this confirmation in itself was an indica-tion that the Emir of Bauchi lacked either the will or the wherewithal to resist the British, or both. At any rate, it foreshadowed the absence of military resis-tance to the British when they finally arrived to occupy Bauchi town forty-two months later. In addition to this experience of British power and willingness to use it, account should also be taken of the British defeat and occupation of the emirates of Kontagora, Bida and Yola, all in 1901, which occurred between the sack of Wase and the final invasion of the Emirate of Bauchi. There is no ground for doubting that in spite of the serious Gwaram incident in 1900, the Emirate followed the fate of these other emirates with a keen interest, having itself had such a direct and costly experience in the hands of the British. Thus, in spite of the fact that the Emir of Bauchi had refused to acknowledge receipt of Lugard's "Proclamation,"[97] when the British finally invaded her, Bauchi offered no physical resistance in spite of the deeply-felt bitterness with which the Emirate, chiefs and people alike, regarded the invasion.[98] After the occupation of the town, even though the chiefs made a fairly protracted attempt to retain Umaru as Emir, as we shall see below, they finally gave way to the British demand that he should be deposed. Thus we can conclude that internal contradictions had reached such an advanced stage and British military superiority over the emirates had been so repeatedly confirmed that Bauchi found itself unable to repeat the daring heroism that the southern emirates had demonstrated; and Bauchi's response to the invasion set the pace for most of the emirates invaded after her.

Gombe

In the case of Gombe, apart from the fact that so many other emirates had been defeated with heavy losses and that Bauchi, just next door, had paved the way for non-resistance, the Emirate's internal situation was also such as to produce paralysis. The salient points of this internal situation were as follows: From c.1887, a Mahdist military outpost had been established at Bormi,[99] under a local Mallam, Jibril Gaini, whom Hayat b. Said appointed his *Amir al-Jaish*, a title which, significantly, the Emirs of Gombe also bore. Shehu Uthman dan Fodio had conferred it upon its first Emir, Buba Yero.[100]

Attempts by successive Emirs of Gombe, with whose permission the mallam had initially settled at Bormi, to dislodge him, proved unsuccessful over a period of fifteen years.[101] In resisting Gombe, Mallam Jibril used a combination of both military strategy and diplomatic deceit, and was favoured by the inability of Gombe to win the aid of neighbouring emirates after the initial aid they gave her on the orders of the Sarkin Musulmi.[102] Indeed so successful was Mallam Jibril in resisting Gombe that to save his own capital from falling to the Mallam, the Emir of Gombe, Umaru (1898–1922), made a peace agreement with him around 1900, recognizing him as the ruler of the territories he had captured from Gombe.[103]

The ability of Mallam Jibril to withstand such a prolonged attempt by the Emirs of Gombe to dislodge him should serve as a pointer to the existence of some other serious problems for the Emirate, since it would seem that the Mallam did not dispose of large numbers of forces.[104] Pending a proper study of the history of the Emirate, not much that is definite about the number and nature of such problems can be said.[105] In the meantime two such problems should be pointed out: one is the external relations of the Emirate and the other is its internal contradictions.

The external problem existed in the first one or two years of Gombe's struggle against the Mallam and was in fact the factor that helped to deprive the Emirate of further assistance from neighbouring emirates after the initial one they gave her. This was the existence of a border dispute between the Emirate and the Emirate of Missau.[106] In spite of the fact that all the emirates were within the same Caliphate, this dispute continued right up to the British invasion and led to a confrontation, on Gombe territory, between the two emirates.[107]

It was the existence of the other internal contradiction alluded to above in the Emirate of Gombe that made it possible for Missau forces to bully into Gombe's territory and confront her forces there. This internal contradiction was constituted by a dispute between the then new Emir of Gombe, Umaru, and Buba, the Galadima of Akko.[108] As to the reasons that led the Galadima to revolt in the first place, Adeleye finds that they "are still shrouded in mystery."[109] However, in the light of the subsequent conducts of the Emir and the Galadima on the arrival of the British, especially during the momentous events that followed the entry of the fugitive Sarkin Musulmi in the emirate, while accepting Adeleye's opinion that the causes of the Galadima's revolt "are still shrouded in mystery," I have not found it necessary to accord the opinions of contemporaries like the Sarkin Dillari, the Sarkin Nafada and the Emir of Kano, all of whom gave the Emir of Gombe an implicit support against the Galadima, much weight.[110] Nor would one attach much weight to the fact that, the Sarkin Musulmi, Abdurrahman finally asked the Galadima to go to Gombe and apologize to the Emir.[111] In this regard, suffice it to say that the Sarkin Musulmi did *also* write to the Emir asking him to accept the Galadima's apology. In fact, it would seem that it was the attempt of the Emir of Missau to exploit the situation that helped to gain sympathy for the Emir of Gombe from both the Sarkin Musulmi and the others mentioned above. Besides, given the general situation in the Caliphate at the time, with her enemies closing in on her from all sides, exigency alone would have dictated to the Sarkin Musulmi that settling the dispute quickly was better than taking time to decide on whose side justice lay, the Emir or the Galadima. It is for this reason that I feel that we should not attach much importance to the issue of whose side the various third parties in the dispute seem to have taken. These attitudes were dictated by exigency rather than equity. Nor were these attitudes contrary to justice as laid down in the Shari'a, exigency here very much approximating to the pivotal concept of *maslaha*, the wider interest of the Muslims.

Hence, we propose that pending a thorough investigation of the what and the wherefores of the quarrel between the Galadima and the Emir, we should, on the basis of the conduct of the Emir and the Galadima during the subsequent British invasion, give the benefit of our doubt to the Galadima. In this regard, it should be said that the Emir of Gombe, far from resisting the British in February 1902, welcomed them.[112] However, while the Emir of Gombe and, along with him most of his chiefs, including the Galadima, did not resist British invasion of the Emirate, Mallam Jibril, with Toungo as his base, resisted the British on March 1, 1902, was defeated with heavy losses, and was himself captured on 15 March and deported to Lokoja.[113]

However, when, in July 1903 the erstwhile Sarkin Musulmi, Attahiru Ahmadu, arrived in Gombe, it became apparent that the surrender of the forces of that Emirate seventeen months earlier had been mainly the handiwork of the Emir to which some of the chiefs at least, including the Galadiman Akko, had acquiesced. They did so simply because they felt it was hopeless to resist when the Emir himself was surrendering. Hence with the appearance of the Sarkin Musulmi on the scene, these chiefs hastened to join him while the Emir, at least to all appearances, remained on the side of the British.[114] This way, it happened that both the Galadiman Akko and the Emir were present at Bormi on the day of the final battle between the Sarkin Musulmi and the British. The Galadima inside the town was on the side of the Sarkin Musulmi – the Emir, by this time a British stooge, was on the outskirts of the town helping the British by turning back the people of Gombe, who were still hurrying towards Bormi to reinforce the Sarkin Musulmi.[115] The only other "Emir" who was at Bormi on the side of the British on that day was the "Emir" of Missau, Alhaji, whose rival and predecessor Ahmadu was inside the town on the side of the Sarkin Musulmi.[116]

This way the two "Emirs" of Gombe and of Missau, Umaru and Alhaji, stood out even among the collaborators who either submitted to the British and agreed to continue to serve under them, or were actually appointed by the British themselves. It was probable that the two of them were brought to Bormi by the British, not merely because of the proximity of their capitals, but primarily because they were more genuinely loyal to the British than all of the others; for in terms of proximity the Emirs of Bauchi and Katagum at least could also have been summoned to be present at Bormi to help the British with discouraging their people, who were also trooping to Bormi in large numbers. It is also pertinent to point out that the two of them were among the Emirs of the first generation to serve with the British who died in office, while most of the others of this set of British-appointed Emirs were later to be deposed.[117]

We ought to hesitate to brand them out and out traitors to the Sarkin Musulmi and the cause of the Caliphate only because the chances are there that at the same time as coming to the aid of the British against the Sarkin Musulmi, they might also have earlier on encouraged or at least deliberately overlooked the flight of people to the Sarkin Musulmi. Only research specifically dealing with the two emirates along the lines of those that dealt with the emirates of Fombina and Katsina, for example, can settle the issue conclusively.

Yet, while leaving this opening for the vindication of his conduct, along with that of Alhaji of Missau, one would like to restate that our inclination is to believe that the conduct of the Emir of Gombe in 1902 to 1903 was more than involuntary and went beyond the bounds that are permitted by the Islamic concept of *Taqiyya*, namely dissimulation. To say the least, dissimulation is supposed to be verbal, rather than actual "support," except in trivial matters.[118] And to say that the Emir's collaboration was involuntary is to make the power of the Emir's circumstances over him absolute, which is an extreme exaggeration in point of fact, in the sense that the weakness of the Emir of Gombe vis-à-vis the British, in 1903 at least, was not much greater, if at all greater, than, say, the weakness of the Emir of Bauchi, nearby. Such, then, was the man that the Galadima had fallen out with earlier on; hence the reason for giving the benefit of the doubt to the Galadima.

Zaria

Perhaps more than in any other Emirate, in Zaria it was British activity in the Sokoto Caliphate that led to non-resistance to them when they arrived in March 1902. Thus, when the British ousted the Emirs of Bida and Kontagora in February 1901, the latter of the two, with a very large following, moved into Zaria and Katsina territory.[119] Under those circumstances the Emir was either unable or unwilling to impose discipline on his followers. Thus western Zaria was ravaged by the fugitive Kontagora contingent.[120]

In the meantime Lugard had, since early 1900, been pressuring the Emir of Zaria, Muhammadu Lawal, who had allowed Bishop Tugwell to settle at Girku within the Emirate, to accept British friendship and a British garrison.[121] With the unwanted visitors on his territory, the British pressure became more persistent; and when both the Emir and the Sarkin Musulmi failed in their attempts to get the Emir of Kontagora to control his contingent, the Emir of Zaria deemed it necessary to accept the British offer of "assistance." Hence, when the British entered Zaria territory in March 1902, it was as the "allies" of the Emir against the fugitive Emir of Kontagora that they did so.[122] But even after effecting the arrest of Ibrahim Nagwamatse, the British remained put and established a garrison outside the city in April 1902, with Captain Abadie as Resident.[123]

By now the Emir of Zaria had lost the initiative to the British. Hence although he openly expressed his regrets to Abadie[124] for allowing the British to come in the first place, and although he felt deeply troubled about the now certain prospect of Zaria being used as a base for British invasion of Kano and Sokoto,[125] he could take no action against the British. It was in vain that Muhammad Lawal tried to dissuade the British from reinforcing their garrison at Zaria with additional troops from Bauchi, Yelwa and Lokoja;[126] and when, in desperation, he put his own troops in a state of alert[127] soon after the arrival of the reinforcement that was sent from Lokoja, Muhammad Lawal was arrested by the British and sent into exile.[128]

Resistance in Kano and Sokoto, and the Surrender of Gwandu and Katsina, February–March 1903

Kano

After the occupation of Zaria, the British invaded and occupied Kano;[129] and unlike in Zaria, the British met with resistance in Kano. However, the factors that led to resistance in Kano were not quite the same as the factors that had led to the resistance of the southern emirates. For while the resistance of the southern emirates was, at least substantially, inspired by the hope of defeating the British, in the case of Kano such hope had been abandoned at the latest by the end of 1902. In fact it was a combination of this very hopelessness which, by the time the British arrived had turned into fatalism, and the circumstances that prevailed in Kano at the time the British arrived, that helped to produce resistance to them.

To start with, it should be noted that when Bishop Tugwell and his mission visited Kano in 1900, the Emir did think of executing them but was dissuaded from doing so by his Waziri, Ahmadu, who pointed to the French occupation of Zinder as an example of what Europeans could do to any African ruler or town that defied them.[130] Then there is the story that sometime in 1902, Hamza, the Chief of Garko, feeling concerned with the British invasion of the emirates of Bida, Kontagora and Yola, went to Kano, warned the Emir of the impending danger, and advised that the Kano walls should be strengthened and fortified.[131]

It is said that the Emir was at the point of accepting the idea of mending the walls when Waziri Ahmadu, a senior brother of the Emir, urged the Emir not to entertain the idea of resisting the Europeans in view of the fact that powerful places like Damagaram and Bida had failed to resist them successfully; and the Emir believed the Waziri and dismissed the idea of fortifying the city walls.[132]

It would seem that it was not only the success of British arms against Bida that impressed Kano chiefs like Waziri Ahmadu. Such chiefs were also impressed by the fact that the British were willing to work with the erstwhile rulers of the Sokoto Caliphate if only the latter were willing to accept a subordinate role. In fact, to propagate the idea that they were not out to destroy the position of the rulers of the emirates, the British had got the man they appointed as the Emir of Bida, Muhammadu, to write to other Emirs informing them of British willingness to preserve them and cooperate with them.[133] Indeed, it is even alleged that British agents, especially Adamu Jakada, had distributed bribes among leading figures in the emirates to induce them to push the idea of accepting British rule and cooperation with the British.[134] In our view, such claims should not be dismissed lightly and need to be thoroughly investigated if our understanding of the attitude of the rulers of the Sokoto Caliphate is to be complete. Investigation should be made to find out how, first, the Royal Niger Company, and then the "protectorate" administration of the pre-conquest days, related not only to the caliph and Emirs but also to leading princes and officials in both Sokoto and the emirates.

Yet, with the establishment of a British garrison at Zaria in April 1902, Kano started rebuilding the walls of the city and instructions were sent to the authorities of subordinate towns between Kano and Zaria to repair their own town walls.[135] By this time, the repeated messages of the British puppet in Bida were falling on deaf ears. Besides rebuilding the city walls, the Emir of Kano also redoubled his efforts to secure arms, his sources being Tripolitanian merchants and runaway mercenaries from the West African Frontier Force, and by October 1902, it would seem that the Emir of Kano was even willing to take war to the British at Zaria, a project which, Lugard claims, he abandoned only on receipt of the news of the death of the Sarkin Musulmi, Abdurrahman.[136] And when, in November, Magaji Yamusa arrived in Kano after killing the British "Resident" at Keffi, the Emir treated him as the national hero that he was,[137] the Emir being greatly inspired by the Magaji's action.

However, in the light of subsequent events, the significance of these preparations on the part of the Emir of Kano are apt to be exaggerated. As for these subsequent events that later confirmed the fatalistic disposition of the Emir, we would first single out the fact that Aliyu, like his uncle Muhammad Bello

(Emir 1883–1892), was a believer in the evacuation of Hausaland;[138] and his departure from Kano with most of his chiefs and contingents[139] for Sokoto, at a time when British invasion of Kano was known to be imminent, even though its exact timing could not be predicted.[140] One would argue that if the Emir had really been hopeful of offering a successful military resistance to the invasion, then, his departure from Kano, taking along with him almost all his chiefs at this time, cannot be excused – not even by the lack of knowledge of the precise date when the British would invade. If anything, this lack of definite knowledge should, under the circumstances then prevailing, have persuaded the Emir to remain at home. Nor was the departure necessary in terms of precedence in the relations between Kano and Sokoto. Thus, even though it had been the practice for all Emirs to visit Sokoto soon after their own appointment and soon after the appointment of a new Sarkin Musulmi, the necessity of these visits was not absolute. That is to say, if there was sufficient ground for an Emir not to go in person, he could send a delegation with his excuses, and this had been done before both by Kano and other emirates.[141] Certainly, if ever there was a valid ground for an Emir to excuse himself from visiting a new Sarkin Musulmi or presenting himself to the Sarkin Musulmi after his own appointment, the circumstances prevailing in Kano in 1902 to 1903 constituted such a ground. Hence the Emir of Kano's departure for Sokoto in January 1903 should at least be ascribed to indecision on his part about whether to resist the British or not. Better still, it should be ascribed to a conscious decision on his part either to offer what he knew to be both a futile and costly resistance, or to submit to a conqueror whose pretentions he abhorred.

Then there was the fact that when, while on his way back to Kano, the Emir learnt for certain that the remnants of his forces in Kano had been defeated by the British, he, rather than continue with what was Kano's main force to meet the British, decided to avoid them and escaped.[142] It might be argued that the Emir thought that since he was not able to meet the British with his combined force, and since a substantial part of his force had already been defeated and his ammunition dump captured, it was futile for him to meet the British with the other part, though it was the main part. In response, one would point out that, in that case, he had the option of hurrying back to Sokoto and combining his forces with those of the Sarkin Musulmi. Thus, the fact that instead of taking this second option, the Emir took a third one and escaped from the Caliphate should be credited to a decision taken long before the capture of Kano, that resistance was futile.[143] Adding weight to this view is the fact that the Emir did not even risk being held back from his flight by his chiefs. He avoided the possibility of having his hands forced by some of his chiefs, by simply leaving in secret with only one of his wives and five trusted servants.[144] In taking this course, Aliyu at once followed the dictates of his conscience, unilaterally absolved himself from responsibility for any course of action that his chiefs might later take, and by the same token absolved those chiefs, collectively and severally, to follow the dictates of their own conscience.[145]

Similarly, the behaviour of his chiefs after the departure of Emir Aliyu goes to support the thesis that the prevalent view in Kano was already that resistance was futile. Thus, when, in the morning it was discovered that the Emir had fled, his chiefs divided into three groups.[146] The first group was made up of the Wambai, Abbas, and a few followers. It avoided the oncoming British and headed straight for Kano to submit to the Resident, a clear and simple confirmation of the belief of this group in the futility of resistance to the British. A second and very small group under the Galadima, Mahmudu, a full younger brother of Emir Aliyu, and including the Alkali and the Liman, marched back to Sokoto. The intention of this group could have been one of several. On the one hand, it might have returned to Sokoto in order to participate in Sokoto's defence. On the other hand, the mother of Aliyu and the Galadima, a daughter of Sokoto's fourth caliph, Aliyu b. Bello (1842–1859), had been living in Wurno since the death of her husband Emir Abdullahi b. Ibrahim Dabo, in 1883;[147] and the Galadima might have gone back there with the sole intention of living in comparative obscurity as a maternal "nephew," with some comfort and no responsibility. This was an option which, under the circumstances, might have appeared more attractive to him than that of going back to Kano, where he might have become the target of any hostility that the conduct of his brother, Aliyu, since he became Emir, but especially on the eve of the British invasion, might have aroused. In point of fact the Galadima remained in Sokoto for about fifteen years before returning to Kano to accept the office of a District Head under Emir Abbas.[148] Therefore, while the conduct of this second group does not add weight to the thesis being advanced here, it does not detract from it either. It has been narrated here both to make our account more complete and to invite further investigation into the matter.

The third group was in fact the largest,[149] and was led by Waziri Ahmadu, the very man who tried to dissuade the Emir from rebuilding Kano's walls. This group neither went back to Sokoto nor tried to avoid the oncoming British. Instead it marched straight to meet the British, which it did at Rawayya near Kwatarkoshi. It charged against them and lost its leader, the Waziri, and some others. The rest scattered and made for Kano in small groups.[150] Every evidence about this group and its behaviour points to a conscious search for martyrdom on its part. First, there was its leader's early sense of fatalism. Then, there was the fact that by now it must have been known for certain that a military encounter between itself and the British would lead only to its own defeat and decimation. Then, there is the fact that as the group was about to approach the British, a number of its members, including the Waziri, dismounted and performed ablution before remounting and charging the British column.[151]

Yet the question remains as to why the force that the Emir left behind in Kano offered the invading British a physical resistance rather than opening the city's gates and letting them in. In answer to this question, one would suggest that the officials that the Emir left behind, namely the Sarkin Shanu, Muhammadu dan Gwari, and the Sallama, Jatau, both of them slaves of the Emir, must naturally have been the most loyal to him, for otherwise he would not have left them behind. Hence we should expect them to take their duty towards him very seriously and avoid by all possible means letting down the Emir or appearing to betray his trust. They were also most likely to have been among the few chiefs who might have remained convinced of the possibility of a successful resistance by Kano against the British, in spite of the failure of all the emirates that had resisted them. It makes sense to leave behind officials with this conviction even on the part of an Emir who was already more than inclined towards accepting the futility of resistance, assuming that his belief in this futility was not absolute. Leaving behind officials with some measure of confidence in the efficacy of resistance was a way of enhancing the possibility of success, very dim though the Emir's own perception of such a possibility might have been. Then there was the added conscientious advantage of not having imposed the responsibility for the resistance on those who had little or no faith in resistance.

The loyalty of the Sarkin Shanu and his assistant to the Emir, and their trust in the efficacy of military resistance apart, there was also the sanction of the possibility that even if they surrendered without a fight, the Emir, with his larger force, and better still the Emir, in combination with Sokoto, might, after all, succeed in defeating the British. If this happened, the Emir might have visited retribution not just on the vanquished aggressors but on the traitors who gave in to them without a fight. Finally, there was the element of surprise contained in the timing of the British invasion of Kano.

Thus we have already pointed out that though it was known in Kano that the invasion was imminent, its exact timing was not known, an ignorance which argued against the Emir's departure for Sokoto in January if he had any real intention of resisting the invasion. Then there was the fact that just before invading Kano, the British had marched up to Katagum from their base at Gujba in Borno and then gone back, a maneuver which is said to have misled the Sarkin Shanu to feel that the British invasion of Kano was after all not all that imminent.[152] Hence, when the British finally invaded Kano at the beginning of February, the invasion to some degree came as a *surprise*;[153] and the Kano forces, had to, and did, act on the spur of the moment, as it were. And given both the violent posture of the British as well as the posture of "readiness" of the Kano forces, the only possible action on the part of the forces, in the absence of deliberation, was resistance, as actually happened.[154] That is to say, in spite of the long period of foreknowledge of the British invasion, and because of the element of surprise it carried under the immediate circumstances in which the invasion was launched, the resistance on the part of the defenders of Kano was to a certain measure automatic rather than deliberate.[155]

Gwandu

Like Bauchi, Gombe and Zaria, Gwandu did not offer physical resistance to the British when they finally invaded it on March 12, 1903.[156] The explanation for this non-resistance should be sought for in Gwandu's relations with Argungu up to that time, the fate of the emirates that the British invaded earlier, and Gwandu's own experience of British aggression prior to this final invasion. Concerning Gwandu's relations with Argungu, it should be noted that in 1849 Argungu was re-established as the traditional successor to the old kingdom of Kebbi, on whose territory the Emirate of Gwandu had been carved out in the first decade of the nineteenth century. Ever since then, this kingdom had, with a few periods of truce,[157] kept up military confrontation with the Caliphate generally and Gwandu Emirate in particular, right up to the British conquest of both the Caliphate and Argungu. Thus, to a great extent, at the same time as consuming the energies of the two protagonists, the mutual hostility between them did help to make it impossible for either of them to pay due attention to the growing British danger until it was too late. Besides, as far as Gwandu was concerned, there is the fact that from 1898 the rulers of Argungu were inclined to treat the Europeans generally as allies against Gwandu and Sokoto, their 'common' enemies,[158] an inclination which made it impossible for the two antagonists to close ranks against the British.

As for Gwandu's experiences with the British prior to the invasion of 1903, the fact is that apart from the diplomatic relations that the Emirate had with the RNC between 1885 and 1897,[159] Gwandu had a history of military confrontation with the British, especially in the years since 1897. It is only in the light of the history of this confrontation between the Emirate and the British that we can fully grasp the significance of Gwandu's non-resistance in March 1903.

In this regard it should be remembered that it was in 1897 that the British first invaded Bida and Ilorin, two emirates which were under the immediate supervision of Gwandu.[160] Following these two acts of aggression, the Emir of Gwandu, along with the Sarkin Musulmi, refused to accept the yearly *jizya* that the RNC had paid to him ever since 1885, but other events in and around the Caliphate[161] rendered it impossible for Gwandu, with the aid of Sokoto or without it, to take military action against the RNC. Indeed, as we have already seen, far from mounting a military action against the RNC, Gwandu as well as the emirates neighbouring on Nupe and Ilorin, suffered a psychological shock, now having seen a practical demonstration of the Company's military capacity, and willingness to employ it.

Then soon following on the British attack on Bida, the French established military posts at Bussa, Yagha, Botu, Karimama, Illo and Gwamba, all either in Gwandu or very close to it,[162] a move which put Gwandu and Sokoto in a great dilemma. For it means they had to decide which of the two invading powers was the lesser evil and temporarily ally with it against the other if they could; and the RNC took advantage of this dilemma to achieve a measure of conciliation with both Gwandu and Sokoto. Hence, from the end of 1897 to May 1898, Gwandu and Sokoto continued to pay greater attention to the danger which the French posed towards the Caliphate.

However, when Marius-Gabriel Cazemajou, who had tried to visit Sokoto in January 1898 but was successfully ordered back by the Sarkin Musulmi, was killed at Zinder on May 5 of that year, Gwandu and Sokoto were relieved, and once again turned their attention towards the danger that the RNC posed to the Caliphate. For this reason, an attempt in May by the RNC to station a garrison at Jega in the Emirate of Gwandu under the pretext of protecting the Caliphate against the French was forcefully rebuffed[163] by Sokoto; but the British were able to establish seven garrisons in Borgu and at Yelwa in Yawuri, an independent kingdom having treaty relations with Sokoto, through Gwandu.[164] The establishment of these garrisons, and the fact that the British had written to inform the Caliph that by his refusal to let them establish a garrison at Jega he had declared his enmity towards them, ensured the permanence of the rupture of friendly relations between the Company on the one hand and Gwandu and Sokoto on the other.[165] Then in August 1898 the British established another military post at Illo. The combined hostility of the Emirs of Gwandu and Kontagora, especially the hostility of the people of Illo which led to skirmishes between them and the garrison on 25 September, during which both of the two British officers as well as all the fourteen mercenaries manning it were killed, forced the British to abandon the garrison.

When Lugard issued his "Protectorate Proclamation" in January 1900, he sent Arabic translations of it to the Sarkin Musulmi and all the Emirs. At Gwandu the messenger who brought the "Proclamation" was told verbally that there was no need to reply Lugard after the British had already seized some Gwandu territory.[166] It was against this background that the British went ahead to reoccupy Bida in 1901 and to occupy Kontagora, Yola, Muri, Bauchi, Gombe, Zaria and Kano and oust their Emirs between 1900 and September 1901. In the immediate hinterland of Gwandu town itself in March 1901 the British, operating from their post at Illo,[167] attacked and burnt the towns of Raha and Kalgo,[168] both ruled by members of the Gwandu ruling house.[169] Yet the Emir of Gwandu took no punitive measure against the post.[170] Hence, when the British planned a second attack on Kalgo in April 1901, the chief, Halirun Abdu, sent and invited Captain Keyes, the commander of the post, to pay a friendly visit to Kalgo. Captain Keyes paid the visit and was warmly received by the chief.

There is no specific evidence that Haliru invited Captain Keyes on instructions from the Emir of Gwandu, nor is there any evidence that the Emir penalized him in any way. The issue of authorization and punishment by Gwandu is raised here because normally, one would expect a minor chief, such as the Sarkin Kalgo, to enter into friendly relations with such an important enemy of Gwandu Emirate and the Sokoto Caliphate generally, only under specific instructions from the Emir. It is also reasonable to expect that if the Emir decided to arrange a local truce with the British at Illo, he should, himself, enter into negotiations with them, instead of allowing a minor subordinate to do so. This carried the dangerous consequences that allowing the British to fraternize with minor chiefs could very well augur for the unity of the Emirate. Similarly, one would normally expect that if a minor chief, such as Haliru of Kalgo, entered into friendly relations with the British on his own, he would be recalled to Gwandu. Hence, it would seem that the passivity and seeming indifference of Gwandu connotes either some abnormal situation in the Emirate itself or a decision even at that date to submit to the British, which was not yet communicated to the latter for some reason, such as non-clearance from Sokoto.

Yet, apart from its confrontation with Argungu and the fact that the Emir of Gwandu, Bayeron Aliyu, was already an old and sick man who was preoccupied with winning paradise in the next world,[171] there was no indication of an internal crisis in the Emirate. Hence one is left only with the conclusion that by early 1901 Gwandu's rulers had already lost heart and were prepared to accept British subjugation together with the "guarantees" for the rulers that subjugation allowed;[172] for by this time the British had already repeated several times over that they were willing to accommodate the rulers of the Caliphate in their *Raj* and had demonstrated this willingness in the retention of the Emir of Ilorin and the appointment of the Makun, Muhammadu, as the Emir of Bida on terms that, under the circumstances then prevailing, did not appear too repulsive. This willingness to retain the erstwhile rulers of the Caliphate was also to be seen in the fact that Resident Burdon at Bida allowed the agent of the Emir of Gwandu to collect Gwandu's yearly tribute in Bida in March 1901.[173] Far from stopping the collection of this tribute, Burdon expressed "happiness" to see the customary relations between Gwandu and the Emirate of Bida being kept up. [174] Burdon even sent a letter to the Emir of Gwandu through this agent and received a friendly letter from the Emir in return. In addition, there were the letters that he got the Emir of Bida to write to the rulers of the Caliphate, urging them to reach an accommodation with the British.[175] Thus, it would seem that only the uncompromising stand of Sarkin Musulmi Abdurrahman against surrender forced the authorities in Gwandu not to come out openly and capitulate to the British as early as the beginning of 1901.[176]

Hence one finds it easy to accept the claim in May by Captain Keyes that the Emir of Gwandu had surrendered by March 1901, and that by that date only the Caliph remained hostile, a claim which P.K. Tibenderana, for example, doubts.[177] At any rate it would seem that the successful occupation of more emirates by the British between April 1901 and February 1903, in many cases with heavy casualties for the emirates, only went to lend weight to the authorities in Gwandu in the decision not to resist. Hence with the death of Sarkin Musulmi Abdurrahman in October 1902, a disputed succession to the office of Caliph, the profound doubt that had gripped Sokoto itself by the end of 1902 about the wisdom and legality of resisting the British in the face of certainty of defeat, and the arrival of a British force in Gwandu, all combined to make it easy for the Gwandu authorities to capitulate on March 12, 1903, as soon as the British arrived there on their way to Sokoto.

Sokoto

As in the case of the emirates, to understand the conduct of the Caliphal authorities in Sokoto, when the British finally arrived there on 15 March 1903, we need to review relations between the Caliph and the British from c.1890, but especially since the conquest of the Caliphate by the former started in 1897. In this connection, it should be pointed out that news of the conquest of Segu in 1890 to 1891 reached Sokoto possibly before the end of 1891, and certainly by 1894.[178] And although by this time the Sokoto authorities had some idea that the French and the British were different, it was known that both had designs on the Caliphate. Then the Sokoto authorities witnessed with apprehension the rivalry between the French and the Royal Niger Company in Borgu, Yawuri and Nupeland in 1894–95, during which the French established Fort d'Arenberg, at Bajibo on Bida's territory.[179] This was the case, even though the threats posed by Rabeh, now established in Borno, seemed more imminent and preoccupied the attention of Sokoto in the years 1895 and 1896.[180]

Not that Sokoto, either directly or through Gwandu, would have attacked the French or the Royal Niger Company. Indeed Sokoto did not contemplate attacking even Rabeh. But in accordance with her traditional strategy, Sokoto sent support to the emirates directly threatened by the latter in order to combine and repel him;[181] and in the case of the French in Nupe, it was their rivalry with the Royal Niger Company that forced them to give up their fort in Nupeland in September 1895. Similarly, when hostility between Bida and the Royal Niger Company itself reached a point of crisis in the latter half of 1896, all the Emir of Gwandu did was to send to both the Emir and the Company, appealing for a peaceful settlement of the differences between them.[182] The Emir of Gwandu sent a message, informing the Caliph, Abdurrahman, about his stand. There is no evidence that the Caliph either sent to order a more positive stand by Gwandu on the side of Bida or offer his own aid.

When the Company mounted its aggressive offensive, first against Bida in January 1897 and then against Ilorin in February 1897, the Caliph would only send letters to the riverain emirs asking them to expel the Company from their territories.[183] Though the Caliph himself refused the Company's tribute for that year, the tribute was accepted for 1898.[184] Underlying the passive nature of the Caliph's hostility towards the Royal Niger Company in 1897 were the fact that the Royal Niger Company was not the only enemy the Caliph had to contend with, Rabeh's threat was still real, while the French threat once more attracted the Caliph's attention, with the arrival in Sokoto of the ousted Amir al-Muminin of Segu at about the same time as the Bida and Ilorin expeditions were mounted by the Royal Niger Company. Furthermore, the French forced themselves back on to the scene by the establishment of military posts close to Gwandu at Karimama, Illo and Gwamba.[185] Finally, Goldie played up the fact that even though the Royal Niger Company invaded and defeated Bida and Ilorin, it neither replaced the local ruling dynasties nor stationed its troops in the capitals of those emirates.[186]

In fact, so threatened by the French expedition under Cazemajou did the Sarkin Musulmi feel in January and February 1898 that the Royal Niger Company was able to send a force towards Sokoto under the guise of helping the Sarkin Musulmi against the French.[187] The real aim of the Company was to establish an advanced military post near Sokoto and to get the Sarkin Musulmi to accept a British Resident in his capital. The Sarkin Musulmi was well disposed towards the expedition so long as the French threat was there. But when Cazemajou agreed to withdraw from the Caliphate and yet a part of the Royal Niger Company force, with the Resident designate, continued towards Sokoto, the attitude of the Sarkin Musulmi altered. He sent the Emir of Kontagora as the head of a force of 7,000 horsemen to tell this British force to go back or be attacked.[188] The force chose returning to Yelwa, where it reinforced a garrison it had left behind there. The Sarkin Musulmi vehemently objected to this garrison too, though he was not able to dislodge it. Similarly, when the Company established another military post at Illo in August 1898, the Sarkin Musulmi objected to it, an objection in which, according to Adeleye, he was supported by Sarkin Yawuri and which yielded positive result when the Royal Niger Company found the situation of the Yelwa post so untenable that the post was abandoned in September 1898.[189] Soon afterwards, the people of Illo in a popular uprising annihilated the whole of the Illo garrison on 25 September 1898.[190]

Nor did the Sarkin Musulmi, Abdurrahman, even again relax his hostility towards the British. If anything, his attitude towards the Royal Niger Company stiffened so much so that by 1900 he formally suspended relations between himself and the Company.[191] It was in spite of this suspension of relations with the Royal Niger Company that Lugard sent his "Proclamation" to the Sarkin Musulmi.[192] Needless to say, the Sarkin Musulmi rejected British pretensions to sovereignty over the Caliphate. In fact he did so out of hand, merely dismissing the British messenger and warning him to bring no more messages from them.[193] He did not even find it necessary to give Lugard a written reply.

But our real interests here are: firstly, in the extent to which the attitude of the Sarkin Musulmi was typical or atypical of the attitude of the whole central leadership of the Caliphate, though from a legal point of view his attitude was adequate on its own;[194] secondly, the manner in which the Sarkin Musulmi intended to meet the British threat should Lugard move to give effect to his claims; thirdly how the conquest of the various emirates affected official opinion in Sokoto about how to meet this British threat and, finally, the point at which the decision to evacuate the territories of the Caliphate was finally taken at Sokoto.

On the first issue, for the period up to October 1902, it is very difficult to determine the extent to which the Sarkin Musulmi's attitude was typical. This is because Abdurrahman, who was Sarkin Musulmi throughout that period, seldom sought or accepted advice on any matter.[195] Specifically on the issue of the British threat, Kiari, the British messenger, reports that the Sarkin Musulmi received and read the "Proclamation" in the presence of his councilors; but he neither asked Kiari to withdraw so that he could hold consultations with these councilors nor asked their opinion about the contents of the letter. The Sarkin Musulmi simply turned round to them and said in Fulfulde, which he wrongly assumed Kiari, a Kanuri, could not understand, that if this was the sort of message the British would send him, he would never again receive and read letters from them. It was then that he turned round and dismissed Kiari.[196] Hence we can assume that the opinions of his councilors over the matter, whether they harmonized with those of the Sarkin Musulmi or differed from them were not elicited and in all probability were never expressed, out of fear of the Sarkin Musulmi.

However, as far as the short period of October 1902 to March 1903 was concerned, it would seem that the Sarkin Musulmi's attitude which, from the outset was inclined towards migration, as opposed both to accepting British rule and to fighting them,[197] was a reflection of what at the time appeared to be a consensus of opinion, but what in the course of events turned out to be the opinion only of a section of the Sarkin Musulmi's advisers. The attitude of Sarkin Musulmi Attahiru is deemed to reflect what appeared to be a consensus of opinion because he is reported to have sought the opinion of his advisers over the issue, a course which should be expected from a new ruler whose accession to office was surrounded with dispute.[198] Besides, the bitterness which, after the British occupation of Sokoto, the Sarkin Musulmi felt towards those among his advisers – the majority – who refused to follow him but instead submitted to the victorious British, we must assume, arose out of a sense of betrayal not only of those advisers' oath of allegiance to him, but also of a decision to which those advisers had been party.[199]

It was also the fact that the majority of his council remained behind. This indicates that they could not have acceded to the decision to emigrate out of conviction. They did so merely out of the fear of opposing what they felt was the popular opinion among at least a very significant section of Sokoto's population. Besides, there is the fact that the Waziri later attributed intellectual responsibility for the Sarkin Musulmi's *hijra* to the Chief Qadi, Abdullahi b. Ali, who emigrated with the Sarkin Musulmi.[200]

As for the manner in which Sokoto hoped to cope with the British threat, we have noted above that from the time of the accession of Attahiru, the intention was to emigrate; but then, we have also noted that as late as early 1898 Sarkin Musulmi Abdurrahman was fully willing to meet British aggression with force. This was evidenced by the fact that he actually sent a force under the Emir of Kontagora to meet and send back the British "Resident" and his escort, an act which convinced the Resident to turn back.[201] Hence the issue is reduced to the point at which, between 1898 and the end of 1902, the decision to embark on a *hijra* rather than stand and fight was taken. Certainly, with every British military success against an emirate, the proposition to stand and fight them lost a measure of its credibility, except purely as an act of martyrdom. But there is little evidence that Abdurrahman personally ever lost his willingness to stand and oppose the British with force. If anything, his letter to Lugard in May 1902 following the latter's report to him of British occupation of Bauchi showed that this resolve had neither flagged nor was based on a pure desire for martyrdom on his part, as evidenced by his assertion that "there is no power or strength save in God on high."[202] Nothing happened between May 1902 and Abdurrahman's death in October 1902 to shake this determination. Therefore, we should assume that until Abdurrahman's death, the official policy in Sokoto was to stand and fight the British, and to do so not only in order to embrace martyrdom, but also because the possibility of victory over the British was still entertained. But this official policy was only based on the views and determination of the Sarkin Musulmi, and perhaps a few of his advisers. Hence, immediately after his death, the policy was abandoned apparently in favour of a *hijra* but, judging from subsequent events, in favour of submission to the British as far as a majority of the Sarkin Musulmi's advisers were concerned.

It is here that the issue of the impact on Sokoto of British military successes against successive emirates, as well as their subsequent policy in those defeated emirates, comes in. As far as the military successes are concerned, we have hinted above that every success tended to further discredit the theory of the possibility of a military victory over the British, if not in the eyes of Sarkin Musulmi Abdurahman, at least in the sight of his less heroic advisers. In making this suggestion one would point out that among the emirates that were subdued between January 1900 and the middle of 1902 were some of the most powerful emirates in the Caliphate, which included Bida, Yola and Bauchi. In fact we would suggest that after the fall of Bauchi, which in fact did not even fight, the capacity of the British to defeat any force in the Caliphate must, for the majority of the Caliph's advisers, have been demonstrated beyond doubt. Whatever the British — who until then were partly ignorant of the history of the Caliphate[203] — might have said about people thinking that Kano was going to be the final and most conclusive test, the fact is that in the actual history of the Bauchi Caliphate, which repelled El-Kanemi in 1826 and helped to curb the power of Buhari in the 1850s, played at least an equally prominent military role as Kano in the history of the Caliphate.[204] In fact the only time Kano militarily stood out above all the other emirates was in 1891 during the notorious battle against Argungu.[205] But as is well known, it was more in loyalty towards the Sarkin Musulmi, Abdurrahman, rather than in military capacity, that the Kano contingent, under Galadima Tukur, who was angling for the Emirship of Kano, excelled over all the other contingents. This includes that of Sokoto itself, whose commanders were known to have been conspiring to get rid of the Sarkin Musulmi, and hence ran away from the battle field, in an effort to abandon the Sarkin Musulmi to his enemies.[206]

Hence, we should dispense with the claim that everybody in the Caliphate awaited the defeat of Kano as the most conclusive test of British capacity, a claim made by Lugard and nurtured by later writers who should have been more critical.[207] It can certainly be pointed out that since it repulsed El-Kanemi and frustrated Buhari, Bauchi had bled itself to weakness in a civil war. But so also had Kano bled itself in a civil war, in fact much later than Bauchi. Hence we should assume that by the middle of 1902, though official policy in Sokoto, better still the opinion of Sarkin Musulmi Abdurrahman, remained optimistic, in spite of all evidence to the contrary, the majority of the central officials of the Caliphate had been convinced of the futility of military resistance to the British, though they lacked the courage to own up to it.

However, as we have seen in the case of Kano, with particular reference to the attitude and conduct of Waziri Ahmadu, conviction about the futility of resistance did not automatically lead to an abandonment of such a resistance which, under certain circumstances, Muslims were duty bound to offer even if their defeat was certain.[208] It is here that British policy in the occupied emirates, namely that of retaining the services of the native aristocracy and of giving Islam a measure of recognition, comes in. This policy was indeed dictated by the imperatives of British colonialism in the emirates, but it did have the effect of reassuring the rulers of the Caliphate, and of relieving them of the religious duty to resist. This policy, in short, consisted in retaining the emirates' ruling dynasties in office and letting them carry on very much as before, except in certain matters, such as waging the *jihad* and enforcing the *Hadd* in cases of theft, adultery and murder. The Caliphal officials, it seems, were able to rationalize both of these matters as inessential to their allegiance to the Islamic way of life; and from a strictly legal point of view those officials had a basis, especially with regard to the punishment of theft and adultery, the injunction on both of which had hardly ever been enforced in the Caliphate, because the rules of evidence about them, and the circumstances surrounding their commission, were so stringent.

To be sure, the restrictions on the powers of the rulers of the emirates were not intended by the British to remain so few and so light, but quite naturally they did not announce their intention to further curb and restrict the powers of the Emirs, thus deliberately misleading the Emirs and the Sokoto central chiefs about their full intentions. On the contrary, as we have seen, the British kept on pointing out to Sokoto and those emirates they had not yet occupied, how well disposed they were towards the ruling classes and Islam;[209] and this had the effect of reassuring the less heroic elements, especially among the *ulema*,[210] and to encourage them in their inclination to accept British conquest. Particularly reassuring to the officials in Sokoto was the fact that the British allowed the emirates they occupied to continue sending customary gifts to Sokoto. They even allowed central officials such as the Waziri in Sokoto and the Magajin Gari in Gwandu to tour such emirates as hitherto and collect the gifts themselves.[211]

Thus, we are inclined to conclude that by the middle of 1902, the majority of the officials in Sokoto had privately come to favour staying and submitting to the British, on the basis of the guarantees that the British, by their policy in the occupied emirates and by repeated protestation, seemed willing to offer as to the position of the Caliphate's rulers. This is not to say that even these officials welcomed the advent of the British. Far from that, they definitely saw it as a calamity for the Muslims in general and as a humiliation to themselves in particular, and hoped that it was very temporary. The Qadi of Gwandu, and the Waziri of Sokoto were later to write down these sentiments as movingly and eloquently as anyone could.[212] But our argument still remains that from all indications, submission was their choice among four difficult alternatives, the other three being *shahada*, the *hijra* and withdrawal from the towns to conduct a guerilla-type resistance.

Yet, in point of fact, Sokoto did offer a battle to the British. It was only after losing that battle that the Sokoto leadership divided into two camps, one opting for submission and the other for the *hijra*, each in accordance with the true individual conscience of its members who, until the arrival of the British, could not be known for certain to others. Our explanation for the fact that the central leadership of the Caliphate did ultimately fight is that it was overtaken by events which seem to have had a logic that was independent of the individual, and indeed even the group will of the actors. That it was the momentum of events that compelled a battle on Sokoto is made clear by Waziri Junaidu who says:

> And when they received the news [about the capture of Kano] they discussed the matter amongst them. Some of them counselled peace with the whites, should they arrive, others favoured fighting and some resolved on migration. The *amir al-muminin* was inclined towards migration, and people began to prepare for the journey. They bought shoes, mules, donkeys and other necessary

things. They even fixed the date of departure, but while thus engaged they suddenly heard that the whites had arrived. Thus the determination to depart gave way and fighting ensued.[213]

An Exceptional Situation in Borno

Like Bauchi and Gombe before it and Zaria, Gwandu and Katsina after it, the Sheikhdom of Borno was occupied without resistance from its erstwhile rulers. This lack of resistance too can be explained in terms of the internal situation in Borno and her external relations during the previous decade. In fact the situation in Borno was exceptionally complex and peculiar, much more than the situation in any of the emirates of the Sokoto Caliphate. This is because the indigenous rulers of Borno, the El-Kanemi dynasty, which had effectively ruled it from c. 1810 to c. 1893, and which alone at the time of the British invasion was in a position to give Borno an organized leadership, had been forcibly evicted in 1893 and kept out of power and in dispersal and destitution up to 1901 by Rabeh, who, though a Muslim and an African, was himself a foreign invader in Borno.[214]

Thus, to understand the lack of resistance by the "traditional" leadership of Borno to British occupation, a summary of events from the ouster of the El-Kanemi dynasty up to the coming of the British occupying force in March 1902 is necessary.[215] In this regard it should be pointed out that after the execution of Shehu Kiari by Rabeh at Gashagar in the summer of 1894, members of the El-Kanemi dynasty dispersed in all directions in groups and bunches. A group went to Damagaram, some to Kanem, others to Kano, a number to Mandara, while others went into hiding inside metropolitan Borno itself.[216] In fact as many as twenty-three members of this dynasty, including two later Shehus, Abubakar Garbai and Umar Sanda Kiarimi, accepted an invitation which Rabeh sent out to all the members of the dynasty to come and live with him in Dikwa.[217]

It would seem that the group that took refuge in Damagaram was the largest and the most important of all these groups, for it was its leader, Umar Sanda Ibn Ibrahim alias Sanda Kura, that the other princes recognized as Shehu when the French overthrew the Rabeh regime in 1900 to 1901.[218] In fact, by the time the French came into contact with any of the Borno princes, their various groups had already started to regroup, an indication that the liberation of Borno from the yoke of Rabeh was more than a task that the French performed on behalf of a passive Borno populace. Thus it was at Begra rather than at Zinder that the Foureau-Lamy expedition, which arrived at Zinder in November 1899 and left in January 1900, overtook Umar Sanda Kura and the other princes that had taken refuge at Zinder.[219]

Indeed, as early as February 1898, the Royal Niger Company had reported Umar Sanda and about 670 of his followers to be living on the border between Damagaram and Kano, soliciting for the Company's assistance against Rabeh.[220] The British, who were busy trying to secure an alliance with Rabeh, ignored these solicitations.[221] From all indications Umar Sanda never went back to Zinder after 1898, for if he had done so and had witnessed either the killing of Cazemajou by the Sultan of Damagaram or had participated in Damagaram's battle against the Joalland expedition, during which the Sultan was himself killed, the French would not have accepted his offer of alliance against Rabeh as they did.[222] Similarly, by the time the French met the princes, at least some among the twenty-three who had gone to live with Rabeh, including its most important figure, Abubakar Garbai Ibn Ibrahim, had already defected from Dikwa and linked up with Umar Sanda's group.[223]

When the Foureau-Lamy expedition overtook the Borno princes at Begra, Umar Sanda asked for their recognition of him rather than Rabeh as the ruler of Borno. So widespread and deeply felt was the respect in which Umar Sanda was held by the Borno aristocracy and gentry that the expedition later on decided it would be a good bargain on their part to give him the recognition he sought from them.[224] Thus, according to Foureau, all the local dignitaries in the vicinity of Begra came to welcome the French expedition, bringing foodstuff for its members and expressing the hope that the expedition would help the people of Borno lift the yoke imposed on them by Rabeh.[225] To demonstrate their recognition of Umar Sanda as their leader, the Bornoans formally installed him as the Shehu of Borno on 14 January 1900 in front of the expedition and a huge and jubilant crowd.[226]

Earlier on the French expedition under Captain Joalland, which occupied Zinder in July 1899, had preceded the Foureau-Lamy expedition along more or less the same route, while in March 1900 a third French expedition under the overall leader of the French expeditions, Colonel Gentil, left the Congo on its way to Kanem, using the River Shari.[227] By April, all the three expeditions had arrived in Kanem.[228] It was only after his arrival in Kanem that Gentil realized that Dikwa was in "German" rather than "French" Borno and that the French were bound by "international" convention not to enter there.[229] It was at this point that the availability of Shehu Umar Sanda acquired an international as opposed to a purely local importance for the French. Thus to give their invasion of "German" territory a legal basis, Gentil got Gwarang, the Sultan of Baghirmi, to write Shehu Umar a formal letter of protest against Rabeh's aggression in

Baghirmi and to ask the Shehu to take measures to restrain Rabeh. The Shehu, doubtless acting on French prompting, replied Gwarang that his protest was legitimate, but that he himself did not have sufficient forces to deal with Rabeh. He, therefore, authorized Gwarang and his "allies," the French, to enter Borno territory and join him in defeating their common enemy.[230] So, armed with this legitimate invitation from the erstwhile ruler of Borno, the French entered the "German" section of Borno, and with the assistance of Umar Sanda Kura and Gwarang, defeated and killed Rabeh on 22 April 1900 at Kusseri.[231]

At the time when Rabeh was killed, his son, Fadl-Allah, was at Logone. On learning of his father's death, Fadl-Allah retreated to Dikwa, where he collected his father's family, and all the family's property that he could carry with him.[232] Together with a force of 5,000 he retreated further south with the French in pursuit. When the French pursuit ceased, he stopped at Kopchi and then moved on to the vicinity of Mubi in the Emirate of Fombina where he rested for sometime before moving on to Kilba, from where he dispatched a messenger to Hewby, the British "Resident" at Ibi asking for British recognition of him as the ruler of Borno.[233]

Meanwhile Shehu Umar Sanda Kura had installed himself at Dikwa. The French, pretending that in helping to defeat Rabeh they were merely serving the Shehu rather than helping to secure themselves in Kanem and Baghirmi, demanded a fee of 30,000 Maria Theresa dollars from him.[234] The Shehu, either out of genuine gratitude to the French in helping him to defeat the foreigner that had humiliated and dispersed his family, or because he felt he could not successfully resist the French demand, dispatched his agents to all parts of Borno to collect the sum from the peasantry.[235] Then the French went further and demanded that the Shehu allow them to drive away all the Shuwa Arabs living west of Lake Chad into Kanem.[236] At this time, it seems Umar Sanda was very bitter against the Shuwa, the bulk of whom had defected to Rabeh on the advent of the latter in 1893 and even now reserved their allegiance, not to the Shehu but to Fadl-Allah.[237] However, despite his bitterness towards the Shuwa, the Shehu knew, as doubtless did the French, that the Shuwa were the owners of an enormous wealth in the form of cattle and sheep. Hence the Shehu rightly refused to accede to this French demand. The French, on their part, withdrew their "recognition" from the Shehu, and transferred it to his more pliable younger brother Abubakar Garbai who, as it turned out, was ready to supplant his senior brother. To facilitate Abubakar Garbai's security in the office of Shehu, the French deported Umar Sanda Kura to the Congo in October 1900.[238]

Having helped Abubakar Garbai to replace his brother as the Shehu of Borno, the French withdrew their forces from Dikwa, leaving behind only one officer, Lieutenant Robillot, to collect their fee from Abubakar Garbai.[239] This fee was increased by an additional $50,000,[240] the addition possibly being intended as a fee from Abubakar Garbai, for the help the French gave him to supplant his brother; but there is no evidence that Abubakar Garbai had also accepted the earlier French demand that they should be authorized to drive the Shuwa to Kanem.

In the meantime Fadl-Allah's request for British recognition had met with favourable consideration from Hewby and Wallace. Accordingly, a British Officer, Major McClintock, was sent with an escort of half a company of troops to interview him.[241] Major McClintock visited Fadl-Allah at Birguma, two days' march north-east of Gujba. This was between May and July 1901. The Major was highly impressed by Fadl-Allah and on his return to Lokoja, he recommended that the British should without delay recognize Fadl-Allah as the ruler of "British Bornu".[242] But Lugard had gone to Britain on leave and Wallace, who was acting for him, did not feel competent to take that step. [243]

Fadl-Allah was not destined to live long enough to receive formal recognition from the British. For, emboldened by McClintock's visit to him and French withdrawal from Dikwa, he sent a force under one of his lieutenants to go and recapture Dikwa from Abubakar Garbai.[244] The latter fled before this force could arrive but was pursued to near Kusseri, by now renamed "Fort Foureau" by the French. Abubakar Garbai appealed to the French to come to his aid. The French, no doubt prompted both by the desire to earn another fee from Abubakar Garbai, and by the realization that while Fadl-Allah still had military capacity they themselves were not secure in Kanem, accepted Abubakar Garbai's invitation. With troops mainly supplied by Abubakar Garbai himself, they first defeated the detachment that ousted Abubakar Garbai from Dikwa and then marched further west to Gujba where they fought and killed Fadl-Allah on August 23, 1901.[245]

Significant enough, the retreating French found their path out of Borno blocked by some Shuwa Arab clans and they suffered two "disasters"[246] with the loss of one officer in the hands of the Shuwa at Uda Taib.[247] When the French finally got reinforcements from Fort Foureau in December 1901, they avenged themselves on the Shuwa, killing many and forcing others with no apparent sanction from Abubakar Garbai, together with their herds and flocks, into Kanem.[248]

Meanwhile, Abubakar Garbai had left a garrison under the *Digma*, Mammadu, at Gujba which, prior to 1893, had been a border post, and had himself returned to Dikwa, where he settled together with a French Officer, Captain Dangville and a French force of thirty-two men. He had sent back his agents to collect the French fee of $80,000 from the peasantry.[249]

This was the situation in Borno when Lugard returned from leave. Naturally, he was much angered at the fact that Fadl-Allah, after receiving a friendly visit from a British Officer, was destroyed by the French, and of all places on "British" territory.[250] He regarded this French act and the circumstances that surrounded it as an insult upon British dignity. Hence, at the same time as reporting the event to the Colonial Office and requesting them to take up the matter with the French Government, he hastened the sending out of the so-called "Lower Bornu Expedition."[251] It was this same expedition that also occupied Bauchi and Gombe.[252] As far as Borno was concerned, the pertinent portions of his instructions to the expedition were as follows:

1. To march to Gujba (via Bauchi) and locate a garrison in each of these places and so restore British prestige which must have received a severe blow owing to the reported incursion of the French into this Protectorate and their defeat of Fadl-Allah after he had been recognized by this Government in a friendly manner.

2. To report the action of the French when in British territory, whether they appointed any chiefs.

3. To ascertain what has become of the remnants of Fadl-Allah's force and what can be done with them if in British territory. They might perhaps be located near the garrison at Bauchi.

4. "Proceeding from Bauchi... collect all possible information regarding the best place where to locate the garrison and to form the capital of Lower Bornu Province... The primary object is to be in close touch with the most powerful local chief. If you find yourself compelled to appoint a chief you will do so on the conditions of the letter of appointment."

5. "You may find it necessary ... to break the power of Mallam Jiberella or you may find that he is a useful man to recognize as a sub-chief or even as a principal chief in Lower Bornu."

From numbers two and three of these instructions, it looks as if Lugard was not aware of the existence of Abubakar Garbai as Shehu at Dikwa. In fact, Lugard was fully aware of the Shehu's existence.[253] Hence, what we can infer from the way he ignored him is that either he thought that the Shehu, who was stationed in "German" territory, was not available to the British, or that Lugard was not willing to avail himself of the services of a man who was partly responsible for French incursion into "British" territory.

We should assume that Abubakar Garbai for his part was not aware, as a matter of definite information, of the instructions that Lugard gave the expedition concerning Borno, and how these instructions did not take his existence into account. However, Abubakar Garbai had known about Major McClintock's visit to Fadl-Allah at Birguma, as well as the implications of the visit for his own position. Indeed, he had in fact sent a letter to the Major asking that the British recognize him rather than Fadl-Allah, as the ruler of British Borno, but his emissary arrived to find that McClintock had already left Birguma.[254]

Hence, in spite of the destruction of Fadl-Allah, the question of the possibility of Abubakar Garbai resisting the British should be ruled out. For one thing, the fact that the French had found him more amenable than his brother, Umar Sanda Kura, rules him out as the patriotic type of an African ruler. For another, it is simply impossible that Abubakar Garbai had any illusions about the capacity of the rulers of Borno, of whom he was by 1902 the head, to organize a military resistance against the British. Thus, Abubakar Garbai was over thirty years of age when Rabeh arrived in 1893, and he was, therefore, a fully mature witness of the ineptitude and treachery that marked and marred Borno's attempts to resist Rabeh.[255] Then, given that he himself lived at Dikwa with Rabeh, he must have been able to appreciate the full extent of Rabeh's military power, which must have struck him at first as being impossible to surpass. Yet he saw how the French, with the aid of the same traditional forces that Rabeh had so utterly humiliated, were able to effect the complete destruction of Rabeh's power within the space of two years. Next he witnessed how the French, whom he knew from his own experience and the experience of Umar Sanda Kura, did not keep promises with weaker parties, and were very eager to respect the agreement they had made with the British concerning the division of Borno. Hence, it is not absolutely necessary to speculate whether Abubakar Garbai knew how the British had, by the time they invaded Borno, broken so many emirates of the Sokoto Caliphate including Bauchi and Yola, about whose *puissance* the house of El-Kanemi needed no lecturing on.[256]

Thus, when the British expedition arrived at Gujba, it was received by Digma Mammadu, who informed Morland that Abubakar Garbai was awaiting his arrival at Maifoni.[257] Already, Morland had learnt at Bauchi that not only did the Shehu living at Dikwa regard himself as the ruler of British Borno; he had also already placed a lieutenant of his at Gujba;[258] and if it was anger with Abubakar Garbai that had caused Lugard to ignore the existence of Abubakar Garbai when instructing his expedition, by the time the expedition arrived at Gujba its commander could see no reason to keep up the anger and overlook him. For one thing, the British did not see much of the remnants of Fadl-Allah's forces. For another, Mallam Jibril, far from coming forward to be "recognized" by the British as the ruler of any place at all, had distinguished himself as the only ruler in the whole of the area between Ibi and Gujba that stood up against Morland's expedition.[259]

Thus, Morland's only worry when he arrived at Maifoni was that he did not find Abubakar Garbai there. Instead, he found a message from him saying that Captain Dangville would not let him leave Dikwa until he had paid up the balance of the French fee which, at that point, stood at $65,000.[260] Accordingly Morland sent to Dikwa Captain Murrough, who spoke some French, to secure the release of Abubakar Garbai and to offer him a formal invitation to "come over" and be the Shehu of "British" Borno.[261] Once Captain Murrough arrived at Dikwa, Dangville did not hesitate for long before allowing Abubakar Garbai to go and meet Morland. As we have already seen, the French knew quite well that Dikwa was in "German" rather than "French" territory. Hence, Dangville knew that even if he refused to allow Abubakar Garbai to cross over into British Borno, the Shehu was in the end going to serve another European power and not the French. But to make sure the Shehu would pay up the balance of his "debt" to the French, Dangville made him leave most of his entourage and property behind. Abubakar Garbai left these under the care of another Umar Sanda, a brother of the late Shehu Kiari of Gashagar fame.[262]

The Shehu left for Maifoni with 300 horsemen and 200 foot soldiers, an indication of the extent of his wealth and power at that point.[263] There is little doubt that Abubakar Garbai left Dikwa with no intention of returning. But Dangville was somehow convinced that he would come back, possibly on account of the fact that the Shehu had left most of his property behind; and much to the indignation of the French captain, Abubakar Garbai never returned to Dikwa, either to pay up the balance of his "debt" to the French or to collect his followers and property. Instead, it was Captain Murrough that Morland sent back to collect these for the Shehu[264] and, needless to say, Dangville confiscated some of the property and managed to persuade many of the Shehu's followers to remain at Dikwa. Among those who elected to remain behind were the two Umar Sandas, the brother and the son of Shehu Kiari. The French appointed Umar Sanda, the uncle, as the next Shehu of "German" Borno;[265] and at Maifoni the result of the meeting between Abubakar Garbai and Morland was that Abubakar Garbai accepted British recognition of him as the Shehu of British Borno.

Conclusion

We can conclude this chapter by stating that, the technological superiority of the British apart, conditions in the Sokoto Caliphate favoured British victory over the forces of the Caliphate. Thus, there was the fact that the emirates adopted the same tactic of dealing with their erstwhile enemies – namely of each Emirate undertaking its own defence – against the British who indeed represented an enemy far superior to any the Caliphate had ever faced. Then, there was the fact that in each Emirate there were internal contradictions even among the ruling class, apart from that between the ruling class and the commoner class. Though contradictions had always characterized both the internal and the external relations of the emirates,[266] these contradictions seem to have acquired new dimensions in the last two decades of the nineteenth century leading in at least three emirates, Bauchi, Kano and Muri, to very bitter civil wars among members of the ruling dynasties. Other aspects of these contradictions included disputed successions that did not involve bloodshed, such as at Katagum, Zaria and indeed Sokoto; the alienation of the *ulema* in a number of the emirates, including Yola and the emergence of Mahdist states in at least two emirates, namely, Yola and Gombe; and whereas the authority of the Caliph continued to be upheld throughout the Caliphate, as shown by the continuity of the practice of sending yearly tributes to Sokoto from all the emirates without exception and the paying of yearly and other occasional visits by all Emirs to Sokoto, yet in the event of intra and inter emirate disputes the views of the Caliph were often quietly ignored, as was done, for example, by Umaru, the Emir of Bauchi, during his dispute with the Chief of Gwaram, and by the Emir of Missau, Manga, when he intervened militarily in the dispute between the Emir of Gombe and his Galadima at a time when the Caliph was mediating in the dispute.

Another aspect of the situation in the Caliphate that helped to facilitate British conquest was the existence of threats from external enemies other than the British. In addition to the threat posed by remnants of the regimes that were substantially destroyed by the jihad – such as Argungu and Gobir against Gwandu and Sokoto itself, a multiplicity of such old regimes against Yola, and the Borno regime against all the emirates bordering on Borno – there were also threats from the African adventurer, Rabeh, who had occupied Borno from 1893, the French who tried to carve out portions of Bida and Ilorin, and the Germans who threatened Yola. Finally, it should be borne in mind that the British threat to the Caliphate acquired a local character from the time when, in the 1880s, the Royal Niger Company turned its trading posts at Lokoja and other places on the Niger and the Benue into military bases from which it could mount its attacks on the emirates. While these factors combined to ensure British victory over the emirates, some of the emirates, the first to be invaded, such as Bida, Ilorin, Kontagora, Lapai, Agaye and Yola, offered physical resistance, each with a progressively diminishing hope of defeating them. The later emirates to be invaded, with the exception of Kano and Sokoto, owing to a hopelessness bred by the success of British arms and tactics over the first emirates to be invaded, and partly owing to a realization by large segments of the ruling classes that the British were going to retain their services, chose to submit without a fight.

4. Shehu of Borno, Abubakar Garbai El-Kanemi (1902–1922) in 1906.

2

The Nature of the British Occupation
and Its Immediate Impact

Introduction

This chapter examines the claim that the British conquest of the Sokoto Caliphate and its neighbours was characterized by minimal violence and the absence of large scale destruction of property. Proponents of this view assert that much of the little violence recorded, and the destruction of property occasioned by it, was forced upon the British by troublesome emirs or their truculent subordinates. On the contrary, in the chapter, we will argue that this view is a complete negation of the reality on ground, contradicting the official reports of the British, and especially, reports by commanders of the various military expeditions. The eagerness of the British to use overwhelming military force at the slightest provocation, and even when confronted by a numerically inferior opponent bearing less sophisticated weapons, was overwhelmingly self evident. This, as we will show in the present chapter, was the case during the British invasion of Bida, Kontagora, Wushishi, Ilorin and Lapai, among others. The available evidence shows that the mercenaries under the British did not use violence sparingly, as it is erroneously asserted; rather, they bombarded and set houses on fire even after subduing the anti-colonial resistance. Such was, for example, the case with the occupation of Yola on 1 September 1901, which we will attempt to show in greater detail. The same was the case, as we shall equally demonstrate, with the battle of Bormi when the town was first surrounded, and later, stormed by the British on 27 July 1903, killing the Caliph and 600 people, and burning the town completely in the process.

Furthermore, we shall argue in the latter part of the chapter that, apart from the emirates where the British met active resistance, even in emirates where there was little or no physical resistance, as in Bauchi, the British tried to provoke the people into violence through bellicosity. In addition, we shall attempt to show that the British military expeditions also visited unprecedented violence upon the less powerful non-Muslim groups outside the emirates, particularly in Adamawa, Bauchi and Nassarawa Province, subjecting the people to bloodshed, arson and looting in order to terrorize them into complete submission. We shall also draw attention to the fact that apart from the officially sanctioned violence of the British, there was the unofficial violence by mercenaries of the West African Frontier Force, perpetrated alone or in the presence of British officers, as reported in Adamawa, Sokoto and Zaria Province, among others. Similarly, we shall highlight the role played by criminal elements who, taking advantage of the general disorder occasioned by the British invasion, engaged in acts of brigandage and lawlessness in Ilorin, Sokoto, Bauchi, Yola and the Kano-Zaria boarder areas.

We shall examine another important dimension of the British occupation that is often over looked which we shall examine. This has to do with the widespread emotional distress suffered by the people in the Caliphate after the violent conquest, manifesting itself in mass emigration that resulted in demographic change over a large area. This, as we will argue, was caused by a multitude of factors and made worse by the wholesale deposition of emirs and chiefs, affecting not only those deposed but also a multitude of their followers in diverse ways. Thereafter, we shall proceed to examine the measures taken by the British to consolidate their hegemonic control through a relentless programme of confiscating weapons from the emirs, and through boundary adjustments, desired by the colonizers but destructive of pre-existing political identities. The consequences of all these on relations between communities on either side of the new boundaries will also be examined. We shall finally conclude the chapter with an account on the actual reasons behind the abolition of the office of the Sarkin Musulmi by the British, prescribing limits on the powers of the Sultan and erection of tariff barriers between the conquered emirates.

The Conquest of Bida and Ilorin

There is a tendency among writers on the subject, often only implicitly, to represent the British occupation of the Sokoto Caliphate as a very speedy and more or less bloodless and indeed non-violent process during which the British went out of their way to avoid using force and to spare life and property.[1] However, an examination of even a few episodes in that process should suffice to show that the occupation involved copious violence, bloodshed and destruction.[2] Thus, to start with, it should be emphasized that during its invasion of Bida in January 1897, the Royal Niger Company deployed a force consisting of 32 European officers and non-commissioned officers (NCOs), and 507 mercenaries with one 12-pounder and one 9-pounder whitworth guns, twelve 9-pounder guns, five 7-pounder mountain guns, five .45 Maxim automatic machine guns, Snider rifles for all the troops "plus ample stores of ammunition."[3] This was the force the British mobilized against a Nupe force estimated at 30,000 foot and 1,000 mounted but armed with "Snider and Remington rifles, flintlocks, spears and swords." Far from using this force sparingly and with caution, the Company went out of its way to impress its military capacity on the rulers and people of the emirate. Thus, when these troops arrived Bida on January 27, they heavily shelled the town from morning until 4 pm, and when they entered the town after the resistance of the defenders had been broken, the British fired houses with incendiary rockets.[4] In the process the British, who suffered a casualty of only one officer and one mercenary killed, and nine wounded, inflicted a casualty of 600 to 1,000 killed and wounded on the defenders.[5]

Similarly, the Company's aggression against Ilorin in February of the same year, using the same force as it had used against Bida, was not a simple affair by any stretch of the imagination. Thus, during this battle, which lasted two days, namely February 15 and 16, Ilorin town was shelled and partially burnt down and the defenders, who numbered 8,000–10,000 including 800 mounted, suffered a very heavy casualty, the cavalry alone losing 200 killed.[6]

The Occupation of Agaye and Lapai

Even for the occupation of the small emirates of Agaye and Lapai in June 1898, an exercise which the commander of the occupying forces, Lieutenant Colonel. T.D. Pilcher, merely referred to as "Field Operation," the British mustered a force consisting of 31 European Officers and NCOs, 410 mercenaries, 450 carriers, three 7-pounder guns with 20 rounds per gun, and 4 Maxim guns with 1,000 rounds per gun, apart from rifles for the troops.[7] As for any assumed "restraint" of the force, a summary of its own account of its conduct given in Pilcher's report is a sufficient refutation. Thus the force, which left Lokoja on June 8, arrived at Barro on June 14. Here, it learnt from its spies that the combined forces of Agaye, Lapai and Bida were camped at Galoo, a day's journey from Barro. Accordingly, Pilcher took 22 European officers and NCOs, 291 mercenaries, each with 100 rounds; two 7-pounder guns with 20 rounds per gun, 12 rockets, and 3 Maxims with 1,000 rounds per Maxim. He left the remainder of the force at Barro as a "precaution." The desire of the

British was to surprise the forces of the emirates. They achieved this as they were not sighted by the latter's scouts until 4:30 pm when they were only 30 minutes march away from the latter's camp, outside the walls of Galoo.

The British formed a square on approaching this camp and continued their march in that formation. They were within only a few hundred yards of the camp when they attacked it with rifles, Maxim guns and rockets. The forces of the emirates, after a few minutes stand, found the barrage too overwhelming. They therefore fled, leaving their dead and wounded behind.

To teach the "natives" a memorable lesson, the British "systematically burnt" all villages in the vicinity of Galoo as well as the town itself, before they resumed their pursuit of the remnant of the defenders' forces. Having adopted a scorched earth policy in reverse, the British did not even have to leave a small garrison behind. Hence "the whole force" marched to Sanfada, 14 miles away from Galoo and 5 miles from Lapai, Pilcher conveniently "believing" the Emir of Lapai was going to defend his capital "fiercely."

At Sanfada, the Colonel gave his troops an extended rest of one week, a fact which shows that the initiative in the war was entirely in British hands. On June 21, the British got ready to attack Lapai. On approaching the town the force formed the usual square, and advanced to within a very short distance of the town. There, the British saw what the Colonel estimated to be only 60 horsemen taking up position outside the walls of the town, and yet they fired 200 rounds from a Maxim gun at them. The defenders, who allegedly escaped being hit, fled the field. Next, the British shelled the town and then proceeded to occupy it, understandably "without resistance." Yet in spite of the absence of resistance, the town as well as "several villages" in its neighbourhood were burnt before "the whole force" once again moved on, this time for Badegi, some 9 miles away.

Pilcher's alleged object was to reach Badegi before daybreak, surround it and capture the Emir of Lapai, "who was believed to be concealed there." For this purpose of springing a surprise on Badegi and its supposed guest, an advanced party under a Lieutenant Carrol had been dispatched from Lapai much earlier ahead of the rest of the force, which was still going round burning villages near Lapai. However, owing to "bad guides," the advance party was unable to reach Badegi before daybreak. Hence, Badegi's inhabitants were able to evacuate the town before the arrival of the British. Thus, the latter found Badegi empty, but nevertheless treated it in the same fashion that they had treated earlier towns and villages, before moving on to Agaye, 17 miles further on. Agaye was still inhabited when the British arrived, their "arrival being a partial surprise." So the Colonel sent "an order" to the Emir "to come out and confer." Realizing that the

Emir would sooner evacuate the town than "come out and confer," the British decided not to allow a peaceful evacuation. Hence at "the request of Mr. Drew," the political officer accompanying the force, "few rounds from the 7-pounder gun and one rocket" were fired at the inhabitants while they "were flocking out" of their town. At 5 pm the British entered the town and a company proceeded to the Emir's palace, which was found unoccupied. Because the Emir had earlier on not come out to meet the British "as was expected," "foraging parties" were sent out and "some horses, sheep and corn were brought in for the benefit of the troops." For some obscure reasons, Agaye, unlike Lapai before it, merited a garrison. Hence Colonel Pilcher left behind 50 men and one Maxim gun under a Lieutenant Skinner to garrison the town "at the request of Mr. Drew;" and having ousted the Emirs of Lapai and Agaye, as well as looting and burning their capitals and the villages surrounding them, the main body of the British force returned to base at Lokoja.

The Occupation of Kontagora and Bida

Nor did the British send a small or disciplined force to occupy the emirates of Kontagora and Bida which fell in January and February 1901 respectively.[8] On the contrary, the British force that effected the conquest of these two emirates consisted of 14 European officers and NCOs, 433 native mercenaries, with 275 mm and 3 Maxims guns, under the command of Colonel Kemball, at that time Acting commandant of the West African Frontier Force (WAFF). Certainly, compared to the force sent against Agaye and Lapai, and especially bearing in mind the fact that Kontagora and Bida were militarily more powerful than Agaye and Lapai, the force sent against Kontagora and Bida was not impressive, especially as concerns the number of European officers and NCOs; but when the relative technological and organizational capacities and competence of the two emirates, on the one hand, and of the British on the other are taken into account, the British force sent against the two emirates was still impressive. This force left Jebba on January 19; an advance party had earlier left and captured the village of Udara, 4 milies north of Kontagora, in order to foil any attempt on the part of the Emir to escape; but the Emir and the inhabitants of Kontagora had evacuated the town before the arrival of the party. Hence, it was a "completely deserted" Kontagora that the British captured. Yet they burnt sections of the town.

As for the fugitive inhabitants of the town, as soon as Kemball arrived Kontagora, he sent a party under a Captain Graham in pursuit. The latter, on sighting some fugitives, "brought the guns into action," and he inflicted a casualty of "probably … 50 killed." This party, the British later learnt, did not include the Emir, who was further ahead, reportedly heading towards Zaria. Hence, another party was detailed specifically to pursue the Emir. The latter party, after marching for 4 days without catching up with the Emir, returned to Kontagora.

Meanwhile Lugard himself had moved to Wuya, about 8 miles away from Bida together with "an escort" of 100 mercenaries, under the command of Captain Cochrane. Hence, after leaving a garrison at Kontagora, Kemball moved on to Wuya to join Lugard. Together they moved on to Bida, which they reached after a 3-hour march. As we saw in the last chapter, the British had already managed to engineer a division within the ranks of the Bida aristocracy and had secured the neutrality of a section of the town under the leadership of the Makun.[9] As a result of this division the British did not expect a battle. Yet, they made sure that they arrived at the town in an impressive array. Hence "the whole force, including the heavy guns, arrived in compact formation," though allegedly "no shot was fired" before the town was entered.

Even if we accept the last claim,[10] the fact still remains that the final occupation of Bida in February 1901 was not an isolated event but the culmination of a long drawn out military confrontation between the British and the Emir, going back to 1897 when the British temporarily succeeded in ousting him,[11] a confrontation which the British had stepped up since July 1900.[12] For the purpose of stepping up the level of this confrontation, the British had established a garrison at Wushishi after a severe battle during which the British burnt half of the town and expelled the chief, a nephew of the Emir of Kontagora.[13] From July 1900 to January 1901, the British tried to break down the combined resistance of the Emirs of Kontagora, Bida and the fugitive chief of Wushishi. To overcome the stalemate between them and the two Emirs, the British had in July reinforced the Wushishi garrison and posted a new commander, one Major O'Neill, with the order to "patrol the country and repel raids" which the British had the guts of describing as "more and more aggressive."

By December 1900, Major O'Neill had tipped the balance in favour of the British and mounted an offensive against the two emirates, Bida in particular. In the process, his garrison inflicted repeated and heavy casualties on Bida Emirate. Thus, for example, on December 14, a detachment under a Sergeant Edwards "defeated with heavy loss a force estimated at 100 horse and 700 foot." On December 15 and 16, a detachment under O'Neill himself attacked and defeated a Bida force which "lost 50 killed at least." On the night of December 17, O'Neill again "marched on the hostile forces … and surprised them at dawn." He estimated "the enemy at 500 horse and 1,000 foot" and inflicted on them a casualty of "at least 200." By this time, the garrison had already burnt all the villages around Wushishi, occupied a farm belonging to the Emir of Bida, and reduced the whole population between Wushishi and Bida to "living in great fear."[14] Then, on December 18, O'Neill advanced towards Bida "with 13 mounted and 25 dismounted men, driving parties of the enemy before him." These he "pursued up to the walls of Bida, and actually entered the town with a handful of men and endeavoured to seize the Emir with his own hand."[15] After this act of bravado, even Lugard could not help concluding that O'Neill was mentally unhinged. Hence, he forced O'Neill to take "his accumulated leave" and sent him home to Britain.[16]

In the light of these facts, Lugard's emphasis on the "fact" that Bida was taken bloodlessly in February 1901 becomes very much of a mockery of reality and an abuse of language.

The Occupation of Yola

Yet in 1901 the British attacked and occupied Yola.[17] For this purpose they deployed a force of 22 European officers and NCOs and 365 mercenaries, 275-mm guns and 4 Maxims, under Colonel T.N.L. Morland, the substantive commandant of the WAFF. This force arrived at Yola on September 1 in two steam boats. The bigger of the two boats was deemed too big to leave the main river and pass through the flood water connecting Lake Njuwa near the town to the main river five miles away at that time of the year. Hence this ship, together with 25 men under a Lieutenant, was left at the river with the instruction "to seize all canoes … and prevent any of the enemies from crossing the river" to Girei, a *ribat* fifteen miles north of Yola. The remainder of the invading force was carried in the second ship and in another one "lent" to Morland by the agent of the Niger Company at Yola. These two steamers were piloted up to within half a mile of the town and anchored near a baobab tree locally known as Bokki Hampeto. This was at 10 am of September 2.

After forming up the troops in the usual square formation, Morland sent "a trustworthy messenger"[18] with a letter "to the Emir containing the terms" of the British. The "trustworthy messenger" returned to Morland within three minutes and reported that the Emir had refused to receive the letter and had turned him out. This caused Morland to move his troops nearer the town before sending the messenger back to the Emir with the threat that if the Emir "again refused" to open the letter, he would "take steps to compel him to do so."

Before the messenger returned from this second errand, people "on horse and foot" had started to come out of the town and gather in front of the British square. When the messenger returned, it was with basically the same report as before, namely, that the Emir still refused to receive the letter and was additionally warning the British that if they did not at once re-embark, he would push them into the water. Meanwhile "horse and foot" continued to "stream out of town." Morland, like a man working on some lifeless objects rather than about to kill human beings, calculated that it would in fact be to the advantage of the British to let the people of Yola attack the British in the open. That was much better for the British than fighting the defenders in the narrow streets of the town where British "superior arms would not have full play." Hence, Morland decided to await the attack of the people of Yola, a wait which lasted until "about 1 pm" when, "after much shouting and exhorting from their mallams," the people of Yola "advanced to attack on our front and right." Even then, instead of immediately ordering his men to fire, Morland made a calculated decision to "reserve our fire till the leaders were within 200 yards" before he ordered the Maxims to open fire. "In 10 minutes the attack melted away, some fanatical footmen getting close to the square before they were killed ..."

After repulsing this "attack," the British went over to the offensive. From "900 yards away" on top of Bokki Hampeto, the British forces burst a shell over the Emir's palace. Although "2 shells [were] fired in reply" from the palace, they "fell wide." On entering the gate of the town, the British confirmed what Morland had all the time feared, namely, that Yola had not yet benefitted from British ideas about town planning. Hence his complaint that "the streets were narrow and winding" and the British "could only advance on a narrow front." Besides, though the British met with "little resistance" till "the neighbourhood of the palace was reached," the palace itself and the Friday mosque "near it were strongly held" by "the enemy." Morland himself was wounded, and of all weapons, "by an arrow from the mosque." Further, "the rifled guns of the enemy hidden round a bend of the road, were fired at 30 yards' range blowing off one man's leg and severally wounding several others."

Even after "Major McClintock led a charge and captured the guns" and a Captain Baker "drove" the defenders from the mosque,[19] "the walls of the palace were still obstinately defended." So Morland ordered up "the 2 75-millimetre guns," which were "well served under Lt. Henvey." Understandably, "the close range fire of these guns was too much for the defenders and they began to leave the walls." Next, the British "rushed the gate" of the palace "in a gallant style and in a few moments the whole palace compound was cleared of the enemy."

When the British turned round to count the casualties on their own side and "estimate" those of the defenders, they discovered that Morland and McClintock were "slightly wounded, 2 men killed, 6 dangerously, 8 severely and 23 slightly wounded," while "enemy losses were put at 50 killed and 150 wounded," which, given the admitted ferocity of the resistance, we must regard as an underestimation.[20]

The destruction of life and property caused by the British in Yola on the day of the battle could be excused on the grounds that it was done "in the heat of battle", that is, during actual combat between the two antagonists. In that case it should be added that "early on the morning" of the day following the capture of Yola, which was now completely empty of its inhabitants, "the audience chamber of the palace," which somehow had escaped destruction on the day of the battle, "was blown up," before the British went round the town burning other important-looking houses in what can only be described as a spree of unprovoked vengeance.

Nor did the districts surrounding Yola escape destruction in the hands of the invading British force. Thus, for example, on learning that the Emir, who escaped alive from Yola after the battle of September 2, was somewhere in the vicinity of Gurin, forty miles east of Yola, Acting Commissioner Wallace, who had arrived at Yola on September 3, hastened after the fugitive Emir. He took with him one steam boat, 8 European officers and NCOs including Morland, 150 mercenaries, one 75-millimetre gun and 2 Maxims. After a journey of twenty six hours in the Benue, the Faro and the Heso rivers, the British arrived at Gurin only to be told that the Emir had not been there. Being in doubt as to whether Gurin was in "British" or "German" territory, the British turned back, apparently without any "encounter." Next, the British got another piece of "information," namely, that the Emir was at Ribadu, fourteen miles behind them and clearly within "British" territory.

Hence, while Wallace himself returned straight to Yola to see to the "appointment of another Emir," Morland stopped at Ribadu only to find that the fugitive Emir had not been there either, and that, at any rate, the people of Ribadu would have nothing to do with the British. Instead of proceeding to Yola, Morland spent the night offshore at Ribadu so that he could settle accounts with the inhabitants the following morning. This he did by shelling the town before returning to Yola on the morning of September 7.

The Pursuit of the Sarkin Musulmi and the Battle of Bormi

Another episode in which the violent and destructive nature of the British conquest of the emirates can clearly be seen is their pursuit and final battle with the Sarkin Musulmi, Attahiru, who attempted to undertake a *hijra* after he had lost the battle for Sokoto town. The Sarkin Musulmi left the battle field at Sokoto on 15 March 1903, with the British close on his heels, killing those of his followers that they overtook.[21] In an attempt to head him off, the British made a detour and reached Tureta ahead of him to await and surprise him there. However, the Sarkin Musulmi was warned of this ambush at Rini and hence avoided Tureta.[22]

Having thus missed the Sarkin Musulmi, the British went back to Sokoto where Burdon, the Resident, mistakenly decided that the fugitive Sarkin Musulmi was not worth worrying about.[23] Hence, no other force was sent against the Sarkin Musulmi until three weeks later, by which time Burdon had realized that Attahiru was still a force to reckon with. The force that was sent after the Sarkin Musulmi as a result of this realization was made up of only 50 men with one Maxim; but this was simply because that was all Burdon could spare from the British garrison at Sokoto, so soon after the occupation of that town. This force headed for Gusau where the Sarkin Musulmi was reported to be resting.[24] However, the force arrived Gusau one week too late and, being satisfied that the Sarkin Musulmi was "no longer in Sokoto Province", went back to Sokoto.

It was the Acting Resident at Zaria, Popham Lobb that sent out the next British force to pursue the Sarkin Musulmi. This force too missed the Sarkin Musulmi, but it overtook fifty Zaria horsemen who were trying to join him. It engaged these and inflicted "a considerable loss on them" before returning to Zaria.[25] Then Featherstone Cargill in Kano sent a force of sixty mounted troops to head off the Sarkin Musulmi, by now passing through Kano Province and drawing a large following. This force was instructed either "to capture or kill" the Sarkin Musulmi, but it never overtook him. However, it kept up the pursuit up to Missau and fought "6 engagements" against parties of Kano people trying to join the Sarkin Musulmi. In two of these engagements alone, the British killed 35 people.[26]

Nor did the British detachment from Kano return from Missau, which was the last emirate in Kano Province. Instead, it waited for another force that had been sent out from Bauchi by Resident Temple. This latter consisted of two British officers, seventy mercenaries and one Maxim. It made the junction with the detachment from Kano at Missau on June 9. The combined British force then marched on after the Sarkin Musulmi, killing off stragglers it overtook until it reached the town of Bormi in the Emirate of Gombe on June 13.[27] This town was supposed to have fallen to the British in February 1902, when a British force had ousted its Mahdist ruler, Mallam Jibril Gaini, and appointed another ruler, Mallam Musa, who was wrongly assumed to have accepted British overlordship.[28] Yet, on this occasion too, the British attacked Bormi when Mallam Musa refused to answer their summons. This attack resulted in a "heavy loss" for the "enemy" and among those killed was Mallam Musa himself. But a British attempt "to enter the town was checked by heavy arrow fire."[29] After repeated British attempts were repulsed in this way, the invading British decided to withdraw to Bauchi lest the "enemy" mount a successful counter-offensive and finish them off. Already the British had sustained a casualty of two killed and fifty six slightly wounded while the defenders of Bormi had a casualty of "at least 150 killed" who were "lying in heaps in front of the gate."[30]

Meanwhile Captain Hamilton Browne, the British commander at Gujba in Borno, had received news that the Sarkin Musulmi had reached Bima near Gwoni, on the left bank of the Gongola River, some 30 miles west of Gujba which the Sarkin Musulmi had in fact by-passed only by "a few miles."[31] The "same night" that Hamilton Browne received this news, he left Gujba with one other officer, 51 mercenaries and one Maxim. This was on May 12, but because the force had to fight its way through defiant villages that lay on its way, it did not reach Gwoni until May 17.[32] On this date at 9 am, the British sighted the Sarkin Musulmi's camp close to the river. His people "were completely taken by surprise." The British opened Maxim and rifle fire "at once" and the Sarkin Musulmi's party fled across the Gongola to the west, leaving behind their "entire baggage, 63 guns, a quantity of powder, many camels, horses and donkeys," and, we should assume, a number of dead. The Sarkin Musulmi went back in the direction of Bormi and at the same time wrote to Temple at Bauchi telling him that "he had no wish to fight [and that] all he asked for was to be allowed to travel in peace." To this Temple replied "demanding an unconditional surrender."[33]

Meanwhile, Hamilton Browne, having learnt of the check and retreat of the British from Bormi, did not dare to pursue the Sarkin Musulmi to that place. Instead, he returned to Gujba leaving a patrol on the left bank of the Gongola "to watch the enemy." At about the same time, Major Barlow had left Zaria on May 8 together with 2 other British officers and 60 mercenaries, all mounted.[34] He reached Gombe on May 23 and on 26 received news both of the British repulse from Bormi and of the Sarkin Musulmi's presence in the latter town. Possibly with the aim of gaining the glory of succeeding where others had failed, Barlow "decided to push on to the vicinity of that place so as to be in a position to capture" the Sarkin Musulmi "if he attempted to leave it."[35]

On May 31, Barlow reached Ashaka on the Gongola River, two miles east of Bormi, and occupied it with a heavy casualty for the defenders. It was here that the patrol which had been left behind by Hamilton Browne joined him on the following day. With this combined force, Barlow "proceeded to reconnoiter the town of Bormi without attempting to force an entrance." However, he "succeeded in drawing the enemy into the open and killed a large number of them." Another attempt to draw the "enemy" out on June 4 failed, but from the 4th to the 18th Barlow "continued to harass the Burmi people by cutting off their cattle and food supplies," sent in from Bauchi. This blockade sufficiently annoyed the defenders of Bormi for them to send some men on the May 13 to attack the besieging British. This attack was, after a long battle, repulsed with 18 of the "enemy" killed.[36]

In the meantime, news of the earlier British repulse from Bormi was received at Zungeru on June 6.[37] Consequently, an additional force of two British officers, half a company of mercenaries and a large supply of ammunition was ordered to march from Zaria to Bauchi. Another force of 9 European officers, 165 mercenaries with one 75-millimetre gun under Major Marsh was sent from Lokoja, leaving on June 13, in a steamer and reaching Bauchi on July 12. But even before the arrival of this force at Bauchi, another force of 2 European officers and 50 mercenaries under Captain Sword left Bauchi for Bormi arriving there on June 19.[38] The same day, Hamilton Browne, with 30 mercenaries and one Maxim, arrived at Bormi from Gujba. The new arrivals brought British troops at Bormi to a total strength "of 7 officers, 180 men." This force attempted to storm the town on June 22, but was repulsed with a casualty of 4 people "slightly wounded."[39]

On June 27, the reinforcement from Bauchi arrived, bringing the force up to 270 "Rank and File." The new arrivals brought an order from Wallace that no more attacks were to be made on Bormi until the other reinforcements had arrived. Nonetheless, on June 30, Barlow proceeded with 130 mercenaries and a Maxim "to visit" various villages in the vicinity of Bormi.[40] He was accompanied by Resident Temple. During this "visit," the British sacked and burnt down a town called Birri, in the process of which they themselves sustained a casualty of two men severely wounded and fifteen others, including 2 European officers slightly wounded, an indication that the defenders must have suffered very heavy casualties indeed. In the meantime, the rest of the force besieging Bormi had to engage "a party of 200" of the defenders "who came out and attacked it while it was cutting off food supplies." Fifty of the defenders were killed, and the British lost one horse killed and several mercenaries wounded.[41]

Finally, on July 24, the awaited reinforcements, together with Barlow's party, which they met at Nafada, arrived at Bormi, and on July 27 the attack on the town started at 11:30 am.[42] During this battle, we are told, "the [Maxim] guns did excellent execution" and at least "over 600 of the enemy," including the Sarkin Musulmi "were killed and the town burnt," a very eloquent and grim reply to the theory of British restraint.

The Occupation of Bauchi[43]

In case there is some doubt that the British resorted to violence, killing, arson and looting only where they met with physical resistance, it should be pointed out that even where British occupation was "peaceful" it was the people of the places concerned that absolutely refused to accept a battle. A good example of a place where the British did their utmost to provoke the people into a fight but the people refused to be so provoked, and hence made British occupation "peaceful," was Bauchi in February 1902.[44]

The British force which occupied Bauchi was accompanied by Acting High Commissioner Wallace and consisted of two Colonels, Morland and Beddoes, seventeen other European officers, and 1,400 mercenaries, of whom 900 were carriers, relatively a very large force indeed. This force disembarked at Ibi on the Benue on January 31 and made the overland journey via Dul, "a Fulani town" some 50 miles south of Bauchi. From there it moved on to Kanna, a "pagan village" under Bauchi, all the time collecting intelligence of a type that convinced the British of the inevitability of a battle with Bauchi. Thus, for example, they allegedly "learnt" at Kanna that the Emir of Bauchi "had formed a camp outside but close to the town of Bauchi and that he had called up his people to assist him to repel our advance." As if to stiffen the attitude of the Emir, Wallace sent a threatening letter to him from Dul. It reads:

> a few months ago I wrote to you from Ibi advising you to send your representative to salute the Governor, to that letter you have not deigned to reply, so I am coming in person to see to the matter. If you and the Bauchi [people] want war, we are prepared, if peace then you should send one of your chiefs, a man of wisdom, to meet me on the way. I have also to inform you that on reaching Bauchi we shall take charge of the province and leave white men and soldiers to keep order and guard it from enemies, same as we have done with the provinces of Nupe, Muri, Ilorin, Kontagora and Yola.

On receiving this letter, the Emir sent a representative to meet the British, but before the representative met them, Morland had dispatched yet another letter to the Emir from Katagum, 19 miles from Bauchi. This second letter preempted the possibility of negotiations between the British and the Emir, leaving the Emir only two options, namely to surrender and abdicate or to fight. The contents of the letter were summarized by Wallace thus:

> That having taken no notice of my previous letters, hearing from many sources that he was oppressing his people, that he had refused to allow Resident Cargill to approach Bauchi, that he had treacherously murdered the chief of Gurum and afterwards massacred the people, he was unsuited to rule over his people so that on taking over Bauchi we would depose him and install a new Emir, the choice of the people.

It was after they had dispatched this letter that the British met the Barayan Bauchi, Bello, nine miles from the town.[45] According to Wallace himself, the Baraya stated that the Emir and his chiefs had agreed to the terms stated in the first letter which had been read and discussed in the mosque, adding that the people had no intention of fighting the British. The only request which the Baraya made of the British was that they should halt where they were until the Emir could make adequate preparations to receive them "in a fitting manner." Yet Wallace was not mollified by this olive branch. Instead he informed the Baraya of the contents of Morland's second letter of which the Baraya had not heard until then. He "clearly made" the Baraya to understand that "we intend to adhere to what had therein been written." The request to halt was also rejected out of hand. Instead Wallace informed the Baraya that "the force would advance and camp close to Bauchi and would expect that the chiefs would come to discuss matters" with him.

The Baraya correctly refused to reply to this ultimatum one way or the other but promised that that same night a messenger would bring back the reply of the Emir and chiefs regarding the question of deposing the Emir. The messenger did in fact come – with a message which, it seems, was designed to gain time for the people of Bauchi during which to make up their mind in the light of the new ultimatum. The message was that they were willing to do all the British demanded and that they would meet the latter at the gate of the town. Yet, in spite of this extremely conciliatory attitude on the part of the people of Bauchi, the following morning, Colonel Morland's troops "moved up in square to the city wall" only to meet with no opposition and to find the gate, the south gate in fact, open, ready to let them in. Quite needlessly the British "took charge of the gate."

Here they met the emirate's chiefs headed by the Chiroma, Muallayidi. The British reiterated their intention "to depose" the Emir and "install another." The Bauchi chiefs, in a desperate effort to retain the Emir, rather pathetically asked if he "might be allowed to come and salute" the British.[46] To this plea the British contemptuously replied that they did not care whether he came or not, that if the people would bring him a prisoner they would "take him out of the country," but that otherwise they would not "seize him treacherously." Perceiving the futility of trying to plead with the British for the Emir, the chiefs finally just asked to be given until 5 pm that evening during which time they would nominate someone to succeed the Emir whom the British had rejected for them. To this request the British "acceded."

The 5 o'clock meeting drew a much larger assemblage of people than the previous meeting, and many of the Bauchi people turned up armed. Morland took an exception to the presence of these armed men and they had to with- draw from the scene. After that, when Wallace asked the chiefs their choice for a new Emir, the chiefs made a final but half-hearted attempt to retain their actual Emir. Thus, they claimed that they were "quite satisfied and prosperous" under the Emir but that since the British insisted on his removal, their next choice was the Chiroma, Muallayidi. The British accepted this choice because in the patronizing words of Wallace "all the reports we had heard concerning Muhammadu were in praise of him." Wallace then announced that the Chiroma would be installed the following morning "in the square in front of the palace."

In order to salvage some dignity for the erstwhile Emir, the chiefs begged that he should not be deported and undertook to be responsible for his "good behaviour." The British refused to accept even this request, saying that they would not decide until they had "seen him," as if it was he that had refused to come and meet them. Hence, rather than await further insult and indignity, the Emir withdrew from the town at night and "was followed by thousands," a clear testimony that his deposition was not the decision of the people of Bauchi, and that the people preferred a rather erratic Emir to the foreign invaders.

Even after all this, the British would not forego their martial antics. Thus on the morning of February 17 it was "in full force" that they marched to the square. The alleged reason for this show of force was that a report "was being circulated that it was the intention of "the Emir's party" to fight. This time, however, the "reports" came very near to being true, for the bellicose posture and attitude of the British was starting to boomerang. The previous night the town had been evacuated of women, children and the infirm, and as the British marched through the town they "were surprised to find every man and boy armed." But the British easily outmatched the people of Bauchi in willingness to fight. On reaching the square Morland "occupied" it in a manner that was "a revelation" to Wallace, it being done "in less than a minute, all the thoroughfares leading from the square being guarded, and the Maxims and millimetres being trained on the masses of the people." The palace compound was then "seized," searched and found empty, before the British proceeded to "install" the new Emir.

British Violence against Non-Muslim Communities

It might be thought that the British expended so much force and behaved so violently during the occupation of the emirates simply because they felt that unless they so behaved they might fail before the military might of the emirates which, in comparison to the non-Muslim communities that they subordinated, were fairly strong and well-organized. However, it should be pointed out that the British were not less violent and destructive during their occupation of these non-Muslim communities themselves than they were during the occupation of the emirates. If anything they were more violent and more destructive against these communities than they were against the emirates.

A good example of British violence and destructiveness towards the non-Muslim communities on the peripheries of the Sokoto Caliphate can be seen in an "operation" which they undertook in January 1903 against some such communities in what was then known as the "Chukkol Division" of Yola Province on the border between Adamawa and Muri emirates.[47] During these "operations" a force consisting of one major, one British NCO and 78 mercenaries was mobilized, with Lt Crawley as commander while Barclay, Resident Yola Province, himself, acted as political officer. This force arrived at Gengle, about 50 miles west of Yola, on January 21. This village was "quite deserted" when the British arrived, but it seems that the British somehow expected to be welcomed and feted. Hence "as there was no sign of the villagers coming in, the town was burnt and its supplies destroyed." However, no sooner did the British begin to march away than "the enemy begin to crown the hills" to their rear. "So a few rounds were fired from the Maxim" and the British proceeded to other villages without even bothering to "estimate enemy losses."

The people of the next village, Temneh, in all probably having learnt what the British did to Gengle, neither came forward to submit nor waited for the British to arrive and burn down their own village. Instead they started a bush fire in front of the British in order to impede their march while they were evacuating the village. The British were particularly angered by the fact that the fire had been "timed accurately." Predictably, these "visitors" who had burnt Gengle without provocation did as "a consequence" of this act of "provocation" burn Temneh, which they found deserted, and, on top of that, destroyed its supplies. The majority of the villages after Temneh were situated in hills and that fact alone saved them from the fate of their neighbours. The British also found the first village they came across in the plains deserted. Yet, after "supplies for the men were drawn from it," this village too was burnt down. The British commander then sent ahead a messenger into the next village, ordering him to tell the head man to "come and see" him. In fact two headmen with about 30 villagers did come in, but the commander was not at all conciliatory or appreciative – though he thought he was, for their cooperation. He told the villagers that he had "come to punish" them for "murdering and plundering" traders on the Yola–Lau route, but as they had obeyed his summons, their punishment was that each headman "must bring in" by evening "2 head of cattle", 20 sheep or goats, 20 bundles of guinea corn and 6 bows, arrows and spears." He then cautioned them that if they failed to comply with this order "their villages would be burnt and their crops destroyed." To make sure the order was complied with he kept "three of the minor chiefs" as hostages.

In order to get away from the British, the villagers lied, telling them that they would meet the commander's demands and he sent them away. This tryst was made at 9 am, but soon the commander grew impatient. During the course of the day, he claims, he sent three times asking them to bring in the fines and "reassuring" them that the hostages he took would not be hurt, if the fine was paid. To buy time the villagers sent saying that they were collecting the "fine" and would bring it the following morning. Instead of doing so the villagers attacked the British camp at 11.30 pm. Their aim, it seems, was simply to cause enough confusion to enable their imprisoned compatriots escape. This they partially achieved when, during a stampede by the carriers, one of the chiefs and some two "guides," who the British had earlier on abducted elsewhere on their way, escaped. Inevitably, the next morning "the villages in the vicinity of the camp were destroyed as a lesson to the others," before the British proceeded, as late as 1 pm, taking the remaining two chiefs along with them as "guides." On the way, the British came across 25 cattle and captured them without even bothering to find out to whom they belonged.[48] The second day, January 24, the commander sent a colour sergeant with 20 mercenaries to the next village, Kudaku, with orders to destroy it on the alleged ground that its headman had failed to come in and see the British. The colour sergeant burnt down the "entire village" and, in the process killed 12 of the "enemy." The following day the commander himself, with 15 mercenaries, proceeded as a matter of course and "destroyed the villages in the vicinity of Koodakoo." This he did in spite of the fact that "no resistance was met with" during the destruction of the villages.

The same day, the headman of another village, Nanke, was summoned and "ordered to pay a fine of 10 sheep and 10 bundles of guinea corn," allegedly after the commander had "previously explained to him why he was being punished and the reason for the leniency" of the "punishment." This was partly because the commander had "good reason to believe" that the 25 cattle captured the previous day belonged to Nanke. So "purposely" the fine was made "a nominal one." As should be expected, the people of Nanke could perceive neither the "justice" nor the "nominality" of the fine. Hence the chief failed to bring in the fine. This failure met with prompt retribution on the following day, January 26, when a column left for Nanke at 8.20 am under the commander himself. The British found the village deserted, the villagers having retired on to a big hill "which commanded the whole place." Hence it became "necessary" to "clear" this hill before undertaking the inevitable destruction of the village. This clearing was done with a loss of 7 dead to the "enemy." Nanke was then burnt down.

The next group of villages to be "visited" was Danko, Zante, Panna, Labani and Koko. At Danko the villagers were taken by surprise by the sudden appearance of the British. No doubt aware of what had befallen the other villages, the villagers "immediately began to drive their cattle away." But the logic of British colonialism was not to be cheated. This was a "cause" which had automatically to be followed by a necessary "effect." Hence "in consequence" the commander ordered the Maxim into action 'at 500 yards' range." The villagers fled to some nearby hills; but the colour sergeant with 20 mercenaries was sent to "clear" the hills. This he did and captured fifteen head of cattle for the British. Danko was then set on fire. Meanwhile, Crawley himself, with 10 mercenaries, made for Koko, another of the villages. He allegedly found the people of this village in an "aggressive" posture, even though on their own territory. "Some sharp fighting immediately took place." Even though the British were reinforced by 21 more mercenaries, the people of Koko gave such a good account of themselves that the British commander was later to lament that "the enemy were numerous and well posted." For once, the British had to beat a retreat without either dislodging the villagers or burning down their village. It was only afterwards that the commander learnt that the villagers suffered 23 killed in the encounter. In addition to inflicting that heavy casualty on Koko, the British captured "17 head of cattle and 60 sheep and goats" belonging to its inhabitants.

By this time it had dawned on Crawley that he had moved too far away from the "base," Yola. Hence, the next village the column "visited" was also the last village it "visited" on this particular "pacification" exercise. This was Bubon, "the largest non-Muslim village met with during the expedition." By the time the British arrived there they were quite exhausted; but it would seem that this was unknown to the villagers who must have been following events between their neighbours and these thoroughly unwelcome "visitors" with an involved interest. Hence, instead of standing up to the British, the villagers preferred to pay the "fine" imposed on them. This was made up of "2 head of cattle, 10 sheep, 10 goats and 10 bundles of cloth." From Bubon the British returned to Yola, which they reached on January 31 with enormous booty and much greater blood on their hands.

Other good examples of the violent and destructive methods by which the British reduced the non-Muslim communities in and around the emirates to submission are furnished in the "operation" which the "Resident" Zaria Province undertook against the Gada and Kaje peoples in the "south-east of the Province,"[49] in March 1903. With the sanction of Acting High Commissioner Wallace, the Resident took a force composed of 11 European officers and NCOs. and 195 mercenaries, a very large force if we consider the military weakness of these communities. This force arrived at Sherifi on March 19 and "arrested" the chief because he had refused "to hold any communication" with the visiting Resident. We are not told the casualty suffered by the village during this arrest. The following day the British arrived at Karigi where "several arrows" were fired at some soldiers who had been sent into the town "to collect food which the inhabitants had refused to bring out." This gave the British the opportunity to chase the inhabitants out of their town and to loot it afterwards. They also captured forty "prisoners."

When the British arrived at Gadas on March 21, they found the town deserted except for a few men "who fired" on their approach and fled. But hearing that most of the people of Gadas had retired to Tudun Wada, the force followed them there. On arrival, the force surrounded the town and had all its gates blocked before sending for the chief "to come out." The chief refused to do so and the British entered the town and captured 60 prisoners and 6 horses. On March 30, the force arrived at Amo "where the enemy showed slight resistance." When the British opened fire the town's people retreated "up the hills on the far side of the town;" but the British were able to capture 30 prisoners after a battle during which 5 of the "enemy" were killed. They then looted the town and burnt it down, before moving on to "the first of the Rokoba towns" where "very much the same sort of thing occurred." In precise terms, the British "captured ten prisoners and burned the town."

Having learnt of the fate of their neighbours, the people of the next town, Zangon Katab, refused to invite a fight which was always only too readily offered by these "visitors." Instead, the people gave the British the submissive treatment they demanded. But when the force reached Kamkandan, "one of the head Kaje towns", it met with "considerable resistance." A pitched battle lasting two hours took place. During this battle a certain Lieutenant Bosher did "useful work with an M/M gun, constantly placing a shell among parties of the enemy who had fled to what they considered a safe distance from us." As a result, "23 of the enemy were killed and several wounded." In addition the

British captured 10 prisoners and burnt down the town. The British found deserted the next two towns they "visited." These were Madakia and Kadun, both of which they burnt down. The third town, Gidan Soro, was not even given the chance to choose between war and "peace." Instead, it was taken by surprise and 59 prisoners were captured. At the next town, Zonkwa, which the British found deserted, three prisoners and three horses were taken, the latter as a "fine." At Fadia "the last of the Kaje towns," the British killed two men. From there the force returned to Zaria, which it reached on April 13, after 41 days of "tour of pacification" during which, through sheer brigandage and after many villagers had been killed and thousands of them rendered homeless, it had been able to establish what must have been a very tenuous and fragile "authority" of the British over "south-east Zaria Province."

Yet, other illustrations of the pain, destitution, death and bereavement which the British inflicted on the non-Muslim communities of the emirates during their occupation and "pacification" of this part of Nigeria can be seen during the so-called "Tilde Expedition,"[50] of 1904. This expedition was jointly undertaken by the Residents of Nassarawa and Bauchi Provinces. The expedition set out from Jama'an Daroro in the then "Nassarawa Province" on November 7. Some of the Kagoros of Jama'a Emirate, against whom this expedition was partly taken out, must have known of the "visit" and its purpose. Thus, on this day, they kept at home in the mountains. Hence, though the British passed through "several farms belonging to the Kagoro villages," they did not see any people. Nor indeed did the British have any illusions about the feelings of the Kagoro towards them, for the Resident admits that "the Kagoro tribe [was] hostile both to Hausas and English." However, luckily for the British, the village of Karshire, "belonging to the Attakar" offered to allow them to spend the night in a camp near it. They were also able to spend the nights of November 8 and 9 as barely tolerated "guests" at Assala, "the chief town of the Kibbu tribe" which, in many ways, was "extremely hostile," the people manifesting "in their attitude that they wished [the British] to quit their place" as soon as it was morning.

The first engagement the British had with villagers during this expedition was on November 9 at Daniawara. When the British demanded food, the villagers refused "outright" and insisted that the British "leave their country." Even before then the "hostile intentions" of the villagers, who had come out in a body numbering "some seven or eight hundred men," were "clear" to the British. Hence with "promptitude" the British opened fire and the villagers "were thoroughly defeated." They suffered a casualty of "over 100 killed and wounded, 43 being counted in front of the square alone." In the face of such heavy British fire the villagers fled, "food was obtained, and some ponies of which they possess[ed] a great number were captured."

Four days later, on November 14, the British got another opportunity to drive a lesson home to the "natives", this time against the people of Gyel near Bukuru, at that time in Bauchi Province. On arriving there, the British sent back some of the curious people who had come out to watch them to go and call the town's chief. After waiting for "an hour" without the chief appearing, Resident Temple of Bauchi entered the town with six men and "arrested" him. However, while being interrogated, the chief uttered a "war-cry" and "armed men hurried up from all sides." The British opened fire on Temple's orders. The villagers were first driven back into the town and then out of it. Having in this way expelled the people of Gyel from their town, the British burnt it down. Then they spent the next four days going round burning "the remainder of the N'Giel[Gyel] towns." On November 18, the column moved on to Kunkuru, which it found deserted. But two men came down from a hill behind the town to tell the British that the people of Gyel were hiding among them and had refused to leave. This misled Temple into imagining that the chief of Kunkuru would seek British "aid" against the people of Gyel. To anticipate the chief, he sent the men back with a message to say that if the chief came down, the British "would spare his town." The men returned to say that the chief was coming; but having waited for half an hour, Temple decided that the men were lying. So he "requested Captain Gallagher to attack and burn the town." This was done but the British did not know how many casualties they had inflicted on the town.

Yet, in spite of the heavy bloodshed, arson and looting that the British inflicted upon the Kagoro, the Gyel, and other peoples in the area, they were not able to claim that their expedition had been a success or that the "natives" had been reduced to submission to them. Thus, Temple lamented that "a body of four or five hundred was seen out of range retreating in the direction of N'Giel[Gyel]. The combined tribes of Kunkuru and N'Giel[Gyel] must be able to put several thousands into the field; they possess a great number of horses and are courageous fighters. One company of infantry is not adequate to cope with them. Mounted infantry would be required in addition, if they are to be absolutely defeated and driven from the country," an indication of more British visits to follow. Nonetheless, for the communities involved, this British "visit" to their villages, like British "visits" to other villages and against the capitals of the emirates, was indeed a visitation that brought in its wake death, pain, poverty, destitution and very traumatic shock. There should be little doubt that if a careful count was done of those who died as a direct result of the British occupation of the emirates, through being killed outright on the day of the occupation or dying a few days after, as a result of the immediate hunger and exposure that the looting of towns and villages brought, the figure would run into hundreds of thousands. This is by no means a "slight" figure for any population anywhere.

"Unofficial" Violence by Mercenaries

Though Lugard would like us to believe the contrary,[51] besides the officially sanctioned violence that characterized British occupation of the Sokoto Caliphate, there was also the violence that mercenaries in the WAFF indulged in on their own both while alone and even when in the company of British officers. Thus, for example, in September 1902, Barclay in Yola reported that "a lot of mischief" had been done "through the Fulani country by soldiers and carriers."[52] According to him the "whole country" between Daware and Goila, a distance of about 60 miles, was practically deserted, "the people having fled to the bush on hearing of [British] approach." The Resident admitted that it was difficult to keep carriers in check "even when accompanied by white men."

The immediate occasion for Barclay making his report was that during a "tour" from Yola to Borno, his own carriers stampeded a flock of sheep "and drove them through the camp, clubbing them; and tearing them to pieces before our eyes, amid a scene of indescribable savagery." Similarly, Barclay reported that when two British officers, Watson and Deverell, camped inside Goila with 150 mercenaries "the place was completely ransacked unchecked." There was also "a case of looting by the men in charge of 100 bullocks sent down [from Maifoni in Bornu] to Wamdeo by Captain Cochrane to meet Dr Watson and Lieutenant Deverell."

From Sokoto in April 1903, one month after the occupation of the town, Burdon reported that many "serious charges" were brought against the men of the WAFF detachment."[53] According to one of these charges, a villager was murdered by a soldier one night, "being shot by a small bore bullet." Yet, the Resident was unable to find out anything to "enable" him make an arrest.

In fact there had been many complaints of highway robbery on "the caravan road which passed close to the barracks." These robberies were generally at night and were carried out by "a party armed with sticks and machetes." Worse still for the people of Sokoto, whenever some of the traders went to the Resident with their complaints against these mercenaries, they were "a good deal knocked about" by the mercenaries. The Resident found it very hard to see what could be done to stop the robberies. Significantly, he was afraid to send an armed piquet out of the road "lest the remedy prove worse than the disease." It is indicative of the anarchy that British occupation created in the emirates that

Burdon's "only hope" was that "the people, traders, farmers and so on" would "pluck up enough courage to offer armed resistance and capture some of their assailants." In the meantime, he admits, "the people [lived] in such mortal terror of the soldiers they [dared] not resist."

The British officers could not do anything against their own troops in spite of the fact that the violence of these troops was having "a very bad effect," in spite of the fact that "Numbers of farms and villages round Sokoto [were] deserted," and in spite of the fact that "fear of the soldiers [was] one of the things which [were] causing people ... to desert their homes and follow the ex-Sarkin Musulmi." In fact so serious was the situation that "three times lately, in broad daylight and within half a mile of the camp" soldiers, armed with sticks, attacked Burdon's own political agents when the latter were escorting to the Provincial Court some Sokoto women who had been abducted by soldiers but had been identified and claimed by "their masters." The soldiers seized back the women and "severely handled" the complainants.

As late as May 1905, Burdon reported that on his "march down the Banaga road" he heard "constant complaints" as to the behaviour of passing police escorts.[54] On three occasions, he was told that some constables fired their rifles inside towns, twice to enforce their demands for food, and in the third instance merely to show off. In this last case, the constable fired at a tree and the bullet, passing through, wounded an old woman so badly that she died two days later. Needless to say the constable escaped and had not been arrested up to the time of Burdon's report.

Again in November Burdon received reports of serious outrages on "the Kano road" committed by three Kano policemen returning to their stations in Kano Province.[55] This time "steps were taken for their arrest" and the case was going "to be dealt with judicially in due course." Yet, still in December of the same year, Burdon received reports of "serious outrages" culminating in murder, "alleged" to have been committed by a patrol of three mounted infantry soldiers from Katsina.[56] In this case too "the proper judicial steps" were "being taken" and the case would "be dealt with in due course."

From Zaria, the Resident reported as late as February 1906 that "a gang of nearly 120 carriers," en route from Zaria to Zungeru were reported to have sacked the local market at Koriga, and that one of them had tried to set the house of the chief of that town on fire before being overpowered.[57]

Criminals Come to Their Own

In addition to the violence and lawlessness of native mercenaries employed by the WAFF, there was also the brigandage of lawless elements in the societies of the emirates, elements that took advantage of the violence of the British and their mercenaries to come to their own. A brief account of some of the reported activities of these local lawless elements is necessary to give as near an accurate picture as possible of the atmosphere of violence and insecurity that accompanied the British occupation of the emirates. Thus in July 1900, P.M. Dwyer, the Resident for Ilorin Province, reported that the Emir of Ilorin was "complaining very bitterly of the amount of crime that was taking place in Ilorin town, murder and theft being the most common forms of it."[58] It is indicative of the hindrance that the presence of the British constituted to the checking of this wave of crime and violence, and of the frustration that the Emirs felt, as a consequence, that the Emir of Ilorin requested Dwyer "to give him permission to catch the thieves and kill them."

Lugard himself in his first Annual Report as High Commissioner, the report covering the period from 1 January 1900 to 31 March 1901, lamented that "throughout the Protectorate but especially in the southern provinces, the crime of extortion or personation is very prevalent." He reported that "a man wearing a fez and a pair of trousers comes into a village and announces that he has been sent by the white men. He may remain there for months, levying blackmail from the natives. He will often not content himself with demanding horses, cattle, fowls and grain (sometimes in large quantities), but by threats that he will bring against the people some serious charge which (he informs them) will result in their extermination by the forces of the Protectorate, he may terrorize them into yielding to him their wives and children."[59]

And in January and February 1904, Acting Resident C.W Orr from Sokoto, once more gave prominence to the question of robbery in that "Province."[60] He owned up to having received "many complaints" of caravan raiding on the Sokoto–Kano road in the neighbourhood of Kwotorkoshi. The Acting Resident, through his political agent Kiyari, got all the headmen of the towns around Kwotorkoshi to come into Sokoto where they told him that the "marauders were Goberawa from Maradi" and were led by a man called Magajin Hassan. Attempts to get both Sarkin Gobir na Tsibiri and Sarkin Katsina na Maradi as well as Magajin Hassan himself to come into Sokoto failed, though they were at that point still within "British" territory. Hence, Orr decided that the matter could not be settled until he himself went to Tsibiri and Maradi, something he hoped to do "in due course."

Indeed, the Annual Police Report for 1905 documents the prevalence "as in 1904" of "robbery with violence," stealing "in the various forms known to law," and extortion "generally accompanied by intimidation or impersonation."[61] In that year, 100 people were tried for highway or other robberies and 278 for extortion or impersonation or similar offences in the various "Provincial Courts."

As late as March 1906, Resident Arnett at Zaria was reporting robberies on the Kano road near the border between the two provinces.[62] Arnett blamed these robberies as well as the burning down of the British Rest House at Anchau on the son of an Ex-Magajin Anchau, whose father the British removed as chief in 1905. But whether the acts of lawlessness were politically motivated as Arnett claimed or not, the fact remains that lawlessness was endemic in that area of Zaria. Similarly, as late as 1907, Dwyer reported from Ilorin that "over twenty men had been shot in farms near Jebba by hunters."[63] Dwyer too tried to attribute these murders to political motives. Thus, according to him, "rumour had it that the chief of Ajia was responsible for this massacre." Yet, he admitted that "though the DSC made many arrests (in fact the lock up at Jebba was filled with hunters), no evidence could be got to pin down the crime to the Ajia or any of the hunters under arrest." Dwyer then went on to plead that had the province been "properly patrolled such crimes as this one and the several midnight attacks on outlying farms" would not have taken place. He pleaded that the police in his province were too few in number to carry out this duty in addition to "their ordinary duties," and begged that if no soldiers were to be left in Ilorin Province "at the very least" there should be 100 policemen. "Less than this [was] worse than useless." This way, Dwyer testified to the fact that the British, after breaking the power of the Emirs, failed to make adequate arrangements for the protection of the lives and properties of the inhabitants of the emirates. Not that the presence of soldiers and more policemen in Ilorin would have made the difference that Dwyer imagined it would have, judging from the experiences of Yola, Sokoto and Zaria, among other places, with these British agents of "law and order."

Nor was Yola free from the violence of local anarchic elements. Indeed, as late as March 1908, the Acting Resident was reporting that Captain Browne had just been to "inspect the Pella detachment," to the north of Yola.[64] The latter found a number of traders waiting at Song, afraid to go on. They took advantage of his escort as far as Pella; and indeed between Song and Goila when some lagged a mile behind, "they were robbed and some of their number badly wounded." Captain Browne himself saw groups of armed men sitting on skopjes along the road "apparently waiting for likely prey."The Acting Resident ended the "judicial section" of the Report by admitting that "crime is ... very prevalent in Yola, the most prevalent forms [being] kidnapping and theft."

Indeed, though Mary Smith may not have realized this, the central theme of the story that Baba of Karo narrated to her was the violence and anarchy that British military activities in Bida and Kontagora unleashed in north-western Zaria.[65] Her story could have been repeated almost word for word, except for the names of persons and villages, by narrators from other parts of the Sokoto Caliphate who went through the traumatic events of the period. The simple truth of the matter is that the British who "took over" the "administration" of the emirates and disarmed their authorities, physically and legally,[66] woefully failed to control both their own mercenaries and the erstwhile criminal elements of the subjugated society. In this way the population of the emirates suffered untold insecurity, molestation, robbery and death, quite at random and right inside its own towns and villages.[67]

Lest anyone doubt that it was the British occupation that activated the lawless elements of society in the Caliphate, we will here point to the fact that in the Emirate of Fombina, for example, throughout the nineteenth century there was only one occasion when a brigand was captured and his arms amputated. That this brigand, Abdulkarim b. Hamidu, was a grandson of Modibbo Adama and a nephew of the then ruling Emir, Lamido Zubairu, is itself a strong indication that it was the rarity of brigandage rather than an indulgent attitude on the part of the Emirate's authorities that accounts for the absence of more amputations or executions of brigands.[68] Yet the Emir himself, after his ouster, fell a victim to robbers at one point in the course of his wanderings before he was finally killed.[69]

Similarly, attention should be called to the conversation that took place between the Emir of Bauchi, Hassan, and Resident Temple on the prevalence of crime in Bauchi after the British occupation of that emirate. Thus, according to Temple himself, the Emir taxed him point blank with aiding criminals against honest men. Bearing in his mind the typical British colonialist hypocrisy that it was better to tolerate a certain level of crime than to resort to the methods that Emirs had used to stamp it out in the pre-British days, methods such as the amputation of the hands of thieves, the Emir promptly assured the Resident that he, the Emir, an old man at that time, could remember only three occasions when the hands of thieves were amputated.[70] That is to say that in the emirates of the Sokoto Caliphate, crime had been so rare that though the Shari'a permitted the amputation of the hands of thieves and the execution of armed robbers, the authorities seldom ever had to invoke these sanctions.[71]

One must add that in conversation with elders during the few field trips made, one was always told that before the coming of the British the hands of thieves were amputated while robbers and adulterers, as distinct from fornicators, were executed. Yet when one asked them if they knew of specific examples of the amputation of the hands of thieves or the execution of robbers and adulterers, they invariably confessed to knowing no specific examples. No doubt, in the case of adultery, it is the amount of evidence needed for establishing it that prevented the fulfilment of this injunction;[72] but in the case of theft and robbery, the infrequency of their occurrence must have been among the factors that made the implementation of the Shari'a's injunctions on them to have been so infrequent that today hardly anybody remembers the practical implementation of those sanctions. To an extent, this is a comment on the British claim to have "humanized" "native law and custom," but our intention here is to contrast the minimal existence of crime or violence in the Sokoto Caliphate with its prevalence during and immediately following the British overthrow of that Caliphate.

Attitudes Towards the Sarkin Musulmi's Hijra

Contrary to Lugard's boastful claims,[73] the British occupation of the emirates was also attended by a deep-felt emotional distress by the people of the emirates, of all classes and by attempts on the part of very many of them to flee from what al-Qadi Ahmad Saad of Gwandu described as "the abode of affliction and travail."[74] This emotional distress and the attempt to escape from it — as distinct from attempts to run away from specific British policies — are to be seen in the response of large sections of the populations of the emirates to the *hijra,* on which the Sarkin Musulmi, Attahiru, embarked after the British had occupied his capital. Thus, when the Sarkin Musulmi embarked upon this *hijra,* the people through whose districts he passed saw him as capable of leading them to a place where they would not have to submit to Christian rule and, for this reason, they elected to leave home, follow him and submit to his leadership. Thus, several weeks after the Sarkin Musulmi had left Sokoto "the farmers [of Sokoto Province] were still trying to make their way to him."[75] In fact, the peasants were leaving to follow the Sarkin Musulmi in such large numbers that Burdon forebodingly predicted "short crops" in the following year.

By the time the Sarkin Musulmi reached Zaria territory he had "some hundreds of horses and footmen and about 2,000 women" in his train.[76] In Zaria itself: "the presence of the Ex-Sarkin Musulmi had a very disquieting effect ... for malcontents and the enemies of the new Emir made preparations to join

Attahiru, and were only prevented from doing so by the prompt measures taken by the Emir." In fact, "the King and headmen of Maikarfi [joined] Attahiru, and four of the disaffected headmen from Zaria also, taking with them several hundreds of their people and all their property."[77] In the course of only four days, between Bebeji and Kogo in Kano Emirate, the Sarkin Musulmi "quadrupled his following." Sarkin Karaye, "the most important chief in the district," joined him and "most of the sarikis" followed suit. Each town he passed through ... "half the population ... tied up their bundles and joined in his train."[78] Resident Cargill realized that "to allow Attahiru to sit down even for a week in Kano territory would practically mean the population joining him en masse." In fact as it was, "half the population of the districts" he had traversed, including "the majority of the Sarkis," had joined him, "his following growing larger the further he [went]." In Kano city itself "the princes" were "disaffected and awaited developments."[79] Cargill had to "call them together and inform them that anyone joining the movement would have his property confiscated." The Emir had to send a circular round his territory, warning people that all who left their farms or towns and followed Attahiru "would be punished on their return."[80]

By the time the Sarkin Musulmi entered Katagum Emirate "the people appeared to rise en masse at the Sultan's call, men, women and children," leaving their towns and villages to follow him, thus showing "a fanaticism" which Wallace for one "never for a moment thought they possessed."[81] The popularity of the *hijra* was "a bit of a mystery" to Wallace. By now it had dawned on the British that "to the mass of the people Attahiru was still the rightful head of the Musulmans and not the successor whom we had installed at Sokoto."[82] As the Sarkin Musulmi marched through Katagum and Missau "people began to go daft, and joined the throng in a blind unreasoning sort of way." For a moment it "looked as though the madness would engulf all." "Everybody" joined in "the pilgrimage including the halt and the blind."[83] All this occurred in spite of constant harassment of the rear of the Sarkin Musulmi's train. Indeed, "the further" he went from Sokoto "the greater his prestige ... and therefore his following."[84] This following took "from sunrise until midday passing,"[85] two emirs, those of Missau, and Jama'are joined the Sarkin Musulmi,[86] who, by now, had "with him 600 horsemen ... 40 camels, 1,500 head of cattle, 100 transport bullocks, 1,000 donkeys and countless thousands of men, women and children on foot."[87]

Meanwhile, the people of Yola awaited the arrival of the Sarkin Musulmi with expectations and eagerness. But when, after some time, he did not arrive there, this expectation "appeared to have subsided," only to be rekindled when "a messenger arrived from the direction of Kano with two flags, round which the supporters of the Sultan were to rally."[88] The Resident's only hope about the situation in Yola was that the Sarkin Musulmi would not be able to make his way through the "pagan" territory between Yola and Gombe, the same area in which it was claimed Lamido Zubairu had been killed three months earlier.[89]

Even those who were not immediately able to join the Sarkin Musulmi did try to facilitate his escape, so much was his cause appreciated. Thus, for example, while the Sarkin Musulmi was at Rinji resting, the day after he had left Sokoto, "messengers from the Headman of Rini came saying that the Europeans and soldiers were out after him but had passed on to Tureta."[90] Then, while the Sarkin Musulmi was at Shinkafi resting, "a messenger came from Abubakar, the Emir of Katsina, bringing gifts of eighteen bales of cloth to him."[91] And two days after leaving Shinkafi, the Sarkin Musulmi, who was heading towards Ruma in the Emirate of Katsina, met the Emir's messengers once more. They warned him that the British had left Katsina the previous day and "it seemed as if they intended to make Ruma on that day."[92] Once more the Sarkin Musulmi was enabled to avoid the British with the help of an Emir who was outwardly on the side of the British.

In fact, throughout the *hijra* the Sarkin Musulmi was kept in touch with the movements of British columns that were bent on heading him off and destroying him, by people who had decided, for one reason or another, not to join him. One of such "informers" was in fact discovered by the British. That was the chief of a town whose name Captain Sword gave as "Keardah" in the vicinity of Birnin Kudu in Kano Emirate.[93] Needless to say, the chief paid with his office and liberty for this "betrayal."

And Temple reported with "regrets" that "a certain amount of disloyalty in Bauchi had come to light."[94] He had "the clearest evidence" that a large caravan of 200 donkeys loaded with corn arrived at Bormi a few days before "the [final] engagement." They were from Maimadi in Bauchi Emirate. Besides, "a large number" of the arrows discharged by the Muslims at Bormi were "undoubtedly made in Bauchi and charged with Bauchi poison." Temple was sure this would not have taken place "without the influence of some important chief." He made "allowance for the strain on their loyalty caused by the proximity of the Sarkin Musulmi ... as a fugitive and outcast" but all the same insisted that "at all events the sending or the fact that they did not prevent the sending of provisions to Burmi must be punished" if "the chief or chiefs" responsible "could be discovered."[95]

Even at the moment of his death the Sarkin Musulmi was not abandoned by his followers. Thus, according to Temple, even after the British had been able to storm the gate of Bormi on the day of the final battle, "street fighting continued until nightfall, the last stand being made at the mosque at about 6.30 pm."[96]

Meanwhile, the Sarkin Musulmi had been praying inside the mosque. When he heard the fighting just outside the mosque "he very bravely came out ... and was killed at the spot." Around his body were piled "the corpses of 90 of his followers."[97]

The death of the Sarkin Musulmi ended the attempt at escape for some of his followers but large numbers did go on to the Sudan under the leadership of Attahiru's son, Muhammad Bello Mai Wurno, whom the contingent came to regard as the new Sarkin Musulmi.[98] Among these were the Emir of Missau, Ahmadu, and a son of Waziri Buhari, Shehu Mai Rugga.[99] These migrants set a pattern for the Muslims which was taken up and which lasted right until the end of the colonial era.

The Wholesale Deposition of Emirs and Chiefs

The British occupation of Northern Nigeria was accompanied by a wholesale deposition of Emirs and chiefs as well as their officials. Indeed, there were very few Emirs who were not deposed. Notable among these were the Emirs of Ilorin, Shuaibu (1896–1915) and Gombe, Umaru (1898–1922), who died in office after collaborating with the British for sixteen and twenty one years respectively. Others were the Sarkin Kebbi of Argungu, Samaila, and the Emir of Katagum, Abdulkadiri. In the case of some emirates the British deposed not one but two or three successive Emirs. Good examples of where the British had to remove or kill not only one Emir but two or more successive ones were Katsina and Yola where they removed two and three respectively. As far as the Emirs that the British found in office were concerned, some were in fact killed in battle by the British. These included Sarkin Abuja, Ibrahim, the Sarkin Musulmi, Attahiru Ahmadu, and the Emir of Adamawa, Zubairu, who spent eighteen months after the British capture of Yola fighting or eluding the Germans and the British, and the Emir of Hadeija, whose showdown with the British came only in 1906, after the Satiru revolt. Others who barely escaped with their lives were the Emirs of Bida, Abubakar, that of Kontagora, Ibrahim, and that of Missau, Ahmadu.[100]

However, the impression should not be gained that the British went out of their way to reject the Emirs they found in office. The only Emir they rejected in spite of a willingness on his part to carry on under them was the Emir of Bauchi, Umaru.[101] In all the other cases where the British deposed the Emirs, it was the unwillingness of the emirs, more than premeditation on the part of the British that led to the depositions. This was the case in Zaria, Kano, Katsina but especially in Yola, Bormi, and Sokoto where the British seemed particularly keen to secure the "services" of the incumbent Emirs and the Sarkin Musulmi and were forced to appoint other men, almost in spite of themselves.[102]

In the case of Emirate officials, those who lost their offices, and this happened particularly in Gombe, Kano, Zaria and Sokoto, did so because they went with the fugitive Sarkin Musulmi Attahiru, and were either killed with him at

5. Abdullahi Bayero, eldest son of Emir Muhammadu Abbas of Kano, was demoted from the post of Waziri to Chiroma by the British in 1908.

Bormi, or continued the *hijra* under the leadership of his son, Muhammadu Bello Mai Wurno, or returned home to find that they were unacceptable to the British and the Emirs they appointed.[103]

Two of the Emirs who refused to accept the British, the Emirs of Bida and Missau, fought at Bormi on the side of the Sarkin Musulmi, and after the battle, the Emir of Missau continued on the *hijra* to the Eastern Sudan. The Emir of Bida as well as the Emirs of Kontagora and Kano, plus the Emirs of Bauchi, Umaru, and Zaria, Muhammadu Lawal, were arrested by the British and sent into exile to other emirates like Ilorin and Yola, but ultimately to Lokoja or Zungeru. Similarly, the two Emirs of Katsina that were later deposed viz: Abubakar and Yero, the Emir of Gwandu, Muhammadun Aliyu, and the second Emir of Adamawa to be deposed, Bobbo Ahmadu, were sent into exile either at Ilorin or at Lokoja. Given that these Emirs were people with large personal followings and large families, their being sent into exile meant an unsettling in the lives of very many people besides the Emirs themselves. This fact was remarked upon even by the British who, for example, recorded that the Emir of Kano, Aliyu, went into exile with about 300 followers, while the servants of the Emir Zubairu after his death allegedly contributed to the lawlessness that marred the lives of the people of Adamawa in the first decade of British colonial domination.[104]

This suffering for the families of the deposed Emirs was increased by the fact that whether the Emirs were killed or exiled, they lost their properties which were taken over by the British. This was particularly the case with the properties of the Emirs Zubairu of Yola and Aliyu of Kano. The cattle and grains of Zubairu, for example, were taken over by the British, who fed some to their troops and sold off others over a number of years.[105] Indeed, the Emir had only one wife and one child, a daughter, Kingi, who was married in Yola and had property in her own right;[106] but then, the Emir left several concubines who had been dependent on him and who would very much have appreciated being given a share of his property.

In the case of Aliyu, who is reckoned to have been the richest Emir Kano has ever had to date, his property was shared between the British and his successor Abbas;[107] and while Zubairu left only a daughter, Aliyu had scores of children, many of whom, along with some of his wives, followed him into exile.[108] He had to keep all of them on a "mercy" allowance of a few pounds a month. Besides, there must have been worse cases of destitution among the wives, children and followers of the other Emirs and officials that were killed or exiled by the British.

Disarming the Emirs

One of the immediate consequences of the British occupation of the Sokoto Caliphate was the disarming of emirs and chiefs including the new Sultan. Thus, whereas in the Caliphate Emirs were first and foremost military commanders,[109] the British policy was that while retaining and using the services of these Emirs, they were to be deprived of their military powers and be disarmed of all modern weapons.[110] This was promptly done with the occupation of each emirate. Thus, the British retained all the arms and ammunition that they captured in the various capitals of the emirates,[111] while at the same time, they made the handing in of weapons by the forces of each emirate the most vital part of surrender on the part of those forces.[112] Similarly, among the non-Muslim as well as small Muslim communities, apart from capturing all the weapons that they could lay their hands upon in the process of "pacifying" these communities, it was the usual practice of the British to impose fines to be paid not only with so much grain, so much cloth and so much livestock, but also with specified numbers of bows and arrows.[113] Inevitably the process of recalling the emirates' weapons was a little drawn out, some minor chiefs attempting to retain theirs.[114] Yet the collection was quite relentless. Thus, although in some places such as Borno the Residents were able to secure permission for the Emirs to retain a few flint locks with some rounds of ammunition, in others Lugard would not permit even this concession.[115] Indeed, in at least one case, a chief who held too tenaciously to his firearms was apparently killed and the firearms recovered. This was Kachalla Ari Afuno, District Head of Manga District in the Sheikhdom of Borno. He was known to possess many guns but refused to hand in any of them, the British recovering nineteen of the guns only after he was killed in May 1904.[116] But it is not clear from the records who killed him and for what reasons. Our deduction that he was killed by the British and for his refusal to allow himself to be disarmed is based on the fact that it was not likely for such a powerful man to be killed by any other force in Borno except the British, and on the absence of any other crime being levelled against him. However, in spite of the fact that there were some small attempts by some minor chiefs to hold on to their weapons, British collection of weapons from the Emirs and the officials was thorough. The Emirs all but lost their military capacity, even though that it had been great relative to British military capacity.

The Territorial Implications of British Conquest

An aspect of the European occupation of the Sokoto Caliphate and neighbouring territories that is apt to be overlooked is that concerning the physical structure of each of these erstwhile states. The impression which a reader will get from the literature dealing with the destruction of these states at the turn of the twentieth century is that they merely lost their sovereignty, passing more or less in a piece under the British. It would seem that the rather casual manner in which the territorial side of the destruction of these states is treated is due to three factors. First, and perhaps most important of these is the difficulty of establishing the extent and boundaries of these states in the days of their political independence. This difficulty, in its turn, derives from the fact that the borders of these states, though fairly stable, had not been static. The territory of each was disputed by one or another of the other states right up to the time of the European occupation. The second reason for making light of the issue is a definite, if not openly articulated assumption, that these and other precolonial African states, being "primitive," "medieval" or some such other "non-modern" phenomena, were without a clearly defined concept of territoriality.[117] While this assumption is on the whole confined to Western European and North American writers, it is to some extent shared by even African writers.[118] The third factor responsible for the neglect of the territorial implications of the occupation of these and other African states seems to be a deliberate shying away from the issue of the present boundaries of African states. There is a feeling that any suggestion that whereas the state system in Africa predated European colonialism, the borders of the states as presently drawn were the imposition of the Europeans, is also a suggestion that these borders should be revised to what they had been in precolonial days.

As for the second factor mentioned above, the chauvinistic assumption that the concept of territoriality was foreign to African political thought hardly deserves a specific rebuttal. However, for the attempt to shy away from the issue for fear of encouraging irredentism and attempts at territorial aggrandizement, it should be pointed out that where territorial ambition or irredentist yearnings exist, fictitious grounds can be concocted to support them. Indeed, European colonialism in Africa was itself the worst form of territorial aggrandizement. Although Europe did not have the remotest historical claims to any part of Africa, Europe was able to grab the whole of the continent and construct a whole corpus of legal and philosophical "justification" and "rationalization" for the act of absolute piracy. Then there is the fact that, in a real sense, to expose the foreign origin of present African boundaries is to emphasize the essential unity of the continent, and thus to refute the theory of its disunity, a disunity which may soon enough require force by imperialism and its local lackeys to maintain. It might also be added that to point out that precolonial African boundaries were different from the ones present African states inherited from colonialism in no way implies arguing that those precolonial borders would have remained the same if Europe had not intervened to alter them. Indeed, it has already been emphasized that precolonial African boundaries were so dynamic that the dynamism has discouraged almost all scholars from trying to demarcate them, while it made it easy for European chauvinists to dismiss them as non-existent.

Yet, in spite of the fluidity of precolonial African boundaries, it is possible to fix them, from time to time, since their fluidity did not exclude periods of stability. Specifically in the cases of Sokoto, Borno and Argungu, it is possible at least to indicate the emirates, provinces and principalities they each included, at the time when the Europeans intervened and both terminated their sovereignties and altered their physical structures. Hence, it is possible to assess fairly accurately the territorial implications of their occupation by European powers.

Thus the Sokoto Caliphate, for example, was approximately 150,000 square miles in area, had superseded wholly or partially at least 32 hitherto sovereign polities,[119] contained numerous linguistic groups and was organized into 30 emirates.[120] The larger and linguistically more heterogeneous of these emirates such as Fombina, Zaria and Bauchi, each had a number of sub-emirates. Thus Fombina, with an area of about 40,000 square miles, had over 42 sub-emirates of varying sizes, some of which were fairly autonomous.[121] Bauchi had nine fairly large and autonomous sub-emirates, in addition to numerous less autonomous districts.[122] Zaria had eight fairly large sub-emirates, three of which were large enough to be constituted into emirates by the British after the occupation.[123] Borno, for its part, was spread over a fairly large area, the size of which we have not been able to establish. However, from c.1810 to c.1893, that is, from the time of Muhammad al-Amin al-Kanemi to the time when Rabeh overthrew Borno's government and established his own dominion over parts of its territory, Borno included what for convenience we may call 'metropolitan Borno', administered directly by the Shehu and those of his officials who lived within easy reach from him, including the Galadima, who was resident at Nguru.[124] In addition to metropolitan Borno, the Sheikhdom included about a dozen fairly autonomous provinces and principalities.[125]

However, when the boundaries between British, French and German territories were finally demarcated both on paper and on the ground between

1898 and 1907, much of Sokoto was included in British territory. But the French acquired eight of her thirty emirates[126] as well as a number of districts around Wurno and Gwandu town excluding Sokoto town, while the Germans acquired virtually the whole of the Emirate of Fombina except for its capital, Yola, and a few districts in its immediate vicinity, which remained with the rest of the Caliphate under the British.[127] As for Borno, most of its metropolitan provinces and districts were acquired by the British while the French took all of her semi-autonomous provinces and principalities and the Germans snatched a few districts around, including Dikwa and Bama, districts which had formed part of metropolitan Borno.[128] Argungu, the extent and organization of whose territory as it was between 1849 and 1900, Rikon Kebbi, we have not been quite able to reconstruct, at any rate, saw all of that territory handed over to the French, while the British occupied "the district around Argungu [town, the capital] and the Kengako's district."[129]

In this way, while the capitals and the heartlands of the Sokoto Caliphate, the Sheikhdom of Borno and the Kingdom of Argungu were occupied by the British, each saw a substantial part of its territory occupied by the French, or the Germans, or both. The fraction of territory each lost in this way are reckoned to be about 35 to 40 percent for the Sokoto Caliphate, over 50 percent for Borno and over 70 percent for Argungu. Nor did the British uphold the political unity of its shares of these states, except in the case of Argungu, where the territory that the British acquired was too small to be carved up, and was, therefore, administered as a single Emirate. Thus, in the case of Borno a portion, Gumel,[130] was detached right away and constituted into an emirate, independent of the rest of the Sheikhdom. In the case of the Sokoto Caliphate, each emirate was made "independent," and "metropolitan" Sokoto was constituted into an emirate, with a Sultan as its Emir, the Sultan in theory being the successor to the former Caliphs.[131] In the case of the individual emirates, we have seen how Bida was deprived of all her territory south of the Niger.[132] Then four sub-emirates of Zaria were detached, three of them being constituted into an emirate, each autonomous of Zaria;[133] while two of the sub-emirates of Bauchi, namely, Wase and Lafiya, were constituted into emirates on the same footing as Bauchi.[134]

Indeed, not only were individual emirates broken up into several emirates; the new emirates so formed were often put into different Provinces from one another. Thus, for example, three extra emirates carved out of Zaria, namely, Keffi, Nassarawa and Jama'a, were put under Nassarawa Province while Zaria, the parent emirate, was constituted into a province almost all by itself. In the same way, of the two extra emirates carved out of Bauchi, one, namely Wase, was put in Muri Province along with Muri Emirate, while the other, Lafiya, was included in Nassarawa Province. Bauchi, the parent emirate was, along with Gombe Emirate and the formerly independent kingdom of Ningi, constituted into a Bauchi Province. This way the British attempted to destroy the old identities without necessarily creating new ones, since within each province, each emirate or chiefdom was encouraged to be conscious and jealous of its identity from, and "independence" of the other emirates and chiefdoms, the British Resident and Assistant Residents alone being in contact with all of them.

However, the territorial division of the Sokoto Caliphate, probably because it took so long to finalize on the ground, took some time before dawning on the emirates and peoples affected. This division must have presented a very serious problem for both the Emirs and the people concerned, although there is little record of this difficulty except in the case of the Emir of Adamawa, the most affected by the division. We shall discuss the reaction of the Lamido of Adamawa in the next chapter. It remains here to note that many of the minor chiefs in Adamawa who were seriously affected by the territorial settlement between the British and the Germans adopted an attitude to the settlement which might well have been adopted by all chiefs and peoples who were similarly affected by the partition. In this regard, the reaction of one such chief, Yerima Babbawa b. Hamidu, a grandson of Modibbo Adama, was not atypical though a little accentuated. In the nineteenth century, the father of Yerima Babba, namely, Mallu Hamidu b. Modibbo Adama, had been put in charge of a large chunk of territory occupied mainly by the Chamba and Verre peoples, with his headquarters at Nyibango, about 30 miles south-west of Yola. On the death of Mallu Hamidu the administration of the territory was taken over by his sons. Of these, Yerima Babbawa was the one in office by 1900. The Anglo-German boundary gave the greater part of this territory, together with its population, to the Germans while Nyibango itself was taken by the British.

At first, it seemed, Babbawa was willing to remain in Nyibango and content himself with exercising whatever little influence he could over the "German" portion of his territory.[135] But his son, Hamman Bello Maigari, "a pushing go ahead man,"[136] when he returned from Marwa, to which he had accompanied his grand uncle, the fugitive Lamido Zubairu, the only royal prince to stick to Zubairu for so long, was not willing to surrender effective control of what constituted virtually the whole territory of his father. Hence he went over to the "German" side and got himself recognized as ruler by the local population. "Having accomplished this he set about trying to induce his father and the people under him" to leave the "British" sphere and join him on the "German" side.[137] In the end he succeeded in over-coming his father's inertia, and the latter, with a very large following of Fulani as well as Chamba and Verre, crossed over to the "German" side.

After abandoning Nyibango, Babbawa founded another town, Nassarawo, on the "German" side. Next he "entered into negotiations with the Germans, sending presents of horses, cattle and guinea corn to the German Resident" at Garwa.[138] This secured him the recognition by the Germans but at the same time alienated the British, who accused him of "coercing Fulanis and pagans under him to cross the border against their will," of "abducting slaves" and of sending "a band of Chamba to a farm in British territory" to carry off a quantity of guinea corn. To put an end to "these criminal activities", Barclay issued a "warrant" for Maigari's "arrest" and dispatched mounted troops to go and abduct him. The troops succeeded in "catching" him "near the border but, unfortunately, while being brought in he managed to escape from custody and got into German territory."[139] So, on 20 February 1909, Barclay, Resident Yola, met the German Resident at Garwa, Captain Strumpell, in order to urge him to curb Babbawa.[140] This, Strumpell promised to do, but in fact the Germans were either unwilling or unable to curb him effectively.

Meanwhile, the British had appointed a nephew of Babbawa, one Hammawa b. Iyabano b. Hamidu, as ruler of the "British" portion of the territory, with headquarters at Nyibango.[141] With this appointment, what started off as a direct confrontation between Babbawa and Maigari on the one hand, and the British on the other, degenerated into a pathetic family feud, a feud which involved a lot of bloodshed and bitterness, and lasted up to the First World War[142] with which it merged.[143] Further to north of Nyibango, the dismemberment of the emirate presented the people of Gurin town with a land problem. While the town remained in Nigeria, many of its farmlands, specifically those on which it used to grow rice and a specialized flood-land corn known as *muskuwari,* were handed over to the Germans. The inhabitants of Gurin thereby automatically lost the right to cultivate their farms which lay less than half a mile away from their town, across the River Heso which formed the border.[144] Luckily for Gurin, however, the first towns of importance on the German side of the border, namely Turwa and Beka, were about ten and fourteen kilometres east and south-east of Gurin. So the towns people were able to get the Resident Yola Province to write "an application" to German Resident Strumpell at Garwa on their behalf asking "for permission to rent and cultivate" these farmlands, specifically an "island lying between the Rivers Heso and Faro." They promised "to pay the German Government 5 percent of the crops on the island, as a rental."[145] Though we have not been able to locate the reply of the German

Resident, we assume that such permission was granted, the war between Britain and Germany still being five and a half years away.

Indeed, to this day, the farmlands which still lie in the Republic of Cameroon, the adjustment of the border following the First World War not affecting the area in the vicinity of Gurin, are still cultivated by the people of Gurin.[146] Still further north, the chief of Uba not only lost some of his villages to the Germans; but, even his town through which ran the River Yadserem (Mayo Bani) was divided right in the middle, his half, the western half remaining in Nigeria and renamed Uba Hosere while the eastern half was occupied by the Germans and became known as Uba Mayo Bani. Worse still for the people of Uba, while the British regarded the Mayo Bani as the boundary, the Germans claimed that it was its tributary, the Mayo Mubi, which formed the border before its junction with Mayo Bani.[147] This way the people of Uba Hosere lost not only their farms to the east of the town but also those to the southeast of it. This point was driven home to the inhabitants when, at the end of 1906, German troops confiscated all their livestock and slaves to the east and southeast on behalf of the chief of Uba Mayo Bani, Jelani, and threatened to shoot anyone from British territory attempting to harvest the produce of the farms they had cultivated in German territory.[148] By February 1907 this had led to the onset of a famine, the price of guinea corn rising to one shilling (1/-) for 16 mudu as compared to 1/- for 26 mudu in Yola. Not to be outdone, the chief of Uba Hosere, Ardo Ilyasa, with British support, confiscated 114 cattle belonging to the people living on the German side but which happened to be on the British side at the time of the final demarcation in March 1906.[149] He also allegedly mounted an armed attack across the border, abducting slaves belonging to the people on the German side of the border, in the process of which his men dared to pitch a battle with German troops commanded by Resident Strumpell himself.[150] Even after mutual seizures of each other's property seemed to have stopped, there still continued to be "a considerable amount of discontent" among the peoples on the two sides. For the people of Uba Hosere this was due to "the three percent levied by the German chiefs on all flocks and herds" that crossed the border "when grazing or travelling even if only a few minutes."[151] When Resident Webster of Yola approached Resident Strumpell for "mutual concessions," the latter "regretted he could do nothing as this rule was enforced even between neighbouring districts in the Kameruns."[152] All Resident Webster could do in the light of that reply was to suggest to the Governor that "either our District chiefs should be allowed to levy a corresponding grazing fee or that German cattle grazing on British territory should be taxed by us, and a slight remission granted to the cattle owners who have to pay the double tax."[153] The Governor endorsed this suggestion but still hoped that the "Resident Yola [would] be able to arrange with the German authorities for the pasturage on both sides of the border."[154]

Elsewhere, a similarly bitter reaction to the imposition of the colonial boundaries was reported from Argungu, where Resident Gwandu Sub-Province said "from Yelu to the Eastern bend North of Chibiri, bitter feuds over wells and farm lands and the payment of tribute" were the result of the imposition of the border, which at the time the Resident made this report, October 1905, was still being demarcated on the ground.[155] So also did the border between British and German Borno become a cause of friction between, and difficulty for, the chiefs and people living on the two sides. Thus as early as May 1902, the Resident Bornu Province was reporting mutual recrimination between Shehu Abubakar Garbai of British Borno and Shehu Umar b. Bukar of Dikwa in German territory who, in fact, were first cousins, both being grandsons of Shehu Umar b. Muhammad al-Amin al-Kanemi.[156] The two chiefs took to raiding each other's villages, each with the tacit support of the European power on his side.[157] Thus we can conclude, however tentatively, that the dismemberment of the Sokoto Caliphate, as well as the Sheikhdom of Borno and the Kingdom of Argungu, did have a great and negative impact on the peoples divided by the borders imposed, leading to confiscations of properties and abductions by chiefs, with the three European powers, Britain, Germany and France doing little to restrain them. That the chiefs took to visiting their vengeance on one another, rather than combining to harass those who had forcibly divided them is a measure, not of any innate propensity towards violence by Africans, nor of the supposed tenuousness of the unity of these political systems. It is a measure of the degree to which the chiefs and their people had lost the initiative to the invaders, becoming pliable tools in the latter's hands.

Abolition of the Office of Sarkin Musulmi

The question of the position of the Sarkin Musulmi in a British-occupied Northern Nigeria was raised for the first time, it would seem, in August 1901.[158] This was in a dispatch from Wallace, then acting High Commissioner, to the Colonial Secretary. In this dispatch, he informed the Secretary that he had sent an Arabic copy of the "Proclamation of 1 January 1900 and a letter from Sir F. Lugard" to the Sarkin Musulmi, Abdurrahman. In the letter, he was "informing him" of the British occupation of Kontagora and Bida, and the appointment of Muhammadu, the Makun, as the Emir of Bida, and asking him to nominate an Emir for Kontagora. Wallace also said that he himself wrote another letter to the Sarkin Musulmi "informing him that it is our wish to place a Resident at Sokoto." Thus, Wallace was here hinting to the Sarkin Musulmi, Abdurrahman, that if he would accept British overlordship, the British were willing to rule the emirates through him. However, as Wallace should have expected, "to these letters [the British] never received answers verbal or otherwise." But in spite of the "non-cooperation" of the Sarkin Musulmi, Wallace still remained "of the opinion" that the Sarkin Musulmi should be told that the British were "determined to take and rule his country through him and the Fulani if they are agreeable, through others if the Fulanis resist." He suggested that Britain should not interfere with "the tribute now being paid to the Sultan by his emirs excepting that no slaves should form part of it."

Then in April 1902 Burdon, by this time installed at Bida as the Resident, expressed similar views regarding the position of the Sarkin Musulmi.[159] This was in connection with the "arrest," chaining and humiliation of Ibrahim Na-Gwamatse, the Emir of Kontagora. He urged Lugard that Ibrahim had committed "offences" against "native law" and "most grave offences too." For this reason, he should be "tried by native law and by the suzerain against whom he has offended viz: the Sarkin Musulmi." He argued that "the universal desire" in Bida "was that Ibrahim should be handed over to the Sarkin Musulmi for trial." He believed "most strongly" that such a course was not only "the most just one, but also by far the most politic." In his opinion, such a course would, "by its recognition of the Emir of Sokoto, bring about his friendship at once and would induce a feeling of confidence throughout Hausaland that nothing else could effect." He alleged that he was "not alone in this conviction" and that Captain Abadie, "who has had special opportunities of judging the feeling in the interior thoroughly," agreed with him.

Later on Lugard himself sent a letter to the Sarkin Musulmi, Abdurrahman, informing him that he "had been compelled" to occupy Bauchi.[160] He indicated that Umaru, the Emir of Bauchi, might be ousted, but insisted that he did not wish "to drive out the Fulanis and Mohammadans" and that for this reason, in the event of his ousting Umaru, he would "endeavour to find his proper successor and install him," as Emir. This was certainly not an invitation to the Sarkin Musulmi either to sanction the ouster of Umaru or to nominate a successor to him, but it was at least a nodding acknowledgement of the existence of the Sarkin Musulmi and of his rights in Bauchi. Then, when a fortnight later, the troops Lugard referred to above occupied Bauchi, Wallace promised Muallayidi, the man whom the British appointed to succeed the ousted Umaru, that the British would neither stop him from sending the "Gaisuwa" to, nor indeed prevent him from answering the summons of, the Sarkin Musulmi if the latter were to summon him to Sokoto.[161]

It seems that Lugard never received a reply from the Sarkin Musulmi. But the Sarkin Musulmi did allegedly write to the new Emir of Bauchi expressing his happiness that Umaru had been ousted.[162] He was alleged to be happy because Umaru had "refused on two occasions to proceed to Sokoto when summoned, and further had fought and treacherously destroyed the Muhammadan population of Gwaram, contrary to the orders of the Sarkin Musulmi." Significantly, the arrival of this letter "was the occasion for great public rejoicing" in Bauchi. Temple too was elated that Sarkin Musulmi Abdurrahman, while not communicating directly with the British, had tacitly endorsed their action in Bauchi. Similarly pleased was Abadie in Zaria when, late in March 1902, in spite of the presence of the British near the town, the Waziri of Sokoto, Mallam Buhari, came to Zaria and collected the "annual tribute."[163] But more relieved by this visit was Muhammad Lawal the Emir of Zaria. So honoured was he by the visit that when, on learning of the arrival of British troops in the town, the Waziri threatened that "he was leaving at once," the Emir protested to Abadie that "if the Waziri went he would go with him." And when, in order to avoid meeting Abadie, who was pressing for a meeting between them, the Waziri left by night a few days later, the Maajin Zazzau was "greatly relieved" that the Waziri had been able to escape with most of the tribute.

Five months later, in September 1902, Temple allowed the Emir of Bauchi to send "his contribution to Sokoto, the first he has dispatched" since the British occupation.[164] This "contribution," which was shown to Temple, "consisted of 15 loads of native cloth."

But when Sokoto fell to the British in March 1903, Lugard, in his speech on the occasion of the installation of Attahiru b. Ali b. Bello,[165] made it clear that the office of Sarkin Musulmi as a political, administrative and judicial institution for the entire Caliphate, was to cease, and that the new Sultan, far from being allowed to supervise the emirs, was himself to be placed under the immediate supervision of a British Resident.

Thus, regarding final power, which, in the nineteenth century, had been exercised by the Sarkin Musulmi, Lugard said, "the Fulani in old times under Dan Fodio conquered this country. They took the right to rule over it, to levy taxes, to depose kings and to create kings. They in turn have by defeat lost their rule which has come into the hands of the British." The chief representative of British power in Northern Nigeria was going to be the High Commissioner, Lugard himself, while the immediate representative of this power in each emirate was the Resident or the Assistant Resident. The Sultan, theoretically the successor to the highly esteemed Caliph office, which was once filled by men such as the Shehu and Muhammad Bello, was patronizingly told by Lugard "you must not fear to tell the Resident everything and he will help you and advise you."

Concerning the appointment of Emirs and other state officials, Lugard announced that henceforth "every Sultan and Emir and the principal officers of state will be appointed by the British High Commissioner throughout all this country." There was not even a promise that the Sultan would be consulted before an appointment was made. Far from that, in fact, "when an emirate or an office of state becomes vacant it will only be filled by the High Commissioner and the person chosen will hold his place only on condition that he obeys the laws of the Protectorate and the conditions of his appointment."

About the legal system of which the Sarkin Musulmi had been the head, Lugard conceded that "the Alkalis and the Emirs will hold the law courts as of old." However, "sentences of death will not be carried out without the consent of the Resident." Besides, it was "to the Resident," and not to the Sultan that "every person … [had] the right to appeal." As for taxation "the government [held] the right of taxation and [would] tell the Emirs and chiefs what taxes they [would] levy, and what part of them must be paid to government." Finally, concerning war which, in the nineteenth century the Sarkin Musulmi alone had the power to declare, Lugard warned that "henceforth no Emir or chief shall levy war or fight but his case will be settled by law and if force is necessary Government will employ it." Thus Lugard did not outlaw all war, as is often claimed, but only those that the Sultan or the Emirs might want to undertake. The right to wage war, be it noted, was not abolished. It was merely transferred from the Sultan to the High Commissioner. And to symbolize the Sultan's subordination to the British, he was made to accept investiture with a gown and a turban by the High Commissioner in sharp contrast to the fact that hitherto the Caliphs of Sokoto, while investing Emirs were never themselves invested, a fact which Lugard fully knew and consciously contradicted, for emphasis.[166]

But while the British refused to recognize the Sultan and in fact reduced him to the level of an Emir, the scope of whose authority, subject to the supervision of a British Resident, was limited to a relatively very restricted area around Sokoto town, in reality his political authority as Sarkin Musulmi continued visibly to flicker up to about 1910, and his spiritual authority in the emirates never in fact died out. Evidence of this influence was noted by the British themselves on several occasions and, in fact, they found it convenient to exploit it on some occasions and necessary to be vigilant about it always.

Thus in May 1903, Gowers reported the arrival in Yola of two messengers with two letters to the Emir, Bobbo Ahmadu, one each from the new Sultan and Waziri Buhari.[167] The letters announced the ouster of Attahiru b. Ahmad by the British and the appointment by the latter of Attahiru b. Ali b. Bello. The Emir told Gowers that the letters were written on the instruction of Burdon and that similar ones had been sent to all the other emirates. But one would not infer from this, as Adeleye has done, that the letters were circulars announcing the abolition of the office of Sarkin Musulmi.[168] For one thing, it had been the practice in the nineteenth century to write and inform the Emirs whenever a new Sarkin Musulmi was appointed, and this might have been the intention of the Sultan and the Waziri. For another, by getting the Sultan to dispatch these letters as of old, Burdon, far from intending to spread word about the demise of the office of Sarkin Musulmi, might well have been hoping to help consolidate the position of the British in the emirates by using the prestige of that office. His hope, we suggest, was that these letters would both create the impression of continuity and show the Emirs that even Sokoto was now loyal to them. Besides, getting the new Sultan to write and tell the Emirs of his own appointment was likely to have been seen by Burdon as a good way to help isolate the erstwhile Sarkin Musulmi, who was still alive and active within the Caliphate. So, far from interpreting these letters as an announcement of the demise of the office, one is inclined to see them as an attempt by Burdon to make the Emirs feel that the office of Sarkin Musulmi was still there and was in alliance with the British. In short, the British were both eating their cake and having it.

Indeed, this was how Gowers himself reacted to the letters. Thus he insisted that:

> the question at once arises: what is the position with regard to Sokoto as to the tribute formerly paid by Yola and other places? Now that the British have installed and acknowledged the new Emir of Sokoto does it not unnaturally suggest itself to the Fulanis that the Government will support him in claiming the tribute formerly paid to his predecessors by vassal states?

He asked Lugard for guidance on the matter, stating that he himself "imagined that though the Sarkin Musulmi is still to be regarded as the spiritual suzerain of Mohammadans, the temporal suzerainty is to be considered to be now vested in the British, and that any presents sent to the Emir of Sokoto must be considered as voluntary offerings to the religious head and not as a tribute enforceable by the sovereignty of the country." He had in fact "conveyed this view without definitely committing myself as to the further policy of the Government." Lugard, who had said nothing specific about this aspect of the relationship between the Sultan and the Emirs during his speech at Sokoto, equivocated in reply to Gowers. Thus, according to his political assistant, "His Excellency concurs in your view. He objects to a tribute, to a state which does nothing whatever in return. At the same time His Excellency would encourage the voluntary contribution to the religious head." Clearly Lugard, who was not about to brook another sovereignty in the North, was not quite sure it was in the interest of the British to try and eliminate completely the influence of the Sultan in the emirates.

While Gowers would rather keep the Sultan's influence in the emirates to a minimum and Lugard would rather have no definite policy about it, Burdon in Sokoto was even willing to efface himself somewhat and let the Sultan handle the Emir of Gwandu for him. Thus, in his May 1903, report he informed Lugard that Bayero, the Emir of Gwandu, was dead and that the Dangaladiman Gwandu, Muhammadu had been "duly approved by the Sarkin Musulmi as the new Emir."[169] In fact, though Burdon went to Gwandu, he went there only to witness the installation of the new Emir whom he found had "in accordance with custom" already "taken possession of the late emir's house." Indeed Burdon arrived in Ambursa with the Sultan's messenger "bearing the letters of appointment." The following morning Burdon was merely "present" at the installation ceremony, which he "insisted should be carried out entirely in accordance with native custom." It was letters "brought by the Sarikin Muslimin's messenger" rather than a British letter of appointment that were handed to the Alkali "who read them aloud in Arabic and then translated them into Hausa and Fulani." There were four letters, two each from the Sultan and the Waziri. The first from each was to the new Emir and the people of Gwandu condoling them on the death of the late Emir. The second from each was "to the people nominating Muhammadu to be Emir of Gando and inculcating loyalty and obedience."

When these letters were read "relatives and headmen" came up in succession to pay homage to the new Emir, who then made a speech "calling on all to be loyal to him as he had been loyal to his predecessor" and "promising to rule justly and according to the Koran, telling his people that he had promised to obey the Government and ordering them to do the same." The Emir, who had been wearing old clothes, then retired into the house returning in a few minutes "in the new gown, cloak and turban sent by the Sarikin Muslimin." It was only at the end of the ceremony that Burdon "asked leave to address the people" and this "was readily granted." Thus, except for the Emir's mention of "loyalty to Government", which could later turn out to be sheer dissimulation, but for the presence of Burdon and the fact that he managed to squeeze in a speech of his own into the ceremony, this installation ceremony, in every other detail, might have been taking place before the British occupation. It was the Sultan that appointed the Emir of Gwandu; it was he that sent the letter of appointment and the regalia of office, and it was his representative that performed the ceremony, with the assistance of the Alkalin Gwandu. And, as formerly, it was the Dangaladiman Waziri, in this case Muhammadu Ambo, that deputized for the Sultan, all this, Lugard's speech at Sokoto a month earlier notwithstanding.

Also when the "need" to remonstrate with the Emir first arose, it was the Sultan that Burdon called upon to do the remonstration. Thus, he reported that although he had "particularly insisted that no officials were to be appointed without" his sanction, on his way back to Sokoto he heard "by accident that the Emir had, with due ceremony, appointed Shehu to be his Yerima, second man in the state and heir to the Emirate."[170] Hence on his arrival in Sokoto he "reported the whole affair to the Sarkin Musulmi, and requested him as suzerain of the Emir of Gando to deal with the matter." Of course "the Sarkin Musulmi was very upset," such action being "the reverse of the line he himself followed and he condemned it most strongly." The Sultan went on to console Burdon by informing him that he too had been ignored by the new Emir of Gwandu, "for the customary message announcing the accession and sending tribute of homage have on this occasion been omitted," alleged omissions which Burdon clearly did not approve. With Burdon so willing to believe him and rely on him, the Sultan went on to beg Burdon "not to degrade the Yerima now that he was made, promised to get me an ample apology from the Emir of Gando and was most grateful to me for leaving the matter in his hands."

Burdon was satisfied for the moment, but at the same time, he started to look for a way of supervising the Emir of Gwandu without having to rely entirely on the Sultan. So he suggested to Lugard that "the sooner a Resident can be put there the better." However, he "would not advocate making it a separate Province" because such a course would "inevitably make the Emir of Gando independent of the Sarkin Musulmi and so further reduce the status and the prestige of the latter."

As late as July 1905, both Burdon and Ruxton, the Assistant Resident posted to Gwandu, were still relying on the Sultan in their bitter relations with the Emir of Gwandu.[171] This time Ruxton got the Sultan to say that "Shehu was the last man" to select for the successor to the office of Emir, and that "it would be perfectly lawful from the native point of view to deprive him of his rank." It was the Sultan that Ruxton asked to nominate another man to succeed the Dangaladima, and he was very delighted when the Sultan "at once named those three whom either the Resident or myself would have named as being most likely to make efficient rulers viz: Basharu Hanafi, Haliru of Raha and Haliru of Kalgo. Asked to name one of those three, he chose Basharu Hanafi." Three months later, Burdon announced with pride that "the Sarkin Musulmi, the Waziri and all the best opinions in Sokoto thoroughly appreciate the leniency with which the Emir of Gando has been treated, and recognize that patience has its limits, which have now been reached." When, finally, in February 1906 the British deposed the Emir of Gwandu in favour of Haliru of Kalgo, it was again the Dangaladiman Waziri that went and installed him at Ambursa, though this time the Resident took a more active part in the ceremony than he had done in 1906.[172] On this occasion, as on the one in April 1903, the Dangaladima took with him the regalia of office and carried from the Sultan two letters, of which one announced the deposition of Muhammadu and the other the appointment of Haliru.

Meanwhile, Cargill in Kano so worried Abbas about what the latter thought about the Sultan that the Emir told him what we assume he believed the Resident wanted to hear, namely that he owed the Sultan nothing since both of them were British appointees.[173] This message was conveyed to Resident Sokoto. Accordingly, in July 1903, Captain Lewis, then Acting Resident, solemnly "visited the Sarkin Musulmi and informed him that the king of Kano did not wish to send presents or tribute to Sokoto, also of the reasons given by" the Emir.

Residents like Festing in Kano and Palmer in Katsina did not like the continuation of the influence of the Sultan in any form in "their" province. Hence in 1906, "when the present Emir of Katsina Muhammad Dikko was installed," Palmer "requested the Acting High Commissioner to make no allusion whatever in his speech to the Sarkin Musulmi." This request was made on the ostensible ground that "if told, Mahama, who is a Tejani that the Sultan of Sokoto ... had been consulted as to his selection, would not have understood and would probably have [taken] offence." Festing and Palmer were very pleased when they were told "here in Katsina that, when the new Emir on election sent round the customary present of kolas to all his brother Emirs, he treated the Sultan on an equal [basis] with all the others."

It was definitely with the purpose of playing his influence down that Festing and Palmer neglected to have the Sultan consulted before they removed the family of Mallam Ishaqa from the Emirship of Daura and restored the pre-jihad dynasty that had survived its eclipse at Zangon Daura.[174] Instead, it was the Emir of Kano that was "informed of his Excellency's decision." The latter, doubtless realizing that he was merely being "informed" rather than consulted, and that the possibility was very slim indeed that his dissent might alter "His Excellency's decision," quickly "wrote saying that the move would be a most popular one" and that "no one could refuse to accept Mallam Musa as a brother Emir."

In spite of Festing and Palmer's efforts to stamp it out, the influence of the Sultan visibly persisted among the "princes" of Kano. Thus, as late as September 1907 the sons of the late Emir Tukur were "intriguing with the Sarkin Musulmi to get one of them substituted for Abbas."[175] Similarly, the Sultan was in "intrigue with the Yero faction in Katsina." In February 1907, secret investigations conducted by Arthur Festing on the instructions of the High Commissioner helped to throw some light on the position of the Sultan in the emirates. He discovered that Burdon's most trusted agent, Kiyari, "was widely regarded as the agent of the Sarkin Musulmi", and that he was one of the channels through which "constant communication and friendly relations were kept up between the Sarkin Musulmi and the other Emirs, notably Nupe, Ilorin and Yola." Festing, as indeed Palmer, was positive that "undoubtedly some intrigue did go on without Burdon's knowledge." As an illustration of this, he cited a letter that was sent by one of Burdon's interpreters, one Mainasara, to the then Emir of Katsina, Muhamman Yero, just after the Satiru episode, a letter which the bearer at first mistakenly delivered to the then Durbi, and later Emir, Muhamman Dikko. The letter was admittedly written by Mainasara himself, presumably with the aim of making money out of the Emir. But Mainasara claimed "to be writing on behalf of the whiteman and the Sultan." He wrote that "the Sultan intended to give him the Provinces of Kazauri and Daura as a token of approval." Thus, while Mainasara was definitely an impostor purporting to represent the British and the Sultan, the fact that he tried to invoke the name of the Sultan at all, and his suggestion that the latter could still give and take away emirates, was indicative of the extent to which the Sultan still continued to be regarded as the real ruler of the emirates.

Festing also discovered that in both Kano and Katsina, though the Emirs attached no importance to the fact that the Sultan was the head of the Qadiriyya, the two of them having by then abandoned this *tariqa* in favour of the Tijaniyya, throughout Kano Province. This was at that point made up of Kano, Katsina, Hadeija, Daura, Kazaure, Katagum, Missau and Dambam as well as Gumel. A great importance was attached "by the ruling classes" to the fact that the Sultan was "the head of the house of Shaifu." And although of these emirates, "only Daura continued to pay what can be called the '*Gaisei*' as we understand it, ... undoubtedly some mild intrigue and the accompanying exchange of presents are still carried on" between these Emirs and the Sultan.

But when all is said and considered, what was essential after the British occupation of Northern Nigeria, was the fact of the abolition of the office of

Sarkin Musulmi. Thus, the extensive and extended tours of the emirates by the Waziri and other Sokoto officials completely ceased immediately after the occupation of Sokoto town, never to be resumed throughout the colonial era. It was only towards the end of that period that the Sultan sometimes sent the Waziri to the emirates for the purpose of offering condolence or congratulations on the occasion of the death or appointment of an Emir.[176]

Similarly, the regular visits to Sokoto by the Emirs stopped altogether. In fact, the first time that the Sultan met Emirs from outside the Sokoto Province after the occupation was in December 1925, when all the Emirs and chiefs in Northern Nigeria, including the Sultan, Muhammadu Tambari, journeyed to Kano to greet the Prince of Wales during a stopover in that city, on his way to South Africa.[177] After this gathering, it was not until five years later, in December 1930, that the Sultan, Hassan dan Mu'azu, met the Emirs again, and that was during the first Conference of Chiefs to be organized by the British.[178] This meeting became a more or less regular yearly occasion over which the Sultan formally presided. These meetings continued until 1947, when the House of Chiefs was established under the Chairmanship of the Lieutenant Governor. But it is noteworthy that these conferences took place at Kaduna rather than Sokoto. Some Emirs used to proceed to Sokoto to visit the tomb of the Shehu and greet the Sultan at home after each of these meetings.[179] But these visits to Sokoto were voluntary and received no encouragement from the British. The only time that the British got the Emirs to visit Sokoto was in 1939, during the opening ceremony of a Women's Training Centre there, the first that the British opened in the North.[180] On the other hand a few months earlier, when Sultan Abubakar was installed by the Governor, not a single Emir from outside Sokoto Province attended the ceremony.[181]

We also have no evidence of an appeal being lodged at Sokoto against the decision of an Emir, while there were several such appeals against the decisions of both Emirs and Residents that were lodged with the High Commissioner.[182] Similarly, though the British undertook countless bloody expeditions against recalcitrant villages and districts, right up to the time they left Nigeria, we have only one example of an Emir undertaking an expedition against a village after the occupation of his emirate by the British.[183] That was the Emir of Muri, Hassan, in 1903 and as a result of undertaking this expedition he was promptly deposed "for slave raiding."

Rather than themselves deal with a defiance of their authority the Emirs, including the Sultan, relied on the British whenever they felt it necessary to deal with an emergency. Thus for example, it was to the British that Sultan Attahiru reported when a "Mahdi" appeared in Satiru and was going round burning villages that refused to acknowledge his authority. It was only after the British had attempted to put down the revolt and had been routed that the Sultan was allowed by the Resident to deal with the rebels. He sent a very large contingent of horsemen under the Marafa, Muhammadu Maiturare. This contingent in turn was "routed" without putting up a fight. In fact, as we saw in the last section, the British did not merely forbid the Sultan and the Emirs from waging war, they also deprived them of their weapons, in some cases including bows and arrows.

Thus, we can conclude that while the British did not try to completely suppress the institution of Sarkin Musulmi, in its original status as a Caliph, they allowed it to exist, more as a semblance that they could manipulate or ignore at their convenience than a self-supporting, autonomous political reality. But even if they had tried to suppress it completely, they would not have succeeded, for the institution did continue to enjoy a considerable measure of prestige among the aristocratic classes of Northern Nigeria.

Erection of Tariff Barriers Between the Emirates[184]

As we shall see in Chapter 7, one of the first acts of the British after occupying each emirate was to erect caravan toll stations. We shall deal with the caravan tolls as a means – one of many such means – of creating a colonial political economy in the emirates, and with the extent of its success in helping to create that political economy in these emirates. So, here we shall confine ourselves to pointing out the political significance of the erection of the toll stations. We see their erection as a retrogressive step, like almost everything else the British did in the emirates. We make this contention because the stations, at which a very high rate of taxation on trade on goods – first locally produced goods but later both local and European goods – was collected, by 1904 as high as 15 percent of the value of the goods, discouraged long distance trade. By the same token, it discouraged the movement of people from one emirate to another. By discouraging the movement of both people and goods among the emirates, it ipso facto weakened the unity of the emirates, creating disunity where there had been an appreciable measure of economic, political and cultural unity in at least the one hundred years preceding British occupation. Thus, the introduction of these tolls can be said to have taken the emirates if not exactly to the position where they had been before the creation of the Sokoto Caliphate, the means whereby the people of a very large area had substantially overcome their disunity, at least to a situation not far from that position. It should also be remarked, in this connection, that the introduction of these hated tolls alone could be sufficient to expose the hollowness of British claims, which were later to be echoed by politicians and scholars alike, that they had united the "peoples" of Northern Nigeria. The introduction of these tolls exposes the hollowness of such a claim because the establishment of customs barriers, which was what the stations amounted to, is the very antithesis of the steps taken to create nation states. These steps consist in the abolition of customs barriers and the unification of weights, measures and currencies among others, as witness the histories of France and Germany, to mention two European examples. It might be argued that at the same time as establishing the customs barriers among the emirates, the British did introduce a uniform currency and uniform weights and measure. We regard the latter claim as only partially true. That is to say that whereas the currency, weights and measures were uniform, it is not quite so true that it was the British that unified these in the emirates. As far as currency is concerned, it should be pointed out that, while several items had been used as currency, all those items had legal tender throughout the emirates, and this legality of the tender of all of the items that were used constituted the monetary unity of the emirates in precolonial days. As for weights and measures, it should be pointed out that their standardization was at least a major concern of the founders of the Caliphate, though in the absence of consistent attention to the study of the issue in the currently existing literature, one cannot categorically assert that such standardization had been practically achieved. Suffice it to say that such standardization had at least been accepted as a desideratum in the emirates.

Conclusion

We have shown that the British occupation of the Sokoto Caliphate and neighbouring states was a very violent affair involving incalculable loss of life and property as well as large-scale destitution. In the process of the occupation, towns and villages were looted and then burnt down, animals were either driven away by the invaders or destroyed. We have also shown that even where there was no fight, it was the people of the towns concerned that went out of their way to placate the British and avoid a battle; and that, in addition to the violence that British military and political officers sanctioned, there was the violence caused by their mercenaries, both troops and carriers, for a long period after the occupation of the Caliphate. They did not mostly engaged in such violence when travelling alone only, but also very often even while in the company of British officers who did little to restrain them. So also did erstwhile criminal elements of the indigenous population such as kidnappers and brigands, who

6. British troops and the infamous Maxim guns used in the conquest of Northern Nigeria.

had hitherto been held in check by the Caliphate's authorities, come to their own as a result of the general disturbance created by the British occupation, and thereby added to the people's suffering and woes.

We have also shown that far from welcoming the British, as the latter claim, the people of the emirates were filled with fear and hatred for them. This fear and hatred were expressed in the large scale response of the population to the *hijra* that Sarkin Musulmi Attahiru Ahmadu embarked upon, in the subsequent increase of pilgrims towards the East.

Finally, we have also shown that the occupation was followed by immediate political consequences, and that these included the territorial break-up of the Caliphate, Borno and other neighbouring states, a break up which was made necessary by prior agreements among the British, the French and the Germans to share these territories among themselves. Other very important and imme-diate political consequences of the occupation were the deposition of almost all those Emirs who had escaped being killed in battle, the abolition of the office of Caliph, the appointment of a Sultan for a new "Emirate" of Sokoto, with no po-litical authority beyond this new Emirate; and the imposition of tariff barriers between one emirate and another, a step which, in effect, took these emirates back to the international situation that had existed prior to the emergence of the Sokoto Caliphate, early in the nineteenth century.

7. Lieutenant-Colonel, later General, T.N.L. Morland led various invasions in Yola (1901), Borno (1902), Kano and Sokoto (1903).

8. Mr. W.P. Hewby, who was the agent of the West African Frontier Force at Ibi and led the attack on Wase, later Resident Bornu Province

9. Shehu Abubakar Garbai of Borno.

3

Relations Between the New Emirs and the British

Introduction

In this chapter, we shall devote our attention to an examination of three important outcomes of the British invasion that were also closely related with one another. These are: passive resistance to the British by emirs, attitude towards the British appointed emirs by the emirate population, and popular hostility towards the British. Naturally, one would assume that the British would have a smooth working relationship with the emirs they newly installed after deposing the previous ones who, either actively resisted the occupation, or were unwilling to collaborate with them after the invasion. On the contrary, many of the newly installed emirs, as we shall show in this chapter, rather than showing gratitude, through loyalty and obedience, for ascending the throne, decided to engage in passive resistance to the British for one reason or the other. This was the case in almost all the emirates, with the possible exception of Emir Umaru in Gombe, Alhaji in Missau, Haliru in Gwandu and Muhammad Dikko in Katsina. We shall attempt to find out the causes of the passive resistance in the affected emirates, examine the nature of such resistance by the respective emirs, and ascertain the reaction of the British to the challenge. We shall then proceed to examine the attitude of the people to the newly installed emirs in some of the emirates, particularly in Ilorin, Yola, Gombe, Sokoto and others. We hope to show that a majority of the newly installed emirs were held in contempt by the people, who resorted to varying measures, sometimes even extreme measures, to express their contempt for, and rejection of, the imposition of such emirs. Finally, we shall argue that the people of the emirates were not only hostile to the new emirs, they were similarly resentful of the British for many years after the occupation. We shall attempt to demonstrate the nature and extent of the resentment with specific cases in Ilorin, Yola, Bauchi, and Sokoto, where the extreme resentment led to the outbreak of the Satiru Revolt in 1906.

Abuja, Bauchi, Keffi, Ilorin and Nassarawa

As indicated in the last chapter, relations between the British and the Emirs they appointed or allowed to continue in office under them were often so disastrous that, in some places, they had to depose several emirs in succession before they could get one with whom they could establish the minimum rapport necessary for even a modicum of cooperation. Indeed in the first one or two decades of their domination over the emirates, there was hardly an emir, with the exception of Umaru in Gombe, Alhaji in Missau, Muhammed Dikko in Katsina and the possible exception of Haliru in Gwandu, with whom the British were able to work in harmony. On the contrary, even in the case of those emirs who did not go out of their way to oppose British policies openly, what the British called "passive resistance" was very common.

Thus, from all accounts, Suleiman, the Emir of Ilorin that the British found in office and allowed to continue in that office till his death in 1915 was a pliable character, a puppet in the hands of his *Baloguns* before the imposition of colonial domination, and a creature of the British after the imposition. Yet, even he was far from being as docile to the British as one would accept an Emir whose internal position was weak. Indeed, far from being "grateful" to the British for rescuing him from his powerful Baloguns, the Emir complained to Resident Carnegie that since the British occupied his emirate, headmen of outlying villages had refused to pay any rent, giving an excuse that they had been ordered to take all their produce to the British at Jebba.[1]

Nor did Suleiman confine himself to merely voicing his grievances against the British. He did also try to avoid cooperating with them whenever such avoidance seemed feasible to him. Thus, for example, in July 1900 Colonel Morland, who was passing through Ilorin, required two horses to replace two of his that had gone sick. Resident David Wynford Carnegie requested the Emir to hire the colonel two of his horses, but the Emir flatly denied having horses. It was only when the Resident converted the "request" into a preemptory order that the Emir supplied Morland with the two horses.[2] But, on the following day also, Suleiman refused to supply food to a party of British soldiers that arrived in Ilorin and Carnegie had to allow the soldiers to enter the town market "for themselves," an allowance which certainly must have taught the Emir and his people that the consequences of refusing to bring food to British troops could be very unpleasant.

Similarly, on the day that Carnegie was finally to leave Ilorin, he indicated his wish that the Emir should go to the barracks and meet him and his replacement, Dwyer. The Emir refused to go, pleading that he was not well. As usual when Carnegie received this evasive reply from the Emir, he sent to tell him that "he must be in the Barracks before mid-day," supplementing this order by pointing out the "folly" of "persistent disregard of the wishes of the whiteman."[3] Only through such cajoling did Carnegie get the Emir to go and meet him and Dwyer.

After their very bloody capture of Abuja in 1902, the man the British installed in place of Ibrahim, the ruling Emir whom they killed, was Muhammadu Gani. We have not been able to trace an account of the reasons for which he was appointed Emir, but one could assume that at the time when they appointed him, the British were deluded that Gani was going to be pliable and cooperative, "amenable" – as Lugard would put it. Yet by 1910 the British were thoroughly disillusioned with him. Thus Morgan found him "of little practical value."[4] Sciortino, assessing him in 1914, lamented that "he did nothing unless driven," that he was "a clog on progress," that he constituted "a danger to the administration" and that he openly approved "malcontents;"[5] and in 1915 Pembleton endorsed "all the previous reports on the Emir."[6]

In fact, in 1914 Sciortino did suggest that Gani be deposed, a suggestion which was dropped mainly because the British were not quite sure of Musa Angulu, the only man they had with whom they could possibly replace Muhammadu Gani and who, indeed, succeeded him on his deposition and exile to Zaria in 1916.[7] Musa, a son of the Emir Ibrahim (1876–1902) that the British had killed in 1902, was at this stage "an active nervous, eager individual." Another reason for letting Muhammadu Gani to carry on until 1916 was that his deposition "would undoubtedly be regretted by all people, both pagan and Hausa" – the fact being that Gani was liked. For, he had "always been absurdly generous" and had "never ruled and never oppressed,"[8] in short never cooperated with the British.

In order somehow to ensure some "administration," a British obsession, for which Gani's contempt verged on the absolute, Morgan, in 1915, came up with the plan of appointing a Waziri to be adviser "to the Sarki." The man appointed to this post was an outsider to Abuja, one M. Gambo, a relation of ex-Alkalin Kano, Suleiman, who ironically himself originally came to Abuja as fugitive from British colonial domination in Kano.[9] The British intended M. Gambo "practically to undertake care of administration." But Muhammadu Gani, far from sighing a sigh of relief that someone had taken over "administration" from him without his being deposed, became openly contemptuous of M. Gambo, being "apt to slight him whenever occasion [offered]," a practice which no doubt contributed to his own deposition a few months later. This was the extent to which the Emir of Abuja, Muhammadu Gani, abhorred British policies.

Next door to Abuja, in Keffi, the British, after attempting to "reorientate" Ibrahim, the Emir they found in office, to serve their policies, finally gave up and forced him to abdicate in December 1902, subsequent to the killing of Molony, the first Resident of Nassarawa.[10] To replace him they appointed Abdullahi, alias Mallam Angulu, a man they felt better suited to answer "the needs of the time." But this judgment turned out to be utterly subjective. Soon enough the British discovered that Abdullahi had used them to facilitate his own succession to the Emirate without having any more desire to execute their policies than the man they helped him to replace.[11] Abdullahi tried to escape working for the British by taking refuge in religious devotion. Thus Larrymore found him to be "a very holy man" who "had no concern for worldly goods." Fitzpatrick was "sorry to say that [Abdullahi] was not a success as an Emir" though he was "a scholar, very kindly and easy going and personally charming." It is both a clear indication that in pretending to shun this world, Abdullahi was merely trying to avoid being a British tool, and a very good comment on British conception of "administration" that the man whom they regarded "a failure as an Emir" was known to be very keen in initiating and supervising community development projects. Thus, he was reported by the British to be "very skilful as a bridge builder" and to be in the habit of personally turning out to supervise road building works, a practice which the Assistant Resident did not approve.

That was not the attitude that the British were looking for in a "successful Emir" or an "efficient administrator." Hence Abdullahi rated very low in their estimation. The complaint that he was "not of much assistance to the administration," became a refrain in every report on the Emir. Down to 1916, Abdullahi remained "a man of charming manners and a scholar [but] absolutely useless as an administrator [though] useful as a bridge-builder," a man who could "not be made to exercise any authority," as the British understood that authority. By 1917 British judgment of the Emir had become harsher for, by now, they had decided that he was "a deadweight on efficiency, most disinclined to assert his authority as a paramount chief." Yet up to 1920 when the *Nassarawa Provincial Gazetteer* was compiled, Abdullahi was still Emir. Beyond doubt Emir Abdullahi of Keffi and the British had different and perhaps mutually exclusive scales of values. Hence his survival in office was something the British suffered rather than desired.

Nassarawa's first Emir under the British was Sarkin Kwatto, Muhammadu, who had been in office at the time when the British occupied Nassarawa.[12]

There is nothing in the comments that British officials made on him to suggest that he was a friend of their government. Thus in 1910, D. Cator reported that Muhammadu was not cooperating with him to effect the arrest of some "wanted men" and, as a reprisal, urged that the Emir's salary be "drastically reduced."

In 1911, B.E.M. Waters overreached himself in expressing his contempt and bitterness for, and towards, the Emir. The Emir was, he said, "as cunning as a fox, a consummate liar, grasping, avaricious, with all the faults of a blackman." Muhammadu earned this superlative denunciation because he had refused "to exercise authority, keep his Districts Heads and others up to the mark nor ... ever travel his Emirate." Worse, the Emir would not even own up to his refusal to actively cooperate with the British. On the contrary, he was "always full of promises," ever repeating that he was "most anxious to carry out ... any wishes of the Government." In 1910, Cator had suggested giving the Emir "only £50 a month." In 1911, Waters did not "think he [was] worth a penny over £25 a month."

Nor did Muhammadu ever change his attitude, though he did change his tactics. Thus, in 1913 also, he was "a disappointment" to Assistant Resident Fitzpatrick. This was because while he helped the Assistant Resident with "great apparent readiness," it nevertheless took "a very long time to get any orders carried out in his country." It would seem by now the Emir's tactic was to "cooperate" with the British in the open while secretly frustrating their efforts and policies. This way, without pretending to shun this world, as Abdullahi of Keffi did, and without feigning senility as Gani did in Abuja, Muhammadu, the Emir of Nassarawa, who was still in office in 1920, managed to avoid serving British policies, at least, during our period of study.

In Bauchi, after the early death of their first appointment as Emir, Muallayidi, in 1903, the British appointed Hassan to succeed him, with the hope that they got the man who would conform to their idea of a good and loyal Emir. Yet within five years Resident Howard was recommending the deposition of Hassan. By this time the Resident was definite that the Emir "was" making the task of administering the Emirate through him an impossible one. [13] Howard alleged that not only had the Emir adopted "an attitude of passive resistance to all reforms," he had also "on more than one occasion ... threatened his Sarakuna for rendering assistance to the Government," a move which "compelled" the Resident to by-pass the Emir and issue orders directly to the Emir's subordinates. In fact, Howard went as far as to suggest, in a special memo, that not only should Hassan be deposed but that the High Commissioner should "break the Yakubu succession altogether." For, according to him, "the whole reigning family [were] impossible" while the Emir himself positively had "no other occupation than intrigues levelled against the Government." Indeed, so miserable had Howard become in Bauchi that he took to excessive smoking of opium, from which he died on 20 September 1908, one day after he failed in his desperate bid to persuade the High Commissioner to remove the Emir.[14]

Resident Gowers, who was sent over from Kano to take control of the "grave situation" that Howard's death supposedly created, was able to make excuses for Hassan, charging that during Howard's Residency the Emir had received "casual and improper treatment" from the Resident's messengers while Howard himself had been in the habit of keeping the Emir waiting a long while before receiving him.[15] This way, Gowers charged, Howard made Hassan's position unenviable. Above all, Gowers argued, Howard should have taken into consideration the fact that it was "too much to expect a Muhammadan chief to submit gladly to the control of a Christian power, however beneficial this control may be to his people and to him personally." Because of this initially sympathetic attitude which Gowers adopted towards the Emir's case, Hassan was able to retain his office until his own death 71 days after the death of Howard, his bitter enemy.[16] Yet there is no reason to suppose that Gowers himself would not have changed his attitude towards the Emir had the latter lived longer.

Borno

The first political officer to be appointed Resident for Bornu Province was W.P. Hewby, until then the Resident of the "Upper Benue" or Muri Province.[17] However, he did not arrive in Bornu Province until September 1902, and in the interim the Residency was held first by Captain McCarthy Murrough and then by Captain Cochrane.[18] It was Captain Cochrane that first discovered that the Shehu neither really regarded himself subject to British control nor regarded British stay in Borno as a lasting one.[19] For soon enough the Acting Resident's political agents started to bring in reports alleging that people in the Shehu's service were already out collecting taxes and collecting them by methods that the British always objected to when employed by people other than themselves. Accordingly Cochrane, in his first report to Lugard, complained that on his arrival in Borno in May 1902, he found the Shehu's tax-collectors out collecting taxes all over the districts, and that during the *Sallah* festival, which occurred in June, messengers from the Shehu were sent with letters to all parts of the Sheikhdom, ostensibly with the purpose of summoning in the *Bulamas* and *Lawans*, but with the purpose of collecting taxes. In many places, Cochrane alleged, mounted men with "soldiers" were sent and "general looting" was the result, because the messengers were afraid to return to the Shehu without a certain number of dollars or their equivalent in kind. He cited as an example the village of Daura, north of Gujba, where he claimed the Shehu's "tax-collectors" went and collected as many as 300 gowns from the inhabitants who numbered less than 500.[20]

In particular Cochrane took an exception to the alleged activities of four men whose names he gave as Bulama Musa, Renasco, Sarkin Fulani and Fugu Muhamma.[21] Bulama Musa and Renasco, he insisted, were leading slaves of the Shehu while he believed Sarkin Fulani and Fugu Muhamma to be working for the Shehu, though they were not his slaves. He says that his attention was first drawn to Renasco by Captain Dunn of the Gujba Garrison who, on June 6, 1902, reported that Renasco was two days north of Gujba with a large armed following raiding Shuwa Arab camps and small Kanuri villages, and had by that date collected over 100 heads of cattle and captured a number of slaves.[22] Later, Dunn reported that Renasco had established his headquarters at Kupti, 20 miles north-east of Magumeri, from where he had again started to raid Shuwa Arab camps and Kanuri villages, robbing those who had cattle or money to be robbed and capturing or killing those who were too poor to give him anything.[23] Sarkin Fulani, whose headquarters were said to be at Shani, three days north of Magumeri, was claimed to be "probably the largest raider in the province." He was said to be "a more powerful man than the late Mallam Jibrilla," a claim which Cochrane himself could not credit, though he accepted that Sarkin Fulani had some 1,000 armed men with him.[24] This man was said to concentrate his raids on Fulani and Shuwa Arab camps. In one attack on one unnamed Shuwa village, he was said to have captured "93 cows, 600 goats and sheep, 2 horses and 7 slaves."[25] In another raid, this time on a Fulani village called Gidum, 80 miles from Magumeri, it was claimed that he captured 257 cows, 1,607 goats, 9 horses, 1 donkey and 1 slave, and to have killed 3 men in the process.[26]

It is not easy to evaluate these reports and claims, some of which sound fantastic. This is because the British were, in those early days, utterly dependent on their political agents for information about what was going on in the emirates, and these political agents were a most untrustworthy lot who were not above fabricating information or distorting it in order to implicate a local official who had incurred their displeasure. Besides, in addition to our observation about the character of political agents in general, we should note that Cochrane's agents furnished him with figures which were too exact to be true. It was one thing for a political agent to know that a raid had been carried out in a locality but quite another for him to know the number of cattle, sheep, horses, goats, and men captured, with as much exactitude as shown in some of the figures quoted above. But given the fact that the government of the Shehu had for some time been in decline before 1893 and the fact that Rabeh's seven-year rule over Borno was of a violent character, it is quite plausible to assume that both armed robbery and "legal" forms of violence were rife in Borno in the period immediately following the overthrow of Rabeh. Thus, we may accept Captain Cochrane's reports as exaggerations of true acts of violence against villages by men of whose status he was not quite sure.

The existence of violence in Borno does not necessarily presuppose the blessing of the Shehu. Yet, that the Shehu was the mastermind behind these raids was Cochrane's main contention; so convinced was Cochrane that these men were acting for the Shehu that he taxed him with the matter.[27] The Shehu understandably denied that they were working for him but allegedly admitted that they used to come into Monguno from time to time to see him.[28] Even after being told that the activities of these men were objectionable to the British, the Shehu was reported to have admitted receiving a visit from Bulama Musa and allowing him to go free.[29]

If it was true that the Shehu admitted that he received occasional visits from these men, then it is a strong indication that they were his servants. But in that case their activities were "legal" since the terms on which the Shehu was recognized by the British did not forbid him from collecting taxes. Nor was Cochrane quarrelling with the fact that the Shehu might be collecting taxes through these men. It was the methods the men were said to be using and the amounts involved that he ostensibly objected to. And it was to these that Lugard also took an exception, as was shown by his instruction that whenever the Shehu was found collecting heavier taxes than the Acting Resident thought he should collect, only the excess should be returned to the community involved.[30]

In fact, what the British really overlooked or were unwilling to concede was that if the Shehu was to re-establish his authority in Borno, which he had to if he was to be of service to them, he had to punish those who had actively collaborated with Rabeh during the latter's occupation of the Sheikhdom. The British themselves had admitted that some tribes, Shuwa tribes in particular, had collaborated with the Sudanese conqueror and stood with him to the last, even after his cause had been already lost. Nor were Lugard and his men known to be the opponents of retributive punishment, certainly not in those days in Borno and the emirates as we shall soon see. Hence we have to look for an alternative reason as to why they refused to consider the possibility that these alleged agents of the Shehu were engaged not so much in forcible collection of taxes, as in selective punishment against those tribes and villages which the Shehu believed had collaborated with Rabeh. The reason that readily suggests itself is that the British were unwilling to allow the Shehu to re-establish his authority to an extent that he could dispense with them or even threaten their position in Borno, and this suggestion is quite in keeping with the British attempt to detach certain groups from the Shehu's control.

Having decided to hold the Shehu responsible for the activities of Renasco and Co., and having decided that only the desire to extract money from the populace made the Shehu to be violent, the British went on piling pressure and threats of deposition on him until he finally arrested Bulama Musa, Renasco and Sarkin Fulani, and handed them over to Hewby soon after the latter's arrival in September 1902.[31] The British themselves effected the arrest of another Bulama, one Hamje, who was said to specialize in confiscating the property of traders on the Yola road.[32] Renasco, Bulama Musa, and Bulama Hamje were each sentenced to three years in jail.[33] The Sarkin Fulani was allowed, however, to go scot-free because Hewby felt he could be useful in helping to reconcile the Mbororo with British rule,[34] a clear subordination of "natural justice" to British colonialist interests. The other "tax collector", Fugu Muhamma, who was said to have recognized the authority of neither the Shehu nor the British, and who Hewby felt had been "collecting taxes," from his fellow Fulanis on his own behalf, voluntarily surrendered himself. He too was allowed to go unmolested on the conditions that he would stop raiding and would help the Shehu and the British to control the Fulani.[35] The next man to be caught "collecting taxes" with violence was captured early in 1903. This was one Mala Bukar, whom Hewby claimed was "a much trusted slave of the Shehu."[36] It is not clear from the records exactly what he did, but it seems that his activities had led to the death of some people in a village called Kiri Kagu in what was soon to become the Manga District.[37] Hewby, with the approval of Lugard, decided to make an example of this man who seemed to be of no use to the British and so condemned him to death and publicly hanged him in Maifoni.[38]

But Hewby had already decided that the only way to end armed activity by the Shehu's "servants" was to ask the Shehu and his followers to hand in all the firearms that they possessed. This was in fact a standard practice of the British in the emirates. To get the Shehu's cooperation, Hewby assured him that he would be materially compensated and the British would enforce his authority and maintain law in the Sheikdom.[39] Having received these assurances the Shehu started to collect the guns in the possession of his chiefs. On the first occasion, he handed in a total of 714 guns of several sorts, saying that he was yet to receive 600 more from chiefs living outside Monguno.[40] These other guns kept on being sent to the Shehu for many years after 1902. The collection of the guns took so long because, in spite of a mixture of threats and promises from the British, many of the chiefs were understandably very reluctant to hand in their guns.[41] Yet, although the Shehu cooperated in the collection of the guns, he received no compensation except that he was given back 50 flintlocks with which to arm his bodyguard for ceremonial purposes.[42]

At the same time as he was pressing the Shehu to capture and hand over those he claimed were the Shehu's servants, Hewby was also pressing him to move to Kukawa and make it his capital. However, while eagerly accepting the idea of reviving Kukawa, the Shehu kept on postponing the date of his leaving Monguno. It was normal for the British to assume, as they did, that Abubakar Garbai would be very happy to restore Kukawa, for he was over 30 years old when Rabeh sacked the town in 1893,[43] that is, old enough to have developed some attachment to it. Yet it was not until Hewby served him with the harsh notice that if he did not move to Kukawa by the end of November 1903, his house in Monguno would be burnt down, that he did move. He did not even start to rebuild the old palace at Kukawa until after he had arrived in the town.

The Shehu's reluctance to move to Kukawa should be seen in the light of his general attitude towards the British presence. In this regard it should be pointed out that, in October 1902, Hewby "discovered" that the Shehu and the people generally believed that British stay in Borno would be very short, perhaps a year or two and,[44] as a result, the Shehu felt that he could postpone the execution of all his plans until after the departure of the British. Nor was this belief about the imminent departure of the British as naïve as it may sound, looked at from the point of view of Borno's previous experience. There was much in this experience to encourage such a belief. For one thing, it seems Abubakar Garbai had been quite aware of British attempts, through the Anglo-Egyptian Government and the Royal Niger Company, to reach a settlement with Rabeh,[45] and of how these attempts were brought to naught for reasons which might not have been apparent to him. Second, he must have been impressed by the fact that in spite of European rivalry in the area, metropolitan Borno had escaped a serious dismemberment and had been restored to his family almost in a piece. Third, he was an active witness of the failure of Fadl-Allah's attempt in 1900–1901 to secure firm British support, in spite of the latter's eagerness to recognize him and use him to effect their projected occupation of Borno. All this could not have failed to convince the Shehu, assuming he had a deeply religious outlook, like some of the early Shehus, that after a short period of tribulation his family was once again being favoured by Providence; that the British, like the French before them, were mere instruments of this Providence and were therefore not going to stay long after the restoration of the family to its former position in Borno.

And given that British stay was in his eyes bound to be short, it was under-standable for the Shehu to want to postpone his re-entry into Kukawa until he would do so as an independent ruler, which, he knew, he was not while the British were around. The Shehu's resentment of the position to which the pres-ence of the British had reduced him was frankly expressed by him in front of the Resident on more than one occasion. For example, a little after the British had collected his arms, he reminded Hewby that the British had reduced him to merely obeying their orders,[46] and lamented that the Resident was trying his chiefs and imprisoning them instead of leaving the question of their discipline entirely in his own hands.[47] This, he said, was destroying his prestige in the eyes of his followers, who were starting to feel that he could neither harm nor protect them from injury. On another occasion he enquired from Hewby an explanation why, in 1901, the British contacted Fadl-Allah.[48] Finally, in 1922, towards the end of his life, he told Palmer a bit of his mind. Among other charges, he accused the British of having misled him in 1902 into understanding that all they required from him in exchange for recognition was to put an end to slave raiding and to consult the Resident on any matter on which he felt the Resident's advice would be valuable. He added that he was aware that the Brit-ish accepted him as the Shehu of Borno only because the French had removed Fadl-Allah from the scene.[49] These occasional outbursts must have been minor in comparison to the deeper feelings of the Shehu.

Gwandu, Kano, Katsina, Yola and Zaria

In Zaria, after the ouster of Muhammad Lawal in October 1902, the Brit-ish appointed Aliyu dan Sidi as the next Emir of Zaria.[50] As is well known,[51] he too was deposed in 1922. An account of his deposition lies outside our period. But it should be pointed out here that relations between Aliyu and the British prior to 1922 were never quite smooth nor really involved trust between them. What the British never at any point doubted was Aliyu's "capacity" and "organi-zational ability."[52] Thus, in 1911 the Resident bore witness that "he [showed] a wonderful capacity for taking the measure of men with whom he [was] brought into contact." He was "a natural organizer" who was "not afraid of difficulties and [knew] how to meet them."[53] This observation became a refrain in every subsequent report on him. Yet, always mixed with this admiration for Aliyu's "capacities" were suspicions concerning his motives and his acceptance of many of the changes introduced by the British. In the same report just quoted above, it was also alleged that "his love of power made him an opponent of the system of District Chiefs and subsequently made him to rely on the confidential slaves and Jakadas of his immediate entourage rather than on his *hakimai*."

The following year Fremantle, who found him "delightful to talk with," also insinuated that "he [showed] to better advantage in discussion than in action afterwards." He was "admirable in expression but rather disappointing in execution." Three years later, Goldsmith found him "undoubtedly clever" and possessing "a strong personality" but at the same time "cunning" and "inclined towards dominance," that is, over British officials. Also, while believing Aliyu "to be sincere in his loyalty to the British Government", he thought that the Emir had been "given too much licence by Political Officers in the charge of the Province" and that he had "not always been treated with sufficient firmness." Allegedly, "this [had] led Aliyu at times into dictating to the Political Officer what line of action should be pursued." In short, the Emir required "a tight reign and must not be allowed to run the show." In 1916, Arnett too advised that the Emir required "a firm hand always and close watching."[54] Therefore, it can be seen that the distrust and fear of Aliyu by the British which, in 1922, assumed paranoid proportions for officers like Byng, Sciortino and Arnett, had not started suddenly but had been building up for at least a decade.[55] By 1922 he became a fearsome "monster" to the British, so to speak, but he had always been a source of anxiety and worry to them and never "a friend" to be at ease with.

As we have seen earlier, after occupying Kano, the man who the British appointed to succeed the ousted Emir Aliyu, was his younger brother the Wambai, Muhammadu Abbas. In appointing Abbas, the British relied on the advice of the commercial community in Kano who passed on their advice through Adamu Jakada, alias Baran Nasara, a Kano trader who doubled up as a British agent.[56] But whatever reasons the British had for accepting this advice and selecting Abbas from among relatives who, at that point included two of his uncles, scores of his brothers of whom at least ten were senior to him, and hundreds of his cousins and nephews,[57] before long they were at loggerheads with him. Thus, according to Arnett, "during the first five years of his reign the Emir was out of sympathy with the ideas of our Government and was at times considered a reactionary."[58] In fact Arnett put the matter a bit too mildly. Relations between the Emir and the British in this period were decidedly bitter and, by September 1907, Palmer knew that "the Sarkin Kano and the Residency staff (who are *all* in his pay) look on Adamu [Jakada] with little love and would ruin him if they could – since he is a whiteman's man."[59]

In the same month Palmer, then Assistant Resident in Katsina, wrote to remonstrate with his superior in Kano for being too lenient with Abbas. He charged that "the actions of Serikin Kano are in direct opposition to our policy and prestige." He reminded the Resident that three years earlier "Lugard and Cargill told [the Emir of] Kano that certain reforms were to be carried out. What is the case now? Not only are they not carried out, but the system then condemned is more rampant and vicious than ever. The out-districts will not progress let alone keep up the reforms instituted, unless [the Emir of] Kano is made to toe the line not only in theory but in fact."[60]

Palmer further claimed that it was "only commonplace" that the Emir had ruined a number of

> Hakimai simply because they had intercourse with the Barracks. It is invariably said ... that complainants who go down with letters are insulted in the Emir's presence and often beaten for going to the *kaffiris*. Mallam Bawa (your messenger) was treated with an indignity which Serikin Kano would not put on the messenger of an inferior ... Adamu Jakada is watched day and night by 40 men and it is said all the barrack staff are in the Emir's pay...

He mockingly asked the Resident "do these things happen when the Emir is friendly to Government?" He went on to call on the Resident to "look at the Maigatakarda – a man known all over the country for his anti-whiteman's views. He is the most powerful man in Kano." Still in the same mocking vein Palmer asked Festing whether "a man who is friendly to Government [would] keep over 100 mallams to pray for that Government's destruction." Palmer warned that the "net result" of the Emir's hostile attitude towards the British was that "in the Emirate our prestige is low ..." He admitted that nothing would be gained by changing the Emir but thought that "a more direct administration and the destruction of the Gidan Serikin should be carried out *at all costs*." He saw no need for any qualms in doing this for, according to him, "the Fulani are only sojourners like ourselves ...," asking "why should they take the meat off the bone we have taken from them?"

In fact Festing needed no prodding from Palmer, for he himself was "disappointed from the first to realize how antagonistic Abbas is to our rule and how bitterly he resents anything we do ..."[61] He alleged that it seemed

> quite impossible to get him to grasp the fact that, were he honestly to throw in his lot with the administration as other Fulani rulers have done, he must in the end be a gainer. His only attitude to myself during the last year [1907] has been one of passive resistance. It has been only by the constant changing of Dan Rimi's underlings, our interpreters and even my own personal servants that I have been able to at all keep in touch with the headmen and the people. At times one's position has been little short of untenable.[62]

Indeed as far as Festing was concerned, Abbas was not able to learn from what had befallen other Emirs. Thus, he wrote:

> during the past few years Abbas has seen many of his brother rulers go to the wall. During the past two years he has seen two Emirs of Katsina deposed, severe punishment meted out to Hadeija and has himself been instrumental in causing the ruling house of Daura to be effaced, yet he persistently continues to intrigue against us …

Just two months earlier, Festing had deported one of the Emir's slaves for being party to "the Emir's intrigues" against the British.[63] This was "Mairunfa [who was] a sort of go-between between the Residency and the palace clique. In other words a sort of spy upon all those who approach the Residency." He was "to reside in Quarra Town until he learnt sense."

In March 1908, Walter Miller of the Church Missionary Society (CMS), by then stationed in Zaria, charged "that the Emir was preparing for war against the British and that he had sent emissaries throughout Kano ordering the people to arm themselves …"[64] Consequently "the garrison at Kano was put on the alert for about a week, and groups of native horsemen were in constant evidence watching camp, and there was a well-oriented report to the effect that the Emir and a body of horse one morning before dawn left the town in the direction of the camp as if for the purpose of effecting an escape." In fact Miller's alarm was baseless and it would seem he was merely trying to precipitate a crisis between the Emir and the British for his and his Mission's benefit. But the fact that such a crisis was nearly precipitated is in itself a measure of the extent to which the British and Sarkin Kano Abbas distrusted each other. However, though the Resident himself realized the baselessness of Miller's alarm, he felt the need to punish somebody. Accordingly, in June he removed the Treasurer, Maaji Sadikum, and exiled him to Lokoja for "exercising a baneful influence on the Emir."[65] In addition, he demoted the Emir's eldest son, Abdullahi Bayero, from the post of Waziri to that of Chiroma and removed his second son Abdulkadiri from the post of Galadima and sent him to Hans Vischer's School at Nassarawa.[66] To the post of Waziri he appointed one Allah Bar Sarki,[67] and made him all but independent of the Emir and very much the man in charge of central and District Administration.[68]

Yet three years later, in 1911, Arnett had to confess that he had "never been able to effect reforms after consultation and with the concurrence of the Emir simply because he has invariably adopted an attitude of *non possumus* towards all proposals though always intimating his willingness to accept a direct order upon the subject …."[69] Hence the Resident "got into the habit of giving him direct orders without consulting his judgement, and it [was] likely that this also [had] tended to upset his sense of the dignity due to his position."The Resident, "however always felt that nothing would ever be accomplished at Kano unless one acted independently of the wishes of the Emir and his household." Arnett reminded the Governor that "he had to depose two Emirs of Katsina and sweep out their households before we could get anything done there." But all the same he urged "patience" with Abbas for whose deposition both Festing and Miller were clamouring. This was because he felt "sure that the deposition of an Emir greatly derogate[d] from the dignity of the position and that the successor of the deposed Emir never enjoy[ed] quite the same prestige or influence." Besides, Arnett had "lately seen all the possible successors to the Emir and [felt] the more convinced that in the Emir himself [the British had] the most capable man of his family."

The fact is that Abbas was never on good terms with any Resident and his death in April 1919 in Kano was held to be the result of a violent quarrel he had had with a British official ten days earlier.[70]

Perhaps the best illustrations of the mutual hatred that generally character-ized relations between the British and the first generation of Emirs to serve under them are those provided by their relations with the Emir of Gwandu Mu-hammadu Aliyu, the Emir of Hadeija Muhammadu, the Lamido of Yola Bobbo Ahmadu, and the first two Emirs of Katsina, Abubakar and Muhamman Yero. Of these the Emir of Gwandu was, in a very real sense, neither a nominee of the British nor their appointee, though he acceded to office a month after the sub-mission of Gwandu to the British.[71] However, Burdon did claim that the even-ing before the Emir was installed, he had a long talk with him and explained to him "most carefully the conditions of his appointment following exactly the lines of H.E.'s address on the appointment of Attahiru at Sokoto."[72] He also said that he was "able to claim his loyalty to Government on the score of gratitude for benefits received, namely the relief of Gando and the surrounding country from constant raids by Argungu." He further claimed that Muhammadu admit-ted this "indebtedness" himself, besides fully accepting "the conditions of his appointment and promising loyal obedience to Government."[73]

But, as we saw earlier on in the second chapter, no sooner was Muhammadu installed than he started to act in a way which Burdon considered a breach of his undertaking to him. This was the "breach" concerning the appointment of the next Dangaladima.[74] Burdon claimed that he "had particularly insisted that no officials were to be appointed without my sanction."[75] He went on to claim that in spite of the Emir's "breach" of his undertaking, he determined not to take any direct action on the matter because "action would be a serious indignity to the

Emir, would sap his authority, and would cause the same tendency to anarchy as is evident round Sokoto — more serious in its effect here than there where the Resident is present to check it." Hence he conveniently turned the matter over to the Sultan for handling.[76]

In spite of the apology that Burdon claimed the Emir submitted through the Sultan in February 1904, Acting Resident Orr claimed he was unable to "report favourably of the Serikin Gando", who "did not behave well to Captain Green of the Medical Department who went there two weeks ago to purchase horses."[77] He too felt the "necessity to post a Resident Officer shortly to Gando for a month, as the Emir appears to need a little careful handling." During March 1904 the Emir paid a visit to Sokoto to greet the Sultan and, according to Acting Resident Hillary, "the former spoke to him very severely on various matters where his conduct had not been satisfactory, commended his recent improvement and gave him much good advice."[78] This, Hillary hoped, "would facilitate matters for Captain Ruxton," the man he finally posted to Gwandu with temporary headquarters at Jega.

Hillary's hope in fact did not materialize; for soon enough, in May 1904 in fact, Ruxton was complaining to Burdon that he was "knowing little and seeing less of what [was] going on outside of Jega and its immediate vicinity. Messengers from the two Emirs [Gwandu and Argungu] come and go; the Emir of Gando's son, Aliu, [had] been living in Jega and in daily attendance a great part of the time, but this [was] very different to seeing things for oneself and personal interviews."[79] That is to say that while the Emir of Gwandu was keeping a watch on Ruxton through his son, Ruxton was ignorant of what the Emir was up to, the reverse of the situation the British wanted to create. By August 1905, Ruxton was becoming decided in his ill-will towards the Emir of Gwandu.[80] He complained of the absence of "that mutual confidence between the Administration and the Native rulers which exists at Sokoto," the Emir of Gando being "a hopeless case; old and intelligent, under the influence of evil councillors." He was positive "under the present regime [there was] no chance of improvement." He therefore urged that Basharu Hanafi "be appointed heir apparent." He claimed that Shehu, the Dangaladima, "would give no trouble and could either continue to reside in Gando or in his own village of Dodoro." Burdon approved this plan, the aim being that the new Dangaladima should become the effective ruler of Gwandu while the Emir would be tolerated to continue as a figure head until his death which Ruxton hoped was not far away, he being over 70 years of age.

Meanwhile, Ruxton also reported the burning of his house and office at Jega on 14 July, but he felt that the man who was convicted for the burning was in fact acting on his own. Burdon, on the other hand, felt the man must have been "instigated by someone in authority." By October 1905 both Ruxton and Burdon had changed their minds concerning the appointment of another Dangaladima and leaving "administration" in his hands.[81] Ruxton urged "the advisability of [outright] replacing the present Emir by a more loyal and competent man." He boasted that "it would be easy though lengthy to draw up his 'dossier,' easier still to say that on no single occasion has he loyally assisted me, in fact the very idea of assisting has never entered his mind, his one idea being to thwart the political officer by every underhand means in his power."[82] Ruxton went on to make other charges against the Emir which even Lugard had to warn him were "too sweeping."[83] Further, Ruxton explained that the Emir's enforced stay at Ambursa was probably the "sorest point of all with the Emir not because he dislikes the locality but because he is in contact with the whiteman (spies inform me that we are always referred to as *Kaffirawa*)." Besides "none of the duties devolving upon an Emir as regards tribute are in fact carried out by him" and "the assessment and collection in all their details devolve upon the political officer."

Burdon, for his part, claimed that "from the accession of the present Emir in May 1903, I have foreseen the probability of his deposition becoming necessary. Mr. Hillary, Captain Ruxton and myself have all done our best to avoid it by patience, guidance and repeated warnings. The Sarikin Muslimin has done everything in his power to assist us, but all to no purpose."[84] Thus, he too was "reluctantly forced to the same conclusion as the Resident Gando that a new Emir is an immediate necessity for the good government of the Gando Emirate."

Not sure of Lugard's reaction to this suggestion, Burdon sought to strengthen it. He stated that the "half measure of a new Dangaladima might perhaps achieve the required object and would be less drastic than the deportation of an Emir. But now that it is evident that the Emir is an active power for evil (he was formerly thought more fool than knave), I think it would probably fail. It is a risky half measure at best, and if it fails would make things worse than before." Burdon had "therefore to request Your Excellency's authority for the deposition of Muhammadu, Emir of Gando, not for any specific offence but for general misrule, oppression and covert hostility to Government extending" over two and a half years, "oppression" being a charge stolen in by the Resident, there being no record of complaints against the Emir from the people of Gwandu. Meanwhile there had been "further cases of incendiarism at Jega during the [previous] two months. On 25th September when Mr. R. McAllister was alone in Jega the Resident's house was set on fire, and on September 27th Captain Ruxton being back at Jega, a boy's hut was fired."[85] This time the British refused to entertain any doubt about the "culprit." "Both Captain Ruxton and [Burdon] believe[d] that the guilty parties must be looked for in the Emir of Gando's entourage." Though Lugard found Ruxton's charges against "the old regime" "too sweeping," he did not object to the deposition of the Emir. In fact he went further than his lieutenants in Sokoto. He instructed them that "if a new Emir is appointed a letter of appointment in different terms will be necessary and Gando be declared 'Public Land.'"[86] Thus, by the middle of November 1905, the fate of Muhammadu Aliyu as the Emir of Gwandu had been sealed. His removal from office had been proposed by Burdon, Hillary and Ruxton and accepted by Lugard, all of whose claim to be his overlords the Emir could not accept, pretences to the contrary notwithstanding. The sequence of events between November 1905 and February 1906, when he was actually ousted, followed naturally from this decision taken in November, but it is worth recounting nonetheless.

The next step taken by Burdon was to "strongly" recommend to Lugard that the military detachment at Jega should be transferred to Ambursa "especially in view of the proposed deposition."[87] To buttress this recommendation, he told Lugard that "common rumour in Sokoto credits the Emir with an avowed determination to kill the Resident and his Political Agent next time the Resident speaks hard words to him." Lugard authorized this transfer of troops and cautioned Burdon that it was "a very dangerous thing to retain an Ex-Emir close to his own Emirate. In case of a crisis he is a focus of trouble. It would be much better to send him to a distant place."

Lugard's reply was dated 19 February 1906. By this date, still unknown to him in Zungeru, events had already taken a "disastrous" turn for the British in Sokoto. For, five days earlier, on February 14, Acting Resident Hillary, two other British officials and 27 mercenaries were killed at Satiru where they had gone to "pacify" a Mahdi and his followers. Whatever the feelings of the Emir of Gwandu about this turn of events he did send troops under one of his sons to join the contingent that was sent to Satiru by the Sultan.[88] However, after wiping out Satiru on March 10, the British marched straight on to Gwandu,[89] to effect the deposition of the Emir, as earlier decided. The troops that went to Gwandu consisted of two infantry and one mounted company and were commanded by a Major Goodwin, who had been sent up from Zungeru to command the troops that were then congregating to deal with Satiru. With the troops went Goldsmith, Acting Resident for Gwandu, who had been withdrawn to Sokoto for his own "safety" after the Satiru "disaster" of February 14.

Goldsmith clearly hoped for a chance to use the troops in Gwandu. Thus he claimed that "on the march to Gando [he] received news that there was a possibility of the Emir preferring to fight rather than submit to arrest." However, to his disappointment, Goldsmith, "on nearing Gando learnt from our Secret Service Agents [that] Serikin Mohammadu was unable to rely upon his immediate followers supporting him in the event of his attacking the column." Thus cheated of an excuse to sack Gwandu, Goldsmith blamed the decision of Gwandu not to fight on the "report that Mallam [the Emir's son] had, only the day before, brought back to Gando after visiting the battle field at Satiru," about the fate of that unfortunate but very gallant town.

When the British "arrived at Gando at 7 a.m. on March 20 ... it was easily seen that there would be no fighting, as fugitives from the town with their goods and chattels were clearly visible going over the hill in the direction of Ambursa."[90] Nevertheless the British troop "formed square on some rising ground to the East of the town and commanding the Emir's compound." The excuse for this belligerent posture was a repetition of past allegations, namely that "before the Satiru incident the Emir had given out that the next unkind word that he heard from the Resident he would kill him and then kill himself." Goldsmith further alleged that "for that purpose it [was] well known that he carried daggers on his person and he [was] also stated (authority Kiari) to be in possession of a revolver of modern pattern which he kept loaded. He had made public to his followers that he was an old man now and valued his life of little account and his one ambition before he died was to kill a whiteman."[91]

Consequently no "risks" were taken. The Emir and his three followers were "summoned" to come out, and "before being brought into the square they were all disarmed." The Emir was then told of his "crimes" for which he was going to be deposed. These "crimes" are interesting in that they emphasize both the Emir's refusal to reconcile himself with British presence as well as the extremism of which Lugard and his team were capable. These "crimes" necessarily included "general misrule and oppression." The others were:

1. "Overt hostility to Government extending over 2½ years".
2. "Secretly aiding and abetting Dan Makafo at Satiru".
3. "Allowing Yoli, a subordinate town close to Gando, to forcibly expel the Political Messenger who had been sent to enquire about the Jangali Assessment."[92]
4. "Residing at Gando when he had been expressly ordered to remain at Ambursa ..."
5. "Lately refusing to transport any more Telegraphic material from Jega to Argungu."

The three followers of the Emir arrested with him were his son, Mallam, his chief Messenger, the *Turawa*, and a slave, Nda. They for their part were arrested because "it was considered necessary to rid the Sub-Province [of them] for the time being as successful administration by the newly appointed Emir would be out of the question if the chief instigators of Mohammadu's hostile regime were to remain at Gando."[93]

When the Emir was informed that he would be taken to Zungeru to answer summons from Lugard, he allegedly declared that "he would rather die than submit to the same fate that had befallen Etsu Abubekri, Serikin Kano and Serikin Zozo and consequently he had to be forcibly put on his horse by a posse of soldiers." In view of the charges of oppression and misrule, it should be pointed out that his arrest "caused much wailing in the town," and Goldsmith "thought at one time that the men of the town would be encouraged on by the women to attempt his rescue." However, probably noticing the disposition of Major Goodwin's force, the towns-people thought better of it and allowed their Emir, under a strong escort, to leave his Province without any major interference." Thus the Emir of Gwandu, Muhammadu Aliyu preferred banishment or even death to "loyalty" to the British.

Relations between the new Emir of Yola, Bobbo Ahmadu, and the British started with an illusion at least on the part of the British. Thus Resident Cargill of Muri Province, who was the first British official to be put in charge of Yola, was "very favourably impressed" by the Emir.[94] He thought the Emir "thoroughly realize[d] and [was] strong enough to make his people conform to the new order of things." Similarly in his February 1902 Report, Ruxton, the first Assistant Resident in charge of the "Yola District" of the "Upper Benue Province," was satisfied to be able to report that Bobbo Ahmadu's "conduct and example [had] been all that could be desired. He was allegedly fully sensible of the new state of affairs."[95] The Emir appeared to him "as the best type of Fulani prince."

However, Ruxton was at the same time aware that the Emir was "very sore at the partition of his dominions leaving him about one tenth of them and no town of any consequence, especially as it [was] only quite lately that he [had] come to realize this." Two months later Ruxton came to realize rather bitterly that "this man" had been playing "a double game the extent of which was not known to me till revealed by Captain Dominik [the German Commandant at Garwa]."[96] According to the latter, who made the "revelation" during a visit he paid to Yola in April 1902, the Emir had on two occasions sent large presents of horses and cloth to him. Ruxton admitted that the first present was made with the consent of Cargill "on Captain Dominik's first visit to Yola and, as explained by the Emir, with a view to ingratiating himself with the Germans and being acceptable by them as titular head of German Adamawa as well as British. The second, however, was sent secretly to Garuwa accompanied by a letter stating his willingness to leave the British if the Germans would make him Emir of their territory." Unfortunately for the Emir, the Germans rebuffed him. Both presents were allegedly returned and he was informed that not only would he not be accepted under any circumstances by the Germans, but also if he left [the British] he would not be afforded any asylum in their country.

Regarding the attempts by Bobbo Ahmadu to be suzerain of the whole of Adamawa, Ruxton moralized that:

> one can of course sympathize with the Emir in taking his view that he has been deprived of all but a moiety of his province ... but at the same time it must be presumed that in accepting the Emirate of Adamawa he was fully aware that it referred to the British portion only.[97]

The Emir's "double-dealing" made Ruxton feel that it could not "be [too] strongly impressed upon him that his loyalty must be unquestioned or he must make way for someone who is." As it happened that Morland was in Yola at that time, Ruxton took the opportunity of summoning the Emir to the camp where Colonel Morland spoke to him "plainly." As a result of this "plain talk" from the man who commanded the troops that "broke" Yola in September 1901, Ruxton mistakenly assumed that the Emir "now recognizes quite clearly the necessity of accepting the inevitable and the futility of kicking against the bricks."[98] In fact, for a while, the re-emergence of the erstwhile Emir, Lamido Zubairu at Gudu,[99] about 60 miles to the north of Yola, had the effect of making Bobbo Ahmadu submissive to the British. Acting Resident Gowers was able to see through this "friendliness". He stated that the "Emir of Yola I believe to be friendly in the sense that he sees on which side his interest lies; but his friendliness is largely due to the fact that he is personally unpopular with his Fulani subjects."[100] Lugard could see no alternative at that point to the policy of accommodating the Emir. Hence he ordered Gowers to "try and show the Emir of Yola how his power and wealth may increase" adding that it was "worthwhile trying to gain over the Fulani."

However, Gowers, almost immediately, did the opposite of what Lugard ordered.[101] He convicted and imprisoned the Kofa, a "favourite slave of the Emir and his most trusted agent" for "contravening the slavery proclamation." This act was, in fact, a deliberate attempt to insult the Emir. Thus Gowers observed that it was "notorious in Yola that neither the Emir nor the Alkali will hear a word against [Kofa]." The latter had "consequently been able for some time to do exactly as he pleased, no one daring to bring any complaints against him even to the Resident." In fact Gowers believed that one of his own interpreters, one Adamu, whom he had dismissed in May, had been "in the pay of the Emir" and he was "satisfied that on one occasion at least" Adamu had "assisted in the interception of a letter" written to the Resident by a minor chief near Mayine complaining against the Kofa. Hence the pleasure with which Gowers convicted the Kofa for allegedly having removed "some slaves" from the household of this minor chief. He was sentenced to 2 years in prison and to rub it in he was publicly flogged 40 lashes.

By this time, the danger which the existence of Lamido Zubairu had posed to Bobbo Ahmadu had apparently been removed by the latter's alleged death in March 1903.[102] Hence, predictably, "the conviction of Kofa, and especially the fact that he was not given the option of a fine on one charge, in spite of the representations of the Emir, [caused] the latter considerable annoyance and [made] him somewhat obstructive." This made Gowers repeat Ruxton's earlier advice to Lugard. He too thought "it would be as well to inform [the Emir] that if he [was] not prepared to accept" British overlordship with its vaunted "impartial justice to all persons irrespective of their position, he ... [would] be deprived of his emirate, and someone [would] be appointed who [was] willing to fall in with [British] ideas and methods."[103]

Lugard, more pragmatically, refused to accept this suggestion. On the imprisonment of the Kofa he ordered that "this matter must be referred to the Resident on his return." Meanwhile, Gowers must "try to keep affairs running smoothly." Concerning the reaction of the Emir, Lugard showed an uncharacteristic empathy. Thus, he said: "of course and naturally the Emir is much annoyed at the drain of his labour (carriers) which labour should rightly be employed in the field especially looking to the great scarcity of food this past season."[104]

As if to warn the Acting Resident that he had other channels of information from Yola, he added that "the accounts" he had been receiving seemed "to indicate that Bobbo has done very fairly well, and we might do much worse"; and apart from this he had a "great aversion at present to ousting Emirs and so causing a misgiving among all Fulani Emirs."[105] Also, when the Kofa was sent to Zungeru to serve his sentence, Lugard released him and sent him home, adding that the public humiliation that he and the Emir suffered when he was publicly flogged was sufficient punishment, confessing that the British could not "afford to alienate the feelings of loyal Emirs and to raise a great hatred and bitterness by too drastic an administration of justice at present."[106] However, perhaps in order not completely to dampen the "zeal" of Gowers, Lugard made some concessions to him and permitted him to "say to the Emir that if he remains obstructive you would have to 'speak badly of him' to the Governor. This would probably suffice. His sulkiness is not unnatural in the circumstances."

Meanwhile, Gowers, even before receiving Lugard's reply, beat a hasty retreat on that issue, but at the same time as doing this he held on to his views about the "need" to tamper with the "injustices" of the indigenous system. Thus in his next report he observed that "last month I had occasion to report rather unfavourably on the attitude of the Emir in minor matters. He has now become much more reasonable."[107] However, he "felt strongly that the principle must be insisted on that every native should have the right of access to the Resident and of laying any complaint before him." He was quick to admit that "this course is distasteful to the ruler and still more so to his principal agents," whose alleged "power for oppression" was thereby "much diminished." In fact "at present any chief who visits the Resident becomes an object of distrust and displeasure of the Emir." Indeed Gowers feared that "as yet" it was "impossible to place implicit confidence in the fairness and impartiality of Fulani methods of administration and rule," and it seemed to him desirable that "the Resident should be in touch as far as possible with all sections of the population, and not be dependent solely on the reports" which reached him through "the probably untrustworthy medium of Fulani officials."[108]

However, while the "whiteman's burden" was taken more seriously by Gowers than by Lugard, Gowers himself was not altogether lacking in a patronizing attitude. Thus he "assured the Emir that the Government [did] not desire to interfere with his power over his subjects and that in fact his authority when legitimately exercised [would] be strengthened rather than weakened by British rule" something he claims to have shown the Emir "in practice."[109] At the same time he insisted that "open dealing" on both sides was "essential to good understanding." But Bobbo Ahmadu could neither perceive the truth of the first claim nor accept the wisdom of the second suggestion.

However, for quite some time he held his peace with Barclay, the substantive Resident. In fact Barclay himself was for a year more occupied with the flamboyant presence in Yola of Aliyu, the ousted Emir of Kano, and the activities of Yerima Babbawa on the "border" with "German" territory, and with pacifying a score of "pagan" tribes than with the "obstructions" of the Emir. However, soon enough the British and the Germans collaborated to contain the activities of Babbawa.[110] By the middle of 1906 Barclay had got the High Commissioner to remove Aliyu of Kano to Lokoja, and had himself reconciled to the fact that no amount of violence could "finally" "pacify" the "pagan" tribes.[111] Thus, by the beginning of 1907, the Resident could once again turn his attention to his relations with the Emir. Hence, in his Annual Report for 1907, Acting Resident Fremantle complained that "the process [of forming homologous districts] received little forward help from the Emir."[112] In fact "in some ways [the Emir deserved] to be called obstructionist." Yet still he felt that "by patient and sympathetic yet firm treatment [the Emir could] be made to execute the policy of the Government on the lines laid down," adding that the attitude of the Emir could readily be understood when it was realized that "the closeness of his link with the past, it [being] remarkable that the ... Emir [was the] son of the founder of Adamawa who received the flag from Shehu Othman while the latter's great grandson now reigns at Sokoto and is thirteenth of the dynasty."[113]

In August 1908 Barclay, when asked by the Colonial Office to submit a special report on the "attitude of the Fulani" towards the British, repeated that Bobbo Ahmadu's "attitude [was] precisely what it [had] been throughout i.e. mildly obstructive."[114] This time too he excused the attitude of the Emir, arguing that:

> brought up under conditions and with views diametrically opposed to those among which he now finds himself, it is hardly to be expected that an old man (he is 64 years) can at once change his nature and adopt a regime wholly antagonistic to that which he imbibed with his mother's milk.[115]

Barclay believed that:

> a good deal of patience and tact [were] necessary in handling the Emir. He [was] intensely suspicious as [were] all Yola Fulanis and [imagined] the whiteman's laws [were] framed with the object of undermining his authority and eventually reducing him to the position of a mere puppet.

Also in spite of "repeated assurances (confirmed by actions) to the contrary," he imagined his "position and tenure of office to be insecure." This feeling, "owing to the nature of the man himself," it was "impossible to combat." He seemed "unable to disabuse his mind of the idea that Government [had] intentions, as soon as the opportunity [offered] of deposing him and appointing another Emir." By these means he [succeeded] in making himself supremely unhappy and miserable." Besides, the Emir was "not much use in the matter of collecting tribute."[116] Yet the Resident could not agree with Fremantle who by now was urging the deposition of the Emir. Such a step, he generously argued, would be:

> both unfair and impolite. Unfair because having taken the country we must, I submit, be prepared at the outset to face difficulties and not expect everything to be cut and dried according to our own views and convenience; impolitic because it would never do to let the idea to get abroad that the position of a loyal Emir under us was insecure. Moreover the immediate successor in this case [Yerima Iyabano] would be no improvement on the man he supplanted.[117]

However, within two months of writing this report, Barclay successfully recommended the deposition of Bobbo Ahmadu.[118] His sudden decision to have the Emir removed was occasioned by the murder of the District Chief of Mbilla Malabu, Ardo Jabbo, by the Batta of Vamgo Malabu a village in the Ardo's district. Barclay was of the opinion that this Ardo was the best friend the British had in Yola Province and that it was the Emir that engineered his murder on account of the Ardo's friendliness with the British. Barclay and his staff adopted this view about the complicity of the Emir almost immediately they received news of the murder.[119] However, during the trial of the murderers by Barclay, some of them alleged that they had taken part in killing their Ardo only because they had been told by their chief, the Arnado of Vamgo Malabu, that the Emir would be very much gladdened by the Ardo's removal because the Ardo was "a friend of the whiteman."[120]

To make sure Girouard acted on his recommendation, Barclay insinuated that Bobbo Ahmadu was threatening other chiefs that he Bobbo considered too pro-British. Thus, according to him, soon after the death of Ardo Bello, the Emir "said to Lawan Gwoni, the District Head of Yola [District] 'there are four men I hate in this country, Bello was one of them, you are another, Serriki Shanu of Yola is the third and Bobero [Bobboi Yero] District Head of Gurin, is the fourth. You are all friends of the White man. Bello is dead and I know what I shall do with you others. So let his death be a warning to you."[121]

After some hesitation the Governor approved the deposition. The Emir was deposed in April 1909 and exiled first to Lokoja, and then he stayed in Zaria until 18 months later when his own son, Muhammadu Abba, became Emir and had him brought back to live out the seven remaining years of his life in Yola. Meanwhile, just a few months after removing Bobbo Ahmadu, Barclay himself was drowned in the Benue,[122] an event which Bobbo Ahmadu's supporters in Yola interpreted as God's dramatic and swift vengeance on behalf of the banished Emir.[123]

Attitudes Towards the British-Appointed Emirs

It is also on record that the ordinary people of the emirates as well as a large number of minor chiefs held the men that the British appointed or confirmed as Emirs in low esteem or even outright contempt. Both the hostility of the people towards the British and the low esteem in which the Emirs appointed by the British were held are documented in the Residents' Reports that we have been referring to. Thus, for example, in his report for June 1900 Resident Carnegie in Ilorin remarked that a certain village head Ajidumgari, was supposed to be "a tributary to the Emir of Ilorin" but he had to tell "him that he must continue to pay a tribute to the Emir, a matter he [had] neglected of late. This [was] not an exceedingly exceptional case – many smaller bales [had] given up paying tribute saying that they had instructions from the whiteman to do so …"[124]

Carnegie pointed out that "formerly the system of tribute to the Emir of Ilorin was carried out with far greater regularity" than after British occupation. In fact the Emir complained that since the occupation of his emirate many of the headmen of outlying villages had refused to pay any tribute, giving as an excuse that they had been ordered to bring all their produce to Jebba.

And in the August report on Ilorin, Dwyer, Carnegie's successor, reported that the authority of the Emir was so fragile that he himself had to take:

> every opportunity in impressing on the people I came in contact with and sending word to the chiefs that I would only recognize the Emir as possessing any authority in the town and that if the Emir gave an order for the good of the town, and if the order was disregarded, I would help the Emir with my advice as to what he was to do and hinted pretty strongly that I would help him with force also if necessary.[125]

Dwyer went on to contrast "the poverty and weakness of the Emir" with "the enormous power possessed by the Baloguns," especially Balogun Alanamu, a revealing fact if it is borne in mind that the Emir had been a puppet in the hands of the Baloguns. Each of the Baloguns and chiefs in fact acted "as if they were independent chiefs," and treated "with contempt any orders the Emir [might] give unless it [suited] them to obey and then they [did] so." Dwyer added that it was "the same way with all the Towns of the District. The Chiefs [were] declaring [that] since the Niger Company's Expedition [to] Ilorin the Emir [had] no authority. Before this event they had to pay tribute to the Emir, the amount being in proportion to the size of the town. This they [had] ceased to do now and [were] backed up by the chiefs in this town who [were] most anxious to prevent the Emir having any power. They [wished] him to be a mere figure head, " in their hands as hitherto.

It would seem that the Emir, Suleiman, who reigned up to 1916 never recovered from this weakness. For as late as 1911, the Resident was reporting that the Emir lived in "dread of falling under the sway of Oyo: certain Natives of Southern Nigeria constantly warning him that this must occur sooner or later."[126] Hence he did not act "as quickly or as sternly as might be desired when dealing with his border villages especially those in Oke Moro." The Resident added that:

Suleiman was appointed Emir prior to the conquest of Ilorin. He was a mere puppet in the hands of his chiefs. Since the British occupation he has been little else. He has merely exchanged the tyranny of his chiefs for the more insidious influence exercised by his numerous sons and favourite slaves.

On top of all this the Emir was "despised by the people for his alleged miserly habits, and he is very deeply disliked because of the lack of control over his sons and slaves ..."[127]

Similarly, in Yola Bobbo Ahmadu who, unlike Suleiman in Ilorin, was an outright British appointee, had to put up with a certain amount of contempt from the people right up to the time of his removal by the British in 1909. Thus, according to Barclay, the period following the "breaking of Yola" was a "troublous" period to which he could "personally testify."[128] From the end of March 1902:

> until the death of Zubairu in February the following year, Yola town and the whole Fulani country was seething with sedition. Zubairu's spies were everywhere, the people's sympathies were with their old king while they detested our nomination and Zubairu did his utmost to influence the fanatical passion of the people. The Liman going to the mosque for early morning prayers would find a letter from Zubairu in the hollow of a guinea corn stalk that had been mysteriously placed in the mosque during night. The letter would mention the Emir, Alkali and principal notables by name, calling them dogs and Kaffirs, heaping the foulest abuse upon them for submitting to the Kaffir's rule, pointing out they were doomed to perdition if they continued to submit to it, while paradise awaited the faithful, and calling upon them and the people to rise and drive the infidel out.[129]

Barclay went on that:

> it was a time of real danger, for Yola was like a slumbering volcano liable to break out any moment and strong executive measures were necessary to stamp out possible rebellion. On several occasions I had to confiscate to Government the property of prominent men found communicating with Zubairu and sending him arms and supplies.

When news of Zubairu's death was received, the Resident exclaimed that "the political situation as regards the Fulani of this Province has been greatly relieved."[130] He felt that Bobbo Ahmadu was:

> now a ruler *de jure* as well as *de facto* whereas previously the general opinion of his coreligionists regarded him as a usurper, and he himself felt some anxiety lest he should be called to account by his elder brother should any unforeseen event restore the latter to power.[131]

But Barclay celebrated the death of Lamido Zubairu too early, for in December 1904 he still had to report ruefully that Bobbo Ahmadu was "not popular with the people, one reason being that he was appointed by us, but chiefly because, being a poor man, he is not in a position to lavish presents on all and sundry with the free hand of his predecessors," whom Barclay conveniently imagined had been in a position to "make and break men at their will, enriching some at the expense of others, according to which intriguing party happened to be in the ascendancy."[132]

So strong was the desire to see a return of Zubairu that as late as January 1908 Webster found himself obliged to transmit to the High Commissioner "alarming rumours" concerning the ex-Emir's continued existence not only physically but also as a political force, reports which Barclay, who had, five years earlier, reported the death of Zubairu, was not inclined "to believe", but which he could not reject out of hand either.[133] The rumours which were "persistent" held that "Zubairu was not dead, but had done the hadj and was now returning to turn us out." These rumours were not only "alarming" and "persistent" but also "widespread as we received a warning from the Military Commandant at Fort Lamy that Zubairu was said to have passed through Wadai and was making a descent on Yola." This was, among other things, a clear indication of the degree to which Zubairu's resistance against the British had captured popular imagination, not just among his own people but far and wide in the Central Sudan. Hence, though "there seems no doubt Zubairu was killed and his body identified," a Lieutenant Jones was "keeping careful watch" at Pella, no doubt to the gratitude of Barclay and the Emir.

Another Emir who suffered a loss of prestige on account of his being identified as a "whiteman's man," in contrast to bolder characters in his emirate, was Umaru, the Emir of Gombe. His abject acceptance of British rule contrasted sharply with the uncompromising stance of his Galadima, the Galadiman Akko, and cost him a measure of prestige. Thus, in November 1904 he was reported to be "rather anxious about the effect which a man Buba at present staying at [Dewu] in Bautsi may have on Ako, an important centre in Gombe Province."[134] The Resident pointed out that Buba was "formerly Galadima of Gombe and lived at Ako;" he took "a lot of his people with him and fought at Burmi." After "the fight there he fled to Kano;" and was "now living within 3 days journey of Ako and the Emir fears he may try to induce the Ako people to desert the present Galadima and follow him." The Resident added that his own view was that the Emir was right in his view and "it would be a good thing if Buba were made to reside at some place more distant from Ako than his present quarters." The fears of both the Emir and the Resident were ostensibly for the

British-appointed Galadiman Akko but it is more likely to have been on account of the Emir's own prestige as well.

The lack of prestige of the British-appointed Emirs did not spare the Sultan of Sokoto either. As we have discussed,[135] his new position vis-a-vis the emirates, earlier on in the second chapter, we shall here discuss only the lack of authority under which he laboured within his own Sultanate. In this respect, Burdon, in his very first report on the Sokoto Province, submitted on 31 March 1903, informed Lugard that Attahiru had "some difficulty in obtaining recognition and obedience from his people."[136] Hence Attahiru was "averse to the idea of the Ex-Sarikin Muslimin living in Sokoto territory" even if the latter were to submit to the British. Attahiru feared that many of the people would "refuse to recognize him as the whiteman's nominee, and [would] intrigue with the other Attahiru as the real Sarikin Muslimin." Burdon had no doubt that Attahiru was "right and that the Ex-Sarikin's return to [his farm at] Chimola [would] cause much unrest." Hence, he expressed a strong desire that in the event of the erstwhile Sarkin Musulmi being captured he should "be given somewhere to live outside the Sokoto Province." In his second report a month later, Burdon reported that the Marafa, Muhammadu Maiturare, a younger brother of the erstwhile Sarkin Musulmi, was "setting a splendid example of loyalty both to his Emir and to Government" but that there were "indications that some of the officials (the 'princes')" were "not too loyal to either one or the other."[137] He admitted that "it would hardly be otherwise just as yet especially with the Ex-Sarikin Muslimin still at large." As for the peasants, Burdon had to report that they took no notice of the Sultan. On the contrary, there was "a good deal of unrest among the middle classes especially the farmers due to the Ex-Sarikin Muslimin having been allowed to remain at large."[138]

And if Burdon was willing to regard even the Marafa as being loyal to the British-appointed Sultan and to the British, Lugard was not. Thus, his private secretary warned Burdon, "His Excellency says without doubt Maiturare is for the Ex-Sultan but was wise enough to sit on the fence when he heard of the Ex-Sultan being driven. He is not to be trusted."

The Sultan's lack of prestige was also reflected in the attitude of some of the towns under him. Thus, in the Report for July 1903 Captain Lewis, who wrote the report while Burdon was away on tour, reported a rebellion at Kanoma.[139] This, he stated, was "a pagan town in the south of the Province [which] answers to the Sarkin Musulmi through Banaga." Early in the month, he heard that "these pagans had cast off their allegiance and refused to recognize Sokoto." He pointed out that he wrote to the Kanoma people telling them that "the Sarkin Muslimin was to be obeyed" and that "his power had not been taken away from him by the Government." He got no reply to this letter. Earlier on, the Sultan himself had complained to the Resident that "outside Sokoto he does not meet with the recognition and obedience that is his due."[140] The Sultan reported that the Sarkin Kiawa of Kaura Namoda had "disobeyed his order in a matter of doing justice to certain of his people," that the Sarkin Kebbi of Yabo had 'failed to contribute his quota of materials or workmen for the Residence as ordered by him" and that "other minor headmen" had "ignored him similarly."[141] Hence Burdon "found it necessary to impress" on the people that "so long as the Sarikin Muslimin was loyal to the Government", his authority over his people "would only not be interfered with but would be upheld," and "when necessary" he would assist the Sultan to "depose disobedient headmen and appoint others." In the case of Kwotorkoshi he had to send "Kiari with a small escort to persuade them" to withdraw their threat "that as the whiteman had all the power now they would have nothing to do with the Sarkin Muslimin or their immediate superior, the Sarkin Zamfara."

As the years went by, openly mutinous attitudes like those of Kanoma and Kwotorkoshi ceased, but Attahiru, up to his death in 1915, never enjoyed the prestige that the nineteenth century caliphs had enjoyed. Thus, as late as 1913 he was reported to be "always in difficulty" with "a certain quasi-irreconcilable element in the Sokoto people," whom he had "endeavoured to carry with him but has not altogether succeeded."[142]

Popular Hostility Towards the British

However, the impression should not be gathered from all this that the people, in showing so much contempt for the new Emirs, had transferred their allegiance to the British, as some of the reports seem to indicate. In fact that was far from the case. Far from feeling that they owed the British any loyalty or trust, the people of the emirates, including those who lived in the capitals of the emirates, continued by and large to be hostile towards the British and their troops long after the cessation of military hostility. Thus, for example, in June 1900 Carnegie, at Ilorin, reported that during Colonel Willock's passage through Ilorin to Lagos, "as soon as the townspeople heard soldiers were coming they all ran away, taking their market goods or hiding them, the reason of their fear being that the soldiers bully them and take things without paying."[143] Similarly, "many villages [were] being depopulated along the Jebba–Buda-Egba road – by reason of people leaving them for fear of being taken as carriers or of being robbed by soldiers and carriers, and more particularly by the latter on their return journey."[144]

In July Carnegie reported as follows concerning the unfriendly attitude of the people of Ilorin:

1. The traffic through the gate nearest the Barracks has been diverted and now passes through the next gate.
2. Persons entering the town, with food acknowledged to be for sale in the markets refused, until ordered by me, to sell to the Telegraph Clerk who reported difficulty in obtaining food.
3. A man sent to buy food by the Telegraph Clerk was beaten because he had or appeared to have a soldier's cap on.
4. One of my carriers was beaten in the market ...
5. There is the least doubt that in Ilorin people have an excellent idea that the Ashanti trouble has taken away many solders out of the country and it is conceivable that some order or act on the part of the Assistant Resident might tempt them into open hostility.

Dwyer, Carnegie's successor, confessed to Lugard that "at one time I was afraid that my first appointment under Your Excellency would have been a failure and that I would have been forced to report my inability to keep the town in order or even to remain in Ilorin.[145] He said all his agents "gave similar report as to the animosity of the people towards the Government." Some of the things reported by these agents were:

1. [The people] were going to throw me out of town.
2. All the troops at Jebba had gone to Ashanti and had been drowned. Therefore it was time to attack Jebba.
3. They would wait till the Bida affair was finished and if the Government got the worst of it they would then attack it.
4. Your Excellency sent a large present to Bida to stop the war.
5. Bida had sent messengers to ask the aid of the Emir of Ilorin which was refused, the town people angry at this refusal.[146]

He said the last item he thought real enough "to inform your Excellency by wire." Dwyer had no doubt at all that "had the Emir given countenance to this request the discontent would have flared up into hostile acts." In August, he warned Lugard that "the people still maintain that all Europeans are shortly to leave Northern Nigeria."[147] Nothing would "convince them to the contrary till they see our troops return." In order to get "people at the market to stop insulting soldiers and to sell to their wives," he had to institute market guards and patrols of police and men appointed by the Balogun, in whose part of the town a given market was located.[148] The job of these combined teams was "to bring before me any case in which a soldier or a soldier's wife seizes articles without payment, or in which when these men having offered a fair price have been refused to be supplied."

In December 1901, Ruxton reported from Yola that the town had not yet resumed its normal activity.[149] In what he called "the Foulanee portion of the town" there were "many deserted compounds, in most cases the property of the adherents of Zubairu ..." He added that the destruction of the central mosque of Yola "by accident" at the time of the occupation "was one of the grievances of the Muhammadans and, in Zubairu's letters to the people instigating them to rise against us it was made the chief point of his denunciations." To defuse the situation "and show the Muhammadans" that Government had "no intentions inimical to their religion," Ruxton offered to assist in the rebuilding of the mosque and, towards this end, he handed cloth to the value of £2:15:10 "to the Emir, Liman and Mallams."

From Bauchi, Temple reported that he could not get labourers to help build the British fort.[150] Besides, the Emir had to direct the town crier "to forbid the people in his name to curse the soldiers in the streets." When the Resident sent for "some of the chiefs to come to discuss the matter of the building of the fort", the Emir answered him that "Bauchi would be emptied" if he insisted on getting them to go and work for him.[151] In Yola too C.I. Wilson, foreman in charge of works had to write to Lokoja to request that labourers should be sent to him as they were "not to be obtained in Yola."[152]

Acting Resident Lewis in Sokoto reported in July 1903 that there was a rumour among the soldiers that "a man in Sokoto town was trying to induce the Sokoto people to attack us.[153] This rumour came to the ears of the Sarikin Muslimin who paid me a visit" to say that "he was sorry that such a rumour should have been started" and that "any man caught by him in the use of traitorous language would be severely dealt with" This promise had little value given the Sultan's own tenuous authority and dependence on the British.

During a tour which Burdon undertook to Gwandu and Argungu emirates in July, August and September, he had "a curious experience" at Sambawa, a little village between Jega and Kalgo.[154] Camping there on his return voyage, one of his escort overheard some people, "a woman and four boys planning to kill" his whole party. The member of the escort followed and identified these people, and Burdon reported the matter to the village head of Sambawa who "was a woman and the daughter of Sarkin Jega." The culprits were captured and Burdon sentenced them – excepting the woman, whom he discharged – to twenty lashes and eight months in prison each. He saw the "affair as a warning and a proof" that it was "those we think we have come to benefit who at present hate us most." In February 1904, the Sultan reported that "a mallam was endeavouring to set himself up as a Mahdi in the south of the Province and to induce the people to rise against the whiteman."[155] This was "the mallam of Satiru, a village near Tureta." The Sultan had the man arrested by the Sarkin Kiawa of Kaura Namoda, a chief who lived far from Satiru. This indicated that the arrest involved some military mobility on the part of the Sultan. The mallam was brought to Sokoto where "he died in jail while the matter was being investigated." And "A few mallams" who had joined this "Mallam of Satiru" had to swear on the Koran that they were "merely reading with him" before they were released.

Meanwhile, in Gwandu there was a section of the population which believed in "the early departure of the whiteman."[156] This faction in 1905 pointed to the telegraph line which was being constructed from Zungeru to Sokoto "as final and incontrovertible proof of the truth of their prediction." It was being put up "simply to prevent the whiteman from losing his road when he has to run away."

One of the best illustrations of the hostility which the common people had for the British was to be seen during the tragic event that the British themselves referred to as the "Satiru Revolt."[157] According to Burdon, Satiru and the villages around it belonged to the Sarkin Kebbi of Birnin Rua, 18 miles south-west of Sokoto, who, knowing the temper of the people, "had feared to demand taxes from it, declare it for assessment, interfere with it in any way, or even report its existence" to the British. Yet, on 13 February 1906 just after Burdon had left Sokoto for Zungeru en route home for a leave, the Sultan reported to Acting Resident Hillary that Mallam Isa, the "headman" of this town, had proclaimed himself a Mahdi, and called on his people and those of the surrounding villages to rise in a jihad against the British. In fact, Mallam Isa had already started to act against those who ignored his call and had allegedly killed 14 people in an attack on one neighbouring village, Tsomo.

When Hillary's move against the town on the following day was roundly rebuffed with a loss of 27 mercenaries as well as Hillary himself and two other officers on the British side, the "rebels" gained considerably in prestige and in strength from the accession of "small parties of malcontents." And there were "signs of unrest amongst the *talakawa* in many directions." It took "the firm attitude of the Sarikin Muslimin and the presence in the field of his chiefs and their troops" to prevent the "spread of the rising or any wholesale defection" of the people. Even though Mallam Isa, the erstwhile leader of this jihad died on February 17 from wounds he had received in the abortive British attack of February 14, "his place as leader" was taken by one Mallam Dan Makafo, a fugitive from "French territory" who, some two months previously, had allegedly "murdered two French officers in Zebarma." Soon "wild rumours" were current in Zamfara that "all Europeans and troops in Sokoto had been killed, their rifles having become useless." The people of Zamfara were elated at these rumours and the "result was considerable unrest amongst the *talakawa*." Several Zamfara towns, whose rulers had gone to Sokoto to answer the summons of the Sultan, began "to fortify themselves" in readiness for battle with the British. So earnest was the mood of the people in Zamfara that Burdon, who hurriedly returned to Sokoto on hearing of the rout of the British troops, "sent back all Zamfara chiefs, as they came in, to look after their districts and keep the country quiet." Burdon had to confess that the defeat of the British on February 14, had "shaken the belief of the native in the invincibility of British arms [and] revealed a readiness to rise against all authority on the part of the unofficial classes." Even "the *talakawa* in Sokoto [town] reverted to the sulky looks I formerly had to report."[158]

While the Zamfarawa were strengthening their fortifications and the residents of Sokoto were reverting to their sulky looks, the Sultan reported that yet another Mahdi had arisen, "one Mallam Mai-Layu." He too was able to mobilize large sections of the *talakawa* and take them from Rabah "into the heart of the Dajin Gundumi", where he "started to build a village and call on the religious to join him." It was a reflection of the extent to which these revolts were directed against the British rather than "against all authority" that when Burdon "directed the Sarikin Muslimin to arrest" Mallam Mai-Layu, the latter "obeyed the Sarikin Muslimin's summons without hesitation." Burdon himself realized as much when, in a covert criticism of the hapless Hillary, he observed that the rise of Mallam Isa was "not the first in this Province since its establishment." He pointed out that the Sultan had arrested "this very man's father in the same village, Satiru, in February 1904." Had "the same procedure been adopted in this case," Burdon believed, "a peaceable arrest would have been equally well effected, and nothing would have been heard of the matter outside the Native Court reports." Short of an abject confession, there could be no more candid admission of British lack of authority with the *talakawa* than this admission by Burdon.

Less than two years later, Fremantle in Yola was writing to warn the High Commissioner that "another cause for reflection" was the possibility of unrest being spread by propagandists or so called mallams";[159] that though the "two risings in German Adamawa last July were promptly dealt with," and: "the Germans following up their action by a systematic policy of expelling all who fall under suspicion; there is already sign that Yola is becoming a harbor of refuge for such men and must be carefully watched."[160]

There was "always possibility of some adventurer raising a following among ignorant folk." Hence "Mr Barclay has always kept a sharp look out in these matters." In August 1908, Barclay admitted that "it would be idle" to say that the people of Yola loved the British and that "we should be the first to despise and suspect them if they did or pretended to." On the contrary, the people of Yola did "not grovel in the dust as [they] would to one of [their] own Emirs," nor would one of them "get off a broad road into the bush when an European passes by." This was full six years after the occupation of Yola.

Conclusion

We have seen that relations between the British and the very men that they themselves appointed as Emirs after, one way or the other, ousting the majority of the erstwhile Emirs, were far from cordial. With one or two exceptions, these relations ranged from hostility and contempt on the one side, to the downright hostile and violent on the other. As a result, in some of the emirates, the British had to depose two or even three Emirs before they could get an Emir with whom they worked out a working relationship of some sort. However, while some Emirs more or less readily worked with the British and some others found it absolutely impossible to work with them and had to be removed, a majority of the Emirs adopted what the British themselves called "passive resistance", a tactic whose most usual form was to be very civil and cordial towards the British, to express a verbal approval of most of what they proposed but, at the same time, find one excuse or another for being unable to help in the execution of those proposals.

We have also seen that the British-appointed Emirs enjoyed little prestige in the eyes of the common people. Thus, on the one hand they very unfavourably compared to the erstwhile Emirs who resisted the British, and who were either killed or deposed and banished, thereby acquiring the aura of martyrdom. On the other hand, it was known that these British-appointed Emirs were more or less puppets with no autonomous power – either military or legal, in both respects being visibly subordinated to the British Residents. This applied to the Sultan of Sokoto as much as it applied to the other Emirs. The Sultan's subservience to the British and indeed the readiness with which he accepted office under them, stood in sharp contrast to the courageous resistance to the British by his two predecessors, Abdurrahman and Attahirun Ahmadu. Further, we have also shown that the claim expressed in the writings of Lugard and later writers like Margery Perham to the effect that the people of the emirates transferred their allegiance from the Emirs to the British is baseless. The people of the emirates regarded the British, their troops, police, carriers, clerks and messengers with extreme hostility throughout the period covered in this book.

10. Emir Aliyu Babba of Kano (1894–1903) refused to surrender to the British after the invasion of Kano in February 1903. The Emir and his large contingent attempted to migrate to the East but were captured by the French and subsequently handed over to the British. The Emir died in exile in Lokoja in 1926.

4

The Extension of British Administrative Control to the Small Towns and Villages of the Emirates

Introduction

As soon as the British had finished occupying the emirate capitals and even while the 'pacification' of towns and villages in the emirates was still going on, they began to extend their colonial control to these towns and villages. This exercise, which was drawn out, was referred to as the "formation of 'homologous' districts". Before going on to examine the details of this exercise, which made a great impact on the pre-existing administrative and political structure of the emirates, it is necessary first to gain an idea of local administration in the emirates in the nineteenth century and to show how that system failed to meet British purposes. Then, after examining the exercise in some detail, we shall go on in this and the next chapter to examine the success or failure of the exercise from the point of view of British purposes. Thereafter, we shall assess the nature and magnitude of its impact on the administration, politics and society of the emirates.

Precolonial Local Government Versus British Aims

It was a lack of coincidence between the structure of local government in the emirates, on the one hand, and the British aim of having a few, rather than many people, to hold responsible for law and order in the rural areas and through whom to collect their taxes, and all that at minimal financial costs, on the other, that necessitated the reorganization of that precolonial structure of local government. Thus, in the precolonial days there were very few territorially compact districts with the district chiefs residing therein. In Kano, for example, there were only four – namely, Rano, Karaye, Gaya and Dutse.[1] In the Sokoto hinterland there was hardly any compact district, although many important chiefs lived outside the capital as commanders of border posts.[2] In the Emirate of Fombina, whereas the big sub-Emirs such as those of Bamnyo, Koncha and Bibemi had compact territories, there were few districts with resident chiefs in the hinterland of the capital, Yola which was the only part of the emirate that fell to the British.[3]

Instead of compact districts with "resident" chiefs, the British found that most of the big chiefs, including the former garrison commanders, lived in the capitals of the emirates, from where each controlled a number of villages, not concentrated in one locality but scattered over different parts of the given emirate. Hence, the highest authorities living outside the capital of an emirate were, in the majority of cases, town chiefs, or Sarakunan Gari.[4] These Sarakunan Gari were in most cases of equal status with one another; only occasionally did a Sarkin Gari have authority over villages neighbouring his town. Not only were the Sarakunan Gari in a given single locality equal among themselves, but they were each subordinated not to the same chief residing in the capital but to different chiefs. Between a major chief living in the capital and his towns scattered in various parts of the emirate were messengers known as *jakadu*.[5] Among the functions of a *jakada* were the collection of taxes, the settlement of cases that a Sarkin Gari was unable to settle and bringing to the capital cases that he himself could not settle. They were to be settled either by the chief in whose employ the jakada was or, in particularly important or difficult cases by the Emir. The jakada was also responsible for listening to complaints against the Sarkin Gari, settling them or reporting them to his master in the capital. If a complainant was dissatisfied with the jakada's decision he could himself take his complaint to the capital to the major chief in charge of his town or to the Emir himself.[6] In some cases, including the case of the capitals of the emirates, the inhabitants of a single town owed allegiance, not to a single Sarkin Gari but to several communal leaders within the town.

As an example of the situation depicted above, the chief of Ribadu in the Emirate of Fombina, who was an important border commander, had authority only over a few other villages in the vicinity of his town, the other villages owing allegiance either to chiefs resident in Yola town or to chiefs resident in other parts of the emirate,[7] including a chief living as far away as Uba, over one hundred miles away to the north of Ribadu.[8] On the other hand, the chief of Ribadu himself had authority over Huyum and a few other villages in the vicinity of Uba.[9] Similarly, the border post of Namtari, about twenty miles west of Yola was under the Kaigama of Fombina, who also controlled many of the villages between the Batta chiefdom of Demsa about fifteen miles further to the west of Namtari and the very outskirts of Yola town. But within this area were very many settlements of serfs who, for all purposes, owed allegiance not to the *Kaigama* but to their masters, all of them important officials living either in Yola or in Namtari, in most cases owning houses in both.[10]

Within the hinterland of Sokoto town, that is, in those areas which were so close to the town that the Sarkin Musulmi himself was in effect the Emir, it should be pointed out that the border posts, very many of which were commanded by members of the Caliphal House, and which in many cases were very close to one another, were co-equal in status, all owing allegiance direct to the Sarkin Musulmi.[11] Consequently, there was, for the British, a "great confusion of territories, fiefs and districts which never [existed] in any orderly geographical arrangements."[12] Thus, for example, the Sarkin Sudan of Wurno had no authority over Chimola, just three miles across the river, the latter being under the Sarkin Zamfara who, as a rule, was the senior member of the house of the third Sarkin Musulmi, Abubakar Atiku, just as Wurno was, as a rule, commanded by the most senior member of the house of Bello, the second Sarkin Musulmi. Similarly, Goronyo and Shinaka, about three miles from each other, were independent of each other. So were Gandi and Tsamiya, and Yabo, Dendi and Danchadi, all three within a radius of about six miles.[13] In the same way, even on the very outskirts of Sokoto "the towns, villages and farms belonging to the various headmen [were] mixed up."[14] Sokoto town itself was "not divided into wards."[15] Instead, there were Sarakuna including the Alkali, the Magajin Rafi, the Magajin Gari, the Galadiman Gari, the Waziri and the Sultan himself,[16] "who the people 'followed' ... and who [were] to some extent responsible for such followers."[17] Besides, "this division into following [was] neither by localities, trades [nor] any other recognized classification."[18] Rather "it [was] partly based on historical connection and custom, and for the rest apparently on inclination." From the British point of view "it [was] in no sense a *system* on which [they could] base anything like an elaborate scheme of taxation."[19]

The towns and villages immediately surrounding Gwandu too were, in the same way, controlled by members of the Gwandu ruling house, each of whom owed direct allegiance to the Emir of Gwandu.[20] Here, too, there were single towns which had no single overall sarakuna, an example being Ambursa, which had "no less than six headmen."[21] Similarly, in Kano Emirate, in what later became Kura District, the British found that the town of Chiromawa contained 309 "compounds or families," of which 179 paid taxes to the headman of Kadama, 30 to the headman of Ringimawa, 21 to the headman of Garun Baba, and 16 to the headman of Mallam.[22] In Mallam itself there were 454 families, of which only 303 paid taxes to the chief of the town. Of the remaining families

23 paid to the chief of Kampawa, 28 to the chief of Ringimawa and 104 to the chief of Jobawa.[23] In the same way, in the town of Bebeji 335 compounds paid taxes to Sarkin Bebeji while the rest, 330 in all, paid to Sarkin Kiru, the chief of a neighbouring town.[24] Similarly in Zaria Emirate "the towns owned by the various headmen" were "dotted at random about the emirate and the headmen all [resided] in Zaria [town], and had little or no knowledge of their towns", according to Resident Charles Orr.[25]

On the other hand, the aim of the British, according to Acting Resident Goldsmith of Sokoto, was to have a system that would facilitate "better control"[26] of the rural areas of the emirates by the British and that would "simplify ... Administrative supervision"[27] of local chiefs by them. In other words, the British wanted to be able to "fix responsibility on [some] local chief,"[28] rather than a multiplicity of chiefs, in each and every town and district in an emirate. More than that the British wanted to do away with the large body of jakadu as agents for the collection of their taxes, and to employ instead a smaller number of people, thereby reducing the amount of the proceeds of these taxes that was "embezzled."[29]

The Formation of Homologous Districts

To adapt the pre-existing structure of local government in the emirates to their aims, the British decided to alter that structure. This alteration, they decided, was to take the form of making all the inhabitants of a town or village pay British taxes through a single chief of that town and through no other similar chief. All the towns and villages in a given locality were to pay these taxes through a single major chief, who was to reside in that locality rather than in the emirate capital or in another part of the emirate. In other words, the British decided to secure their aims by outlawing extra-territorial lines of organization and rigorously upholding territoriality as the basis of controlling the rural population. Inevitably, this entailed the subordination of some chiefs to other chiefs with whom they had been equal in status. It also entailed a large scale "withdrawal" of recognition, not only from the jakadu, but also from some chiefs, since a necessary corollary to the territorial rationalization of the system was a reduction in the number of District Chiefs. Hence the exercise was bound to meet with resistance in one form or another; and the British, realizing this, went rather cautiously about carrying it out.

Thus, for example, when, early in 1903, Hewby in Borno asked the Shehu to submit the names of his "fief-holders," the Shehu, while submitting a list of sixty-one officials, pointed out that only thirteen of them lived outside

Monguno, at that time Borno's temporary capital, and registered his opposition to the idea of the others being sent out of the town.[30] Lugard felt that the move made by Hewby was premature, especially at a time when the Shehu was also being pressed to "share" his income with the British and to move to Kukawa, the nineteenth century capital of Borno.[31] Hence, Hewby suspended the move until May 1904, over one year later, when Acting Resident Howard started rearranging these fiefs so that every fief holder would have "all his villages in one locality rather than scattered."[32] By September 1904 there were thirty-one districts, each with a resident *Ajia*, this term being adopted on Lugard's own suggestion, in preference to the more revealing term "superintendent" – by which Hewby wanted to refer to them.[33] However, while effecting this change, Hewby took care not to abolish all fiefs belonging to people residing in the capital, in particular sparing the fiefs of royal women, such as the *Magira*. He also winked at the fact that the *Ajias* spent much of their time in the capital.

In Sokoto, it was not until July 1905 that Resident Burdon started "devoting much time and thought" to the introduction of the system of "homologous districts," and even then only in the Zamfara areas of the Emirate.[34] As far as the Gobir areas were concerned, "districts and rights of property [were] so much more complicated" that the Resident preferred to reserve the formation of homologous districts there for a later period.[35] That is to say he chose to devote "most of his energy to Zamfara [because] conditions [were] less difficult, knowledge easier to obtain and the experiment less liable to cause trouble."[36] What gave Burdon a welcome opening in Zamfara was the fact that the chief of Bakura had just previously deposed the chief of Baraya Zaki, a subordinate town of his, without seeking permission from the Resident.[37] Burdon took this opportunity to get the Sultan to deprive Bakura of the villages of Baraya Zaki, Moda and Warmu. All of these had, allegedly, been placed under Bakura only in c.1893 by the late Sarkin Musulmi, Abdurrahman, after taking them away from Anka, whose chief, the Sarkin Zamfara na Anka had revolted against the Sarkin Musulmi.[38] The Resident restored the three villages to Anka and then went on to suggest to the Sultan that all the towns taken from Anka by the late Sarkin Musulmi, or ruined as a result of the suppression of Anka's revolt, should be rebuilt and restored to Anka. Accordingly, the villages of Sabon Gari, Damri and others, whose inhabitants had been enslaved or had deserted, were repopulated with these former inhabitants whose "self-redemption" was effected, and who were made to move back to their original villages. The rebuilt villages were then restored to Anka.[39]

It was while the Resident was taking these cautious steps in Zamfara that the Satiru revolt and its brutal suppression took place and afforded Burdon the opportunity to introduce territorial changes much nearer to Sokoto. Thus, before the revolt, "Satiru and the surrounding villages" belonged to Sarkin Kebbi na Birnin Ruwa [Silame]."[40] After the bloody suppression of the revolt, the Sarkin Kebbi was "deprived of this piece of territory which was separated by several miles from the bulk of his district."The Sarkin Kebbi lost "Satiru"[41] and the villages neighbouring it, allegedly because "knowing its disaffected state he had feared to demand taxes from it, declare it for assessment, interfere with it in any way [nor] even report its existence."[42] These villages were now placed under the Sarkin Baura of Denge "with whose district it" adjoined.[43] Similarly, the Dan Kogi of Damaga, who had "treated Major Green D.S.O. disgracefully on the return of the latter with the Mounted Infantry to Kano" from Satiru, was deposed. His town deprived both of its autonomy and of its subordinate towns, and added to the territory of Sarkin Kaya of Maradun "with which [they] adjoined."[44] Also "for similar neglect on the march of the Mounted Infantry to Sokoto," the chief of Rara was deposed and his town "transferred from the Bakura district, with which it was not homologous, to the neighbouring district of Raba."[45] In this way "loyal chiefs [were] being rewarded and disloyalty punished while, at the same time, districts [were] being extended and made homologous ...;"[46] and by September 1906, the Resident had been able to reduce Sokoto from an unspecified number of British-created districts to forty-six.[47]

Maintaining the momentum during the next three months, Acting Resident Goldsmith made eight major transfers of villages before December. The benefactors of these transfers were Raba, which got another three "important towns," Talata Mafara, which got an additional town, Badarawa, to which was added one town, Kauran Namoda, which was given an additional town; Goronyo, which gained seven "important towns," Maradun was given four additional towns, Maru gained one town, and one town was transferred to Moriki, but the total number of districts in the Sultanate still remained at forty-six.[48] In addition to these forty-six districts with "resident" District Heads, there were smaller districts mainly around the town of Sokoto still belonging to officials living in the capital including the Galadima, the Magajin Rafi, the Alkali, the Waziri and the Sultan himself. In all there were nine of these additional districts.[49] In 1907, the Resident was still "chiefly engaged in arranging transfers of towns and villages from one headman to another." By the middle of that year, the Resident felt that eight districts had taken a final shape. These were Kebbe, Gumi, Bukwium, Anka, Pauwa, Kotorkwoshi, Dogon Daji, and Kilgori. A ninth district, Tambawal, had also taken a final shape except for the fact that there were "certain towns in the district which belonged to Gwandu and which [the Resident] propos[ed] to put under Shehu of Tambawal."[50]

By 1912 seven of the forty-six major districts had been abolished. These were Badarawa and Bazai which were amalgamated with Isa District; Bodinga which was absorbed by Sifawa; Dinawa and Kwargaba which were incorporated into Wurno District, Wababi which was amalgamated with Denge; and Banaga which was absorbed into Maru. At the same time, Fauwa District was transferred to Katsina while Chafe, which had been transferred to that emirate in 1906, had been returned to Sokoto in 1908 and made into a district. So had Kwiambana which, in 1907, was transferred from the then province of Kontagora to Sokoto also set up as a district; thus by December 1912 leaving Sokoto with forty consolidated districts. Of the smaller districts in the vicinity of Sokoto town, four had been abolished, leaving only five such districts, one each controlled directly through the Sultan, the Waziri, the Magajin Rafi, the Ubandoma and the Sarkin Zamfara;[51] by this time the Galadima, a very important member of the Sarkin Musulmi's council from the time of the Shehu up to the British occupation, had himself been posted out as a District Head.[52]

Changes in the territorial structure of the districts in Sokoto continued right through our period and beyond, the last major adjustment to occur in our period taking place in 1915. Thus, with the appointment of the Marafa, Muhammadu Maiturare, as the Sultan in succession to the deceased Attahirun Aliyu, the Marafa's large District of Gwadabawa was broken into two districts, Gwadabawa and Tangaza.[53] The former was put under his oldest son, Muhammadu Tambari, with the title Sarkin Gobir, while the latter was put under his second son, Abdurrahman, with the title Marafa.[54]

In the Emirate of Gwandu, the number of unconsolidated "Districts" was seventy-six up to February 1906, a number which Lugard found "absurd" in a "small sub-Province," instructing that these districts "should be grouped into half a dozen if possible."[55] By December 1907, Gwandu had been constituted into "14 distinctive homologous, Districts."[56] By this time only Gwandu District, out of which the Emir had just moved to Birnin Kebbi, which thus became the capital of the Emirate, remained to be consolidated. The difficulty with the district stemmed from the fact that most of its sub-district heads were important princes, "much older" than Muhammadu Bashari, who had been made District Head of this symbolically important district by his father, the newly appointed Emir, Halirun Abdu. Though the Emir was able to put Bashari in charge of the district, he was not able to reduce these important princes, among who were Guruza and Basharun Hanafi, both of them contestants with Haliru himself for the office of Emir, to subordination to Bashari. Hence, although "for record purposes the District of Gwandu" was by now "regarded as a homologous whole" with "various sub-districts" such as Kardi, over which Basharun Hanafi ruled with the title of Sarkin Kebbi, in practice the various sub-district heads were allowed to deal direct with the Emir rather than through Bashari, the official District Head. However, the Assistant Resident sanctioned this arrangement only "as a temporary measure."

From the Emirate of Bauchi, Resident Howard reported as late as February 1906, that is, four full years after the British occupation of the Emirate, that he was "bound to confess that, although [he] at first entirely disagreed" with the views of his predecessor, Resident Temple, about the "impracticability" of "making the fiefs homologous", he was "now persuaded that any sudden change would entail a serious loss of revenue for some years to come. And it would probably dislocate the whole system of Native Administration to such an extent that it would never fully recover, as the Fief holders' or District Headmen's power [depended] mainly upon tradition and personal influence."[57] Howard argued that "the principal Fief holders [were] men of birth" rather than slaves as was "often the case in Bornu."[58] They were in fact "the grandsons of the men who received their fiefs from Yacubu and their fiefs [had] remained unaltered since that time."[59] He had "spoken often to the Emir of [the] subject" of making the districts homologous and abolishing the jakadu, and had "done [his] utmost to present [the High Commissioner's] views on the matter;" and, in spite of the fact that he was "persuaded that [the Emir would] do his utmost to bring about the change gradually," he would advise further temporizing even on the issue of cutting down the number of the jakadu. For a jakada was "useful not only in the collection of taxes but as a secret service agent."[60]

However, by March 1908, the Resident had started consolidating the Districts. For example in this month, the "Jarawa sub-district", which was a "fief" of the Sarkin Kudu, was so rendered "by the inclusion in it of several small towns formerly under petty office-holders or slaves."[61] This "was done ... to ensure that the trouble which [had] been taken in settling this very difficult tribe should not be wasted due to a lack of efficient local supervision."[62] By 1914, the emirate had been consolidated into fifteen Districts, of which eleven were still within the emirate while four viz: Warji, Ari, Burra, and Dass, had been made "independent."[63] The "Emirate Districts" were Bauchi, Ganjuwa, Lemme, Lere, Kirfi, Galembi, Darazo, Jama'a, Fali, Toro and the "Plain Angass."

In Gombe too, by 1908, homologous districts were in the process of being formed. Thus in March of that year, the District of Akko was broken up into two, with the Galadiman Akko keeping "the whole of Ako proper" while the Yeriman Gombe who, in former days had been Akko's Kofa[64] in Gombe, was placed over "Deba Habe with the neighbouring pagan towns and Waja," which had formerly been under the Sarkin Yaki before being merged with Akko by the British.[65] However, when, in December of the same year, the Yeriman Gombe was convicted of accepting bribe from an alleged slave dealer and sentenced to a year's imprisonment, his district was broken up and shared among the Galadima, the Ajia and one Maina Musa.[66] The districts in Gombe were in fact so much "rationalized" that by December 1914 there were only eight districts. Of these, only four were left under the Emir of Gombe, namely Nafada, Gombe, Akko and Dukku. The other four – namely Tula, Ture, Tangaltong and Chum, had already been made independent of the Emir.[67] By this time "all the districts [were] self-contained" and "there [were] no tax-gatherers, other than the district and village heads, and no fief holders" living in the capital.[68] In 1915, the number of the Emirate Districts" in Gombe was further cut down to three by the merger of Dukku and Nafada Districts, supposedly "as was originally intended," but in fact in order "to effect savings by replacing the higher salaries" of the two District Heads "by those of village group-heads, with pay not exceeding £36 p.a each,"[69] a rather confused argument.

In the Emirate of Adamawa, by the end of 1907, the policy of grouping "the Fulani districts into homologous units [had] been gradually" effected, but up to this time "many places still [owed] allegiance to some chief other than the District Headman or [followed] the Emir direct."[70] This was "especially" the case with the "hill pagans whose inclusion in a Geographical District under a Fulani headman was in most cases nominal."[71] By this time there were still as many as "twenty Districts under the Emir" plus three new ones acquired as a result of a recent adjustment of the border between German Adamawa and British Adamawa.[72] In addition, certain "pagan areas had not yet been assessed." While some of these twenty-three Districts were tiny and "uneconomical" to run and for that reason were fated to be merged with others, some were very large. This was especially the case with the District of Lamdo Kabi which, in 1908, was split into two, Mayine and Mayo Balwa Districts.[73] By the end of 1909, the number of Districts was cut down from twenty four to twenty, "in addition [to] the Chamba [Binyeri] and the Nyandang-Waka areas which were yet to be brought under effective British control."[74] By June 1910, this number was further cut down to nineteen, with the merger of Holma, most of whose territory lay in German Adamawa, with Zummo, which had also suffered a loss of villages as a result of the imposition of the colonial boundary.[75] Then, in March 1911, yet another district, Njoboli, was abolished and merged with Yola District.[76] The number of districts stabilized at eighteen up to the end of our period. However, soon after the First World War, Adamawa regained part of the territory that she had lost to the Germans. This entailed the creation of new Districts. But even in that portion of the emirate that had never been under the Germans, "District reorganization" was resumed after the war. Thus, for example, between the end of the war and the early 1930s the Districts of Daware, Huyum and Gola were abolished while the Districts of Binyeri and Nyandang-Waka were created.

In Zaria too, up to the end of 1905, the Resident found himself "unable ... to inaugurate the reform laid down in Memo 5 as regards the Division of the Hausa portion of the Zaria Emirate into districts."[77] This was partly because it seemed to him "necessary first to fix the exact assessment of each town and village in order to see that each fief holder [was] fairly dealt with," and partly because of opposition from the Emir and his chiefs. However, by now "the ground" regarding assessment had "been cleared" while "the Emir and his headmen [had] begun to grasp what [was] about to take place." One year later, i.e. up to the end of 1906, it had still "not been possible to divide the Zaria Emirate into districts though ... an important step in [that] direction [had been] taken by the appointment of the Ma'aji of Zaria on the Emir's nomination to take charge of a large tract of pagan territory in the south of the Province", with his headquarters at Kachia.[78] And even though the scheme apparently took off in Zaria in 1907, up to 1912, the process of district reorganization was still going on. Thus, in this year the Kaura's District lost the sub-district of Zangon Katab to the Katuka's District.[79] The following year the District of Limanin Kona was abolished and its three "villages" divided between the Madaki and the Limamin Juma'a.[80]

In the Emirate of Kano, "District Reorganization" was only being mooted as late as the last quarter of 1907. Thus, although the Resident was of the opinion that the Governor's "scheme ... for the amalgamation of the smaller districts and placing the lesser ranks of the Hakimi under the more important ones will ... be of the greatest assistance to the administration of the Province," and during the previous year "one of the greatest difficulties in [the Emirate had] been to get individuals to accept responsibility," and the Resident knew that "under the new system [the British would] have a few really big men to deal with" apart from the Emir, all the Resident had done up to the end of the year was merely to "explain" the scheme to the Emir.[81] And as late as 1915, new districts were still being carved out. In this year   the District of Bichi was carved out of the District of Dawakin Tofa and put under the Chiroman Kano, Abdullahi Bayero, who had formerly resided in Kano city without any defined function since his demotion from the office of Waziri by Resident Cargill in 1908.[82] Similarly, Gwarzo District was carved out of Karaye District and placed under the Sarkin Dawaki Maituta.[83]

In Katsina too, new districts were being formed as late as 1915, in which year, for example, a district was carved out of the Galadima's District and placed under the Makama.[84] In the same year, a whole emirate, Dambam, was reduced to a district and merged with the Emirate of Missau, which was at that time in Kano Province.[85]

Resident District Heads

Simultaneous with making the districts territorially compact, the British were sending the officials in charge of them out of the emirate capitals to go and reside, each in his district. The policy of sending the chiefs out could not be hurriedly implemented owing to opposition from the Emirs and some of the chiefs, as we shall see later, and also because the British themselves felt the necessity of retaining some of the officials in the capitals for purposes of "Central Administration." Yet this policy was as fully as possible implemented within about two years of introducing the British policy on district administration in each emirate. In fact, in the Sultanate of Sokoto the sending out of District Heads preceded even the formation of homologous districts, the former taking place almost at one go in April 1905 when, according to Burdon, the Sultan ordered all the various fief holders, former garrison commanders, etc that had been living in Sokoto to go and live "in their chief towns and perform their [new] duties." These absentee headmen so sent out in April included the Sarkin Baura, who was sent to Denge, the Sarkin Kebbi, who was sent to Shebra, the Sarkin Burmi, who was sent to Jabo, the Sarkin Sudan, who was sent to Kwargaba and the Sai, who was sent to Kilgori.[86] Similarly, in Gwandu, where the district rearrangement as a whole started only in April 1906, by December 1907, the Assistant Resident there was able to report that the emirate had been rearranged in fourteen "homologous districts ... each administered by a Resident Headman."[87] In fact, by this time, there was only one official charged with responsibility for administering a district that was still living in Birnin Kebbi. This was the Waziri, Muhammadu Raji, alias Mallam Baba, who was also the District Head of two districts, Aliu Wanta and Bakwoi.[88] But even he was in Birnin Kebbi only as a "temporary measure," until another person who could "satisfactorily fill his place" as the principal adviser of the Emir of Gwandu could be found. This suggestion clearly shows where the British placed emphasis, between central and district "administration," with the assertion that this *mallam*, allegedly was "one of the most intelligent natives" the Assistant Resident had "ever met."[89] It was he that would be sent out to be a District

Head, while his substitute, who presumably would be of inferior caliber, was going to be retained in Birnin Kebbi as principal adviser to the Emir.

Similarly, in the Sultanate of Sokoto, Burdon claimed that "practically the only fief holders" that were living in Sokoto town after April 1905 were "the Waziri and other members of the Emirs council."[90] The Resident claimed that "their presence [was] necessary here for the conduct of native government," and that he considered their position as representatives at court of [their] sub-District Headmen [was] a sound constitutional arrangement." However, in 1907, C.L. Temple reported that non-Resident District Heads included the Sultan, the Waziri, the Magajin Rafi, the Magajin Gari, the Galadiman Gari, the Alkali, the Ubandoma, the Sarkin Zamfara, the Sarkin Adar and the Ardon Shuni. While the first seven were all resident in Sokoto town, the Sarkin Adar lived in Dundaye while Ardon Shuni lived in Shuni.[91] The latter two were regarded as non-resident District Heads because, although living outside Sokoto town, their districts were not yet "consolidated." He also reported that the real reason for the stay of at least some of these chiefs at Sokoto was not that they had to be in the Sultan's council but that the nine of them had villages scattered "haphazardly" around the town. So strong was the British policy of having "homologous districts" with "Resident District Heads" by now that Temple found himself forced to explain his continued exemption of this area from the policy. Thus, he had to plead that in the area around Sokoto town "villages and farms belonging to the various men [were] mixed to such an extent [that forming] homologous districts would be attended with the greatest difficulties."[92] He also pointed out that even in the case of a homologous district, the Resident District Head did "not live in all his towns but in only one of them, and that no town or village in this area was situated at a distance of more than one day's journey" from Sokoto, Shuni or Dundaye where the "District Headmen" lived.[93]

In fact, the policy of getting all District Heads to live in their districts had been implemented so successfully by the end of 1907 that in some emirates, even the practice which the Emirs had adopted in response to this policy, namely, getting all District Heads to come into the emirate capitals during the Id-el-Fitr, had been discontinued by this date. This practice had been discontinued in Katsina, for example, in spite of the fact that the British policy on district administration started to be implemented only in the second half of 1906, after the deposition of Muhammad Yero and the appointment of Muhammed Dikko as Emir.[94] It was hoped that the policy of discouraging visits by District Heads to the Emir during this festival would eventually be extended to all emirates. This can be inferred from the fact that Resident Festing, while reporting the discontinuation of this practice in Katsina, did point out that Katsina was a general pacesetter.

Even in Kano, where the British policy on district administration started to be implemented rather late and took a relatively long time to implement in all its aspects, the aspect of it concerning making all District Heads to reside in their districts was completed as early as the middle of 1908. Thus, by June of this year, Resident Cargill was said to have "done away with the three remaining slave districts" which had been controlled by the Emir through the agency of servants resident in Kano City.[95] Similarly, the Resident had done "away with the Waziri's District, and made the latter an office holder in Kano."[96] This was when Abdullahi Bayero was removed as Waziri and given the title of Chiroma. His position as Waziri and the title itself were given to Allah-Bar-Sarki, a slave of the Emir, who was nonetheless not allowed to be in charge of any district.

Thus, we can conclude that, although throughout the period under study, there continued to be a few non-Resident District Heads, such as the Limamin Juma'a in Zaria,[97] such exceptions were rare even by the end of the first five years of British colonial domination over the emirates of Northern Nigeria; so great was the importance that the British attached to superintending the rural areas of the emirates.

Duties of District Heads and Basis for Assessing Them

As for the duties of the District Heads, these included the assessment and collection of the Kurdin Kasa and the Jangali, carrying out periodic censuses and keeping record of emigration from and immigration into their districts.[98] It also included helping in arresting thieves and "bad characters," and generally in maintaining law and order.[99] Accordingly, in addition to general loyalty to the British, the basis upon which the British assessed the effectiveness and usefulness of District Heads included the "firmness" with which they controlled their districts[100] and "honesty" with the British.[101] It also entailed the ability to conciliate the people in their districts,[102] vigour in assessing and collecting taxes and executing British projects generally,[103] and the ability to suppress theft and lawlessness.[104] However, hardly any District Head was ever able to fulfil all these requirements. For example, any District Head who was "energetic ... and prompt to execute orders" was almost invariably also "very unpopular", sometimes "even among his own clan", and apt to be "causing a good deal of emigration" away from his district.[105] Similarly, any District Head who was "thoroughly loyal" to the British was also invariably "disliked by his people."[106] In the same way, a District Head who was always "prompt and efficient" in supplying British demands such as for labour and corn, and who also had "a good hold over his district" was found not above "harbouring a gang of thieves" or above being "privy to the theft of some £400 cash from a West Indian trader."[107] Another one who was always prompted in responding to "constant calls' to supply "labour and material" to the British was known to be "corrupt", and in one year alone was reported for "some 12 cases of rape."[108] Similarly, the District Head whom the British considered "the ablest man in Bornu," Digma Mammadu of Gujba, was also ranked as "the most unscrupulous." By 1916 "he [had done] well – both for Government and for himself," having already "made a fortune over his 'job'".[109]

Thus, the qualities that the British looked for in District Heads were so contradictory that hardly any one District Head combined all of them. Hence, the question arises as to how the British resolved the "contradictions" that the behaviours of very many District Heads displayed. That is to say, the question does arise as to where the British laid a greater emphasis between efficiency and loyalty to them, on the one hand, and a lack of "probity," and tact and popularity with the people, on the other. We shall take up this issue later on in this chapter.

Qualification for District Headship

In the meantime, we shall examine the qualifications and personal qualities of the people that the British appointed District Heads in this section. The single most important quality that the British looked for in a District Head, or Emir, or any other type of chief for that matter, was amenability to the British.[110] In addition, he should be "honest" and if possible, rich so that, according to the Residents, he would not be tempted either to embezzle the proceeds of British taxes or to extort from his subjects.[111] He should also be a disciplinarian by disposition, but without being unjust.[112] These were all qualities that the Dambon Ingawa in Katsina, for example, was said to possess in ample measure. Thus, for example, in 1907, he was reported to have done "literally" what he was told concerning assessment and collection of the Kurdin Kasa. He was trumpeted as "the most straightforward Fulani" Resident Arthur Festing had ever come across in the Kano Province, with the singular exception of Muhammed Dikko, the Emir of Katsina. In fact, the *Dambo* was "the ideal of what [the British] required as a District Headman." As for his relation with the people, we are informed that he was a "good disciplinarian and lover of order",[113] and it was claimed that only in his District were the *talakawa* successfully made to turn in all their weapons to the British.[114]

As for background, among those that the British appointed District Heads were members of the Emiral families who formed a large group among District Heads. In fact, having been a District Head was one of the qualifications that a candidate for the office of Emir had to possess. Others appointed District Heads were members of the leading families of the emirate capital, such as the family of the Waziri of Sokoto, a son of Waziri Buhari, being among those appointed District Heads in this early period.[115] So also were the leading slaves of the Emirs appointed, especially in Borno.[116] In many cases, people with "ordinary" backgrounds who attached themselves as clients either to the Emir, to his central officials or to District Heads, were appointed. Such appointments were made, provided that during assignments to collect taxes or to accompany a Resident on a tour, such persons exhibited the qualities that the British required in a District Head. Further, it should be pointed out that throughout our period, the British did not insist on connection with the locality to which he was posted as one of the necessary ingredients in a District Head's background. District Heads with connection to their districts, though there were quite a few of them, especially in Adamawa Emirate, were a minority among District Heads. Indeed, there was not even insistence that a candidate should hail from the emirate concerned. The first generation of District Heads in Adamawa, for example, included immigrant Arabs from Wadai and Dar Fur.[117]

Grounds and Non-Grounds for Deposing District Heads

Among the grounds on which District Heads were deposed were abetting acts of rebellion on the part of the peasantry, or even a refusal to give active assistance to its suppression. Among those who were deposed partly on this ground was the Sarkin Kebbi of Silame, Ahmadu Rufai, in December 1906.[118] Others were Sarkin Jega, Junaidu, and the Sarkin Yamma of Dogon Daji,[119] both in March 1906. The latter two were accused of sympathizing with the Satiru uprising and were so deposed. The Sarkin Jega was, for example, accused of adopting "a hostile attitude" towards the British during this "affair," specifically of "allowing spies to be sent to Satiru [by the people of Jega town], and the consequent circulation in his district of false reports regarding the annihilation of all the whitemen in Sokoto ..."[120] It was also for similar reasons that Baloguns, Ajikobi, Alanamu and Fulani were deposed and exiled to Yola early in 1907.[121]

Another common ground for deposing District Heads was refusal to assist in the assessment and collection of the Kurdin Kasa and the Jangali.[122] Still, more frequent as a ground for deposing them was the embezzlement of the proceeds of these taxes. An example of such deposition was that of Hammawa, the Sardauna of Nyibango in the Adamawa Emirate in July 1909.[123] Another case was the deposition of the District Head of Bazai in the Sultanate of Sokoto in the same year.[124] So were the depositions in 1909 of Ahmadu, the Sarkin Dawaki Maituta, and Haladu, the Sarkin Dutse, both in the Emirate of Kano.[125] So also were the depositions of the District Heads of Azare and Gadau in the Emirate of Katagum in 1914.[126] In 1915 Wambai Saidu, District Head Jaji and Madaki Saidu, District Head Soba, both in the Emirate of Zaria, were deposed on the same ground.[127]

Yet another reason for which District Heads were frequently deposed in this period was connivance with slave dealers or failure to report them to the British. It was on this ground that Burunde, the Galadiman Akko, in the Emirate of Gombe, was deposed in 1905.[128] It was also for the same offence that Burunde's successor was, in his turn, deposed in 1908 and Burunde re-instated.[129] So also was the Yeriman Gombe deposed on the same ground in 1908.[130] In the Emirate of Gwandu the Sarkin Dendi was deposed on the same ground in 1910.[131] However, while noting that connivance in slave dealing was one of the grounds for which the British removed District Heads, we should also note that rivals for an office did often take advantage of British opposition to slave dealing to frame up one another. This was easily done, especially when the framer was in a powerful position, say a District Head or an Emir, against a subordinate official. For, in those days, it was the Emir or the District Head that "sent witnesses" to the Resident or Assistant Resident hearing such cases. Hence, it was very easy for an unscrupulous District Head, or Emir bent on securing the conviction of his rival, to send as "witnesses" people who actually witnessed absolutely nothing but were willing to collaborate with their master or patron to eliminate his rival or the rival of his sons.[132] This might well have been what happened in the case of the Yeriman Gombe who, at the same time as being in charge of Gombe District, was also "a brother of the emir, [and] the next heir to the Emirate."[133] In addition, the Yerima "had been very well re-ported on by the officers in charge of the Gombe Division and by the Resident ..."[134]

Another ground on which District Heads were often deposed was that of demanding or accepting gifts from the people of their Districts. Two notable depositions in this regard in 1908 were those of Sarkin Yaki, Yakubu and Sarkin Yamma, Yakubu, both in the Emirate of Bauchi.[135] The two were deposed one after the other for allegedly accepting cattle as gifts, each soon after his ap-pointment as District Head, for Jarawa and Toro respectively. Not only were they deposed on that ground but they were also imprisoned, twelve months in the case of the Sarkin Yamma. In fact, at the time when Emir Hassan died in November 1908, both were still serving their terms in prison. They were released from jail by the Resident expressly so that they could seek succession to the emirate along with other members of the Bauchi ruling house, a competition which was easily won by the ex-Sarkin Yaki.[136] This was a good comment on what the Bauchi selectors thought of conviction in a British court.

Additional ground for which District Heads were very frequently deposed was that of general inefficiency. An early victim of such general "inefficiency" was the Chiroman Katsina, a son of Ex-Emir Abubakar. He was deposed in the last quarter of 1907 for being "quite hopeless," but, presumably on grounds of "mercy," he was made the Village Head of a single town.[137] Similarly, the Sarkin Kebbi of Yabo, was deposed in December 1909 "as a result of a long series of charges of incompetence and neglect of duty."[138] It should be pointed out, as an evidence of the fact, that Indirect Rule was a myth. While the deposition was said to have been the act of the Sultan in "the presence of the Resident," the Resident was forced to complain that "in this deposition and in certain other minor matters the Sarkin Musulmi [showed] a lack of strength and a shrinking from responsibility which detracted from his value as a ruler."[139] This was a clear indication that the deposition was the work of the Resident, who almost literally had to force the Sultan to pronounce it in his presence. Six months later, the Sarkin Kebbi of Silame, still in the Sultanate of Sokoto, was deposed "for general contumacy and refusal to obey the orders "of the Emir."[140] In the Emirate of Bauchi, Sarkin Yaki was deposed in 1908 on the same ground, specifically for being "quite incapable of controlling his turbulent pagans on the frontier …"[141] Again, in the Sokoto Sultanate, as many as four District Heads were deposed in the last quarter of 1911. These were Sarkin Bodinga, "for inefficiency," Sarkin Zamfara of Gummi "for neglect of duty and inefficiency," and Sarkin Burmi of Bakura "for inefficiency." Only the fourth District Head, the Barade of Wamako, was deposed on a ground other than "inefficiency," namely, extortion.[142] It was also more or less on the ground of "inefficiency" that early in 1913, the Limamin Kona, Haruna, in the Emirate of Zaria, was removed as a District Head. Specifically, he had "for 15 years suffered from elephantiasis and [had] only twice visited his district during [the previous] six years."[143] Furthermore, during "a fracas" which occurred in his quarter in Zaria City in the previous September, the Liman was said to have shown himself "quite incapable."[144] Again, to consolidate district administration, the Liman's tiny district of three villages was abolished and shared out between the Madaki and the Limamin Juma'a with whose districts it neighboured. The following year, 1914, the Magajin Zazzau who was in charge of the Home District was also removed "for general incompetency."[145] So also was the Limamin Juma'a who "was found to be too old to be of use as a District Chief..."[146]

One ground on which District Heads were seldom deposed was unpopularity among their subjects. Thus, for example, though Yerima Isa of Gassol in the Emirate of Muri was known to be "impetuous, hot tempered," to "rule by fear," inclined to rule "by violence" and to be "disliked by his own people," he was allowed to hold office from 1907 to 1915 simply because, in spite of his unpopularity and violence, he was "very loyal to the government," could be "relied on in an emergency" and was "the most efficient District Head" in the Emirate.[147] In fact, when he was finally deposed in 1915 and deported to Ilorin, it was for various charges which did not include his violence and unpopularity with the people. Similarly though Sarkin Tambawal, Shehu, in the Sultanate of Sokoto, was "prone to high-handed actions and liable to lack in proper respect for his traditional suzerain, the Sarikin Muslimin;"[148] though in 1907 "a large number of complaints" reached the Resident from the *"talakawa"* of his District "to the effect that [Shehu] had held runaway slaves to ransom, [had] appropriated their goods and cattle for no reason and [had] 'fine' them without trial;" though the Resident was "satisfied that the Sarkin Tambawal [had] been since April 1906 guilty of many acts of oppression;" and though as a result of the chief's oppressiveness "ten to fifteen Fulani settlements [had] been deserted" in 1906, the Resident made no move to depose him. All he did was to hand over Shehu to the Chief Alkali's court in Sokoto where "a great majority of the cases were given in favour of the plaintiffs," the Court ordering Shehu to pay £150 as compensation to the plaintiffs. Indeed, because Shehu had rendered "a remarkably good service [to the British] at the time of the Satiru rebellion" and because Shehu's "friendship for the whiteman" was "well known," the Resident, with the Governor's approval, granted him £100 "in order to enable him to meet [the fine]."[149] Temple considered this grant "an act of justice as many of Tambawal's acts of oppression were ... due to his having gone to great expense in assisting the garrison at the time of the Satiru Revolt."[150] In fact, though the Sarkin Tambawal never changed his attitude towards the *"talakawa,"* he remained in office and continued to enjoy British support until his death in 1919 and was succeeded by his own son.[151]

Relations Between the District Heads and the Residents

To ensure that the District Heads performed the duties required of them, the British closely supervised them, especially with regard to the assessment and collection of taxes, as we shall see in a later chapter.[152] To the extent that this supervision was "limited", it was the paucity of Assistant Residents rather than a "respect" for "native institutions" that imposed that "limitation."[153] As is to be expected, British supervision was resented by most of the District Heads who almost invariably saw that supervision as interference. In fact, far from this supervision leading to understanding and trust between the District Heads and the British, it more often than not led to distrust and fear on the part of the former. Hence, it was often the case that a District Head, whose district was on one of Northern Nigeria's borders, would "decamp" into "French" or "German" territory on the approach of a British Touring Officer.[154]

Indeed, as can be gathered from the preceding sections, there were some District Heads who established and maintained "warm relations" with the British. These were, however, in a minority and were either people who had bad relations with their subjects and therefore had consciously to cultivate British support, or members of emirate ruling houses who were angling for appointment as Emirs. Typical examples of the first type of District Heads were the Sarkin Tambawal in Sokoto and the Yerima of Gassol in Muri, as discussed above. A good example of the District Heads who quietly cooperated with the British in the hope of ultimately being appointed Emir was Halirun Umaru, the Dangaladima of Raha in Gwandu.[155] In fairness to the Dangaladima, it should be pointed out that his cooperation was neither brazen, nor ultimately successful. When, on the personal instruction of Lugard, the Resident skipped the Dangaladima and appointed Muhammadu Bashari of Gwandu District as Emir of Gwandu in 1915, there was some demonstration in Birnin Kebbi and other parts of the emirate in support of the Dangaladima, who was, in fact the choice of the Gwandu council of selectors. The demonstration led to the dismissal of some of these selectors, among them the Magajin Gari of Birnin Kebbi, Muhammadu bi Jam.[156]

In fact, even among royal princes with ambition for Emirship quiet collaboration seems to have been the exception. Thus, to the Dangaladiman Raha, we can add such other names as Muhammadu Maiturare of Gwadabawa, Sarkin Raba, Ibrahim, and Sarkin Baura of Denge, Moyi, all in the Sultanate of Sokoto; and Muhammadu Tukur (Emir of Muri, 1953–65), who served as District Head for fifty years under the alias Jauro Bawuro, and got very good commendations from the British during our period.[157] The list of those District Heads who did not succeed, apparently for lack of the attempt to impress the British, includes the subsequent Emirs of Bauchi Yakubu II and Yakubu III. Both were once jailed for "embezzlement,"[158] and the subsequent Emir of Kano, Abdullahi Bayero who, as District Head of Bichi, was almost consistently reported as "conceited," "different," and "uninterested in his job."[159] So unsatisfactory did the British find the first generation of District Heads generally that, by 1908, they gave up hope of ever turning those chiefs into the totally pliable tools of their policies that they had hoped to make of them.[160] Instead, they pinned their hopes on the next generation which, they believed, would be more amenable to "progressive government" that the British believed their administration was.

The Cost of District "Administration"

When District Heads were first sent out to the Districts, they were allocated as their pay, 20% to 25% of the proceeds of the Kurdin Kasa and the Jangali collected in their respective districts.[161] Given that the yields of these two taxes kept on rising,[162] it follows that the income of the District Heads as well as those of Emirs and Village Heads would have continued rising, almost indefinitely. But this was not to be, for, in 1907, the Assistant Resident for Katsina Division in Kano Province, Palmer, suggested that "it would be a good thing if the whole distribution of shares was reconsidered and ... all office holders (possibly including the Emir) were put upon fixed salaries."[163] The Assistant Resident's grounds for making the suggestion was that some District Heads got too huge an income while others got too little, and that Heads of small villages hardly got anything.[164] It is obvious that the chief, if not the sole beneficiary of that proposed arrangement, was going to be the British, who appropriated the yields of these two taxes, except for the percentages allotted to the Emir's and District and Village Heads. Yet, the Governor failed to realize that the Administration was going to be the beneficiary of Palmer's proposition, and instead of approving the proposal outright, minuted asking how Palmer's proposed scheme should be implemented, "remembering that if we pay the salary it is subject to Imperial audit and would have to come from Protectorate funds, i.e. our fixed half million."[165]

It would seem the correspondence was suspended here, as far as the payment of District Heads was concerned, until 1912 when we read that steps had been taken "to secure the payment of fixed salaries to the officials of the Central Native Administrations in the smaller emirates" of Kano Province, and that the Resident hoped that the following year it would be "practicable to extend the system of fixed salaries to all the district heads."[166] This time, the real reason for taking the step was admitted when the Resident stated that otherwise "on the percentage basis" the incomes of some of the District Heads would "in the near future become ... unnecessarily large."[167] However, until the end of 1913 the "detailed scheme" was still only "being prepared" while its implementation, in Kano Emirate at least, was put off until 1915,[168] when it was promptly done.[169]

The salaries ranged from £160 to £1,000 per annum. The recipient of the latter being the Chiroman Kano in charge of Bichi District and the Madakin Kano in charge of Dawakin Tofa District, while the next highest figure of £800 went to the Makaman Kano in charge of Wudil District.[170] The Resident was honest enough to point out that "in 1915 the Hakimai or District Heads had very much less money than in 1914," suggesting that in his opinion "none of the District Heads in Kano Emirate should have less than £420 p.a.," if "peculation or illicit exaction" was to be punished.[171] At the same time, he insisted that some chiefs e.g "Chiroma, Madawaki, Makama, of Kano [drew] salaries which should satisfy all reasonable demands, and they [had] little excuse for receiving unauthorized amounts." The essence of his submission was that some District Heads were getting too much rather than that some were receiving too little.

Meanwhile, in the Emirate of Zaria, all District Heads "were placed on salaries as from January 1st, [1913]."[172] For this purpose, the District Heads were classified into six grades, with salaries ranging from £100 per annum.[173] It is significant that in the case of Zaria too, the Resident pointed out that "no District Head [now received] a share in excess of his requirements, as far as [could] be judged," adding that he "could not have said the same had the scheme been delayed, for with the increased Land Revenue, the proportionate shares on the old basis would have become too great."[174]

The following year, Acting Resident Migeod revised his judgment and "submitted a recommendation for the reduction of all District Chiefs' salaries over £400 per annum," suggesting that "anything above this sum [was] ... excessive." But he made no recommendation for raising the salaries of the lowest paid District Heads.[175] Besides, in his opinion, the two recipients of the highest salaries of £600 per annum were "slacker and [took] less interest in the administration of their Districts than any of the other District Chiefs."[176] This reduction was not effected because the Lt Governor instructed that the issue be shelved until the return of Mr. Goldsmith, the substantive Resident from leave.[177] The latter, as we shall soon see, took a less stringent view of the matter than had Migeod. In the Sultanate of Sokoto in November 1913, District Heads' salaries were introduced "in place of the share of taxes hitherto taken by them."[178]

Lest we get carried away by the Residents' claims that the new salaries paid to District Heads were adequate, it should be pointed out that up to that time, the District Heads had no established staff and had to employ their personal servants in the performance of their duties. In fact the only other paid officials in the districts were sub-District Heads and Qadis, where there were Native Courts. It follows that the sums paid to the District Heads were not salaries in the usual sense of that term. They were in fact the total cost of running the "administration" of their respective districts. It was out of these "salaries" that the District Heads paid their messengers, scribes and policemen. Hence if 25% of taxes collected in the districts were allegedly too high a sum to be returned to the District Heads, the average "salary" sum of £300 per annum was in fact too little. Indeed this was recognized by the British soon after they had put the District Heads on fixed salaries. Thus, Resident Goldsmith, for example, pointed out, in 1914, that: "the staff of the District Chiefs [required] strengthening especially in the direction of providing salaries in the Native Treasury Estimates for their numerous messengers they [employed] between the district Headquarters and scattered villages and hamlets."[179] He calculated that every District Head needed a staff of twenty-one, including one scribe, three "envoys," a "Recruitor of labour," a "collector of materials for Public Works," a Superintendent of Roads, and three "Marshallers of Labourers."[180] He argued that "the present scale of salaries" paid to District Heads did "not permit of a regular wage being paid to these people" by a District Head, and that unless these servants of a District Head were "properly appointed and paid" there would be a tendency for them to live off the villages.[181]

One has not been able to see the response of the Lieutenant-General to this suggestion. But certainly, by 1917, District Heads were given salaried staffs, including one District Mallam,[182] and one superintendant of markets per district.[183] However, even after the establishment of these district officials, the total amount paid to a District Head and his staff bore very little relation to the revenue that the British derived from taxation in his district. Thus, for example, in 1917 Balala District of Adamawa Emirate was assessed at £1,087:0:0, while the cost of administering the district was made up of £96:0:0 per annum for the District Head, £18 per annum for the District Scribe plus £4:2:6d per annum for all the Village Heads in the district put together, making a sum total of £164:2:6d for the whole year. In addition, there was one Sarkin Kasuwa who collected £48:3:0 as market dues for that year and was paid an annual salary of £16:10:0d.[184] Similarly, in the same year, 1917, the neighbouring district of Daware was assessed at £876:0:0, while the total cost of administering the district was £139:16:0, being made up of £72:0:0 per annum for the District Head, plus £43:16:0 per annum for all the Village Heads in the district put together, and £24:0.0 per annum for the Scribe.[185] In 1918, the District of Gurin, still in Adamawa Emirate, was assessed at £2,834:0:0, while the total cost of administering the district amounted to £297:14:0, the breakdown being £120:0:0 per annum for the District Head, £141:14:0 for all the Village Heads in the district put together, £18:0:0 per annum for the District Scribe, £12:0:0 for a Sarkin Kasuwa and £6:0:0 for two market sweepers.[186]

The difference between the revenue derived from taxation in a District and the cost of running that District would still be very much greater for large Districts like Dawakin Tofa in Kano and Gwadabawa in the Sultanate of Sokoto than the tiny Districts whose figures have been used above. The difference would still be greater if we consider the total revenue derived from a District and the total cost of running that District and collecting the revenue. Other important sources of revenue were the so called Native Courts, which are the subject of Chapter Six, and some other taxes, the assessment and collection of which emirate officials had nothing to do. These other taxes, along with the Kurdin Kasa and the Jangali, form the subject of Chapter Seven in this book. However, the material presented in this section should be sufficient to warrant the conclusion that the district reorganization, resulting in a District "Administration" with which the British extended their control to all parts of the emirates, was an exercise which entirely paid its way and produced huge revenue for the British.

Conclusion

We have shown in this chapter that the British were dissatisfied with the inherited structure of district administration because it was at variance with their declared principles of putting in place a simplified and effective administrative system at minimal cost. Consequently, they reorganized the structure of district administration by establishing homologous districts and streamlined the number of people to be held accountable for tax collection and enforcement of law and order. In this way, the principle of territoriality was enforced as the basis for controlling the rural population. However, we have argued that resistance by emirs and district headmen affected by the reorganization compelled a review of the exercise by the British, who opted for a more cautious approach. Similarly, implementation of the requirement that District Heads should reside in their districts was delayed, with the exception of Sokoto, because of similar resistance by emirs and the affected headmen. We argued further that there is enough evidence in the available sources to conclude that the British singled out loyalty, followed by honesty, rather than indigeneity or familiarity with the community, as the basis of qualification for appointment as District Head. Such District Heads were then assigned the responsibility for tax assessment and collection, conducting periodic population census, keeping records on migration and immigration, arresting thieves and maintaining law and order. These extensive duties and the powers associated with them, made some of the District Heads corrupt, incurring the wrath of the British and making such

District Heads unpopular with the people. Hence, many of them were eventually deposed for failure to live up to the standards set by the British. However, we have also made it clear that the British seldom deposed District Heads on grounds of unpopularity with their subjects, for fear that such may ultimately undermine their hegemonic position in the emirates. In addition, the fact that the Residents directly supervised the District Heads in the performance of their duties, as we have demonstrated, exposes the notion of indirect rule as farce. In summing up our findings in the chapter so far, we emphasise that the British were keen on bringing down the cost of administration in order to make their colonial territory a profitable venture. Consequently, District Heads in the emirates were placed on fixed but meagre salaries, while the British retained a huge chunk of the large surplus generated from taxation for the benefit of metropolitan Britain.

Map 5. Northern Nigeria and its provinces

5

The Impact of District Reorganization

Introduction

This chapter is a follow up to the preceding one, where we examined the creation of analogous districts by the British in the emirates. In the present chapter, we intend to examine the numerous consequences produced by the creation of the districts. One of the most noticeable and far-reaching consequences was the creation of widespread redundancies among previous office holders in the emirates. We shall attempt to find out the nature and extent of such redundancies, and the category of officials they affected in the different emirates, together with the various measures taken by some of the emirs in mitigating the impact of such redundancies on their powers and influence. The nature of the relationship between the emirs and newly appointed district heads after the district reorganization of 1905 is another important issue we shall examine at length. Among the tasks we shall pre-occupy ourselves with in relation to this matter is ascertaining the nature of the reaction of the emirs to the policy of dispatching their high officials to reside and work in outlying districts under direct British supervision. We shall try to address the question whether the emirs were enthusiastic, apprehensive or resentful of this particular policy. If the latter was the case, as it would seem to us at this initial moment, we shall seek to demonstrate the nature and extent of their resentment, with a detailed examination of the documented case of Lamido Bobbo Ahmadu in Yola, and how the resentment affected his relationship with the District Heads. Similarly, there is a need for us to question whether, in spite of the expressed resentment of the emirs, we can make the apparently simple conclusion that relations between the emirs and their District Heads were never cordial. As we shall find out in due course, this issue is not as simplistic as it seems because, there were also instances of cordial relations between emirs and their district heads.

We shall consider these relations in order to establish their nature, prevalence and the various conciliatory methods of control devised by some of the emirs. Finally, the attitude of the British to the conciliatory methods devised by the emirs, together with the nature and basis of popular hostility in general, and recorded incidences of open protest that greeted the district reorganization in Adamawa Province, Gwandu Emirate and Bornu Province, in particular, will also be examined.

The Creation of Redundancy

One of the immediate consequences of the District Reorganization that we examined in the last chapter was to create a redundant group of people, mainly made up of the erstwhile *jakadu* but also including former "fief holders." Thus, for some time after the imposition of British domination on the emirates, the *jakadu*, who, in the precolonial days, had been the link between the various chiefs in the capitals and their towns and villages in the countryside, were retained and given a stipend by the British. This was because, as Howard put it, they were "useful not only in the collection of taxes but as Secret Service Agent[s]."[1] But already, by the beginning of 1906, the British had started dispensing with these *jakadu* "from the government point of view,"[2] though they still had "no objection" if the Emirs retained the *jakadu* for their own assistance. Even this latter concession was withdrawn by the end of that same year when Acting Resident Goldsmith at Sokoto, for example, started to "explain" to the Sultan how "necessary" it was to "abolish entirely" the *jakada* system, and for emirs to "deal directly" with their village Heads "without the assistance of jakadas." According to him, he received "most loyal and hearty cooperation" from the Sultan with regard to getting rid of the *jakadu*.

It was not only the *jakadu* that lost their status and income with the District Reorganization. So also did those *kofofi* who were not sent out into the countryside as District Heads. A very good example of a *Kofa* who lost his position in the Emirate of Gwandu was Basharu Hanafi. Prior to the District Reorganization, he had been the Maigari of Kardi in the vicinity of Gwandu town as well the *Kofa* for the Jagwadawa Fulani, who occupied the districts of Bakwoi, Matankari and Kauran Aliyu Wanta. With the Reorganization, his own town of Kardi was incorporated into Gwandu District over which Basharu Haliru, the eldest son of the Emir, Haliru, was appointed District Head. The Jagwadawa districts, on the other hand, were incorporated into one district under Basharu as non-Resident District Head or *Kofa*. Now, Basharu Hanafi, a son of Emir Hanafi b. Khalil b. Abdullahi b. Fudi (1875–1876) had, until the end of 1905, been the

Residents' favourite candidate for the office of Emir from which the British had already decided to remove Muhammadun Aliyu.[3] He had so much expectations to be appointed Emir, and had so much contempt for Halirun Abdu that when the British finally decided in favour of the latter, Basharu was visibly reluctant to go forward and render the *Bay'a* to the new Emir. The Emir, for his part, in spite of his victory over Basharu, a fact which might have predisposed a more generous person to forgive Basharu's jealousy, set himself to destroy the latter. Thus, at first, the Emir intrigued with Political Agent Kiyari to get Basharu removed from office as *Kofa*.[4] The intrigue failed when the Emir and Kiyari failed to agree on the bribe the Emir would pay the former.[5] However, with the new British zeal to simplify the chains of command and to cut expenses in the cost of "Native Administration," the Emir seized his opportunity to suggest to the Assistant Resident that Basharu should be relieved of his position as *Kofa*.[6] The Assistant Resident, after some hesitation, possibly because Basharu was of an exalted birth and the British might yet need him one day, agreed. Hence, he informed Basharu that "he had no recognized status in the Native Administration from the government point of view", "that he could have no share in the native portion of the revenue of these [Jagwadawa] districts and that they would be directly under the Emir."[7]

Presumably, Basharu was left with the Village Headship of Kardi. Even if he was removed from that position, the relevance of that removal lies elsewhere rather than here. More relevant here is the fact that, in using British rejection of the *kofofi* system to effect the downfall of his arch-rival, the Emir was not by any means convinced of the need for that rejection. That he was not supporting the British in their bid to end the system can be seen in the fact that after "a short lapse of time," the Emir requested the Assistant Resident if he might appoint his Waziri, Muhammadu Raji, as "Kofa of the Jagwadawa District."[8] In a fit of apparent absent-mindedness, the Assistant Resident consented to this request, but remembered soon enough that it was "not a very good thing having a non-Resident District Headman."[9] So he withdrew his recognition of the Waziri's position as *Kofa* for the District and made the *Jagwadajin* Bakwoi, who was one of three Resident sub-District Heads in the District, its Resident District Head.[10] However, to justify continuing giving the Waziri "a share in the taxes," he appointed him District Head of Ambursa.[11] This way the British made it clear to the Emir that in accepting the Emir's suggestion that Basharu Hanafi should be removed as the *Kofa* for Jagwadawa District, they were not merely helping the Emir to break a rival but, much more important, effecting another "reform" in District "Administration."

As the years went on, more *kofofi* were eased out of employment, among them Ahmad, son of Emir Maliki b. Muhammad b. Abdullahi b. Fudi (1876-1888), better known as Guraza, another of the four candidates for the office of Emir in 1906, and the preferred candidate from the point of view of the aristocracy.[12] Up to March 1906, he had been the leading *Dan Sarki* after Muhammadu Daniya, the Dangaladima or heir apparent, whom the British had made clear they did not like any more than they liked Muhammadun Aliyu, the Emir. In fact, after the deposition and deportation of Muhammadun Aliyu and the simultaneous but coincidental death of Daniya on that same fateful day, and pending the appointment of Haliru as Emir, it was Guraza, a resident of Gwandu, who the whole town looked up to for leadership. There is no specific information concerning which towns he had been the *Kofa* of; but, whatever these might have been, he clearly lost his rights over them. For, he was never appointed a Resident District Head and by the time of his death around 1920, he was living a retired private life in Gwandu.[13] In fact, none of the "numerous yan Sarki"[14] that the Assistant Resident reported to be living in and around Gwandu town ever got appointed District Head. Assuming that most of them had all been *kofofi* prior to the inauguration of the District Head system, their disemployment was a measure of the redundancy that District Reorganization created in Gwandu.

There has been a tendency to attribute the disemployment of these *yan Sarki* to the change of dynasty which the appointment of Haliru Abdu almost amounted to. This was hinged on the fact that, unlike all the other Emirs of Gwandu since the death of Abdullahi b. Fudi, neither his father, Abdulkadir, nor his grandfather, Hassan b. Abdullahi b. Fudi, had been Emir of Gwandu.[15] The argument of those who hold this view is that, if Haliru was to consolidate his position as Emir, but especially if he was to consolidate the position of his own immediate family as the ruling family – a move he tried very hard and succeeded in doing by appointing only his sons, and non-royal supporters, to office.[16] While this view is correct as far as it goes, it should be pointed out that it does not go far enough. Specifically, it omits to point out that even if Haliru did not have the need to cripple numerous cousins having more prescriptive rights to the office of Emir, many of these were bound either to be thrown out of job or at least be subordinated, as Village Heads, to officials other than the Emir, namely the newly created District Heads. The inevitability of this eventuality lay in the fact that the British-created Districts that were relatively large and tended to contain more towns and villages than it had been customary to place under any one *kofa* in the precolonial system. Such necessitated that the number of District Heads had to be smaller than the number of *kofofi* had been.

In Katsina, the disemployment of the *kofofi* was on a massive scale and was undertaken simultaneously with the inauguration of the District Reorganization. Thus, by June 1907, within two years of the inauguration of the system, Palmer had "succeeded in abolishing fifty out of the former title holders" there.[17] This represented "a large reduction" in what he called "the class of people, mostly Fulani who simply lived on other people."[18] The suddenness with which the British dispensed with the former *kofofi* was, in some emirates, not as precipitate as was the case with the Katsina Emirate, where Palmer was Assistant Resident at the material time. In Gombe Emirate, for example, Assistant Resident F.B. Gall "deemed [it] unwise to discard suddenly too large a number of the former office-holders."[19] Instead, he decided to place a majority of these *kofofi* on salaries in order to "prevent cause for intrigue and dissatisfaction" among the aristocracy.[20] "In return for their salaries they would help the District Headmen in whatever they were required to do."[21] However, even so the Assistant Resident warned these *kofofi* that "they were superfluous and [that] their retention was … only an act of policy."[22] Fortunately for these *kofofi*, Gall continued to be in or around Gombe for the next ten years, and the policy of employing them as sub-District Heads, etc, and paying them salaries continued throughout that period. It was only when one or another of them offended British interests and was dismissed that his vote was closed down, as no one else was appointed to replace him, a clear indication that they were actually redundant.

It was in this way, for example, that in 1915 Gall, who was by then Resident Bauchi Province, withdrew recognition from the Madakin Gombe, until then District Head of the small District of Dukku, which was then merged with Nafada District "as was originally intended."[23] Similarly, he dismissed Sarkin Magi, until then sub-District Head of Toungo, and Sarkin Debe, until then sub-District Head of Gombe town.[24] Their sub-Districts were both reduced to the level of villages and put under village heads with lower standing and salaries than sub-District Heads. It is an indication of the extent to which Gall feared the aristocracy or sympathized with it that, even after withdrawing British recognition from the Sarkin Debe, he granted the latter an allowance of £36 per annum. This was because the Sarki "had not been guilty of any irregularities" but was merely "retarding progress."[25] In fact, Gall was so eager to keep former *kofofi* employed and paid that he sometimes even overlooked acts of irregularity of the sub-District Heads whose official recognition was solely in order to keep them gainfully employed. Thus, at the same time as reporting the dismissal of the chiefs named above, Gall also reported that the Sarkin Bage, who had been retained as sub-District Head in Nafada District, had "confessed to an irregularity."[26] Yet, instead of dismissing him at once, "the Emir" gave him a choice between "taking his trial [and] having his salary reduced from £120 to £100."[27] Of course the Sarki "accepted the reduction,"[28] and Gall went on to justify the action of "the Emir" by claiming that the Sarki's record had "been good" and that he was a "true" as opposed to a "superfluous sub-head."[29] However, in the emirates, taken as a whole, it would seem that the fate of the *kofofi* in Gombe was fortunate and rare, a deviation from the norm. Hence, after having thus duly noted it, we should reiterate that one of the consequences of District Reorganization was to disemploy a large number of the former *kofofi* and *jakadu*, indeed a great majority of them.

The emphasis which the Residents so frequently placed on the fact that the abolition of the *jakadu* and the *kofofi* was only "from the British point of view" is correct because, in fact, there is evidence that as far as the Emirs and the District Heads were concerned, the two groups retained their validity even after the British had withdrawn their recognition from them. Thus, for example, in the Sultanate of Sokoto, the Galadiman Sokoto, while being recognized by the British as a member of the Sultan's Council and the District Head of a number of villages scattered around the town, had in their eyes, lost his nineteenth century status as the *Kofa* for the Emirate of Katsina and some villages in Zamfara.[30] But as late as 1909, Assistant Resident G. Malcolm discovered that the Galadima was still "in the habit of sending his representatives" to Gusau and Chafe Districts "to assist in the collection of taxes."[31] On confronting the Sultan about the matter, the Assistant Resident found out that it was "a more or less private arrangement between him and the Galadima."[32] Since the "assistance" of the Galadima and his *jakadu* did not cost the British any extra money, and in the absence of complaints of interference from the two District Heads or of extortion from the people of the two Districts, the only objection that the Assistant Resident could raise against this "private arrangement" was that, whereas the British were "anxious to make an estimate of the actual incomes of all Sarakuna", they would never get it "in any way accurately" if such "private arrangements" were to continue to be made without the British being even informed about them.[33] Hence, far from suggesting that the Sultan should be "advised" to end the "private arrangement", all the Assistant Resident suggested was that the British should insist on knowing that it was the Galadima that derived the Sultan's "share of taxes" from Gusau and Chafe, and that "it should not on paper appear as the income of the Sarkin Musulmi."[34] Though other cases have not been documented by the British, we should assume that just as the Sultan made a "private arrangement" with the Galadiman Sokoto concerning the continued supervision of areas for which the latter had been *kofa*, so did he make other "private arrangements" with the other *kofofi*, through whom the nineteenth century caliphs had supervised the other districts of the Caliphate that now formed parts of the Sultanate of Sokoto.

As for the *jakadu,* one other way the Sultan, and presumably the other Emirs as well, tried to retain them was to employ as many of them as possible as *dogarai*, the organization from which Native Authority Police forces later developed. Hence, by 1911, the Resident "after consultation with the Sarkin Musulmi" arrived at the conclusion that the number of *dogarai* was "excessive."[35] Significantly, he blamed the "excessive" size of the organization on the fact that the "Sarkin Musulmi had a rooted objection to *dogarai* being used for what one may call 'General Service' as against being attached to one particular district."[36] Thus, for example, the Sultan "was of the opinion that a number of messengers should be used to carry orders to such a District and that they should not be used to convey messages to any other District, even if it lay on the way to the District to which they were detailed."[37] However, it seems the Resident was sharp enough to realize that all the Sultan was trying to do was to put as many as possible of his former *jakadu* on the Native Treasury's payroll. However, if the Resident did in fact see through what Attahiru was aiming at, he nonetheless decided to defeat the latter by pretending not to realize what he was up to. Thus either cynically or with dull innocence the Resident "enabled" the Sultan "to largely reduce the number of *dogarai* that would be paid from the Native Treasury."[38] The Resident was able to do such through "considerable discussion" and by trying to get the Sultan to see the advantage of using any *dogarai* "for service to any District or Districts."[39] This way McAllister curbed the attempts of the Sultan to mitigate the plight of a group which had had a function and a status in the nineteenth century government of the Sokoto Caliphate. And no doubt, similar attempts by other Emirs were also frustrated by other Residents and Assistant Residents. Hence our thesis stands that the District Reorganization undertaken by the British from around 1905 led to a large scale unemployment and loss of position among the former *kofofi* and *jakadu.*

Relations Between Emirs and the New District Heads

When considering relations between Emirs and the British — established Resident District Heads, the important fact is that the Emirs never accepted the idea of sending out some of their Sarakuna to live in the countryside except with the greatest of reluctance. In fact even the very idea of the British entering into direct relations with the Sarakuna while they were still living in the emirates' capitals was accepted by the Emirs only with a great apprehension. Nor for that matter did the Sarakuna themselves accept the idea of direct contact with the British with any amount of enthusiasm. Thus, for example, when Resident Temple in Bauchi in March, 1902, one month after the British occupied the town, informed the Emir that he would "maintain the Emir and chiefs in their present stations" and then insisted that he would "have personal relations not with the Emir only but with the chiefs also," he found "some difficulty" in winning his point. For the Emir was "extremely nervous of his influence [over the *Sarakuna*] being impaired," while the latter for their part were "afraid of the inspection of the whiteman" into what Temple adjudged "their somewhat doubtful proceedings."[40] Similarly, when the British instructed the Emir of Bida to divide his emirate into Districts and send his Sarakuna to reside there, the Emir was at "first pessimistic as to the results fearing that the District Chiefs would collect large following and undermine his authority."[41] Similarly, when Resident Charles Orr introduced the idea of "the scheme" to the Emir of Zaria, Aliyu dan Sidi, in 1905 "it was evident that [the Emir] viewed it with dislike and distrust."[42]

Lamido Bobbo Ahmadu's Resentment

A very good example of the hostility of the Emirs towards the District Reorganization was that of Bobbo Ahmadu in Yola. Thus, we are told that the District Reorganization scheme received "very little forward help from the Emir", who was "averse to delegating authority to others." Acting Resident Fremantle, oblivious of the situation that European intrusion created, attributed this aversion to "instinct."[43] Yet, significantly, the Emir's aversion to "ruling through successive links of responsibility" applied "less to the chiefs who [inherited] a Sokoto flag than to those formed since [British] advent."[44] This is to say that whereas both the "Sokoto"[45] flag-bearing chiefs, who always lived in their territories rather than at Yola, and the new District Heads that the British were sending out of Yola, were very likely to take advantage of their living away from Yola, and of the British presence, to assert a measure of autonomy from the Emir. The latter, nonetheless, resented the possibility of the new District Heads acquiring some autonomy than the possibility that the nineteenth century territorial chiefs might enjoy even more autonomy from him than hitherto. Hence, the Emir's resentment was bound up with the realization that the imposition of British colonial domination, far from allowing him to continue with the successful policy of his predecessor, Lamido Zubairu, of imposing a greater subordination on the territorial chiefs, did in fact entail the extension of autonomy to those of his chiefs who, in the nineteenth century, did not have any base or basis on which to aim at acquiring autonomy.

In a very real sense and at one level, the attempt by the Emirs to continue using *kofofi* and *jakadu* for the purpose of administering the new districts, was an attempt by them to retain control over these districts and their new Heads. This is said, without prejudice to our interpretation in the last few pages of this attempt, as an effort to ensure the *kofofi* and the *jakadu* a gainful employment and social status. The contention that the Emirs' attempt to retain the active involvement of the *kofofi* and the *jakadu* in local government was an attempt to preserve their own control over the districts too can be seen in the conduct of Lamido Bobbo Ahmadu. Thus, according to Acting Resident Webster, the Lamido employed his "slaves" and "*ajeles*" for all work "to the exclusion of the aristocracy," in other words the British created District Heads.[46] The Acting Resident continued that though nominally "all slaves" had been removed from their "old Ajeleships" and the whole emirate "divided into homologous districts under resident District Heads", he found out that in "nearly every district" there were villages which still, "against the Resident's orders," paid through "one of the Emirs' slaves."[47] Not only that, the Emir openly and "strongly" objected to any interference with these men, and was "continually" trying to get more appointed to various offices."[48] The Acting Resident gave an example with the District Headship of Verre, which was brought under British control only in 1905. The Emir "first proposed a slave as District Head."[49] It was only when the British turned this proposal down that the Emir proposed another man, an Arab named Lawan Goni.[50] Thus, it becomes clear that the Emir saw the institution of resident District Heads under direct British control as an evil, a threat to his authority. And, to circumvent it, the Emir adopted the double strategy of first getting people with no customary rights, people whose social status very much depended on him, to be appointed as Resident District Heads. Second, where the first strategy failed, he bypassed the District Heads as much as possible and controlled the districts through these personal clients.

Inevitably, relations between Bobbo Ahmadu and the District Heads were at best lukewarm, very often unfriendly, and in a number of cases decidedly hostile. Thus, for example, we have seen that after failing to get a slave of his appointed District Head for the Verre District, he successfully proposed an Arab, Lawan Goni. In doing this, he was no doubt working on the assumption that Lawan Goni, being an immigrant Arab, might feel dependent on him for support. If this was his belief, Bobbo Ahmadu was mistaken. Lawan Goni, it seems, felt the need to have a patron. But it was the patronage of the British, rather than of the Emir, that he sought to cultivate, something very logical for an opportunist to do under those circumstances when real power was in the hands of the Resident and his Assistants. However, while Lawan Goni "proved a good man" to the Resident, in fact precisely because of that, he quickly fell out of favour with the Lamido who, according to the Resident, withdrew his recognition of Lawan Goni as a District Head, and refused "even to forward his reports to the Resident."[51] Instead, the Lamido tried to "get [the Lawan] into trouble." If we next take the Lamido's relations with Ardo Jabbo of Mbilla Malabu and Bobboi Yero of Gurin, we shall find that they were both very bad. However, of the two sets of relations, the Emir's relations with Ardo Jabbo were the worse and had tragic consequence for both of them. Thus, the bad relations between Ardo Jabbo and the Emir encouraged the "pagans" of Vamgo Malabu, a village in Mbilla Malabu District, to murder the Ardo[52] and thirteen of his followers. This murder was in turn used as a pretext by the British to depose and deport the Lamido to Lokoja.[53]

In the case of all the three District Heads, it is clear that relations between them and the British were the cause of the hostility between the Emir and them. We have already seen that the Lamido's relations with the British were hostile.[54] Hence, he came to regard seriously the conduct of any of his chiefs that he felt had friendly relations with the British, and these included the Waziri, Abdulkadiri Pate, the Sarkin Shanu, and the three District Heads mentioned above. Apart from the praises that these chiefs received from the British, and praise was something which, in those early days the British showered on almost anybody who did not come out openly to oppose them, we have no evidence to show that Bobboi Yero, the Waziri, the Sarkin Shanu or Lawan Goni, were overly eager about the British. However, in the case of Ardo Jabbo, there is evidence that he was in the habit of invoking the name of the British whenever he met some opposition. In fact, even at the scene of his murder, one of Ardo Jabbo's followers, his Baraya, tried to frighten the would-be murderers by reminding them that they were "incurring the displeasure of the government by [their] actions, and the probable consequence," to which the leader of the group, the Arnado of Vamgo Malabu, allegedly "replied that he did not care as his hills and caves were impregnable."[55]

As for the Emir's involvement in the elimination of Ardo Jabbo, the evidence we have for it includes the alleged testimonies of the "pagans" involved in the killing. There were fourteen such testimonies. It was alleged that soon after the murder, the Emir went out on a "tour" with no apparent purpose, travelled in the same direction in which the Arnado fled, finally stopping and staying sometime at Song, a few hours' walk from the "pagan" village in which the Arnado and his accomplices were alleged to have gone to hide.[56] Another testimony is that the Emir did not seem to assist in the arrest of the murderers.

There was also the alleged testimony of Lawan Goni, alleging that soon after the murder, the Lamido said to him:

> there are four men I hate in this country. Bello [Ardo Jabbo] was one of them; you are another; Sarki Shanu is the third and Bobboi Yero is the fourth. You are all friends of the whiteman. Bello is dead, and I know what I shall do with you others. So let his death be a warning to you.[57]

As for the testimonies of the murderers and other residents of Vamgo Malabu, it was that just before the murder, the Arnado had visited Yola and Malabu, a District neighbouring on Mbilla Malabu District, and returned with promises of protection from the Lamido and the District Head of Malabu, Ardo Iyawa, and that after Ardo Jabbo was killed, his clothes, including the ones he was actually wearing at the time of his death, were sent by the Arnado to the Lamido.[58]

Arguing against the Lamido's involvement are the facts that even before they made a single arrest, the British had come to the virtual conclusion that he was the instigator of the killing. The testimonies of the murderers and others merely confirmed them in that prejudicial conclusion. Although many of the witnesses claimed to have seen the dispatch of the Ardo's clothes to the Lamido by the Arnado, hardly any of them claimed to have been with the Arnado when he visited Yola and Malabu, and got the alleged promises of protection from the Lamido and Ardo Iyawa respectively. In addition, Lawan Goni had a personal interest in the downfall of the Lamido. Finally, there was the fact that the period is generally remembered as a period of intrigue when the Yerima, Iyabano (Emir 1909–1910), was scheming to become Emir with the assistance of a notorious British Political Agent, Bello Wuro Hausa.[59] Under the atmosphere created by such intrigue, it was easy for the opponents of the Lamido, both those who feared for their own offices and those who coveted his office, to use his known hostility towards Ardo Jabbo, to falsely implicate him in the latter's murder. Yet, on the whole, one is inclined to believe, on the strength of the unanimity of the testimonies of the people of Vamgo Malabu themselves, that the Lamido had some foreknowledge of the plot to murder the Ardo. Whatever the case, it is clear that the Lamido had very hostile relations with Ardo Jabbo, by all indications a District Chief who sought to take advantage of the presence of the British in Adamawa to ignore the Lamido, as several other District Heads tried to do.

Meanwhile, the Lamido tried to contain Bobboi Yero of Gurin by setting up some local dignitaries, including the Qadi of Gurin, Hamman Djere and one Ardo Mammadi, as rival authorities to the District Head. In early 1909, a few

months to his deposition, the Lamido visited Gurin and it seems the supporters of the Lamido tried to organize a demonstration against the District Head
whose official title, was interestingly Khalifa.[60] This attempt failed when Bobboi
Yero marshalled his own supporters. As a result of the mutual readiness of the
two rival factions, "party feeling ran high and there was constant risk of a brawl
between the followers of the different factions."[61] Apparently, on the British
learning of the situation created by the Lamido's visit, an Assistant Resident
rode to Gurin, and Bobbo Ahmadu, "in discussing [the] matter promised to issue orders that the Khalifah must be given due difference."[62] Yet, so bitter was
the Lamido towards Bobboi Yero that instead of waiting till the following day
to issue the promised order, he "left the town in the middle of the night warning none [presumably including the Assistant Resident] of his intended departure."[63] However, he did take leave of the Qadi, who accompanied the Lamido
out of the town, a fact which the British interpreted as "showing that [the Qadi]
was in [the Lamido's] eyes the senior man in the town."[64] The Assistant Resident
had no doubt which side to support. Accordingly, "that afternoon the people
were called together and the leaders of the opposition were called upon either
to swear on the Koran in the Mosque to be true to the Khalifa and follow him
properly, or else leave the town and District at once."

With his patron out of town, the Qadi decided that the safest thing to do was
to comply with the British demand, but Ardo Mammadi was unrepentant and
was "ordered to leave the district."[65]

Neither did Lamido Abba, who became Emir only eighteen months after
the deposition of his father, Bobbo Ahmadu, and subsequent to the deposition
of Lamido Iya, Bobbo Ahmadu's immediate successor, escape having bitter relations with several of "his" District Heads. Thus, for example, we are told that
he was "not on very cordial terms"[66] with Ardo Jijji Adama, the man whom
the British appointed as District Head Malabu after they deposed Ardo Iyawa
on grounds of his alleged involvement in the murder of Ardo Jabbo of Mbilla
Malabu. Significantly, it was his "great cordiality towards Europeans" that caused
Jijji Adama to be "looked upon rather in the light of a renegade"[67] by the Lamido
and others in Yola. This was both ironic and significant. It was ironic because
the Lamido himself was to do a lot of collaborating with the British, especially
during the First World War.[68] Besides, the Ardo's collaboration with the British
was not substantial, for the Resident complained that while the Ardo "like[d]
to be popular [with Europeans]" and while "his Rest Houses and the catering
connected with them [were] well run" the Ardo was "inclined to consider that
this surface display should excuse him from the serious work of administration."[69] In fact, the Ardo, who suffered from some ailment which the Resident

thought might be gout, made "an exaggerated display of bodily infirmity when required to put in any personal supervision in his district, or to present himself at Headquarters."[70] In fact "of all District Heads", he was "the hardest to move and the most prone to subterfuge." He was "essentially of the 'old school' – a prince and not an official." Yet, from the Lamido's point of view, the important fact was that the Ardo tried directly to ingratiate the British, an effort which might have been accompanied by a corresponding insubordination towards the Lamido.

Similarly, Hama Gabdo, the Dangaladima of Mayine was "on very bad terms" with Lamido Abba right from his own appointment in 1911.[71] Though in the Dangaladima's case, the cause of the hostility was not an attempt on his part to befriend the British and ignore the Emir, the fact remains that the hostility was a result of the Lamido's loss of control over local government. Thus, Hama Gabdo was a son of Yerima Hamman Ali Kura, a grandson of Mallu Bakari, a great grandson of Modibbo Adama and therefore, a nephew of the Lamido. In precolonial times, Hama Gabdo's branch of the royal family, which consisted of the descendants of the full brothers Mallu Hamidu and Mallu Bakari, ruled the whole of the territory from Verre in the south-east to Mayo-Balwa in the south-west, exclusively, but also on the tacit understanding that they were excluded from the Emiral Office itself.[72] However, their monopoly of control over that territory was broken with the inauguration of the resident District Head system when a non-royalist former warrior, Lamdo Kabi, was posted to Mayine to control much of the territory that remained in "British" Adamawa. Hammawa Alikura, who was one of the two heads of this branch of the family, was recognized only as a village Head for Mayine town.[73] Similarly, it was Lawan Goni, an Arab, that was posted to Gogra as District Head Verre.[74] Hence, the only portions of the vast territory that were left under the descendants of Mallu Hamidu and Mallu Bakari were that portion that fell to the Germans with headquarters at Nassarawa, and a small portion around the town of Nyibango, the precolonial headquarters of the territory. Besides, both the German part and the portion around Nyibango were under the descendants of Mallu Hamidu as distinct from Mallu Bakari, the head of the former being Yerima Babbawa.[75] Thus, the descendants of Mallu Bakari, at least from the official point of view, were left out in the cold, as it were.

The situation remained such until 1911, when the Lamdo Kabi fell foul of the British over the proceeds of their taxes. Instead of waiting to be arrested and humiliated, he absconded into the German part of the former Emirate, thus creating a vacancy at Mayine.[76] Although the descendants of Mallu Bakari had no official position except that of the Village Headship of Mayine town, they collectively and severally, still had substantial property in the form of farms, serfs, cattle and horses. With the creation of the vacancy at Mayine, Hama Gabdo decided to convert a portion of his property for the District Headship of Mayine. He knew where to look for the office – from the British, hence the intrigue with the notorious "Political Agent Bello for the appointment."[77] Bello made him to understand that he was going to get the whole of the territory formerly administered by Lamdo Kabi. "A considerable sum changed hands." In the meantime, it seems, Bello was also accepting bribes from another person interested in the appointment. This was one Dalil, a former servant of Lamdo Kabi, and a member of the Kesu'en clan of the Fulbe, a clan which was concentrated in the area. Hence, neither of them got the entire territory which, in all probability, on the suggestions of Bello, was broken up into two districts, Mayine and Mayo-Balwa. Hama Gabdo and Dalil were appointed District Heads of Mayine and Mayo-Balwa respectively. Hama Gabdo felt cheated and Bello cunningly "played off his dupe ... against the Emir, throwing the blame for the miscarriage of the plot" on the latter.[78] Out of indignation, Hama Gabdo withdrew "his considerable following from Yola town to Mai-Ino", thus causing a "great dismay" to the Emir and sealing their enmity, which lasted until Hama Gabdo's death in January 1913 during the long trip to Kano to welcome Lugard back to Nigeria.[79]

However, while the case of Yola might have been a little extreme, hostility between Emirs and District Heads was not confined there. Thus, in the case of Argungu, for example, we are told by Assistant Resident Brackenbury that the Emir of Argungu had a "passion for intrigue, often at the expense of his own District Chiefs," a passion that had "constantly to be guarded against" by the Assistant Resident.[80] Among other things, the Emir encouraged "immigrants" from "French Argungu to adopt a kind of independent attitude towards [the] District Heads" of Arewa Yamma and Augi Districts, thereby causing "a bit of trouble" for those two District Heads and the British.[81] In fact it took "the reduction of his salary and the warning that it might be necessary to [deport] him to Lokoja" to make the Emir see "the folly of this policy" and of intrigue against his chiefs generally. Even Emir Haliru of Gwandu, whose predisposition to accept changes introduced by the British was one of the most remarkable among all the Emirs, was averse to "consulting his District Heads," and did "not give his Sarakuna much chance to be themselves."[82] This was eight years after the Reorganization and in spite of the attested fact that he was "very loyal, decidedly able, and, in very many ways, very progressive."[83] The report does not say through whom the Emir implemented his wishes in the districts, but it is safe to assume that it was through his now "personal" servants.

Conciliatory Methods of Control

Yet, it cannot be said that relations between Emirs and their District Heads were never cordial. Indeed in one or two emirates they were, a good example being the emirate of Katagum where Emir Abdulkadir "always support[ed] these men and [was] unwilling to punish them, if any case [was] brought up against them and [was] too willing to make excuses on their behalf."[84] However, emirates in which relations between Emirs and "their" District Heads were so cordial were definitely in a small minority among the emirates of Northern Nigeria. Hence, the existence of such emirates need not subtract much from our thesis that in the first and a half decades of British colonial domination over these emirates, relations between Emirs and District Heads were generally lukewarm, very often unfriendly and sometimes decidedly hostile. However, the Emirs did not restrict themselves to "intrigues" against District Heads as a means of checking the possibility, often the reality, of their being disregarded by District Heads. In addition to these "intrigues," all the Emirs also adopted other and more positive, methods of retaining some control over these former Sarakuna. One of these methods was to require the presence of the latter in the emirate capitals at Muslim festivals like the two Eids.[85] Even at Katsina where, following the appointment of Muhammad Dikko as Emir, it seemed that at one point the practice was going to be allowed to lapse.[86] But by 1911 it was so much revived that "the Emir summoned [not only] all his District Headmen [but also] most of the Alkalai – both district and market – and a great number of town and village heads."[87] These, with their "many retainers" were "entertained by the Emir for about a week."[88]

Another means whereby the Emirs tried to control their District Heads was that of marrying off their daughters to them.[89] The temptation to dismiss these marriages as none out of the ordinary is there. Hence, it should be pointed out that in some cases there were obvious connections between the marriages and the wishes of the Emirs to control the District Heads to whom they gave their daughters. Such a connection may legitimately be seen in the marriage of a daughter of Shehu Abubakar Garbai to Abba Mallam, the Ajia of Monguno. The latter, who had very good relations with the British, and who, in view of his being a descendant of Ahmad Gonimi, was by no means entirely their creature, had, prior to his marriage to the Shehu's daughter, been consistently reported as being on bad terms with the Shehu, upon whom he tended to look down.[90] It should further be noted that at the same time as the report came out that the Ajia had been betrothed to the Shehu's daughter, it was also reported that there was "a great improvement" in the relations between the two men, though

there is no mention of which came first – the betrothal or the improvement
in relations. Similarly, in Zaria, though it is unclear which had come first – the
appointment of the Makama Babba, Alhassan, or his marriage to the daughter of
the Emir, Aliyu dan Sidi – it was asserted that he "owe[d] his position to having
married Gimbia the Emir's second daughter."[91] In fact, he was reported "to be
the puppet of his wife and [to have] the appearance of a weak man," so much
so that up to 1911, over four years since his appointment in 1907, Alhassan
remained "more or less on probation" as far as the British were concerned.[92]

It should further be pointed out that the British, far from aiding contact between Emirs and District Heads, often acted to curtail such contacts. In this regard, it should be pointed out that Lugard, for example, frowned at the idea of
Emirs undertaking tours, describing one such tour as "a mistake."[93] Especially
in the case of Bornu Province which, for a period of six years, was divided up
into three administrative divisions, with headquarters at Maiduguri, Gaidam
and Gujba, there was some attempt, though not necessarily a conscious one,
to restrict contact between the Shehu and the Ajias in two of these, namely
Gaidam and Gujba Divisions. Thus, for example, during the celebration of the
coronation of King George V in 1911, only Ajias from the Maiduguri Division
attended the Durbar that the British caused to hold at Maiduguri. The Ajias
from the other two Divisions, including the Ajias of Gujba and Gaidam, Umar
Sanda Kura and Abba Rufai, both of them brothers of the Shehu, attended the
Governor's Durbar at Zaria.[94] Similarly, it would seem that in 1906 there was
a demand, probably from the High Commissioner, that the Sultanate of Sokoto
be split into a number of Administrative Districts. To this demand the Resident
replied that he did:

> not think that the Sokoto [Sultanate could] be split up into Administrative
> Districts for the sole reason that if, for instance, a Political Officer was to make
> Zamfara his administrative headquarter, all complaints and political matters
> would be taken in the first place to him and thereby undermine the authority
> now exercised over his subordinate chiefs by the Sarkin Muslimin.[95]

Quite possibly, the Resident was merely repeating an objection raised by the
Sultan or he might only be invoking the latter's name to protect his own authority. Whatever the case, the fact remains that the idea of dividing the Sultanate
and reducing the frequency of contact between the Sultan and some of "his"
District Heads was mooted. The British also took an exception to the exchange
of gifts that took place between Emirs and the District Heads on occasions like
the *Ids*. The British took this exception ostensibly because such exchange of
gifts would encourage extortion.[96] Yet, there is evidence to suggest that the

objection was on the political ground that relations between Emirs and District Heads should be entirely in accordance with rules laid down by the British. Thus, in 1911, it was pointed out that the Shehu of Borno had "constantly been forbidden to receive presents from Ajias and Lawans,"[97] and that "in December after 'Salla Laia' he accepted presents of horses from Ajias and Lawans and when taxed with this he stated that he gave handsome presents of gowns and burnouses in exchange." Yet, while "this [was] correct," it was unacceptable in the eyes of the British because the exchange "of the presents constitute[d] a defiance of orders."[98]

Popular Hostility Towards the Reorganization

We have noted above that District Heads that were "energetic" and "efficient" were also unpopular among the common people. Indeed, the dispatch of District Heads to live in the rural areas as a whole was unpopular with the people. To a very large extent, this unpopularity was tied up not just with the dispatch of the formerly capital-bound Sarakuna, but also with the nature of the duties that the District Heads were required to perform, the collection of taxes in particular. This is why the unpopularity affected not only District Heads who were sent out of the capital only after the British occupation, but also those Sarakuna that had even before then been domiciled outside the capital, in the areas that were later to become their districts. But the unpopularity of the system tended to be much greater in districts whose chiefs had been sent out from the capitals. This was on account of the fact that the arrival of the chiefs imposed on the areas concerned burdens that they had not been bearing before and quite apart from the British taxes. Among such additional burdens was the building of houses for the chiefs and their clients and, in quite a number of cases, the payment of extra demands by the chiefs.[99] We shall in a later chapter see the reaction of the people to the imposition and collection of British taxes.[100] Hence, here, we shall register only some evidence of the unpopularity of the new system, quite apart from the nature of the duties of the District Heads.

In the first few years following the reorganization, it was usual for people living in one district to prefer to have dealings only with the chief of another district or even a *Basarake* who had not been appointed a District Head, the preference being on the basis of precolonial arrangements and usages. For example, Resident Fremantle of Yola was testifying to this when, in 1907, he reported that in spite of the formation of "homologous units", "many places still [owed] allegiance to some chief other than the District Headman, or follow the Emir direct, especially the hill pagans whose inclusion in a geographical district under a Fulani headman [was] in most cases nominal."[101] He added that although people were "becoming more willing to pay their taxes directly or indirectly through the appointed District Headman", they still might "regard him merely as the official tax collector," and nothing else.[102] Later on, people adopted emigration as a form of protest. Thus, in 1912, Resident Sharpe in Yola reported that two districts, Daware, east of Yola, and Nyibango, west of Yola, were emptying because the people were emigrating into German Adamawa.[103] In the latter district, for example, the local "market [was] in ruins" and Nyibango town "was especially in a ruined state, and deserted." The District Head had "no authority and [was] unable to improve his district" and there were "endless complaints of high handedness."[104] In some places, the people simply adopted a contemptuous attitude towards the District Heads. This was the case, for example, in the Emirate of Gwandu where in 1913 Assistant Resident McAllister had to endeavour "to strengthen the authority of the Emir and Headmen throughout the emirate against a growing indifference on the part of the proletariat."[105] In yet other places, the people even resorted to killing the District Heads. This, for example, was the case in Bornu Province, where late in 1906, Lawan Adam of Marte District was killed by the Asale clan while engaged in the collection of Jangali.[106]

Conclusion

We have seen that the District Reorganization exercise had a great impact on the pre-existing political and administrative structures. For example, the exercise led to the disemployment of a large number of the former *kofofi* and *jakadu*. This was in spite of efforts by the Emirs to retain the services of these agents, by various means that included employing very many of them as *dogarai* and messengers. The reorganization also led to generally bad relations between the Emirs and the new District Heads, relations which, in a number of cases, were very bitter. This was the result of the fact that many District Heads tried to ignore the emirs and to secure themselves in their positions by a direct reliance on the British Residents. Finally, the reorganization which involved the settlement of the District Heads with many followers in areas that had formerly been directly only under village and communal chiefs, led to demands being made on the rural populace of a type which was new and burdensome. Such demands led to hostility on the part of the populace towards the reorganization.

6

The Establishment of the Native
and Provincial Court System

Introduction

Before British colonisation, the judicial system of the emirates was integrated into the administrative structure, devoid of separation between the executive and judicial arms of government. After colonial conquest, as we will consider in detail in this chapter, the British undertook an elaborate and far-reaching judicial reorganization for the purpose of entrenching their hegemony, generating revenue, enforcing law and order, and meeting other demands. The chapter will discuss the establishment of "Native Courts" and their uneven distribution, powers, jurisdiction, periodic reorganization, imposition of fees and fines, and the impact of the Courts on the people of the emirates. While exploring the structure of the Native Courts, we shall endeavour to find out whether, as argued by the proponents of Indirect Rule, the emirs appointed the Qadis and their Assistants with the mere advice of the Resident, or it was actually the Resident who wielded the power of approval. Such inquiry would, we hope, make it sufficiently clear that the emirs were mere nominal heads of the Courts, while the British retained powers of effective control. This much would be demonstrated with the particular example of Sokoto, where the Resident was granted wide powers over the Courts.

Furthermore, we shall examine the problems and volume of work the Courts were saddled with, and find out why the British employed Qadis as judges in the Native Courts. Pursuing this line of inquiry is important because there are indications that seem to suggest that the British were keen on foisting a veil of legal independence over the Native Courts in order to conceal their desire to dominate, control and regulate the lives of the people. While examining this matter at length in the chapter, we shall back our arguments with particular reference to the trial of those arrested in connection with the Satiru Revolts near Sokoto in 1906. Furthermore, our examination will be accompanied by a consideration of the methods, forms and degree of control exercised over the Courts by the British through the appointment and dismissal of Qadis, receipt and evaluation of periodic reports, together with the various problems encountered by the British in the process. In the course of our exposition on these and other related matters, we shall refer to the operation of the Courts in Bauchi, Sokoto and Gwandu emirates. The chapter will also try to highlight the important role played by the Provincial Courts in the judicial system of the emirates, such as their usurpation of the powers of the Native Courts and the hegemonistic character of the sentences they imposed. We will finally conclude with an examination of the nature of the clashes between the emirs and the Qadis over the judicial administration of the emirates.

The Precolonial Judicial System of the Emirates

At the time of the British conquest of the emirates, there was no strict separation between the 'executive' and the judicial arms of government, both at the emirate level and at levels below it. Thus, in Ilorin Emirate, for example, the British found that the town chiefs held courts while in Ilorin town itself, the ward heads, numbering between sixty and seventy, also held court and settled minor cases including petty debts, petty thefts and matrimonial disputes.[1] In addition, community chiefs such as the Sarkin Hausawa also held court. From all these courts, namely, the ward and communal courts in the capital as well as the town courts, appeals went either to the Emir of Ilorin or to the Qadi of Ilorin, either of whom could handle the appeal or refer it to the other.[2] Similarly, both the Emir and the Qadi did act as courts of first instance, plaintiffs having the choice of either going to their ward, communal or town chief first. Alternatively, they took their cases direct to the Qadi or the Emir; but one would assume that direct references to either the Emir or the Qadi must have been uncommon, because people making such direct references must have had to wait longer than they would have had to if they had gone to the courts of their immediate chiefs. Thus, the Qadi and the Emir had the whole emirate and therefore larger number of cases to settle than any one communal or town chief. From the point of view of British desire to take control of the judicial system, a noteworthy fact about all these courts is that they kept no record of cases.

Similarly, in Yola, the British found that in the important towns there were Qadis appointed by the local rulers, these Qadis and the local rulers, mostly sitting together, constituting the courts of first instance.[3] In addition, there were appeal Qadis at Yola, Girei and Namtari, all appointed by the Emir.[4] As far as Yola town was concerned, the British found four people who were competent to hold court.[5] These were the Emir himself, the Qadi and two other mallams. The two mallams, as a rule, sat with the Qadi and assisted him, but each of them was competent to try cases alone without the other and without the Qadi.[6] Similarly, the Qadis who constituted the final court of appeal in the emirate handled such appeals either alone, or in conjunction with the other three Qadis and other mallams[7] In all probability, not only the Emir and the three mallams had judicial competence; other chiefs in the town such as the Magaji, the Galadima, the Waziri and the communal chiefs residing in the town, such as Lamdo Kabi, Lamdo Kasina and Lamdo Adar, each had jurisdiction over his section of the town or the community of which he was leader.

In the Sokoto metropolis, all the important towns had designated Qadis,[8] but all these were designated by the chiefs of those towns who might give them a free hand or reduce them to the role of legal advisers to themselves. The chiefs themselves were responsible to Sokoto for the settlement of cases in the towns.[9] At Sokoto itself, while there was a Qadi, the Alkalin Gari, all the important chiefs such as the Waziri, the Magajin Rafi, the Magajin Gari and the Galadiman Gari also had judicial competence over their "followers," and had among their subordinate officials, Qadis, such as the Alkalin Waziri.[10] In addition, ethnic communities such as the Arabs, the Tuaregs, etc, had their Qadis.[11] Appeals from all these chiefs, whose courts acted as courts of first instance, as well as appeals from the courts of the surrounding towns, went either to the Alkalin Gari or to the Sarkin Musulmi[12], while appeals from the major emirates were lodged with the Sarkin Musulmi.[13] In practice, however, at the time the British occupied Sokoto all appeals, whether lodged with the Qadi or with the Sarkin Musulmi, were actually heard and decided by the Qadi. In such cases, one or two representatives of the Sarkin Musulmi always attended the Qadi's court to witness how he settled cases and report back to the Sarkin Musulmi.[14] Here too, as in the emirates, it would seem that no records of cases were kept as a matter of course. The only time the disposal of cases was put down in writing was when it was necessary to inform a superior or a subordinate court of how a case involving an appeal was originally or ultimately settled.[15] Thus, the judicial system in the emirates as the British found it was totally integrated with the administrative system.

To bring this judicial system under their control and make it serve their purposes – viz to maintain their law and order, to compel obedience to British ordinances, and to help generate a revenue for 'Native' and 'Government

Administration', the British found it necessary to distinguish between the judicial and the administrative structures, and to introduce a rigid formality that, among other things, included the keeping of regular records of cases for British inspection in its procedure. The British, in their records, referred to these two processes, the separation of the judicial from the administrative structures and the introduction of rigid formality as the "establishment of Native Courts." It is these two processes, together with their concomitants and combined impact on the people of the emirates, that we are going to examine in the rest of this chapter under appropriate sub-headings.

The Establishment of Native Courts

The establishment of Native Courts in the emirates was uneven in its pace. The first Native Court to be established by the British in the emirates was that of Jebba in Ilorin Emirate. This was in October 1900. This court was 'established' by Assistant Resident Dwyer, rather grudgingly, after he realized that the people of Ilorin generally preferred to go to the local Alkalis rather than bring their cases to his 'Provincial Court'.[16] Of course, Dwyer rationalized the people's avoidance of his court. It meant "either crime [was] non-existent or ... the people afraid of the chiefs [did] not come to [him] for advice but [bore] with any injustice that [might] be done them." However, while so rationalizing the situation, Dwyer also understood its implications, namely that he could not ignore the Qadis, and therefore, the sooner he brought their courts under his control, the better. Hence, in October he "established" and "constituted" the Qadi's court at Jebba as a Native Court, by issuing a warrant in accordance with "section 2 of 'the Native Courts Proclamation 1900.'"[17] The warrant spelt out the membership of the court, its jurisdiction, and the punishments it could inflict.[18] In the same month, Dwyer "established and constituted" five Native Courts for Ilorin, one under the Emir's Qadi and one each under the four leading Baloguns in the town.[19]

In Yola, no Native Court had been established as late as the end of February 1902, six months after the British occupation of the Emirate.[20] Up to then the position of the Qadi courts, including the ones in Yola town, still remained anomalous as far as the British were concerned. Meanwhile, the Resident's 'Provincial Court' received only "few petty cases."[21] The Resident's alleged reasons for not "establishing" a Native Court was that he did not know Lugard's "views and wishes" on the matter.[22] To this allegation Lugard retorted that "the memo and proclamation ... would not have been written if it were intended they should be a dead letter." He ordered the Resident to "set up the court at once."[23] Lugard's order was signed on May 8, 1902, yet by June 1902 Resident Barclay had a 'Native Court' in Yola, to be followed by one each at Song and Girei in November, and others at Namtari and Malabu in December.[24]

Similarly, in Borno it was only in December 1902, nine months after British occupation, that Hewby even "discovered" that the Shehu had a court, and that there were courts in several places in the Sheikhdom "presided over by the local Alkali which try minor cases under Mohammedan law, referring big cases to the Shehu."[25] Predictably, in Hewby's opinion, these courts were in "no sense at present courts of justice." Yet, he proceeded to "establish" the Shehu's court as a "Native Court" by issuing it with a warrant.[26] Meanwhile, the other courts remained "non-existent" as far as the British were concerned. On the other hand, in Sokoto, within a month of the occupation of the town, Burdon had not only "established" the Alkalin Gari's court into a "Native Court" but had already started receiving reports of cases from that court and forwarding some of them to Lugard.[27] Within the next eleven months the Resident and his Assistants had "established" "Native Courts" at Gwandu, Jega, and Argungu.[28] Meanwhile in Yola up to March 1903, nine months after the "establishment" of the Yola "Native Court," only the four district "Native Courts" listed above had been established.[29] It was not until February 1904 that a sixth "Native Court" was "established," at Gurin.[30] Similarly, in Bauchi and Gombe emirates only one "Native Court" in each of the two emirates had been "established" up to November 1904, almost three years after the occupation of the two emirates.[31] And in Borno after the "establishment" of the Shehu's "Native Court" in December 1902, it was not until May 1904 that Hewby "established" four more Native Courts.[32]

Meanwhile, in Sokoto Province, by December 1906, eight district "Native Courts" had been established in the Sultanate.[33] Gwandu still had only three "established" Native Courts – namely, at Gwandu town, Jega and Ilorin, the latter being a "judicial council,"[34] while Argungu had only one.[35] Yet within twelve months, that is, by December 1907, "established" Native Courts in the Sokoto Province as a whole had jumped from fourteen to twenty-nine.[36] In the meantime, by the end of 1906, there were fifteen Native Courts in the Sheikhdom of Borno, all of them "judicial councils" and two of them at the capital.[37] In Bauchi Emirate, there were only eleven district "Native Courts" by March 1908, which is six years after its occupation.[38] In Sokoto, on the other hand, the number of Native Courts jumped from twenty-nine at the end of 1907 to forty-three by December 1909.[39] By December 1910, there were forty-seven Native Courts in the Province, of which thirty-two were in the Sultanate, fourteen in Gwandu, and only one in Argungu.[40] This distribution worked out to 1 court to 30,000 people in the Sultanate, 1 to 15,000 in Gwandu and 1 to 45,000 in Argungu.[41] Theoretically, each court in the Sultanate and in Gwandu served 800 square miles; but, in fact, the distribution of the courts within each emirate was very uneven. Some courts were very close to one another while some places were over forty miles away from the nearest court. This was because the courts were established only at district capitals.[42] Meanwhile, Yola Emirate had only seven district "Native Courts" by the end of 1909, eight years after the imposition of British domination.[43] In Kano, up to December 1911, that is nine years after the imposition of that domination, there were only ninety Native Courts for all the eight emirates included in the Province.[44] In Yola, the number of courts increased to twelve by June 1911.[45] By the end of 1912, Native Courts in Sokoto Province had further increased, though slightly, to 39 for the Sultanate, 15 for Gwandu and 2 for Argungu.[46] However, the following year, 1913, the number of Native Courts for the Sultanate was cut down to 25, while those for Gwandu were drastically reduced to 8.[47]

Similarly, the number of Native Courts in Yola was recommended to be reduced by three by March 1912, the warrants of those of Gola, Kilba and Song being recommended for withdrawal on the economic ground that "the small amount of work done by them did not justify their existence and salaries."[48] Similarly, two Native Courts, those of Ribadu and Gurin, were merged into one to be known as Fombina Mayo Native Court and the "Native Courts of Malabu and Daware were left in abeyance" and their functions added to the Native Court at Girei."[49] Hence, by the first quarter of 1912, there were practically only six Native Courts in the whole emirate of Yola. Meanwhile, in Zaria up to the end of 1912, eleven years after the British occupation of the emirate, there were only nine district Native Courts.[50] And at the end of 1915, there were only seventeen Native Courts, including those of the Emir and the chief Alkali in the whole province, which, admittedly, was very much coterminous with Zaria Emirate.[51]

The Structure of Native Courts

Though the Native Courts were sometimes referred to as "Alkalis' courts", the impression should not be gathered that they were "constituted" even in a formal sense each by a sole Alkali, any more than the precolonial courts were constituted by sole judges. On the contrary, each "Native Court" was a bench, as also had been the precolonial courts. Thus, for example, the Jebba "Native Court," which Dwyer set up in 1900, was made up of four members, one of whom, Abdul Mumini, was designated "judge", while the three others were designated "members".[52] The court could not sit unless at least two members were sitting together. Significantly, the warrant did not make it necessary for the "judge" to be present before the court could hold.[53] Similarly, the four courts constituted by the Baloguns were each made up of the appropriate Balogun and two other members "not less than two of whom sitting [should] constitute the court."[54] The chief Alkalis' court too was made up of three members, including the chief Alkali, the court being constituted only when two members, not necessarily including the Alkali, were present.[55] In Yola, the chief Alkali's court was made up of "the Alkali of Yola," Hamman Joda as "president," Bakari and Jabbo as "Fulani" members, and Usman as "Hausa" member of the court.[56] However, in the case of Yola, the report does not include how many of the judges had to be present before the court could sit, or whether the Qadi had to be one of those present. In the case of Sokoto, the warrant appointed Almustapha "to be Alkali of Sokoto, and Malam Mamodu and Mallam Abdullahi to be his assistants."[57] The number of assistants was limited to two because, at this time, "the other mallams available for appointment [had] not yet returned to Sokoto." In the case of Sokoto too, there is no indication as to the number of "assistants" who had to be present before the court could sit, nor whether the presence of the Qadi himself was absolutely necessary. However, Burdon did note that in precolonial days, "the Alkali [had] never been in the habit of disposing of cases by himself."[58] Instead he had "always been accustomed to have one or more of his Almajirai, learners or assistants, present."[59] In fact, "in any important or difficult cases, all the principal mallams of the town [were] summoned."[60]

As to who appointed the Qadi, it should be noted that at first it was either the Resident or the High Commissioner that "established and constituted" the Native Courts and appointed the Qadi and their assistants, though often this was done "on the advice" of the Emir concerned. Thus, for example, in October 1900, it was the "Assistant Resident of the Province of Ilorin" that "established and constituted [the] Native Court for Jebba" and "appoint[ed]" the "judge" and other "members" of the court. It was also the Assistant Resident that "established and constituted a Native Court" in each of the four "quarters" in Ilorin town and the Alkali's court there, and "appoint[ed]" the "members" of these courts, as well as the Alkali.[61] Indeed, although in the letter reporting the setting up of these five courts, the Assistant Resident portrayed the Emir of Ilorin as fully participating in the events that led to the establishment of the courts and the selection of their members, the warrant itself did not mention the Emir except in his capacity as the titular head of each of the four courts. That is to say, the warrant did not bother to state that it was "on the advice" of the Emir that the members were appointed by the Assistant Resident. In Sokoto also, it was "the Resident with the approval of the High Commissioner" that [appointed] the "alkali of Sokoto" and "his assistants,"[62] but in this case it was "on the recommendation of the Sarkin Muslimin" that the judges were appointed.

However, as time went on, the fiction was often concocted that it was the Emir that appointed the Qadi and his assistants either "on the advice" of the Resident or with his approval. Thus, for example, when the Qadi Usumanu of Girei died in October 1903, it was "the Emir" of Yola that "appointed" Mallu Hama Jam as "Alkali and President of the Girei Native Court." It was done with the "approval" of Resident Barclay.[63] However, in Gwandu in March 1903, it was the Assistant Resident, Goldsmith, that "dismissed" the Qadi of Jega for "refusing to try the Dan Gima for actively preventing two Satiru spies from being arrested," and it was the Assistant Resident that appointed a new Qadi on the advice of Sarkin Jega, with no reference to the newly appointed Emir of Gwandu, Haliru.[64]

The Role, Functions and Powers of the Native Courts

In order to understand the role that the "Native Courts" played in British colonialism in the emirates, we should examine the jurisdiction of these courts, their powers and the volume of their work.

Jurisdiction

The "Native Courts", as their name indicates, had jurisdiction over "natives" living within specified areas, which could be whole emirates, one or two districts or even a single town or area of a town, like the market place.[65] However, within these areas, the "Native Courts" handled only cases involving "natives" or "natives against natives."[66] Therefore, the courts had no jurisdiction over "non-natives"[67] or indeed over "natives in government employment."[68] Often, those over whom the "Native Courts" had jurisdiction were defined as "people owing allegiance to the Emir," that is, owing allegiance prior to British occupation.[69] In fact, with the establishment of the Sabon Garis or "Native Townships," the residents of these "townships," who were made up of "foreign natives of African descent" and "natives" who were "employees of the Government or trading firms," were removed from the jurisdiction of the Native Courts and placed under the jurisdiction of the Provincial Courts.[70] These often included people recruited by the British within the emirates themselves. In Kano, for example, "petty litigations between Native Foreigners" so took up the time of the Provincial Court that: "[had it not been] that the bulk of [the] important Native cases [were] settled by the Kano Native Courts, the Provincial staff would [have been] quite inadequate to cope with the judicial work in Kano District."[71]

Yet, instead of suggesting that the Native Courts be permitted to handle litigations from the "Native foreigners," the Resident went on to suggest that "an experienced officer to do nothing else but legal work [was] required at Kano."[72]

Yet, even in the case of people "owing allegiance" to the Emirs, it was not all cases that were handled by the Native Courts, although by the end of our period, the most important ones among these courts handled virtually all cases involving such 'natives'. Thus, for example, the Native Court which Dwyer "established and constituted" at Jebba in 1900 could try civil suits only when "the debt, damage or demand [did] not exceed £10," though it could also handle "all suits and matters relating to the succession to the goods of any deceased native within [its] jurisdiction."[73] As far as what Dwyer referred to as "criminal" cases were concerned, the Jebba Native Court was empowered to handle only "petty assaults" which did "not involve danger to life or serious injury to the body and limbs of person assaulted."[74] The court also handled "criminal" cases of defamation, "juju," "disobedience" of "any lawful order of the Headman," seduction and "extortion or cheating," provided "the property involved did not exceed £5." On the other hand, the five "Native Courts" established in Ilorin town, for each one of which the Emir was the nominal president, were empowered to handle cases of highway robbery, impersonation, rape, arson, communal fights and disturbances, theft in general, debt in general, "ownership of slaves," matrimonial cases in general, and "cattle questions."[75] Yet even these courts, the chief Alkali's court included, were prohibited from handling cases involving murder, slave raiding, deposition of "a chief or Headman" and "land cases in which a large tract of land [was] in dispute."[76]

In Sokoto, however, Burdon gave the "Alkali and his assistant" authority to "judge all matters in the same way as before," though the court could "not try any man employed by Government except by permission of the Resident."[77] In fact, as Burdon later pointed out to Lugard, none of the courts "originally established in this Province", namely the Native Courts at Sokoto, Gwandu, Argungu and Jega, "were limited in their powers in any way (except in the matter of Report to the Resident of death sentences)."[78] Indeed, as time went on, the Native Courts throughout the emirates were allowed to try more and more cases. For example, the Resident in Yola in 1902 and 1904 discovered that Native Courts, including District Native Courts, were handling slavery cases.[79] Up to this time the position was that only the Provincial Courts could handle such cases.[80] However, it turned out that the Native Courts "caught out" handling such cases actually decided the cases in favour of slaves trying to establish or obtain their freedom, and dealt harshly with those seeking to "prove" that the plaintiffs were their slaves.[81] This being the case, the Residents found no ground for ordering the Native Courts to desist from handling such cases, except the purely technical ground that such cases were outside their field of competence. Hence, the Residents allowed the Native Courts to continue handling such cases and Lugard gave his approval to this allowance.[82] Similarly, by 1906, other Residents were coming round to Burdon's view that the British should, on their own initiative, transfer more and more cases from the jurisdiction of the Provincial Courts to that of the Native Courts. Thus, Resident Howard of Bauchi, for example, felt that the Bauchi Native Court should "be trusted to deal with cases in which the Sarakuna were involved."[83] By 1909, almost all the major Native Courts, namely, those located in the emirate capitals and presided over by those Qadis who were locally known as *Alkalan Alkalai*, were already trying homicide and highway robbery cases;[84] and by 1910 these courts were expressly deemed "competent to try every class of case."[85]

Powers

As for the powers of the Native Courts, we have seen that the Sokoto Native Court was, right from the beginning, empowered to impose any sentence it deemed fit provided that "no sentence of death [should] be carried out unless it [was] first reported to the Resident." The Resident reserved the "power to be present at any trial, to rehear any case [in his own court], to order a new trial or to alter any sentence."[86] Hence, while the Sokoto Native Court was supposedly "unlimited" in its powers, in effect the power to give a verdict and impose a sentence lay with the British Resident. This fact should be borne in mind as we discuss the "powers" of the other Native Courts over the years covered in this book. Whatever "powers" they were given, minor or major, they were subject to this very important proviso. It is also important at this point to emphasize that the Sokoto Native Courts were granted these powers by Burdon, more against the opposition of Lugard than with his blessing. Thus, according to the High Commissioner's view, "it [was] better for a Native Court to learn its work in lesser cases, and when it [had] proved itself efficient it [could] be trusted with larger powers."[87] The power to impose up to, and including the death sentence, was also exercised by three other Native Courts in Sokoto Province, namely, those of Gwandu, Jega and Argungu.[88] These courts could also administer strokes of the cane up to a maximum that varied from court to court, thirty six in the case of the Jega court, a limit which the Alkali regarded as "grotesque," the Resident Gwandu agreeing with him.[89] Elsewhere, the main Native Courts in the emirate capitals could also impose the death sentence.[90] Native Courts were also "empowered" to impose fines,[91] a form of punishment that, at least in theory, had been alien to the precolonial judicial system.[92] In a sense, jail terms[93] – with or without hard labour – was also an innovation introduced by the British, in that hitherto people had been sent to jail, not for specified periods but until, in the opinion of the Emir – not the Qadi – the culprit had reformed.[94] Alternatively, people were detained indefinitely as a means of saving society from their menace.

Fees and Fines

It should also be pointed out here that the introduction of fines as one of the punishments that Native Courts could impose was obviously designed by the British to make these courts not only "pay their way" financially but also to be a source of revenue for the British. Hence, not only were the Native Courts made to impose fines, but also to exact fees from litigants. Thus, for example, Resident Dwyer in Ilorin required the Native Court of Jebba to impose the following fees:

"On every criminal complaint - 1/-."

"On every case of debt or demand heard 1/- per £ on the value of matter in dispute."

"In all cases of damages a hearing court fee of 1/- to be paid by plaintiff and a fee of 2/6d to be paid by the unsuccessful party."[95]

Significantly, at first, "all fines imposed and fees exacted [should] be carefully noted and paid over to the Resident."[96] However, this directive was altered by October when Dwyer issued warrants to the Qadi of Ilorin and the four Baloguns in Ilorin town. In these warrants, Dwyer directed that "all fines lawfully imposed to be divided between the Emir and the Balogun in whose district the case was tried."[97] This way, Dwyer hoped both to pay members of the Native Courts and to be able to hold them liable if they accepted bribes.[98] In Yola, Barclay gave no elaborate list of fees because he was, "not sufficiently *au fait* with the subject."[99] However, from the point of view of litigants, what Barclay did was worse than giving an elaborate scale of fees, for he fixed "a minimum" fee of 2/- for all cases.[100] Then he went on to request Lugard himself to "fix them in accordance with those laid down for other Native Courts;"[101] and the High Commissioner promised to ascertain "from all Residents scale of fees so as to ensure uniformity of charges throughout the Protectorate ..."[102] In the meantime, the interim "minimum" of 2/- fixed by Barclay had the immediate effect of scaring litigants away from the Native Courts. Thus, according to Barclay, the "cause list" for September, October and November 1902, was:

> a very light one, owing, as the Alkali informed me, to the fees charged which have the effect of keeping down the number of vexatious cases which used to be common under the previous system; litigants now take care they have a sound case before rushing into law. [103]

The last part of this quote is a clear indication that Barclay had missed the point about the impact of the fees. For, the important point is not that people with petty cases were discouraged from rushing to court, but that the poor, however great their grievance, were prevented from going to court. This way the British made sure that social relations would deteriorate and the propensity to settle accounts by resort to violence would be a permanent feature of society. Besides, this way the British made it easy for Qadis and other "unauthorized" persons to settle cases outside court at no fee or at smaller fees than the British "minimum," and thereby, defeated their own desire to appropriate and control the indigenous judicial system.

Yet, while scaring litigants away from the Native Courts, the fees and the fines, of which the Qadis were allowed to keep a fraction before they were put on token salaries, [104] did become stable and fairly lucrative sources of revenue for the British — sources of revenue that appeared on the list of the sources of monthly, quarterly and yearly government revenue with perfect regularity. [105] So also did another court-derived source of revenue, namely death-duty. [106]

Volume of Work

As to the volume of work done by the Native Courts, all one can say is that compared to the number of cases disposed of by the Residents' own "Provincial Courts," the Native Courts disposed of a very large number of cases. More than this one cannot say, for while absolute figures, that is, figures seen in isolation from comparative figures handled by other courts, are useless, we do not know the number of cases that were settled outside of court. That the Native Courts handled the bulk of the cases that were handled by the colonial "administration" can be seen from a random selection of figures for Provincial and Native Courts, as shown in Table 6.1. [107] However, while the figures in Table 6.1 show quite conclusively that a preponderant number of all the cases tried in court in the emirates were tried in the Native Courts, it would be incorrect to infer from this that these cases were settled by 'native' or 'traditional' authorities on behalf of the British. Such inference would be incorrect in view of the fact that the day to day functioning of these courts was very much controlled, directed and checked by the Residents and Assistant Residents.

Table 6.1. Cases Handled by Courts by Province, 1907 to 1915

Province	Period	Native Courts	Provincial Courts
Bauchi	1907	1206	134
Sokoto	1907	1254	141
Sokoto	1908	3160	128
Sokoto	1909	4459	101
Sokoto	1910	6062	70
Sokoto	1911	11028	72
Sokoto	1912	14331	89
Sokoto	1913	15438	66
Kano	1912	44602	111
Kano	1913	48116	351
Kano	1914	50874	499
Zaria	1912	3150	121
Zaria	1915	5836	748
Yola	1914	3666	29

Hence, in the final analysis, and in a very literal sense even the cases handled by the native courts were settled by the British. So the correct conclusion should be that while the British Residents settled a number of cases without involving the Native Courts, that is, while the British settled a number of cases in the exclusively British Provincial Courts, the British involved the native courts in the settlement of the majority of the cases that were brought before them. This was the full extent of "Indirect Rule" as far as the administration of "justice" was concerned.

Relations Between the British and the Native Courts

The need to establish Native Courts arose out of British desire to control the operation of the erstwhile Qadis. This, in turn, arose out of British desire to use these Qadis to give effect to their policy of employing "legal" means to dominate, control and regulate the lives of the people of the emirates. This desire for such use of the Qadis can be seen in the manner in which the British handled the first "Mahdi" they captured in the Sultanate of Sokoto.[108] Instead of trying him in the Provincial Court, the British handed the man to the Sokoto Native Court. Yet, instead of letting the court handle the case in the light of its understanding of the situation, the Resident directed that he should be kept informed about the progress of investigation into the case and ordered that no sentence was to be passed without reference to him "for the consideration and information" of the High Commissioner. Clearly, the Resident intended both to settle the case in the light of British understanding of it and in their own interest, and at the same time to make it appear that it was the Alkalin Sokoto that settled it. As fate would have it, the unfortunate Mallam fell sick and died even before investigation into the case began.[109] Similarly, after the Satiru Revolt of February–March 1903 and its bloody suppression by the British, the Resident refused to try Mallam Dan Maikafo "and his lieutenants."[110] Instead, he forced the Qadi of Sokoto to try the case, without at the same time allowing him to use his own discretion in handling it. Clearly, the reasons for handing these patriots to the Native Court were political. Burdon claimed that it was "owing to the difficulties and delay connected with murder trials before a British court, and also *because of the tremendous political advantage* to be gained from the *open condemnation* of the false Prophet by the acknowledged Head of his religion ..." that he handed over the men to the Native Court.[111]

The British desire to use the Native Courts as tools of their policy can also be seen from what transpired between the British and the Qadi of Jega in the Emirate of Gwandu in February 1906, about one month before they removed the Qadi, allegedly for blocking the arrest of two "Satiru spies."[112] Thus, according to Burdon, a man and his wife were stoned by the people of Jandutsi and the wife died nine days later.[113] Assistant Resident McAllister "directed the Jega Alkali to try the case."[114] The Qadi fined the headman of Jandutsi 200,000 cowries, a fine which the Acting Resident at Sokoto considered too light. Hence he directed Assistant Resident McAllister to *induce* the Alkali to retry the case "*and fine the Inami,*" i.e. the village head, whom McAllister had already deposed, "*1,000,000 cowries* – money to be given to Dakarkari man" – that is, the man whose wife died after stoning; and "*if the Alkali objected to retry the case it was to be taken out of his hands* [and] an Executive Fine of 1,000,000 cowries inflicted." It is precisely because this latter option was open to the British that the need for the "Native Courts" becomes clearly political. That is to say – the Qadis were "established and constituted" into Native Courts rather than being abolished outright, primarily because the British had a political function for them, namely that of camouflaging British administrative and judicial decisions as the decisions of the indigenous *ulema*.[115] And if the Native Courts were to serve British policy at all, it was necessary for the British to control and supervise them. Lugard stated as much in one of his comments on the Sokoto Provincial Reports.[116] Thus, he urged the Resident that: "since the Sokoto Courts have been given very large powers, and the tendency seems to be to transfer to them all possible cases … a strict supervision becomes even more than usually imperative.[117]

He pointedly added, "I look upon this administrative work as of more importance, and more the work of the Resident, than the Historical Research which you say has occupied so much of your time."[118] To drive the point home, Lugard, later in his comments, added "emphatically" that "the practical needs of Administration" seemed to be "more represented by a close supervision of the Native Courts than by almost any other form of work, except touring (with the objects it is undertaken for)."[119]

The Methods, Forms and Degree of British Control

The primary means by which the British controlled the Native Courts included the power of appointment and dismissal of Qadis, but the forms which British control and supervision of the Native Courts took was that of the receipt of monthly reports from them by the Resident or Assistant Resident, as the case might be.[120] In fact, in some places and in "serious cases no sentence [was] pronounced until the case [had been] fully reported [to the Resident] and [he was satisfied] as to the justice of the verdict."[121] The Qadi would then "tell [the Resident] the sentence he [proposed]."[122] The latter would "after much discussion and reference to Law books," and "with [as] little appearance of ordering as possible" persuade the Emir "to persuade the Alkali to pronounce the sentence which [the Resident] consider[ed] … [met] the necessities of the case."[123] Some of the cases, the verdicts on them and the sentences imposed, were sent by the Resident to the High Commissioner, either to seek his confirmation of the sentences or merely to keep him informed about how the Native Courts were being made to serve British policy.[124] In yet other places, the Residents made "a point of discussing cases as often as possible with the Alkali [and his assistants] and in having them in the Provincial Court when a case of interest [was] being tried" by the Resident.[125] Residents often even "found it necessary to call for weekly returns" of cases from the Native Courts.[126]

However, although what deserves to be emphasized, on account of its being substantial and basic to the relations between the British and the Native Courts, is the reality and effectiveness of the former's control over the latter, this control can be exaggerated unless the factors that *per force* limited its degree and magnitude are acknowledged. Among these limiting factors were physical barriers between the British and a majority of the courts, linguistic barrier between the British and the Qadis, and passive but often open resistance by the Qadis to such supervision. To understand the importance of these factors

in imposing limits on British manipulation of the Native Courts, we shall take
them one by one starting with:

The Physical Barriers of Distance

That distance between some of the Native Courts and Provincial and
Divisional Headquarters did constitute a physical limitation on British supervision was acknowledged by some Residents very soon after the "establishment"
of these courts. For example, in his report for December 1902 in Yola, Barclay
complained that it took a week "to get returns" from Song and four to five days
from Namatari and Malabu "i.e. it would occupy those periods for the clerks
of the various courts to come in and submit them and return."[127] Yet Song was
only 45 miles away from Yola, Malabu 30 miles and Namatari 15 miles. While
some other parts of the emirate at that time were as far as 130 miles away from
Yola, Malabu was about 30 miles and Namatari about 15 miles, while some
other parts of the emirate at that time were as far as 130 miles away from Yola.
Hence, if Native Courts were to be established in such places, in Wuba, for example, one can only imagine how long it would have taken for *muftis* to bring in
"returns" to Yola and take back the Resident's comments. In view of this "serious loss" of British time "every month," Barclay begged Lugard that "it would be
more convenient therefore if your Excellency would let me send in quarterly
returns of Native Court cases instead of monthly."[128] By implication, the Native
Courts too were to be allowed to send their "returns" only once every three
months, a suggestion with which Lugard, surprisingly, concurred.[129]

The Linguistic Barrier

The Native Courts from their inception until the end of British colonial
domination over the emirate in 1960, and indeed even after the exit of the
British, kept their records either in Arabic or in Hausa.[130] Hence, if the British
were to go over every case, these records had to be translated into English. This
was especially the case in the early days of British domination when the majority of courts kept their records in the Arabic language. Hence, even after a
Resident or Assistant Resident might have learnt Hausa, translation from Arabic
into Hausa was still necessary. This necessity and the impossibility of meeting
it in each and every case constituted a second and very important limitation on
the degree to which the British could supervise the Native Courts. That this
constraint was a real one is obvious from the Provincial Reports. For example,
"owing to the want of a proper interpreter [Barclay was] unable to submit records of Native Court cases" for the month of January, 1903.[131] He "wasted a

lot of valuable time attempting to get returns through the medium of a man brought up by Assistant Resident Erskine but had to give it up as hopeless."[132] Similarly, Burdon reported in 1903 that if he were to recognize every one of the 200 or so courts that existed within the Sultanate of Sokoto, "the translating and tabulating of [their] reports would take the entire time of a whiteman [an] interpreter and [a] Mallam to get through."[133] Hence his suggestion, which Lugard rejected, was that: "some system [was] needed whereby the Emir or the Alkali of Sokoto [could] be made responsible for the subordinate Alkali courts, receiving from them reports of all cases tried and reporting only important cases to the Resident."[134] Only a fraction of those 200 courts were ever "established and constituted" into Native Courts. Nonetheless, by October 1905, Burdon was complaining that the Resident for Gwandu had reported that: "the Jega Court Returns [the Gwandu Native Court presided by the learned Alkali Ahmad Sa'ad was not yet cooperating] ... this month [consisted] of thirty cases, taking the best part of a day to translate and compile."[135]

Besides, Burdon himself had "just received for distribution nine Native Court Warrants for the Sokoto [Sultanate]."[136] And this would "entail the translation entering and copying of nine more monthly returns."[137] There was "already great deal more work than the Resident and his staff [could] cope with." Hence, Burdon pleaded, it would "be a sheer impossibility" to attempt "this further burden" unless his staff was increased.[138] Burdon then went on to report that "no returns [had] been received from Argungu for October," an "omission" which, he said, was "probably a protest against Sarkin Arewa trying cases in Beibei and not being called upon [by the British] to render returns." He said there was "no means at present of stopping [the Sarkin Arewa from trying cases] even if I wished to."[139] Hence "the obvious remedy" was "to apply for a warrant for the Beibei Native Court"; but owing to the problem that the translation of returns from "established" Native Courts already posed, he could not see his "way to do so."[140] As long as his staff was "inadequate for the practical needs of administration," he could not "see how it [could] be right to fritter away its energy on compilation of [court] statistics."[141] In effect, what Burdon was impressing upon Lugard was that it was not in his power either to decree away pre-British courts or to bring all of them under British control.

However, it should be pointed out that Lugard, who offered Burdon no additional staff, refused to free him from closely supervising all the Native Courts in the Sultanate. Instead, he told him that "elsewhere" Residents and their "Arabic writer and a Clerk or Interpreter" were able adequately to handle the necessary translation.[142] He said he could not see how a Resident could "supervise his Native Courts unless he [went] through the cases." He offered that no duplicates of the translations were needed "as the originals are sent back to you." At any rate, according to Lugard, "since the Sokoto Courts [had] been given very large powers, and [since] the tendency [seemed] to be to transfer to them all possible cases ... a strict supervision [became] even more than usually imperative."[143] Yet, to record Lugard's refusal to understand Burdon's difficulties in closely supervising all the courts in the Sultanate is not to suggest that Burdon's limitations vanished. In all probability, he did what was possible for him to do under those circumstances, and went on fooling Lugard that he had all the Native Courts in the Sultanate under "strict supervision."

Passive Resistance by the Native Courts

It would seem that the Qadis as a group took very seriously the British promise not to interfere with religion, which the Qadis, in accordance with their own world outlook, understood to include the whole corpus of Shari'a. Hence, they found it very difficult to submit to British supervision and control. Thus, according to Dwyer, although the Emir of Ilorin, his Baloguns and the Qadi of Ilorin readily accepted the idea of "establishing and constituting" Native Courts in Ilorin, there was one suggestion from Dwyer that did not meet with their approval: the suggestion that the courts should give him "written reports" of cases at "[the] end of each month which were tried and the decision arrived at."[144] This, Dwyer "could not get them to promise to do." In fact, "at once the idea seized them [he] had some deep motive in making this request and anything [he] could say would not remove it."[145] He "did all [he] could in a quiet way to gain [his] point but it was no good." The Emir, the Qadi and the Baloguns could volunteer only "to give a verbal report everyday of the cases heard and the decision."[146] Unless Dwyer "was satisfied with this they [had to] ask [him] not to force a court on them but to hear the cases [himself];" and Dwyer had to accept such verbal reports, for a beginning.[147] To some extent, Dwyer was a bit lucky in that he got the Qadi of Ilorin to go and see him at all.

Temple did not fare so well in Bauchi. In his case, he "had the greatest difficulty" in persuading the Qadi even to go and see him.[148] Indeed, when Temple "suggested that the Qadi [Mallam Salihi] should do so the Emir was extremely alarmed, and spoke of writing to [Lugard] about the matter," his reason being that Wallace, at the time of the occupation of Bauchi, "had promised that the native customs should not be tampered with."[149] Nor was the Emir gratuitously protecting the Qadi from meeting Temple. On the contrary, the Qadi's own "scruples ... were even harder to overcome."[150] Temple "had to inform the Emir that if the [Qadi] should continue to refuse to see [him] a new [Qadi] [would] be appointed." And when "at last very reluctantly" the Qadi went to see Temple, it was 'with his face completely swathed" that 'he arrived.'"[151] Even after the Qadi had accepted a warrant from Temple, and even though the latter had "succeeded in persuading [him] to report his cases in writing," the attitude "of both the Emir and Alkali with regard to interference with the courts" was such that Temple thought it not "yet advisable to insist on [his] being present either personally or by proxy when cases [were] being tried."[152] Similarly, in 1906, the Qadi of Jega "openly encouraged rebellion and disorder while the Satiru rising was on."[153] He remonstrated with members of his court for "objecting to the procedure adopted by him" and "declared [that] he would have nothing to do with the whiteman or his orders."[154]

The Resident of Gwandu, by July 1905, was also complaining that "the Alkali of Gando Court [was] as bad as the Jega one," the latter having been found "incompetent and useless ... weak and unjust, disliked by the people and endeavouring to thwart [the Resident] in all reforms," and having been recommended for removal.[155] The Alkali of Gwandu was "as bad as" the Qadi of Jega allegedly because the Qadi, Ahmad Sa'ad, "never endeavoured to meet [the Resident's] wishes and he [was] a mere tool of the Emir," Muhammadun Aliyu, whose relations with the British were disastrous.[156] However, in order to sufficiently poison the ears of Burdon and Lugard, the Resident of Gwandu added the fiction that the Qadi's court was "a force" and that "no one unless compelled to" would take their complaints before the Qadi,[157] The Resident, therefore, proposed "to reconstitute this court after the appointment of a new Emir", which was then being discussed.

Yet, again early in 1906, "the Resident Gwandu report [ed] badly on the Gwandu Native Court," and again proposed to "reconstitute it" with new men "as soon as he [had] the necessary information and the new Emir [Halirun Abdu was] in a position to make recommendations."[158] The bone of contention between the Qadi and the Resident, this time, was that the Qadi had "failed" to send in any reports for the very crucial months of February and March 1906.[159] In fact, the court was not "reconstituted" possibly because Ahmad Sa'ad's reputation in Gwandu and Sokoto was too high for Haliru to want or dare to humiliate him.[160] In the meantime, not only did the Qadi move to Birnin Kebbi with the new Emir, but he managed to find a measure of acceptability with the Resident, for we are told in the June Report that his court was "working fairly satisfactorily."[161] In fact Resident Stanley of Gwandu was even "very well satisfied with the Alkali here;"[162] and went on to contradict his report of August 1905 by admitting that the Qadi "administer[ed] justice according to Mohammedan law and is incorruptible ..." However, it should not be assumed that Ahmad

Sa'ad had suddenly become amenable to British supervision, for Stanley also admitted that the Qadi "may not sympathize with the Administration."[163] In the same way, in 1906, the Resident Bauchi found the Gombe Native Court not satisfactory in the way it recorded its cases and sent in its returns.[164] The Nafada court too was similarly "unsatisfactory;" the Ningi court "unsatisfactory and practically useless" and the Duguri court "quite useless."[165] And in 1907, the Qadi of Zaria so resented the visit of Resident Dupigny to his court that he agreed to try in the Resident's presence only one manslaughter case and one other, but "very minor case." After this, he suspended court till the Resident had withdrawn.[166]

Conflict of Laws and Procedures

Subject to the final word lying with the British, the law that was enforced in the Native Courts was the Shari'a that had been enforced in the precolonial days, and the book used was mainly the *Mukhtassar* of Khalil.[167] Other books used were the *Tuhfat al-Hukkam*, the *Risalah* and the *Qawanin* of Abu al-Qassim Muhammad ibn Abi Jaafari.[168] Hence, because the ultimate decision lay with the British, who were committed to the Shari'a only to the extent that it served their purposes, conflicts over law and procedure did arise frequently between the Qadis and the British. We have already referred to the conflict between Alkali al-Mustafa and Resident Burdon over the handling of the case of the rebels of Satiru in 1906.[169] We have also referred to the introduction by the British of fines, court fees, and death duties, though we have seen no record of an objection by a Qadi to that departure from the Shari'a. However, there was an attempt to resist the British notion of punitive and specified imprisonment. Thus, according to Resident Barclay of Yola, he had to insist that "imprisonment, fine or flogging should also be awarded in all cases of theft," that is, as opposed to the precolonial custom of the courts in Yola which was "merely to compel restitution," a practice which the Resident believed had "no deterrent."[170]

Similarly, Resident Barclay had to break another precolonial legal practice according to which parents and slave owners were held responsible for the behaviour of their sons and slaves. Thus, according to him, the custom was to put down in the record books "only the names of the heads of households" "such as Malam Bakari's son or slave accused of theft." He had to instruct the court "always to record the names of interested parties."[171] The Resident was especially anxious that the principle of "individual responsibility" be recognized because, according to him, slaves were "the chief criminals", and by "Fulani law," slaves incurred "no responsibility beyond being flogged or otherwise ill treated for their misdeeds" while "[their] master solely was responsible for the return of the stolen property."[172] So entrenched was this custom that "the individual responsibility of the criminal was a difficult matter to impress upon the native judges."[173] It was only gradually that they accepted the "principle of how [the British] wish[ed] the law administered" and started to reward "quite respectable terms of imprisonment for certain classes of offences, especially theft."[174]

Another example of the Native Courts' resistance to the British notion of imprisonment is furnished from Jega in Gwandu Emirate. Thus, according to Resident Gwandu, the Alkali convicted and sentenced to three months imprisonment two men that the Resident had himself referred to his court to be tried for extortion.[175] However, the Alkali released them after 24 days' detention at the instigation of the Dangaladiman Jega "whose slaves they were." When the Resident questioned him over the issue, the Alkali "averred [that] they had completed their three months;" but the final word lay with the Resident. Hence, "after some" delay, the two prisoners were surrendered by the Dangaladima and resumed their imprisonment. The Alkali, on his part, was warned "in the strongest terms," and the Resident informed his own superior in Sokoto that he "would advise his dismissal on the next occasion." And in fact he did later.[176]

Similarly, the British took an early exception to the custom of paying *diyya* as a punishment for murders, a practice which, we must say to his credit, failed to "commend itself greatly to His Excellency."[177] As Hillary, who favoured the retention of this custom, noted, the concept of *diyya* was predicated on the view that "crime [was] a wrong done to the individual and not to the state." Not only was this custom in existence; but it was invoked at least once in a Native Court in Sokoto. In fact it was this invocation that led Lugard to task Hillary to "explain fully" regarding the "idea."[178] Yet, although the "dia" did "not commend itself highly" to Lugard, it was not immediately abolished by the British, as can be seen from the fact that in August 1905, the Resident Gwandu was reporting that the Jega Native Court had sentenced an accused murderer to death "as the parents of deceased would not accept 'dia[*diyya*]'."[179] However, as this latter case will show, the issue of *diyya* was not the only cause of British dissatisfaction with the Native Courts handling cases involving life. According to the Resident, after the Jega court had sentenced the accused to death, "the matter was then reported to [him] and confirmation of the sentence requested." However, "on enquiry", he found that no witnesses had been called "but [that] the father of the deceased had sworn fifty times that he had believed the accused to be the guilty party." The Resident then "fetched in all possible evidence and heard it in full" and found it to be "purely circumstantial but sufficient to convict." Hence, he "recommended" to the Native Court a reduction of the sentence to one of imprisonment. He did this more because he had already made up his mind on the basis of similar occasions that the Alkali of Jega was "incompetent and useless ... weak and unjust."[180] He sought the permission of Resident Sokoto for the removal of the Alkali, a permission which was granted.[181]

However, the Resident Gwandu was either too slow to act on this permission, or he acted on it but chose a Qadi with a similar disposition as the deposed one. For, in October, that is, two months after this incidence, the Resident was once again reporting the Jega Native Court over an unsatisfactory handling of a homicide case; and in this case too, the issue of "diyya" came up.[182] Thus, according to the Resident, the Native Court found the accused "guilty of murder." At first, the court requested the Resident "to allow the prisoner to be transferred as a slave to the relatives of the deceased." However, later on, he was asked "to sanction decapitation", presumably because the relatives of the deceased did not want the accused as a slave; but when the Resident "made inquiries as to how the trial had been conducted," he found that "it had been most irregular; no proof had been adduced, the prisoner had not pleaded guilty as stated and the Court Scribe was not present." Hence, he transferred the case to his own court. Thus, we have seen that there were several fundamental points of law over which the British and Qadis differed. These differences persisted not only through our period, but right to 1948.[183] But at least in the period of our study they were always resolved in accordance with British rather than the Qadis' views.

Provincial Courts

From the foregoing, it should be obvious that the British Provincial Courts played an important part in the British colonial judicial system in the emirates. For, very often, it was through the transfer of cases from the Native Courts to these courts that the Residents and their Assistants preempted or overrode the decisions of the Native Courts, in spite of the fact that no appeal was allowed from a Native Court to a Provincial Court. Hence, the work of the Provincial Courts merits some detailed examination. Perhaps, the first thing that should be said about these courts is that their names were misleading, in that there was not only one such court for each province, as the name would imply, but several. Every Assistant Resident had the power to hold such court in his area of jurisdiction. Thus, for example, in Yola Province, in 1907, three Assistant Residents had judicial powers, each with respect to his area of jurisdiction, though in theory there was supposedly only one Provincial Court in the Province, at Yola.[184] Similarly, in Sokoto Province by 1910, seven Assistant Residents each held "commissions conferring on them judicial powers," though in theory – there were only two Provincial Courts in the Province, at Sokoto and Gwandu.[185] Next, it should be pointed out that the Provincial Courts did not constitute an attempt by the British to introduce into the emirates the British tradition of jury and legal defence, for these courts did not use the jury system, nor did they admit lawyers.[186]

The British arrogated to the Provincial Courts the powers of receiving litigations from subjects of the emirates who might prefer to take their cases direct to the British,[187] to transfer cases from Native Courts, and to ask Native Courts to alter verdicts or sentences that they had already handed down. In an emergency, these courts also had the power to confirm and carry out death sentences imposed by Native Courts, although under normal circumstances death sentences imposed by both the Native Courts and the Provincial Courts were referred to the High Commissioner for confirmation.[188] In addition to having jurisdiction on all cases over which the Native Courts had jurisdiction, the Provincial Courts also had exclusive jurisdiction over cases in which emirs and other important chiefs were involved as defendants. A very good example of such cases was the trial of Lamido Bobbo Ahmadu of Yola,[189] and in cases in which 'non-native' Africans and 'natives' employed by the Colonial Administration, foreign firms and by the officials of that administration and the firms, were involved.[190] The Provincial Courts also had exclusive jurisdiction in cases involving breaches of proclamations in the enforcement of which only the Colonial Administration was involved, proclamations such as the Native Liquor Proclamation, the Caravan Proclamation, and the Firearm Proclamation.[191]

Also, on the whole, cases of highway robbery, extortion, kidnapping and slave dealing tended to be handled exclusively by the Provincial Courts, although, very often, these cases were handled by Native Courts as well. Among sentences that the Provincial Courts imposed was the death sentence, often even in cases of manslaughter, as distinct from murder.[192] At least this was the sentence that Resident Barclay imposed on a press-ganged carrier who killed a soldier at Girei during a journey by a British official from Yola to the northern parts of the province.[193] The Resident's excuse for imposing the death sentence was that if "the nice distinctions of English law between murder and manslaughter" were to be applied in "a still unsettled and out of the way place like Yola," the "results [might] be serious and [would] create disaffection and certain amount of alarm among soldiers and civil officials who [might] have orders to apprehend a person."[194] The Resident went on to make the sweeping allegation that "the Fulanis [were] very ready with a knife" and used it "on the slightest provocation whether in the right or in the wrong."[195] Hence, "an example [had to be] made that should have a deterring influence on their propensities in this direction."[196]

Though Lugard refused to confirm the death sentence, the mere fact of the Resident's handing down the sentence is a clear indication that the Provincial Courts were not bound by the "niceties" of English law. In fact it is significant that Lugard's reason for not upholding the sentence was that his Attorney General "held the opposite view,"[197] about the "propensity" of the Fulbe for violence and about their lack of capacity to appreciate the "niceties of English law," which Barclay also alleged. This is to say that if the Attorney General shared Barclay's views about "Fulani character," Lugard would have confirmed the death sentence, in spite of its "repugnance" to English law. It should also be recalled in this regard that it was partly "owing to the difficulties and delay connected with murder trials before a British Court"[198] that Burdon handed the Satiru prisoners over to the Sokoto Native Court. That meant that whenever the "niceties" and "difficulties" of English law seemed likely to cause inconvenience to the British, either those "niceties" were put aside, or the British allowed Native Courts to use their "less humane" methods to secure what British interests in the emirates dictated should be secured.

Still in this regard, it is instructive to note that Lugard's only comment on the procedure adopted by Burdon after the suppression of the Satiru revolt was to point out to Burdon that "a capital sentence [could] be summarily executed in such circumstances" and that "it was not equally necessary that the subsequent executions should have been by the Native Courts." Thus, although Lugard disagreed with Burdon in 1906, as he had disagreed with Barclay in 1902, it was on two contradictory grounds that he differed with them. In the case of Barclay, Lugard's position was that Barclay did not have sufficient grounds, namely, the killing of a single mercenary, for setting the "niceties" of English law aside. Whereas in the case of Burdon, Lugard's position was that the circumstances – an outright rebellion and shedding of British blood – warranted much less "caution" than Burdon exhibited. In the light of the foregoing, we can conclude that the moral fervour with which the British frequently censured Native Courts for "harshness" and "inhumanity" was little more than attempts by the British to justify their domination over the emirates in terms of the infamous "civilizing mission." Our conclusion will be all the more valid if it is added that it was only in cases that did not involve "flagrant" challenge to British authority that the British exhibited this moral fervour. However, when it served their interest to do so, the British did not hesitate to avail themselves of the "inhumanity" of the Native Courts.

Among other sentences imposed by the Provincial Courts was public flogging, which was not a particularly "civilized" form of punishment.[199] It should, in fact, be noted that flogging was such a regular form of punishment that a "Flogging Regulation Proclamation" was enacted and the specifications of flogging "instruments" spelt out. Each such instrument had to be inspected and approved by the High Commissioner.[200] Another form of punishment awarded by the Provincial Courts was imprisonment, which these courts were specifically instructed by the High Commissioner to resort to, as often as possible, as a means of securing labour for the British.[201] So also did the Provincial Courts regularly use fining as a means of increasing government revenue.[202] These fines were at least once as heavy as £15:0:0 for a single offence, in this case the "illegal" possession of firearms.[203] Yet another form of punishment inflicted by the Provincial Courts was that of deportation.[204] This was the usual punishment imposed on deposed Emirs and other chiefs, as well as people engaging in "conduct dangerous to the peace" of their area.[205] Most of these deportees were sent to Lokoja, but, especially in the first few years of colonial domination, deportees were also sent to Yola as was the case with the Emirs Ibrahim of Kontagora, Aliyu of Kano and Muhammad Lawal of Zaria or to Ilorin, as was the case with the Emirs Umaru of Bauchi and Abubakar of Katsina.

Needless to say, the Provincial Courts commanded little authority among the people of the emirates who, in the bulk majority of cases, avoided these courts unless they were arrested, or were, by other means, forced to appear in these courts. This avoidance by the people can be seen, for example, in Resident Ilorin's complaint in July 1900 that his work had "almost been nil," and that, apart from hearing and deciding "a few paltry women palavers" he did "nothing else."[206] Of course, the Resident did go on to speculate that "this [meant] either crime [was] nonexistent in Ilorin or that the people afraid of the chiefs [did] not come to [him] for advice but [bore] with any injustice that might be done to them," but we have no ground for sharing his assessment of the situation. Indeed, in view of the generalized and massive hostility with which the British Resident was regarded in Ilorin at this time,[207] it would be correct to reject that assessment as wrong and very wishful.

Similarly, in March 1902, Resident Temple complained of the "extreme timidity of all classes of natives" — timidity that he found a "great obstacle to our administration."[208] Among the events that led him to make this complaint was "the trial of a Fulani for slave dealing [which] took place in the Provincial Court, ... the result [of which] was that three entire families, relations of the accused, numbering about 150 persons, left their houses and went to Kano territory," a clear rejection of the Resident's authority.[209] Similarly, in Yola in

1904, the Resident reported that "no complaints regarding any decision [of the Native Courts] reached" him.[210] To the Resident, this meant that the people were fully satisfied with the decisions of the Native Courts, but there is every possibility that the absence of complaint to the British from these courts signified a lack of confidence in the British, more than it signified a trust in the Native Courts. Similarly, for the whole of 1910, no civil cases were reported to the Yola Provincial Court, a fact which supports the view advanced above that people went to these courts only when taken there.[211] Indeed, it was this lack of confidence by the people in the Provincial Courts that was partly responsible for the small number of cases handled by the Provincial Courts as compared to the Native Courts, as we observed above. The other factor, of course, is the paucity of Provincial Courts compared to Native Courts.

The Role of Emirs in the Native Judicial System[212]

In view of the simplistic theory of "Indirect Rule," it should be pointed out that though Emirs were assigned a role in the British judicial system, this role essentially excluded both supervision and regular mediation between the Qadis and the British, the relations between the Qadis and the British in fact being as regular and direct as we have depicted in earlier sections of this chapter. In this regard it should be noted that the step taken by Dwyer in Ilorin, in 1900, of making the Emir the nominal head of each of the five courts in Ilorin town and making the consent of the Emir, rather than that of the Resident, necessary before sentences passed by these courts were valid,[213] turned out to be isolated, false, and short lived. The general and enduring practice was that the Resident, rather than the Emir, was the pivot and head of the 'native' judicial system in each emirate.

Rather than consisting in the supervision of the Qadis or mediating between them and the British, the role of the Emirs in the British 'native' judicial system consisted primarily, and among others, in the fact that the Emirs themselves had courts, the so-called emirate Judicial Councils. The establishment of these courts, better still recognition of them, was suggested as far back as 1900 when Dwyer referred to the main court in Ilorin, the one presided over by the Qadi of the town as the Emirs' Court, in contradistinction to the *Balogun*'s courts,[214] and in 1902, when Lugard suggested that the Lamido of Yola should have a court separate from that of the Qadi.[215] However, except in Borno where Shehu Abubakar Garbai sat on the Qadi's court and was nominally considered its head right from its inception in December 1902,[216] the existence of these Emirs' courts remained a fiction until about halfway through the period covered in this book. Thus, Acting Resident Arnett, for example, pointed out in October 1905 "the separation of the executive and the judiciary ... [had] been for several years in this province a *fait accompli*."[217] And it was not until 1908 that an attempt was made to define the functions of the Judicial Councils, among them the Kontagora Judicial Council.[218] Thus, the Resident Kontagora, W.S. Sharpe, suggested that "there should be a broad distinction between the cases heard by the Emir's and Alkali's courts."[219] The Emir's court he argued, should "as a rule" hear all land disputes and deal with communities refusing to carry out public works, supply transport, etc. The Alkali's court, on the other hand, "should deal more with individual cases of theft, assault, divorce and affecting Muslims and requiring knowledge of Muhammadan law." The Resident "certainly [thought] the ransoming of slaves should be dealt with and fixed by the alkali only." Similarly, Resident Edward John Arnett from Zaria suggested that the Emir of Zaria "should be encouraged" to keep "in his own hands" "certain matters" which, until then, had been dealt with by the Alkali's court, but dealing with which had in precolonial days been primarily regarded as the "function of the Sarauta, rather than of the Sharia."[220]

Of these "matters," the most important were disputes about land and landed property, matters which in the districts were, even under the British "almost invariably" settled by District Heads rather than the Native Courts. Indeed, even in Zaria town, the fact is that it was the Emir himself that referred land matters to the Native Courts, not that the people took such matters direct to the court, or that the British had reserved such cases for it. Further, unlike Sharpe in Kontagora, Arnett felt that the emancipation of slaves "by ransom or otherwise," was another "class of matters" that "might well" be transferred from the "Alkali's to the Emir's control." However, Arnett advised against giving "the Emir too many judicial responsibilities for it was desirable that [the Emir] should not devote too much attention to semi-judicial matters," which Arnett considered being of "lesser importance" than what he called the Emir's "thorough supervision of the District Headmen," a job which "necessarily [occupied] ... much of his time." If the Emir was burdened, or allowed to assume too many judicial and semi-judicial responsibilities, there was "the danger" that District Heads would "tend to look for support to the Resident rather than to the Emir," an eventuality which, Arnett claimed, was "opposed to His Excellency's policy of rule through the native administration," a "policy" which our findings, as contained in the preceding chapter and chapters to follow would show, was more of a fiction than a reality. In view of his own recommendation from Zaria, it is perhaps ironical that it was Arnett that, seven years later, in 1915, had "the honour" of reporting from Sokoto that: "the Sarkin Musulmi [sent to the Alkali] every case for decision even where, as in charges against District Chiefs, the Sarkin Musulmi [had] held preliminary investigation and was naturally interested in the results."[221]

It should be pointed out that in 1908, the Residents were clearly writing in response to a general inquiry from the Governor to all Residents about the division of functions between the Judicial Councils and the Native Courts, following a spate of reports from Residents of clashes between the "executive and the judicial arms" of the Native Administrations, that is between Emirs and Qadis. These clashes were consequent on the hitherto anomalous situation in which the existence of Emirs' courts were acknowledged without their areas of jurisdiction being defined, clashes with which we shall deal in some detail just below. By 1913, the Emir's courts were handling minor cases involving District Heads,[222] but this was a function that the Judicial Councils took over in a formal sense from the Provincial Courts rather than from the Alkali's Courts.[223]

Clashes Between Emirs and Qadis

Among the places from which friction between the Emirs and the Alkalis were reported were Sokoto and Bauchi. Thus, as early as April 1903, Burdon was reporting that his own "direct interference with the Alkali and [his] demanding reports from him [had] caused him to evince signs of an independent spirit towards the Emir and [had] caused the latter some concern." Burdon "feared" that the "independence" of the Native Courts "as regards the Emir [was] unavoidable," though he hoped "by care and tact to smooth over the difficulty."[224] Similarly, Acting Resident Arnett of Zaria reported "serious difficulty between the native judiciary and Executive," difficulties arising as a result of the "action of some of [Emir's] native servants."[225] Specifically the Emir of Zaria, Aliyu dan Sidi, reported to Arnett on July 22, 1908, that one of his messengers had been assaulted and abused at the town of Gimba.[226] The messenger had gone to Gimba to convey the Resident's [sic] orders that the people there should send in their surplus corn for sale in Zaria. It was one of them, a man who allegedly had large stores of grain, that assaulted both the Emir's servant and the village head of Gimba who had gone with the servant to the grain owner's house. When the man was arrested and brought to Zaria, the Emir "proposed and [the Resident] agreed that the case should be heard by the Native Court as an ordinary case of assault."

Two days later, the Emir sent a messenger to inform the Resident that the man had been sentenced to only ten days of imprisonment. Yet, when, on July 27, the scribe of the court "brought up the usual weekly report of cases" to the

Resident, this particular case was not included. When the Resident enquired why it was excluded from the report, he was informed that the Alkali had found the accused innocent both of assault and of hoarding surplus corn. From this, the Resident concluded that the Emir had "illegally and unjustly kept the man under arrest and had sent me a false message as to the finding of the court in order to cover his action." The following morning the Resident brought the Emir and the Native Court together and the Alkali gave the Resident "a detailed account of the evidence heard and his finding." Thereupon, the Resident discharged the man and released him.

Later Arnett "discussed the matter" with the Emir and spoke to him "very plainly". During this "discussion," the Emir allegedly did "not defend his action" but pleaded "in extenuation" that the Alkali did not sufficiently recognize the Emir's executive responsibilities in policing the Province." He cited an instance of the non-recognition by the Qadi of the Emir's responsibility in another incident which occurred even while "the Gimba case was under discussion." In this latter incident, "three strangers" arrived at the town of Anchau "under suspicious circumstances," at a time when "a series of thefts occurred there." Though the chief of Anchau could not find clear evidence to connect "the strangers" with the thefts, he sent them to the Emir "for further enquiries." The Emir, for his part, sent them to the Native Court. The court "finding not good evidence against them had them forthwith released." The Emir felt, and Arnett endorsed his feeling, that the men should either have been remanded in custody "for further enquiries or that the Emir's officials should have been given the opportunity to discover their destination and address and to have them watched if not surety for their good conduct were forthcoming." Once more Arnett arranged a meeting between the Emir and the Qadi and "pointed out that it [was] essential that [the two] should work in harmony and that the court must be prepared to assist the Emir in the prevention of crime."

Such was the extent to which the British had become the masters of the situation in the emirates. It was they that radiated between Emirs and native officials, a fact which makes utter nonsense of the theory of "Indirect Rule." At the time of making the above report, Arnett claimed that after his intervention, the Emir and the Native Court were "now working satisfactorily" and that he did not anticipate another clash between the two, but Resident Goldsmith reported once again, in 1914, that the Alkali was blaming the Emir for delays in the Native Court, complaining that the Emir delayed the service of summons, especially when witnesses had to be served "in the outlying districts of the Province." Goldsmith agreed with the complaint; and in spite of all the definitions in the past, Goldsmith found it "somewhat difficult to know how far

to go in defining the powers and jurisdiction of the two courts in Zaria viz: the
Judicial Council and Alkali's Court."[227] Yet, despite his "not knowing how far to
go" and in contradiction to Political Memo No.8 which, by now had laid down
that the two courts should have concurrent jurisdiction, Goldsmith suggested
that the Judicial Council "should only hear cases where the native executive
[was] concerned," such as "revenue cases, boundary disputes, offences by *dogarai*, appointments and depositions of District Chiefs and Village Heads, cases
dealing with [the] Agriculture, Forestry and Roads Proclamations." He also suggested giving the Judicial Council jurisdiction over cases dealing with breach
of peace when this is "serious" and the "native state" was concerned, and cases
dealing with breach of the "Hunting and Wild Animals Proclamation." Though
the Emir now "preferred" cases involving the "division of property and inheritance," Goldsmith "in particular" recommended that the Alkali's court should
"hear all cases of inheritance", as well as all civil and criminal cases apart from
those reserved for the Judicial Council. In addition, the Alkali's court was to sit
as the Appeal Court for the District Native Courts. One finds the Lieutenant
Governor's comments on these suggestions vague and somewhat irrelevant.
Thus, he commented that "the question of jurisdiction is 'subjudice.' As the
law now stands the two cannot exercise jurisdiction in the same area."[228] He
added, "we must wait for His Excellency's ruling on the subject generally." This
comment suggests that from 1st January 1914, final ruling on "native affairs"
came not from Kaduna but from Lagos. However, in spite of the Lieutenant
Governor's mumbling on the matter, the fact that the issue of the relations
between the Emir of Zaria and the Alkali of Zaria was as current in 1914, as
it had been in 1908, shows how intractable and perennial the problem was in
Zaria throughout our period. Thanks to the fact that power had now effectively passed from the hands of the "native-rulers" as a whole into the hands
of the British Resident. Doubtless, it must be conceded that the problem was
particularly acute in Zaria. But as far as the existence of the problem is concerned, Zaria was not atypical among the emirates. Throughout these emirates,
contempt and hostility constituted the general aspect of the relations between
Emirs and Qadis from the time of the "establishment" and "constitution" of the
Native Courts.

The Role of District Heads

As for the role of District Heads in the Native Court system, it should be
observed that at the time of the setting up of these courts, many of them took
the form of District "judicial councils" and were presided over by District

Heads. In fact in the Sheikhdom of Borno, probably owing to the particularly chaotic situation that existed there at the time of the British occupation, all the first Native Courts were in the form of "judicial councils."[229] Elsewhere, the judicial conciliar form was the form usually taken by Native Courts in districts with large or wholly "pagan" populations.[230] However, where Alkali's courts were established, the theory was that the Qadi was "a judicial officer pure and simple", while "the executive should be the District Headmen."[231] According to this theory, "the Alkali should inform the District Headmen as to their orders, and the latter, who should control the *dogarai* should execute them." Also, "the collection of 'Judgement debts,' 'fees for the administration of Estates,' and all the rest [were to be] effected by the District Heads acting on the orders of the Alkalai." To "check on misappropriation," the Alkali was to keep the record of "all his orders and [send] them from time to time to the Beit el-Mal." In theory, this arrangement gave Qadis the independence to try cases according to their own lights, without having to take dictation from possibly corrupt District Heads. Yet, in reality, the Qadis could not have this independence since the District Heads had a hand in their selection, while the consent of a District Head was virtually deemed necessary for the continued residence of a particular Qadi in his district.

Hence, all that this arrangement did was to create mutual resentment between Qadis and District Heads in many cases. In this way, the arrangement enabled the British to be the arbiter and master of the situation. In fact, in the early years of British colonial domination over the emirates, many an Alkali was forced to wander from one district to another on account of friction between them and district heads, the Qadis insisting on their right to try and punish criminals, irrespective of the latter's relations with District Heads, and District Heads insisting that their servants and protégés be exempted.[232] Except in a few cases where both Qadis and District Heads saw a need for fair and even-handed justice for all and sundry, subject to limitations imposed by colonial conditions, whenever there was concord between the Qadi and the District Head in the colonial days, we should assume that such concord was achieved at the expense of justice and on the District Head's own terms.[233]

Another important aspect of the Native Court system was the fact that the courts, in addition to bearing certain legal and political relations with the British, the Emirs and District Heads, did also bear definite legal relations with one another. Thus, right from the inception of the system, the district courts were, in some emirates, put under the tutelage of the courts in the capitals. This was the case in Sokoto, for example, where Burdon at first wanted to make the Qadi of Sokoto "responsible for the subordinate Alkali courts, receiving from them reports of all cases tried, and reporting only important cases to the Resident."[234] As we have already seen, this arrangement was never formally effected and soon enough Burdon had to accept the responsibility of receiving and examining reports on all cases from all courts. However, the seniority of the Sokoto Alkali's court received some recognition by it being made the custom to attach newly-appointed District Alkali's and their assistants to his court for training purposes.[235] Besides, by 1907, the Alkali of Sokoto was given appellate powers over the District Native Courts, [236] without prejudice to the power of the Resident and his Assistants to transfer cases to the Provincial Courts. This power was also accorded to the central Alkali courts in other emirates, Bauchi for example.[237] By 1915, some of the emirate courts even had the authority from time to time to call in the district Qadis "for the purpose of enquiring into their work and discussing matters generally with them."[238] At about the same time, the British also gave the courts grades ranging from "A" to "D".[239] The "A" grade was accorded to all native courts that had "full powers," that is, powers to try all cases up to and including murder cases; the "B" grade was accorded to the central courts of emirates in which no court was accorded "full powers", as well as to some District Native Courts in the bigger emirates. But, apart from possibly enhancing the status of the central courts and introducing further delineations in terms of power and pay among the lower courts, this grading did little to alter the relations that by this time had already existed between the central courts and the District Courts.

Conclusion

Thus, we can conclude that by 1915, the British had appropriated the pre-existing judicial system, adapted it to the interests of British colonialism, and assumed the role of recruiting, supervising and discipling Qadis. We can also conclude that though Emirs were given functions within the colonial judicial system, functions which became quite definite by the end of our period, the Emirs did nonetheless lose the control that Emirs had over the precolonial judicial system. So also did District Heads lose their substantial role in the precolonial system.

7

The Imposition of British Taxes

Introduction

Tax assessment, levy and collection were among the earliest measures the British undertook shortly after the occupation of the Caliphate. It is self evident that taxation occupied the topmost position on the priority list of the British colonial administration because it was critical for the day-to-day operation and sustenance of the system of colonial domination. Therefore, an elaborate study of the theory and practice of the colonial taxation system is absolutely necessary for understanding the nature and operation of British colonialism in the emirates. This is the task we shall undertake in the present chapter. In so doing, we will begin with a consideration of the underlying factors responsible for the British disdain for the precolonial taxation system after its occupation, and how a comprehensive reorganization, in line with the interest of British colonialism, was undertaken. Our examination will be accompanied by a detailed account on the formulation of the initial British taxation policies, the difficulties encountered in different emirates, and the periodic modifications undertaken in order to streamline its implementation. Such modifications were necessary for curbing tax fraud and possible tax revolts.

The chapter will also examine various taxation rates, methods of collection and justification of the imposition of the various taxes like Kurdin Kasa, Customs Duties, Jangali, Caravan Tolls, Hawker's Licence, Native Liquor Licence and Kurdin Su. Perhaps, it is needless to point out that the British faced a series of determined and protracted resistance against taxation in many of the emirates, resulting, in some cases, in emigration or tax revolts, as recorded in northern Kano in May 1908. Therefore, it is appropriate for us to examine the various precautionary measures taken by the British to avoid or minimize public disaffection over taxation, and why the cautious policy was later abandoned.

In order to demonstrate our arguments in this regard, we shall refer to specific developments related to this issue in Yola, Borno, Kano, Katsina and Sokoto Provinces. Similarly, the chapter will draw attention to the peculiarities of the colonial taxation system, owing to differing historical and cultural conditions in some of the emirates, and critically analyse the basis for assessment, rates and incidence of Kurdin Kasa and Zakka or Jangali, and the factors that compelled the British to continuously review the latter tax between 1904 and 1913. In the last section of the chapter, we will exhaustively consider the use of forced labour by the British for the construction of roads, river beds and railway lines, bringing out the various reactions of the victims of force labour, including resistance by some emirs to the mobilization and use of force labour.

The Kurdin Kasa and the Jangali

The justifications the British gave for introducing taxes were several and included the "prosperity" of the country. Of these taxes, the Kurdin Kasa and the Jangali, which were collectively referred to as "Land Tax" or "tribute," were by far the most important. They were imposed among other reasons for the alleged "benefits" which the British conferred upon the people of Northern Nigeria by the sheer act of occupying their country, and because the people were allegedly expecting to be taxed and would not understand why the British occupied the country if the latter did not exact a tribute. This could well have been true.

At the time of the imposition of the Kurdin Kasa, no attempt was made to relate it to any pre-existing taxes except in a few emirates, notably Kano and Katsina. In fact, it was categorically stated by one of Lugard's Residents that the Kurdin Kasa "was not taking from the Emir any of his previous income derived from tithes, etc, but actually an addition thereto."[1] It was only after the decision to impose the Kurdin Kasa that the British started to investigate into the pre-existing system of taxation, and it was only then that they tried to rationalize the Kurdin Kasa as a British share of the proceeds of the precolonial taxes.[2]

The myth that the Kurdin Kasa was truly a continuation of the precolonial taxes has its origin in the fact that by the time they occupied Kano, Gwandu, Sokoto and Katsina, the British had already veered round to this view of the Kurdin Kasa.[3] Hence, in these emirates, unlike in the emirates of Ilorin, Nupe, Yola, Gwandu and Bauchi, which the British occupied earlier, the Kurdin Kasa as well as the Jangali were introduced. It was not a new tax imposed by the British, but as a rationalization, "humanization" and summation of the precolonial taxes, theoretically levied and collected by the Emirs for traditional native purposes, with the British being given a share for benefit conferred.

Similarly, it should be pointed out that the introduction of both the Kurdin Kasa and the Jangali in the first emirates to fall to the British was undertaken with some caution and a measure of fear that the purpose of their introduction might provoke. However, this caution and fear were relatively absent in the manner in which the taxes were introduced in the last emirates to be occupied. The point made above can best be illustrated by some detailed account of the manner of introduction of these taxes in some of the emirates mentioned.

Yola

Though Yola was occupied in September 1901, up to February 1902 Acting Resident Ruxton was not sure he could implement the provision of "Political Memo No. 22 paragraph 9" and introduce "direct or indirect taxation as a *quid pro quo* for benefits conferred" on the "natives" by the British.[4] His uncertainty stemmed from the fact that he was under the mistaken view that in Yola "the majority of the population [were] Fulani;" that is members of the "ruling aristocracy," and because he was honest enough to admit that "no benefits can be said to have accrued to [the Fulani] by our presence, at any rate none that they at present can be expected to realize."[5] In fact, Ruxton believed that: "anything in the form of regular direct taxation would be injudicious and misunderstood, while the native method of personal dashes and return dashes might be made to supply large quantities of food stuffs."[6]

Lugard, rather meekly, accepted Ruxton's views about the risks involved in introducing direct taxation in Yola in the circumstances then prevailing, especially in view of the fact that Kano and Sokoto were yet to be reduced to submission. Hence, he ordered that "direct taxation should not be instituted among Fulanis at present at any rate."[7]

However, by June 1902 Resident Barclay was prematurely reporting that he did not "see any difficulty in making each pagan village not under the Emir pay an annual tribute in grain or other produce," adding that "the same should be levied on all Fulani farms which are numerous and extensive."[8] He also suggested that a proportion of the taxes paid to the Emir "should be directed into Government coffers and a tool of so many heads of cattle should certainly be collected upon all herds in the province." He reiterated an earlier report that "in farm produce and cattle Yola is rich and will prove a valuable acquisition in the near future."[9]

By now the Resident had come to believe that in the matter of instituting direct taxation, "the old adage of striking while the iron is hot is the easiest and safest course to pursue, and that taxes should be imposed immediately a race is conquered." For: "in the face of defeat people will gladly acquiesce to any reasonable terms from their conquerors which, if imposed after a long period of immunity they may be disposed to grumble at or even rise against."[10]

It was at this point that he also came up with the fabrication that the people were in fact very much expecting to be taxed. He asserted, "To put it vulgarly they do not know what game we are playing. They are, therefore, awaiting with curiosity and a good deal of anxiety a declaration of the Government's policy and intentions."[11]

While Lugard, who felt that pending the defeat of Kano, the position of the British in those emirates that they had up to that point occupied was still precarious, continued to hesitate about the imposition of direct taxation in these emirates. Hence, rather than countermand his earlier order that no direct taxation should be introduced "as yet," he simply suggested that the "Fulani should be allowed to go on collecting their rents giving in return their greater intelligence as judges and rulers."[12] In fact, Barclay was ordered to do nothing about direct taxation until he had received "full instructions when the matter has been fully considered and law enacted."[13] However, Lugard would be glad if the Resident was "able without difficulty to exact a tribute from the Emir of a certain number of horses annually to supply the waste in our Mounted Infantry, etc." But the Resident "must go very cautiously in this matter as I do not want either to have disaffection or trouble in [Yola] Province at the moment nor yet to drive the Fulani into the German sphere."[14] Lugard was not willing to accept responsibility for any unpleasant turn of events that might result from haste on the part of the British to extract direct revenue out of the population of Yola. Hence, he very much invoked Barclay's judgement in the matter by stating that:

> If you judge that a small tribute of this kind is feasible and would be readily accepted, you can arrange it as a temporary measure. Similarly a few cattle can be exacted from the large herd owners, but remember it is not a settled tax yet and I rely on your discretion as to its temporary imposition.[15]

By this time, flushed by the successes of British arms and possibly more conversant with the ruthlessness of German methods in their portion of Adamawa, Barclay was ready to take some risks and also refused to share Lugard's fear about people defecting to German Adamawa. "The Germans," he informed Lugard, "are held in too great awe for emigration to be probable, many Fulanis having come over from there and settled in British territory."[16] Yet, in spite of his greater willingness to take risks in the situation, the Resident could not yet start making the demands suggested by Lugard, thanks to continued resistance by the fugitive Lamido Zubairu. Thus, he reports:

> Owing to a want of Maxim Zubeiru has been enabled to settle in the Province and the Yundam difficulty delayed while the Gongola exploration must be taken in hand as soon as possible. So I think it advisable to postpone the taxation question until these matters are settled and the troops back in the Fort with no prospect of their being called out again for a definite period.[17]

By February 1903, however, Barclay had decided to institute a direct tax to be collected by the Emir "for the benefit of the Government from all Fulani, Hausa and Beri-Beri towns under the Emir's rule – the Emir himself retaining one quarter of the amount so collected."[18] However, "for some time to come it will be impossible to collect any tribute from the pagans who occupy the greater portion of this Province."[19] To this decision Lugard gave his assent but warned that the tax should not take the form of a poll-tax. This assent having been given, Yola paid its first direct tax to the British in October 1903, two years after its occupation, seven months after the final disappearance of its erstwhile Emir Lamido Zubairu, as well as the occupation of Sokoto.[20]

For the years 1903 and 1904, the British-imposed tribute remained an additional tax, distinct from and coexistent with the pre-British taxes collected by the Emir.[21] In 1904, the British attempted to make this tribute the sole "legal" tax, to be presented to the people as a consolidation of the pre-existing taxes.[22] This way the British attempted to change their posture from that of foreign rulers imposing a new tax to that of dutiful and faithful allies of the Emir advising him on how to tax his people and being given a share in the proceeds of that taxation as a kind of consultation fee.

However, on protest from the Emir, he was allowed to continue to collect the Zakka as a distinct and independent tax, a concession which further exposed the British tribute for what it was – an additional imposition.[23] The extra nature of the new tax, which, apart from being new, was in fact a poll-tax, was further revealed when the British insisted that the Emir should give them a share of the proceeds of the Zakka, that being the only condition on which he was allowed to go on collecting it.[24]

Borno

In Borno, it was the apparent activities of the Shehu, Abubakar Garbai, that the British used as an excuse to introduce their taxation. Thus, in May 1902, three months after the British had occupied Borno and recognized Abubakar

Garbai as the Shehu, Cochrane, the Acting Resident, reported that the Shehu's tax-collectors were already out collecting taxes all over the Sheikhdom.[25] While not disputing the Shehu's right to collect taxes, Cochrane questioned the methods used by the Shehu's tax-collectors claiming, with nauseating self-righteousness in view of later British activities, that these methods were violent and the demands made on the people exorbitant. Accordingly, when the substantive Resident, Hewby, arrived, he got the Shehu to disown these alleged tax-collectors as robbers, and to arrest and hand them over to the Resident for trial and punishment in the Provincial Court. Further, Hewby did to the Shehu what was done to all the rulers of the Sokoto Caliphate after defeat. He collected all the Shehu's guns except flintlocks, and through him collected all the guns of his chiefs both in Monguno, which was then the temporary headquarters of the Shehu, and elsewhere.[26] Having in this way rendered the Shehu incapable of being violent against the population of his Sheikhdom, the British undertook to "help" him collect his taxes, using this pretext to pacify the country-side and to break the resistance of villages that were not predisposed to acknowledge British authority — which is to say, almost every village they sought to have direct dealings with.

When giving sanction to the Resident's action in sending troops into the villages to collect taxes, Lugard took the opportunity to suggest to Hewby that he should ask the Shehu to share the proceeds of these taxes with the British. However, Hewby did not feel secure enough in Borno to make such a categorical demand. Instead, he confined himself to making occasional demands from the Shehu to give some horses or some cattle to the Colonial Administration. For example, in March 1903, he asked the Shehu to furnish that administration with 25 "good horses," a horse at that time costing between £8 and £15 in Borno.[27]

But unlike in the case of Yola, Lugard, even before the occupation of Kano and Sokoto, refused to share Hewby's caution and fear about making material demands on the Shehu. Doubtless, he felt the rulers of Borno, who had been so thoroughly humbled of recent by Rabeh's occupation of the Sheikhdom, and who owed their restoration to power to European action, though not British action specifically, were not likely to start a quarrel with a European power over the issue of sharing the proceeds of taxes with the latter. He argued, in a manner typical of him, that the Shehu did not need all his income, since he no longer had an army to maintain. He went as far as to suggest that since the British had to be involved with collecting taxes at all, they might as well collect them for themselves rather than for the Shehu — and he ordered Hewby to warn the Shehu that if he could not rule he would be deposed "and that soon."[28]

In fact, irrespective of how the Shehu behaved, Lugard was at first unwilling to allow him to collect any Jangali at all. He was under the wrong impression, conveyed to him by Hewby, that the Fulbe and the Shuwa Arabs, who owned virtually all the cattle in Borno, had been independent of the Shehu prior to the coming of the British. He maintained that such "independent people should pay their taxes direct to the British."[29]

Finding his master so cock-sure about British "rights" in Borno, Hewby stopped putting up any fight on behalf of moderation and caution; and accordingly, in September 1903, he informed the Shehu that he had to share the proceeds of his taxes with the British on a 50–50 basis. However, contrary to Lugard's calculations, the Shehu resisted sharing his income with the British on such a formula. Among his reasons why he would not accept the British demand, he advanced the need for him to rebuild Kukawa, the old capital of the Sheikhdom, and to rehabilitate his family and supporters. Hewby found these reasons compelling enough to drop the demand for a 50–50 sharing of the Shehu's income and, instead, contented himself with a flat 5,000 dollars for the year 1903.[30]

To increase British income from Borno, Hewby proposed levying a special and additional tax on grain for the benefit of the British alone.[31] But Lugard, who was by now realizing the need to avoid imposing what was a direct tax, not only in reality but in appearance as well, vetoed this proposal, avowedly on the ground that the peasants were already being overtaxed. Not willing to let either Lugard or the Shehu have the last word in the matter, Hewby tried next to increase the amount of money the Shehu's taxes would yield, by asking the latter to conduct a population census.[32] He did this in the belief that the census would show that Borno had a larger population than was in fact indicated by the tax returns as they then stood, and in that way showing that the Shehu could raise a higher income than hitherto, and thus be able to give more to the British. The Shehu complied and conducted the census, but the 'natives' too were able to see what Hewby was aiming at. Thus, when the figures were returned, it was obvious to Hewby that the Shehu's officials had falsified the figures on the side of undercounting.

Thus, the British were left with no alternative but to demand an increase in the rate of taxation. So, in May 1904, by this time clearly having overcome his 'pity' for the overtaxed Borno peasantry, Lugard approved Hewby's decision to double the rate of the Kurdin Kasa which, in Borno was referred to as *Haraji*, from 1 dollar to 2 dollars per household.[33] This approval by Lugard was quite in keeping with our contention above that his objection to the imposition of a new grain tax for the benefit of the British was motivated, not by any 'pity' for the peasants, but by a newly gained realization that it was not wise for the British to introduce their taxes without a suitable 'native' disguise. Introducing their taxation in the guise of an increase in the rate of the Shehu's taxes provided this taxation with the necessary cover. The British would get their income alright while the Shehu would reap the unpopularity that the added taxation was bound to incur with the peasantry.

To make sure that the British received every dollar yielded by the increase, Hewby stipulated that the *Haraji* would now be shared according to the formula: the British 50%, the Shehu 25%, District Heads 20%, Village Heads 5%.[34] This way the British and the Shehu reached a settlement, without the Shehu's actual income being diminished; that is, assuming that he had, even before this arrangement, been allowing his tax-collectors to retain as much as Hewby now gave to the District and Village Heads.

The British, similarly, extended their taxation to cattle by slightly increasing the Jangali. The increase took the form of making a herd owner pay 1 cow for every 30 heads of cattle instead of 3 cows for every 100 as hitherto. The proceeds of the Jangali were then shared among the British, the Shehu and the Jangali collectors, with each taking one-third.[35]

Kano

The manner in which British taxes were imposed on the emirates that were grouped together by the British to form the Kano Province cannot be recounted in the same manner that the imposition of these taxes in Yola and Borno has been recounted. This is because the documents relating to the period of the introduction of these taxes were burnt by the first Resident of Kano, Cargill, presumably in a fit at the end of his stay there in 1908.[36] However, we can gain a fairly clear idea from records of the period after 1908 what the British did in these emirates by way of imposing their taxes.

From these later records, it emerges that in Kano Emirate, in addition to the Kurdin Kasa and Jangali, the British also collected the *shuka* and *karofi* from 1903 up to 1909.[37] It also emerges that these taxes, all of which the British found in existence, were sufficiently suitable to the purpose of the British to have been taken over without alteration either in theory or in practice. All of the taxes had been regarded as rents for the use of agricultural or grazing land, as distinct from residential land which had not been taxed. Of these taxes, while the Kurdin Kasa had been levied on farms producing the staple grains of the emirates, namely, guinea corn and *gero* (millet), the *shuka* and *karofi* had been levied on special crops such as cassava, henna, onions, etc.[38]

The taxes, being agricultural rents, were assessed and collected up to 1909 by the District and Village Heads in whose territories the farms were located, irrespective of the places of domicile of the owners.[39] This custom inevitably gave rise to a situation in which an individual might be living in one village but paying his taxes in a different village, or even living in one district but paying taxes in another district. Resident Temple found this situation undesirable because it allegedly tended to weaken the authority of Village Heads or even District Heads over the people living in their villages and districts.[40]

Apart from this administrative objection, Temple had another objection to the system, which was that the *shuka* and the *karofi* did not yield as much as he believed they could yield, blaming the deficit on refusal on the part of the District and Village Heads to declare all they had collected under these two headings. His additional contention that he also objected to the *shuka* and the *karofi* because they discouraged agriculture, which might very well be true, could not have been more than an excuse. It sounded too much like the familiar apologia that the British colonial domination over Northern Nigeria was for the sake of the welfare of the people. Besides, in the report to which we are here referring, this "concern" was obviously added as an afterthought by Temple in an effort to get the Governor to give sanction for a new scheme of taxation that the Resident was about to put forward.[41]

Temple's suggestions were that the *shuka* and the *karofi* be abolished, and, obvious enough, that the "loss of revenue" to be incurred by the abolition of these two taxes be made up "in other ways." Both to make up for this "loss" in revenue and to ensure the "necessary establishment of the authority of the village heads," Temple suggested that the Kurdin Kasa had to be levied on both "the land on which [people had] their houses situated as well as the land which they [farmed]."[42]

According to this new scheme, the people would then have to acknowledge the authority of both the village heads in whose territories they lived and the village heads in whose territories they farmed. For, while continuing to pay the rent on his farms to the village head in whose territory it was situated, an individual was to pay the newly imposed rent on his house to the village head in whose territory he was domiciled. The "loss" in revenue would also be remedied because while the *shuka* and the *karofi* combined had brought "only" £11,000 in 1908/1909, the compound rent, which Temple suggested should be 2/-(shillings) per compound, was estimated to yield a revenue of £20,000 in 1909/1910. Besides, "none of this would be embezzled" as it was "so easy to verify compounds that the village heads would not take the risk of doing so."[43]

Among the objections that Temple thought might be raised to his scheme were that: "(1) it might be said that this was a compound tax, (2) that it partook of the nature of a capitation tax, (3) that it was [a matter of] substituting a mechanical system for an elastic one, (4) that it could not by any stretch of the imagination be termed Zakka."

It is clear why the first objection could be raised. The second objection had its origin in the British wish to equate their taxes with those of the precolonial days which did not include taxes on dwelling houses.

In spite of all these "objections," which he listed, Temple went on to brush aside the contention that the imposition of the compound tax was the only way administrative "reform" could be facilitated and some "honesty" injected into the system of the collection. As to the "non-elastic" nature of the tax, he proposed that, in Kano city, the size of the compound should be taken into consideration, and expressed "every confidence that this system once established at the capital, could, when we have village authorities, rapidly be extended all over the division and applied not only to compounds but to farms [as well]."[44] Besides, while the compound tax bade fair in fact to be a capitation tax, Temple admitted with revealing candour, that the previous taxes that the British had been collecting, namely "the Kurdin Kasa as well as the *shuka* and *karofi* [were] collected in the form of a capitation tax." Thus, the compound tax was not going to be the first tax in Kano to flout the "legal" theory behind British taxation in the emirates.[45]

Perhaps, it was in trying to relate the compound tax with the Zakka that Temple demonstrated, to the most remarkable degree, the ability of British colonial officials to divorce terms from their true meaning, and to apply preexisting terminology to phenomena of their own invention. Thus, he says:

> with regard to the impossibility of connecting the rent for compounds with *zakat*, I see no reason why when this rent and the rent for farms have become proportioned to the area occupied, the two should not be calculated on the basis of one-tenth or one-twentieth as the case may be, of the crops that can be produced on such areas, and it could then be strictly termed a *zakat*.

Thus, Temple was proposing in written words what the British had already started to put into practice and were to standardize later, namely that the Shari'a was what they said it was and not what Muslim jurists might have said it was.

As for the Kurdin Kasa, Temple suggested that a readjustment be undertaken – to assess it more strictly than hitherto in accordance with the size of the holding. He added that "if the people [could] be taught to pay rent on their compounds according to their areas they [would] very quickly learn to pay on the farms according to their area also." This way Temple obliquely hinted that a strict adherence to the payment of the Kurdin Kasa in accordance with the sizes of holdings, would help to check extortion by unscrupulous officials, a "protection" which the British were very eager to extend to the peasantry, for obvious reasons. However, Temple failed to recommend to the Governor that the British should, in their solicitous "desire" to help alleviate the burden of the peasantry, abolish a practice which was clearly unjust, namely the payment of Kurdin Kasa "on all occupied land tilled or untilled." In fact, far from taking a righteous exception to the fact that the tax was paid even on land lying fallow, Temple saw this fact as "one good point about" the Kurdin Kasa.

These "reforms" were approved by the Governor without "amendment" and were instituted with effect from the financial year 1909/1910. The compound tax was in that year collected at the rate of one shilling and six pence (1/6d) per compound in the Districts and at halfpenny (½d) per square foot in Kano City.[46] This was in spite of a large scale revolt in northern Kano against British taxation in May 1908, as we shall see in Chapter 8.

It now remains to examine the role of the Emir of Kano in the institution of this "reform." Temple claims that he had "spoken on the subject of reform to the Emir and all intelligent natives," among whom was the then newly-appointed Waziri, Gidado, and that they had all confirmed him in his suspicion that "only about half the *kurdin karofi* and *kurdin shuka* actually collected [was] declared." Before submitting his proposals, he had "talked the matter over at length with the Emir and the Waziri and other natives" and had not "heard one word said in favour of the *shuka* and *karofi*," and that they all said "that a small rent would be welcomed in their place."

That Temple would consult the Emir, the Waziri and "other intelligent natives" before instituting his reforms ought to be assumed a foregone conclusion. This was so given their positions and local knowledge; they could effectively, though surreptitiously, frustrate the implementation of any "reforms" with which they were completely out of sympathy. Yet, it was one thing for Temple to sound the opinions of these people, and quite another for them to assent to the suggested "reforms." Nonetheless, we are inclined to credit his claim that they told him that they were in favour of this "reform," for the following reasons. In the first place, these proposals were made in 1909, when the Emir had had too many near show-downs with the British for him to relish the prospect of another one. We have touched briefly on his crises with them in a previous chapter, but a more detailed treatment of them is available in C.N. Ubah's study to which the reader may refer.[47] Second, following from the reasons just advanced, a verbal assent was not necessarily a sincere assent, duplicity being freely practised by Emirs and their officials in their dealings with the British. This fact was later copiously acknowledged and illustrated by Temple in his book *Native Races and their Rulers*.[48] In fact, that duplicity should govern relations between the Emir and their "Christian" overlords was the main burden of the letter which the Waziri of Sokoto Muhammad al-Bukhari b. Ahmad wrote and circulated after the British occupation of Sokoto in March 1903.[49] Third, the "reforms" proposed here by Temple, while not the type of "reforms" a Muslim might have instituted under the circumstances, do not seem to have been utterly counter to the letter of the Shari'a. Besides, these reforms might well have provided the Emir and his officials, collectively and severally, with an opportunity to retain their traditional sources of income, without having to share them with the British, a prospect that they would certainly welcome. That is to say, it was possible that while acquiescing to the "abolition" of the two taxes, *shuka* and *karofi,* the Emir and his officials went on collecting these "abolished" taxes, say, at a reduced rate, and where possible, in lieu of the compound tax, but "failing" to account for the proceeds. The cooperation of the people could be assured, especially in view of the fact that the rates of the British taxes tended to rise with every passing year while the precolonial rates tended to be static.

Hence, it is possible to accept Temple's contention that the Emir and other native officials gave their assent to the "reform" without at the same time accepting his implied contention that they accepted the "reform" proposals both in letter and in spirit, openly and secretly. In fact, the "acceptance" of these proposals might have been given by the Emir and his officials, as readily as Temple claims, not because they supported the "reforms", but because they were quick to see how they could turn them to their own advantage.

Katsina

In Katsina Emirate, in addition to the Jangali, the precolonial taxes which the British continued to collect up to 1907 were the Kurdin Kasa on farms producing staple crops, *karofi* and *shuka* on farms producing special crops, *al'adu,* which was a tax on industrial establishments, and the Zakka.[50] The Zakka here referred to was more of a fixed capitation tax on the whole population than the stipulated fraction of certain agricultural products and livestock that it was supposed to be. It was assessed at the rate of 1,000 cowries and one bundle of corn on each married man per annum, and was known as *dubu da dami*, literally "one thousand and a bundle." In addition to this compulsory Zakka, the British allowed the giving of what was known sometimes as *sadaka* or Zakka by individual Muslims voluntarily to a Mallam of the individual's own choosing, or to the Village Head, or District Head, or Emir.

In 1907, an attempt was made to merge the compulsory Zakka with the Kurdin Kasa which, in this emirate, unlike in Kano, was levied only on land which was both actually under cultivation and was of a certain minimum size or bigger. The British "reform" of 1907 sought in effect to impose the system of taxing all farmlands irrespective of whether they were under actual cultivation or lying fallow, and irrespective of size, though assessment was to be based on the size of each farm. Apart from bringing more revenue to the British, the proposed "reform" was also aimed at consolidating the position of the British currency. For, whereas up to 1907 the Zakka had been paid in kind, the "new" combined tax, to be known as Kurdin Kasa, was to be paid in British money only.

However, these proposals met with opposition from the Emir and the District and Village Heads, who Assistant Resident Palmer suspected had in fact been collecting the Kurdin Kasa on all farms behind the scene, handing over to the British only those collected in accordance with the procedure outlined above. But the British had to temporize until 1909 when Palmer again reintroduced this "reform" in a slightly disguised form. The tax now took the form, not of a tax on farm land, but of an agricultural tax on the agricultural productive "capacity" of each village. Temple does not mention whether or not, as in Kano, this "capacity" was assessed on the basis of all land irrespective of size or actual cultivation or non-cultivation; but one suspects that this was what the British actually did. For, otherwise the "reforms" would have brought little additional revenue to them. Furthermore, to cushion the impact of the reform, Palmer called the new combined tax Zakka rather than Kurdin Kasa. So dressed, and so called, the tax was accepted by the Emir. A compelling reason for the acceptance by the Emir of this "reformed" tax might well have been an awareness on his part of the relative power of the British vis à vis the Emirs' authorities generally and vis à vis himself in particular, in view of the fact that he very much owed his position as Emir to them.

Even after this "reform", the shuka and karofi were allowed to be collected as formerly, although Temple intimated that "if during the next year or two there is a falling off in the cultivation of special crops" which were taxed after harvest, "it will certainly show that the taxes on special crops are being abused." In that case, he hinted, he would have to replace them or "reform" them in order to ensure that not only did revenue not decline, but also that it progressively increased. The al'adu tax was also allowed to continue, though Palmer, avowedly because he realized that the rates levied were too high, and because the tax fell on people who also paid the other taxes, reduced the rates on weavers – from 1/6d per annum to 6d per annum, for example. Commendable though his action was, one would be naïve to accept his avowed reason as the sole or even the main reason for this act of "magnanimity." As an alternative to the reason Palmer advanced, or at least in addition to it, one would propose two further reasons. First, the British feared an uprising similar to that which took place in parts of Kano Emirate the previous year.[51] Second, right from the beginning, it might not be the aim of the British to perpetuate this tax at all but to phase it out once it had served its purpose, which was to help depress native industry to the advantage of British imports. In this connection, it should be pointed out that, as we shall see in a later chapter, already at about this time, the ascendancy of British imports in Northern Nigerian markets had been established, and the necessity to discriminate in favour of these imports was already disappearing.

Sokoto and Gwandu

In Sokoto and Gwandu, the British tried both to impose a tribute immediately after their occupation and to graft it to the pre-existing system of taxation. By now they had virtually completed their military occupation of the emirates. Lugard both felt secure enough to abandon the caution with which he had approached the question of taxation of the emirates in general, and had realized the value of disguising British taxes as Emirs' taxes.

However, understanding a situation in its general aspects is only a beginning, though a major beginning, in understanding all aspects of that situation. For, every particular aspect has its peculiarities the understanding of which is essential to a genuine grasp of the whole situation. Hence the British, to their dismay and chagrin, discovered that no Kurdin Kasa was levied in Sokoto or Gwandu, and that the Zakka was the only tax levied.[52] This discovery meant that in Sokoto and Gwandu, unlike in the emirates, it would not be easy to smuggle in British taxes under the guise of familiar precolonial taxes. Lugard decided that the best way out of the situation was simply to ask the "Emirs" of Sokoto and Gwandu as well as that of Argungu to give the British a share of their incomes, whatever these were and without delay. But Burdon was not willing to do this; for, to him:

> the question of contribution to the Government from the existing revenue of chiefs is in this Province a very difficult one. There can be no denying the poverty of the Emirs of Sokoto and Gando [Gwandu] as compared with those of Bida and Kano. And there is no adequate system of taxation in existence here as in those two Provinces which without altering or offending native custom can be tapped by us. I am enquiring into and tabulating all such sources of

native revenue as I can elucidate and hope to report fully on this point. In the meantime I have only to urge the danger of acting without full understanding.[53]

But Lugard, never for a moment forgetting the status of the British as conquerors, was not willing to delay the imposition of the tribute even for a short while. He insisted that the Sultan and the Emir of Gwandu had to start paying a share of their revenue to the British immediately, stating "for tribute read taxes if you like, an emir's revenue however got is the matter in question."[54] Thus, without actually saying that a poll-tax should be introduced if there was none already in existence, Lugard left Burdon in no doubt that this was what he wanted him to do. He warned Burdon that "no other Resident presents this non-possumus attitude. This law must be enforced and the legal taxes collected even if Sokoto [town] has to be left without an officer at times."[55] With Lugard in such a highly imperious mood, Burdon decided not to put up further resistance. But all the same, he took his time consolidating his hold on the Province and studying how best to go about introducing the "legal" taxes that Lugard was insisting on. Hence it was not until January 1905, i.e. twenty months after the occupation of Sokoto, that the Kurdin Kasa, together with the Jangali, was imposed on Sokoto, Gwandu and Argungu. As usual, these were levied and collected in the name of the Sultan and the two Emirs.[56]

The Kurdin Kasa: Basis of Assessment

When the so-called Kurdin Kasa was imposed by the British in most of the other emirates apart from Kano and Katsina, it was introduced essentially as a poll tax rather than as rent for the use of agricultural lands as Lugard, his assistants and successors, would have us believe. In this sense, it approximated more to the *jizya* than to any other of the precolonial taxes. As such, it was assessed, initially, on villages as a lump sum in accordance with the estimated size of the population of each village and independent of its productive capacity. Also, the claim of the British to the contrary notwithstanding, the assessment was at a rate higher than the rate at which precolonial taxes generally, taxes on non-Muslim communities included, had been assessed.[57] However, in comparison with rates that the British were later to impose, these first rates were indeed low or even "token." For example, the first assessment in Yola was one horse, worth about £5 per 100 head of population, the British depending entirely on the Emir and his chiefs for estimates of the size of the population of each town and village.[58] In only a few cases were communities simply ordered to pay at the rate at which they had been assessed before the imposition of British domination.

However, from about 1906, the assessment tended to be individual rather than communal and such factors as the size of a person's house, the number of rooms, and the size of his household, were taken into consideration. In cases where a man was a craftsman, say a carver, a dyer, a tanner or a butcher, in addition to being a farmer, his estimated income from these other sources was also taken into account. Often, a man was taxed separately for himself, his household, his farm and his income from other sources, but paid all in a single sum. This was particularly the case in Sokoto and Gwandu emirates.[59] Thus, in these emirates the Kurdin Kasa, which started as a poll-tax, became both a poll-tax *and* an income tax from about 1906, and remained so until about 1911.[60]

For some time after 1911, there was a tendency to go back to the system of a flat assessment, ignoring the incomes of individual payers.[61] But at the end of the period under study, i.e. from about 1916, there was a tendency to return to basing the tax on general and individual productivity.[62] It is worth dwelling on why the British did not stick to one policy with regard to assessment. The explanation is that in the first days of their rule, the British imposed only a poll-tax, and a disguised one at that, because they were in fact partly putting out feelers to find out how people would react to the idea of paying taxes to the British. Hence, they deemed it wise not to make the assessment rigorous; for in fact they reasoned that in the immediate wake of military defeat at the hands of the British, the people of the emirates might not reject out of hand the very idea of paying taxes to the British. They knew the possibility was there, nonetheless, that if the taxes were imposed and assessed with rigour, people would revolt, at least against the rigour if not against the very fact of the imposition. However, by 1906 they felt confident enough, in spite of the existence of endemic, if sporadic, revolts against the payment of taxes, to dare to be less cautious and more thoroughgoing in enforcing their demands on the people. This tentative abandonment of caution took the form of insisting on taking into account a man's income and taxing it over and above the general rate.

The return to the flat rate system from about 1911 was partly also an expression of the further growth of British confidence in their mastery of the military situation. As we shall see below, what the return to the flat rate meant was not the abolition of additional tax for those who had occupations other than farming, but the assessment of the whole community at the same rate, the rate being that at which only the "rich" were formerly assessed. That is to say, in their own presentation of the case, taxes on industries were "removed" and all people were required to pay "only" a general rate, as a concession to native industry and to hard work.[63] In fact, the general rate was reintroduced not positively in favour of those who had other occupations in addition to farming, but negatively at the expense of those who depended only on farming. It should also be remarked that this return to a poll-tax, pure and simple, coincided in time with the obvious decline of the indigenous economy generally and of its industry in particular.[64] That meant that the decision to return to a flat rate was taken at a time when the British were running out of "men of substance" to assess above this flat rate. Thus, this pattern of now imposing an additional tax on crafts and now "removing" it by extending the rate of the "rich" to everybody, which we have seen to recur throughout our period, was the principal means of both increasing British revenue and stifling local industry without killing it outright.

Kurdin Kasa: The Rates

As we have seen above, at the time of the imposition of the Kurdin Kasa, the rate was high in comparison to precolonial rates. However, if we assume a household to contain five people on the average, in comparison to rates the British were to impose later, these first rates were not high at £5 per 100 head of population in Yola, for example, and even less in Borno where it was $1, i.e. about 3/- for each household. In some places, including Sokoto and Gwandu, the first rate was in fact 6d per adult male.[65] However, in some emirates, by 1907 the rate was as high as 3/- per adult male with or without a house, and with or without a known source of income, a rate which even the Governor found too high.[66] This was in addition to the taxes collected on industries. By 1909, the rate had in some emirates reached 5/8d per adult male.[67] In addition, in Zaria, for example, if people planted crops other than guinea corn, they paid an additional 5/- per plot on sugar cane, 2/6d per plot on tobacco, and 3/1½d per garden on cassava.[68] All these were in addition to the Zakka and industrial taxes. The industrial taxes were 3/1½d per smith, 3/1½d per dyer, 1/10½d per carpenter, 1/7d per hunter, 3/1½d per "tapper," 1/7d per beekeeper, 3/1½d per "bori" dancer, 7½d per basket maker, 1/3d per bamboo-door maker; 1/- per cotton spinner, 1/- per "gammo" maker, 6/3d per native doctor.[69] There were also separate market taxes.

The decision in the first few years to keep to a comparatively low rate was a deliberate policy on the part of the British to avoid a general uprising that might have completely dislocated their still shaky hold on the country. In the words of Gowers in Yola, this low rate was simply what "seems fairest and most practicable at present."[70] It was correctly stated by Barclay to be "purely a temporary [rate] to test the temper of the people."[71] For Burdon in Sokoto: "this rate, though in these first two years of its collection exceedingly small, is I am convinced as large as it can be without causing discontent. As it is, there have been cases where protest was made and remission allowed."[72]

But even in those early days, the aim of the British was "that the assessment should be gradually raised year by year till what on a more intimate knowledge was considered to be a fair amount [was] reached."[73]

Besides, as Burdon pointed out, most of the people were so poor that a yearly rate of say 3/- per adult male and 2/- per adult female, as Lugard was suggesting even for that early period, would be a patently unfair imposition even from conquerors. Burdon stated that: "No such sum is within the bounds of possibility in this Province. The bulk of the people have no money, they live from hand to mouth, sell a bundle of corn to buy a little meat for next day or a domestic animal to buy a new cover cloth."[74]

In fact, Burdon "rather frightened the Sarkin Musulmi by suggesting 1/- per man for Sokoto" town and had to reduce it to 6d though on the "distinct understanding that it [would] be gradually increased in future."[75] So insistent was Lugard that Burdon had to plead:

> I am afraid Your Excellency would regard this as far too small, but I venture to think that it is the most I could have laid down. And for political reasons, the certainty that this tremendous innovation could be started with a low amount without causing friction or discontent was the strongest of arguments for not increasing it against the Sarikin Muslimin's advice.[76]

As for the rather steep rise in the rate after 1906, but especially after 1910, this is explained both in terms of the greater degree to which the British felt they had subdued the country; and in terms of the need to compensate themselves for ceasing for the time being, in most of the emirates, to assess income additionally, and for officially "abolishing" the Zakka, in whose proceeds they had a share. In fact, increasing the rate of the Kurdin Kasa was only one way they "compensated" themselves for the "loss" of revenue they "suffered" by "abolishing" income tax and the Zakka in most of the emirates. Another way they "compensated" themselves was to start assessing women too for the poll-tax, a practice which they had hitherto confined to non-Muslim communities, as we shall see in the next section.

Kurdin Kasa: Incidence

As we have seen in the last sub-section, Lugard suggested, at the time of the imposition of the Kurdin Kasa, that the rate should be 3/- per adult male and 2/- per adult female. However, apart from rejecting the rate he proposed for adult males, the Residents, under pressure from the Emirs, spared women the incidence of this tax until later in the period under study, except for non-Muslim communities, both inside and outside the emirates. Thus, Burdon "carefully left out women, for the mere suggestion of women paying offended the Sarikin Muslimin, very naturally in a Mohammadan country."[77] Women excepted, the incidence of the Kurdin Kasa fell on "every man, slave or free, rich and poor, or beggar, even to the Waziri himself."[78] However, "unattached young men, 'masterless men' are escaping this year and the net amount will probably increase automatically as the net is drawn tighter in future."[79] But while theoretically every adult male could be held responsible for paying his rate, in practice, it was only the householder that was held responsible for payment by his slaves, servants, adult sons and other dependants. This was in keeping with the structure of responsibility in the emirates in the nineteenth century when a householder was generally held responsible for the behaviour of all his dependants. It was also in keeping with the precolonial practice of taxing only "the cultivator and the artisan" but exempting chiefs, "minor craftsmen, hireling labourers" and the unemployed or *banzan gari*.[80]

In the non-Muslim areas, women were separately assessed right from the time of the imposition of the Kurdin Kasa on these communities. This was, as a rule, much later than its imposition on the Muslim communities on account of the fact that the non-Muslims in their mountain fastness were able to resist the British longer than the Muslims did.[81] The reason given for this assessment of women was that in these communities "the women hold property in their own right,"[82] as if women among Muslims held no property. However, women were assessed at half the rate of the male adults, and it was their husbands that were actually held responsible for paying for them. That meant that, in reality, the non-Muslim communities paid a poll-tax that, until 1910, could be 50% higher than the poll-tax paid by Muslim communities.[83]

By 1910, however, women were being assessed even in the Muslim communities, at least in some of the emirates.[84] In this case, however, we are not told the reason for separately assessing the womenfolk. It was possibly in the name of "justice" and British "hatred" for discrimination, the rationale being that by extending the non-Muslim system to the Muslims, the British were in fact rationalizing an anomalous situation that had been unfair to the non-Muslims. But that anomaly could also have been rectified by freeing the non-Muslim women from the yoke of the Kurdin Kasa. A more plausible explanation for extending the Kurdin Kasa to cover Muslim women as well is that the British never in fact rejected Lugard's suggestion, made at the onset of British taxation, that women too should be assessed. They merely delayed the implementation of his order until they felt more secure in their grip on the Provinces.

Jangali: Incidence

At the time of its imposition, the Jangali which, in strict terms was a *zakat*, was generally paid only on cattle, excluding sheep, goats, horses, etc. Also in some emirates, only cattle belonging to nomads, as opposed to those belonging to people living sedentarised lives in villages, were assessed, though the cattle of sedentarised people too were included among the property to be considered when a man was being assessed for the Kurdin Kasa.[85] Further, in these first few years, not all nomadic herds were assessed for the Jangali but only those which were large enough to qualify for the payment of the *zakat*; that is to say — herds numbering at least 30 heads of cattle.[86] During the course of the period 1903–1912, the above situation was altered step by step. That, in effect, meant that by 1912, not only cattle but sheep and goats as well, were assessed for the Jangali; by this date the cattle of both nomads and sedentarised people and all herds, irrespective of size, were assessed.

It was in 1904 that the Jangali was extended[87] to sheep and goats. In 1910, the system of levying the cattle "zakat as laid down by the Koran ... [was] abandoned in favour of a tax on all cattle irrespective of the size of the herd, or the age and sex of animals" in most of the emirates.[88] In other emirates, including Borno, this "reform" was in fact effected much earlier.[89]

Jangali: Rate

For a few years after its imposition, the Jangali was assessed in terms of percentage of the herd or flock concerned. In some places, the percentages were 10% for sheep and goats and 7% for cattle, payment for the cattle being in bulls only. In other places, it was collected at the rate of the *zakat*, i.e at 1 bull for a herd of 30, 1 cow for a herd of 40, etc with herds of less than 30 exempted. With the decision to collect the Jangali on all herds irrespective of size, the rate was initially set at 1/- per head for the cattle of sedentarised people and 1/6d per head for the cattle of nomadic people.[90] The differentiation was justified on the grounds first that the nomads pastured their cattle under conditions "more favourable to the cattle both as regards reproduction and freedom from disease," and second, that "the expense of herding was less for them as they did not approach lands when the crops were standing" and therefore seldom had to pay damages to farm owners.[91] Another reason was that the nomads paid no Kurdin Kasa, a very weak reason in view of the fact that in the case of herds of 10 or more, the extra Jangali they paid on their cattle was much more than the Kurdin Kasa they would have paid.

The Fate of the Zakka

At the time of the imposition of British taxation, an attempt was made to suppress the payment of the Zakka even where the payment was voluntary. When informed that apart from those taxes sanctioned by the British, no other ones were to be collected, the Emirs protested. The Shehu of Borno, for example, argued that stopping him from collecting the Zakka would amount to a departure by the British from their undertaking not to interfere with religious matters. He added that at any rate, the peasants themselves would object to being relieved from paying it.[92] The Sultan also, when informed of the intention of the British to make the collection of the Zakka "illegal," requested Burdon to write to Lugard and appeal against interference with the Zakka.[93] Presumably, the other Emirs also made a similar appeal. Hence, the British relented and allowed the continued collection of the Zakka on two conditions. These were, namely, that its payment on the part of the peasants and cattle owners should be voluntary and that the British would be given a quarter of the proceeds.[94] The Emirs acceded to these conditions and the collection of the Zakka continued for some years with the active assistance of the Residents and Assistant Residents. The British share of it was entered in the "Tribute Register" and the "Blue Book" under a heading separate from the other taxes. This was an attempt, on the part of the British, not to go back on their promise to the Emirs that they would never merge this canonical due with the "general tax."[95]

However, the British were not able to rise above their prejudices and tolerate for long this continued expression of a desire on the part of the Emirs to retain a measure of autonomy. Thus, by 1906, Goldsmith in Sokoto was reporting that in his record at least, he was no longer able to accord the Zakka a separate recognition and that he had granted it under the heading "Tribute,"[96] that is lumping it together with the Kurdin Kasa and the Jangali. The following year, on instruction from the Governor, the Emirs and District Heads were informed "clearly" "that the [increased] General Tax includes the Zakka and is not in addition to it."[97] As should be expected, this order was not in fact obeyed by the District Heads, no doubt with the support of the Emirs. Thus, for example, the same year that the collection of the Zakka was made "illegal" by the British, two District Heads in Sokoto were caught collecting it and the Sultan was promptly ordered to depose them on that account, an order which he obeyed. The two District Heads were the Sarkin Burmi of Bakura and the Ardon Dingyadi.[98]

On the other hand, it seems it was not the case that the British meant their order "abolishing" the Zakka consistently to apply throughout the emirates or at all times. Thus, in 1909, two years after the order "abolishing" the Zakka, the Resident Kano was reporting that: "the zakka actually paid in [to the British] is ... roughly 1/10 of the crop. I should think that probably an amount about equal to ½ of the amount paid in i.e. about £8,000, is embezzled." He added that "this embezzlement will only disappear after the village heads are strong enough to collect the rents without the aid of *jakadas*."[99] And as if to emphasize that he had forgotten about the "abolition" of the Zakka, he suggested that "the institution of farm measuring and the inclusion of the Zakka in the rent charged will put a stop to embezzlement."

Similarly, as late as June 1911, Webster in Yola was reporting that "corn Zakka is paid by a large percentage of the population over and above the regular taxation."[100] He added that he had informed people of the "abolition" of the cattle Zakka in favour of a per capita rate, but that "several people anxiously enquired if they might also pay the Zakka to the District Head. What became of it was not their affair, but pay they must as a matter of religion. I do not pretend that this feeling is the universal spirit, but I think there is a strong local feeling of the religious importance of the payment of Zakka." Seeing that the desire to continue paying the Zakka was so strong on the part of the people, Webster urged that the British "recognize its payment [once more] and take our share." In "this case" he thought, "a percentage of the total tax should be laid aside for charity act," as he thought "the tax [was] not nearly so frequently misapplied as it is often thought."

By this time the Governor's resolve to suppress the existence of the Zakka as a distinct tax, voluntary or involuntary, was stiffening. Hence, he ordered Webster that "the system of taxation in Yola should as far as possible be brought in line with that which has been approved for other Provinces ..." He thought that if it could be explained to the people "that zakka is included in the general tax which they are asked to pay whether it be on land or on income, their religious susceptibilities will be satisfied."[101] Thus, henceforth, under the British the Zakka remained "illegal" and those chiefs caught demanding or accepting it were liable to being accused of extortion and punished accordingly. But this did not stop the Emirs, District Heads and Village Heads from accepting it throughout the colonial period.[102] However, demanding the Zakka henceforth involved hazards because, in the event of the individual or community involved being not favourably disposed towards paying it, the official making the demand could be reported to the British and be tried for extortion.

Other British Taxes

Though the other British taxes do not merit as lengthy a discussion as the Kurdin Kasa and the Jangali, both because they directly affected only certain classes of the society, and because some of them were abolished after some time. However, they still deserve some consideration both because while they lasted they proved a burden on the classes affected, and because they contributed, severally and collectively, to crippling the economy of the emirates and consummating its incorporation into the British imperialist economy. We shall study these other taxes in terms of the time of their imposition, alleged reasons for imposition, the rates at which they were assessed and collected, the role of Emirs in collecting them, and their impact on the particular trades affected and on the economy generally.

The Caravan Tax

Of the other taxes, the most important was the Caravan Tax, which was imposed by the British at the same time as they were occupying the emirates, extending it piecemeal to each conquered emirate. The alleged reason for the imposition of this tax was that the British had rendered trade routes safe and that traders had to demonstrate their gratitude by contributing towards the costs of maintaining law and order.[103] Another alleged reason for the imposition of this tax by the British was that even before their occupation of Northern Nigeria, customs dues had been collected by Emirs and other chiefs.[104] As we saw in an earlier chapter, this was a fabrication. But even if it were true that some form of customs had been collected within the Sokoto Caliphate, we should consider this "reason" as being secondary at best. The fact was that the British never allowed anything to exist under their regime simply because it had been in existence before their advent. It was the requirements of their administration that made them continue with some pre-existing institutions and practices, to discontinue with other institutions and practices, and to reintroduce institutions that had been superceded. They in fact did not find any institution or practice too hallowed to escape interference from them one way or another. Their habit of reverentially referring to institutions and practices they wanted to retain was sheer tactical hypocrisy. Hence, we should regard the imposition of the British Caravan Tax solely as answering to their own fiscal and economic needs, the prior existence or nonexistence of such a tax in the emirates being in the final analysis irrelevant.

The rate of the Caravan Tax varied from a minimum of half percent of the value of the taxable goods in 1900 through 3% and then 10% in 1903 and finally 15% in 1904.[105] When the decline in trade, made inevitable by this high rate of taxation, started to manifest itself, this rate was allowed to fluctuate between a minimum of 5% and a maximum of 10% – depending on the commodity involved and the distance covered by a caravan. The shorter the distance the higher the rate, and the disposition of traders in a given locality to retaliate to a high rate by suspending trading.[106]

Among commodities liable to the tax were native salt, ivory, kola nuts, rubber, potash, native cloth and cattle.[107] European goods were at first exempted from this tax on the alleged ground that Europeans paid import duty before entering the Protectorate of Southern Nigeria.[108] However, this could not be the real reason for excluding foreign goods, since those native products which, like ivory, kolanuts, potash, cattle, and native salt, were often imported into the Protectorate from "German" and "French" territories, are levied both Customs Duties and the Caravan Tax.[109] In fact, the real reason for exempting European imported goods was to be seen in the pressure which the Niger Company brought to bear on the Colonial Government, whose *raison d'etre,* the Company insisted, was to support British industry against native industry.[110]

The policy of taxing traders dealing in native goods while exempting trade in European goods was one of the means by which the British ultimately converted the indigenous commercial class into a total appendage of British imperialism, the hawkers of its goods pure and simple. This was so effective in stifling trade in native goods that, by the end of 1904, trade in these goods had sufficiently declined for the British to realize that they were hurting their own financial interests by their blatant discrimination against it. Hence, in October of that year, it was decided that European goods too were made liable to the Caravan Tax. However, it is questionable that the British extended this tax to European goods in order to save native industry from total extinction, or only because by this time trade by indigenous traders in European goods was so large that the Colonial Administration felt that it would be losing substantial revenue by exempting those goods. One is inclined to the latter view. At any rate, the extension of this tax to European products was a reflection of the measure of confidence that the British had come to feel by the end of 1904 about the entrenchment of their products in the markets of the emirates. These goods no longer needed to be supported against local products.

Perhaps the most important aspect of the method of collection of the caravan tolls was the fact that neither the Emirs nor the District Heads had any role in it at all. They were neither invited to help nor did they offer to do so. Rather than invite the Emirs or their officials to help, the British, with the aid of their African clerks and constabulary, undertook the collection. In fact, the actual collection was done by African clerks at various centres designated as Toll Stations or ports of entry in the case of those on the boundaries with "French" and "German" territories. For example, in Yola Province, such stations in 1905 included Bing Kola, Malabu, Gurin, Girei, Pakorgel, Wuro Yolde, Uba, Jimeta, Yola town, Nyibango, and Chukkol.[111] In Sokoto Province at this time, the stations included Jega, Sokoto town, Isa, Kaura Namoda, Yelu, Bengui and Beibei.[112] Apart from stationing clerks and sometimes even British Revenue Officers at these toll stations, the British had patrols of police and army personnel roaming villages surrounding these stations. This was intended to make sure that traders did not succeed in avoiding them, and that they called in at the stations even if doing so would divert them far from their intended route and destination.[113]

So bent on excluding Emirs and other chiefs from the collection of this tax were the British that, even though they were never at any point able to secure enough clerks to place in all the stations, they would rather leave some stations vacant than empower District Heads to collect the tolls for them or get the Emir to send some of his central officials to do so. Similarly, in spite of the inadequate number of policemen and soldiers available for patrol work, the British never asked the Emirs to use their *dogarai* to do the patrolling. It was only when the patrols became too expensive that District Heads were asked to assist by reporting toll evaders,[114] and we have not come across a single mention of any District Head so obliging.

However, there is evidence that some of the chiefs on the border areas between the former Sokoto Caliphate and its neighbours continued to collect their own tolls from traders as they did in the days before the coming of the British. In all probability, traders, for their part, preferred to pay much smaller amounts to Emirs and District Heads to paying the much higher rates to the British. This might explain the refusal of the British to enlist the aid of the Emirs in the collection of the tolls. The Emirs were suspected to be in league with the traders. The evidence that came to the notice of the British that chiefs were surreptitiously collecting tolls was significant in Argungu, where the Magajin Argungu was sent to Yelu by the Emir to collect "the original native tolls that had lapsed since our advent."[115] This took place from May to July 1905 "shortly after" the clerk managing the station was temporarily withdrawn to Sokoto to fill a gap in the Provincial Office left by another clerk who had gone on leave.

Soon after this was discovered in July, Captain Ruxton sent for and arrested the Magaji, who was taken to Jega. He informed Ruxton that he was acting on behalf of the Emir of Argungu. Hence, Ruxton took him to Argungu, where "the Emir admitted the fact and said he was merely continuing the ancient practice now that Governments were no longer collecting tolls; he did not know he was doing wrong." Captain Ruxton could not pretend moral indignation at extortion by a "native ruler," for the rate collected by the Emir compared extremely favourably with the 5% to 15% collected by the British, and for that reason redounded to the credit of the native system. Ruxton admitted that "the fito" taken by the Magaji was very small in amount, about 3 *lingai* of salt on a donkey load, and one *lingai* on a man's load (a lingai being a "small packet worth roughly ½d").

Nonetheless, or perhaps because the Emir of Argungu not only dared to act like an independent ruler, but also to levy a rate of taxation that exposed the British rate for the very extortionate rate that it was, Ruxton felt constrained to punish the Emir. He fined him the sum of £5:0:0, being the approximate value of the probable amount of salt collected in three months in a station where the British collected £234:0:0 in one month alone.[116] This fine was to be paid in British currency in spite of the "total lack of cash in Argungu" at the time. The Emir was, in recognition of this "difficulty," given 15 days in which to pay up the fine.

Customs Duty

Very similar to the Caravan Tax was the Customs Duty. The difference between the two was that the customs duty affected European products more than it affected local products. The obvious reason was that most of the local products were produced within the Protectorate, only a few being imported from "German" and "French" territories. As the customs duty affected mainly European products, its rate was very low indeed compared with the rate of the Caravan Tax,[117] seldom ever exceeding 2%. However, while the Caravan Tax remained in force only until 1907, the customs duty remained in force throughout our period. But it must be emphasized that in reality it was the indigenous population that ultimately bore the whole burden of taxation on trade, though perhaps not in "legality." This was so because the Niger Company and other European firms took care to add the customs duty on their goods to the selling prices of these goods. We can also be sure that in buying local products to export, these firms took into account not only the weight of the sacks, the weight of water contents of the products, the weight of dirt, etc., but also the export and import duties they would have to pay for the products at Nigerian and European ports. Thus, the customs duty too boiled down to a tax on the local population right from the start.

The method of collecting the customs duty was similar to that of collecting the Caravan Tax, as far as local products were concerned. That is to say, the duties were collected at specific "ports of entry" by clerks of the Colonial Government, and without the assistance of the Emirs. Not only the methods of collection but even the stations at which the collection was done, and the clerks who did the collection, were the same for the customs duty as for the Caravan Tax.

Canoe Tax

The Canoe Tax was also imposed at the onset of British colonial domination in the emirates. At first, Lugard decreed that only canoes capable of carrying half a ton of goods were subject to it. But when some of the Residents sent to complain that "there were very few [canoes] in this Province that would reach the lowest weight rating,"[118] and that "the majority of boats would barely hold three men,"[119] that "very often the canoe was merely a hallowed out palm log,"[120] he replied that "all canoes [were] taxable [because] small canoes used for fishing earn[ed] money,[121] and for that reason could not be exempted. Not only was the Canoe Tax imposed on all canoes, its rate was unbelievably high, ranging from 5/- to £3 per canoe per annum,[122] in spite of the fact that the canoes "generally looked as if 5/- would buy them outright."[123]

In the collection of this tax too, Emirs were not involved, though Burdon, at one point at least, evinced a desire to ask for their help in its collection. For some reason which is not obvious, as far as Lugard was concerned, the collection of this tax was neither the duty of the Emirs nor of clerks, but of the Residents themselves. His instruction was that each year, a Resident was to collect all the canoes in his province in one place and collect this tax from them in a day or two.[124] In practice, however, it was clerks that were detailed to do the collection; and, instead of collecting them all in one place, a clerk with one or two policemen travelled along the rivers stopping canoes and collecting the tax.[125] This practice must have placed the canoemen under great insecurity during the collection season, which usually lasted the whole of December. However, it also enabled them receive advanced warnings from friends and so hide their boats until the hateful team had passed. This way, many of them were reckoned to have evaded the payment of this tax.[126]

As time went on, the difficulty involved in the collection of this tax became greater as the canoemen became more and more adept at avoiding the collectors, and some of the Residents started to question the financial wisdom of collecting it. Burdon called it "a bad tax, giving the maximum of trouble, causing among those affected the maximum of discontent, and bringing to government the minimum of revenue", and called for its suspension if not outright abolition.[127] However, it was not until April 1st, 1907 that the Canoe Tax, along with the Caravan Tax, was abolished on the permission of the Colonial Secretary.[128] The inevitable subsequent "loss" of revenue to the Colonial Government was recovered by raising the rate of the Kurdin Kasa and making its collection more efficient.

Needless to say, the abolition of these taxes was very welcome to the local population, although the rise in the Kurdin Kasa was later to be greeted by revolts of which the revolt in Dawakin Tofa in Kano Emirate was an example. The relief that people felt at the abolition of these two taxes was, for example, expressed in a letter which the Emir of Bida, Muhammadu, wrote to Wallace, the Acting High Commissioner. The letter was "one of many received from Emirs and [went] to show with what universal joy and satisfaction the receipt of [His] Lordship's decision in this matter [had] been received throughout [the] Protectorate."[129] The only objection lodged against the abolition of either of these two taxes came from P.M. Dwyer, then Resident Ilorin, who objected to the abolition of the Caravan Tax.[130] He received an appropriate reply from Wallace, who informed him "nothing you can say in favour of this tax can possibly upset the worldwide objections to it. It was millstone to the trade of the Protectorate and helped to keep our prisons full."[131] Ominous enough for the local population, Wallace urged the heartless Dwyer, "now is your chance to show what can be done with the Land Revenue which is the legitimate tax of the future."[132]

Game Tax

Another tax imposed by the British on the local population was the Game Tax. This tax took the form of paying a fee to obtain a licence for hunting game. But it is very doubtful, indeed, that this measure was ever successfully enforced. It was "the extent of the territory to be dealt with, the smallness of the staff available for collection"[133] of the game fees and Lugard's unwillingness to leave the issuing of the licences in the hands of the Emirs that combined to make the attempt to impose this tax on the local population somewhat ineffective at the beginning. Nor would Lugard have succeeded in enlisting the cooperation of the Emirs had he tried to do so. This was demonstrated by the failure of Burdon to enlist the active, as opposed to the verbal, cooperation of the Sultan. The latter "promised all the assistance in his power" and Burdon, on account of that promise, judged him "capable both of appreciating and carrying into effect the law," of being: "intelligent enough to appreciate the danger of extinction of game and to realize that as the possibility of this arises from our action in giving the land peace, we are thoroughly justified in our endeavour to prevent it."[134]

However, even while being taken in by the Sultan's profuse protestations of appreciation and generous promises to cooperate, Burdon was realistic enough to perceive that interfering with the people's rights to hunt game "must always be a very delicate subject", and that "it would be a mistake to endanger the loyalty of the people to their ruler by too much pressure."[135]

Lugard also was aware that the imposition of the licence was "a most arbitrary act"[136] on the part of the British, but disagreed with Burdon that Emirs had to be rewarded if they helped to collect it; for he disliked "the principle of constant rewards for doing one's duty." Lugard reminded Burdon that it was not out of love, sentiment or altruism that the British retained the Emirs. In fact "they were retained as rulers [so that] as a quid pro quo they [had] to enforce the law. Otherwise they [were] useless,"[137] and might as well be sacked. That was to say, either the Emirs were to help in collecting the Game Tax without being given a share in its proceeds, or they should not be asked to help. He took the loyalty of the Emirs to the British for granted. That the Emirs did not help in collecting the Game Tax is plain from the proceeds of this tax, which were very meagre in the first three years of British rule. As to the reason why the Emirs did not assist in its collection, one would suggest much the same reasons as we suggested for the caravan and canoe taxes. This is to say that the Emirs refrained from assisting, partly because the British, who were eager to avoid having to share its proceeds with them, never made any serious effort to enlist their assistance. This was partly because at 5/- per licence they regarded the rate as exorbitant, and partly because, as Burdon suggested, an attempt by the Emirs to help in rigorously enforcing this tax would have caused them to forfeit the loyalty of a very significant section of their population, the hunters who, until the coming of the British, had been an important element in the armies of the emirates. This is so especially bearing in mind that the belief was widespread in the emirates that the British would not stay for more than a few years, a belief which must have been accompanied by fear that British withdrawal would restore the necessity to resolve the old conflicts, the resolution of which the British occupation had interrupted. One can easily understand the Emirs' refusal to cooperate in enforcing a tax the enforcement of which would have caused a real disaffection among the hunters.

Native Liquor Tax

An additional tax the British introduced in the form of licence was the Native Liquor Licence. However, as far as most of the emirates were concerned, as a means of raising revenue the tax was unviable, and as a means of depressing a native industry it was unnecessary. Both the tax's lack of viability and its lack of necessity stemmed from the virtual absence of the industry in the emirates, except possibly in parts of Adamawa, Bauchi, Gombe, Zaria, Ilorin and Nupe. Even in this case, one would emphasize the doubt. This is because it would seem that the widespread drunkenness in the non-Muslim section of the emirates, which was a palpable feature of the colonial era, was not a carry-over from pre-colonial days, but on the contrary a result of the colonial situation itself. That is to say, judging from the career of this tax, it would seem that drunkenness, like mysticism, quietism and crime, was only adopted by sections of the population of the emirates after the emirates had lost control over their situation to the British and therefore had to withdraw into something, as it were. The assumption that drunkenness was part of Nigerian "culture," that it was a phenomenon independent of the existence of colonialism rather than an inevitable creation of that colonialism, ought to be considered as one of the theories concocted by the British and their sympathizers, in an effort to absolve themselves from responsibility for creating a situation in which it was impossible for the bulk of the population to uphold the dignity that was a necessary part of being human.

But while we can only hypothesize about the prevalence of drunkenness, in parts of some of the emirates we have evidence, supplied by the British themselves, that drunkenness was foreign to many of the emirates at the time of the imposition of British rule. Thus, in April 1903, Burdon reported that:

> the Emirs of Sokoto and Gwando prohibit the manufacture of liquor in their own towns, and as far as possible throughout their territories. It certainly exists only to a very slight extent and by stealth in their principal towns ...The same applies to Argungu the people of which though called 'kafirai' by the Fulani are as good Mohammedans as any.[138]

The latter claim by Burdon might well be an exaggeration, but it does not render invalid Burdon's claim about the status of drinking and brewing liquor for the three emirates. In fact, what Burdon had to say about Jega helps to establish the objectivity of his claim. Thus he went on to admit that:

the exception is Jega, where owing to the numbers of Nupe and Yoruba traders, the sale of liquor, though disapproved of, is allowed. It would in fact be almost impossible to stop it. But the manufacture is confined to a certain section
of the inhabitants, Kambari people...[139]

Similarly, Resident Orr in Zaria, in 1905, reported that in his Province
"these licences again [were] collected chiefly in Zungeru," while "a few [were]
issued to the wives of police and soldiers, but the licences [were] far more useful as a prevention of drunkenness than as a source of revenue."[140] Be it noted
that neither Zungeru nor the "wives of police and soldiers" could at this time be
said to form part of an emirate or its society.

However, even where this tax could be levied, the British could not summon
the courage in those early days to ask the Emirs to help in its collection. The
situation simply did not provide them with a leeway through which to approach
the Emirs. Thus, as Burdon again pointed out, "though some liquor brewing
went on in the outlying pagan towns of the Sarikin Muslimin, in accordance
with Islamic custom he does not interfere with their morals any more than
with their religion." Hence, Burdon found himself "unable to ask the Sarikin
Muslimin's help in this matter."[141] Lugard did not like the idea that his Liquor
Tax could not be collected by the Native Authorities, but it would seem that by
and large, without actually withdrawing the tax, its collection was left in abeyance and the item only rarely appeared among other items under the heading
"Revenue" in the Provincial Reports.

Hawker's Licence

Even hawkers had to pay a special tax in the first four years of British rule,
a fact which, like many other facts, made British colonial domination over the
emirates more like a restoration of the pre-jihad system of government, with
its multiplicity of taxes,[142] than the improvement on the emirate system of
government that the domination was claimed to be by the British and their
protagonists.

A hawker was virtually any person who preferred being gainfully occupied
in petty trading to either being idle or going away to work on the mines and
other British projects during the dry season. Hence, this tax amounted to a
punishment against those who refused to be idle during the dry season or to
drift away to centres of intense British economic activity, there to surrender
themselves to the latter's exploitation. Its rate was 5/- per month,[143] in return
for a licence to be a hawker.

That the hawker's licence too was a very unjust imposition, some of the Residents, Burdon in particular, were able to realize. Thus, in the case of Soko-to, which he took over at the time of its occupation, Burdon thought it was "not advisable to attempt this tax for some time."[144] He correctly thought that among those to be affected by the tax were those who had already paid the Caravan tax; but, being afraid to come out and suggest that such a double taxa-tion should not be attempted, he confined himself to merely suggesting that if this tax was to an extent a duplication of the Caravan Tax, "it need not be con-sidered until this latter is established."[145] He went on to suggest that this would "also be in the nature of an experiment on the popular feelings for which I am certain the time is not ripe in Sokoto," as if the British colonial regime in the emirates was particularly concerned to court popular approval. To these and similar suggestions about other taxes, Lugard gave Burdon the reply to which we referred earlier in the chapter, namely that "no other Resident presents this non-possumus attitude," and went on to warn that "the Law must be enforced and the legal taxes collected …"[146]

In the collection of this tax too, the Emirs were not involved. It was govern-ment clerks and policemen that were used to collect it. This was the case even in Yola Province, where there was "no special staff available for the collection of taxes."[147] Yet the tax had a short life, ostensibly because by 1904, the Kurdin Kasa and the Jangali had become effective British taxes. But one suspects really because its collection was very difficult and was, by the time of its abolition, uneconomical. Besides, it might have started to discourage trade to a point which was against the interests of even the Niger Company, which relied to a great extent on native traders for the distribution of its goods.

Kurdin Su

However, as late as 1914, another "class tax" was introduced by the British. This was the Kurdin Su, which was payable by fishermen.[148] It was assessed on the basis of the number of nets a fisherman possessed, at the rate of 30/- per net per annum. The receipt issued to each fisherman for paying this tax served as his "licence" to earn his living. The Kurdin Su, like the Kurdin Kasa and the Jangali, was collected, not directly by British clerks, but by Village and District Heads. It would seem that by this time, the British had come to prefer reliance on the cooperation of the Emirs to rely on the inadequate exertions by their own officials.

Forced Labour

To the taxes listed above should be added one other measure by which the British Colonial Administration made the people of the emirates to express their subordination to them and contribute towards the execution of their projects. This was the extraction of forced labour, generally with a token pay, but often without any pay at all. Among projects that were undertaken by forced labour were the clearing of roads, the building of Rest Houses for the British along their routes, the clearing of riverbeds in some areas, the building of market stalls, and the planting of trees in European quarters. Examples of projects executed through forced labour abound. But a few should suffice to establish that, contrary to the myth and claim that the use of forced labour was foreign to British colonialism as distinct from French colonialism, the British did indeed employ forced labour to execute their projects, especially in the early days of their domination over the emirates. Thus, as early as February 1902, the Emir of Yola, at the behest of the Acting Resident, got "several lengths of road" widened and cleared – notably the roads to Girei, 15 miles away and to Tepe 70 miles away.[149] The Resident believed that such undertakings would be made "with little trouble" whenever required, and at that point preferred them to outright imposition of taxation. Hence, prior to the imposition of "direct taxation", an individual could be "called upon to liquidate [allegedly] legitimate Government claims by personal service in default of other means" of doing so.[150] Hence the Resident made it "compulsory on the people to come to the assistance of Government in an emergency."[151] It was on account of this stipulation that people were pressed-ganged into carrying for the British in Yola during pacification trips to "pagan" areas and other resistant districts, and to carry to Borno goods meant for the British in that Province, such goods being first brought to Yola by steamers and barges.[152]

To this stipulation Lugard, did in fact minute that forced labour may not be exacted in any circumstances, but that in a great emergency, the law may demand any man's help, e.g forest fires, etc. This does not include ordinary transport. The Protectorate law does not allow it and "you have no power to go outside the law."[153] However, this stipulation did not carry much weight with the Residents in the field and, as we shall see below, Lugard himself was obviously not sincere in his repeated warnings against the use of forced labour. The Resident Yola excused himself from obeying the "Protectorate law" on this issue on the ground that "the number who voluntarily contract to take loads from Yola to Borno is very small," the pay being extremely small, 16/- for the 700 mile journey to and from Maiduguri.[154] Besides, British currency, in which all British payments were made, was not yet in demand.

With the arrival of the Anglo-German Boundary Commission in Yola in August 1903, the problem of transport "reached a somewhat acute stage owing to the large demands for transport made by the Commission."[155] Hence, the Resident was able to state "with conviction" that "without forced labour these demands for transport [could not] possibly be complied with."[156] This gave him the opportunity to challenge Lugard to give "clear instructions as to whether in the event of stores arriving here for Bornu, or of other urgent demands for transport, I am to wait until willing carriers can be procured, which will mean that stores will be indefinitely detained in Yola, or impress carriers either directly or through the Emir."[157] Lugard could only equivocate in his reply, hoping that "things will resume their normal state and supplies go through as before."[158]

Clearing of Roads and River Beds

Meanwhile, roads continued to be cleared through compulsory and unpaid communal labour. In effect, this compulsory labour was used to punish those communities which had submitted to British colonial domination while those which did not submit to that domination were left alone as the following report indicates:

> Throughout the part of the Province inhabited by the Fulanis the main roads have been thoroughly cleared to a width of from 12 to 20 feet. The only pagans who have been ordered to clear the roads are the Kilba tribe on the Yola-Bornu road and the Yundam and Manna Mumuyes on the Lau-Yola road.[159]

The other "pagans" had not been asked to do any clearing partly because they were truculent and partly because they were not occupying areas traversed by "roads that were strategic" to the British.[160] The last phrase quoted above should be an effective answer to any contention on the part of historians that projects like road building were undertaken for the benefit of the indigenous population. And in Zaria, by the end of 1904, i.e. within two years of the occupation of the Emirate, forced labour had been used to build roads "fit for wheeled traffic" both from Zaria city to Zungeru, and from Zaria city to the border between Zaria and Kano Provinces.[161] In the same period, forced labour had also been used to build barracks for the British mounted infantry "consisting of accommodation for 10 officers, 10 NCOs, stabling for 250 horses, orderly room, guardroom, stores, veterinary stores, mess house, etc."[162] Inevitably "the amount of labour and material required was very great", but these were "admirably arranged for by the Emir."[163]

In Sokoto, within 11 months of British occupation, the Sultan had built for the British, using forced labour, the Provincial Court House, houses for the Resident, Revenue Officer and Police Officer, a government jail, police and army huts, and houses for the African staff of the Residency.[164] Similarly, the Emir of Gwandu, in spite of his general hostility to the British, had "loyally carried out Major Burdon's orders as to the clearing of the river bed, and in many cases, a channel had to be cut through heavy ground."[165] This enabled provisions for Burdon and his officers to be brought by boat "from the Niger right up to Sokoto, and it [remained] for the problem of the rapids at Bussa to be solved for Sokoto to be brought into direct communication with Lokoja and the coast."[166] At the same time, "the cleaning, widening and opening up of roads [went] on apace."[167]

In fact, the clearing of the Rima river bed was a semi-permanent affair in those early years of British domination over the emirates. In April 1905, Ruxton reported that in his "interview with the Emirs [of Gwandu and Argungu, the chief point made was the clearing of the river."[168] Burdon admitted that the clearing of the river was a "far more labourious task than road clearing," and suggested that in view of the fact that there already had "been two clearings without pay ... at least £1 a mile be allowed for the work done to date."[169] Replying to this request, Lugard once more pretended not to be aware that forced and unpaid labour was the means by which the British had been executing their projects in the emirates. Thus, he irrelevantly asked:

> what cost has been incurred in clearing the Gulbin Gindi? It was, I suppose, sanctioned and money provided? Of course no forced labour is used. Work, however urgent, must not be undertaken without sanction and provision for pay. There are many urgent projects in the Protectorate, including housing for Europeans.[170]

Naturally enough, this hypocritical reprimand drew a sharp rejoinder from Burdon, who wrote to inform Lugard that:

> the method of getting the work done is the same as was reported in my report No.8/1903 which was passed without comment by Your Excellency. I have got all the towns from Bunza to Argungu at work clearing the grass and digging out the channel. The work done and the success achieved was again reported by Captain Orr in Report No.11 where the phrase 'Major Burdon's orders as to the clearing of the river beds' showed plainly the means by which the carrying out of the work had been effected. While commenting on the utility of the work Your Excellency made no comment on the method employed. The original cutting out of the river bed and the second annual clearing was again reported in the annual Report for 1904 and passed without comment by Your

Excellency further than enquiring as to whether any use had been made of the result.[171]

He went on:

> I am afraid that in the literal sense it is undoubtedly forced labour that has been used – though in no sense the violent catching of people and physical compulsion that that phrase commonly conveys. I can only say that by no other means than by orders to headmen and their authority over their subjects can any work be achieved in this Province whether paid or otherwise and without any reference to the question as to whether those working are slaves or free. And if I have committed an error in using such means for the improvement of transport I can only say that I have done so in the spirit of the Roads Proclamation, and in the absence of any adverse comment on the full and unconcealed reports on my action quoted above, in the full belief that my methods had your Excellency's approval.[172]

By October 1905 the following roads, all of which were of particular importance to the British, had been cleared and brought up to a standard acceptable to the British through compulsory labour:[173]

a)   Tambawal to Jega and Bunza,
b)   Jega to Gwandu and Argungu,
c)   Jega to Giru and the boundary between Sokoto and Kontagora Provinces,
d)   Jega to Ambursa and Birnin Kebbi,
e)   Bunza to Bengu, and
f)   Bengu to Tsibiri, running along the border between British and French territories.

Though none of these roads were then "available for wheeled transport, it would take comparatively little to make them so."[174] In addition to clearing these roads, the people also had to plant trees along them to reduce the chances of Burdon and company suffering sunstroke.

That the British employed compulsory labour only on projects that had direct benefit to them is made simply clear in an opinion advanced by Burdon about a suggestion made by Lugard – that chiefs should be instructed to get people to clear their towns. Burdon's opinion on this suggestion was that the Sultan would not pay the people after making them clear their town and that until the Sultan was ready to make a payment for such work, the cleaning of the towns had to be left alone. Thus he says:

> any scheme for paid sanitation is absolutely impossible for the present. The Sarikin Muslimin would not grasp the fact that if he orders his people to work in the town he must pay them for it. Any immediate move in this direction

would be a grave mistake. And the very idea of sanitary works must be given time and approached with caution. The loyal and peaceable attitude of Sokoto and its rulers is too valuable an asset to be endangered.[175]

This is to say that when it came to making them work for themselves, the feelings of the people had to be taken into consideration, a point which was not raised by Burdon when the people were being made to work on projects in which the British had an obvious and immediate interest. This passage also shows how low the British rated the moral capacity of the Emirs; for here we see Burdon, of all the British, questioning the moral calibre of none other than the Sultan himself.

Yet, the authority of these Emirs was indispensable to the British. Burdon suggested that even if sanitation were:

to be carried out and paid for by Government officials [in the European station] it could only be done by utilizing [the] Sarikin Muslimin to provide labour, i.e. by ordering him to order his people to turn out and by eventually paying them through him. It is the only method by which labour, whether free or slave, can be obtained at present in this Province.[176]

Tellingly enough:

the sanitation of Sokoto, a mile and a quarter from the European lines is not of sufficient urgency to impose on the people, even for their good, tasks and regulations which would be in the highest degree vexatious to those concerned and disturbing to the political equilibrium.[177]

Only projects affecting British welfare and interests were "of sufficient urgency to impose on the people [such] tasks and regulations."

The Building of the Nigerian Railway

The single most important project on which forced labour was undoubtedly used in our period was the construction of the Nigerian Railway from Lagos to Kano and Jos. This can clearly be seen among other records in the Zaria Provincial Reports during the period when the construction was passing through that province. Thus, for example, we are told that during the first quarter of 1910, the entire "Political staff in the Province," that included the Resident and all his assistants, "were fully occupied in supplying the needs of the Railway." And that "supplies of labour had to be maintained well into the months of May," that is quite some time after the ploughing and planting season had begun.[178] Even then, the British "were fortunately able to dismiss" not the whole conscripted labour but only "large numbers of men to their farms after the fall of the rains."[179] In the Western Division of the Province in particular, which included "the area in which the most active Railway (Bridging) work was in progress from the commencement of the year," we are told that:

> all ... District Heads were actively employed in superintending the numerous buildings required at the Kaduna Station, or in clearing the Telegraph Track or in providing the labour required for maintenance and repairs of the many washaways on the line caused by the heavy rains.[180]

It should, however, be pointed out that the Resident supplied all this information, not for the purpose of putting on record the contribution of the indigenous population to railway and other constructions but, in order to explain why he and his staff had not done much to carry out the policy of "close assessment" for taxation. Indeed, far from "regretting" the hardships imposed on the indigenous population by such a heavy demand on their labour time, Withers Gill found it possible to extol the "civilizing influence" that this demand made on "native character."[181] It was ostensibly "with a view to extending the area of this influence" that the Resident "had several levies made from various backward tribes in the Southern Division," through which the railway was not passing at all.[182] And he looked "forward to the contemplated extension of a Branch Railway to Naraguta as a further civilizing influence amongst these pagans in teaching them discipline, widening their narrow outlook, and in showing them the desirability of earning money."[183] He averred that British "efforts to encourage them to have trade relations with Hausas, to open markets and get away from the Hills to settle on the plains" – in short British "efforts" to further integrate these people into the British imperialist system – would "doubtless be accelerated by the experience they [had] gained in Railway work and from people outside their tribal boundaries,"[184] a claim which was substantially true but one-sided.

In the event Withers Gill, or rather his successors, got more than what he so eagerly looked forward to in 1910. For when "the Bauchi Light Railway Extension was completed, as far as Zaria Province was concerned," in May 1913, "active preparations [became] necessary at the end of the year for the commencement of earthworks" on yet another extension "the Eastern Railway."[185] Such provided another opportunity to the British to "civilize" the "pagans" by demobilizing them from their farm and other necessary economic activities, and mobilizing them to participate in railway construction work. However, as far as Resident Gill's views about the benefits of the indigenous population's participation in this work were concerned, it is obvious that the population itself did not perceive such benefits. Thus, Fremantle remarked that "in 1912 it was feared that demands for labour for public works such as the railway were causing a number of families to emigrate to Kano,"[186] where, ironically, such demands were soon to catch up with them. He went on to admit that "that such emigration exists," i.e even in 1913, "there is no doubt." But he went on to attribute it, albeit "partly," to "the nomad character of the Maguzawa Pagans,"[187] quite a novel claim. Emigration or no emigration, Fremantle assures us that "the labour required on the new capital site [at Kaduna] will cause great demands on the resources of the Provinces ESPECIALLY DURING THE RAINS ..."[188] And so it was, for even pending the mobilization of labour for building the capital, during the June quarter of 1914, that is, at the height of the rainy season, an average of 4,537 forced labourers were employed on such other projects as the Eastern Railway, the "Open Lines," the Military Camp at Kaduna, the "Kaduna Deviation," "Trading firms," "Public Buildings at Zaria" and "Zaria Station Repairs."[189] But as we shall see in chapter 11, a general famine, which had been on in the emirates since 1911, attained calamitous proportions in 1914. In Zaria "the scarcity of food [had already] been severely felt in the Northern portion of the Province." The Resident anticipated that "in a few weeks' time there [would] be no corn left" in Zaria town. And that "unless native traders [imported] food from other Provinces, for a few weeks before the gero crop [was] reaped the people of Zaria [would] be in a bad way."[190] It was this tragedy that helped to ensure that desertions by the labourers were: "comparatively few owing to the prompt payment of subsistence money to the labourers on their arrival on the work for the number of days taken by them from their homes, and the regular weekly issue of corn."[191] Nonetheless, it was "with the greatest difficulty [that] the greatest strength of labour [could] be maintained,"[192] so unrelated were the projects on which they were employed to the interests of the labourers. That this is how the labourers saw it is clear from the September Quarter Report. In this Report, it is clear that while there was "a considerable increase in the number of enlisted labourers," there was also "a great many desertions."[193] One of the reasons given by the labourers on interrogation was that "they were hungry," although the Resident insisted that there was "always a plentiful supply of food at the labour camp."[194] Yet other labourers, especially those from Kajuru and Woinya Districts, protested that the forced labour was taking them away for too long from their farms. The Resident conceded to them that they were "to work for two weeks instead of four" but also that "they must see that their relief [arrived] promptly."[195] Thus was the Nigerian Railway built "by the British."

It is understandable why the British should want to undertake projects serviceable to their purposes and why they should want to achieve those projects by using compulsory and often unpaid local labour. The question to ask here is: why would the Emirs agree to cooperate in supplying such labour, particularly at a time when the British were giving out that it was a cardinal aim of their occupation of the emirates to end the enslavement of man by man? To this question we can only offer speculative answer. For, even if the events were current events, it is unlikely that the actors would be clear in their minds why they acted the way they did. The impossibility of a clear and definite answer to the question is made all the more unavoidable by the time lapse and the death of the original actors in the situation, and of their contemporaries.

The answer one would suggest as to why the Emirs cooperated in the execution of these projects by compulsory labour is first that they were fully aware of the certain consequences of refusal to cooperate with the British. They were all witnesses to what had happened to their bolder predecessors, the erstwhile emirs, who were almost, to a man, ousted and in several cases killed, for refusing to accept British overlordship. Besides, although the terms of their own appointment by the British did not include an explicit requirement that they should compel people to work free of charge for the British, they must have been aware that these terms were so general that they could be interpreted to include the supply of forced labour if the British should need such labour.

Second, the Emirs and the people were aware that in many cases the British called upon them to work on projects which were clearly useful to the people themselves. The clearing of roads and river beds, and the planting of trees along roads and avenues, could not have been construed as being useful to the British alone. This realization about the benefit of such projects to the indigenous population played some part in making the Emirs cooperate with the British to undertake them. This is underlined by the fact that some of the Emirs – Muhammadu Aliyu, the Emir of Gwandu and the first two Emirs of Katsina to serve under the British, Abubakar and Yero, while cooperating on such projects – did refuse to cooperate with respect to those projects whose benefit was for the British alone. Such projects were the building of rest houses, forts and barracks.[196] But the fear of the consequences that would have followed refusal to cooperate must be held to have been the ultimate and overriding cause of their cooperation. Indeed, the relevant point about the imposition of forced labour on the population of the emirates is that, whatever benefits might have accrued on this population as a result of such forced labour were incidental and nowhere comparable to the military and economic benefits that accrued to the British from such labour.

11. Sir William Frederick Gowers, Resident Yola Province and later Lieutenant-Governor of Northern Nigeria (1921–1925).

13. H.W. Goldsmith, Resident, Zaria Province by 1914.

12. Sir Richmond Palmer, Resident, Kano Province (1915–1916).

14. Sir Ralph Moor, Consul-General of Niger Coast Protectorate (1896–1900) and High Commissionner of the Protectorate of Southern Nigeria (1900–1903).

15. Sir E.P.C. Girouard, Lieutenant Governor, Protectorate of Northern Nigeria, 1907–1909.

Conclusion

We can conclude this chapter by stating that the taxes imposed by the British, far from being fewer, more rational and lighter than the precolonial taxes, as was claimed by the British, were, in fact more in number and heavier in incidence than the precolonial taxes. Many of them were baseless and arbitrary, some having as their primary purpose not the provision of revenue to the Colonial Administration and the Native Authorities, but the creation of a colonial economy devoid of an indigenous industrial base and geared towards the production and export of unprocessed raw materials. We have also seen that throughout our period, British Residents and Assistant Residents were much involved in the assessment and collection of these taxes than people are led to believe by the theoreticians of "Indirect Rule."

8

The Attitudes of the Various Classes
Towards British Taxation

Introduction

In this chapter, we shall examine the attitude of the various social classes towards British taxation, particularly by the emirate aristocracy and the "commoner classes." We will begin by exploring the basis of the generalized resistance against British taxation, highlighting the dilemma faced by the emirate aristocracy and the predicament of the "commoner classes" in their active resistance to British taxation. We shall endeavour to show that the aristocracy largely engaged in passive resistance while the commoners resorted to active resistance. However, as the British increasingly utilized vicious suppression, both forms of resistance declined, but did not altogether disappear throughout our period of study and beyond. In discussing the attitudes of the emirate aristocracies, we shall show the nature of their varying disposition to the introduction of Jangali and Kurdin Kasa, and the factors that influenced their bent, together with the British response to it. An important dimension of the tax issue that warrants closer examination is the marginal involvement of the emirs in the administration of taxes. We shall highlight how such generated "bad faith" between British officials in Bauchi, Sokoto, Zaria, Gwandu and Kano Emirates.

Next, the chapter will address the response of the common people to the imposition of Kurdin Kasa and Jangali. Here, we shall attempt to find out, in view of the false claim by Lugard that the people of the emirates welcomed such taxation, whether the evidence for the claim exists in the colonial sources. As it will turn out, we shall attempt to provide evidence of both passive and active resistance against such imposition, dwelling at length on the resistance in Gwandu Emirate, and the Dawakin Tofa tax revolt of 1908, which broke out in Kano Province. Other cases of active anti-tax resistance that we shall highlight include those in Sokoto, Adamawa, Abuja and Borno Emirates.

Grounds for Resistance to British Taxation

As should be expected, the population of the emirates offered resistance in all known forms, passive and violent, to the introduction of the taxes discussed in the last chapter. It was the ruling classes – the Emirs and their officials – that generally confined themselves to passive resistance while the "commoner" classes frequently resorted to armed resistance. As time went on and the willingness of the British to respond with dismissals, depositions and military expeditions to acts of resistance and defiance became established beyond doubt; even passive forms of resistance became rare among the rulers while the ordinary people resorted less and less to armed resistance and tended to confine themselves to passive forms of resistance. But resistance to these policies in one form or another never ceased right up to the time of Nigeria's achievement of formal independence in 1960.

The tendency of the Emirs and their officials to confine themselves to passive forms of resistance all along can be explained partly by the fact that these Emirs and officials were appointees of the British. Virtually all the original Emirs and a large proportion of their officials had been killed or sacked at the time of the imposition of British rule and prior to the introduction of specific British policies. It can also be explained in terms of the weakness of these Emirs and officials. Thus, physically, there was the fact that the British took away their firearms, and, morally, there was the fact that these rulers lacked the prestige and authority that their predecessors had enjoyed by virtue of being the appointees and agents of a foreign occupier.

In view of their weakness and dependence on the British, it can validly be asked: why did these Emirs and officials resist British policies at all in any form whatever? The answer to this question lies in the complexity of the situation that followed British occupation of the emirates. Thus, at one and the same time, the new Emirs were the appointees of the British, were British agents, but they were not that alone. They had something to gain from accepting British rule but also something to lose from accepting each and every one of their policies. The British had been honest with them in announcing that ultimate authority was going to reside with the High Commissioner and that the Residents were to oversee how they administered their emirates. But the British had not been honest with them to the point of telling them that the terms of their appointment could be interpreted in ways different from the way they might have understood them when they accepted these terms.

By way of elaboration: the complexity of the situation can be restated thus: while it was the British that appointed the Emirs, these Emirs partly owed their appointment to being the traditional rulers of their communities. Both the Emirs and the British knew that the latter could not indefinitely impose upon the people an Emir or official to whom the people were totally opposed. Similarly, while the Emirs had their position to keep by accepting British policy by and large, they would utterly compromise the modicum of prestige and authority they had in the eyes of the people if they accepted British policies in all their aspects and details. For, the British were Christians while the Emirs were Muslims, and not all that the British in their interpretation of Christianity, or in their essential disregard for it, considered legitimate, could the Emirs regard as permissible. Similarly, while the British were total aliens who were in the emirates temporarily — in the belief of the people — and for material gain alone, the Emirs were native and had not only a material but also a spiritual and moral stake in the welfare of the people to whom they were related by blood, language, history, a common future, religion and outlook upon life.

Nor should the divergence between the British and the local interpretations of the terms on which British occupation was accepted be underestimated. This divergence became clear to the Emirs and their officials only when the British started to make specific demands of them, as we have seen in the previous chapters. Given their differences with the British and their similarities with their own peoples, the Emirs and their subordinate officials were bound, in spite of their reduced and subordinate status, to find considerable aspects of British policy objectionable, and were equally bound to express their objections one way or the other, however hesitant and feeble the manner of giving those objections an expression.

The ordinary people, in contradistinction to their rulers, confronted a substantially different situation. At one level British policy was, for them mainly, if not entirely negative. The British taxes were heavier than the pre-existing taxes, more systematically and efficiently collected, and lacked religious sanction, or any other tangible justification for that matter. At another level, they had no position to keep. Hence, the contradiction between them and British colonialism was much more resolved and clear than the contradiction between the British and the Emirs. Their situation was at once simpler and more brutal than the situation of the official classes. It was clearly and consistently a matter of antagonism with the British.

The fact that it was often through their own erstwhile leaders that the British conveyed and enforced their policies on the people served either to mitigate or to aggravate the bitterness with which the people received these policies, depending on the attitude of the officials. If the particular officials enforcing these policies seemed to feel that the policies were unjust impositions, that by agreeing to implement them they were merely choosing the lesser of two evils both for themselves and their people; if they were lenient with those who were unable or unwilling to comply beyond a certain point, the people were relatively conciliated and more willing to cooperate; all these were presumably, to help an essential friend keep his position, and to save themselves from the inevitable wrath of the foreign imposter. If, on the other hand, the officials concerned presumed to believe that the demands of the foreigners were just, that the people owed it a duty to the British to comply with these demands, and for that reason displayed zeal in enforcing these demands, the bitterness of the people was compounded and their opposition stiffened. Not only were they being imposed upon by foreigners; but people whom they felt to be their own were betraying them and siding with the enemy, not just in the presence of the enemy, but even in his absence.

The situation as a whole was in fact much more complex than the above arguments may have succeeded in presenting it. For, neither the reaction of the official classes nor that of the ordinary people was in all cases true to expectation. Thus, for example, there were many cases in which officials incurred the displeasure of both the British and the common people. Two types of officials found themselves in this situation. There were, first, the officials who sought to take advantage of their relations with the British to lord it over the common people for their own, as distinct from British, benefit. This type of official was rejected by the people because he was oppressive, and by the British, because he was "dishonest" with them. Very often in such cases, the people did not hesitate to take advantage of the contradictions between the British and such officials to get rid of one enemy by using another enemy.

The second type of official who lost his position as a result of concerted action between the British and the common people was the official who tried to behave as if the British were both there and not there. For example, such officials tried to collect for the British their taxes and to collect for other purposes, often legitimate in the Shari'a, the canonical taxes, in particular the Zakka. Such people, as we have already seen, usually had the support of the generality of the people who on their own felt obliged to go on paying such dues, and were ignored or even aided by the British, for the latters' benefit, in the first few years of their rule. However, the position of such officials became very vulnerable when the British became totally opposed to the continued collection of such dues. On the other hand, there were always elements among the Muslims who, without renouncing Islam, were opposed to paying the Zakka unless they could not avoid doing so. Such people never hesitated to report any official who continued to collect the Zakka whatever he did with the proceeds, as soon as they realized that the British would listen to such complaints and punish the officials involved for "extortion." Therefore, what follows is a reflection of a complex historical situation.

The Emirs and District Heads vis-à-vis the Kurdin Kasa and the Jangali (1903–1914)

When, even before the occupation of the emirates was completed, some Residents started to report that "the Fulani" were "awaiting with curiosity and a good deal of anxiety a declaration of the government's policy and intentions,"[1] they were in fact referring only to the aristocracy who, in the eyes of the British, were synonymous with the Fulbe. It was also to this class that Lugard was referring when he minuted that there was "no reason why the Fulani should not still form the well-to-do-class and collect their rents giving in exchange their greater intelligence as judges and rulers."[2]

Judging from these reports, it would seem that the Emirs did in fact expect the British to levy taxes either on the Emirs or directly on the people. It would also seem clear that this expectation was the result, not of a naïve trust in British justice and good intentions, either towards all classes of the population or towards the Emirs in particular, but, in fact, the result of a realistic and logical distrust of British intentions. By the account of the British, in spite of their own protestations that they had come to put the world right, to end wars and strife, to establish peace, justice, etc., the Emirs assumed that they had in fact occupied the emirates only for the gain they expected to make out of these emirates; that their declarations of intent notwithstanding, the British were bound to exact some dues from the people of the emirates.[3] In fact, far from being reassured by British declaration of the "purity" and "honesty" of their intentions, the Emirs regarded these declarations as an attempt to lull them into false sense of security. They felt that the British were "up to some game" in making all the statements of good intent that they were wont to make in the early days of their rule.[4]

The British sounded a little surprised, even though somewhat pleasantly, to discover that the Emirs nursed such scepticism about their intentions. However, it was this British surprise that was naive. The Emirs' refusal to swallow British propaganda wholly was far from being out of the ordinary, or, as one Resident suggested, the result of the inability of harsh rulers to understand that others were capable of benevolence and justice towards those they defeated.[5] Their refusal was the only attitude they could logically adopt as a result of their observation in the previous five years of the practical conduct of the British, as opposed to their verbal protestations. These Emirs were all living witnesses of the destruction of life and property, arson, rapine and looting in which the British and their mercenaries engaged during the occupation of the emirate capitals and during their "pacification" expeditions to the outlying districts. Such conduct could not inspire trust and confidence in any normal person; and, in choosing to judge the British by what they did rather than by what they kept on declaring about their "intentions", the Emirs were displaying, not cynicism but a healthy strain of realism.

The only ruler who seems to have been at first taken in by British declarations was the Shehu of Borno, Abubakar Garbai, and that was because of his lack of experience in the ways of the British. The circumstances of Borno at the time of its occupation, and the activities of the French and the Germans in the vicinity, combined to deprive the British of the opportunity to behave in Borno as they did in the emirates. However, even the Shehu did not retain his naivety about the intentions of the British for very long. Their disarming him, attempts by them to detach some of his subjects from his authority and curb that authority over the rest of his subjects, as well as the conduct of the British towards defenceless villages during "pacification" expeditions, combined to rid him of his illusions about the British by the middle of 1903, less than 18 months after their occupation of Borno.

Thus, the imposition of the Kurdin Kasa and the Jangali, when it came, did not come to the Emirs as a surprise. They were able to link it directly to the very fact of British conquest. Hence, they generally received the news with calm and apparently made no request for a delay in its timing. Besides, although British records give no indication of this, we should assume that the fact that right from the time of the imposition of these taxes the British became very intimately involved with their assessment and collection, while at the same time spreading the myth that the taxes were collected for the Emirs rather than for the Colonial Government, could not have fooled the Emirs. They could not have failed to notice that the British were a bit too "eager" on their behalf. The businesslike manner in which the British went about assessing and superintending the collection of these taxes could not have failed to suggest to the Emirs that, ultimately, the British would relegate their interests and their services very much to the background, an eventuality which might be hastened if they tried to resist. It was this fear that must have contributed to the apparent "readiness" with which the Emirs "welcomed" the virtual British takeover of taxation.

However, the fact that the Emirs as a group accepted British interference with taxation does not mean that there were no emirs who did not accept this interference and found it difficult to pretend that they did. Prominent among the Emirs who did not do a good job of pretending to welcome the British interference with the system of taxation were the Emir of Gwandu, Muhammadun Aliyu, the Emirs of Katsina Abubakar and Muhammad Yero, the Emir of Hadeija, Muhammadu and the Emir of Keffi, Ibrahim, as well as the Sarkin Zazzau of Abuja, Muhammadu Gani. The inability of these Emirs to pretend successfully that they "welcomed" this interference was part of their inability to reconcile themselves with British presence generally. They suffered deposition and even death in one case as a result of this refusal. To these Emirs should be added the Emir of Kano, Muhammadu Abbas, the Emir of Ilorin, Shuaibu, the Emir of Keffi, Abdullahi and the Shehu of Borno, Abubakar Garbai. The resistance of these Emirs to the imposition of British taxation was much less open and therefore did not lead to the deposition of any of them; but their attitudes are nonetheless noteworthy, even if only because they did embarrass successive Residents and Assistant Residents.

It should also be noted that the fact that the Emirs were not, as a rule, invited by the British to play a very active role in the assessment and collection of these taxes did help many of the other Emirs escape having openly to betray their hostility. Had they been required to be actively involved in either the assessment or the collection of the Kurdin Kasa and the Jangali, a few more might have come into open conflict with the British over the issue.

However, and in spite of the myth of Indirect Rule, perhaps the most striking thing about the Emirs' involvement with the assessment and collection of these taxes was that it was minimal, in many cases much less than the role of the Residents and Assistant Residents.[6] Thus, it was these British officials that either summoned the District Heads into the emirate capitals or went themselves on tour round the districts for the purpose of assessment. In fact, the work of assessment of the Kurdin Kasa and the Jangali and their collection was, according to Lugard, "almost the most important" work of the Resident and his staff.[7] It was the Residents, rather than the Emirs, who issued books to District Heads for entering the names of tax payers, and it was the Resident or his Assistants that went round checking such.[8] Even when the District Heads brought these books to the emirate capital, it was to the Resident or Assistant Resident that they passed them direct: sometimes in the presence of the Emir's representative; often not, and seldom in the presence of the Emir himself. Not even the assessment of the emirate capitals was left in the hands of the Emirs. In fact, far from taking advantage of the presence of the Emirs in these capitals to leave their assessment in the hands of the Emirs, the Resident and the Assistant Residents took advantage of their own presence in them to assess these towns, down to apportioning to individual households the amounts they were to pay.[9]

Thus, the role of the Resident and his Assistants might be confined to deciding how much each district was to pay; or, it might extend to apportioning this lump sum among the various villages in each district. Each Assistant Resident would also select a number of villages whose lump assessment he would personally apportion among the households they contained. This way, quite a number of districts were assessed and surveyed village by village by Assistant Residents by 1910.[10]

Even where the Resident or Assistant Resident limited himself only to deciding what each district was to pay, it was the District Heads and not the Emirs who decided what each village was to pay. A District Head too might limit himself to apportioning to each village its lump sum or he himself, might go to the extent of apportioning this sum to the households making up each village, depending on the size of his district, his own energy, and the degree to which he felt he could leave affairs in the hands of his village heads. Similarly, it was the village heads that did the actual collection of the taxes, which they would then take to the District Heads who would, in turn, take the proceeds to the Emir or Resident.[11]

The Emir's role in the Assessment was limited to: receiving complaints from the Resident or Assistant Resident against individual District or Village Heads concerning non-cooperation in the assessment or collection of the taxes, concealment of cattle or households, under-statement of the population of their districts, etc; and administering the disciplinary measures, more or less exactly, that the Resident or Assistant Resident might "recommend." It was very seldom for an Emir in those early days to undertake a tour of his emirate in connection with the assessment or the collection of the Kurdin Kasa and the Jangali. In fact, in spite of all the claims about ruling the emirates through the Emirs, such occasional tours by the Emirs were regarded by Lugard as "dangerous precedents."[12] Assessment, according to him, was to be done by the Resident, rather than the Emir, going round the province or emirate, deciding on the basis of the size of the human or cattle population and the productivity of each district what the various districts, and if possible, the villages, were to pay.[13] Where it was not possible for the Resident to undertake such tours, the District Heads were to come to the provincial or emirate capital with the data, so that the Resident could do the assessing. Even after Lugard had left Nigeria, the precedent of Emirs very seldom undertaking tours in connection with taxation was adhered to.

However, although the Emirs did not go out on tours for assessing or su-perintending the collection of the Kurdin Kasa and the Jangali, Residents or their Assistants always took representatives of the Emirs with them when they went out on tour. But these representatives were not high ranking officials of the Emir. They fell in the category of messengers, and were known as *Yaran Sarki* (sing *Yaron Sarki*) in the emirates and *Iyalema* in Borno. Theoretically, they went with the British officials partly because the latter were unknown to the District Heads and as such had to be introduced to them. However, even after an official had become known to the District Heads, he still went out only in the company of these Emirs' representatives. In this way, it was impossible for a District or Village Head to insult the British official without at the same time insulting the dignity of the Emir. Similarly, any disobedience to the British official involved a disobedience to the Emirs. Hence, by taking these repre-sentatives along, the British were able, most of the time, to insulate themselves from unpleasant reception; in the cases where the presence of a *Yaron Sarki* failed to afford an effective insurance against insult for a British official, the British were able to represent the insult as an insult upon the dignity of the Emir, thus presenting opposition to themselves in terms easily comprehensible to the local rulers.[14]

From the Emirs' point of view, the presence of these representatives with the British helped them both to know what the touring British officers were up to, and to coordinate the reaction of the District and Village Heads with their own ideas about how the District and Village Heads should react. Similarly, the presence of the Emirs' representatives with the British officers made it easy for each District Head to know in advance the type of questions an official was likely to ask. This was made possible by the fact that there was usually a pause between the touring party's arrival in a district capital and the time when an interview would take place between the British official and the District Head. This pause was normally used by the Emir's representative to brief the District Head on the type of questions this official had asked in districts previously visited as well as to suggest to him the sorts of answer that the Emir wanted him to give.

The fact that the District Heads were the principal local officials involved with both the assessment and the collection of the Kurdin Kasa and the Jangali, coupled with the fact that there were more of them than there were Emirs, made it inevitable that cases of "bad faith" came to light more among the District Heads than among the Emirs. The existence of "bad faith" by District Heads towards the British with respect to taxation in the first decade of British rule, can be illustrated by the following few examples.

In Bauchi in 1906, Resident Howard was, throughout the collection season, "discovering concealed cattle", so much so that by the end of the season, Jangali in the province was collected on 30,000 more cattle than had been assessed for the previous year. Especially disheartening to the Resident was the fact that "the worst case of concealment was by the Emir of Bauchi's brother Mallam Namuda, Hardo Bauchi", that is, the District Head in charge of Bauchi town. He was discovered to have concealed over 1,200 cattle, was deposed as District Head by the Resident and handed over to the Emir for any additional punishment the Emir might want to inflict. The Resident himself could not inflict any further punishment on this Ardo or on the other "guilty ones because the Hardos and collectors [were] difficult people to deal with. They [were] easily frightened away, and if dealt with too severely they [could] make the collection of Jangali an impossibility."[15] From Zaria, Resident Arnett reported, in March 1906, that there had been "many cases of embezzlement by village headmen. In some cases they spent the proceeds [of the Kurdin Kasa] for the benefit of themselves and friends." Those of them who were arrested were sentenced to terms of imprisonment under the Revenue Proclamation 'but several others [escaped] capture."[16]

Similarly, in Sokoto in December 1906, the Sarkin Kebbi of Silame, Ahmadu Rufai, was discovered to have "instructed his hakimai and owners of rugas to conceal the number of their cattle" from the British.[17] The Acting Resident reported the Sarkin Kebbi to the Sultan, who summoned him into Sokoto where, according to the Resident, "it was proved to the Sarkin Musulmi's satisfaction that Ahmadu Rufai had undoubtedly instructed his subordinates to keep back certain information from the Assessment Officers." Now it so happened that it was this same Ahmadu Rufai that Burdon had held partly responsible for the Satiru uprising in February of the same year, on the ground that he had not declared to the British the existence of the village or the turbulent history of its people.[18] In February, he had been punished by the removal of the villages around Satiru from his district and their transfer to the District of Dange. Hence, this time the Resident "requested" the Sultan to depose Ahmadu Rufai, and the Sultan obliged. Ahmadu Rufai was deposed for "withholding his assistance and more or less obstructing progressive administration."[19]

Similarly, in March 1907, Resident Temple, during a tour of Jega in Gwandu Emirate "wished to make a reassessment of the town which appeared to [him] to be paying a very small tribute considering its size."[20] However, the Sarkin Jega, a man the British had appointed only in April 1906 after deposing the erstwhile Sarkin Jega for "disloyalty," together with "his principal men lied to the Resident persistently for about three hours. Finally they owned to 700 compounds as existing in the town. A careful counting of the town revealed 1,400 compounds."[21] As a result, Temple ordered the Sarki and his headmen to Birnin Kebbi, where the Emir of Gwandu had settled late in 1906. He "handed them over to the Emir to be dealt with", but could not demand their dismissal, probably because it was the British themselves that appointed the Sarkin Jega and the Resident was not sure how deposing him so soon would be interpreted by the local population. Hence, all that happened to the Sarki and his chiefs was that the Emir "thoroughly berated them and fined them in his court £5 a head."[22]

In June of the same year, Temple again had to depose another District Head in Sokoto, for refusal to cooperate in the assessment of the Kurdin Kasa.[23] This was the Sarkin Zamfara, Abdullahi, who lived in Sokoto town and controlled a number of villages around the town. At first Temple believed the Sarkin Zamfara was merely "unable to assist [him]." He blamed this inability on what he believed to be the Sarkin Zamfara's lack of "knowledge of his people or towns." However, it soon became clear to temple that the Sarkin Zamfara "not only evinced a lack of administrative capacity, but there was a distinctly no-ticeable lack of desire to assist."[24] What finally made Temple have him deposed by the Sultan was a refusal by the Sarkin Zamfara to obey promptly Temple's order that he should "recount separately the compounds etc of two villages which he had included in one in spite of having been several times corrected for this mistake." Impatient and perhaps looking for an excuse to remove the Sarkin Zamfara, Temple made the order extremely preemptory. Apart from resenting the preemptory manner in which the order was given and gener-ally being averse to helping with the assessment, the Sarkin Zamfara might have delayed action in order to avoid the loss of face, "the order having been given in the presence of several chiefs and their followers." But the fact that he gave the order in public made Temple also feel that if he let the chief get away with his disobedience, he too would lose face and his authority weakened; for indeed the Sarkin Zamfara's "lack of obedience was patent to everybody and commented on." Besides, *agents provocateurs* were not lacking to point out to Temple the consequences of not punishing the Sarkin Zamfara. One such was the *Majidadi* who was the Sultan's "principal messenger to the Resident." He "was much put out and represented to [the Resident] that if this kind of thing was allowed [the British] should not get on with the assessment very quickly."

Hence, in order to maintain the authority of the Resident and "show the chiefs that this [was] not the kind of thing [the British] wanted to occur or [intended] to allow," the Resident: "called in the Marafa [a close relative of the Sarkin Zamfara] and after consulting him, the Sarkin Musulmi and Waziri, [he] decided on their advice to recommend the Sarkin Musulmi to allow Abdullahi to retire into private life." Actually, he was appointed "Headman of a small town called Bunzalega", as a way of providing him with pension.

Six months later, Temple had to secure the dismissal of another District Head, the Ardo of Shuni, for refusal to cooperate in the assessment.[25] The Ardo's non-cooperation occurred during a visit by the Resident to Shuni for assessment purposes. The Ardo "not only gave [him] no assistance but had evidently told all people to withhold all information. [The Resident] had the greatest difficulty in obtaining guides: the Headmen of the villages would not appear and generally speaking every obstacle was put in [his] way." As well as getting the Sultan to dismiss the Ardo, Temple "had to convict and imprison several of the Village Heads." It was only after this whole-sale dismissal of its chiefs that "a large part of the Sullubewa country" was assessed and mapped.[26]

In fact, it can be claimed that most District and Village Heads were in the habit of at least concealing cattle and understating the population of their areas. That included those District Heads who were sufficiently good at dissimulating and seeming to be able to gain and retain British confidence. Foremost in this group of District Heads was the Marafan Gwadabawa, Muhammadu Maiturare. Evidence that he concealed cattle came to light in December 1907, but the British were so taken in by his posturing that to them this evidence proved the contrary of concealment, namely the transparent honesty of the Marafa. Thus, the Marafa, having observed the vigour with which Temple had tried in the previous year to uncover concealments, "voluntarily" "found and declared 25,000 head of cattle in his district as compared to 12,000 [the previous] year."[27] Unless the Marafa was largely ignorant of his district and its resources, a possibility which all accounts of him tend to believe, he could not have been ignorant of the existence of as many as 13,000 head of cattle. At any rate, he could not have been ignorant of them in 1906 only to discover them in 1907, as Temple naively believed. It would be safer to assume that the Marafa all along knew the size of the population of cattle in his district more or less exactly but, like the rest of the District Heads, saw no reason for declaring more than he absolutely had to declare. And this number varied with the vigour of the Resident and the growing intimacy of knowledge that the British had of the districts.

Another District Head who declared twice as many cattle in 1907, as he had declared in 1906, was the Sarkin Kebbi of Yabo. He "found 18,000 as compared with 9,000 [the previous] year."[28] Also, although the "discoveries" made by the Marafa and the Sarkin Kebbi were "the best [in the Sokoto Emirate], every District Headman, almost without exception [showed] an increase of cattle," that year.

In Kano as well, Temple encountered the same problem of passive non-cooperation from District Heads, complaining that:

> all the tax collectors the jakadas, village heads, sub-district heads and district heads ...[had] all without exception got into a groove of delaying their payments in the hope that by sheer force of inertia they [would] obtain a remission. They [had] been so successful [at this] in the past.

In the financial section of the Report, Temple reported "too large remissions ... applied for," a fact which Temple said necessitated "stringent measures."[29] He singled out two District Heads for special mention. These were the Turaki Manya, a brother of the Emir, and the Sarkin Dawaki Maituta. The Turaki Manya:

> made a complete hash of the Zakka and Jangali collection for 1908/09. Two months after he had been ordered to collect the haraji for 1908–1909, it was found that he had not only taken no pains to do so but had actually interfered with his sub-District Heads and prevented them from doing their work. He was therefore suspended by the Emir.[30]

The Sarkin Dawaki Maituta "also made a complete hash of the collection of the 1908–09 Jangali and Zakka, and the 1907–08 haraji ... He was therefore suspended."[31]

The Response of the Common People to the Imposition of the Kurdin Kasa and the Jangali

In his reports to the Colonial Office in London, Lugard claimed that the imposition of taxes by the British was welcomed by the people of the emirates especially because, he claimed, these two taxes were much preferred by the common people to "the unequal incidence and the arbitrary and tyrannical levies of the past."[32] This was an echo of the reports that were sent to him by his Residents from some of the provinces.[33] However, there is no evidence – in the Resident's reports concerning the attitude of the people towards both assessment and collections, to indicate that they welcomed the imposition of the two taxes. This is not to say that a mass and general uprising followed the imposition of these two taxes. In fact, judging from the lesson which the people had just learnt of the futility of actively resisting the British, it would be unrealistic to expect the people to resist the imposition of these taxes by military means and on a mass scale.

Yet, in spite of the absence of a mass and general uprising against the imposition of these taxes, the Provincial Reports, of which Lugard's Reports to London were summaries, do furnish evidence to show that Lugard's claim that the imposition of these two taxes met with popular approval, for any reason whatsoever, was false. The reports contain a lot of evidence that the Kurdin Kasa and Jangali were resisted in all the provinces by the common people, from the time of their imposition up to the end of the period covered in this book, and indeed beyond. This resistance was manifested in both active and passive forms, and met with corresponding responses from the British. Here, we shall put on record some of the evidence of this popular resistance to British taxation in both its active and passive forms, both for the sake of demonstrating the existence of such evidence and in order to provide a popular comparison and contrast to the attitudes adopted by the Emirs and District and Village Heads.

Among examples of popular active resistance to the imposition of the Kurdin Kasa and the Jangali was that of the village of Yoli Birni, in Gwandu Emirate, in November 1905.[34] According to Assistant Resident Ruxton, it was only in November 1905 that he heard that there was "a very large number of cattle around Yoli Birni."[35] Having learnt this, Ruxton sent "courier Audu accompanied by the Emir's messenger to find out to whom these herd belonged." The Emir's messenger was "a boy of Muhammadu Shafo the *Kofa* of Yoli and who [resided] there."[36] However, the Emir was the same Emir Muhammadun Aliyu, with whom Ruxton had generally disastrous relations, whom he elsewhere reported was doing everything to baulk him in his task of assessment, and whom he was to depose after the Satiru revolt. Ruxton seems to have assumed that because he, Ruxton, was ignorant first of the existence of "a very large number of cattle around Yoli" and then of their ownership, the Emir and Yoli's *Kofa* were similarly ignorant. But, on the contrary, we should assume that the Emir was in fact instrumental to the concealment of the cattle from Ruxton. In allowing his messenger to accompany the Resident's "courier", the Emir was probably trying to cover up his own involvement in the concealment.

However, whatever the role of the Emir in the concealment of the cattle, on the arrival of the messengers at Yoli Birni:

> the local Dikko and the cattle Fulanis collected, chased the courier out of the town, seized his property and told him the whiteman would be served in the same way if he came to look at their cattle. Audu's two boys were beaten as

was also the Emir's messenger. Later Mohammadu Shafo was driven out of the town and his house looted.[37]

Certainly, as a way of further implicating the Emir on the side of the British, Ruxton "left the punishment of Yoli to him." The "Emir had the herds or a part of them counted, imposed a fine of 70 heads of cattle and compensation to be made to the Courier." He collected the Jangali on the 800 heads of cattle counted, the Jangali being 49 heads of cattle, but characteristically indicated his unwillingness to collect the fine of 70 cattle and Ruxton considered it wise not to press the matter further.

Another and even more spectacular manifestation of the ordinary people's active hatred for the Kurdin Kasa is to be seen in the revolt staged by the people of Dawakin Tofa District in Kano Emirate in May 1908.[38] These disturbances, which started from about 10th May and lasted until 20th May, were endemic throughout the district but most intense around the villages of Danzabuwa, Dumbulum and Weri. The disturbances started specifically against a "new" system of assessment introduced in that year. But they later developed into a rejection of all forms of taxation and were directed against those village heads who had been very energetic in the collection of the Kurdin Kasa. During these disturbances the District Head, the Madakin Kano, as well as all his village heads, were "openly defied." Some villages, in Resident Cargill's own presence, refused "to allow their headmen to check their assessment and collect their taxes." The village head of Dumbulum was driven out of his town by its inhabitants, who were wielding clubs, bows and arrows.

The response of the British took the form of punishing any village that joined in the revolt while at the same time relenting on the question of the "new" assessment. Thus, on 10th May, Cargill dispatched mounted troops from Kano under Hamilton Browne and sent off a telegram to Acting Governor Wallace in Zungeru to tell him of the outbreak of the disturbances. To this telegram Wallace replied on 11th May to say that he had the previous week received a letter from the substantive Governor, Percy Girouard, in which he requested "that no undue pressure with regard to taxation be placed on the Kano Province."

In "compliance with Sir Percy's telegram" Cargill "cancelled the new assessment entirely and reverted to the customary taxes without any modification whatever." However, the people "as usual misinterpreted" this "concession as a sign of weakness" and showed "signs of an indication to refuse to pay any taxes at all." Cargill believed that "unless this disposition [was] promptly checked it [would] spread to other districts in Kano." Hence, he asked for a specific authority "to keep moving in the Madaki's district during the collection of this year's taxes in order to make arrests and use force when necessary." Meanwhile, Cargill took the responsibility of ordering a patrol out immediately to Danzabuwa, where the refusal to pay up was decidedly adamant. Wallace sanctioned the patrol asked for by Cargill, but regretted that "this trouble has arisen through new assessment measures as it is the Governor's wish to keep Kano quiet." He added that if the British had "to collect taxes at the point of bayonets our Revenue policy will have to be considerably modified or direct taxation will have to give place to indirect." Thus, if they had to, even the British could call a spade a spade. They imposed a direct taxation on the emirates, all the claim about helping emirs to collect their own taxes being sheer humbug. By this time, the people of Dumbulum had forced their chief out of the village, and to Cargill "all symptoms point to one of sporadic outbreaks of *talakawa* for which the western districts of Kano are notorious."

Playing up this spectra of more widespread disturbances and the attempt to divorce the disturbances from their rational causes, and blaming them on what he saw as the customary irrationality of the "western districts of Kano" were all calculated by Cargill to secure him a stronger backing from Wallace. He was by now no longer content to confine himself to suppressing revolts as they broke out into the open. Instead, he decided to provoke the people, to draw the "enemy out" as it were. He declared he was now "proceeding with a strong patrol to Dumbulum and (proposed) opening fire on villagers immediately if they [appeared] with bows and arrows in hand." By now he firmly believed "a few sharp lessons [were] needed," and he was willing to help manufacture the circumstances that would warrant the administration of such lessons. However, not quite sure about the strength of the reaction his proposed provocative conduct might elicit, he suggested to Wallace that the mounted troops then stationed at Sokoto be moved to Kano to re-enforce him. Wallace sanctioned his proposed conduct and also sent an immediate order to the commandant of the British troops in Sokoto to send his mounted troops to Kano forthwith.

Meanwhile, although Cargill did proceed to Dumbulum with a force of 75 mounted troops with a Maxim, the people refused to be provoked and he met "no opposition." He arrested the "principals" in the recent attack on the village chief. Next, Cargill moved on to Danzabuwa where he, again, met with no armed opposition. Here too, he "effected a large number of arrests" on 18th May. On the 19th Cargill "effected further arrests near Danzabuwa and Weri", and the latter arrests were those of what he claimed to be "a band of robbers who [had] been terrorizing people and instigating them to resist civil authority." This group might have been an incipient anti-colonial insurrection-ary group that had taken it upon itself to inspire the people of the area to an armed struggle against the British, and to punish all those who refused to stop cooperating with the British, including Village Heads. Cargill's reference to the group as a band of robbers was just an attempt to deny this possibility. That the group was the brain behind the revolts is suggested by the fact that soon after its arrest the rebellion subsided.

Yet, even with the cessation of the rebellion, Cargill was so shaken that he would not allow the reinforcements from Sokoto to be sent back. He wanted them to be stationed in Kano "as a precautionary measure." He returned to Kano on 21st May but left Hamilton Browne with 25 soldiers at Dawakin Tofa "to try prisoners and settle up the District." In fact, he advocated keeping the area patrolled until the people were more accustomed to "our milder methods of rule."

The role of the Emir of Kano in this rebellion, either on the side of the rebels or on the side of the British, is not at all mentioned. The conclusion one would draw from this complete lack of reference to the Emir in the British records is that the British, Cargill in particular, being on bad terms with him because of his general attitude towards the British, simply did not trust him enough to invoke his name to justify the measures they were taking against the villagers. They must have felt that the most they could hope for from him was his neutrality. So long as they had no direct evidence that he was on the side of the rebellious villagers, the British must have reasoned, Abbas was best ignored.

However, while their refusal to invite his cooperation or invoke his name is understandable in the light of his generally "non-possumus attitude" towards the British, the fact that they did not assume his connivance with the rebels, needs further speculation. In this regard, we can assume that after their recent drastic measures against the Emirs of Gwandu, Hadeija and Katsina, they felt that unless an Emir openly and unmistakably sided with rebels, they should assume that no connivance existed. On the other hand, because he had been a living witness to the fate of the three Emirs mentioned above, the Emir might have absolutely refused to give the British any ground for suspecting him of conniving with the Dawakin Tofa rebels. It might also be that Cargill's claim that Dawakin Tofa and the neighbouring districts had been accustomed to re-volting against the Emirs of Kano – even before the advent of the British, was true. In that case, the Emir might have seen no wisdom whatever in abetting rebellion in that area. Hence, he refrained from abetting this rebellion, and made sure the British realized this, without at the same time going out of his way actively to side with the British. For whatever reason, Emir Abbas – apparently – did not figure in the episode on one side or on the other.

The Dawakin Tofa uprising had another significance apart from helping to reveal British methods and tactics against people in revolt against their policies. It also showed how completely the British could ignore an Emir if they either felt they did not need him or felt they could not trust him. This additional significance lies in the fact that it took place in a highly Islamised Emirate, an emirate that is one of those whose people are erroneously associated with docile obedience to "authority", whoever may be exercising it and however it is exercised. If any event is capable of suggesting a re-examination of this assumption, the Dawakin Tofa tax revolt of 1908 is such an event, though by no means the only one.

Another resistance to British taxation, though apparently on a small scale, is the one reported in June 1909 by Assistant Resident Malcolm from Buzai, a village in Gwadabawa District of Sokoto Emirate.[39] According to Malcolm, the people of this village, inspired by some of their own number, absolutely refused to pay the Kurdin Kasa until he arrested the instigators, took them to Sokoto and sentenced them to £10 fine and six months imprisonment each. In view of the claim that "these people have given trouble each year over the payment of General Tax," it ought to be assumed that the "trouble" in June 1909 was a particularly serious one, though he does not say how serious a 'trouble' it was or how many troops he had to use in arresting the instigators, and whether there were casualties either on the Buzai side or on his own. Nor does he mention any assistance given to him by either the Sultan or the Marafan Gwadabawa.

A major revolt against the Kurdin Kasa involving bloodshed took place in the Emirate of Adamawa in December 1909.[40] It was staged by the Verre people to the west of Yola. Up to this time the Verre, like most of the other "pagan" tribes in the Province, virtually decided themselves what they were going to pay. But in 1909, when the people of one of the Verre villages, that of Guriga, met to decide what they were going to pay, one of them was alleged to have pointed out that the previous year, 1908, the neighbouring village, Kura, had refused to pay anything, and "nothing happened." They resolved, therefore, not to pay anything. This was, in fact, a challenge to the authority of the Emir, who had sent three messengers to collect the Kurdin Kasa. This was the only way taxes could be collected from the Verre, who "refused to recognize the Resident's authority and had always maintained a defiant attitude towards the Europeans" in spite of the fact that since the British occupation, the Verre had "been visited by a patrol on three occasions."[41]

To emphasize that they were now against even the authority of the Emir, the people of Guriga gave his messengers three days to leave, and at the end of that period executed them. After killing the three messengers, the villagers went round the neighbouring villages trying to garner support, in readiness to meet the British expedition that they knew was going to come. Some of the other villages like Marashi, Marufa and Shambi did join the people of Guriga, but some others refused to join them and fighting broke out between the opposing sides.

It was under these circumstances that Captain Boyle arrived with a company of soldiers from Yola. The arrival of the troops changed the situation, and forged a unity among the Verre. Accordingly, "the patrol was met by armed resistance and defiance" from every village it went to, and it responded in a manner fitting the violent reputation of British troops. It stayed in the area for eleven days, visiting the villages one by one, fighting off the villagers and destroying the villages. Among the villages destroyed were Deledi, Gejipa, Marufa, Guriga, Bati, Numki, Marashi and Shambi. How many people were killed among the local population is not stated, in all probability because the figure was too high. The British themselves suffered three soldiers seriously wounded.

Still in Adamawa Emirate in February 1911, "a section of the Chamba tribe refused to submit to assessment" and the Governor sanctioned a patrol against them.[42] This patrol consisted of 50 rank and file and two British officers. During the patrol, heavy fighting took place at Tibak, where "a sharp lesson had to be administered." The number of dead on the Tibak side was twenty, according to the report, but it could be heavier. The British themselves, whose casualties were usually one for a hundred "natives," suffered a casualty of one private killed and another severely wounded. Apart from whatever casualty in dead and wounded the people of Tibak might have suffered, their town was emptied of guinea corn, sheep and goats and then burnt down. Because of the manner in which Tibak was crushed, "the whole (Chamba) tribe came in, and the patrol also had a salutary effect on other tribes who were wavering."[43]

Yet again in the Emirate of Adamawa in January 1912, the Districts of Lala and Kilba "defied the District Heads' authority, openly stating their refusal to pay tax."[44] To get the Kurdin Kasa collected, "a military patrol had to visit the Districts." It spent twenty-two days forcibly collecting the tax. In the process, a number of villages were burnt down and many undisclosed number of people killed. Even so, not the full amount of Kurdin Kasa estimated from Lala could be collected, although in the Kilba District, the "tax was paid in full, with the exception of £2:5:0d due from two villages, Gungun and Lar, who deserted their villages and removed everything." The British laid part of the blame on the District Head, Hamman Bello, a son of ex-Emir Muhammadu Iya (1909–1910). He was blamed, not for harshness or lack of tact, but for being "utterly incapable." Resident W.S. Sharpe got the Emir to recall him and sent another man who was assumed to be "a much more capable man." Two months later, in March, three other "tribes" in the area, the Hona, the Marghi and the Bura revolted and refused to pay the Kurdin Kasa.[45] In fact, the Bura beat up their Fulani District Head and killed the policeman and three Bura Village Heads who were accompanying the District Head. The Marghi were for their part said to be generally hostile to their District Head, refusing to pay anything, and in one village, Kopri, "the village Head attacked him." A military patrol was sent against all three, but the report of what the patrol did could not be traced out.

In November 1912, in the Emirate of Abuja a number of villages in Pai District revolted against the Kurdin Kasa and started to punish all those villages which refused to join them.[46] Among the revolting villages were Killankwa, Kabbi and Chikuka. In this case the British sent out a patrol from Minna. This patrol occupied Killankwa on 21st November, "after a determined resistance at the foot of the hill. The wall [of the town] was defended under severe fire for more than 15 minutes." Between thirty and forty of the villagers were killed before the villagers fled, but up to the time the patrol left the town, the people never returned to pay their taxes. Instead, the British took away whatever the town contained before burning it down. On 24th November the patrol occupied Chikuka while it was in the middle of rebuilding its town wall, which had been in a state of disrepair ever since the British occupation. Here too, the town was emptied of all food and goats in lieu of the Kurdin Kasa and was burnt down as a punishment. Kabbi was visited on 30th November, but it was found to have been deserted by the inhabitants, who had also removed all their crops. So the patrol could not do more than burn it down.

In this revolt, the local chiefs, including the chief of Pai, were clearly on the side of the British. In fact, by the time the revolt broke out, these chiefs had become thoroughly unpopular with their people. Their own forcible ouster by the villagers was the signal of the revolt. But there is no evidence in the British records that the Emir of Abuja either sided with the British or was an instigator of the revolt. For all the British knew he simply did not exist as far as this revolt was concerned. Nor should this be surprising, the Emir being Muhammadu Gani, whom the British regarded as absolutely useless to them. The fact that he was not accused of complicity with the revolting villages might be either because he was able to conceal his involvement very well or because, after assessing the forces involved in the situation, he decided to have nothing to do with the rebels. What can be stated about him with any degree of certainty is that the Kurdin Kasa was not popular with him and, apart from "personally paying for an odd hundred satellites,"[47] he gave no further assistance to the British either in the assessment or in the collection of this tax, anywhere in his emirate.

At about the same time, another revolt was taking place in Adamawa Emirate. This was by the Yungur who, in December 1912, arrested their Hausa District Head, Magajin Pirambe, and executed his interpreter.[48] The Yungur took these steps against the District Head because "he had seized their cattle" as payment of arrears of Kurdin Kasa" due "from them in connection with the 1911 season for which they paid only £230 out of an assessment of £580." On the inevitable arrival of a British patrol, the villagers of Kento and Kuti, who had executed the interpreter, refused to come into Primbe though they released the Magaji. So the patrol, which was accompanied by Assistant Resident Ryan, "proceeded there and after collecting the tax burnt the village."[49] In the process of "collecting" the tax and burning the two villages "a slight opposition" was met with and the villagers "lost 10 killed." Next, the patrol "visited all the other villages. In most cases the inhabitants took to the surrounding rocks." But Ryan "confiscated enough of their cattle to make a fair tax."[50]

Again, in February 1914, sections of the Verre in Adamawa once more refused to pay the Kurdin Kasa.[51] The inhabitants of two towns were particularly determined, barring the District Head, Eli Jakada, a Darfuri Arab, from entering their towns for the purpose of collecting the tax. These were Kura and Boi; and this time Resident Sharpe took "prompt" action, personally taking a patrol to the District. "After waiting for over a week [at Gogra, the District Headquarters] sending messages almost daily Kura still remained defiant." Hence, the Resident and his troops "visited the town and removed what supplies were necessary in lieu of tax, destroying houses as a punishment."[52]

A very good example of active resistance to British taxation, of British response, and of the rather ambivalent position of the Emirs, is also provided by events in Borno in the period 1902 to 1914. Thus, as we saw above, soon after their arrival the British disarmed Shehu Abubakar Garbai and forbade him from allowing his subordinates to collect taxes by force. Feeling that this order was not being obeyed, the British undertook to do the collecting for him and towards this end, Resident Hewby sent Assistant Resident Cochrane with some troops on a very extended "tour" of the northern parts of the Sheikhdom. This was in November 1902 and prior to the formal introduction of British taxation. The first thing to strike Captain Cochrane was the people's loathing both for taxes and for the British themselves. He sent back to Hewby, stating that he and his troops were attacked and robbed in northern Mava by a party of Tubu coming from "French" territory, and that the people of the District had refused to pay their taxes to him because they believed that after him no European would return to Mava.[53] So uncooperative were the people of Mava that Cochrane lost his composure and sense of balance, and resorted to extreme measures in order to collect the taxes. Thus, he attacked a nomadic Fulbe tribe, seized 2,000 of their sheep as "tax", and in the process, killed the head of the tribe, Ardo Chiroma.[54] Next, he went to a village called Kabi and captured all the stock he found there and burnt down some houses and farms as a punishment for the people's refusal to pay voluntarily.[55]

At the same time, another Assistant Resident, Captain Mundy, was undertaking a similar "tour" in the southern parts of the Sheikhdom and collecting taxes in a similar fashion from villages and tribes who were unwilling to pay voluntarily. In one village, Degdegna, after collecting all the corn and stock he found in it, he burnt it down, dispersed the people and exiled its Bulama to Kukawa for his refusal to help him collect the taxes and for allegedly hiding a gang of "thieves."[56]

The reports sent back by Cochrane and Mundy led Hewby to conclude that " in Bornu [too] there was that same feeling met with on the Benue that the advent of the whiteman means no more taxes or tribute, i.e. a total disorganization of the country."[57] Noting that "in the meantime we [have] disarmed the native authorities and forbidden them to take forcible measures," he urged Lugard that the British should be prepared to "back them up by occasional drastic steps."[58]

Yet, these "drastic steps", some of which we just recounted, far from inducing submissiveness in the Borno population, aroused some sections of it to such a level of resistance that the British were reduced to almost complete military impotence vis-à-vis even individual villages. Thus, for example, in September 1904, Assistant Resident Gall, the political officer attached to the British garrison at Gaidam, sent to tell Hewby that he was experiencing "great difficulty" in collecting "outstanding" tribute from villages on the "French border," adding that villages only a day's journey away from the garrison were in open revolt.[59] He cited as an example Zajibiriri, a Manga town of about 2,000 people just 10 miles to the north of Gaidam. This village had returned a letter he had sent to them without even having opened it and expelled his subsequent messengers. Hewby ordered Gall to proceed against this village, exact the tribute, and arrest Kaigama Musa, the Village Head. But Gall, who had 10 soldiers and

40 armed policemen, admitted that the forces at his disposal were not enough to undertake the expedition and at the same time avoid a "disaster," which was a euphemism used by Lugard and his men for defeat in the hands of the local population. The matter was left there until November when, Kaigama Musa, perhaps on the orders of the Shehu, went to Gaidam to surrender and was sentenced to five years in exile at Kukawa.[60]

Meanwhile Hewby, who had gone out of his way to detach the Shuwa Arabs from the authority of the Shehu, was having trouble with them over the payment of the Jangali. Thus, in January 1903, he complained to Lugard that the Shuwa were not reciprocating his "sympathy" for them.[61] They were, he said, "a difficult lot to deal with satisfactorily ... They [were] largely a dangerous vagabond lot, lawless, paying no grazing due and determined to avoid taxation."

In fact, the British admitted that the Shuwa had not been used to paying the Jangali in the nineteenth century. Thus, according to a research conducted by Lethem, the Jangali had been exacted from the Shuwa only on three occasions in the nineteenth century. These were in 1865, 1894 and 1895.[62] Hence, the Shuwa came to see the 3% Jangali imposed by the British, not as a light tax, which Hewby thought it was, but as a heavy and unusual imposition. When they felt their Chima Jilibe, Lawan Adam, was being over-enthusiastic in his collection of this Jangali, they ambushed and killed him on the border between "British" and "German" Borno in June 1906. In reprisal for this "murder" Hewby characteristically fined the Asala Shuwa, in whose area the killing took place, 500 head of cattle and deported four of their Sheikhs from the area.[63]

From this point onwards the British in Borno adopted a predetermined attitude towards the Shuwa. They became incapable of appreciating the reconciliatory and cooperative attitude adopted by the Shuwa from 1907. From this year, the Shuwa started to pay the Jangali rather promptly, in spite of the fact that the number of cattle for which they were assessed increased enormously with every passing year. Thus, for example, in 1905 all the Shuwa in Borno paid Jangali on only 5,000 heads of cattle, but, in 1907 the Qualmi Shuwa alone paid Jangali on 20,000 heads of cattle and 30,000 goats and sheep while, in 1911, the Shuwa paid a tax of "exactly 300% more than they paid in 1906."[64] Of course, these increases by leaps and bounds in the population of the stock of the Shuwa were an indication of the degree to which they were able to conceal their property from the British, especially in the earliest days of British colonial domination in Borno. Nonetheless, the fact that by their own admission, the British had little difficulty in collecting the Jangali on these enormous herds is proof enough that, by 1907, the Shuwa had decided to put up with the hated Jangali.

Yet, in 1913, Hewby and his staff decided to take an extraordinary measure against them. This was the so-called Shuwa Patrol.[65] The reasons they gave for undertaking this "patrol" were:

a)   The Shuwa had been truculent and had evaded the payment of taxes in previous years;

b)   They had refused to stop burning grass;

c)   They had ignored the Game Preservation Law that made grass burning a crime and

d)   A good many criminals in Borno were Shuwa.[66]

Our concern in this chapter being the reaction of the population to the imposition of British taxation, we shall not discuss the truth or falsehood of the other charges, their relevance belonging elsewhere. We have refuted the charge about the evasion of taxation. What remains is to examine the activities of the Shuwa patrol, the attitude of the Shehu towards it, and how its consequences recoiled on Hewby and his staff.

The patrol was undertaken by Captain Secombe, Assistant Resident in charge of tax assessment. He was assisted by Abba Mallam, then Ajia of Monguno, a staff of sixty mallams and a company of soldiers.[67] Abba Mallam, though a great-grandson of Ahmed Gonimi, clearly owed his position as Ajia not to the Shehu, to whom he was known to be disrespectful, but to Hewby, whom he had served as political agent between 1903 and 1906.[68] It was to Abba Mallam that Captain Secombe largely left the operation, though the instructions he gave him were clear.[69] In brief, Secombe's instructions were for Abba Mallam to gather all the Shuwa and their cattle in a certain area, a few square miles in size, get the cattle into previously constructed *guros,* and count them for the purpose of taxation. He was to confiscate all the cattle of any Shuwa who failed to be within that area by a certain date. As for those who complied and drove their cattle into the area, he was to check the number of cattle that each man actually had against the number for which he had paid Jangali in 1912. Where there was a positive discrepancy between the two numbers, Abba Mallam was to confiscate the extra cattle and make the man pay Jangali on the rest.

To facilitate the execution of the "patrol," the Shuwa Arabs were removed from the jurisdiction of the District Heads in whose districts they were scattered and were placed under Abba Mallam for all purposes. It was not surprising that most of the Shuwa fled into "German" territory. All the same, Abba Mallam was able to confiscate 2,174 cattle, 6,125 sheep, 90 donkeys, and 78 horses, and collected a larger Jangali than had been collected in the previous year when the Shuwa population was larger.[70]

To secure for the "patrol" the consent of Lugard, Acting Resident Thompson had written that Shehu Abubakar Garbai was in favour of it. Yet, when Palmer was sent to investigate the truth about the patrol, he found that the Shehu thought it was a "mistake", and had taken no part in it both because he did not approve of it and because nobody asked him and his Ajias, with the exception of Abba Mallam, to give assistance. However, he did redeem some of the cattle confiscated.[71] It would seem that the truth about the role of the Shehu in the patrol was that like almost everything else that was done in the name of the Emirs in those days, the idea for undertaking it did not originate from the Emir. While it was probable that Hewby or Thompson did tell him of their intention to undertake it, and that knowing that his opinion carried little weight with them, he might have perfunctorily replied that it would be a good idea. During the actual undertaking the British, as in most other things, ignored him, and his real judgment about it being that it was uncalled for, he was only too glad to be ignored and did not try to force himself into it.

At the end of the operation, he performed his duty of converting all tax proceeds in kind into British currency.[72] When Palmer was sent to find out what actually happened and he was questioned, the Shehu told him what he knew Palmer wanted to hear, which also happened to coincide with his own real feeling about the "patrol." Thus, the Shehu found a contradiction between his real feelings about the patrol and what the Resident wanted to hear. This was before the patrol. After the patrol, noticing that the reaction of Headquarters coincided with his real feelings, he spoke up his mind. Hence, while his conduct was not that of a morally brave man, he was able to salvage part of his soul as it were and at the same time keep his position intact. In fact, one of the consequences of Palmer's investigation into the nature of the patrol was to enhance the position of the Shehu and give him a status that the Provincial Administration had denied him up to 1914.[73]

Passive Resistance

As stated earlier on, active resistance was not the only method communities in the emirates adopted for resisting British taxation. In fact, it was not even the most widespread method, because of the obvious risks that it involved. Far more widely and more frequently used was passive resistance, in its many forms. Many instances of passive resistance did come to the notice of the

British and were recorded, but we ought to assume that many more instances escaped their notice and were never recorded.

The most prevalent form of passive resistance to the Kurdin Kasa and the Jangali was migration, especially where the timing of the collection of taxes within two neighbouring provinces did not coincide. In such cases, all the people living on the two sides of the boundary moved to one side of it or the other, depending on which side taxes were being collected at a given time.[74] In some cases, the migration took the migrants much further afield and clearly included the aim of never returning. In the case of cattle owners, the most frequently used method of avoiding the Jangali was hiding most of the cattle in the bush, leaving only a few on their settlement before the arrival of the assessment officials. Yet, other people avoided paying their taxes simply by refusing to be hurried "whatever pressure [might] be put upon them."[75] In this way, collecting seasons ran into one another. Thus, the British were often obliged to remit an earlier season's amount. However, such apparent procrastination on the part of the people was often due to a genuine inability to pay the amount required from them, especially during years when crops did not do very well. Some people have to sell as much as a half of their harvest before they could meet the amount for which they were assessed.

An example of passive resistance to the Kurdin Kasa, and very interesting because of the subtlety of the method used by the people involved, was reported by Assistant Resident Goodair from Gombe in November 1904.[76] Thus, according to him, "the pagans of Bojudi [were] assessed at four hundred bags [£200] per year." Yet, when they "brought the 'equivalent' of this, it actually consisted of five emaciated horses and colts valued £5, and some cloth value £3:5:0, total value £8:5:0." This, the "pagans assured me was worth 200 bags." It was indicative of the relationships between the emirates and their non-Muslim subjects in the nineteenth century that the Emir of Gombe, who was very much beholden to the British, assured Goodair that "this was what they usually paid [in pre-British days] and though he knew the real, still to save trouble he had always accepted it at the fictitious value which they chose to put on it." However, Goodair saw no necessity to allow the "pagans" to dictate the value of the objects they brought in liquidation of "dues" imposed by the British. Hence, he "bluntly" told the people that "any tax brought in would be accepted for just as much as its sale in open market would effect and for no more." Thus, this incident, reported by the British themselves, not only proves the existence of passive resistance to the Kurdin Kasa but reveals a contrast between their system of government and the pre-existing emirate system, to the disadvantage of their own system.

Similarly, in March 1906, Resident Howard reported that: "the town of Pamguru [in Bauchi Emirate] was assessed 100 bags of cowries which was more than it was able to pay, the result of this being that half of the town left and the remainder paid nearly 12/- a hut."[77] This time, however, the British were somewhat willing to understand the situation. Howard then went on to suggest that "the system of assessments in Bauchi was too irregular ..." So much did the people in Bauchi try to avoid taxation that during a journey from Bauchi to Gombe at the end of 1906, Resident Howard: "found three of the towns on the road absolutely deserted and the tendency among the remaining towns to follow this example the result being that for the first two days march ... no food was obtainable."[78] Howard had to leave two of the Emir of Bauchi's officials travelling with him, the Wambai and the Madaki, behind to collect the people, reassure them, and encourage them not to flee before visiting British officials. However, the practice became so frequent on both the Bauchi to Gombe and Bauchi to Zaria roads that Howard made provision for foodstuff to be bought and stocked at various points along these two roads, in order to save travelling British officials from starving.[79]

Another concrete example of passive resistance to British taxation is the case reported from Kontagora in October 1906 — that a whole village, "Waamu, deserted in the hope that they could evade tribute."[80] However, they merely settled in Wushishi territory and all that the Resident did was to alert the Assistant Resident at Wushishi of their presence in his area of jurisdiction. When they realized that the only choice they had lay between paying the Kurdin Kasa in Wushishi and paying it in Kontagora, "they promptly returned [to Kontagora territory] and came into Kontagora [town] where they were warned against non-payment in the future."[81]

The Resident also complained that owing to a lack of sufficient police under him with which to lend Village Heads support in "many villages off the main road the Head-men have the greatest difficulty in getting in the tribute and all along the Niger the islanders and riverain villagers refused to obey orders and defy police going there in couples."[82] This admission, apart from indicating widespread resistance to taxation in Kontagora, also helps to define the boundary between "passive" and "violent" resistance. Judging from this passage, it was the attitude of the British that helped to transform a passive resistance into an active one.

Still in 1906, Assistant Resident Stanley in Gwandu reported the embarrassing situation in which the District Head of Tambawal found himself as a result of the zeal with which he collected the Kurdin Kasa and the Jangali in his district. According to Stanley, it appears that in 1904 and 1905 the Sarkin

Tambawal had collected the percentage laid down for the Jangali in full "while other chiefs were not so pressing or inclined to help the Administration."[83] Consequently, in 1906, the nomadic Fulbe and other herd owners "kept out of the Tambawal District and paid through other chiefs." As a result, "the Sarkin Tambawal lost a large percentage of his income."[84]

In Adamawa, Resident Sharpe, in December 1909, saw "the chief disadvantage of the proximity of the German border" to be in "the continual threat that if the District chiefs press for the full payment of tribute, the villagers will migrate to German territory."[85] In fact much of British officials' time in 1909 was taken up "listening to continual application [from chiefs] for reduction of tribute, owing to the continual migration since the last assessment."[86] Besides people migrating expressly to escape payment of the British taxes, Resident Sharpe was struck by the "increased desire [of people in Adamawa] to make its pilgrimage to Mecca."[87] This was in sharp contrast to the fact that in 1901, the British found that in the whole of Yola Province only one man, the Alkali Hamman Joda, had performed the pilgrimage.[88] Hence, Resident Sharpe himself did not infer from the "increased desire" to go to Mecca on the part of the people of the province that they were partly motivated by a desire to escape British taxation. But one cannot help feeling that such a desire must at least have contributed to the increased inclination to undertake the journey. This inference is valid if we take into consideration the fact that it was reported in another report by Sharpe that many of those who left for Mecca in fact ended up settling at Marwa.[89] This was the last major town to support Lamido Zubairu in his opposition to European occupation of his emirate and which, in fact, remained a centre for those who refused to reconcile themselves to the European occupation of the Sokoto Caliphate, and as such was treated by the Germans with a mixture of caution, deference and hostility.[90]

Similarly, in 1910, the Resident Yola found it necessary to complain rather bitterly that there was little immigration from "German" Adamawa into "British" Adamawa, but there was a good deal of "emigration" into the German portion.[91] According to him:

the Yola Fulani is very fond of using the easy excuse of crossing the Kameroun frontier as a threat against being called upon to pay tribute in a higher assessment, or to escape punishment for offences. He will also move across the border to avoid too close proximity to a newly established station under a Political Officer, and to escape having to submit to reforms or a closer supervision than hitherto. This adds considerably to the difficulty of administering the Districts on the Frontier.[92]

In fact, the constant complaining by Residents of Adamawa about emigration prompted the Governor to demand a full investigation into its causes. This investigation was carried out by Resident Webster and its findings were submitted in June 1911.[93] According to Webster, even before British occupation of Adamawa, there had been "a steady eastward movement of the Fulani to the richer lands round Garwa and Ngaundere." Yet this trend, he admitted, was increased by British policies. The first among these was British taxation for, until 1910 no Kurdin Kasa was paid in German Adamawa, the Germans collecting only the Jangali. It was only in 1910 that the Germans collected an additional levy of two marks per household.[94]

Second, Webster states that, in comparison to German methods, the British method of administration was too direct. According to him, the Germans did "not go into detail as we do. So long as a District Chief stops slave raids and highway robbery he is left to his own devices." Thus, possibly without realizing it, Webster was admitting that the ordinary people preferred to live under their chiefs to living under conditions in which the Europeans, both British and German, took a direct part in assessment and collection of taxes and the administration of justice. The significance of this tacit admission lies, first in the fact that it tends to suggest that the chiefs were much less thorough in their assessments of people's wealth and less pressing in demanding payment, virtually leaving each individual to decide what he was to pay. Second, the admission stands in contrast to the conscious and express claims often made by British officials, and all too faithfully echoed by some writers, that the ordinary people welcomed British taxation because it was lighter, simpler, more rational and more humanely collected than had been the system of taxation prior to their occupation of the Sokoto Caliphate.

After giving further reasons for the rampancy of emigration from "British" Adamawa that neither sound plausible nor are quite relevant here, Webster concluded on a pessimistic note that "unless conditions alter therefore we must expect the wealthier Fulani to continue to migrate in considerable number." He completely overlooked the fact that it was up to the British themselves to "alter conditions" by being less exacting in their tax assessment and collection, and by interfering less directly with the ordinary people, the strength of whose feelings against them the British consistently refused to understand or accept as real and rational. Far from adjusting to the demands of the situation in Adamawa, the British in fact withdrew into self righteousness. Thus, Resident Sharpe, in his 1911 Annual Report, after reporting that emigration into German Adamawa was still going on, explained the phenomenon as follows:

(a) Lighter taxation in the Kamerouns

(b) The fact that their system of administration is not nearly so strict, and if I may say so, not so high principled as ours..."[95]

Thus, the blame was conveniently shifted away from British political incapacity to adjust to a situation in which they were only one factor out of several, to the supposed moral incapacity of the local population to measure up to the much vaunted high moral principles of the British.

However, when, in 1912, in the Zumo District there was "an exodus from three villages into German territory," Sharpe was forced to advise that "the District needed reassessing to make the incidence of the Kurdin Kasa lighter and so hopefully stem the exodus."[96] This suggestion that shows that the British were at last revising their "high [moral] principles" in the light of reality and that the local population, in this case without resorting to violence, was forcing the British to consider that they could be wrong.

Conclusion

We have established in this chapter that, British claims to the contrary notwithstanding, the imposition of British taxation was not welcome by the common people of the emirates. They had absolutely no cause to welcome that imposition. In spite of the absence of an immediate large scale, coordinated and sustained mass uprising against that imposition, British taxation was in fact resisted by the peasantry both through frontal and violent means and by subtler, more devious methods, not just in the first few years following the imposition, but throughout the period under study. Although as the years passed by and British military superiority over the peasants was repeatedly demonstrated, the indirect methods became the preferred methods of resistance. We have also seen that the Emirs were caught up in a contradiction that more or less immobilized them. Sharing a community of interests with the British up to a point, and being nagged by the requirement that they should not side with non-Muslims against Muslims, the Emirs tended not to figure on one side or the other in the open struggle between the peasantry and the British. Similarly, we have seen that District and Village Heads, who were openly and directly employed by the British for collecting the Kurdin Kasa and the Jangali, included quite a number of individuals who found such an employment so unsuited to their interests that they failed to conceal their unwillingness to cooperate and had to be dismissed. Yet others tried to line their own pockets at the expense of both the British and the peasantry, and were often enough caught out by the British or exposed by the peasantry and suffered dismissal as a consequence.

9

Disbursement of Revenues

Introduction

One of the most salient issues in British colonial taxation that we will consider in this chapter is the extent and magnitude of the wealth extorted as tax from the people. Our aim is to disprove the claim by the British that the emirates did not yield enough revenue for their administration. Our argument against this assertion will be made by referring to records on the amount of revenue realized in Yola and Zaria Provinces, even if the available figures contain some missing gaps. The relevant figures that we shall be concerned with are those for Caravan Tolls, Kurdin Kasa, Canoe Tax, Jangali, Customs Duty, Court Fees and Fines, Hawker's Licence, Games Licence and Native Liquor Licence. With regard to the allocation of collected revenues, we shall find out whether the officially approved formula for allocation was adhered to in practice; and if not, we intend to find out the excuses used by the British in misappropriating a preponderant share of the native revenue. In addition, we would try to ascertain whether such revenues were expended on projects that were of benefit to the welfare of the people or not. Furthermore, the chapter intends to critically examine how emirs, District Heads and Village Heads spent their share of native revenue, and how the British actually spent their appropriated share of tax proceeds.

Thereafter, we shall provide an outline of the establishment of Native Treasuries in the emirates and examine the vital question of who actually controlled them. This is important because of the claim by proponents of Indirect Rule that the emirs were fully in charge of their treasuries. We will argue that, on the contrary, the British were fully in control. We shall substantiate our argument by showing the nature and degree of such control. While doing so, our task will be to try to determine whether the British control was limited or extensive, whether it extended even to the preparation of budget estimates and the administration of day-to-day expenditure, and whether Native Authority funds were appropriated for the execution of British projects. If, as it appears, the British used the Native Treasurers to control the Native Treasuries, it will be interesting for us to examine how the emirs responded to their exclusion from the control of the Native Treasury. It is equally significant to examine the nature of public expenditure; and here, we shall argue that the bulk of the funds were used for the payment of salaries of personnel engaged in the maintenance of law and order, necessary for sustaining British imperial hegemony, while the sum allocated to education and public welfare was extremely paltry. We hope to back up our argument on this issue with tabulated figures for Kano, Katsina and Sokoto emirates. Yet, huge cash surpluses were declared based on the statistical returns of a majority of the emirates. It is, therefore, paramount for us to find out whether the surpluses were invested within the emirates or taken abroad for the benefit of the British metropolitan economy.

The Proceeds of the Taxes

In Tables 9.1 and 9.2 below, we have tried to give an indication of the amounts collected for the various taxes in the emirates in the first decade of British rule, both for the purpose of indicating the magnitude of the wealth they directly and openly extracted from the people and to show that the often-repeated British charge that the emirates did not yield enough revenue for the administration was false.[1] For this purpose, we have reproduced the figures of the revenues the British Administration derived from the Yola and Zaria Provinces in the period up to 1913. The choice of Yola and Zaria has been on account of the fact that the figures for these provinces are the most complete of all the sets available. Of necessity even these figures are somewhat fragmentary, owing to the loss of some of the monthly reports, while others give incomplete figures. Hence, the picture of the amounts collected is patchy. But, however patchy the picture may be, it should be sufficiently clear to serve the purposes for which this section has been written.

Among the interesting and pertinent facts that these figures reveal is that up to 1907 the Caravan Tolls, in addition to serving to help depress local industry and trade, were in fact the single most important means which the British had of taxing the native population. On monthly and yearly bases, the revenue of the government derived from the emirates' population often increased by up to 80%.

Table 9.1. British Share of Taxes from Yola Emirate by Years

Year	Total Receipts in £	Kurdin Kasa & Jangali in £	Caravan Tolls in £
April 1903–March 1904	1620:18:3½	287:0:0	908:11:10
April–December 1904	1294:6:0	18:7:4	569:14:6
April 1905–March 1906	2840:0:0	1939:0:0	?
April 1906–March 1907	3872:0:0	2250:0:0	1562:0:0
April 1907–March 1908	2723:18:11	2172:11:3	Nil
April 1908–March 1909	3608:19:2	2717:1:0	Nil
January–Sept. 1910	4686:3:4	1449:3:5	Nil
April 1910–March 1911	5697:12:11	4884:15:7	Nil
January–Dec. 1911	7026:1:11	6254:6:8	Nil
April 1911–March 1912	?	8028:2:0	Nil

*(Culled from the various Provincial Reports on the period). These totals include the revenues derived from all the various British taxes. Apart from Kurdin Kasa, Jangali (in the records lumped together with British share of zakka as "tribute") and Caravan Tolls, the other sources were Canoe Tax, Customs, court fines and fees, Hawker's Licence, Game Licence, Property looted during pacification of villages or confiscated from deposed Emirs and chiefs, and Native Liquor Licences.

Table 9.2. Zaria Emirate, Revenue for Ten Years, 1904–1913*

Year	Total	Kurdin Kasa	Jangali
1904/5	?	£532:5:3	-
1905/6	?	£1,085:6:3	-
1906/7	?	£5,112:10:7	-
1907/8	£9,456:13:10	£6,450:1:1	£3,006:9:9
1908/9	£10,235:13:0	£7,493:5:6	£2,742:7:6
1909/10	£12,040:14:9	£8,872:14:9	£3,168:0:0
1910/11	£15,405:18:8	£13,504:3:2	£1,901:15:6
1911/12	£36,785:12:11	£15,717:10:11	£21,068:2:0

*J.M. Fremantle, "Zaria Provincial Annual Report for 1913," SNP 10 No.107P/1914, NAK. It is not stated whether these totals represent all revenues collected in the emirate or just the Native Administration's share, but there is little doubt, judging from the fact that in 1910–11 Katsina Native Authority's share of revenue was £35,547:13:0, that these figures excluded the shares of the British Administration.

It should also be pointed out that revenues actually realized were often fantastically larger than the estimates made by the Residents, especially in the case of the Jangali, whose yields kept on rising by leaps and bounds throughout the period considered in this chapter. It was a phenomenon which is at least partially able to hide the true population of the cattle, sheep, etc. of their areas from the British.

The figures also show that the abolition of the Caravan Tolls and Canoe Tax coincided with the decline in the yield of these taxes. Such, in the case of the Caravan Tolls, reflected both a decline in local trade and local industry, as well as the increased sophistication of the methods of evasion devised by local traders. Similarly, these figures show that the abolition of these two taxes was a mere ruse, a deception, in that their abolition was followed by rises in the yields of the Kurdin Kasa and the Jangali. Finally, the figures indicate a steady rise in drunkenness as British colonial rule became consolidated, a rise which was reflected in the yields of the so-called "Native Liquor Licences."

Allocation of Collected Revenues

It must be emphasized that the figures for Yola represented those revenues that went entirely to the Colonial Administration, as distinct from the so-called Native Authorities. Even the figures for the "Tribute" or "Land Tax" represented only the Colonial Administration's share of the Kurdin Kasa, the Jangali and the Zakka, which were the only taxes the administration shared with the Native Authorities. The other taxes were exclusively appropriated by the administration. In the case of the emirates, the formula for dividing the proceeds of these taxes between the Colonial Administration and the Native Authorities was theoretically as follows:

a)　*Kurdin Kasa* and *Jangali*: 50% to the Colonial Administration and 50% to the Native Authority.

b)　*Zakka*: 33⅓% to the Colonial Administration and 66⅔% to the Native Authorities.

In practice, however, the Colonial Administration took up to three-fifths of these taxes, leaving two-fifths to the Native Authorities.[2] Hence, the figures under the heading "Kurdin Kasa and Jangali" in Table 9.1. represents three-fifths of the amounts collected for these three taxes.

As for the non-Muslim areas or "Independent Chiefdoms," the Colonial Administration took 80% of the Kurdin Kasa and where possible all of the Jangali,[3] on the pretext that it was collected from people who, prior to the coming of the British, had not been under the authorities of these areas. This claim was false as far as the relationship between the Fulbe in these areas with the host governments of the areas in the nineteenth century was concerned. The claim was all the more false in view of the fact that not all of the cattle belonged to the Fulbe. Some numbers belonged to non-Fulbe, although such owners almost always left their herds in the care of Fulbe. Besides, the Jangali was paid not just on cattle but also on sheep and goats, which were definitely owned by both the Fulbe and the non-Fulbe themselves. At any rate, it should be noted that the desire to maximize their own share of the taxes was largely responsible for the zeal with which the British sought to detach and "protect" as many "pagan tribes" as possible from control by the emirates.

Thus, it should be clear that the Colonial Administration in the emirates had huge financial resources at its disposal, the frequent wails of Lugard about paucity of resources at the disposal of his administration notwithstanding. Those frequent complaints, which are echoed with remarkable faithfulness by many writers on the establishment of British colonial domination over the emirates,[4] were, it seems, designed to forestall any likely attempt by the Colonial Office to demand a direct share in these resources. As to what Lugard and his men did with these resources, while the question is not strictly outside the scope of this book, all one can and should state here and argue with absolute impartiality is that not even one percent of the revenue realized by the Colonial Administration was spent on any project designed to benefit the people of the emirate throughout the period under study. All such projects, and very few of them were initiated during our period, were paid for out of the Native Authorities' shares of the Kurdin Kasa and the Jangali. In fact, even the task of policing the indigenous population was largely left to the Native Authorities, as we shall see in a later chapter.[5] This included patrolling the "Government Residential Areas" at night.

The Native Authorities and the Allocation of Their Share of Revenues

The history of the Native Treasuries, the sources of their revenue, the control of these and how they were spent, will be taken up in the next section of this chapter. Hence in this section our discussion will be confined only to how the Emirs, District Heads and Village Heads spent the revenues left to them in the period up to the establishment of these Treasuries. The logical assumption to make is that the Emirs, District Heads and Village Heads spent these revenues in the same way that Emirs had spent their revenues in the precolonial period, except for the buying of weapons and the equipping of expeditions against the enemies of the Sokoto Caliphate. This expenditure was rendered unnecessary by the presence of the British, their disarming of the Emirs, and the outlawing of all wars except those waged by the British themselves.

The other areas of precolonial expenditure included occasional payments to various officials such as Qadis, *mallams* and messengers, the costs of maintaining law and order in the emirate capitals and in some other major towns, and the provision of aid to the needy.[6] We shall emphasize here two of these responsibilities. This is because when the Native Treasuries were established, the British, who assumed the effective control of the manner in which the treasuries spent their revenues, refused to accept the validity of these two areas of expenditure. The British did not include them among the responsibilities of the Native Treasuries, thus relegating them to the private and philanthropic concerns of those Emirs, District Heads, Village Heads and individuals who had a civic sense of responsibility and the means with which to undertake these responsibilities. These were, first, payments to mallams in their capacity as teachers and general civic functionaries, as distinct from their being occasional Qadis or legal advisers to the British-constituted Native Authorities and, second, the provision of some relief to the needy.

However, that the Emirs did consider it their duty to make occasional gifts to mallams and to provide some relief to the needy is beyond doubt, though the seriousness with which they regarded this duty varied from Emir to Emir. Oral tradition in Sokoto, Kano, Yola and Maiduguri invariably included gifts to mallams, more or less regular alms to blind men, lepers, the lame and destitute travellers among the expenditures of Emirs. And in Borno and Yola, at least, the provision of one meal a day to all those who felt like taking it, was undertaken by Emirs during the first five decades of this century.[7] In fact, with the removal of the Treasuries from their control and the refusal of the British to include these services among the responsibilities of the Native Treasuries, the Emirs resorted to various devices in order to avoid entirely giving up these responsibilities. Among these devices were the intensification of their farming activities,[8] the appointment of several people to do a job that one person could adequately do, and the surreptitious collection of the Zakka even after it had been outlawed by the British. Such practice which, as we saw in chapter 8, earned many District and Village Heads the charge of extortion, and cost them their offices.

While refusing to acknowledge the validity of the two responsibilities of the Emirs, the British did, at the time of the establishment of the Native Treasuries, recognize that "in former days," i.e. before 1908, the Emir not only "drew from the [Emiral Treasury] what he pleased for his private expenses" but also used the revenue allotted to him "for expenses in the public service."[9] Hence while getting the Emir to accept a fixed amount "per mensum for his private expenses," the new Native Treasury was charged with the "expenditure in the Public Service,"[10] minus the social welfare aspects which the British lumped together with the Emir's "private" concerns.

Not only do the Provincial Reports provide us with this information; in some cases we are informed in great detail the nature of the "expenditure in the Public Service" that the Native Treasuries at the time of their establishment took over from the Emirs and District Heads. In the case of Kano, this expenditure included the payment of the salaries of the members of the Emir's Council, of the staff of the Native Treasury itself, of ninety police and night watchmen in the capital, thirteen gatekeepers in the city, forty policemen attached to District Courts, thirty one warders for the city jail, the African staff of the school which the British established at Nassarawa, one official in charge of public works, one expert on the history of Kano, and one expert blacksmith. It also included the feeding of prisoners in the city jail, repairs to the thirteen gates of the city, repairs to markets in both the city and scores of other towns, and repairs to the houses of the Emir and members of his Council.[11] So also did it include the rebuilding of the city jail, the building of court houses in the city and in the district capitals, and of thirty three rest houses for touring British officials as well as the rebuilding of the city mosque. This list, apart from indicating to us the types of the projects undertaken by Emirs and District Heads with the partial aid of the revenue allotted to them prior to the establishment of the Native Treasuries, does also compel us, in conjunction with the information obtained from oral tradition, to conclude that even taking into account the positive nature of some of the items on the list, it was mainly the negative aspects of the duties of the Emirs that the British allowed to be taken over by the Native Treasuries at the time of their establishment. This is a fitting comment on the nature of British rule in Northern Nigeria. It was, with some slight incidental mitigation, the negation of what a good government ought to be.

The Establishment, Management and Control of Treasuries

The revenues of the Native Authorities were made up of the share of the proceeds of the Jangali, the Kurdin Kasa, the Zakka and fees charged by the Native Courts. Of these, the court fees at first yielded comparatively little, though, as we have seen in an earlier chapter, they were sufficiently forbidding to prospective litigants to help curtail litigation in the courts.[12] Hence, to all intents and purposes the Jangali, the Kurdin Kasa and the Zakka were the only

sources of revenue of the Native Authorities in the first five years of British colonial domination over the emirates, and with the abolition of the Zakka around
1908, the Jangali and the Kurdin Kasa became their only effective sources of
income.

Up to 1908, these revenues were handed over to the Emirs, the District
Heads and the Village Heads, with the Emirs taking 50% and the District Heads
and the Village Heads 25% each. Since the total share of the Native Authorities
amounted to less than 50% of the proceeds of these taxes, each Emir's share
actually amounted to less than 29% of the proceeds of the taxes collected in his
Emirate, while the shares of the District Heads and the Village Heads amounted
to less than twelve and a half percent of the totals collected in their respective
Districts and Villages.

Beginning with Katsina in 1908 and then Kano in 1909, Hadeija and Zaria
in 1910, Sokoto and Yola in 1911, Borno in 1912 and Gombe and Bauchi in
1914, Native Treasuries were "set up" in the various emirates.[13] At the same
time, Emirs, District Heads and Village Heads were put on salaries, which in
the case of the Emirs were fixed at about 5% of the revenues of their emirates
at that point and in the case of the District and Village Heads at less than 1% of
the revenues collected in their respective Districts and Villages.

Control of the Native Treasuries

Although some of the Residents claimed and were later to be echoed that
the Native Treasuries were controlled by Emirs[14] and, belying their names,
these Treasuries were under the control and direction of the Residents and
Assistant Residents, rather than of the Emirs. This control resided in the fact
that the Residents prepared Native Treasury Estimates and the Governor approved them. Even day to day expenditure was, in the bulk majority of cases, controlled by Residents and Assistant Residents throughout the period of
study.[15] Thus in Borno in 1911, for example, "the Beit el-Mal [was] under the
charge of the Assistant Resident who [had] to keep the accounts," and "for performing this duty," the Resident asked the permission of the Governor to let
the Assistant Resident "draw an allowance from the Native Administration."[16]
Similarly, in Yola in the same year, it was Resident Bryan that prepared the
"Beit el-Mal Estimates," which, at any rate, he forwarded to the Governor for
approval, an approval which was granted.[17] In the same way in Kano in 1913, it
was Resident Gowers that prepared the "Native Treasury Estimates", though he
explained the "principle of Estimates" to the Emir, who made "comments [that]
were shrewd and to the point."[18] Indeed, so much were the Emirs expected to

be kept out of the preparation of "Native Treasury Estimates" that Gowers had to make excuses for even inviting the Emir of Kano's comments. Thus, by way of excusing himself, he observed that:

> in this as in other matters there is little doubt that the members of the Native Administration will respond cheerfully and efficiently to any reasonable demands that are made upon them provided that they are taken into confidence and encouraged to make their own suggestions.

He went on to allow that:

> it is only natural and even commendable that they should desire to have a hand in and see the results of the Native share of the taxes when it is remembered that five years ago the Emir was subjected to no inquiry in the spending of that share of the taxes which forms the bulk of the Native Treasury revenues, and that when the Native Treasury was organized and his personal income fixed he, like other Emirs, believed that the balance of the Native share of revenue would be spent on public objects within the Emirate which produced it. [19]

This control was also admitted in the case of Zaria where it was not until the middle of 1913 that "the 1914 Estimates were prepared" by the Native Treasurer and his staff, "and submitted" to Resident Fremantle a "feat" which the Resident said was "a logical sequence from the work which they [had] taught themselves to perform." [20] "Formerly" even this initiation of the Estimates "was all done for them and they acted chiefly by proxy." [21]

Similarly, in Borno it was not until 1914 that the Shehu was allowed even "authority for expenditure within the margin of votes sanctioned by the Governor," and even this only with respect of "all Departments except the medical," over whose expenditure the Resident continued to retain such authority. [22] Meanwhile, in the emirates in Kano Province, up to 1915, at least, "European officers [had] a natural tendency to do [Treasury] work themselves in collaboration with the Treasurers rather than risk possible mistakes if the Native Treasurers [were] left to carry out instructions conveyed through the Emirs in the ordinary way." [23] The British officers did the work themselves allegedly because "District Officers found it difficult to make it intelligible to [the Native Treasurer] the adjustments necessitated the sanctioned expenditure not being known till May." [24]

Role and Attitude of Emirs

At least, superficially, the initial attitude of Emirs towards the "establishment" of the Native Treasuries seems to have been favourable. Thus, for example, while reporting the establishment of the Zaria Native Treasury, the

Resident also reported that "in addition to the fees from Native Courts and the share of Taxation formerly known as the Emir's share, the Emir [had] voluntarily surrendered to the Beit el-Mal funds the Kurdin Sarauta and the *ujeran gado* on Fulani inheritances."[25] Similarly, in Yola we are informed that it was the Emir who, with the assistance of a Kano trained mallam, kept the Native Treasury account books and cash.[26] It was he that received "all Native Revenue" and made "all payments" and he was said to have "adhered" to the expenditure "as laid down in the Estimates" that were drawn up by the Resident and approved by the Governor. In Kano too, it was the "Ma'aji and his staff," that is, people in the employ of the Emir, that kept the Native Treasury accounts;[27] and we have already seen how the Emir made "comments [that] were shrewd and to the point" when the Resident explained "the principles of Estimates" to him while the Estimates 'were under discussion' among the Resident and his British staff.[28] It was this, perhaps, that encouraged the Resident to predict that: "the members of the Native Administration [would] respond cheerfully and efficiently to any reasonable demands that [were] made upon them provided that they [were] taken into confidence and encouraged to make their own suggestions."[29]

However, in spite of the civility with which the Emirs seem to have accepted the "establishment" of the Native Treasuries and its control by the Residents, there is enough evidence that the "establishment" and British control of these Treasuries rankled with them. For example, Palmer noted that because British Officers in Kano Province had taken to running the Native Treasuries, "in collaboration with the Treasurers" and more or less to the exclusion of the Emirs, this had "unfortunately" resulted "in the Emir losing interest in the work of the Native Treasury and becoming jealous of and hostile to his Treasurer."[30] Much more clear example of how the Emirs felt about the "establishment" of Native Treasuries were the objections raised by the Emir of Zaria when, at the end of 1913, as usual, "proposals were made for Native Treasuries to supply contributions to various government services in the form of votes-in-aid."[31] Remarkably, "the Emir took strong exception to the idea of contributing funds for uses over which he had no control or which were of a Government rather than Native character."[32] The Emir "therefore begged that the Government take each year whatever [was] required and leave him the rest, so that he [might] know where he [stood]." The Emir was said to have put his views in this conciliatory manner because he was:

> quite alive to the pressing needs of the Government, to which local requirements [might] have to give way; and he [had] no illusions as to the conditions under which the Land Revenue [was then] equally divided between the

Government and the Native Administration namely, at the discretion of the Governor who alone [was] in a position to judge of the respective needs.[33]

As for the response that the Emir received to his request, we have not been able to trace it, though the Resident for his part attributed the Emir's attitude to "the very laudable desire to play a real and not a nominal part in the administration of native finances." And though "loath as [the Resident] should be to see the proportion of shares reduced", the Resident subscribed to the Emir's view that "such a course would be preferable to interfering with the spontaneous nature of the budget."[34] Even if the Governor's reply was positive, it would not be relevant because in fact, control of the Native Treasuries remained in the hands of the Residents and their Assistants, throughout the colonial period, in spite of the "jealousies" and protests of the Emirs.

Directions of Expenditure

We have already noted in an earlier section how the British took over mainly the negative side of the Emirs' responsibilities and left the social welfare side of them. Therefore, what we shall do in this section is to see in greater detail the "services" on which the British spent the Native Treasury funds. These included payment of salaries to the Emir and Native Authority councilors, Treasury and Native Court staff and policemen, the building of markets, offices, jails, court houses and repairs to Emirs' houses;[35] the construction of roads in the GRAs; the building and maintenance of rest houses for British officials and other Europeans on tour;[36] and the holding of durbars and bonfires for the celebration of coronations, visits and returns of important British personages.[37] What positive services there were, were meager, far apart, and cost little. For example, the Borno Native Treasury maintained two leper settlements for a few years.[38] In 1911 the Yola Native Treasury maintained one Native "hospital" of a single room in Yola as well as a leper settlement with twenty one inmates near the town.[39] The Native Treasuries, especially that of Kano, contributed money for the running of the two Nassarawa schools, as well as the schools located in a few of the emirates, such as Zaria, Bida and Bauchi towards the end of the period under study.[40] The Sokoto Native Treasury supported a fairly large leper settlement with 116 inmates in 1911;[41] and by 1913 had employed 4 sanitary inspectors to "tour the Districts and see that the Serikin Muslimin's orders [were] carried out."[42] The point being made here can be illustrated with the Kano, Sokoto and Katsina Native Treasuries' history of expenditure, beginning with Kano's expenditure for 1909–10.[43]

Table 9.3a. Kano Native Treasury Expenditure, 1909–1910

Officials	Monthly Salaries
I. Members of Native Administration Paid from the Native Treasury	
a) Executives	
Emir	£400:0:0
Waziri Gidado (Chief Judge)	£83:0:0
Ma'ajen Kano (Treasurer)	£30:0:0
Liman Ahmadu	£8:0:0
Mallam Faruku	£2:0:0
Mallam Ibrahim	£2:0:0
Mallam Ahmadu Bazazzagi	£2:0:0
Mallam Ahmadu (Wan Waziri)	£2:0:0
b) Native Treasury	
Abdullahi	£4:0:0
3 Junior Accountants at £2 per annum	£6:0:0
c) Police and Town Conservancy	
Ma'ajen Wateri	£30:0:0
20 Town Police at £1 per month (*Dogarai*)	£20:0:0
20 Night Watchmen (*Masu gefia*) at £1 per month	£20:0:0
13 Gatekeepers at £1 per month	£13:0:0
50 Police attached to 13 District Courts at £1 per month	£50:0:0
40 Police attached to 13 District Courts at £1 per month	£40:0:0
d) Gaol	
1 Head Gaoler (*Sankomi*)	£3:0:0
30 Warders (*Kuomawe*) at £1 per month	£30:0:0
e) School	
Ibrahim (Teacher)	£3:0:0
Nagwamache	£1:10:0
Haderu	£1:10:0
Momadu Kukawa (subsidized pupils)	£1:10:0
f) Public Works (Recurrent)	
Sarkin Tafariki	£3:0:0
g) Various	
Historical Export/D/Rimi Nuhu	£1:0:0
Blacksmith Export: Umaru of Fagi (on condition that he keeps 4	£2:0:0
apprentices)	
h) Judicial	
Alkalin Kano	£50:0:0
4 Muftis at £4 per month	£16:0:0
13 District Alkalis at £5 per month	£65:0:0
26 Muftis at £4 per month	£104:0:0
Total monthly, essential and non-essential	£993:0:0
Total Yearly	£12,586:0:0

Table 9.3a Contd. Kano Native Treasury Expenditure, 1909–1910

II. Other Yearly Expenditure Incurred or Likely to be Incurred (Essential and Recurrent)	
a) Public Works:	
Repairs to 13 gates and walls of Kano	£200:0:0
Repairs to Markets	£100:0:0
Repairs to 13 District Heads' Houses, Waziri, Ma'aji and Alkali Houses	£200:0:0
b) Education	£1,000:0:0
c) Various	
Entertainment of Envoys	£300:0:0
d) Gaol	
Prisoners' food, etc; about	£60:0:0
e) Incidentals such as Mallami sent to verify measurements of farms and houses or yield of crops, etc.	£200:0:0
Total Yearly	£2,160:0:0
Grand Total, Yearly & Recurrent	£14,746:0:0

Table 9.3b. Kano Native Treasury Extraordinary Expenditure, 1909–1910

III Extraordinary Expenditure on Public Works incurred contracted for or likely to be incurred before March 31st, 1910	
Rebuilding Kurmi Market (incurred)	£500:0:0
Repairs and "Debbe" of streets (contracted)	£210:0:0
Rebuilding Mindawari Market (contracted)	£100:0:0
Rebuilding Jail (contracted)	£860:0:0
Additional expenditure estimated will be necessary	£400:0:0
Building Court House (contracted)	£200:0:0
Repairing 13 Gates, Kano Town (contracted)	£260:0:0
Repairing Emir's House	£100:0:0
Repairing 13 District Heads' Houses, Waziri, Ma'aji and Alkalis' Houses	£250:0:0
Rebuilding Eighteen Markets at £100 each	£1,800:0:0
Building of 33 Rest Houses at £20 each	£660:0:0
Total	£5,440:0:0

The same point can be illustrated with Sokoto Native Treasury's list of expenses in 1911 as laid out below.[44]

Table 9.4. Sokoto Native Treasury Monthly Expenditure, 1911

(a) Executive:	
Sarkin Musulmi	£400:0:0
Waziri	£83:0:0
Galadiman Gari	£25:0:0
Magajin Gari	£17:0:0
Magajin Rafi	£25:0:0
Ubandoma	£17:0:0
Majidadi	£50:0:0
Shentali	£30:0:0
Alkalin Waziri	£5:0:0
Sarkin Zanfara	£40:0:0
Dagamalle	£3:0:0
Total	£695:0:0
(b) Judicial:	
Alkali	£30:0:0
1 Assistant	£10:0:0
1 Assistant	£3:0:0
1 Assistant	£3:0:0
Total	£46:0:0
(c) Giddan Ajia (Native Treasury):	
Ajia	£10:0:0
Na Mallam	£5:0:0
Amadu	£5:0:0
12 Guards at 20/-	£12:0:0
Total	£32:0:0
(d) Dogarai (Native Police):	
Sarkin Dogarai	£3:0:0
30 Outside: 10 at 20/-	£10:0:0
20 at 10/-	£10:0:0
93 District Messengers: 46 at 20/-	£46:0:0
47 at 10/-	£23:0:0
25 Town Police at 20/-	£25:0:0
Total	£117:10:0

Table 9.4 Contd. Sokoto Native Treasury Monthly Expenditure, 1911

(e) Prisons:	
Yari (Chief Warder)	£3:0:0
20 Warders at 20/-	£20:0:0
Prison Food	£3:0:0
Total	£26:0:0
Total Monthly Recurrent	£916:16:8
(f) Recurrent Yearly:	
Education	£300:0:0
Public Works	£100:0:0
Miscellaneous: Envoys, etc	£300:0:0
Total	£700:0:0
Public Works Extraordinary	£450:0:0
Survey: Salaries to Taki Mallams	£200:0:0
Grand Total Estimated from 30th September 1911 to 31st March 1912	£7,767:16:8

Table 9.5. Katsina Native Treasury Expenditure, 1909–1910[45]

Judicial and Executive Council	
Emir	£300:0:0
Waziri	£41:0:0
Magajin Gari	£20:0:0
Sarkin Fada	£8:6:0:
Bebeji	£5:16:8
Majidadi	£5:3:4
Magatakarda	£2:10:0
Liman Ratibi	£2:10:0
Liman Juma'a	£2:10:0
Ladan	£1:0:0
Native Treasury:	
Mutawalli (Treasurer)	£8:6:8
1 Chief Accountant	£4:3:4
5 Junior Accountants at £2 per month	£10:0:0
12 Guards at £1 per month	£12:0:0

Table 9.5 Contd. Katsina Native Treasury Expenditure, 1909–1910

Police and Katsina Town Conservancy:	
1 Head Police (Messenger)	£1:10:0
20 Mounted Police at £1 per month	£20:0:0
3 Market Police at £1 per month	£3:0:0
Sarkin Pawa	£2:10:0
Sarkin Parayi	£1:0:0
Sarkin Shara	£2:10:0
Gaol	
1 Prison Mallam	£1:0:0
1 Head Police (Gaoler)	£3:6:8
12 Police (Warders) at £1 per month	£12:0:0
Prisoners' Food	£10:8:4
School	
Alhaji Balarabe (Teacher)	£2:10:0
Public works (Recurrent):	
Sarkin Hanya	£2:10:0
Various	
Exiles: Maintenance of Ex-Emirs	£2:0:0
Judicial	
Alkalin Katsena	£8:6:8
3 Muftis at £2:10/- per month	£7:10:0
1 Court Scribe	£1:13:4
Mai Tsaron Gida (Keeper of Court House)	£1:0:0
Mai Bad a Rantsuwa (Administrator of Oaths)	£1:0:0
M. Mohamma (Gado)	£2:10:0
Alhaji Modu (Mufti)	£2:10:0
10 District Alkalis at £2:10/-	£25:0:0
Total Monthly Expenditure being incurred, essential and Recurrent	£582:11:00
Total Yearly Expenditure, essential and recurrent	£6,991:0:0

Briefly, from these lists, it emerges that the bulk of the Native Treasuries' expenditure was spent on the payment of salaries to people whose job, directly or indirectly, was to maintain law and order and keep the people quiet. The salaries of Emirs were extremely out of proportion with the salaries of their councillors, a fact which helped to make them dominate these councillors, as Lugard actually wanted them to do.[46] The sums allocated to education were pitiable both absolutely and in comparison with sums allocated to each of the other items of expenditure. Finally, the bulk of "capital" expenditure was spent on the repair of the houses of the keepers of law and order, the construction of roads and markets to speed up the distribution of British goods, and the collection of raw materials for their industries.

Creation and Disposal of Surplus

The amounts that the various Native Treasuries spent on their various items of expenditure were much less than the amounts they collected from their various sources of income. This is illustrated in Table 9.6:

Table 9.6. Native Treasury Revenue and Expenditure, 1909–1914

Year	Native Treasury	Total Receipts	Total Expenditure	Balance
1909/10	Kano[47]	£32,231:0:0	£20,276:0:0	£11,955:0:0
1910/11	Kano[48]	£35,547:13:10	?	£10,467:7:4
1911	Kano[49]	?	?	£10,854:0:0
1912	Sokoto[50]	?	?	£11:692:0:0
1913	Sokoto[51]	?	?	£14,002:16:9
1914	Bauchi and Gombe[52]	£34,248:0:0	£25,951:0:0	£8,297:0:0

The chief means by which the British got rid of the "surpluses" they unfailingly created in the Native Treasuries was to hand over these surpluses to the Colonial Administration for "investment" in securities abroad through the Crown Agents. This was known as the Reserve Fund and was supposed to be used for financing Native Authority purchases abroad. Thus, for example, in 1911, £5,000:0:0 was so invested from the Kano Native Treasury, a sum which the Resident hoped would be increased to £10,000:0:0 "as soon as possible."[53] In 1912, they sent £4,000:0:0 from the Sokoto Native Treasury to the Colonial Treasurer at Zungeru for such "investments.[54] The following year £3,000 was transferred from the same Treasury for such "investment," "making with £4,000:0:0 of the previous year a total of £7,000:0:0 so invested up to 31st December 1913."[55] Although in 1913, the Native Treasuries in the emirates "invested" £33,000 with the Colonial Government, the total "investment" to that date already being £300,000:0:0.[56] However, with the outbreak of the First World War, a "Nigeria War Committee" was formed,[57] and the committee deemed it that "a fund is required to supply troops and carriers with comforts, to provide for the immediate needs of each draft as they return and to supplement, when necessary, and allowances made by Government to the men and to their families."[58] The Committee further decided that "every native in Nigeria should regard it as a privilege to contribute to the fund, and native rulers are invited to make special contributions."[59] This was because, allegedly: "the natives of Africa [were] especially concerned in [that] war, for on its result [depended] the securing to them of a Government based on principles of humanity and fair play, as opposed to one of military domination and oppression."[60]

Accordingly, on the one hand, the British got District Heads to collect special levies from the peasantry for the Red Cross.[61] On the other hand, part of the surpluses generated in the Native Treasuries was handed over to the War Fund. Thus, for example, in September 1914, the Emir of Zaria, "on hearing that the Native Chiefs of India had come forward and subscribed large sums to the War Fund at once expressed a desire to be allowed to contribute. The sum of £1,750:0:0 was suggested and offered."[62] Further, "the Emir also offered, and his offer was accepted, to supply 500 pairs of sandals for the carriers who were enlisted in Zaria Province."[63] It was alleged that these sandals were paid for out of the Emir's "own pocket,"[64] but we might do well to question this. Then, at the end of 1915, £3,000:0:0 was transferred from the Zaria Native Treasury to the Fund.[65] Conveniently, this too was done on the "offer" of the Emir "with the consent of his council."[66] At the same time, another £3,000:0:0 was "placed to the Investment Reserve account."[67] Similarly, the Native Treasuries of Bauchi and Gombe together, in 1914, in addition to *increasing* their "Reserve" by a sum of £2,000:0:0, contributed £3,500:0:0 to the War Fund.[68] The Kano Native Treasury for its part contributed £7,000:0:0 to the Fund in 1915.[69] This same year the Native Treasuries in the North among them "invested" £38,000:0:0 with the government, in addition to their "War contributions."[70] This sum was much less than the Governor wanted his Administration to take over and use, his own wish seeming to have been to take over all the "Native Treasury balance after the full charges for personal Emoluments had been met."[71] His excuse was that "the urgent needs of the Protectorate in the matter of increase of Political Staff, housing of officials, increase of roads and railways and British staff (Education and Forestry) – were of greater importance than some of the Provincial works on which it was proposed to spend" that balance.[72] By "Provincial Works," the circular was no doubt referring to the markets that were being built and repaired in the emirates.

At any rate, what stopped the Governor from taking all the surpluses generated was that the Secretary of State for the Colonies, Mr. Harcourt "personally took exception to [that] course."[73] Meanwhile, the contribution to the War Fund by the Native Treasuries continued right up to the end of the War. Sokoto and Argungu, for example, paid an annual contribution of £3,000:0:0 and £300:0:0 respectively in 1917.[74] The contributions in that year were converted into interest bearing loans from the Treasuries to the Colonial Government.[75] Nor did the transfer of the Native Treasuries' surpluses to the Colonial Government and for investment abroad ever stop right up to the end of British colonial domination and beyond. In fact later, these surpluses were transferred not just to the Colonial Government in Nigeria and to Britain, but also to other parts of the British Empire, like Australia, New Zealand, and Hong Kong.[76] Indeed, according to one informant, the District Officers that were later detailed to run the more important Native Treasuries were very strict about getting these Treasuries to send abroad as much money as possible.[77] The zeal suggests that those District Officers must have been working not only for the Colonial Office, but also directly for one or another of Britain's financial institutions. At any rate, up to the time of research for this work in 1974, some of these Native Treasuries investments were still maturing.[78]

Conclusion

We have seen that the Native Treasuries which were created in the period 1908–1914 were the creatures of the British, and were throughout the colonial period controlled and directed by the Residents and their Assistants with the help of emirate staff, rather than by the Emirs who had little or no say in the direction of these Treasuries, "Native" though they were said to be. We have also seen that the Native Treasuries which budgeted with very large surpluses spent all the money that they locally spent on the payment of salaries and the erection and maintenance of markets, court houses and prisons for the purposes of maintaining law and order, and facilitating the disposal of British goods and the collection of Northern Nigerian raw materials for export to Britain. Finally, we have seen that the large surpluses generated by the Native Treasuries were used to subsidize the Colonial Government which, to start with, took over 50% of all revenues collected by the Native Authorities, and to export abroad to Britain and other parts of the British Empire.

16. Workers on the Gwari section of the Baro–Kano railway,
Northern Nigeria, 1908.

17. Workers on the Gwari section of the Baro–Kano railway,
Northern Nigeria, 1908.

10

Changes in the Economy of the Emirates and the Influx of European Firms

Introduction

One of the objectives of twentieth century European colonialism in general was to transform the colonies into economic appendages of Europe. This, in essence, was the major factor for the British invasion of the Caliphate and its neighbours. Therefore, our exposition on the subject matter of this book would be incomplete without a comprehensive examination of the process through which the foundations of a colonial economy were laid by the British in Northern Nigeria.

The chapter begins with a detailed account on the nature of the precolonial economy, as depicted in the colonial sources. We shall show how the promulgation and imposition of new policies undermined the precolonial economy. Such policies, as we will demonstrate, were many and ranged from taxation to the imposition of British currency for the payment of taxes. The imposition was gradually extended to cover other transactions. We will argue that as a result of the assault launched by these colonial policies, the inherited precolonial economy began to witness a steady decline. We shall draw attention to the fact that the decline was not smooth or uninterrupted owing to resistance by the people. As the British began recording success in the eradication of the circulation of the predominant currencies in circulation at the time of their arrival, namely, Austrian minted Maria Theresa dollars, German mark and cowries that facilitated local, regional and international trade in the Caliphate, a colonial capitalist economy began to emerge. We will examine the process through which this was accomplished, the various challenges encountered at different stages, and how the British overcame those challenges by the end of our period.

In the latter part of the chapter, we shall focus our attention on the arrival of European trading companies, their commercial activities, trading methods, relations with the colonial state and their impact on the economies of the emirates. It is worthwhile for us to find out whether the influx of the trading firms resulted in increase in the number of non-official European settlers in the emirates. We shall follow this up with an account on the export of cotton, groundnut, tin, hides and skin, and other primary produce in the emirates, and how their volume increased by the end of our period, including the extent to which the production of these primary produce contributed to the outbreak of the 1914 famine. We shall also strive to show how the trading firms, with the apparent collusion of British officials, jettisoned competition and forced a monopolistic price on the produce of peasant farmers, along with other methods of maximizing their economic gains. We shall conclude the chapter by arguing that the support given to the trading firms by the colonial state went beyond fixing monopolistic prices, but included using state funds and mobilization of forced labour for building critical infrastructure needed by the firms.

The Introduction of British Currency

By the end of the period of study, all the British taxes were being paid in British currency. But this was not the case at the time of their first imposition. At that time it would have been utterly unrealistic for the British to demand that payments be made in their currency, which was just being introduced and which was hardly being accepted by the population of the emirates. Hence, at the time of the imposition of these taxes, payment was offered and accepted in kind, and in order to fulfil specific needs of theirs, such as equipping or provisioning their troops, the British did often demand that these payments be made in some specific commodities. The Kurdin Kasa, for example, was, at various times and in various places in the emirates, paid in cattle, horses, sheep, cowries, cotton, native cloth, gum, corn, Maria Theresa dollars, native salt, leather, firewood, labour time, German mark, goats, hoes, shea nuts, gutta.

Some of these commodities like cattle, horses, sheep, goats and corn were either redeemed by the Northern Nigeria Regiment or sold on the market at places like Kano, Jega and Lagos. Others like shea nuts, gutta, cotton, gum, leather were handed over to the Niger Company for redeeming. Very often the cattle, sheep, goats, hoes, native cloth, native salt, when these exceeded their share of the taxes, were given to the Emirs and some District Heads such as the Marafa of Gwadabawa, Muhammadu Maiturare, for redemption at "reduced" prices, as a mark of favour. The cowries collected as taxes were used by the

British to flood the markets and tip the exchange parity between this precolonial currency and the British currency in favour of the latter in an effort to hasten the ouster of the cowrie. Firewood was accepted only along the rivers plied
by steam boats, viz., the Niger, the Benue, and the Gongola, and was stacked
at stations along them for the benefit of the steam boats. Similarly, labour time
was demanded when it was desperately needed and in acute supply such as, say,
for carrying loads for a touring British party at harvest time. The Maria Theresa
dollars were accepted mainly in order to withdraw them from circulation and
give the British shilling an enhanced prestige, and it was for roughly the same
reason that the German mark were at first accepted. But whereas the dollars
were not redeemed by any country, the Mark was in fact redeemed by the
German Colonial Bank in Berlin.[1]

However, right from the time of the imposition of British taxation, the
Kurdin Kasa was assessed in terms of British money. This was because of British
desire to establish their currency as the country's standard currency, a position
which at the time of British occupation was, in the emirates and Borno, occupied mainly by the cowrie and to a lesser extent by the Maria Theresa dollars
and cloth. This desire in turn was subservient to another desire of the British,
and that was to get the people to come forward and work for them for their
money, not just for the Colonial Administration but also for the commercial
and mining firms.[2] Indeed, this desire was often so crudely stated, as we shall
see below. But it was also betrayed on those occasions when the British exclaimed that the people were not casting off their "indolence" and were coming
forward to work for money, or that they were abandoning their local areas and
travelling to such British centres as Lokoja and Naraguta to seek British money
and other benefits of European "civilization."[3]

Thus, British efforts to establish their currency as the sole medium of payment of taxes should be seen as just an aspect of their attempt to subvert whatever residual autonomy the indigenous economy had retained by the end of the
nineteenth century. That is to say that their attempt to establish British money
as the currency of the emirates, in turn, was only a part of a wider process: the
attempt to take over complete control of the indigenous economy. Hence, the
process whereby British currency was established as the medium of payment of
taxes to the British is here studied in its proper context – the establishment of
that currency as the general medium of exchange in the emirates, the "imper-
sonal" instrument with which they could master the labour power of the local
population.

Ousting the Maria Theresa Dollar, the German Mark and the Cowrie

Soon after their occupation of parts of the emirates, the British started to identify the obstacles to the introduction of the British currency. Paradoxically, one of these obstacles was the attitude of the Niger Company which, as we shall see below, for its own exploitative purposes, was very averse to using money as a medium of trade with the local population and preferred to offer local traders its own shoddy goods in exchange for their products. Part of the anger that some Residents expressed against the Company's methods of trade was, doubtless, the result of this contempt which it displayed against British currency. We shall study these methods later in this chapter in a discussion of the company's own contribution to the economic burden imposed on the people of the emirates by the British. The second obstacle to British currency was the non-British currencies, namely the Maria Theresa dollar and the German mark. The former was already the standard currency in the Sheikhdom of Borno by the time the British arrived there.[4] The German mark was introduced into Yola Province by indigenous traders who were forced to accept it by the Germans in that portion of Adamawa occupied by them. The dollar seemed so entrenched in Borno that the British found it necessary to accept it for tax payment by the people both because in many cases the only alternative to accepting it was to suspend taxation, and because accepting the dollar in payment of taxes was the surest way of gathering and ousting it as a currency. However, Lugard at the same time never relented in urging his subordinates in Borno to keep on insisting on British money. In fact, in the eyes of some of his subordinates outside Borno, even this temporary compromise with the dollar was not patriotic. Barclay felt strong enough about the matter to write from Yola and tell Lugard that the recognition of the dollar was "directly detrimental" to English currency that "it militates against our coinage."[5]

Meanwhile, Barclay himself was level-headed enough to realize that British money so much lacked acceptance in Yola that it would be unfair of him to pay his staff in that money alone. So he paid them partly in money and partly in cloth, an act which helped Lugard to snatch the patriotic initiative from him. He warned him that "by paying in cloth ... you check the currency and help to produce the evils you have described."[6] Similarly, Barclay had found it necessary to accept cattle, horses, sheep and corn from the Emir as tribute in December 1902 without Lugard requesting for them. This too Lugard did not overlook. He warned him that "tribute will be in cash where possible" and instructed Barclay to insist on money, the implication being that it was up to the Emir and his subjects to devise means of obtaining the money. With the Company not paying in money, there was only one way this could be done, namely to send people down to Lokoja or Bauchi to enter into British service and obtain the money. But Lugard did not cross the t's or dot the i's. He simply stopped at informing the Resident to "demand payment in coin for all payments and they will soon appreciate it."[7] Hence, by July 1903, the Acting Resident at Yola, Gowers, had decided that "assessment will be on a cash basis and cash only will be accepted from the Emir in liquidation of his liability."[8] That was to say that while the Emir was free to collect the Kurdin Kasa and the Jangali in kind, "the portion of the tribute payable to the Government by the Emir [would] be in cash unless payment in another medium would be to the advantage of Government."[9]

To hasten the ouster of the cowrie as a currency, the Acting Resident suggested that:

> the government should send to Yola a large stock of cowries purchased at Lokoja or on the coast, to be kept in store by the Resident. When the rate of exchange [fell] below 1,200 cowries to the shilling, the Resident would put cowries on the market until this ration was again reached.[10]

The Resident believed that stabilizing the exchange rate between the cowrie and the shilling at 1,200 cowries per shilling would tend to force out the cowrie by making it unprofitable for Nupe traders to bring the cowrie from Lokoja. Up to then, these traders were doing "an extensive and lucrative trade" by being "the sole agents for the introduction of cowries into Yola."[11] They used to drain the province of the little British money that was paid to soldiers and other government employees and in its place brought in the cowries, "their profits averaging at least 100% on each trip."[12] This was a very good indication of the contempt with which British money was regarded in Yola at that time. Hence it was worth the Government's while to incur some loss in money by artificially sustaining the shilling against the cowrie for a short time. In the end the British were going to gain beyond computation by taking over total control of the native economy. For, indeed, once they monopolized the emirates' currency they would get people to do almost anything for them.

Further, Gowers suggested the introduction of small coins, i.e. pennies, half-pennies and one-tenth of a penny made in copper, in addition to the shilling which was in silver.[13] This too would hasten the establishment of the British currency as the standard currency of the country and by that token, put the entire population and its economy effectively at the disposal of the British. Lugard did not hesitate in complying with this request. He at once dispatched 409 bags of cowries on a steam boat and reprimanded the Acting Resident for not having collected "a supply of copper a long time ago," ordering him to "indent for it at once."[14] But a whole society's economy could not be so easily subverted. Hence, up to 1905, the British were still finding it necessary to accept payments in kind throughout the emirates. Yet, paradoxically, this was to an extent a reflection of their very dominance over the emirates' society. As Hillary in Sokoto pointed out, "the monthly receipts in cash from various sources are largely in excess of the payments made by both civil and military."[15] As late as 1909, this was confirmed by Temple in Kano when he pointed out that "we are not paying out as wages half the amount we are collecting in rents."[16] Since payments to their troops, civil employees, labourers and suppliers was the only way the British could inject their money into the emirates' society, the very fact that all these were lowly paid made the pace at which they could inject this money into the society inevitably slow. Meanwhile, the economic life of the society could not be brought to a halt, and hence the cowrie, the Maria Theresa dollar and other forms of currency had to retain their currency.

Besides, the British themselves from time to time found it necessary to demand that payments to them had in part to be made in some of the commodities listed above. Cotton, gum, and shea nuts were among these. The Government wanted to send these back to Britain, but the people were, as late as 1906 not sufficiently desirous of British money or goods to exert themselves to grow or collect these for sale in the quantities required by the British. Hence, to make them either grow or gather them from the forests, the British had to insist that some payments be made in them. In giving this order, the British both slowed down the establishment of their money as the main standard of exchange, and revealed quite glaringly that both the institution of taxation and the introduction of the British currency were merely a means to put the native population at the service of the British.

Yet, in spite of all the factors militating against the availability of British currency in 1906, Lugard and his men deemed it proper to inform the Emirs that the government share of the Kurdin Kasa and Jangali had to be paid in cash unless the British themselves made a specific request for payment in kind. Luckily for the Emirs, the need did recur now and then for the British to demand that payment be made in kind. A good example was when the officer in charge of the British troops in Sokoto requested the Resident that he should be supplied with corn at a low price and the Resident in turn instructed the Sultan that Government share of Zakka for that year, 1906, be paid in guinea corn.[17]

However, the stipulation that unless ordered to the contrary, Emirs must pay the British share of the taxes in British currency epitomizes the subordination of the Emirs to the British. It meant that the British arbitrarily reserved for themselves the absolute freedom to demand payment in kind or not to accept payment in kind, while they put the Emirs in a situation in which they had to minister to what must have appeared to them the shifting and unpredictable whims of the British. They must have felt the pangs of bitterness at being left with neither an independent will nor even discretion, of having to pay in British currency whenever the British demanded this, irrespective of the state of availability of this foreign commodity, and of having to supply corn, cotton, etc whenever the British preferred these. They must have keenly felt the frustration of not being able to predict whether the British were going to demand payment in money alone, or payment in kind, or payment in both money and kind. The British indeed made their prerogatives in the matter so wide that they could not possibly be wrong, whatever they did.

To secure the requisite amounts of British money needed of them, the Emirs mainly took to trading. Thus, for example, the Shehu of Borno, Abubakar Garbai, is on record as having been in the habit of sending cattle to Lagos for sale. The Sultan is said to have relied on Yoruba traders frequenting Jega market to sell cattle and obtain the money. Even the Emir of Kano, in whose capital town many people outside the emirate thought British money was readily available, had to send stock to Lagos for sale in order to obtain this currency.

As far as the status of British money with the ordinary people was concerned, a break-through started to be made from about 1907, when it started to be accepted as a general currency and not just as a means of paying taxes as hitherto. Thus, for example, in Sokoto in September 1906, the exchange value of the shilling was 1,200 cowries, but by January 1907, it rose steadily to 2,600 cowries, which was above the "official" rate of 1,800 cowries per shilling.[18] This steep rise of the value of the shilling in fact coincided with the collection of the Kurdin Kasa and the Jangali. However, even after the end of the collection of these taxes, the rate of exchange did not fall back to the former level of 1,200 cowries per 1/-, but stabilized at 1,500 cowries per shilling.[19] At about the same time, the Resident in Yola was pleasantly surprised when, during a visit by an Assistant Resident to their territory, the Mumuye of Zing "brought food for the troops and received payment in cash."[20] He was delighted that "they appeared now to understand all about cash though their regular currency is iron rods, known locally as "tagi" which are of the value of 6 for 3d. This would appear a sure sign of the acceptance of civilization by these people who have till lately been unapproachable."[21] In Kano, the parity between the cowrie and the shilling in normal times was by 1909 at 1,600 to 1/-, rising to 2,400 to 1/- during tax seasons.[22] Besides, at this season in 1909 "horses, cattle, etc. [were]

put on the market and sold far below their value [in British currency] of a year ago."

With these "hopeful" signs that their currency was now achieving the general acceptance that they wanted for it, the British decided to degrade the Maria Theresa dollar and the German mark. Accordingly, the Governor instructed that "German currency be stopped and that German coins be taken only for taxation and when unavoidable. In this case, coins are not to be received at equal value, but at a reduced scale."[23] In fact "all the German coinage will be collected and sent to Garua in exchange for a draft on the Colonial Bank at Berlin payable to the Crown Agents."[24] But, in spite of all British efforts, and although the subversion of the native economy was becoming clearly obvious, right up to the mid-1930s the cowrie was still in use in some of the emirates including Sokoto.[25] And right up to the coming of the First World War, neither the German mark nor the Maria Theresa dollar had been effectively ousted, and both the Kurdin Kasa and the Jangali were still being partially paid in kind, though the British held Emirs responsible for the conversion of their share of the proceeds unless they had a particular need for some commodity. This state of affairs was a reflection of the ability of the emirates' economy to put up some resistance against efforts to totally subvert its autonomy and therefore constituted a credit to it.

The Subordination of the Old Economy

Quite revealing and in keeping with the Marxist explanation[26] of the purpose of European imperialism in Africa, but in stark contradiction with Lugard's own explanation for British conquest of the emirates,[27] one of the first acts of the British Residents after occupying each emirate was to take stock of its economic resources and the first reports sent back to Lugard by the various Residents were overloaded with information about the economic and commercial conditions of their various provinces. These reports referred to trade prospects, the types of agricultural and other commodities available for export, trade links between each province and other areas both in "British" territory and beyond, the volume of trade, the concentration or dispersal of trade centres within the province, their individual importance both relative to one another and relative to other centres of trade in the emirates, the "ethnic" group or groups in whose hands that trade was concentrated, soil fertility, the methods and implements used in agriculture, the extent to which the province seemed able to meet its own food requirements, the abundance or paucity and type of livestock, the types of secondary industry in existence and the degree of the sophistication of the methods used in each, in particular the degree to which textile industry had developed. Hardly any economic factor escaped the notice of a Resident or was considered too trivial to report to Lugard: so central was the desire to take over control of the economy of the emirates in the calculations and intentions of Lugard and his henchmen.

The Precolonial Economy of the Emirates

The relevance of these early reports to this section is that they provide us with some picture of the economies of the emirates before the imposition of British taxation. For example, in the third report on Yola Province,[28] the Report for December 1901, Acting Resident Ruxton expressed satisfaction for being "able to report that trade prospects [were] all that [could] be desired." He noted that potash was coming into Yola in large quantities and that "a large number of ass-loads of gum, gutta and groundnuts" were "expected shortly from Marwa" in "German" Adamawa. Similarly, the "Ngaundere road was open, small quantities of ivory being brought in."[29] Ruxton also reported "with satisfaction" the widespread use of irrigation for agricultural purposes along the banks of the Benue and its many tributaries. Though he had by this time been in Yola for two months only and was of necessity pre-occupied with "security," he had already visited quite a number of places for the purpose of observing economic activities there. Among such places were Beti, Mayine, Gurin and Dasin. In all these places, he found fairly extensive irrigation using the *shadoof*, a method whose name he did not know and which he could only describe and illustrate with diagram, but which he believed was "a labour saving appliance common in south-eastern Europe." For manure, he found the people using guinea stalk ashes and cow and sheep dung, and among the crops cultivated were wheat, tomatoes, *muskuwari*, sweet potato, onions, lapsur, cassava, tobacco and okra.

In the same way, in his second report on Bauchi, the Report for March 1902, Temple stated that the Bauchi town market was "well supplied on the whole with food and livestock."[30] However, he regretted to have found "no sign of that abundance which might have been expected." He added that he had impressed on the Emir and chiefs the "necessity" of "planting largely this year" while the Niger Company's agent who was with him, also explained to them what [was] required" of the people of Bauchi by that Company, a very important fact to the students of the relations between imperialism and colonialism.

Similarly, in his Report for March 1905 on the Sokoto Province, Burdon gave a detailed account of the dyeing industry at Jega and of Jega's trade links with the "outside" world.[31] By this time he had already concluded that Jega was the predominant trade centre in his province. But even so, he claimed that its trade with the outside world was limited. "Lagos men come up with imported cloths which they exchange against cattle and sheep. Other than this, there is no local trade with other countries." Worthy of notice was the fact that "cloths worn by the people [were] ... manufactured within the limits of the Sokoto Province." However, there was "a considerable transit trade in skin, Morocco leathers." So also was there "transit trade" in native salt. In short, we can conclude that the British Residents in their first reports on the economic conditions in the emirates were generally impressed, and were of the opinion that the emirates were a worthy prize for the money and effort they expended in capturing it.

However, within months of writing these self-congratulatory reports, some of the Residents were reporting a decline in the economies of these emirates and directly linking that decline with the imposition of British colonialism. Most revealing were reports by Barclay from Yola. Thus, in June 1902, nine months after its fall to the British, the Resident alleged that:

> Yola's prosperity as a market centre in the olden days, i.e. before the imposition of British rule was entirely due to the slave and ivory trades of which we have stopped the first and the Germans the latter. Practically the whole of the ivory is now in German hands and they are taking care, it does not pass out of them...[32]

The Resident went on to report that:

> except native cloths and a limited market in hides there is nothing now in Yola to attract anyone beyond the few peddlers shown in the returns... The return to prosperity by the gradual encouragement and influx of trade in other directions than those mentioned above will, I fear be a slow process.

That the Resident blamed the precipitated decline of Yola's commerce on the abolition of the traffic in slaves is only to be expected. The British always insisted on the moral inferiority of the precolonial system in comparison to their rule. However, in spite of this insistence, we need not accept the claim, even if only because it grossly exaggerated the importance of the slave trade to the economy of the emirate, as witness his own Report for December 1901, in which he made no mention of slaves.[33] An alternative, and to this writer, more plausible explanation for the decline is the fact that the British had already and very swiftly started collecting tolls and customs on all categories of native products though at this point the British preferred to regard these two taxes as "charges ... for camping ground only."[34] Seven months later, in January 1903, the Resident was still making the same statement, "no Caravans came to Yola now as there is nothing to induce them to do so ... the trade of Yola with the outside world is now represented by a few pedlars who come in singly or by twos and threes."

However, the decline in trade was not an uninterrupted one. Thus, by February 1903, Yola's trade started to show some revival, the people having been forced to resume trade both by sheer necessity and by a probable realization that the British were not likely to go away as quickly as the people had expected, and that in the meantime the economic life of the people had to be carried on in spite of the intruders' harassments and impositions. Hence, in his Report for that month, the Resident was "glad to state that trade showed a marked improvement and [hoped] that the crisis [had] been passed and steady upward movement [might] be looked for ..." However, with a singular ruthlessness, he went on to assure Lugard that "the establishment of [more] customs posts [would] result in considerable revenue accruing to the Province," a statement which typified the attitude of the British towards local trade in those days, namely that it had to be taxed even at the risk of killing it.

The extent of the damage that British economic and fiscal policies inflicted on the emirates' economy can be grasped with even greater clarity if it is realized that at the time of the imposition of their domination on the emirates, the economy of these emirates was based on indigenous agriculture as well as indigenous industry, with imported goods playing little role. As British policy started to be implemented with ever greater efficiency, this economy correspondingly lost its indigenous industrial base, and had its agricultural base distorted with a growing emphasis on export crops for the benefit of the British metropolitan economy. In fact, by 1904, the decline of the indigenous industrial base of the pre-existing economy was discernible to some of the Residents, especially Barclay in Yola who, even from the British point of view, could not entirely endorse it. Thus, in his March 1904 Report, he stated that "the quantity of cotton available in Yola Province at the present time is inappreciable. I should not estimate it at more than 10 tons at the outside." He went on to relate that "at one time large quantities could have been purchased in any of the markets of the Province but the introduction of British cotton goods killed the trade and only sufficient is now grown to meet the diminished demand." However, at this stage, what particularly worried Barclay about this decline of the local textile industry was not that British manufactured goods were killing it. He was warned that the people were not doing what the British expected of them, namely grow as much cotton as hitherto and sell the newly created surplus to the Niger Company – thereby turning their country into an ideal colony, i.e a country which served both as a dumping ground for British goods and the source of raw materials for her industries.

According to Barclay, this "ideal" situation had not come about because the Niger Company had shortsightedly discouraged its realization. The company was, in fact doubly underpaying those who sold their cotton to it. Thus, the company, on the one hand, had insisted on deducting "transportation money" from the price of the cotton and thereby buying the cotton at 1½d per lb, which was "about 1d per lb less than the present retail prices here." On the other hand, the Company was not paying even this price in full, but instead was paying for "its nominal value in trade goods ... which the cotton traders sold in the market at a considerable loss."[35]

However, while urging the Company that it should pay the 1½d per lb in full, Barclay was also performing his imperialist duty of "impressing on the Emir and the people the far-reaching effects cotton growing [was] likely to exercise in promoting the progress and prosperity of the country and urging one and all to plant as they possibly can." But at that point, he was meeting with little success for "the attitude of the people ... [was] ... apathetic and discouraging." He believed that it was improbable that any quantity "would be grown this year," fancying that cultivators would be "cautious and try experimental patches only so that in case of results not coming up to expectations they [would] not stand to lose much." To discourage this caution and make sure that at least in future years "quite as much [cotton] as the Niger Company [could] conveniently undertake the transport of" was produced, Barclay told the Emir that he could "pay his taxes in cotton delivered at the Company's stores," an offer he hoped might "stimulate the Emir's energies." But a plot suggested by Lugard failed to work because the Emir immediately recognized it for what it was. Lugard's plot was that the Colonial Administration should compel the people to grow cotton by advancing them money to be repaid in that commodity at the time of harvest. When the suggestion, complete with its camouflage of lies about British "desire" to "help" the people was put to the Emir by Barclay, the Emir politely rejected it. And, as if not to be outdone in pretence, the Emir told Barclay that his concern was with British interest. He said he knew that people who borrowed the money would "waste" it, rather than invest it for cotton production, in which case the British would have either to write off the loans as bad debts or imprison the people. As the British were not keen to do either, the plot fell through and, in fact, up to the end of the period under study, the people of the emirates had not yet taken to farming for British markets on a scale that would completely please the British.

Meanwhile, trade generally started to decline once more. Barclay attributed this decline to the harsh treatment that he alleged the Germans were in the habit of meting out not only to traders from "British" Adamawa in particular, but to all indigenous traders in general. Barclay accused the Germans of adopting the policy of "exploiting [indigenous traders] to the utmost extent and by such methods to acquire large and immediate returns with no consideration whatever for the future." He lamented that this was "killing the goose with the golden egg with a vengeance", though it "would not be of any consequence if it were not for the fact that [the British] suffer as a direct result of [the German] short sighted policy." However, reading between the lines of Barclay's reports, it emerges that the decline in trade was not as absolute as the returns of the Caravan Tolls from which he made his deductions indicated. Nor were the poor trade figures necessarily a true reflection of the extent to which local industry had declined. It would seem that while there was an absolute decline in the volume of trade, the British perception of this decline was magnified by the fact that traders had by then perfected methods of eluding British patrols and avoiding the toll stations. One way of doing this was to break up a large caravan on entering the vicinity of a toll station and regroup at an appointed place outside that vicinity, for "an individual trader might ... manage to steal pass a toll station but no caravan of any size could possibly pass through the Province without my knowing it." Another way in which the decline in the proceeds of Caravan Tolls tended to exaggerate the absolute decline in trade was "that traders [took to] more largely trading in European goods on which no tolls [were] collected." However, this discovery of the Resident about the local traders' compulsive preference for European goods as opposed to local products and manufactures further confirms what we said earlier in this section about the adverse effects of British taxation policy on local industry and agriculture.

Yet so determined to uphold their interests at the expense of the indigenous population were the British that rather than relent and let the local economy revive a bit, Barclay was looking for ways of further tightening British control over that trade. Thus, he noted that a "few traders from Kano are now coming and taking cattle from the Gongola valley but I have no staff for dealing with a toll station in that district yet." He went on to state that "in the meantime I have written to the Residents Kano and Bauchi advising them of the fact so that the caravans may be intercepted when passing those provinces."

However, at this point, a contradiction emerged between the interests of the Colonial Administration and those of the Royal Niger Company. Whereas the interests of this firm demanded a continued exception of British manufacture from the Caravan Tolls at the same time as local products remained subject to these taxes, the interests of the Colonial Administration demanded that the tolls be extended to cover British manufactures, now that a sizeable number of local traders had switched to trading in them on account of their immunity from the tolls. Luckily for local industry, the interests of the Colonial Administration which, at this point, happened to coincide with the interests of local industry, prevailed and the Caravan Tolls were extended to traders dealing in British goods as well. Normally, one would assume that this extension of the tolls would give some boost, even though inevitably temporary one, to local industry – by making it commercially indifferent whether a trader dealt in British manufacture or in native products.

It would, however, seem that the hypothetical effect of Lugard's new decree was very slow to materialize in practice. For, in August 1904, Barclay was, on the basis of statistics at his disposal, still reporting that "the rapid spread of our rule and the bringing of European goods within reach practically of everybody has brought about a greater demand for imported articles to the detriment of local manufactures …" This need not imply that Barclay was completely correct. For, as we indicated above, Residents' knowledge of conditions in their provinces was nowhere near total and could not possibly have been, given both the limitation of the resources at their disposal and the fact that the situation was not static. Hence, the success with which British manufactures supplanted local products might not have been as great as Barclay believed. On the other hand, the mere fact that he was able to say what we quoted above was in itself an indication of the injury already done to indigenous industry in Yola by the middle of 1904.

Henceforth, the decline of that emirate's economy was the essential fact about it, the revival in trade that was occasionally reported being incidental, temporary, and of a minor significance. In this connection, it should be noted that after reporting some slight "improvement" in trade in September and October 1904, Barclay found it possible and necessary to report in November that "it looks as if the trade in native goods to Yola is gradually approaching its end."[36] At the same time, he expressed the hope that the "new proclamation will put an altogether new aspect of affairs," that "it will have the effect of reviving native industries some of which, such as cloth weaving and dyeing, are well worth preserving, but which were threatened with extinction."

However, in this same report Barclay relayed to Lugard that:

> Mr. Lenthall of the Niger Company at the same time he was protesting most strongly any taxation that might even remotely affect the Company, told me that the 15% caravan tolls on native manufactures was not nearly high enough and that the object of the Government should be to crush native manufactures

by prohibitive taxation for the benefit of Lancashire in particular and British goods in general.

To his credit, Barclay added that:

Patriotism judiciously displayed, is undoubtedly a fine attitude but it is possible in this instance that patriotism has less to do with influencing Mr. Lanthall's personal interest in the Niger Company and I informed him I was quite unable to look upon the matter from his standpoint.

Barclay might "refuse to look upon the matter" of the Caravan Tolls from the standpoint of the Company, which he found too narrow and myopic, but the High Commissioner could not indefinitely refuse to adopt the Company's point of view, and it was as a result of the Company's pressure that the tolls were altogether abolished in 1907. Indeed, it was a measure of the extent to which local industry had declined that the tolls were completely abolished, rather than merely abolished for British goods alone. By this time, the trade in local products was relatively so insignificant that it was worth neither a specific tax nor holding down in favour of trade in British goods.

So far, we have concentrated on the discriminatory tolls as the factor responsible for the decline of the emirates' economy. However, there were several other important contributory factors – all forming part of British economic and fiscal policies. Among these others were the hawker's licence, taxation on industry itself as opposed to trade, i.e. taxes on weaving, dyeing, tanning, etc. In this respect too, it should be noted that the fiscal "reforms" of around 1908 which "did away" with taxes on industries by generalizing them, coincided with the point in time at which the decline of these industries was becoming clearly discernible. In fact, the bogus "abolition" of the taxes was specifically justified by some Residents in terms of a desire to save these industries from extinction. That is to say, the taxes were "removed" only after they had effectively stunted local industry and assured their remaining tame and safe to British manufacture ever after. The industries never became extinct, which is a compliment to their resilience. But they remained in a pre-industrial stage in their organization, non-innovative in their methods, and a little more than marginal in their effect, thanks to the success of British fiscal measures and open collusion with European companies against these industries.

Also, there was the periodic link in some emirates between the size of a man's farm and the Kurdin Kasa he paid. Similarly, the fact that Jangali is also levied on sheep and goats, and at a high rate, must have discouraged the keeping of these animals. For, if they were kept for a few years, the total amount in Jangali that would have been paid on them would exceed their market value, which was not high in those days. Finally, among the factors that obviously tended towards the destruction of the emirates' economy was the introduction of the British currency. We have in another section pointed out that the manner of introducing this currency had among its effects the forcing of people to abandon their farms and crafts, and to gravitate to places like Lokoja and Naraguta where they led a proletarian existence working in European mining and commercial establishments. Yet others were forced to abandon their villages and communities to go and enter British service as soldiers, policemen, casual labourers, cooks, stewards, etc.[37]

Still, in connection with the impact of the introduction of British currency, it should be pointed out that at the time of the payment of the Kurdin Kasa and the Jangali, the emirates' economy was further weakened not in one but in three ways. In the first place, there was the wealth that was given away to the British absolutely for no return except the much vaunted but highly illusory Pax-Britannica. Second, as Barclay observed with regard to the 1905 season: "the effort to obtain cash [to pay the taxes with] has resulted in a great cheapening of marketable commodities. Horses and cattle scarcely procure half their proper price when put on the market".

It would be both superficial and partially false to argue that it was not the British that bought these commodities. This argument would be partially false because, in fact, both the Colonial Administration and the British firms did purchase in markets, though they did so through local agents. Hence, they were direct and immediate beneficiaries of this seasonal wholesale cheapening of local commodities. Then, this hypothetical contention would be superficial because the mere fact that the British were in ultimate control of the currency, the necessity to procure, which made people sell their commodities at cheap prices, meant that the British were the *ultimate* beneficiaries of that cheapening, even if they were not its immediate beneficiaries.

The third way in which the collection of the Kurdin Kasa and the Jangali seasonally aggravated the decline of the emirates' economy was paradoxically in contrast to the second manner just enumerated. It is the fact that not everybody finally succeeded in obtaining the British currency and that payments for these taxes all too often had to be accepted in kind as shown in the previous section of this chapter. In the early years at least, the British themselves had to accept commodities other than their currency as their share of taxes and these were accepted at fictitiously low values. Then there were the confiscations they made during raids on villages. Hence, after handing over some of these commodities to the Niger Company and some to the Northern Nigeria Regiment, the Colonial Administration was always left with large stocks of cattle, cloth, cowries, etc. in the emirates. The Residents often tried to get rid of these by selling in the local markets, but as soon as these were "put on the market price(s) at once fall." However, while some of the Residents, like Barclay and Burdon, recognized the bad effect of the Colonial Administration's selling of commodities like cattle and cloth in the local markets, hardly a single of them ever acknowledged the greatly adverse effects of their periodic and deliberate flooding of the markets with cowries.

The Influx of European Firms

We have so far in this chapter merely alluded to the Royal Niger Company, and still less, to other British and European firms. Hence, we shall devote this last section of the chapter to a more detailed though brief examination of the presence and distribution of these firms, their activities and methods, their relations with the colonial regime, and the impact that their establishment and activities in the emirates had already had on the latter's economy by the end of the period under study. In this connection, it should be pointed out that at the time when British colonial domination was established over the emirates at c.1900, the Royal Niger Company was the sole company directly operating in the emirates.[38] And even that company had stations only in the riverain emirates, namely, Bida, Ilorin, Muri, Adamawa and the Zaria sub-emirate of Nassarawa.[39] Elsewhere in the emirates, the operations of the Company, like those of other European commercial firms, were carried out by North African and local traders, some of whom doubled as spies for the British.[40] This situation, except for the Niger Company's establishment of one or two other stations within the riverain emirates, notably in Kontagora, and partly for reasons we shall see below,[41] remained so until the second decade of the century. However, between 1911 and the end of our period and, no doubt because of the extension of the Lagos Railway up north, the Niger Company and other European firms rapidly made an influx into the more northerly emirates, notably Kano and Zaria. Thus, for example, up to the end of 1910, there was virtually no European company in Kano, though there were large numbers of Arab traders in the province.[42] However, four firms had established in the province by the end of that year.[43] This number grew to nine by the end of 1912.[44] The figure seems to have remained at nine with no reports of new leases being taken in the years 1913, 1914 and 1915, in all probability because of the outbreak of the First World War. In Zaria too, except for the existence of the Niger Company and the British Cotton Growing Association (BCGA) at Zungeru – then part of the province, it was not until 1911 that four firms opened stations at Zaria.[45]

By the end of 1912, seven more firms had opened stations there, making a total of eleven.[46] The list of firms in the province during the following year, that is 1913, included thirteen trading firms and nine mining companies, but it would seem that the nine mining companies were just branches of the Nigeria Tin Company, which was included among the thirteen other firms.[47] The following year, 1914, three of the twelve firms folded up while five "non-European" firms were established.[48] It is not clear under what circumstances one of the three firms closed down, but it is clear that the other two, Messrs Gaiser and Pagenstecher, which were German, were "closed" as a result of the outbreak of the First World War.[49] Indeed the following year, 1915, the stocks of both of them were put on auction and the premises of one of them, Messrs Gaiser, were "temporarily sublet to Messrs Ollivant and Company."[50] At the same time, two more European firms were opened while one "non-European" firm, Messrs Francis, folded up, leaving a total of thirteen European and four "non-European firms in the Zaria Province at the end of 1915.[51] In Bauchi Province, up to the end of 1914, the only firm, apart from mining companies, was the Niger Company which, by this date had stations at Nafada, Gombe, Bauchi, Jos and Naraguta.[52] Although the 1914 Report was supposed to include detailed tables of mining properties and Europeans employed there, we have not found such a table in the Report; but we are informed in the Report that there were in 1914, 185 exclusive prospective licences, covering an area of 726 square miles, and 193 alluvial mining leases covering 58,636 acres.[53] Of these, only six of the licences and eighteen of the leases were issued in 1914, the others having been issued earlier.

Increase in European Population and Expansion of Export Trade

With the increase in the number of firms in the far northern emirates, there was also a sharp increase in both the volume of the export trade and in the number of non-official Europeans living in these emirates. Thus, for example, in Kano the number of Europeans working for commercial firms jumped from two in 1911 to sixteen in 1912.[54] If we take all "non-official non-Africans" into account, the number slightly increased from 113 in 1911 to 122 in 1912; but it is significant that whereas in 1911 the figure of 113 included 14 women, in 1912 the figure of 122 included only 4 women.[55] Although we are not given the figure for 1913, it is stated that there was "a great influx of traders both European, Asiatic, and Native to Kano."[56] In Zaria, the number of non-official Europeans in the province rose from zero at the end of 1910 to 33 by March

1913, a figure which compared favourably with 26 European officials in the province.[57] By the end of that same year, 1913, the number of Europeans in the province had more than doubled to 130, an increase of 71, almost all of whom we can reasonably assume to have been non-official. As for 1914, it is ironic that the provincial figure has been torn from the Annual Report, although we may have some idea of this figure from the fact that Zaria Town alone had 44 Europeans.[58]

From the point of view both of the preoccupation of the European population, as well as that of the social implications of the presence of the Europeans in the province, it is significant that there were only seven European women in that year.[59] The rest were all male, probably on tours of a few years each, many of them probably living with mistresses, some of whom they might have enticed away from their husbands. As for Bauchi, though we have not been able to see the figures for Europeans, either official or non-official, for the province, we can get some idea of these figures from the fact that there were 421 licensed firearms, with 45,429 rounds in the province in 1914. Almost all of these licences were granted to Europeans. In this respect, it is especially significant that in this particular year "there was a rumour that the Europeans at a mine in the south of the Naraguta Division were in danger of being attacked by pagans."[60]

As for the volume of the export trade from the emirates, it should be pointed out that in Kano Province, for example, by the end of 1911, apart from the fact that Arab traders were exporting 16 tons of skins a month, the London and Kano Company, which gained a new vigour in that year, was already doing "a large export trade in dressed skins."[61] In fact, the Resident estimated that the number of skins exported from the province was half a million per annum.[62] The only other export was cotton, of which the BCGA purchased only 2,500 lbs in a temporary station in Kano city. The Association did so poorly because the 1d per lb that it was willing to pay was "too low to obtain any quantity at Kano."[63] However, the Association was able to buy large quantities of cotton at Maska and Malumfashi in Katsina Emirate, a fact which caused it to open stations in southern Katsina against the following year.[64] For 1912 as well, the Resident had no reliable figures for the export of skins, but he was able to report that the trade in skins was "showing a very satisfactory increase."[65] This year also saw the beginning of the export of groundnut, of which some 5,000 tons were bought by European firms at a price that the Resident estimated to be between £15,000 and £20,000.[66] So also were 26 tons of tin exported in this same year, 1912. Though this figure is relatively small compared to later figures, it is significant to note that the influx of miners and their employees did help cause "a considerable rise of prices [of corn] all over the province," and as well aggravate the famine which was already going on.[67]

The following year, 1913, Kano Province exported 16,533 tons of groundnut, 64 tons of tin, 459 tons of dressed skins and 1,059 tons of undressed skins.[68] This represented about four-fold increase for groundnut and more than twofold increase for skins and tin over the 1912 figures. It is also worth recording that "owing to competition among European traders and the high price of groundnut in England," the price paid by the Europeans for groundnut in Kano rose to £10:0:0 per ton, an increase of well over 100% over that of the previous year. In 1914, 4,363 tons of skin was exported, a threefold increase over the 1913 figure.[69] On the other hand, the export of groundnut fell to 66 tons or about 0.4% of the amount exported in the previous year. This virtual disappearance of the groundnut export was due to the fact that the European firms offered only £4:10:0 per ton as against £10:0:0 the previous year, a price which could not compete with prices offered by local consumers in a year of extreme famine. Tin export also fell to 42 tons. Nothing else seems to have been exported in 1914.

As for Zaria Emirate, though BCGA agents came from Zungeru in 1910 specifically for buying cotton, up to 31st December of that year, they were able to get only 2,000 lbs of the item. The reason for their failure was that they were willing to pay only 1d per lb while local weavers from Kano and Zinder were willing to pay 1½d per lb.[70] This figure rose steeply to 346,316 lbs in 1911, and 2,823,608 lbs at a total cost of £11,768:0:0 in 1912.[71] Other products exported in small quantities were ginger, capsicum and bees-wax.[72] During 1913, the export "trade [went] ahead by leaps and bounds," and groundnut and hides were "the chief produce bought."[73] The hides amounted "to several hundred thousand in the course of the year." On the other hand, because of effective competition from local weavers, "it was a bad year for the BCGA," its annual purchase falling to 1,524,705 lbs.[74] At the same time, the firms put together made sales of European goods amounting to £8,000:0:0, while the Bank did "remarkably well," its monthly turnover amounting to £80,000, and its monthly profit £1,000. In the second quarter of 1914 "cash trade doubled that for the corresponding quarter in 1913 and [ran] into several thousand pounds monthly per firm."[75] Similarly, the produce trade showed "a varying increase of from 25% to 150%." In particular, there was "a very considerable increase" in the hides trade and competition among the European firms for that trade was very keen because of "the increased price ... offered in Europe." One trader alone, Messrs Ambrosini, "who [specialized] in hides informed [Assistant Resident] Porch that the average value per month of hides bought during the [previous] quarter by then (sic) was £3,267:0:0."[76] During the December quarter of 1914 hides were "railed from Zaria at 20 tons monthly."[77]

The Business Methods of the Firms

As indicated above, competition by local traders, as well as high demand in Europe for some of the products of the emirates, did combine to force prices of these products up. However, the firms did also "form a ring" to force prices down whenever farmers, in response to a good market in a given buying season, doubled efforts to produce more the following year.[78] We have already seen the firms do this when they temporarily eliminated competition among themselves and forced the price of groundnut from £10:0:0 per ton in 1913 to £4:10:0 per ton in 1914. But, apart from such collusion to lower the prices of local products, the European firms did also practice "a certain amount of fraud ... on native sellers by the use of incorrect scales,"[79] a practice which often forced local traders "to retaliate by treating skins with water or groundnut oil to increase the weight."[80] Yet, another way the firms defrauded local traders was to pay them in European goods rather than in money,[81] a practice which no doubt also helped further to undermine local industries and to make raw materials more available for export.

The Example of the Niger Company in Yola

Whereas Residents from other provinces for some reason did not give the issue of the business methods of the European firms a systematic treatment, the Residents in Yola did. What they had to say about the business methods of the Niger Company, which was the only company there throughout our period of study, is worth studying in some detail. Thus, complaints from Yola against the Company started to be made by the Residents as early as December 1902 when Resident Barclay reported that prices "to natives at the Company's store are so prohibitive as to render money practically valueless to them."[82] He said the Company's object was "to discourage cash sales and get barter goods which yield a higher profit, and up to quite recently the variety they would consent to sell for cash was extremely limited."This way "unsalable stock in Lokoja was foisted" on the people at Yola. He granted:

> it is business of course but hard on the native who is compelled to purchase something he doesn't want. In barter goods it is impossible for a man to tell whether he is getting full value for his things, especially in the case of ivory as the trader knows nothing about weights.

Barclay blamed the Company's conduct on the absence of competition. For, "at present everything is in the hands of the company and the monopoly posed by them is fatal to the development of the country." He pleaded that:

> under any circumstances monopolies are bad and repugnant to English views but when a young country is saddled from the outset with so serious an incubus in this respect as Northern Nigeria has to contend with, the results can only be disastrous to its interests and proper expansion.

Hence, he suggested that "a rival store or two would soon alter all this as a man would be able to judge by comparison whether he is getting his money's worth." He thought small traders "would meet the case better than large companies which could combine in maintaining the present position of affairs." Also "a native who is shy of going to a whiteman's store and receiving cavalier treatment could go to the small trader and haggle and bargain to his heart's content."[83] Lugard, however, ignored the substance of this complaint and his Political Assistant warned Barclay to "please stick to the circumstances of your Province and leave generalities to His Excellency."[84] Thus, to Lugard, what a British commercial company did to the indigenous population was none of the Resident's business even though the Resident was responsible for the safety of the personnel and property of that company.

Indeed, and probably this was not known to Barclay, Lugard had, as far back as 1900–1, made up his mind and very frankly confessed that the Niger Company's monopoly of trade in the emirates was highly desirable and must be supported by his administration. This decision preempted any possibility he might be sympathetic to complaints like those emanating from Barclay. Thus, in his report for the period 1st January 1900 to 31st March 1901, he observed that "much" had been said from time to time, by people who he did not mention, "regarding the absence of trade competition on the Niger."[85] Regarding these repeated calls for competition, he urged that it was "necessary to bear in mind the distinction between European competition (a) in the native markets, and (b) in the supply of necessaries to Government employees," namely soldiers, policemen, messengers, carriers and so on. With regard to competition in the "native markets", that is, for selling to and buying from the generality of the population of the emirates, Lugard had "only two observations to offer."[86] These were, first, that "the argument of those who hold that the policy of amalgamation of European interests in undeveloped countries is preferable to competition in the purchase of native produce deserves to be seriously considered."[87] Simply put, Lugard supported the formation of cartels and "rings" by European companies trading in the emirates, in order to remove competition among those companies and force down the prices of native produce to as low a level as possible. His grounds for supporting such a monopolistic practice were two. These were, first, to encourage the companies to trade by assuring them of maximum profit for their capital, and second, to force the local population both to produce plenty of raw materials and to take up low-paid jobs with the Europeans, by making their earnings from the sale of raw materials insufficient for them. He states this typically imperialist position as follows:

if fair dealing enterprise, and energy be assured, an amalgamation of European interests may prevent the undue enhancement of prices [of local produce] and enable the amalgamated trading corporations to set aside capital for extension and development [that is for the expansion of their businesses] which else would be absorbed in the struggle of competition. While the wants of natives in a primitive state remain few, enhancement of prices [for native produce] no doubt decreases supply, for the producers having acquired all the [European] goods they need will not exert themselves to tap the full resources of the land [for the benefit of the European companies]. For similar reasons it would have an adverse effect upon the supply of labour and would put (sic) up the price of the labour market; and (as I have pointed out), Government being the chief employer of labour (whether for public works, soldiers, or transport) is the principal sufferer, and progress is rendered most costly, and the cost of administration is greatly increased.[88]

Lugard's second reason for supporting monopoly was his alleged inability to get *British* firms to come out to the emirates and offer the Niger Company a competition. Thus, according to him:

in spite of the clamour that the Niger should be thrown open to trade competition, I am unable, after enquiry, to discover any British firms who are willing to enter the field under the principles of free trade without bias or discrimination. The country is now open to them to reap the supposed benefits for which they have for so long agitated, but none have come forward to introduce capital or competition, and so far as I can ascertain, those traders who desired to enter Northern Nigeria have coalesced with the Niger Company, or are debarred either by lack of capital or by pre-existing contracts from becoming rivals.[89]

In short, Lugard is here stating that his own inclination was fully supported by the actual practice of the companies, namely that of merging or buying out one another from agreed spheres, the emirates being the sphere of the Niger Company.[90]

However, when it came "to the question of competition by European firms in the supply of necessaries to Government employees" Lugard was a little willing to consider forcing the Niger Company to sell at "reasonable" prices. The reason was that since these employees were wholly dependent on their wages from the colonialist administration, Lugard could not avoid taking into account prices charged by the Company when fixing their wages. Hence, the less exorbitant the prices were in the case of these employees, the lower would be the wages he would pay them.[91] The prices paid by the native employees of Lugard were, in fact, a charge on his Treasury. Lugard was willing to concede that "no doubt in this field [i.e. as distinct from selling to and buying from the generality of the emirates' population], competition is highly desirable."

Yet, on the absence of cooperation from the all-powerful Niger Company Lugard was, it would seem quite reluctantly, "compelled to undertake the formation of a canteen for the supply of provisions to Europeans" and stressed that "had it in contemplation to import the barter goods necessary for the use of native soldiers in order to reduce prices."[92] In short, Lugard was reluctantly "contemplating" creating an enclave of "fair enterprise" to protect his staff and servants from the unbridled exploitation to which he willingly and insistently submitted the population of the emirates. However, his fundamental and deep-seated support for the unlimited economic power of the Niger Company in the emirates would not let him offer the Company even this mild challenge. Hence, he could not go beyond merely "contemplating" to "import the barter goods necessary for the use of native soldiers ..." He could not go beyond a mere contemplation of this mild alternative to such abject dependence on the company because, according to him, "such semi-commercial transactions are not the proper function of Government, and the Protectorate staff is insufficient to meet the extra work entailed."[93] Another reason for leaving even that mild project at the level of "contemplation" was that Lugard had:

> since learned with great satisfaction that the Directors of the company are willing to come to a satisfactory arrangement with me both on this matter and on the question of freights, which they have already tentatively reduced from 1st January last.

However, should they fail "to effect a thoroughly satisfactory arrangement on this question," Lugard saw "no reason why competition should not be introduced (if necessary assisted by Government) in this department of trade." But he would consider even this only if it could be done "without violation of the principles of fair trade", which it was his "object to maintain." Given that we have already seen him argue that "if fair dealing enterprise, and energy be assured, an amalgamation of European interests" under the leadership of the Niger Company must be supported, we should understand "non violation of the principles of fair trade" to mean the non-infringement of the Niger Company's monopoly of trade in the emirates. This is to say that Lugard was merely using a roundabout way of saying that, come what come might, he would take no steps to protect even his own Treasury from being looted by the Niger Company. And in a real sense he did not have to protect his Treasury from the company since he had the easier, and to him more attractive, alternative of making up for losses imposed on him by the company by doubling and trebling the rate of taxation on the emirates' population. Lugard might or might not have been a physical eunuch but he was certainly a political eunuch where the Niger Company was concerned.[94]

It was to a man of such a disposition towards the Niger Company that Barclay kept on repeating his complaints against the Company. Nor would Barclay allow himself to be discouraged by Lugard's "non possumus attitude", as can be seen in the fact that yet again in June 1904, he found it necessary to call the attention of Lugard to the activities of the Niger Company.[95] He used the occasion of reporting two cases in which the company prosecuted its agents in the Provincial Court to do this. Thus to him, and he hoped to Lugard also:

> the two cases in which the Niger Company appear are instructive in showing up the exceedingly lax manner in which their business is conducted and the methods adopted by the Company and its agents in dealing with [native] traders, and taken altogether the case against Campbell is one that the Company would have been well advised to keep out of Court.

When giving evidence in this case "the Benue District Agent, Mr. Langley, calmly informed the Court that it was the custom at all the Company's stores to deduct from 10% to 20% from the weight of traders' produce to allow for fare, dirt and shrinkage, and that he did not think this was robbing the traders, although in the case of gum the, produce is cleaned before it is weighed. As regards the fare, the weight could of course be exactly ascertained by the simple process of weighing the bags in which the produce is brought after they have been emptied, and I do not think the fare would be more than 3% at the outside." Barclay went on to point out that:

> what with juggling with the scales combined with underpayments to the traders by dishonest agents and clerks, the wonder is not that trade is dwindling and traders complaining, but that any produce is brought to the Company's store at all. It almost looks as if it might be necessary for Your Excellency to devise some means of ensuring the fair treatment of natives at the hands of European traders, but I fancy the disclosures made in Court will have some effect towards remedying the existing disgraceful state of affairs – at least it is to be hoped so.

To this report Lugard made no comment. Lugard no doubt did not forget what Barclay seems to have forgotten when he made this report, namely that creating conditions for unequal trade terms between its traders and native traders was one of the most sacred duties of a colonial regime, the British colonial regime in the emirates included. Hence, Barclay's hope that the disclosures made in his court would make the Company desist from its "disgraceful" activities was never realized as can be seen from the fact that in 1910 his successor, W.S. Sharpe, had to write and complain that:

> trade is not encouraged by the trading firm's paying for produce only in salt and cloth at fictitious prices. Consequently, the Nupe and Kakanda traders are gradually absorbing the trade, by exchanging cloth and salt at more reasonable prices, and by paying in cash. A bag of salt priced at 8/- in the Niger Company's store can now be bought in the market for 2/6d.[96]

Similarly, in December 1911, Acting Resident Elphistone felt that he "must mention again, as has been done so many times from this Province, and also from others, the small prices given by the only trading firm, the Niger Company. An increase in prices would, I am sure, result in a more than commensurate increase in trade. The small amount of cheap and worthless cloth given for shea nuts and gum must be seen to be believed."[97] He went on to say that:

> the practical refusal to pay for trade in cash, hampers the increase in trade which should be accruing annually. If only a fair value in cash was paid for produce the decrease in the direct profit would be more than compensated for by the increase in the total quantity. The people are only too willing to find some means to find cash. It is owing to the fact that the Niger Company have not tried to supply the demands that the trade in gum, shea and groundnuts is not a huge trade ... Although groundnuts are grown in huge quantities none are brought here at all.

This complain too drew no response from the then Governor, Hesketh Bell, who was obviously carrying on Lugard's tradition in that respect.

Yet, the indifference of headquarters would not silence the Residents at Yola. For, it would seem, they were under the pressure of complaints from local traders. Thus, Resident Sharpe again brought up the matter in March 1912 and reported that:

> after a good deal of discussion and several applications, the Niger Company now state their willingness to pay for produce in cash. But the native is not encouraged to demand cash, and says he is 'afraid to ask.' Also the Company do not always have sufficient cash in hand nor do they sufficiently study local fashions and wants.[98]

Table 10.1 shows the different prices that obtain in the canteen and the native market:

Table 10.1. Price Differences in the Canteen and Native Market

Goods	Company's Prices	Market Prices
Grey Baft	13/-	11/-
Bowls	6d	3d
Sugar (Packets)	9d	5d
Salt (Bag)	7/- to 8/-	5/- to 6/-
Blankets	3/6d	2/9d
Dyed Yarns	7/-	5/-

Sharpe's determination to place on record the activities of the Niger Company in his province was as great as the Governor's decision to ignore those reports. After a two-year silence Sharpe, in March 1914, again felt constrained to "draw attention ... to the subject of the Niger Company and trade and the abuses that are still extant."[99]

According to him:

The A.D.O at Numan (Mr James) reports a case of a trader taking a load of gum to the Niger Company's store at Numan.

Gross weight	56 lbs
Deduction for bags	2 lbs
Adultration	3 lbs
Nett weight	51 lbs

The payment for this was 20 'heads' as follows:
½ piece plain grey baft, 12½ heads, Market value 1/6d
1 rice dish, 4 heads, market value 6d
1 deep basin, 3 heads, market value 6d
1 zinc mirror, ½ head, market value 1d
Thus for a man's load of gum he was paid trade goods of local value 2/7d.

The Resident stated that "another case was reported to the ADO at Numan but the latter had been unable to trace the man who sold the produce." The informant stated that while in the Niger Company's store at Numan he overheard the clerk "tell a Bashima pagan that his load of rubber was worth 1/6d." The man said he had "to pay his tribute and asked for cash. The clerk refused, and gave him a small enamelled bowl, canteen value 9d, market value 6d." The man "took the bowl to the market, and then discovered he had been cheated. The ADO concluded that he was prepared to oppose the statement that the natives prefer kind to cash. As for [the claim of] these trumpery goods fulfilling a long felt want the low prices in the markets are a sufficient refutation."

Relations Between the Colonial Regime and the Firms

The relations between the colonial regime and the European firms in fact went beyond the negative one of the regime letting the firms do as they pleased. The regime did also take positive steps and undertook projects to assist the firms in exploiting the resources of the emirates. Among the projects the regime undertook or caused the Native Authorities to undertake in order to facilitate the activities of the firms were the construction of roads, railways and markets, and the dredging of rivers – all undertaken with forced labour. We have already seen these in an earlier chapter.[100] Others were the distribution of cotton seeds provided by the BCGA to peasants,[101] the setting up of experimental and model farms,[102] the use of taxation, including the Caravan Tolls, both to ruin local industries that competed with the European firms for markets and raw materials and to make the local population work for the companies in diverse ways.[103] Other ways were the arbitrary fixing of wages at low

18. The opening of Jebba Bridge in 1916 by Lord Lugard, Governor-General of Nigeria.

levels on the tin mines,[104] the arbitrary restriction of autonomous tin mining and smelting by the local populations of the tin areas,[105] and encouraging people, especially Native Administration officials, to open accounts with the Bank of British West Africa (BBWA), as well as depositing Native Treasury funds there.[106]

Impact of the Establishment of the Firms on the Emirates' Economy

The impact of the establishment of the European firms, their activities and the measures that the government took to support these companies, had many aspects. These aspects did not manifest themselves at the same time. Thus, famine immediately followed the imposition of British colonial domination, and was intensified by the growth in the export of cotton, groundnut, tin and so on;[107] thus partly indicating that labour was diverted from food production to the production of the export commodities, in the case of cotton both to meet the demands of local weavers and partially to meet the demands of the foreign companies. This was admitted by some of the Residents.[108] And whereas some local industrial activity, especially tin smelting and, to some extent, iron smelting, were drastically curtailed by direct government intervention,[109] some of the other industries, especially cloth-weaving, did survive substantially throughout our period. This was responsible for the fact that the European companies were, throughout this period, out-bidden by local weavers in the cotton market.[110] Following the partial collapse of native industry and the need to obtain British money to pay taxes, the European firms were able to pay labourers very low rates, often as low as 6d a day.[111] Similarly, not only did the goods in which traders engaged shift in favour of the European firms; that is, in favour of selling raw materials to the Europeans and buying finished products from them. It would also seem that the volume of trade generally declined and many markets collapsed, or at least shrank in size.[112]

Conclusion

We can conclude that the imposition of British taxation on the emirates in conjunction with the effects of the imposition of forced labour, the forced introduction of British currency, the extension of the Niger Company to the northern emirates, and the influx of new companies together with the "trading methods" of these companies, was destructive to local industry, agriculture and commerce. By the end of our period, local industry had been forced to halt its further development and growth, to mark time and to start playing a marginal role in the economy of the emirates, while the "export" of raw materials to British and other European markets was already becoming very substantial.[113] In short, by the end of our period, British fiscal policy and economic activity in their diverse forms had begun visibly to divest the economy of the emirates of what autonomy they had possessed prior to the imposition of British colonial domination, and to force a large segment of the population of the emirates to place itself utterly at the disposal of the British in their various organizations. However, we have also suggested that the fact that this process of completely emasculating and subordinating the economy of the emirates to that of Britain had only begun to be visibly effective. That it had not gone much further than that is a tribute to the resilience of the economy and a testimony to the relatively high degree of development it had attained before the onset of British imperialism generally and colonialism in particular.

19. Soldiers of the 3rd Nigerian Frontier Regiment of the Royal West African Force aboard the SS Accra, upon arrival in Plymouth, UK, 1937.

11

The Nature, Extent and Essence
of British Social Policy in the Emirates

Introduction

To start our discussion in this chapter on the nature and essence of British social policy after the imposition of colonial domination over the emirates, it is paramount for readers to bear in mind that colonial social policy in general is widely misunderstood and, perhaps, colonial policy on slavery remains the most misunderstood aspect of colonial social policy. The present chapter will critically examine these issues at length and will argue that what the British found in the emirates at the time of their invasion was a form of serfdom, not slavery. We shall then examine the claim that the British abolished what they misconceived to be slavery, and interrogate the paradox of whether British colonialism, which in itself was a form of slavery, was capable of actually abolishing slavery in a real sense. On the introduction of western education by the British, the chapter will argue that contrary to popular misconception, western education was indeed slow to spread in the emirates. We shall probe the reasons for this, with a view to establishing whether it was due to hostility or disinterest on the part of the people, or because the British themselves were not very enthusiastic. It is probable that in some of the emirates, there was reluctance and disinterest in western education, as it was the case with the Emir in Hadeija and the Sultan in Sokoto. However, Emir Muhammad Dikko in Katsina was positively disposed while commoners in Kano and Zaria were reported to be keen on sending their boys to school. Therefore, the question we shall address is: Why was it that the establishment of western schools in these and other emirates lagged behind the establishment of police and prisons, including prisons for lepers by many years, as we intend to demonstrate in the case of Sokoto, Yola, Zaria, Borno and Bauchi? Similarly, we will also explore the quality, funding, accessibility and problems of the schools established by the British, together with the fate suffered by Islamic education after the occupation of the emirates. Such an examination may help us unmask the true nature of the claimed commitment of the British to the spread of western education in the emirates.

In the latter part of this chapter, we will give an account of the outbreak of meningitis, smallpox and famine which killed a large number of people in the emirates, and the British response to these social catastrophes. Here, we shall be concerned with whether the British were prepared for, and effectively intervened in containing the epidemics, given that dispensaries were as rare as schools, while colonial policies in general were at variance with the promotion of the welfare of people. We shall argue that, as a result of poor British response, the emirates recorded unprecedented population decline through deaths and emigration. Finally, we will conclude the chapter by showing how the overall effect of the British policy on inter-communal relations kept the religious and linguistic communities of the emirates physically, culturally and psychologically apart.

The "Abolition" of Slavery

Perhaps, no facet of British colonialism in the emirates has been as misunderstood and distorted by historians, anthropologists, lawyers and administrators as that concerned with their social policies. Of these policies none has been more distorted and misunderstood than their policy on slavery. Thus, the general belief is that the emirates that the British subjugated had been slave-societies hitherto, and that the British did abolish that slavery.[1] We intend to raise some questions regarding the first assumption and then adduce evidence to show that the second assumption was at least an exaggeration if not outrightly false.

Regarding the first assumption, one would like to posit that so far the issue of slavery and the much larger issue of the relations of production and class struggle, have received a very inadequate and incidental treatment in Nigerian historiography, with the consequence that our understanding of Nigerian history at its various stages has been superficial and partial.[2] Instead of paying the necessary attention to the relations of production and to the issues of classes and class struggle, the predominant tendency has so far been to focus attention on tribal and religious groups and the struggles between them, not as expressions of a more fundamental social commotion or as the complicating factors that they were, but as the very driving force of Nigerian and related societies.

With specific reference to slavery, the result of this neglect is that we lack a comprehensive picture of the forms that slavery took in Nigeria and the phases it passed through. We are as well not in a position to say definitively whether slave production was ever the dominant mode of production in Nigeria; and, if so, whether by the turn of the twentieth century, slave production was still the dominant mode of production in our societies, especially in the emirates – in which case these societies were still slave societies, nor whether by this time slave production had yielded the primary position to production by serfs or a tribute-paying peasantry, in which case the society had become mainly feudal, with remnants of slavery.[3]

However, if it is granted that the difference between slavery and serfdom, and indeed the difference between slavery and wage labour, is relative rather than absolute, legal rather than actual, and if it is granted that the categories slavery, serfdom, feudalism, capitalism, wage labourer are valid categories for analyzing European and Asiatic societies, then it should also be granted that all of them, rather than just slavery, are valid for analyzing African societies, unless, of course, it is being contended that the difference between Africa, on the one hand, and Europe and Asia, on the other, was absolute rather than relative. It should also further be conceded that settling the issue of whether Africa at the turn of twentieth century had a slave or a feudal society on an *a priori* basis – that is, on the basis of assumptions rather than on concrete investigation and analysis – is indefensible. Similarly, one will posit that in the rush to conclude that Africa was a slave society until its subjugation to European colonialism, the concrete conditions of "slavery," that is, the rights and obligations of "slaves" in that society at the time just before the imposition of colonial domination, has not been given much attention. Hence, one looks in vain in the bulk of the literature for such crucial information as to whether "slaves" had any right regarding sale, marriage, inheritance, manumission, self-redemption, free-days during which to work for themselves, a share in products, questions the answers to which are indispensable to determining whether a class was slave or serf.[4] In short, the term "slave" has been so indiscriminately applied to Nigerian and African groups that the term has lost meaning when applied to these societies. It is in this imprecise and very malleable sense that the term *slave* should be understood when a claim is made that the British "liberated" slaves in the emirates.

As for the second assumption, namely that the British actually liberated slaves in the emirates, one would like first to posit that such a liberation would have been a veritable paradox, given that colonialism, by its very nature, was a form of slavery imposed on the colonized society as a whole, and then to point out that in fact the British never enacted a law to that effect. The most radical law the British enacted stipulated that no one who was born on or after 1st April 1901 could be regarded as a slave.[5] This stipulation did not include people born before that date, including those born on 31st March 1901. With regard to "slaves" born before 1st April 1901, they remained legally slaves albeit the proclamation granted the slaves "rights", some of which they had enjoyed prior to the imposition of British colonial domination.[6] One thing which the British undeniably did was to outlaw the capture of fresh slaves and the sale of slaves and captives. In fact, so serious did the British take this prohibition and so promptly did they deal with those contravening it, that many innocent persons had been framed up by unscrupulous rivals in British service and falsely convicted in British courts for the offence.[7] The issue as to why the British were so vigorous in stamping out domestic slave trade need not be discussed, partly because it has been adequately covered by the discussion on why the British turned against the trans-Atlantic slave trade a century earlier, and partly because to the extent that the issue is not settled by that discussion, it is metaphysical.[8]

Apart from what the British Proclamation on slavery said or did not say, we have other evidence that the "slavery" that the British found in the emirates continued, often enough with open British support.[9] To start with, we have seen in the fifth chapter of this book that both slaves and slave-owners did go to court throughout our period claiming ownership of a slave or freedom as the case might be. Other examples are that in June 1902, Resident Barclay was reporting to Lugard that "owing to the serf system," the aristocracy in Yola was getting its "farms worked for nothing" and had "no occasion to work for a living."[10] This was thirty months after the promulgation of the Proclamation that is now often assumed to have outlawed slavery, and sixteen months after the British had occupied Yola and imposed their domination on it. Lest it be assumed that Barclay meant serfdom as distinct from slavery, it should be pointed out that he did go on to predict that "the gradual extinction of these serfs through freedom and natural causes [i.e. in accordance with the 1900 Proclamation] will settle the question." After this, he predicted there would be a "general uprising" of the aristocracy "or they will adopt the inevitable and fall into line with the rest of the people."[11] Clearly, in using the term *serfdom*, Barclay was merely being "careless" with his terminology rather than trying to imply that what existed in Yola was serfdom rather than slavery in the classical senses of the two terms. Similarly, in 1906 Resident Howard reported the existence of outright "slave-dealing" in the chiefdom of Ningi in Bauchi Province;[12] and though its existence was "due to scarcity of food among the Warji," this was only "partly" so. The following year, when listing complaints against Shehu, Sarkin Tambawal, Resident Temple included some charges that this chief "had held runaway slaves to ransom,"[13] a complaint which no one would dare lodge with the Resident if slavery had lost its legal status. Much more revealing in 1907, Resident Fremantle in Yola, in commending the assessment of individuals for tax payment, an assessment in accordance with which slaves too paid tax, pointed out that "if slaves [had] to come to their masters to obtain the wherewithal for payment it [might] serve to keep the latter's hold on them." He added that "too great independence [was] not to be encouraged at the present state."[14]

That the British, far from leading a crusade for the liberation of slaves, might actually have been trailing behind the indigenous society and waging a rearguard action against such liberation can be seen from the "interesting case" which Resident Barclay reported from Yola in 1909. It was a case "in which a slave named Abarshi was voluntarily freed by his master as a reward for good services performed."[15] In our view, the fact that this was "the first instance of the voluntary freeing of a slave by a Yola Fulani that [had] yet come to [the Resident's] notice" simply indicates that much happened in Yola and elsewhere in the emirates which the Residents, much as they were in charge in the emirates, did not know, people not being keen to let them know, and their own espionage system being much less than omniscient. So much did the British accept the legal status of slavery and so slow were "slaves" in availing themselves of the Slavery Proclamation that in 1911 Assistant Resident Brackenbury was still pointing out that, except for Namtari town, the villages of Namtari District were "mere farm hamlets inhabited by Fulani slaves of mixed race whose owners live in Yola or Namtari."[16] As late as 1917, an Assistant District Officer was officially recording that there were "2062 slaves amongst the population" of Balala District of Adamawa.[17] It is significant from the point of view of the charge we made above that the British colonialists, historians and anthropologists used the term "slave" loosely. The Officer went on to record that some of these slaves were owned by local residents while others were owned by masters living at Yola and that generally the slaves lived in hamlets by themselves "on the land they till," and "the terms on which locally owned slaves work[ed] 5 days a week from 8 am to 2 pm, Thursdays and Fridays being at the disposal of the slave," while "few [had] to work 6 days a week having only Friday to themselves." On the other hand:

> slaves whose masters [were] in Yola [had] much less onerous terms. Males [had] to give 10 and female 5 baskets of [guinea corn] to their owners per annum. This [was] the maximum and if the harvest should be a bad one the number of baskets [was] either considerably reduced or not demanded at all. Anything a slave [could] farm above this quota he [kept] for himself.

On top of this, some "slaves" had their taxes to the British paid for them by their masters, yet others only partially, while some paid the whole of their own taxes. This information clearly suggests that what the British found in existence in the emirates was more of serfdom than slavery in the classical sense.[18]

Yet, another evidence that the British, on the whole, gave legal sanction to this system — slavery or serfdom — is the fact that the Officer in this same Assessment Report complained that "the conduct of the slaves in many cases [was] causing great dissatisfaction. Many [would] not do a fair day's work at all," "a fair day's work" here clearly being in terms of the "slave" owner's assessment. The Officer then went on to report that "at Solomsi one slave owner asked [him] to see his slaves and order them to work as they refused to do any." So much had slave owners realized that when all was said and done, the British were on their side against the slaves. Far from being pleased as one would expect a liberator to be that the objects of his liberation were stirring themselves, the Officer advised the slave owner to "apply to the Native Court."[19] In case anyone prefers to believe that given the existence of the Proclamations, this could be a "neutral" advice, it should be pointed out that the Officer added that he was told that: "those who refus[ed] to work ... [were] generally strong men in the prime of life. They [spent] their time roaming round the countryside and [he believed were] mainly responsible for the robberies reported on the roads."[20]

Thus, we can conclude that whatever the British found in existence in the emirates — slavery in their view, serfdom in mine — they did not abolish it, contrary to the assumption of many scholars. What the British did was to outlaw, and exert themselves to suppress, slave trade as distinct from slavery, to incorporate into their own laws the right to self-redemption, a right which had been there before their advent, and to uphold the right of masters over "slaves" born before 1st January 1901 who had not for one reason or another secured manumission. In a very real sense, the British did more than uphold the right of masters over slaves; they enslaved the entire society except a tiny minority of "native rulers" whom they employed as foremen. This enslavement of the entire society they realized through the imposition known as forced labour, which we have dealt with in an earlier chapter.[21]

The Introduction of Western Education

Another aspect of British social policy in the emirates which needs to be put in proper context is that of western education. As of now, there is a general agreement that western education — the issue of its aims and content apart[22] — was slow in spreading in the emirates. However, this growth is seen mainly in terms of the pace of its spread in southern Nigeria, where this pace is said to have been rapid – in relation to the pace in the emirates. Thus we are caught in a vicious circle. We intend to break out of this circle by comparing the pace of expansion of western education in the emirates not so much with its pace in southern Nigeria as with the pace of expansion of other aspects of social life both positive and negative. This specifically refers to the rate of expansion of medical services, police and prisons in the emirates.

To start with the introduction and expansion of western education, the earliest attempt to start a British school one has come across was that made by Resident Barclay at Yola in July 1902, ten months after the occupation of the town.[23] According to him, this attempt failed, partly because of objections from the Qadi, Hamman Joda, an objection the grounds of which we shall take up later in this chapter. Another reason this early attempt failed was that there was "a difficulty" in finding "suitable men for the purpose, the difficulty being that they themselves would first have to master the Fulani Language."[24] In the meantime, there were "no Evangelical or other Missions in Yola yet," and Barclay pleaded with Lugard to "veto the advent of any for some time to come." Barclay recalled reading "of some misguided fanatic who proposed forcing Christianity upon these people in the same way that Mohammadanism [was] said to have been forced upon them." He warned that "any attempt at proselytisation just now in Yola would be premature, ill-advised, create suspicions to our bona fides and possibly be fraught with grave political danger." He advised that if any missionary was yearning for:

> distinction and a possible martyr's crown they might be allowed to display their zeal among the ... pagans in the northern parts of the Province, though it [was] possible [the British] should have to kill a number of the unfortunate savages as a direct result of their efforts.[25]

In short, Barclay was not ready to start a school in Yola and was unwilling to allow in missionaries because he felt – quite rightly as we shall see below – that the missionaries were not so much going to educate the people as to seek to convert them to Christianity. Lugard for his part merely expressed his pleasure at Barclay's "effort to start a school at Yola" and informed him that an "ARC mission [was going] to Ibi but none [was] going to Yola."[26]

The British did absolutely nothing further about introducing western education into Adamawa Emirate until December 1911, ten years after the occupation. Even then, it was only to send three mallams to Nassarawa in Kano to learn reading, writing and accounting in the western style.[27] No boys were sent to the school because, according to Resident Elphinstone, there were "no boys

in the Emirs family of sufficient age to proceed to Kano for education," an excuse which is an indication of the restricted and conservative purposes of western education in the emirates. Nor indeed was the sending of the three mallams
such a big "step forward among the Adamawa conservative Fulani," that Elphinstone claimed it was. For, all the three mallams[28] had been taken from what
was then the most famous Islamic school in Adamawa, the school of Modibbo
Murtala b. Raji at Girei.[29] All were in their mid-twenties[30] and very advanced in
their Islamic education.[31] Hence, for the three of them going to Kano to learn
reading and writing in the Roman alphabet as well as elementary accounting
was at most a vertical jump. At any rate, up to December 1911, these mallams
remained the only indigenes of Adamawa in a western school. When, at the
end of the year, the Resident offered "to persuade the leading Native Heads
to send their boys"[32] to Nassarawa, the Governor informed him that the "Nassarawa school [was] too full ... to accept more pupils."[33] This clearly shows that
even if the people of the emirates were very keen about western schools, the
British would not have provided those schools. It was when the three mallams
returned to Yola early in 1912 that the Resident set about looking for others
to take "their places" at Nassarawa.[34] And it is revealing about the priorities of
the British that, instead of opening a school for these mallams to teach in, the
Resident put them to work in the Native Treasury and Native Court.[35]

However, the year 1912 did end up being an important one for the introduction of western education into Adamawa. For one thing, the Resident finally
sent not three but ten mallams to "Nassarawa. For another, a "model school"
was started in Jimeta, Yola's equivalent of the Sabon Gari;[36] but the establishment of this so-called "model school," turned out to be a false start. For,
towards the end of 1913, it was "withdrawn," quite significantly not because
pupils were lacking, not because there were no instructors, but on the ground
that "no provision for its continuation was allowed in the estimates."[37] Given
the fact that the Native Treasury and its estimates were controlled by the Resident, this was equivalent to saying that the Resident had decided to abolish this
"model school;" and, given that at this time the Native Treasury, like all the
Native Treasuries, were generating annual surpluses, it should further be accepted that the Resident refused to provide for even this single school, not on
financial grounds but on other grounds. The following year 1914, eight other
mallams were sent to Bida for training.[38] Indeed, until the end of the period
under study, the emirate remained without a single western school. The whole
province which, apart from the emirate was made up only of Numan, had only
the small SUM school at Numan, with its very limited and religious purpose.
In fact, it was not until 1920 that the so-called Provincial School was opened at

Yola – with nineteen pupils.[39] But that was a development outside our period. The establishment of this school took place relatively late in the colonial period, eighteen years after the British occupation of Yola.

If we next turn to Zaria Emirate, we shall find out that CMS missionaries arrived there almost at the same time as the force that occupied Zaria in 1902.[40] The mission station, however, remained at Girku, about forty miles from Zaria, until 1905 when it was moved to Zaria City, and established at a place "not far from the Emir's palace."[41] At Zaria, Dr. Miller, the man in charge of the station was, by 1906, "superintend[ing] a small school and [keeping] a dispensary,"[42] no doubt as a means of attracting the "natives" so as to be able to convert them to Christianity. This same year when the CMS opened another station at Kuta, which at that time, was in Zaria Province though not in the emirate.[43] However, it would seem that at least part of the reason for opening this station was that of making money by taking advantage of the labour of the Gwari. Thus, the CMS intended "to make it in part an Industrial Mission," while gathering information on "the customs and language of the Gwari tribe." This knowledge, the Resident predicted, would "be of much use" to the colonial regime – "the Protectorate at large" as he put it.[44] By 1910, Dr. Miller had changed the curriculum in his small school from a "secular" one "to one of active proselytisation".[45] The colonial regime, which had up to now established no school of its own in Zaria, either directly or through the Native Authority, quite correctly decided that "the scope of the school [had] become much narrowed and [that] the establishment of a Government school outside the clash of creeds [was] much to be desired."[46] However, while expressing this opinion, the Resident did nothing except warning: "the parents of the scholars who [attended] the school ... that the open encouragement of the government [had] given place to benevolent toleration and that the responsibility for any conversions to Christianity [became] theirs."[47]

The regime failed to open a secular school in spite of the fact that with the shift of Reverend Miller's priorities from providing education to winning adherents only "a few town boys ... [continued] to attend the school."[48] In the meantime, by 1912, it would seem that the proselytisation activities of the CMS had started paying dividends for the Mission and causing division and conflicts within the local community. In his speech on one of the Sallah days in that year, the Emir of Zaria did say, among other things:

> [L]et everyone watch his ways [and] let no one follow another's way; let everyone follow his religion; he who has left his [former] religion will not be forced to return to it, he who is [still] on his [original] one will not be taken out of it by force.[49]

This reassurance indicates that there had been some loose talk to the effect that force would be used either to convert people from Islam to Christianity or to retain within Islam those who wished to abandon it in favour of Christianity. One year later, on the occasion of Eid-El-Fitr, which fell on 2 September 1913, the Emir once again found it necessary to reassure the populace, which was still obviously undergoing a social upheaval. Thus, he advised:

> [E]veryone to attend to his business, everyone to his religion. He who is a follower in the steps of the Prophet will not be forced to leave the path, nor shall one who has left the path be forced to return; to everyone his religion.[50]

Meanwhile, it was not until 1913, twelve years after the British had imposed their domination on Zaria that "a building [was] being created for a Provincial School on the lines of Nassarawa."[51] This school was started under a British official at the beginning of 1914 and was "formally opened" by the Resident and the "Director of Education" on May 8 that year.[52] By June 1914, the school had 64 pupils "of which 36 were boys from Zaria, the remainder having been transferred from [the] Nassarawa school." Thus, it would seem that this "Provincial School" was after all not provincial but regional. Otherwise, the distinction between "Zaria boys" and those "transferred from the Nassarawa school" would have been needless. This number dwindled to 39 by the end of 1914, and this time they came from three provinces, namely Zaria itself, Kontagora and the Central Province.[53] This situation, in which Zaria shared one small "government" school with two other provinces while having two small mission schools in the city and at Gimi, whose interest lay exclusively in proselytisation, was what obtained in Zaria at the close of our period.[54]

In Bauchi Province, there was no western school of any description up to 1906, in which year either the SUM or the SIM – the Resident simply refers to them as the Sudan Mission – opened a station at Kanna, which was regarded by the British as an "independent chieftaincy," that is, not under any emirate.[55] However, the establishment of this station was far from meaning the introduction of western education to Kanna. The man who opened the station, a certain Mr. Burt, by "ordering work to be done [for him] for which no actual payment was made," and by "demanding the Sarkin Kanna's horse as a dash, and making an inadequate return" dash, antagonized the people of Kanna, who told the Sarki that if he agreed to let the missionaries stay "they would leave."[56] The people of Kanna having been antagonized by the missionaries, the latter could render no service, educational, medical or religious, even if they tried to. The Resident recommended to the High Commissioner that the missionaries "could not do much harm at Bukuru and might do good,"[57] which is to say that he supported their expulsion from Kanna. Meanwhile, the Emir of Bauchi went out of his way to express his fear that the British might allow missionaries to settle in his emirate, in the same way that they had been allowed to settle in Wase, which was no longer in Bauchi Emirate or indeed Bauchi Province but in Muri Province.[58] So alarmed were the chiefs in Bauchi about the prospects of missionaries being allowed into the emirate that the Resident cautioned the High Commissioner that "if they [did] ever come to [that] Emirate it would be advisable to increase the military force in order to protect them."[59]

However, in the province as a whole, by December 1908, there were an SUM Mission at Bukuru and a CMS Mission at Panyam, both very well outside Bauchi Emirate.[60] It is not clear, however, whether the SUM Mission at Bukuru was in fact the same one that the missionaries had tried to establish at Kanna. One is inclined to believe so because there was no mention in the Resident's report of any other mission station in Bauchi Province apart from these two. By this time, however, the missions were engaged in some educational work, and the one at Panyam especially "impressed [the Resident] favourably." But it is not clear who they were teaching what. The Resident simply reported that they were "alive to the desirability of encouraging the use of Hausa as a lingua franca and [were] not attempting the premature teaching of English."[61]

By 1911, Bauchi was sending boys to the Nassarawa school at Kano and to the "Provincial" school at Zaria.[62] In 1914, for example, Bauchi Emirate and the several "independent" chieftaincies that, together with the emirate, formed Bauchi Division, had nine boys at Zaria. Gombe Division, which was almost conterminous with Gombe Emirate, had four boys, while the "independent" chieftaincies making up the Naraguta Division had two boys, making a total of 15 boys from Bauchi at Zaria.[63] It was very unlikely that the boys from Bauchi attending the Nassarawa school were as many as 15. The school was more prestigious than the Zaria school, more selective and serving all the emirates rather than a number of them, as in the case of the Zaria school. Hence, in 1914, thirteen years after British occupation, the Province of Bauchi, made up of two large emirates, Bauchi and Gombe, and a large number of "independent" chieftaincies, a province which was so large as to be split into two later, not only did not have a single "government" school, but also had fewer than a total of 30 boys attending elementary schools outside the province.[64] It was only in the following year, 1915, that an "intention" was made to open a school in Bauchi. But this "intention" was "frustrated by the impossibility of the Education Department being able to spare an officer."[65] The lameness of this excuse can be seen in the fact that it did not really need a British officer to start what, in fact, was an elementary school. At any rate, one of the District Officers working under the

Resident could have been told to supervise such a school in addition to his main "duties," viz taxation, taking out "pacification" expeditions, and being a magistrate. That the "intention" to open the school could be dropped for lack of a special "officer," and the "officer" was lacking while administrative and military officers were not lacking, should be accepted as evidence of a lack of will on the part of the British to start the school. In short, throughout the period under study, Bauchi Province did not have a single government school.

Sokoto was luckier than its emirates because Resident Burdon opened a class for boys there as early as April 1905,[66] just two years after the occupation of the town. It was a very small class which, in June 1906, had only eight boys in attendance, six of them sons of Native Authority officials, residing in Sokoto town; the two others sons were of a District chief within the Sultanate. That is to say, the class was almost exclusively for boys from Sokoto town. By 1st January 1907, the school had thirty one pupils, of which 29 came from the Sultanate, while two came from Argungu.[67] At the same time, a "school" for adult mallams was started with four mallams in attendance.[68] Then, in October 1909, Hans Vischer visited Sokoto and recruited 6 mallams for the Nassarawa School.[69] These mallams were known to be "of good intelligence" and were said to be of "good standing." Hence, in all probability, they would have little to learn in Kano. Next, the British opened a class of 8 boys specifically for training "taki" surveyors to help with tax assessment. This was in the September quarter of 1911.[70] By December 1911, the class had 12 "young mallamai."[71] In 1917, another school was opened at Birnin Kebbi, making the number in the province two, the survey class apparently having lapsed by now.[72]

Thus, up to 1917, that is 14 years after the British occupation of Sokoto, Gwandu and Argungu, the three emirates shared two elementary schools. There is no doubt that, in comparison to other emirates such as Bauchi, Yola and Zaria, the Sultanate of Sokoto can be said to have been lucky. But, in absolute terms and in comparison to the proliferation of such negative institutions as prisons, police, warders, tax collectors, British performance in introducing western education into these three emirates, the Sultanate included, was abysmally poor.

Turning to the Sheikhdom of Borno for another example, we shall find that it was not until the end of 1907 that Resident Hewby proposed to open a class for boys. The Governor approved this proposal, asking them to work together with Hans Vischer, who had already been detailed "to begin secular education" and was about to go on a visit to Cyprus and the Sudan to gain some insight into his new assignment.[73] Yet, no school was reported opened in 1908.[74] Even in 1909, the Resident merely reported that four mallams from the Sheikhdom had been sent to the Nassarawa School and that on their return a school would be opened in Borno.[75] In 1910 also, "no steps towards education [had] yet been taken beyond sending mallams to Kano."[76] In 1912, all the Resident could report was that there were nine sons of chiefs, six "pupil teachers" and "14 others" learning and teaching crafts at Nassarawa; and that of the 9 sons of chiefs, three were from Bedde, Fika, and Biu.[77] In 1913, the Resident categorically reported that "no local school had yet been started but [that] 8 boys and 6 mallamai [had] attended Nassarawa during the year."[78] In fairness to the Resident, it should be recorded that he went on to point out that:

> the advantages of education at Kano [were] appreciated by the Shehu and chiefs, but they [did] not like the long absence of the boys caused by the consumption of more than twenty days each way, over forty days in all, in travelling to and from Kano.[79]

We may take this as his timid way of advising the Governor that a school should be opened in Borno. But it might well have been sheer information on the attitude of Borno's native rulers towards western education. In any case, at the end of 1914, a "Junior Superintendant of Education arrived [in Maiduguri] and a start was at once made on the buildings required for the Provincial School."[80] In the meantime, "temporary buildings were also put up in which a beginning could be made,"[81] and "class began on 14th January 1915, the original pupils being those who had previously been to school at Nassarawa."[82] Thus, Borno got its first western school,[83] after a period of 12 years, 11 months of British occupation.

If we take Kano as yet another example, we shall find that it was only in 1907 that Assistant Resident Hans Vischer, then in Borno, was detailed to "begin secular education."[84] But even then, there was no guarantee that whatever school the British might decide to open as a result of this visit which, it was proposed, Vischer should pay to Cyprus and the Sudan, would be sited in Kano,[85] though in fact it was sited there, opening in September 1909 with adult mallams.[86] However, as we have already seen, this school served all the emirates and not just Kano Province. Then, in 1913, a "Provincial School" was opened in Katsina, which was then in Kano Province.[87] As a result, pupils from Katsina who were formerly attending the Nassarawa "primary school, were repatriated to Katsina to form the foundation boys."[88] In the same year, what later came to be known as the Kano Survey School was started on a more formal basis[89] when 18 of the *taki mallams* working under the Kano Native Administration "were handed over to the Survey Instructor for instruction in cadastral surveying."[90] In 1915 a "Kano Emirate Provincial School" was opened on a different site from

the Nassarawa School which, from that year, became an "Industrial School."[91]
This brought to four the total number of schools in Kano Province viz:[92]

i)   The Kano Emirate Provincial School
ii)   The Katsina Emirate Provincial School
iii) The Kano Industrial School and
iv) The Survey School

Thus, we can conclude that Kano Province, which included nine emirates,[93] got only four western schools in the period under study at the tail end of that period. Taking all the emirates together, we can conclude that until the end of our period, most of them did not have a single western school located in them by the year 1915, and the few that had one or two western schools had to share these – all of them elementary schools – with several other emirates.

Police, Prisons, etc.

In order to bring out the sharp contrast between the British attitude towards the education of the "natives" of the emirates and their attitude towards imposing their imperialist "law and order", we shall next briefly examine what the British did within our period of study in establishing prisons and police forces in the emirates.[94] We shall then go on to examine other aspects of British educational policy in the emirates. An objection that is likely to be raised to this approach is that the establishment of a police force and the setting up of prisons predated the imposition of British colonial domination over the emirates. This is granted.[95] Yet the approach we have adopted here is valid and legitimate on two grounds. In the first place, just as there had been police forces, the *dogarai* and prisons, the *gidajen yari*, in all the emirates, so also had there been schools (*makarantun allo*) and higher schools (*makarantun ilimi*) in the emirates. Hence, the mere fact that police forces and prisons had been in existence prior to the imposition of British rule cannot be the reason for taking over and retaining them. If that was the case, why did the British not take over the schools and higher schools, adapting them if necessary to suit their colonialist and imperialist purposes, instead of letting them survive or perish on their own? Indeed, far from merely taking over and retaining these two and other negative institutions of the pre-existing system, all indications are that the British would have founded them if they had found none in existence. Second, our approach is legitimate in that even though police forces and prisons had been in existence, the British not merely retained but also transformed them, if not out of recognition at least very substantially, through increasing both their number and their efficiency.

Thus, as far as numbers were concerned, it should be pointed out that in every Provincial Headquarters, the British Provincial Administration built a jail within the first year of occupying that province.[96] In fact, in some provinces, the British built not one but several "Provincial Jails." Thus, in Kano Province, they built them at Kano, Katsina and Hadeija; in Borno they built three at Maiduguri, Geidam and Monguno, while, in Bauchi, there were provincial prisons at Bauchi, Naraguta and Nafada.[97] These were in addition to the Native Authority prisons that assumed the character of distinct state institutions soon after British occupation. Similarly, with the creation of homologous districts, a jail house or a 'lock up" was built in each.[98] In fact, the British even built prisons for lepers – prisons as distinct from leper settlements.[99] Given that by 1910, there were altogether hundreds of homologous districts in the emirates, it follows that there were hundreds of prisons and lock ups in these emirates by 1910, during which period there were at most five elementary schools in all the emirates put together. Nor were these jails kept empty.

The Provincial Prisons to which only those sentenced in the Provincial Courts were sent and, for that reason, contained fewer inmates than the Native Authority Prisons, each contained a daily, quarterly and yearly averages of inmates that ranged from 15.3 for Zaria in 1904; 21.33 for Sokoto in 1907; 21.33 for Sokoto in 1908, 28.0 for Sokoto in 1911; 28.82 for Zaria in 1910; 40 for Zaria in 1913; 44.9 for Zaria in 1914; 54 for Bauchi in 1910; up to 100 for Kano in 1916.[100] Both absolutely and in comparison with the figures for the inmates of the Provincial Jails which, judging from the above figures, almost unfailing kept on rising for individual Provinces as the years passed and Nigeria "developed" as a British colony, the figures for the Emirate and District prisons were scandalously high. Thus, for example, in 1913, the Zaria emirate Native Authority Jail contained 99 prisoners "throughout the year,"[101] while there were 145 inmates on 1st January 1914 and 159 on 30th June 1914 in that jail.[102] The figure for 1st December 1914 was also 159.[103] In Kano Province, the figures on 31st December 1913, for example, were:[104]

Kano Emirate Prison – 261
Kano Emirate District Prisons – 166
Katagum, Missau and Jama'are Emirate Prisons – 102
Daura and Kazaure Emirate Prisons – 84.

The corresponding figures for 31st December 1914 were 195, 199, 139, 56 and 66.[105] In addition, there was, in 1914, a total of 272 deaths in these Native Authority prisons, spread throughout the four quarters of the year.[106] In

Sokoto, the Sultanate Native Authority Jail had a yearly average of 74 inmates for 1912,[107] while for 1913 the average was 120.[108]

As far as policing the emirates was concerned, it should be pointed out that although the British did not count soldiers among their police, this omission was merely formal. In actual fact, the soldiers, in addition to their various "pacification" expeditions, also did what, in normal colonial parlance, was referred to as "police work." These included guarding prisoners, patrolling the GRAs at night, providing escort to travelling colonial officials, and they carried their arms while performing these police functions. Soldiers performed these police duties almost up to the end of our period of study by which time the native *dogari* forces had been sufficiently "reorganized" to take over these functions from the soldiers and, in some provinces, even from the government constabulary force.[109] One of the consequences of this involvement of soldiers in "police work" was that suspects and prisoners were often shot and killed while attempting to escape.[110] However, the point being made here is that the figures that the British quoted as constituting their constabulary force and the Native Authority *dogarai,* while high, especially when compared to the number of teachers, which for most emirates was zero, and nowhere was up to ten, were nonetheless false figures, in that they excluded soldiers. As for these false figures, they include 86 government constables in Zaria in 1914,[111] 122 government constables in Borno in 1906,[112] 100 organized and salaried Native Administration *dogarai* for Zaria in 1913,[113] and143 *dogarai* for Bauchi Emirate [328 for the whole Province] in 1915.[114] The Sheikhdom of Borno, for its part, had 203 *dogarai*, including 95 mounted, in 1912.[115]

It should also be pointed out that these constables and *dogarai* were far from model men. Thus, at one point, a British Resident found it necessary to complain that it was difficult to recruit "the class of man required" into the force and that it had "often been necessary" to employ men "on regular duty" before they had been "sufficiently trained or received sufficient instruction in discipline."[116] Hence, "they were apt to make use of their position to extort from the people." In fact, "the experiment of sending even picked men to protect villages from the acts of returning carriers [had] proved anything but a success.[117] These complaints which, as it were, came from the horse's own mouth, were repeated throughout our period of study.

The Cost of the Introduction of Western Education

We now return to the introduction and spread of western education. It should be pointed out that its total cost, except for the salaries of the British Education Officers, was paid, for not out of the British share of the taxes, but out of the "Native Share" of these taxes.[118] Another source of funds for the schools was the fees that the British charged the parents of the pupils,[119] a measure which, given the newness of western education and the understandable suspicion in which its introduction was held, seems to have been a calculated attempt to sabotage its acceptance. Although when looked at from the point of view of what we regard as the cardinal point in British educational policy in the emirates, namely that of imparting some western literacy to the aristocratic class, to the exclusion of the commoner classes, the imposition of fees was perfectly logical. It was definitely bound further to discourage artisans and the peasantry from sending their children to school, though to a large extent, the issue of whether it actually did so or not must remain hypothetical, since, at any rate, only a few places were available in the schools, just enough to be filled by the sons of those sections of the aristocracy who, for various reasons, were willing both to send their sons to school and could afford to pay the fees.

Since western education was new in the emirates, and since before they could teach, those who were to teach in the first schools had themselves to be taught, the issue of how the first teachers were obtained becomes as interesting as the largely metaphysical question of which came first – the chicken or the egg. In answer to this question it should be pointed out that the first teachers were in fact either the Residents and Assistant Residents themselves, or clerks from southern and western Africa working in the Provincial Offices.[120] Later, European officers specifically recruited for the purposes of teaching, took the place of the Residents both as directors and teachers in these schools while some of the products of the schools were retained as "native teachers" and others sent to the Native Treasuries, Native Courts, etc.[121] Not that the numbers of these teachers were large. In fact, while in proportion to the numbers of pupils, the numbers of teachers were large, in comparison to Assistant Residents, the numbers of British school officers were tiny, and in comparison to tax collectors or policemen, the numbers of "native mallams" were very insignificant up to the very end of our period. Thus, for example, in 1914 Zaria Province had one Government Elementary School with two British Education Officers, Mr. Oakes and Mr. Walker, and six native teachers, products of Nassarawa,[122] while Bornu Province had one elementary school staffed by one British Education Officer, a certain Mr. Worseley, and five natives, also products of Nassarawa.[123]

The Attitude of the People of the Emirates Towards Western Education

If we next turn to the issue of the attitude of the Emirs and the people of the emirates towards the introduction of western education, one would first suggest that the issue is not very important. This is because the views, feelings and attitudes of both the Emirs and the people were seldom ever accorded more than a casual attention by the British. Suffice it to be pointed out that the attitude of the rulers, especially of the population towards the imposition of British taxation and of forced labour, to cite just two British measures, was downright hostile. Yet, this hostility did not stop the British from going ahead and imposing these measures essential to their colonial domination over the emirates. In the same manner, one can validly argue that had educating the people been essential to the British, they would have gone ahead and introduced that education on a large scale, irrespective of the feelings and the attitudes of the people. Yet, we are going here to set down, as complete as possible, the attitude of the people to the introduction of western education, both as a matter of record and by way of making our understanding of the experience of the people of the emirates during the early days of the so-called colonial era as complete as possible.

Regarding this attitude, it should be stated that it was not uniform even from the word "go", not even among the aristocratic classes. Thus, for example when, in July 1902, Resident Barclay in Yola suggested to the emir, the Qadi "and others," the establishment of a school "under the auspices of government with a Mohammadan at the head to teach the Fulani youths English," the Emir was reportedly enthusiastic about it and said he would become one of the first students, and that adults as well as youths would join the class, while the Qadi raised an objection.[124] The Qadi's objection was that the "Fulanis [were] quite ignorant of English manners and customs." He, therefore, suggested "the advisability of waiting for some time till the people had become better acquainted with the British."[125] Though the Qadi was "practically the only dissentient," his "influence [carried] a lot of weight," and hence, Barclay had to try and convince him. This he tried to do by pointing out to the Qadi that "it was precisely [that] ignorance of [British] ways and customs that necessitated the proposed step being taken;" and the Qadi, who was well conversant with British power, gave way, allegedly saying that "whatever the government chose to do was good and he would cooperate to the best of his ability."[126]

It is significant that although the Qadi did come round to accept the idea of starting the school, and in spite of the fact that Barclay himself knew that "from a political point of view there [could] be no doubt as to the immense value teachers of the Mahommedan faith with a thorough knowledge of English history and traditions would be in the settlement of the Fulani question and assisting to bring about more cordial relations between [the Fulani and the British]", the class was never opened.[127]

The alleged reasons for not opening the class were that although the Qadi gave his consent to the project, Barclay could "see that the idea [was] unpalatable to him", and that it was difficult "to find suitable men for the purpose, the chief disability being that [the teachers] themselves would first have to master [Fulfulde]."[128] Hence, Barclay added that even if Lugard considered the project "feasible", he did "not think it [could] be taken in hand very too soon."[129] For his part Lugard, who was pre-occupied with preparations for his aggression against the far northern emirates and the seat of the Caliph, ignored the issue of feasibility, though he had time to offer the rather cynical view that "the idea of a school [was] unpalatable to the Alkali because it [would] wholly sap his monopoly and sap his rule."[130]

Similarly, when Acting Resident McClintock in Borno suggested to the Shehu in 1907 that a western style class that would have "a curriculum that would not scare Muslims" be started in Maiduguri, the Shehu "thoroughly" understood its advantages and expressed himself willing both to send his own son and to feed all the boys attending the class.[131] As we have already seen, this suggestion also fell through, not because of local opposition, for which we have no evidence, but because opening schools in the emirates was not really part of British policy. However, when the Nassarawa school was opened, the Shehu and some other chiefs did send their sons in spite of the distance between Kano and Maiduguri.[132] And when a school was finally opened in Maiduguri itself at the end of 1914, within six months the number of pupils rose from the eight that originally transferred from Nassarawa to forty-two. Of these the Shehu alone had four sons while the Shehu of Dikwa, who was still legally not in Nigeria, sent a son and three nephews. The Mais of Fika, Bedde and Biu sent a son each. So did the Chief Qadi, Liman Amsami. At any rate, forty-two seems to have been the highest number the school could accommodate, a low number dictated, not by a shortage of pupils, but by British colonialist educational policy in the emirates, as indicated by the fact that the following year the school enrolment rose to 81 when the British decided to raise it.[133] In fact, as far as the Shehu was concerned, he not only sent his own sons, but took a very close and keen interest in the school, paying frequent visits, "listening in an amused admiration at the boys' efforts and [waxing] enthusiastic at some of their performances."[134]

His only quarrel with the school allegedly, was "the use of Hausa, of which neither he nor any of his councillors or Ajias [could] speak a word."[135]

In Sokoto though the school was started with the formal consent of the Sarkin Musulmi, it would seem that some of the chiefs as well as the Sarkin Musulmi and the Waziri held back their own sons and relatives until they had seen the influence of the school on the first batch of eight boys to be sent. Indeed, among this first batch, except for the son and the grandson of the Magajin Rafi, all the others, six in number, were sons or relatives of men who were notoriously pro-British, namely Majidadi Usumanu, who gave a son and two nephews, Mallam Agali, who gave a son, Nagwamatse, who was later to become noted as a teacher at Sokoto itself, Katsina and Zaria, and Sarkin Tambawal, Shehu, who gave two sons.[136] The next person to send his relatives was Haliru of Kalgo, who sent two sons soon after his appointment as the Emir of Gwandu.[137] It was only after the school had been in existence for about a year that Resident Temple suggested to the Marafa, Muhammadu Maiturare, "that as he now [had] had time to see that no attempt to proselytise the boys was being made, he might like to send one of his own sons."[138] The Marafa "answered very well to this appeal with the result that not only he but the Sarikin Muslimin, [the] Waziri and the other members of the royal family sent their sons, grandsons or relations."[139] In fact, the Sarkin Musulmi sent a grandson while the Waziri, Muhammadu Buhari sent a son and grandson.

Thus, between December 1906 and March 1907, the number of boys in the school jumped from nine to thirty-one, of whom two were sons of the Emir of Argungu, two sons of the Emir of Gwandu and the remainder from the Sultanate.[140] From now on the British could not use the alibi that pupils were not forthcoming. In fact, at the end of 1907, Resident Temple admitted that "the feeling against the school which at one time existed [had] quite disappeared;"[141] and by this time a class had already been opened for adult mallamai.[142] Yet, three years later, in December 1910, the number of boys at the Sokoto School was still exactly what it had been about four years earlier in March 1907, namely thirty-one.[143] So opposed to education was British policy in the emirates, and so limited were their needs for people literate in the Roman alphabet.

In Zaria, the story was more or less the same. As we have seen, when Dr Miller opened his school and before he made conversion his top priority, members of the aristocratic and literary classes sent their sons to the school, although most of them withdrew these sons when he resorted to open proselytisation and to teaching with the Bible.[144] Similarly, in spite of their experience in the hands of Dr Miller, when the "Provincial" School was opened on May 8, 1914 as many as forty boys were sent there of whom, in fact, a majority "were found to be sons of the lower classes." This fact of their parentage displeased the British so much that they actually sent away twelve for being "quite unsuitable for education".[145] Yet, by the end of June, there were thirty-six Zaria boys in the school,[146] which is to say that the British were able to obtain ten boys with the requisite background to replace the twelve that they had rejected. In fact, this number was obtained in spite of further "numerous changes which took place among [the pupils] – some boys being withdrawn by their parents because they were unable to pay school fees, others being replaced by District Chiefs' sons," in conformity with British policy.[147] If nothing else, this open, undisguised British aversion against giving sons of the lower classes western education should render irrelevant all allegations that these classes in Zaria and elsewhere in the emirates were prejudiced against that education. It was not meant for them and they were deliberately excluded from it. Hence the impropriety and irrelevance of raising the issue of their prejudices against it as a factor that constrained its growth and expansion.

In Kano as well, there was no shortage of pupils, as both the Emir and his chiefs sent their sons to both the Nassarawa school, which Kano shared with all the other emirates, and the provincial school, which was opened in 1915.[148] Indeed, the Survey School seemed to contain only the sons of the Emir and his brothers; so many of them went there.[149] This is not to mean that the Emir and his chiefs had no reservations about these schools, reservations to which Resident Palmer referred in his report for 1915.[150] However, the reservations to which he referred concerned specific aspects of the educational system, aspects such as control of the school by the Provincial Administration rather than the Native Administration, formal games, the boarding system and the minor role given to Arabic in the schools.[151] In Katsina, which had its own "Provincial" School, the attitude of the Emir, Muhammadu Dikko and his chiefs towards that school, was definitely friendly. They not only "accepted" the school but also "appreciated" it. The "Head Teacher [was] a personal friend of the Emir," and, to be sure, there was "no great difficulty about obtaining pupils."[152] The only place in Kano Province, and about the only place in the emirates as a whole, where the chiefs flatly refused to send their sons to a western school, was Hadeija.[153] But then Hadeija's hatred for the British colonialist generally was particularly intense. At any rate, it should be pointed out that even the Hadeija chiefs did not outrightly reject western education. On the contrary, they were careful to point out that it was sending their sons outside the emirate that they objected to, coupled with the fact that they lacked "knowledge of the objects and methods of the Kano School."[154] Quite possibly, these could have been mere excuses the Hadeija chiefs were putting up against sending their sons to British schools.

But this cannot be proven for our period, since the British did not within this period open a school at Hadeija, by which means alone they could have tested the truth of the chiefs' excuses.

The Fate of Islamic Education

In order to know what resources they could tap regarding the recruitment of scribes and no doubt also for the sake of monitoring their activities, the British did, right from the imposition of their domination over the emirates, try to keep records of the number of Koranic and Higher Islamic schools in these emirates. Hence, even if inadvertently, the British did leave behind some irregular statistics on these precolonial schools. The earliest reference to these schools, we have seen, was the one made by Lugard, significantly in connection with the Native Judiciary. Thus, in his comments on Yola's Report for January 1902, after ordering the Resident to "set up" a Native Court at Yola "at once," he also asked the latter if the "alkali [had] some learners and a designate to succeed him."[155] He then went on specifically to order the Resident to send him "a report ... relative to Mohammedan Mosques and schools in [Yola] Province."[156] Accordingly, in his Report for July 1902, the Resident reported that there were 15 schools in Yola with the "racial" breakdown of 8 Fulani, 3 Arab, 2 Beri-Beri and 2 Hausa.[157] He revealed that the largest of them was an "Arab school" with 20 pupils, "the others average 10 to 15" pupils.[158] The figure of fifteen seems to be too small, especially in view of the fact that the schools to which the Resident was referring were Koranic schools in which "the only things taught ... [were] reading, writing and the Koran."[159] That is to say, according to the Resident's information, there was not a single Higher Islamic School in Yola, but in fact we know from other sources that there were several of such schools in the town. As for Koranic schools, they abound in the households, the elementary education of youngsters having been primarily the job of the womenfolk.[160] It would seem that not knowing what the British intended to do with the information they were gathering on Islamic schools, the Emir and the Mallum'en of Yola decided to return a false understated figure. The next return for schools in the province was for 1911 and gave the number of schools "in the Province" as 414 with 2,704 scholars.[161] Although the Resident neglected either to break down these figures into those of Koranic and Higher Islamic Schools and scholars, or to break them down according to towns and districts, the figures are nonetheless useful. For one thing they support our contention that the figure of fifteen given for Yola town in July 1902 was an understatement. This is because the 1902 figures were said to be for the capital alone while the 1911 figures were said to be for the Province as a whole. At this time, the Province of Yola was made up only of the "pagan" Numan Division and the small fraction of the nineteenth century Emirate of Fombina that fell to the British as opposed to the Germans. And within that area, the position of Yola and Girei 15 miles to its north was absolutely predominant from the point of view of Islamic scholarship.[162]

Hence, Yola's share of the numbers of schools and scholars returned for the province must be at least 35% or roughly 120 schools and 945 scholars, figures the differences between which and the 1911 figures were too great. The 1911 figures were also useful in that they seem to indicate that Islamic education was able to expand even under adverse colonial conditions and in spite of lack of British patronage. We can make this deduction even if we take into account the possibility that the 1902 figures might have been grossly understated. By the same token, there was also the possibility that the 1911 figures were also understated, since we have no evidence of the Mallum'en seeing any tangible benefits in allowing their schools to be accurately counted. The argument here is that the differences between the 1902 and the 1911 figures seem to be too great to be totally accounted for by a greater understatement in 1902 than in 1911. However, lest we celebrate too early, it should be added that for 1914, the figures for schools and pupils in Yola Province were given as 326 and 1,495 respectively, a very substantial fall from the 1911 figures.[163] But we have not found a ready explanation for the fall.

For Bornu Province, the figures of three thousand schools and "something over 10,000 pupils" were returned for 1912,[164] figures which stood in absolute contrast to the zero and about ten for western schools and pupils for the province in that year.[165] But in the absence of figures for earlier and later years in the period under study, one cannot measure the growth or decline of Islamic education in that province, which was more or less conterminous with the Sheikhdom. For Kano Province, the estimated figures of "about 14,000 native schools ... with some 550,000 children of between the ages of 5 and 12" were returned for 1914.[166] These figures were very impressive even when it is taken into consideration that the province at this point in time included the emirates of Kano, Katsina, Hadeija, Katagum, Daura, Missau, Jama'are, Kazaure as well as Gumel, all of them having predominantly Muslim populations. The impressiveness of these figures will be all the greater if we consider the fact that these figures were for Koranic schools alone, that is schools for "children of between the ages 5 and 12." In Zaria Emirate in 1912, a total of 5,443 pupils were said to be attending Koranic schools.[167] Of this figure 2,154 were in Zaria town, while 4,724 were boys and 719 were girls. The number of students in Higher Islamic

Schools in the emirate in that same year was said to be 1,007, of whom 380 were in Zaria town and 49 were female.[168] In 1915, there were a total of 910 schools, both Koranic and Higher Islamic.[169] These schools contained 7,713 pupils – made up of 5,488 boys, 817 girls and 1,388 Higher Islamic students, figures which represented notable increases over the 1912 figures.

The impression that one gets from all the scattered figures quoted for the various provinces mentioned above is that in terms of numbers of pupils, Islamic education in the emirates managed to continue to grow in the period covered by our study. However, the only evidence that we have come across of the British offering to help these schools was in Borno where, in 1912, it seems an offer was made to give school masters some allowance from the Native Treasury, an offer which they declined to accept.[170] Apart from that, there is no other evidence that the British offered any direct help to these schools, though it may be argued that indirectly, the British encouraged Islamic education by making some of its products, Qadis, muftis and scribes with or without additional training by the British. However, the number of those who secured employment this way represented only a fraction, perhaps less than 20% of those who passed through the system. It should also be admitted that the Qadis in particular, sometimes even muftis and scribes, did double as teachers. This practice was made possible by the fact that in those days court sessions used to be in the afternoons, very often at the home of the Qadi, rather than in the morning, and at a special court room as it was in the later colonial period.[171] Hence, to some extent, by paying these Qadis and muftis salaries, the British were subsidizing Islamic education.

On the other hand, it should be pointed out that a majority of the *ulema* kept their distance from the British. Indeed, among the mallams, the incidence of emigration, both successful and abortive, from Nigeria, was substantial.[172] Though the "universal" imposition of European colonialism on the Western Sudan actually meant that the emirates both received and lost mallams through migration into and out of them, it would seem that on balance, it made a net loss of that group as a result of the imposition. This is because even before the imposition of European colonial domination on these parts of the world, the Holy Land was very attractive to the *ulema* and the generality of the Muslims of the emirates and the Western Sudan generally.[173] Hence, even in the hey-day of the Sokoto Caliphate, a period which represented the height of the glory of that class, the rulers of the Caliphate had to resort to exhortation to stop members of the class leaving the Caliphate for the East.[174] With the grievous calamity that the imposition of European colonial domination represented, in fact, a calamity which the *ulema*, aware of the attraction of the Holy Land graphically, even one-sidedly, became much greater than ever before. Hence, even though large numbers of *ulema* and other strata of society from the West entered the emirates after the imposition of French colonialism over their territories, they more or less saw themselves as en route to the Holy Land rather than as permanent refugees in the emirates. And even though they did dilly-dally at Sokoto and other parts of the emirates, once British colonial domination was imposed over the emirates, most of them did continue their *hijra* to the Holy Land. Not only did they carry on their *hijra;* they also took along with them very large numbers of *ulema* and other strata of the population of the emirates.[175]

Hence our contention that in spite of the entry of *ulema* into the emirates after the imposition of British colonial domination, the net result of the demographic movement caused by that imposition was that the emirates lost a proportion of their *ulema*. On this ground, we can claim that Islamic education, in relative terms, suffered as a result of the imposition of British colonial domination, though in absolute terms that education continued to expand even after the British conquest. However, education is measured, not only in terms of the number and size of schools, but also in terms of the quality of education received therein, and in terms of the creativity of the scholars by way of authorship. With regard to quality and creativity, one would contend that Islamic education in the emirates absolutely stagnated and relatively declined after the imposition of British colonial domination. Thus, among the factors that influenced the quality of education in the western Sudan generally in earlier epochs, was cross-fertilisation with North Africa and the Middle East.

However, with the imposition of European colonialism over all the three areas, this cross-fertilisation all but ceased as far as the emirates were concerned. For, while there was emigration from the emirates to the East, most of these emigrants remained in the East. That is to say – they took away their talents, their commitments, etc. to the East and never returned to bring back anything. Nor was there any noticeable immigration of North Africans and Middle Easterners to the emirates, at least not that of *ulema*. As a result, one can hardly find a book that was introduced into the emirates in this period.[176]

If we turn to creativity, our period of study stands in very sharp contrast from earlier periods in the history of the emirates. Certainly, it could not compare with the period just preceding and following the Sokoto jihad when there was such an outpouring of literary creativity in the area covered by the jihad, in short the emirates.[177] For the sake of objectivity it should be admitted that the jihad era stands in a class by itself concerning literary creativity. No other period, as far as we know, matched it. Yet the point can still be made that whereas the difference between other periods in the eighteenth and nineteenth centuries and the jihad period was relative even if great, the difference between that period and the period under review in this study is almost absolute.[178]

Health and Welfare

The period we are dealing with witnessed a number of epidemics, among them a smallpox epidemic which broke out in Yola Province in November 1905.[179] This epidemic was said to have been mildest in Yola town "where there were not many deaths," the number of deaths "as near as Resident Barclay could ascertain being 30."[180] We should regard this account as a measure of the severity of the epidemic in the Districts. In fact, in one town in Gola District in the northern part of Adamawa Emirate as many as 90 people died out of a population of 400.[181] In another village near the Niger Company depot, just outside Yola, as many as 23 died out of a population of 250 people.[182] The Resident had the honesty to admit that this small-pox epidemic, in combination with a famine that had been on for two years and an epidemic of cerebro-spinal meningitis, killed a number of people "impossible to estimate but which must be counted in thousands."[183] And, lest the smallpox epidemic be regarded as a rare occurrence, the Resident further admitted that "smallpox may be said to be in the Province all the year round, generally assuming epidemic form at the end of the year."[184]

Again, in 1909, there was another epidemic, that of cerebro-spinal meningitis.[185] The Resident claimed that it was not reported until his agents discovered it, and that it was confined to only one village, Dakri, on the northern bank of the Benue opposite Jimeta. That it was not reported should not be surprising, since there was little point in reporting, unless it was merely to warn the British and those in their service to take precautionary measures for themselves. However, we should treat with caution the Resident's claim that the epidemic was confined to a single "Batta village;" for just as this village did not report the outbreak, it is quite possible that other villages also refused to report similar outbreaks among their populations. Hence, all that we can accept from the Resident's report is that he knew of only one village that was affected, but even the experience of this single village was tragic enough. Thus, the Resident admitted that "the population of Dakri in the spring of 1908 taken for assessment purposes was 200. At the time of Dr. Dalziel's visit [that is after the ravage caused by the epidemic], it was reduced to 48."[186] In Zaria in 1914, there was a smallpox epidemic which was said to be confined to one district, the Dangaladima's District.[187] Yet the total number of deaths in this district by the end of June, by which time the epidemic was still on, was 509, with 160 cases yet to recover.[188]

Widespread Famine

Our period did also witness repeated famines, both localized and wide-spread. For about six years following the imposition of British colonial domination, there was a famine in Yola Province. The famine which was so severe that people took to pawning their children into slavery.[189] Corn simply stopped being available in the markets in the years 1902–1908 and the British had to import corn from areas where the famine was less severe, such as parts of Bauchi, and ration it among their own troops and employees. By the middle of 1904, the Resident was reporting that "numerous deaths were occurring daily caused chiefly by people eating poisonous leaves and roots. The growing crops have all been consumed without waiting for them to ripen and this of course means greater scarcity than ever next year for it will leave no resources to fall back upon." [190] During a tour of the Gongola valley sometime in 1906, an Assistant Resident, Mr. Liddard, found that:

> from the mouth of Gongola River as far north as Gashi, all the riverside towns and villages and also those inland ones lying to the east and west which I visited viz: Bobini, Bangu, Guburundi, Pitila and Shami were found to be suffering severely from famine which [had] existed for the [previous] three years.[191]

He went on to add that:

> the signs of famine [were] patent. Numbers of ruined compounds, deserted villages, barns empty or containing grass seed. It was a common sight to see villagers starting for the bush early in the morning to collect grass seeds and herbs. At the same time, the natives [reported] that the stress [was] lighter in 1906 than in 1905. Probably this [was] in a measure accounted for by a great number of people having died leaving only the stronger who from their deplorable experience [had] learnt the necessity of storing grass seed and other herbs.[192]

Villagers told Liddard that the previous year, large numbers died in the bush where they had gone in search of food and had not returned. From "a careful census of the population of towns and villages" taken by Mr. Liddard "an idea of the loss of life [could] be gathered." To take Banjeram, for example, the population in June 1906 was 43, whereas a few years earlier Barclay had estimated it at 4,000.[193] Similarly, in what the British referred to as the "Fulani districts" of Yola Emirate, the population seemed to be "very much on the decrease and the small population of children [was] most marked, the number of adults being twice or three times as great." There were numbers of deserted compounds and villages which presented "an air of desolation."[194]

In Zaria, the year 1904 was marked by "such a scarcity of corn that in some districts there was a regular famine and actual hunger was experienced by many of the poorer people," a fact which the Resident described as "an almost unprecedented occurrence in this fertile and thinly populated land."[195] The Resident further admitted that the "scarcity of food was greatly increased by the large demands made on the district round Zaria ... to support the considerable [British] force of Mounted Infantry which was being raised" for the purposes of "pacifying" villages.[196] He admitted that "for feeding the horses alone" eighty bundles of guinea corn "were required daily," while "flour in large quantities" was required for feeding the soldiers and their families.[197] It is noteworthy, as an evidence of the relentless and unconditional nature of British demands, that "notwithstanding this scarcity," the Kurdin Kasa was "with few exceptions ... paid in full throughout the Province."[198] In 1911, food scarcity broke out in Gwandu Division owing to bad harvests of the staple grains in that Division; gero (millet) and guinea corn.[199]

Two years later, in 1913, there was reported to be "a partial failure of crops" in the northern districts of the Sultanate of Sokoto.[200] This same year, a similar "partial failure of crops" was reported to have occurred "throughout [Kano] Province," with the northern and eastern parts of the province being the worst hit.[201] In fact, in "the more northerly districts" of the emirates of Katagum, Missau and Jama'are, "the crops almost completely failed."Worse still, from the point of view of the scarcity of food the same crop failure, which extended into "French territory," forced "large numbers" of people from the latter area south into Kano province.[202] In Borno too, crops were said not to have been "so poor for years" as they were in 1913.[203] This poor harvest, which was said to have followed "on a not very rich harvest in 1912 and upon [a] very large and especially encouraged exportation of corn to Bauchi Province ... raised the price of corn."[204] Thus, the price of one *sa'a* of guinea corn rose from 3d in 1912 to 1/- in 1913.[205] Bauchi, which was so hit by food scarcity in 1912 that the British had to encourage the import of grain from Borno, went on in 1913 to share the "poor harvests" that were suffered by other emirates.[206] This led to "severe famine in 1914 in the Ganjua and Darazo Districts of the Bauchi Emirate and in the northern Districts of the Gombe Emirate."[207]

While the severe famine of 1914 was the result of the crop failures of 1912 and 1913, the year 1914 once again witnessed "poor crops in Fali and Kirfi Districts of the Bauchi Emirate" which, in turn, promised a continuation of famine in 1915, at least for parts of this emirate.[208] The year 1914 also saw "a very prevalent and fatal disease among the cattle of [Fali and Kirfi] Districts and of the Gombe Emirate as a whole."[209] Zaria Emirate also experienced the famine of 1914, as also did Kano Province,[210] where the famine was particularly serious in Katagum, Gumel and Hadeija emirates, and where the famine was accompanied by a great infant mortality.[211] A point that must be emphasized here is that in the midst of this endemic famine, the British did nothing except occasionally organizing the import of grain from one part of the emirates to another such as from Borno to Bauchi, as we saw above,[212] and infrequent and partial remitting of taxes for the worst hit areas of a district or emirate. These remissions were fully recouped by higher taxes as soon as the famine seemed to abate. The callous attitude of the British towards these famines was best symbolized by the fact that in 1910, the Resident of Kano converted into a prison a house that the Emir of Katagum had built for the purpose of storing surplus grain as a precaution against subsequent crop failures.[213]

Medical Facilities

As for the provision of medical facilities, it should be pointed out that in those days dispensaries were as rare as western schools. For example, in the whole of Yola Province throughout our period of study, there was only one government clinic set up in 1902 at Yola, catering mainly for the British and their employees.[214] The only other health establishments were the SUM clinic at Numan, and a leper settlement outside Yola, at which a few lepers were segregated.[215] Zaria Province had only one government clinic, known as "Native Hospital" at Zaria.[216] The only other health establishments were the CMS dispensary at Zaria and a Sleeping Sickness Segregation Camp set up in 1910, also at Zaria.[217] In Sokoto Province, there were a clinic and a leper settlement at Sokoto town,[218] and probably another clinic at Birnin Kebbi. In addition, the Sarkin Musulmi appointed four itinerant Sanitary Inspectors in June 1914.[219] Their job was said to be that of touring the districts of the Sultanate "in turn" to see that the Sarkin Musulmi's "orders were carried out," a very vague definition of the function of the four gentlemen. Evidently, they had no medical training of any amount, and their duties did not include dispensing. Bornu Province had two clinics, namely a Native Hospital at Maiduguri and a "Native Dispensary" at Geidam as well as two leper settlements or *Dirimari* at Maiduguri and Geidam.[220] Bauchi Province did not seem to have even a single Native Hospital as of 1914. The only medical facilities in the province seemed to be the "simple medical facilities" that the Mission Station at Kabwir provided.[221]

Population Decline

With so much disturbances and uncertainty, with such a rhythm of "natural calamities" like famine and epidemics, and while medical facilities were so abysmally meagre in the emirates in the period up to 1915, it is not surprising that there is evidence to suggest that there was a decline in the population of these emirates during this period. Thus, to start with, as mentioned above,[222] the figures of the population of Adamawa Province in 1906 showed a larger number of adults over children. So also did the 1910 figures show a great preponderance of adults over children in the population of Adamawa, children being only 35,801 out of a total population of 181,307, an adult preponderance which suggests a high rate of infant mortality.[223] It should be conceded that these figures were very unlikely to have been accurate. Given the facts of taxation and of forced labour, the tendency was to conceal the adult population, not the population of children. Hence, far from being a more accurate return correcting the imbalance between the adult and children populations, it is more likely to have made the gap between the two even much wider. Another piece of evidence that the population of Yola Province was on the decline in this period was provided in the Assessment Report on Namtari District for 1910–11, in which it was stated that "in many villages there [were] no children at all."[224]

In Kano, a register of "births and deaths" was kept during the years 1912, 1913 and 1914.[225] The figures for the years 1912 and 1913 were:

Table 11.1. Register of births and deaths, Kano 1912 and 1913

Year	Births	Deaths
1912	880	1,212
1913	874	1,181

Source: W.F. Gowers, "Kano Provincial Annual Report for 1913," SNP 10 No.98P/1914, NAK

In 1912, the Resident thought that the figures had been carelessly kept, but in 1913 he changed his mind, conceding that "these statistics [were] more carefully kept than [he] had previously supposed and the figures recorded [were] in themselves by no means improbable."[226] Meanwhile, in 1914 the Kano Provincial Administration estimated that "the death toll ... from famine amounted to 50,000 souls."[227] Of this figure, they estimated that "30,000 at least were French subjects." That is to say, by the British estimation, Kano Province lost at least 20,000 people in 1914 alone, from a famine which neither started nor ended in that year. Some latter-day apologist of British colonialism in the emirates might retort that the British might have exaggerated the death too. There is little reason for their doing so. But it should at least be pointed out that "careful statistics" collected in the Kano Division of the province showed that the Division, at that time made up of Kano and Kazaure emirates, lost 14,025 people to the famine in that year.[228] Of the following figures for the other Divisions in the Province, some were "careful," some "unreliable" and others "uncompleted."[229]

Table 11.2. Estimated deaths from famine

Katsina	5,000
Katagum	10,000
Northern Division	13,025

Source: A.C.G. Hastings, "Kano Provincial Annual Report for 1914,"

The report further points out that Hadeija Emirate alone lost 7,769 out of a population of 142,606. It should be remembered that the report does not give figures for the animals that died in the province in that year, and that whereas, apart from Kano's only a few other Provincial Administrations bothered to take "careful statistics" and make "estimates" of those who died from starvation in 1914, the famine that hit Kano during the period 1911–1915 covered very large parts of the emirates including the Provinces of Sokoto, Bauchi and Bornu. It should also be remembered that the negative consequences of this and other famines for the emirates were not necessarily confined to the periods of the occurrence of such famines. These consequences must have extended beyond these periods in the forms of reduced protein resulting from animal mortality and a decline in the productive, and possibly reproductive capacity of the remainder of the population, just to mention only one or two forms of such extended consequences. Suffice it to point out here that, ominous enough, in this same year 1914, it was stated in the Medical Section of the Annual Report that the "return of births and deaths for Kano City ... [showed] 882 births and 1,215 deaths" and that these figures did "not include deaths from starvation."[230]

Another province whose administration took up the issue of the effects of the 1914 famine on its population was Borno. Here, we are told, "the census of the Province as found by the assessment staff (under Mr. Benton) for [the 1914] taxation [showed] a total decrease in population in the emirate districts [namely those within the Sheikhdom as opposed to other chiefdoms in the Province] of 142,312, or 29% of the total population in 1913." This admittedly "very large decrease" in the population of the Sheikhdom was blamed on "the drought in 1913 and the scarcity of food combined with high prices in 1914."[231] It was this drought and this scarcity of food that "caused the population *always inclined to move*, to migrate out of the Province."[232] Though the British in Borno avoided directly mentioning the number of dead, we can compute it from their statement that "total migration less deaths [numbered] 57,794." Take the latter figure from the figure for the "total decrease in the population," viz 142,312 and the difference – 84,518 represents deaths as a result of starvation. At least for the record, it should also be pointed out that of the 57,794 who emigrated from Borno "24,915 were to foreign countries and [only] 8,069 to other Provinces." Indeed, this is one way of stating that of the 142,312 people that the Province lost as many as 84,518 were lost forever, for both Borno and Nigeria, having died, while a further 24,915 were lost, more or less permanently, not just for Bornu Province but for Nigeria as a whole, these having left the country altogether.

Inter-communal Relations

If we next turn to British policy and practice vis-à-vis relations among the various linguistic and religious communities that they found co-existing, or that they brought together for their own (British) convenience, we shall find that their policy was to keep these communities apart physically, culturally and psychologically, though where administrative convenience demanded, they did allow these communities to share abode or institutions or both. Thus, as far as the local communities were concerned, British policy was to emphasize the differences and exaggerate mutual hostilities between Muslim communities on the one hand and "pagan" communities on the other, and as a rule to keep the latter in "independent" chieftaincies. Even where a "pagan" community had previously formed part of an emirate, the patent desire of the British was to restore the "independence" of the latter.[233] However, as time passed by, the British, on purely practical grounds, tended to leave such communities in the emirates of which they had been a part. They also did this in emirate communities that, prior to the imposition of British colonial domination, had managed to maintain a large measure of independence from the emirates.[234] Nor was religion the only purported basis of separation. Thus, for example, we have seen the attempts the British made in Yola to grant Hausa and Kanuri communities some autonomy in the emirate;[235] but the attitude was much more accentuated in the case of the "pagan" communities. Each "tribe" was seen and treated not just as separate and distinct from the neighbouring Muslim communities but also as independent of, and hostile towards other "pagan" communities. Hence, in provinces like Bauchi and the Central/Nassarawa Provinces, the British established not one but several "independent" chieftaincies.[236]

However, it was with respect to elements they introduced or thought they introduced that the British went to somewhat absurd lengths to enforce separation and autonomy of one community from the others. For example, very early in the era of their domination over the emirates, they introduced the interesting terms of "non-native Africans" and the more general term "non-natives".[237] Minimally, apart from Europeans who came to the emirates for commercial or administrative purposes, these included Syrians, Lebanese, Indians, Lagosians, Ibos, Itsekiris, Binis and people from the three other West African British colonies; and in some cases they include even Ilorin, Yoruba, Nupe, Hausa and Fulbe elements, that moved from one emirate to another, not to set up their own business, but to work for the British administration, or a foreign mining or commercial company.[238] Next, with the establishment of Native Courts and Native Administrations, the British adopted a policy of making the jurisdiction of these on "non-natives", including "non-native Africans", vague and ambiguous, depending, among other factors, on the choice of the non-natives and the specific consent of a British official.[239] While European commercial agents tended to maintain outright that their native employees were beyond the jurisdiction of the Native Authorities and Courts, British Administrative Officers used to equivocate that "the Native Administrations [had] Judicial Power over all including non-natives (i.e. natives from Lagos or other colonies), but in the latter case only by consent of the Resident."[240] This meant that while the "non-native Africans" could and did "avail themselves of the Native Courts for civil cases even [when] they [were] Christians,"[241] nonetheless "they [were] never summoned or arrested [by the Native Authorities] without first informing the Resident [sic], except in cases of emergency."[242] This privilege was extended not just to servants of the Provincial and Divisional Administrations and of European commercial companies, but to all "natives known to be in European employ," as house-boys, cooks, etc., most of whom were originally from the emirates. This was "done for the convenience of the employer."[243]

As a result of this arrangement, "criminal cases against non-natives [were] practically always dealt with in the Provincial Court."[244] Hence, as was "observed on the mine fields, on the railway and in other departments or spheres," there was "always a danger of natives passing out of the authority of the local administration when in the employ of Europeans."[245] In the meantime, up to 1913, the "non-native" Africans lived side by side with the local populations of the emirates either inside the original "native towns" or in new settlements founded near the Government Residential Area (GRA) known as Sabon Gari, all of which were subject to the reservations made above, under the jurisdiction of the Native Authorities.[246] Clearly, whatever one may think of the Native

Authorities and the Native Courts, one must concede that it was natural for them not to like the situation in which they found people who lived in areas nominally under their jurisdiction but who had the option to be or not to be under their jurisdiction; and once this concession is made, the issue of whether it was the Emirs that insisted on the physical removal of the non-native Africans, from the "native" towns loses its relevance. Responsibility for that would squarely lie with the British. At any rate, even the British records do not contain evidence that it was the Emirs that insisted on the physical segregation of this "non-native" African population, whereas some old residents of Sabon Garin Kano insisted that it was the British that initiated the removal of "non-natives" from the city where they had lived amicably with the native population and the Native Authorities.[247]

Whatever was the case, the removal of the "non-native" population started in Kano in 1913. Thus, according to the British authorities, it was in 1913 that first attempts were made to mark out "a non-European Reservation."[248] The "primary object" of the Reservation was "to provide an area within the precincts of the Government Reservation Area or Township" where "such native foreigners as were not ordinarily subject to the jurisdiction of the Native Authority were to be allowed to reside."[249] The people who were originally resettled in the new Reservation were clerks, artisans "and others who ministered while no person was "admitted without a permit from the Station Magistrate." This was a clear indication that the Sabon Gari emerged, not so much as ghetto for social pariahs, but as a suburb for the relatively privileged. Indeed such permits were not given to "carriers, temporary labourers or other indigenous natives." Hence, perhaps, the reference to it as a "Reservation" rather than as a "Reserve," which the City and Fagge became in effect. Indeed in 1917 the Sabon Gari was constituted under the township Ordinance into "the Second Class Township of Kano," that is, second to the Government Reservation Area, and not to the city which it superseded within the British colonialist arrangement. It was "through lack of rigid control [that] the Native Reservation whose specific object had formerly been to provide residential plots for [native foreigners]" came to have a large number of emirate natives" – 2,040 out of a population of 7,619 in 1938–39.[250]

In the meantime, the year 1913, when the Sabon Gari was started, was a year when there was "a great influx of traders both European, Asian and Native to Kano."[251] Hence, "new and improved line of sidings and residential plots," were laid out in the GRA or European section of the Kano "township" and were "allotted at auctions to the highest bidders" among the European traders, the highest bid being £105:8:0 per annum.[252] At the same time, "non-European sites" were also laid out in the vicinity of the GRA and "with railway facilities similar to those employed by the European plots," and four of them were taken by Asian traders.[253] As for the "native foreigners" and "alien natives," "some 250 plots" were allotted to them in the "native quarter of the township" or GRA. However, at this relatively early date, "Natives of Northern Province" who arrived in Kano "were not allowed to settle in this reservation." Instead, they were sent to "the native city where they [were] responsible and controlled by the native judiciary and executive." In the meantime, the Resident suggested that it was "better to dissociate the whole township [rather than just the European section of it] from native authority." He said that this was necessary partly because "otherwise control [would] be divided," and partly:

> as it [was] impossible that the native administration should exercise full and effective control over native foreigners in accordance with Mohammedan Law and native custom, it [would] strengthen rather than weaken the Emir and native administration if the township [was] excluded in practice from their sphere of authority,[254]

The allegation does not sound convincing. Hence simultaneously the township – "European and Native" – was severed from the Kano Divisional Administration and placed under "an officer who discharged functions analogous to those of a Cantonment Magistrate," and who was directly responsible to the Resident.[255] Meanwhile, Yoruba people continued to live in the city, a sign that when the Sabon Gari was founded, living there was optional. This goes to emphasize the privileged position of the "foreign natives" relative to local population, for while the former had the choice of living either in the native city or in the township, the latter had no choice but to live in the native city. Apparently, the British were not pleased with the fact that some of the foreign natives opted to stay together with the "native" population.[256] Hence the following year, that is in 1914, the British raised the "question of Yoruba living in the Native City rather than in the Native Township" with Emir Abbas.[257] Allegedly, the Emir held that "Yorubas who, or whose parents had been born in Kano and who agreed to submit themselves without question to Moslem Law and the Emir's executive authority", and who agreed to give up "the wearing of European clothes" were welcome to continue staying in the city.[258] There is no mention in the report of anybody rejecting those terms and moving out of the city. It would seem that the British were trying to insinuate either the Emir into driving the "foreign natives" from the city, or the latter into pulling out of the city. They were clearly unsuccessful in getting either the Emir or the "foreign natives" into complying with their wishes, which they, at that time, did not dare to issue out as a decree. Later on they were to do just that.[259] It would also suggest that the demand that only Yoruba who or whose parents were born in the city could stay could not possibly be the Emir's, since it was unnecessary to solve his problem, namely that of having to live with a group of people that were above Islamic law and not bound by local customs.

Once people agreed to place themselves under that law and to respect local customs, they ceased to constitute a problem for the Emir, whether or not they and their parents were born in the city. However, the demand that only those who or whose parents were born in the city could continue to live there easily harmonized with the British policy of keeping religious and linguistic communities apart, and we should deem it to have been a British demand that they twisted to sound like the Emir's demand. It was precisely not to compromise this British policy that in the same year, 1914, the British "altered" the western "boundary line" of the township "in order to exclude a small part of the Fagge village which encroached on the township."[260]

In Zaria too "native foreigners" lived side by side with "emirate natives" both in the city and in Sabon Gari, which seems to have sprung up near the GRA from the time of the establishment of the latter, soon after the imposition of British colonialist domination on the emirate. Hence, when the British decided to solve the contradiction between its policy of keeping the "native foreigners" and "emirate natives" apart, on the one hand, and the fact that they were living together in Zaria, on the other, the issue was not that of creating a Sabon Gari, or a native section of the GRA. The issue in Zaria was to enforce the segregation of the two communities by simultaneous expulsions – of the "native foreigners" from the city and of "emirate natives" from Sabon Gari. This was precisely what the Provincial Administration began to do in 1913, the same year the Sabon Gari in Kano was established. Thus in this year, the "Emir" removed "the feeling of distrust between the non-native element and the Native Administration" by "arrang[ing] to transfer to the Sabon Gari all non-natives that had begun to be domiciled in Zaria town."[261] However, in contrast to the situation in Kano, even after the expulsion of the "native foreigners" from the native town, they continued to be theoretically liable to being prosecuted in the Native Courts and to have the option of availing themselves of the services of the Native Courts for civil cases.[262]

Similarly, unlike in Kano, the Zaria Sabon Gari, in which "native foreigners" were forced to concentrate, continued to be under the jurisdiction of the Zaria Native Administration and to be open to "emirate natives." This tended to make the "foreign natives" relatively under-privileged. For whereas the "emirate natives" could reside anywhere except in the GRA proper, the "native foreigners" forfeited the option of living anywhere except in Sabon Gari, but their position was nowhere as under-privileged as that of "emirate natives" in Kano, for their privileges vis-à-vis the Native Courts continued to exist. That is to say, they continued to enjoy freedom from arrest by the Native Courts, except with the permission of the Resident, and were free to go to the Native Courts or not to go there in civil cases, a freedom and an option which "emirate natives" did not enjoy either in Kano or in Zaria, or anywhere else; everywhere the latter were under the full authority both of the British and the native authorities.

At any rate, the following year the anomalies of the situation were removed and the situation harmonized with what obtained in Kano. Thus, in this year by Gazette Notice No. 182 of 9 April the Zaria GRA, including the Sabon Gari, "was declared to be a township within the meaning of the Cantonments Proc- lamation;" and the Governor-General issued orders "reserving a Native Loca- tion in the township for the use of Native foreigners of African Descent and [Emirate] Natives in the employ of government or of non-natives resident in the Township."[263] This "Native Location" was deemed to occupy "the same area as what was known as the 'Zaria Sabon Gari'."This allegedly made it "advisable and necessary to remove [the Emirate] Native community since these natives were directly subject to the Native Administration,"[264] which now lost its juris- diction over Sabon Gari and all authority over "Native foreigners."Therefore, "a site was selected for a new settlement on rising ground between Kubani River and [the] Native town of Zaria, and the Emir named it Tudun Wada."[265] The "emirate natives" were compensated a total of £662:0:0 by the Provincial Ad- ministration for their houses in Sabon Gari which they forfeited. As "the natives were expropriated from Sabon Gari, new plots 100 ft. x 50 ft. were available for selection at the new settlement." Everything happened very rapidly.

The British were bent on removing contradictions between their policy of segregation and the actuality of consanguinity by those supposed to be segre- gated. Thus, it was only in November that payment of compensation to those affected started to be made, and yet at the end of the year, the Resident was able to announce triumphantly that "Zaria Township [could] now be reported as clear of natives directly subject to the Native Administration."[266] This way, Zaria came to have four residential areas namely the Government Reservation Area, Sabon Gari, Tudun Wada and Old City. This arrangement not only practi- calised the British policy of segregating races and ethnic and cultural groups but also established shades of privilege and under-privilege among all those living in Zaria. In fact, this order of listing represents a hierarchy of colonial privilege starting with the GRA at the top, followed by the Sabon Gari, then Tudun Wada and with the old city at the bottom, the only complicating factor being the unavoidable presence in the city of the Emir and his officials. Administratively, Tudun Wada passed under the jurisdiction of the Native Administration while the townships – namely the GRA and Sabon Gari – were put under the Resident, pending the appointment of a "Station Magistrate."[267]

However, it should be pointed out that soon after the establishment of the townships, Sabon Gari started to create some "problems" for the British. This made the idea of direct British administration over them less attractive than it initially seemed. Thus, in Zaria the British Administration, as early as 1915, found it difficult to keep out "emirate natives" who "were not either employees of Government, Trading Firms or other Residents in the townships" from Sabon Gari. Hence, the Administration resorted to the system of issuing "permits" to all residents of this Native Reservation. It issued 1,355 permits, out of which 885 were issued to "non Government" and 470 to "Government" residents.[268] In Kano, the Administration reported that "since the end of July [1915] there [had] been little serious crime in the area of the Station and Township."[269] This "latter area," on the other hand, "unfortunately" seemed to "attract in increasing numbers the most undesirable class of [Emirate] natives of both sexes." This was allegedly owing to "the freedom they [enjoyed] from the restraints and discipline of organized native society and [the] comparative leniency of British law."[270] To deal with the situation, that is, to retain Sabon Gari as a place of privilege rather than a refuge for the criminal and the uprooted, the British first toyed with the idea of appointing a *Bale* and a Council for the area but gave up, allegedly because "in a cosmopolitan community such imported institutions [were] entirely out of the place, and only tended to still greater abuses than those they [were] designed to combat."[271] In actual fact, the British gave up the idea of a Bale and a council either because these would serve as focuses of unity for the "foreign natives" – a possibility which the British were bound to dread, given their policy of segregation and division; or, because they thought that this latter policy of theirs had so succeeded that if they set up a council, the magistrate would have had to spend his time patching up "differences" in the Council and enforcing the authority of the Bale over all the other tribal groupings in Sabon Gari, apart from the Bale's own. However, one is more inclined towards the thesis of the fear of the unifying potentials of the Bale and the council.

To make matters worse for the administration, "the Government Police" showed no great ability to cope with crime in the township.[272] Hence, the British resorted to seeking the assistance of the Kano Native Administration to police the area around Sabon Gari, a measure which prevented the incidence of "much more robbery than [had] occurred," and at the same time somewhat compromised the theory that the Native Administration was to have nothing to

do with administering the Sabon Gari. Though this compromise of the principle of excluding the Sabon Gari from the jurisdiction of the Native Authority
did not develop further after our period until towards the end of the colonial
period itself, the principle of Sole Administratorship was compromised when,
in the early 1940s, Sabon Gari got an unelected council made up of notables
from the various ethnic groups and presided over by a Sarkin Sabon Gari, appointed by the Emir, with the rank of a Village Head (*dagaci*).[273] The first to be
so appointed was a certain Mr. France, a retired clerk from the Gold Coast,
and the second, one Ballard Hughes, a professional photographer from Sierra
Leone.[274]

Conclusion

We have seen in this chapter that it is facile and not necessarily correct to
assume that the society that the British found in the emirates was a slave society
and we have suggested that far from that society being a slave society there were
indications that slavery, whose mere existence in a society does not make that
society a slave society, was, in fact, on its way out giving way to serfdom. We
have also shown that whatever the British found – slavery or serfdom – far from
abolishing it, they preserved it, both in legal theory but especially in practice.
We then suggested that instead of arguing about the British abolishing slavery,
it would be more accurate to argue about the British reducing the whole of
society into their own slaves, complete with foremen and gang drivers.

Concerning the introduction of western education into the emirates, we
have seen that in the period covered by the book, the British did extremely
little, both absolutely and in comparison to what they did in the establishment
of such negative institutions as police, prisons and courts, all of which were
instruments of domination in their hands; and that for every person they sent
to school in this period, they must have sent at least 100 other people to jail.
We have also demonstrated that it was the needs and priorities of British colonialism itself, rather than resistance from the people and traditional authorities
of the emirates that dictated the snail pace of the growth of that education. We
have also shown that, in spite of lack of patronage from the British, Islamic education did continue to survive and perhaps even expand, though there is little
evidence of creativity among the scholars, in sharp contrast to the eighteenth
and nineteenth centuries when that class was very creative.

Turning to health and social welfare, we have shown that during the period
under study the emirates suffered continual famine and epidemics which led to
the deaths of hundreds of thousands of people. The British established virtually

no medical facilities and did little – not even to waive some of their impositions – to provide relief to the people of the emirates during even the worst years of these famines and epidemics, such as the year 1914. Hence, there are good indications that the population of the emirates suffered a numerical decline during this period. Finally, we have shown that far from the British bringing the people of the emirates together, both among themselves and with immigrants from Southern Nigeria, they went out of their way to divide them through the establishment of "independent" chieftaincies, and Sabon Garis and Tudun Wadas in the major cities.

20. Adverts calling on investors to profit 'without delay' from the cotton revolution.

General Conclusion

In an era when imperialism generally, and colonialism in particular, have been thoroughly discredited and are visibly in retreat all over the world, when a literature has emerged that exposes the total bankruptcy of colonialism in other parts of the world, it is ironical that the literature dealing with Africa on the whole tends to, and, in a large number of cases categorically does, idealize colonialism. This stems from two causes. First, there is the fact that the literature has been produced on the whole by conservative pro-imperialist European scholars or by Africans under their supervision. Second, there is the fact that for most of Africa and almost the whole of West Africa, the anti-colonialist struggle was led by bourgeois and petit-bourgeois classes whose quarrel with colonialism was not fundamental, classes which did not question the basic structure and orientation of European imperialism but were simply asking for a share in running the political affairs of the various colonial territories.

Hence, the intellectual challenge that the anti-colonialist movement threw to colonialism was restricted in scope and intensity. Consequently, also, the existing literature is based, not only on an uncritical acceptance of the pronouncements of imperialist proconsuls and ideologues about the purposes of European colonialism in Africa, but also on a superficial interpretation of Africa's precolonial history to the extent that Africa's backwardness in that period is both exaggerated and blamed, not on the true culprit, namely the extremely exploitative nature of the relations between Africa and Europe in the four hundred years preceding the imposition of European colonialism, but on some rather congenital incapacity of Africans to develop beyond a certain level of civilization. This exaggeration and shifting of the blame for Africa's backwardness in the precolonial period have, in combination with the easy acceptance of the imperialists' pronouncements about their intentions, led to a generally implicit, but often enough explicit, conclusion that European colonialism was, when each and everything about it are considered, a blessing to Africa, even though it might have been a curse to other parts of the world which were also subjected to it.

This conclusion, in its turn, helped in no small measure to vitiate serious investigation into the true nature of European colonialism in Africa, as well as the level of the backwardness of precolonial Africa, and the true causes of that backwardness. This has been so much so that much of what passes off as a critique of European colonialism is, on a close examination, nothing but an approval of its nature and objectives, with minor and reluctant criticism of its "methods," "aberrations" and the "cruelties" of some individuals among its functionaries, both European and local. Nor should this be surprising given the basic assumptions upon which such critiques are predicated, for phenomena are judged in accordance with their real or perceived essence and general features and not in accordance with particular details and minor exceptions.

It is in at least tending to counter these prevalent fundamental assumptions and basic conclusions about European colonialism in Africa, especially British colonialism in Northern Nigeria, that this study, which has been deliberately empirical, constitutes a significant though modest contribution to the literature on European colonialism in Africa. Based almost entirely on British records, and *barely* starting with a basic and rejectionist assumption about European colonialism in general, the study has reached conclusions about British colonialism in Northern Nigeria which should compel at least a rethinking in Nigerian and African academic and political circles about the nature and consequences of European colonialism in the continent.

Thus, whereas others have put forward the thesis of a welcome reception of the imposition of British colonialism by the people of Northern Nigeria, the study has found physical resistance and tremendous hostility towards that imposition. Further, contrary to the thesis of peaceful occupation and minimal violence and bloodshed put forward by some scholars, the study has come up with a lot of evidence about the violent and bloody nature of that occupation.

Similarly, whereas others have put forward the thesis of a self-effacing British colonialist bureaucracy hiding behind Emirs and their officials in a system of "Indirect Rule," the study has shown that the British officials were very much in evidence and had their fingers in all aspects of the existence of the people of the emirates. So also, whereas others see the British as *lifting* the burden of multiple and heavy precolonial taxation from the shoulders of the people, the study has concluded that what the British did was indeed to *impose* numerous and heavier taxes and, to collect them with a much greater efficiency and ruthlessness than hitherto; and whereas others would rather see the emirates as a financial burden on the British Imperial Treasury, the study has come up with enough evidence to show that the emirates not only "paid for" their own domination by the British, but also exported "surpluses" to various financial institutions in both Britain and other parts of the British Empire. Equally, whereas others would leave out the role of the imperialist companies when considering British colonialism in the emirates, the study has shown that the inclusion of the role of these companies in such a consideration is both essential and possible, given the availability of some relevant material in the British records.

In the same way, whereas there has been a lot of glib talk about the British *abolishing* "slavery" in the emirates, and about the alleged difficulties that they encountered in a supposed effort by them to introduce western education into the emirates, the study has shown that both in theory and in practice the British abolished no "slavery", and that it was the imperative of British colonialism itself rather than resistance on the part of the people of the emirates or lack of funds that hampered the spread of western education in the emirates. The study has also shown that the British grossly neglected the health and welfare of the people of the emirates, especially during the famines and epidemics which were more or less permanent features of the people's life during the colonial period. So also has the study demonstrated that the British came very near to having converted the emirates into one vast prison and slave camp, complete with foremen, headmen and gang drivers (Hausa: *ganduroba*). It is hoped that the reader will agree that the contents of the book tally with these conclusions.

A Note on Sources

As its title clearly states, this book is essentially an interpretation of British records – official, semi-official and unofficial – dealing with the imposition of their colonial domination over the emirates of Northern Nigeria. Of these, the official records form the basis of the book, first, because they are more numerous and more readily available here in Nigeria. Second, because we consider them to have a more authoritative status. Third, on top of that, they are by far much less inhibited in recording British activities in the emirates and less pretentious in making claims for British colonialism than the semi-official and unofficial records, though this is not to deny that they too contain such claims. Fourth, these official records, especially the Provincial and Sub-provincial Reports, deal with the practical activities of the British in the emirates, and by that token, even if only inadvertently, indicate the impact of British colonialism on the people of the emirates. Other sources used are oral traditions that we collected mainly from local authority official circles in Sokoto and Kano, but to some extent also in Yola; published and unpublished secondary works by both Nigerian and foreign scholars, as well as one or two works of the leaders of the nineteenth century Sokoto jihad. However, we have used oral traditions and secondary works only as a supplement to the British primary sources, for the purposes of explaining or amplifying the points one is trying to make in the interpretation of the British records.

Official British Records

The term "Official British Records" is here used to designate that class of writing that officials of the British colonial regime in the emirates, namely the High Commissioner (later the Governor), Military Officers, Residents, and Assistant Residents (later District Officers, Assistant District Officers and Touring Officers) engaged in during the course of discharging their official duties.

These Records include reports sent to Provincial and Regional Headquarters by the commanders of military expeditions, Monthly, Quarterly, Half-Yearly, and Yearly Reports sent by Assistant Residents to Provincial Headquarters concerning their respective Divisions (or "sub-Provinces," as they were referred to during most of the period covered in this book), similar periodic reports sent by the Residents in their turn to Regional Headquarters concerning their respective Provinces, and the Annual Reports sent by the High Commissioner, or Governor to the Colonial Office in London.

The comments made by the Residents, the High Commissioner and the Colonial Office on the Reports from their respective subordinates, but particularly, the comments made by the High Commissioner and the Residents on the Reports sent to them from below, form integral parts of these Reports. In the case of the High Commissioner's comments on the Provincial Reports, they are distinct from the Provincial Reports but preserved, in almost every case in the same file with the Reports. On the other hand, the High Commissioner's own Annual Reports to London are, indeed, summaries, with factual additions and subtractions, of, and commentaries on, the Provincial Reports. Similarly, the Residents' own Reports to the High Commissioner were summaries, again with factual additions and subtractions, of the sub-Provincial Reports. Occasionally, the Provincial Reports took the form of verbatim quotations of the sub-Provincial Reports with the Residents' views added. This was especially the format of the Provincial Reports from Sokoto Province under Burdon and from Bornu Province under Hewby.

Other forms of British official records are the frequent letters that were sent from one level of the colonial regime to another and from the High Commissioner to the Colonial Secretary, and vice versa; extraordinary reports made necessary by extraordinary events such as the *hijra* of Sarkin Musulmi Attahiru in 1903, the Satiru and Dawakin Tofa Revolts in 1906 and 1908 respectively, the "crisis" created by the death of Resident Howard in Bauchi in 1908, and the Shuwa Patrol in Borno in 1913. Others include Touring Reports, District Note Books, Assessment and Reassessment Reports on each District and, often enough, each village group in the emirates; and finally the various Provincial Gazetteers, which are summaries of the various Provincial Reports up to c.1920. These Provincial, sub-Provincial and Assessment Reports touched on every aspect of life in the provinces, including their agricultural, animal and industrial resources and prospects, dynastic and ethnological histories, taxation, appointments and dismissals, the military activities of the British, the psychological disposition of the chiefs and people, and the work of Native and Provincial Courts.

Location and Identification

Very many of the records from the Northern Provinces have been deposited in the Nigerian National Archives, mainly in Kaduna, but to some extent also at the headquarters of the archives at Ibadan. Since 1971 some have been recovered by the Arewa House at Kaduna which, apart from its excellent library, has a small collection of British and post-British documents. The records in the National Archives are in the bulk "SNP" (for Secretary, Northern Provinces) and "Prof" with the name of the relevant province (or its capital) from which the document was recovered forming a prefix, e.g "Sokprof," "Yolaprof," "Minnaprof," "Maiprof" for documents recovered from the Provincial Offices at Sokoto, Adamawa, Niger and Bornu Provinces respectively. Another classification is "Kadcaptory," referring to letters written in either Arabic or Roman alphabets and exchanged either between an emirate and another, or between an emirate and the British at the end of the nineteenth and the beginning of the twentieth centuries. After each of these classificatory letters is numbered to identify a particular file, e.g "Sokprof No.575/1905" for the file containing the Sokoto Provincial Report for the months of July and August 1905.

Value and Adequacy

However, there is no doubt that the bulk of the official records, especially the District Note Books and the Assessment and Reassessment Reports, are still lying in the former Provincial Offices (most of which have now become S.M.G's Offices in the state capitals); in Divisional Offices, in Native Authority Offices (all of which have become Local Government Headquarters), and in District Offices all over the former Northern Region of Nigeria. Among such scattered records, there are bound to be many that will be directly relevant to the period covered in this book; but the majority of these scattered documents are most likely to deal with the rest of the colonial period. However, while the documents dealing with our period that have not yet been deposited in the National Archives will definitely add greater detail and throw more light on the period, there is very little chance that they will alter the conclusions reached in this book about the nature and operation of British colonial domination over the emirates and the impact it had on the emirates and their people. In fact, not all the documents deposited at the National Archives and dealing with our period of study have been consulted during the course of the research. So many are these records, and among those out of which one made notes, not all have been cited in the book. So much similar and in agreement are the records about the nature of British colonial domination over the emirates. Indeed we will say, without fear of contradiction, that documents from anyone province could have sufficed for the writing of the book and would have led us to the same conclusions we have reached, on the basis of examining records from several provinces.

Regarding the value of these documents, there should be little doubt; but this is not to say that they were devoid of faults. For, the people who compiled them were racists, some more so than others. Hence, blatantly racist views are very often openly expressed, but such are subjective judgments which, while worth taking into account by researchers on the nature of British colonialism in the emirates, need not invalidate the factual material and data contained in the documents – such as on the number of people killed during an expedition, property confiscated, "fines" imposed on whole villages, the number and types of taxes imposed, their yields and the disbursement of the revenue realized from them, the number of Districts formed, and of Native and Provincial Courts established; the number and nature of cases disposed in these courts, the number of convictions, the types of punishment, the number of prisoners, the number of Islamic and British schools, and of pupils in each; the frequency of famines and epidemics and their tolls, etc; namely data concerning the issues which we are preoccupied with in this book.

To be sure, one cannot dismiss the possibility that some of the compilers of these documents might have been aware that one day some Nigerian students of history would, under conditions different from those prevailing at the time of compilation, use these documents to recount the lot of our people under the British. But if there were such officers they must have been very few, or they must have been so taken in by the much vaunted "civilizing mission" of European imperialism in Africa that they felt that anything the British might have done to Africans in the course of accomplishing that "mission" was justified; and would be seen as justified by all historians, including Nigerian historians. We make this point because what strikes me about the documents is their factual candidness and not understatement about the negative nature and impact of British colonial domination over the emirates. This is not to deny that there could have been an understatement of the negative aspects of that domination; or an exaggeration of its positive aspects; or even downright suppression of particularly compromising information, here and there in the reports. That such understatements, exaggerations and suppression would be made should indeed be accepted as axiomatic. Nonetheless, in spite of such distortions of facts the reports provide more than a sufficient basis for concluding that British colonial domination over the emirates was extremely negative. Indeed, that is the only conclusion that these documents allow. It is on this basis that I regard the British official records as extremely valuable and adequate for the reconstruction of the experience of our people during the period under consideration.

The British Official Records versus Oral Tradition

In fact, one should add that these records strike me as being much more useful and much more candid than oral tradition collected from Native Authority official circles. These traditions were obviously coloured by the propaganda work that the British undertook at Katsina College and through the Gaskiya Corporation, painting a rather gentle picture of colonialism – emphasizing the "honesty" of the British Residents, their "humanity," their abhorrence of injustice and so on, in contradiction to the picture that emerges from an examination of the official records. This is not to say that a more realistic – and worse – picture of British colonialism in the emirates could not be obtained from the lower non-official classes of society. In fact, we have had opportunity to compare the accounts that one gets from the official circles and those obtained from members of the lower classes, and we have found those from official circles rather reticent, using the official records as a check. For example, while people in the official circles would either not mention forced labour and "pacification" expeditions, or at best mention them rather casually, members of the lower classes remember these vividly and tend to make them the centre of their discussion, if one gives them a free reign. Yet, even among the lower classes, there is a tendency to blame the negative aspects of British colonial domination, both at the level of policy formulation and policy execution, not so much on the British as on their local agents, while the British records leave one in no doubt that all policy was at least laid down by the British themselves.

As for the execution of policy, because this was largely done by local agents, though not by them exclusively and, given the type of people employed by the British as messengers, District Heads, Village Heads, etc, there was, and indeed there was bound to be, additional injustice on top of that "officially" imposed and sanctioned by the British. But perhaps the most important point about oral tradition is that with present Federal and State Governments' policies over the matter, researchers are all but restricted to the official circles. As far as Government is concerned, there is no difference between a Nigerian doing research, even on his own village, and an American researcher working in Nigeria. Both need "security" clearance which, in some cases, the Americans find it easier to obtain; both have to be sent to the Local Authorities who would then send them to specific people. To be fair to the Local Authorities, the guidance given by them is very helpful in that it helps one break the circle of ignorance about where the old and knowledgeable men are. But, of necessity, this guidance limits one's contacts to people who are either themselves officials or more or less reflect official views about British colonial domination. Besides, occasionally some of the people to whom these authorities direct one flatly refuse to cooperate because they have no faith in the local authorities, or in researchers for that matter. Hence, what one gathers from the lower classes must be done during casual, unofficial contacts, and are limited. Until there is a change in policy by the government about research by Nigerians, and perhaps even after such a change, pending a greater rise in the level of political consciousness of the lower classes, and the growth of trust by them in researchers, the British official records in the National Archives and outside, correctly handled, in our view, remain the best source for reconstructing British colonial domination over the emirates and its impact over the people of the emirates.

Semi-Official and Unofficial British Records

By unofficial British records one is referring to private diaries, kept by British officials during active duty, and memoirs they wrote after retirement, newspaper articles and memoranda written by contemporary British personages having interests in British colonialism in Nigeria but who held no office, or were encouraged to be written by the traditional *ulema* in their employ and, later, by Northern Nigerian elements educated at the Katsina College and the various Provincial Schools and, working at the Gaskiya Corporation or teaching in the various Middle Schools at the time of writing. There is quite a number of these, as will be seen in the bibliography that follows this Note on Sources.

We must, however, state, first, that we have not seen most of these records including diaries and articles deposited in Britain except those in Nigerian archives, essentially because the material gathered in the Nigerian archives was sufficient. Secondly, the memoirs of the British officials deal with non-essentials such as rules of etiquette between British officials and Emirs, personal friendships struck, minor humiliations suffered by junior officers in the hands of their superiors or the obsequiousness of messengers and interpreters towards the British.

Without doubt these unofficial records, together with the publications of Gaskiya Corporation, Zaria, will be very useful in the reconstruction of the history of British colonialist propaganda, which is a vital part of the history of British colonialist domination over the emirates. However, a reconstruction of the history of that propaganda is not the aim of this book. Hence only little use was made of this category of British records in the study.

It should, however, be pointed out that much of the secondary works that are relevant to this topic, whether commissioned by the Nigerian Colonial Administration or not, share the perspectives of that administration and implicitly, if not explicitly, legitimize what the British did or did not do in the emirates. Indeed, in terms of contents some of these works, especially Margery Perham's biographies of Lugard, should properly be classified as primary sources rather than part of the secondary literature on the colonial period. We must, however, state that we found these works useful both as ready sources of information that is scattered in the Provincial Reports, and as sources of contrary opinions to those that evidence from the official records has dictated to us.

Approach and Critique of Anjorin's Thesis

One must state that we do not pretend to have been "neutral" in our approach to the topic of this book which in fact is explicitly interpretative. Far from being neutral, we approached it with the initial hypothesis that British colonialist domination of the people of the emirates, as Lugard claimed and Perham and others later amplified, was for the benefit solely of the British, and that under colonialism British gain was indeed a loss to the people of the emirates. In other words, one approached the topic on the basis of the hypothesis that the sum and essence of what happened in the emirates during the period under study was not development, but its antithesis, namely retrogression, or at best stagnation. We adopted this hypothesis on the basis of our reading of the works of Lenin, Stalin, Mao, Ho Chi Minh, Kwame Nkrumah, Sekou Toure, Amilcar Cabral and Walter Rodney. These works deal either with the general nature of imperialism as in the case of the works of Lenin and Stalin, or with the specific nature of European imperialism and colonialism in Asia and Africa, in the case of the others, especially Ho Chi Minh, whose approach was very concretely tied up with the experience of the peoples of South-East Asia and Africa under European, especially French, colonialism.

However, we did not approach the topic with more than a hypothesis. Nor did we try to invent or ignore essential evidence in the course of our investigation. On the contrary, we let the evidence obtained from the horse's mouth, as it were, confirm or refute this initial hypothesis and, in our view, the evidence absolutely confirmed and strengthened it. It was partly in a conscious effort not to force the evidence that we decided to quote the records as much as possible rather than paraphrasing them all the time. We also quoted often in order, by that means, to question or ridicule the views of those being quoted.

Finally, given that the very topic on which we are writing has already been written on by another Nigerian historian, Anjorin, [see Abel Olorunfemi Anjorin, "The British Occupation and the Development of Northern Nigeria 1897–1914" (Ph.D, London, 1965)]. We must say a word or two about his work and how this one differs from his own and those of others who, while, writing on the topic specifically or not, reached conclusions similar to his own. To start with, Anjorin similarly makes use of British records and did rely on the samples of these records that are kept mainly on microfilm in London, where he did his research. Now, judging from his work and from our own experience when we used material gathered from some of these microfilms for a seminar paper on Borno in May 1973, it is clear that the stuff they contain deal mainly with British officials' discussions of their policy, only secondarily with the execution of policy at the regional level, and rarely with the execution of policy at the provincial and sub-provincial levels. Hence, whoever uses the samples that Anjorin used is almost inevitably going to miss the potential implication and actual impact of the execution of these policies on the people of the emirates.

But, as will become clear in the course of our detailed review of his thesis, Anjorin was not just anybody. As a scholar, he obviously suffers from a bias that precludes the possibility of his correctly grasping the meaning, for our people, of the policies discussed in theoretical terms by the imperialists among themselves. Hence, unlike what we tried to do in this book, he ended up writing a thesis that essentially leaves the people of the emirates out of the discussion. He almost entirely concentrates on the views and problems of the imperialists, their quarrels, etc.; and on top of that, he perceives these views, quarrels, etc in subjective and very idealistic terms, very often contrary to evidence dug up by himself. In the process, Anjorin displayed contempt for, and a hostility towards, the people of the emirates that are both intense and unwarranted by evidence. To put it a little graphically Anjorin has, both because of the sources he used and as a result of his own serious limitations, painted a moving picture that is 99% of the time dominated by imperialist British actors, mostly debating; and the 1% of the time that the people of the emirates, of both upper and lower classes, are dragged into the picture only so that the British would patronize and pauperise them while Anjorin intrudes to castigate them for their contemporary and previous "crimes."

Distortion of Precolonial History

As an illustration of the points we have made above, we would point out that Anjorin, in his discussion of the history of the Sokoto Caliphate, exaggerates the dissensions among the emirates and does so on the basis of incorrect facts. Thus, relying on M.G. Smith, he repeats the latter's mistakes [p.15] in assuming that the practice of newly-appointed Emirs dismissing most of the officials inherited from their predecessors was universal in the emirates rather than limited to certain emirates such as Zaria, Bauchi and Kano during the 1880s, and of perceiving this practice as peculiar to the Caliphate whereas, in fact, it was, for example, the very hallmark of the modern western European and American system, in which every succeeding King, President or Prime Minister comes in with his set of ministers, entirely or partially displacing the preceding King, President or Prime Minister. He also misunderstands the succession of Umaru b. Ali b. Bello (c.1881–1890) to the Caliphate as a "usurpation" of the "rights" of Said b. Bello when, in fact, Umaru's succession was neither illegal nor, for that matter extraordinary, in the light of earlier successions, namely those of Ali b. Bello (1842–1859), Ahmad b. Abubakar (1859–1866) and Ali b. Bello (1866–1867), all of whom held the office before their uncle Ahmadu Rufai b. Uthman b. Fudi (1867–1873). On top of that, Anjorin wrongly attributes Hayat b. Said b. Bello's departure from Sokoto to Umaru's "usurpation" of the Caliphate from the former's father, when, in fact, Hayat left Sokoto three or four years earlier than this alleged "unsurpation." And he wrongly credits Hayat with a successful "incitement of the vassal states of Bauchi and Adamawa to revolt against the Sultan" [p.17], a success which Anjorin deems to have "illustrated the political instability within the Fulani empire," [ibid]. Further, Anjorin misunderstands the military relationship between Sokoto and its emirates when he posits that it was Sokoto that sent military help to individual emirates, specifically citing Adamawa [p.8], against their enemies when, in fact the truth was the direct opposite of this, especially in the case of Adamawa. Directly issuing out of this misconception was another one, namely that the Niger Company, by supplying firearms to the riverine emirates – specifically Adamawa and Bida – made them independent of Sokoto and Gwandu, making them to see the authority of the latter two over them as merely "spiritual" and specifically non-political [pp.18–19].

A Cover up of British Aggression

Second, Anjorin, deliberately or inadvertently, tries to cover up British aggression against the emirates and their neighbours. Thus, he sees the military occupation of Northern Nigeria by the British as "the last of the series of invasions to which the territory had been subjected over several centuries" [p.6]. The other and earlier "invasions" were, according to him, the wars of expansion among the Hausa states from the fifteenth century to about 1800, the Kwararafa incursions into Hausaland and Borno in the seventeenth century, "invasions", by Songhai and Borno, and the Sokoto jihad [pp.6–10]. Even if we were to allow that all these wars were wars of "invasion" we do not see the justification for lumping them with the British conquest of the emirates. We raise this objection both on account of the fact that the states and peoples involved in these earlier "invasions" were either parts of the same state-system in the area or local rebels rising against the authority of their own governments, while neither was Britain part of the state-system of the area nor were Goldie, Lugard and other British officers rising against governments to which they were subject. And on account of the fact that whereas the various local states that struggled against one another were more or less at the same level of economic and political development, Britain was at an entirely different and much higher level of development than the emirates at the time when it invaded them.

Anjorin came very near to stating categorically that the European invasion of the Caliphate was, after all, not even an external aggression. This can be seen in the following passage:

> By the Anglo-German agreement of November 15th, 1893, nearly seven eighths of Adamawa territory was cut off from the Fulani empire to form German Adamawa. The Germans appointed a new ruler (Jerima Abo) for the separate district. Thus, the Sultan of Sokoto could no longer exercise his authority over it [nothing left out]. While stability of the Fulani empire was being shaken *from within* [emphasis mine], it was threatened from outside by Rabeh after his conquest of Bornu in 1893...(p.19).

Thus we can legitimately infer that Anjorin is trying to say that while Rabeh was a foreigner in the emirates, the British and the Germans were not. In fact this inference is reinforced by another assertion of his. Thus he states that:

> For the leaders of the Fulani empire, the year 1897 was a critical one. While Fadl-Allah threatened from the north, Sir George Goldie, the Governor of the Royal Niger Company, launched a military expedition against Nupe and Ilorin, two of their southern vassal states. (p. 22)

Thus Anjorin is reminding us that Goldie was a "Governor of the Royal Niger Company," a vague but nonetheless legitimizing phrase for the aggressive activities of the Company against the emirates; and he is neatly juxtaposing Fadl-Allah's "threat" with Goldie's military "expedition," a perfectly vague and relatively innocent term in this context.

Indeed, Anjorin would never tire of making excuses for the British invasion of the emirates. Thus he informs us, more or less as a matter of fact, that:

> The British claim to Northern Nigeria was originally based on *the* treaties which the Royal Niger Company had made with various chiefs in the country during the last two decades of the nineteenth century. But after Lugard's race to Nikki in 1894, the period of treaty making in the Niger territories was virtually over. From then on, all *valid claims* to any territory had to rest on its effective occupation by the European power claiming it. France forced Britain to adopt the policy for, by her (French) activities in the Niger area during the 1890s, it was clear that she would respect no claims based merely on treaties between native rulers and *Great Britain*, unsupported by any actual occupation by troops and white officials." [All emphasis mine] (p.23).

So much does Anjorin bend over backwards to defend the British and shift any possible blame on to the "aggressive" and "greedy" French. Not that Anjorin is adducing false "facts". In fact there is at least a large grain of truth in what he says in the passage just quoted. Our point is that Anjorin is not being "neutral" in his presentation of facts. On the contrary, he is being intensely committed in his approach; but his commitment is not to Nigerian nationalism but to British imperialism. Seen from the Nigerian point of view, it is not relevant whether the French were more aggressive towards the British or vice versa. The important thing is that the British did mount a bloody and relentless military aggression against the emirates and imposed their military and political domination over the emirates, with a consequent intensification of British exploitation of their human and natural resources. But then, Anjorin was not concerned with the independence of the emirates. He was concerned only with "British rights on the middle Niger" [p.24], the "French threat" to these "rights," he says, "prompted Chamberlain, the Secretary of State for the Colonies, to ask the Royal Niger Company to make their claim effective," [p.23–24]. So innocent and righteous was the cause lying behind British military "expedition" – read "aggression" – against the emirates – in the eyes of Anjorin.

In a nutshell, it should be said that the whole of chapter one (pp.23–220), dealing with "Military Expeditions" (Parts I and II) was consistently written from the British point of view and devoted to highlighting British problems and the justice of their actions, not the problems and the justice of the actions of the emirates, as one would expect from a Nigerian historian. (There were three exceptions, viz p.89, where the problems of the Caliph are given a brief mention, pp.99–100, where the "Fulani" military disadvantage is traced to their lack of central military organization, and pp.101–102, where Lugard is slightly censured for making no effort to win the friendship of Attahiru I after the death of the Caliph Abdurrahman) He did not even attempt a "balanced" presentation of "both sides" as one would expect from a "neutral" but objective historian. Thus, we are repeatedly reminded that every single act of the British against the emirates between 1897 and 1899 was forced on the British, this time by obstinate Emirs. "The West African Frontier Force had to deal with many of them ["revolts' by the emirates] during the next two years" [p.27]. Then we are told in detail British "problems" with regard to recruiting men into the WAFF and maintaining them there, and the "obstructions" they met from the emirates' rulers, whose "objection to the recruitment of slaves was to be expected from people who depended upon slave labour for their day-to-day activities," [p.30]. Thus, for once, Anjorin displays some empathy with the rulers of the emirates, but his was an empathy clearly touched with contempt. However, in conso-nance with Anjorin's line, the events that surrounded the *hijra* of the Caliph At-tahiru and his pursuit and destruction of Bormi were also presented in terms of the "problems" that they posed for the British. These included the great support that the Caliph received from the *talakawa* and minor chiefs (pp.93–94), the fortifications of Bormi town (p.96), the refusal of the local leader of Bormi to support the British against the Caliph (p.97), the fighting ability of the people of Bormi and their tenacity [ibid].

Hostility Towards those who Resisted the British

Then there was Anjorin's allegation that Lugard abhorred bloodshed, "an-ticipated a trial of strength with the Fulani rulers," but could not carry out a quick surgical operation, as it were, because "the Ashanti war broke out" – a cover up phrase for British aggression against the Kingdom of Ashanti – in 1900 and "1,262 soldiers were dispatched to the Gold Coast from Northern Nigeria" (p.32). However, "in spite of the demands upon his troops," Lugard did engage in "some military operations" during his "first year of administration in North-ern Nigeria," (p.33). Yet, in this case too, Anjorin dutifully reminds us that these "earliest" military "expeditions" were "precipitated by local inhabitants who at-tacked some of the survey parties which Lugard had sent into the country to se-lect a good site inland for an administrative capital, and to extend the telegraph line into the interior," (p.33). Not that the "survey party" was such an innocent group. On the contrary, it "was escorted by Captain Carroll and one hundred soldiers," which was not at all a small force given the British technological and organizational superiority over the emirates and their neighbours in those days. That might well be why, [when they entered] "the Tiv country at Udenim, the inhabitants attacked the party and prevented them from reaching Ibi," (p.33). But Anjorin does not — and possibly cannot — see the matter that way. On the contrary, he implicitly endorses the fact that "Carroll sent for reinforcements at Lokoja as the Tiv warriors, who were armed with poisoned arrows, outnumbered his men by twenty to one," [ibid]. Similarly, the British invasions of Bida and Kontagora in 1900 were blamed on intrigues against the British by Emirs of the two places, Abubakar and Ibrahim, as well as on their general intransigence, [pp.35–36].

In the same way, we are informed that in 1901 "Lugard directed his attention also to Bornu because the French were encroaching upon British claims there," [p.38]. Yola, for its part, was occupied for two reasons; partly because "Zubairu, the Emir, had attacked the mission which McClintock led to Fad-el-Allah in June 1901," and partly because of Zubairu's "constant disturbance of the Niger Company's trade in Adamawa." Not only that but we are also told that Yola was able to put a notable resistance — for two days according to Anjorin — because Zubairu's "mercenary soldiers fired on Morland's men" from the palace and the mosque [p.51]. Thus, we are being told that it was the defenders of Yola that were "mercenary" and not the British troops who are simply referred to as "Morland's men." Without doubt, Anjorin has little love for Zubairu whom, he said, "considered all white men as intruders in the country," [p.52] an attitude which Anjorin obviously does not agree with. In fact, he levelled this sweeping accusation against Zubairu because the latter "was ... involved with the revolt which the head chief of Marua was organizing against the Germans,' [ibid]. Thus Anjorin, who supports the British against the Germans, supports the Germans against the Emir of Yola. Let that be the measure of his alienation from Nigerian nationalism.

Another "crime" of Zubairu for which he forfeited Anjorin's sympathy is that "in his messages to the Sultan of Sokoto, he had expressed his deep hatred for the Christian 'unbelievers'," [ibid.]. It was "his intolerant attitude towards all white men [that] cost him his life" [p.53]. In the same way, Magaji dan Yamusa in Keffi was made by Anjorin to bear full blame for the events that led to a showdown between him and Resident Moloney in October 1902 during which Moloney was killed by the Magaji whom Anjorin refers to as a "murderer," [pp.68–69]. Similarly, he describes as "a good reason," [p.68], Lugard's use of the refuge afforded the Magaji by the Emir of Kano as a pretext to invade Kano, [pp 68 and 70], a point which he later emphasizes when he avers that "the Kano expedition failed to accomplish its main objective: the capture of the Magaji of Keffi and the punishment of Aliyu, the Emir of Kano who gave him shelter," [p81]. Similarly, the attack on Sokoto was justified on the "vagueness" of Caliph Attahiru's rather friendly reply to Morland's letter demanding that he handed over the Magaji of Keffi and the Emir of Kano [pp.82 and 88].

Nor does Anjorin mention any of the atrocities committed by the British, such as the burning of the bodies of the defenders of Bebeji. On the contrary, he describes Morland's capture of Kano as a "brilliant campaign," [p.82], and alleges that all the fighting between the British and the defenders of Kano "was done in the two-mile space between the walls and the inhabited part of the city, thus preventing unnecessary damage to buildings" besides "sav[ing] Morland's men from engaging in hand to hand combat along the fatuous alleyways of the city," [p.80]. Similarly, the two battles around Kwatorkwashi between the Kano people returning from Sokoto and the British were dismissed as "skirmishes" [p.87], although in the first battle, the British killed sixty-five of the Kanawa and in the second battle routed them [ibid.].

As for the non-Muslim communities, Anjorin alleges that "between 1901 and 1905 [Lugard] paid very little attention to the 'pagan' districts," [p.103] and that "he only sent punitive expeditions against them whenever they attacked survey parties or the trading posts of the British merchants," [pp.102–103], claims which fly in the face of facts contained in the British records covering this period, especially in the case of what were then known as Yola, Central (Bauchi and Plateau) and Zaria Provinces. Furthermore, "under the administration of Girouard, military operations were gradually replaced with peaceful penetration into the 'pagan' districts," [p.106]. Indeed, the few military expeditions were undertaken – in fact only two, in Bauchi, are mentioned – were the work of a few "unscrupulous political officers," such as Howard, Resident Bauchi, [pp.105–106]. Nothing whatsoever, not a single word is said in this long chapter about the destruction of Satiru and the attack on Hadeija in March and April 1906, which is perhaps as well, since, otherwise, we might have been treated to a nauseating tale about how the hand of the British were forced by religious fanatics and bigots.

Misunderstanding of British Policy

Concerning what the British did with the emirates after capturing them, Anjorin divides the rest of his thesis, apart from the introduction, etc, and the chapter on "the military expeditions" into five other chapters as follows:

Chapter 2: Attempts to Abolish Slavery
Chapter 3: Transportation: the Railway
Chapter 4: The Development of Cotton and Tin
Chapter 5: Background to the 1914 Amalgamation
Chapter 6: The Recall of Lugard from Hong Kong, and the Amalgamation of Northern and Southern Nigeria, 1912–1914.

In the chapter on "Attempts to Abolish Slavery" Anjorin, first of all, reduces pre-British wars in "Northern Nigeria" to "slave-raiding," [p.113], which, he says, "remained an annual event," "even up to 1903 when Lugard finally subdued the Northern Emirs," [ibid.]. However, "after the conquest of the Muslim states in 1903, Lugard successfully stopped slave raiding in Northern Nigeria," an assertion that we agree with in the sense that the British not only disarmed the Emirs and forbade all wars except their own "pacification expeditions," but also, in the sense that, to their great credit, the British ruthlessly suppressed traffic in human beings. Then, Anjorin goes on to aver that Lugard's "measures against the institution of slavery took a much longer time to have effect in the country," a fact which "was due to the importance of slavery in the economic and social structure of the Muslim society" [ibid.]. The main problem with this assertion is that by "other measures," Anjorin was in fact referring to an alleged "liberation of slaves," which he says "was not an unusual thing in Northern Nigeria [ever] before the advent of the British officers," [p.115]. That there had been no general "liberation of slaves" in the pre-British days is a point that should hardly need arguing. Nor in fact does Anjorin really mean that there was such a general liberation; for he goes on to argue, quite correctly, that even in the nineteenth century, slaves had days off and could save money to redeem themselves. This is true and was emphasized in this book, but the right to self-redemption is one thing and "the liberation of slaves" quite another.

As for "the liberation of slaves" by the British, or even an attempt by them to bring about such liberation, Anjorin has not substantiated the point, and cannot do so, because in fact there was no real attempt at such liberation. Again, we have tried to show this in this study. Thus, according to him, "the first attempt [to liberate slaves] was after the Bida-Ilorin campaign of 1897 when the Royal Niger Company made a decree against the legal status of slavery and provided a Home (called the Victoria Settlement) near Lokoja for some liberated slaves," [p.116]. However, Anjorin's quarrel with this measure was not that the phrase "abolition of the legal status of slavery" is very vague and evasive but that "neither the decree nor the philanthropic action of the Company towards the liberated slaves had any marked effect," [ibid.]. Then "by August 1900, [Lugard] had issued his first slavery proclamation" which, by Anjorin's own admission "did no more than reenact Goldie's decree of March 1897. It differed only in terminology" [p.117]. Yet again:

> early in 1901, Lugard drafted a second slavery proclamation which was more effective than that of August 1900. It was intended to make the acquisition and the disposal of slaves a criminal offence, to confirm the abolition of the legal status of slavery, and to declare all children born in Northern Nigeria after March 31, 1901 free.

Even Anjorin had to admit that it only "apparently outlawed slave dealing and provided for a natural and gradual abolition of the institution of slavery," [p.118]. We find this to be a useful admission from a scholar who argues about "the liberation of slaves" by the British. In fact, as Anjorin states without clearly bringing out the significance of the memorandum, Lugard did, under pressure from some of his more reactionary officers, issue a memorandum in which he "explained that he had no intention of abolishing domestic slavery in the same sense as a decree of emancipation would do" [p.119]. Besides, we are told that Lugard was pressurized by the Colonial Office to further modify even his ambiguous 1901 proclamation and bring it more in line with Moore's "Native House Rule" proclamation in Southern Nigeria which, far from abolishing slavery, "legislat[ed] against vagrancy," [p.123]. According to Anjorin, however, "the most outstanding achievement of Lugard with regard to slavery in Northern Nigeria was the establishment of the Slave Homes," [p.131]. Yet by his own account, only two of such "Homes" were established, at Lokoja (later moved to Zungeru) and in Borno. He also admits that less than two hundred children were admitted into each home per year, that often as many as one third of these children died, that as soon as possible these children were handed over to "respectable families" or employees of the British for keeping. At any rate, in 1909, the Homes were handed over to the Sudan United Mission, which transferred the children to Wase and essentially used them for agricultural production on a 60-acre land [pp.124–135], though this is our own deduction rather than Anjorin's way of seeing the facts that he furnishes.

Yet Anjorin himself, after giving a detailed discussion of British attempts to "liberate slaves," ended up against himself as it were, concluding that "neither the efficient running of the Slaves' Homes (that of the Sudan United Mission and those previously established by Lugard), nor Lugard's slavery proclamation brought slavery to an end in Northern Nigeria by 1914." However, to the end he misses the point that the British "failed" to liberate slaves not just because it formed "a cornerstone, in the social life of the people," which in fact is not so manifest a truth, but principally because its abolition was not an imperative demand of British colonialism in the emirates. For, while they needed cheap labour for both the projects of the Colonial Administration and the projects of the imperialist companies, they could obtain it through forceful and semi-forceful means as is shown in this study. And hence the existence of slavery on some scale, far from hindering their own demands for labour, facilitated its mobilization for them. Indeed, even what seems to Anjorin as a prime need for the local upper and middle classes — namely unpaid labour for agricultural production — was in the final analysis the need of British imperialism, first for cotton and later for cotton and groundnut.

Irrelevant Issues

A very good section of the thesis in which Anjorin could see the truth of our claim above is in the next chapter, the third chapter of the thesis, in which he discusses the extension of the Railway from Lagos to Kano and Bauchi. However, of this 40-page long chapter, less than five pages were reserved for a discussion of labour and the discussion was not at all from a Nigerian point of view, as we shall soon show. The rest of the chapter, that is, over thirty-five pages out of forty, was wasted on a rather sterile discussion of the military, economic and political necessity of the railway to the British, the politics of its conception as it involved Lugard, Girouard, the Governor of Lagos, the High Commissioner of Southern Nigeria and various personages in the Colonial Office. Thus, the cost and slowness of transporting military equipment and material by using head porterage was emphasized. In the course of doing such, Anjorin once more reminds us of the military dangers that French and German presence in adjoining territories posed to the safety of British hold on the emirates. This "called for strict measures against possible invasion of the country from outside" [p.143]. He avers, and goes on to point out that "already, the French had stationed a large and well organized force at Zinder, a French 'military zone' near the Anglo-French border," arguing that "although the troops were there *to deal with Tuaregs from the desert,* their mere presence near the northern border of Northern Nigeria made the country vulnerable to attack" [pp.143–4]. Turning to internal "threats" to the British, he laments that "expenses on the Northern Nigeria Regiment were mounting every year as a result of patrols and garrisoned soldiers in many parts of the country" [p.155], and for once he mentions Satiru. But as anticipated earlier, it was only to report "Girouard's view" that "the Satiru revolt of February 1906 was ... a clear indication of the deep rooted hatred which the Muslims had for Europeans" [p.160].

Non-Identification with Nigerian Labourers

The issue of labour was discussed on pages 163–67 and raised here and there on pages 175–78. Thus on pages 163–64 we are told that:

> On August 8th, 1907 the Colonial Secretary informed Girouard that Parliament had approved the construction of the Baro to Kano railway, and the extension of the Lagos line to Zungeru through Jebba. Soon after the announcement, the political officers in Bida began to recruit labour gangs for the railway. On January 7th, 1908 the Emir of Bida performed, at Baro, its formal inauguration at a ceremony which was attended by the Northern Governor, his political officers and the railway officials.

> During the first six months of the year, the average daily attendance of labour gangs ranged between 2,426 and 4,822. *Even some non-Muslims in the Niger district voluntarily sought employment on the railway.* The first group to be employed on May 21st, 1908 were the Gwaris. Girouard was so impressed by *their willingness to work* that he described the incident as 'a notable departure' from the hitherto hostile attitude of the people towards the government of Northern Nigeria. Both labour gangs and technicians were recruited from outside the Protectorate: the former from the Yoruba country in Southern Nigeria, the latter from England and South Africa. The imported labour gangs were engaged on piece work for the earthworks which the local recruits could not cope with. The first group of technicians from South Africa arrived in February 1908 as foremen and surveyors. [Emphasis mine].

Thus, Anjorin is here arguing that labour for the railway was voluntary, although he had evidence to the contrary, as we shall see later. As for conditions under which the labourers worked, he states simply, and without comment, on page 164 that:

> *In order to speed up the earthworks*, two groups of labour gangs were employed daily *for seven days* in the week. The first group would work *from six in the morning to three in the afternoon* with one hour's break. The second group would take over at three and work until *midnight* with one hour's break as well. *In this way, the earthworks for the first one hundred miles were nearly completed towards the end of the first year.* [Emphasis mine]

The first and last sentences are emphasized because they seem to contain Anjorin's main interest, namely British speed and the efficiency of the work. In his preoccupation with British efficiency, Anjorin overlooks the cost of that efficiency even in "human terms", to say nothing of his seeing it in terms of Nigerian lives, or for that matter, in terms of the lives of the Yoruba involved.

Indeed, Anjorin is aware of the forced nature of recruitment and the abuse and ill-treatment of the labourers and he does raise the issue, but he does so in a manner that obviously downplays it and reduces it to the "allegation" of an individual. Thus on pages 164–65, and immediately following the passage quoted above, he informs us that:

> The only protest against the conditions of employment and treatment of the labour gangs came from Bishop Tugwell, the representative of the Church Missionary Society in Nigeria. After his visit to Baro in 1909, he complained to Wallace, the acting Governor, about the ill-treatment of the labourers by their European and African foremen. He *alleged* that many of the labourers had been forced to volunteer for work on the railway by the local chiefs through whom the political officers recruited labour gangs. Secondly, some of the labourers did not receive their full weekly wage of three shillings and six pence. Thirdly, many of the foremen inflicted heavy punishments on the workers for minor offences. Deserters received heavier punishments both from their village chiefs and their foremen after the chiefs had sent them back to the railway site. Lastly there was no compensation for those who sustained injuries – some very seriously at work. [Emphasis mine]

As if to emphasize that these "allegations" were those of Bishop Tugwell and not his own, and perhaps to emphasize that even the Bishop was not too sure about the allegations, Anjorin goes out of his way to point out that:

> Tugwell *made it clear that he was accusing nobody for the alleged malpractices*, but he wanted Wallace to make investigations into them and take steps to improve the relationship between the workers and their European and African foremen, [p.165, Emphasis mine].

This way Anjorin forces one to conclude that he was more reactionary in 1965 than a British missionary had been in 1904. Nor was Tugwell wrong, as Anjorin himself shows, in this "even-handed" statement:

> Although Wallace denied all the allegations with supporting evidence from Father Scherer of the Catholic Mission at Lokoja, the subsequent enquiries made by Eaglesome who was in charge of the railway, showed that Tugwell's allegations were *not wholly unfounded*. [Ibid., Emphasis mine, and meant to expose Anjorin's bias.]

Anjorin goes on to admit that:

> During the year 1908, Eaglesome admitted that some European foremen from South Africa and *some Africans too*, were guilty of ill-treating the labourers. He dismissed a South African *foreman* for beating the men under him. A few were tried in Divisional Courts and fined, while some were served with *warning notices*. As a result of his *stern measures* against *bad behaviour* on the part of the foremen during the first year, there was *a considerable improvement in the relationship of the* foremen and the labourers, [pp.165–166, Emphasis mine].

Similarly, "the report of Goldsmith, the Resident who was responsible for recruiting local labour gangs, went further to prove" what Anjorin now admits to be "the validity of Tugwell's complaints," [p. 166]. Thus:

> With regard to the use of force in recruiting the labourers, he admitted that 'in a sense, labour recruited through the Political Staff is not voluntary,' otherwise there would be 'no means of keeping the work.' Although no physical force was employed to secure the services of the labourers some form of pressure or threat was occasionally used by the village chiefs in order to meet the demand of the political officers. The Resident also confessed that 'a certain amount of ill-treatment of the labourers is bound to occur at times,' since foremen 'from various parts of the world' were employed to control large numbers of labourers, [pp 166–67].

There is clearly an attempt here by Anjorin to put some distance between himself and the views held by the Residents. This he has tried to do by using quotation marks rather than give us a wholesale paraphrase of those views. But this attempt is isolated, both in the thesis as a whole and in the chapter under discussion, and it is insufficiently sustained to put such a distance between him and those views. Indeed by the beginning of page 167, he has abandoned that attempt and reverted to a wholesale paraphrase, and by that means adoption of very objectionable views of the British, specifically Gordon Graham, "the paymaster" of the railway project. Thus, he completes this comparatively brief discussion of the lot of the Africans by stating that:

> The allegation concerning some labourers not receiving their full weekly wages was equally true, *but the fault was not that of Gordon Graham, the paymaster.* He handed the correct weekly wage of every worker to him in person, with a political officer as witness; but *Gordon testified* to instances when village heads would demand portions of the labourers' wages. The village chiefs were required to stay on the railway site while their people were engaged there so that they might help the foremen in making them work. When Gordon queried the chiefs for demanding part of the labourers' money, *he was told* that it was to pay for the food which had already been supplied to the labourers. *The chiefs acted as middlemen for the food-sellers at the railway site.* Since seven labourers from Bida who were interviewed on the matter *said nothing contrary to what their chiefs told Graham it was assumed* that it was a mutual agreement. There were no further complaints of fraud or ill-treatment on a large-scale until the completion of the railway in March 1911. *This was due to the efficient supervision of Eaglesome and his railway* officials, [p. 167, Emphasis mine].

Thus, Anjorin ends the section with his favourite message, namely British "efficiency." Obviously, he has enough material to indict British colonialism vis à vis the peasantry of the emirates and adjoining areas, but instead of doing that he tries to use it to make a case for British colonialism. Hence the attempt to reduce a systematic crime to "ill-treatment" by individual foremen.

Essentially, the last six pages of the chapter viz: pages 174–79 are devoted to highlighting the "benefits" of the railway to the British. These included a "considerable reduction" of "the time spent on travelling within Nigeria," [p.174] by the British and their agents; and a "great increase" in the "volume of freight", which is Anjorin's way of referring to European surplus goods dumped into the emirates, and the latter's natural resources exported to Europe as raw materials. However, even in these pages Anjorin does return to the theme of British efficiency and does push the exploitation of the labour of the emirates' lower classes to the background. Thus he avers:

> Eaglesome deserves special mention in connection with the construction of the Baro–Kano railway, and the branch line to the Bauchi tin fields. The rapidity with which the 356 miles of railway from Baro to Kano was completed in less than four years defied comparison in the construction of railways in West Africa. Instead of the usual method of entrusting the construction of railways in West Africa to the consulting engineers, he made use of the officers of the Northern Public Works Department. Thus, a great deal of money was saved. Whereas the Lagos–Ibadan railway cost £7,800 a mile, and the Uganda line £10,000 a mile, Eaglesome constructed the Kano railway at £3,500 a mile [p.176].

Lest we forget, we are reminded that Eaglesome "was able to cut down the railway expenditure because he *made use of* local materials [such as timber] where they were available," and not because the British ruthlessly exploited the forced and virtually unpaid labour of the lower classes of the emirates. Far from that: "The employment of both the Muslims and the non-Muslims on the railway brought them together without fear of one attacking or enslaving the other. The contract reduced the tension which had previously been characteristic of the relationship between them" [p.177]. So much for the chapter on "Transport: The Railway" during the writing of which Anjorin dug up very significant material but entirely missed its message.

Bias for Imperialist Commerce

The next chapter on "The Development of Cotton and Tin" also suffers from the bias to Britain and against the interests of the people of the emirates. Thus, it concentrates entirely on the needs and difficulties of the British Cotton Growing Association (BCGA), which was formed in 1902, and how the association, by dint of hard work and "luck", overcame these by 1911. The association's "luck" [the term actually used by the writer is "advantage"] was "firstly the political officers in the British territories *were willing* to cooperate with the merchants in encouraging West African farmers to grow more cotton. They were also *prepared* to serve as buying agents and to distribute cotton seeds among the farmers" [p.183]; assertions which at least *tend* to overlook the fact that British colonialism was imposed on the emirates, as on any other part of the world, to serve the purposes of British monopoly companies. The second "advantage" of the association was that it was "able to learn from the experiments which French and German cotton experts had carried out in *their territories* in West Africa" [ibid.], a veritable "luck" this one, if ever there was luck, given the competition among the three imperialisms involved. A third "luck" of the association was the successful addition of its voice to the demands of other commercial interests on the imperial government to sanction extension of the Lagos Railway to Kano. Indeed, "the British Cotton Growing Association played no small part, as a pressure group in urging the British government to provide this railway" [p.195].

Among the "difficulties" of the BCGA was initially transport, then the "pessimism" of Lugard's immediate two successors, namely Percy Girouard and Hesketh Bell, about the prospects of "developing" cotton in the emirates [pp.198–200], competition from local weavers, and finally the preference of the peasants of the far northern emirates to produce groundnut rather than cotton. Concerning local competition, Anjorin laments that:

> although the question of transporting cotton Southwards had been solved [as from 1911], there were *problems facing the British Cotton Growing Association.* Since they began to purchase cotton in Northern Nigeria, *they had to* compete with Nigerian buyers for the native cloth industry ... Although there are no records of the quantity of cotton used locally, some political officers noted that Nigerian cotton buyers usually paid more for seed cotton than the Agents of European firms.

Not that the European firms were at a fault, for "this was due to the fact that the European merchants fixed their buying prices according to the price of cotton in England; and *the* farmers preferred to sell their products to the highest bidder;" a preference that Anjorin seems to adjudge somewhat perverse, in this case. Of course, as stated above "*another problem* [of the BCGA] was that in the northern parts of the Protectorate – roughly from Kano upwards – groundnuts were more widely grown than cotton," for ecological and social reasons – the dietary needs of the people in the case of the latter. For example "up to 1924, it was estimated that "37,000 tons were *still* consumed in a normal year," [p.203]. But it was not the needs of the people of the emirate that interests Anjorin. His pre-occupation is with "the demand of the Lancashire Cotton Industry," a demand which "made the political officers [to] encourage the northerners to concentrate more on the cultivation of cotton than on groundnut during the first decade of this century" [ibid.]. Given the nature of his pre-occupation, Anjorin did not find it necessary to utter a single word on the several famines and deaths that the local population suffered in this same period. On the contrary, Anjorin celebrates [pp.200–201] the fact that the export of cotton from the emirates to Britain grew by leaps and bounds as from 1911. Indeed, he celebrates the progressively weakening resistance of the local economy to the demands of the BCGA and other European firms. Thus, he announces that contrary to Hesketh Bell's "pessimism" from 1905 onwards "fluctuations [in the quantities of cotton exported] did occur, *but they were due mainly to the unusually long periods of drought,*"[p.200] that is, as opposed to the resistance of the local economic system. Perhaps it should be added that after all Anjorin does "take note" of the long "periods of drought" that occurred in the period covered in the chapter. But it was solely from the point of view of the droughts' impact on British commercial interests, not from the point of view — even secondarily — of their impact on the local population and economy.

The section on tin was also discussed from a similar angle and in similar terms, and need not detain us for long. For it to do so will entail a repetition of what we have said before. Nonetheless, we would like to state categorically that Anjorin does not have a single word about the disastrous effect of the activities of the mining companies on the people of the areas affected and their economy. On the contrary, he sees the issue from the British angle, namely that "the rise in the production of tin-ore brought increased revenue for the government of Northern Nigeria in form of royalties" [p.227]. Similarly, concerning the topic of the chapter as a whole, he avers that "the results of the development of tin and cotton between 1902 and 1914 gave a clear indication of a promising economic future for Northern Nigeria" [p.228]. So much does Anjorin confuse the interests of British imperialism with the interests of "Northern Nigeria."

Lengthy Irrelevance

Finally, it should specifically be noted that Anjorin spends eleven pages [216–27] discussing the irrelevant issue of how some colonial officers — especially Wallace — flouted imperialist "morality" by using their knowledge of the emirates to direct their friends in the commercial field towards the most promising tin areas. So seriously does he take imperialist "morality" that he misses and therefore does not bring out the humorous aspects of the issue – namely that at one point there was a perceived danger that a sufficient number of officers might resign from "Administration" into "mining" so as to cause the collapse of the colonial government, thereby defeating colonialism through colonialism's own success. Far from seeing this "funny side" of the situation, Anjorin discusses the whole issue in such a sombre tone as to leave one in no doubt whatsoever that he takes the "white man's burden" or "dual mandate" theory of imperialism literally.

The chapter on the "Background to the 1914 Amalgamation," apart from the pro-British bias that it shares with the earlier chapters, contains hardly any facts worth knowing. It is just a long (81 pages) rehash of the often-repeated "poverty" of Northern Nigeria, the confused and dangerous charge that "Northern Administrators," like Lugard, wanted "Southern Nigeria to subsidize the North, and at the same time to become subordinate to the northern government politically!" [p.245], and lengthy portrayals of the "differing" personalities and perspectives of various colonial and imperial personages like Lugard, Moor, Lady Kingsley, Morel, McGregor and Egerton; including a long discussion of Lugard's relations with his wife and their "struggles" and "labour" "against" the Colonial Office on behalf of the "Northern Protectorate." There is also a long, [pp.277–99] discussion of border disputes between "Northern Nigeria" and "Lagos" which, he says, started with "clashes between the Yoruba and the Fulani" that in turn "started during the second decade of the nineteenth century when Afonja made use of *the* Hausa mercenaries to carve a dominion for himself within the effete Oyo empire" [p.284]. What was totally absent in the discussion was even a single word about the lot of the people of the emirates. In fact, only a passing phrase or two are uttered about the imposition of British colonialist taxes on these people and absolutely nothing about the impact of these taxes on them. Indeed, instead of that Anjorin talks about Lugard's plan to make the Governor-General of an amalgamated Nigeria, "responsible for all legislation and all financial matters, especially the revenue and the expenditure of the whole country, *the distribution of funds and staff to the various administrative units*, and the sanction of military operation" [p.277], as if colonialism, specifically British colonialism in Nigeria, was an agency for *distributing* rather than collecting funds.

Eulogy and "Opposition" to the British

The final chapter, the chapter on "the Recall of Lugard from Hong Kong, and the Amalgamation of Northern and Southern Nigeria, 1912–1914," is a continuation of the previous chapter in both tone and substance, and is very much woven around the person of Lugard. Yet, the chapter contains three points that are worth taking note of because they further highlight the author's bias for the British and against the people of the emirates. Thus, in the first place, he clearly expresses his views about the beneficial nature of British colonialism to the people of the emirates when he observes that:

> As far as Northern Nigeria was concerned, Lugard brought political stability to the territory which for many centuries, had been subjected to series of invasions from outside and to constant disturbances from within. To achieve the stability he [Lugard] first of all conquered the Muslim states one by one, replaced the stubborn Emirs by other members of the ruling family who promised to be of *good behaviour* [p.351, emphasis mine].

He added:

> The political control of Northern Nigeria was only one aspect of the duties of the British officers. *Their intention was to develop its material wealth for benefit of Britain as well as for Northern Nigeria itself.* The promotion of British trade inevitably affected the economic development of the Protectorate. Modern transportation, of which the railway was the most spectacular example, was introduced. *The material wealth of the country steadily increased.* The greater portion of the *territory* which had hitherto looked northwards to the Arabic world for trade and religious inspiration, was gradually brought under the influence of European culture. The link with the Arabic world was reduced to the influence of Islam, whilst *Britain took over the economic and the political development of the Protectorate* [P.52, Emphasis mine].

Not that Anjorin supports everything the British did. He does oppose – from the right – some of the things they did or did not do. For instance, he obliquely takes exception to Lugard's refusal to make either the Rivers Niger and Benue or "racial" and ethnic boundaries the boundary between Northern and Southern Nigeria, and he openly criticizes the British for refusing to impose Christianity on the people of the emirates. Thus, on the border issue, which he discusses at much greater length and in much more chauvinistic terms in the previous chapter, Anjorin has the following to say:

> In his amalgamation report, Lugard commented only on Morel's suggestion for making use of the two main rivers in the country as the provincial boundaries. 'They were wholly undesirable', he said 'because in Africa rivers connect rather than divide people.' If the provincial boundaries had been pushed to the banks

of the rivers, the whole of Kabba province, the greater part of Ilorin and some parts of Muri, Yola and Tiv districts would have been cut off from Northern Nigeria. Obviously, according to Lugard, no frontier demarcation based on ethnic groupings was possible in Nigeria ... [pp. 322–23, Emphasis mine].

The issue of the imposition of Christianity on the people of the emirates is raised by Anjorin, in his discussion of the introduction of western education into the emirates. Thus he observes that:

While a sound foundation for the political and the economic development of Northern Nigeria was laid between 1900 and 1914, the British officers neglected its educational advancement, the excuse being Lugard's promise in 1900 not to interfere with the religion of the Muslims ...

Another reason for the neglect of the education of the Northerners was the suspicion of *the Muslim themselves* that the introduction of European education would mean the imposition of the Christian religion which would lead to 'an indirect attack on their religion.' Thus, *the unwillingness of the people* to be influenced by European education, and *Lugard's undertaking to preserve their religion and customs, impeded the development of education* up to 1909 when Hans Vischer, a political officer, submitted a scheme of education for Northern Nigeria [pp. 353–54, Emphasis mine].

This way Anjorin blames British neglect of western education in the emirates on the religious prejudices of the people, and clearly implies that the British should not have heeded those prejudices.

The allegation that it was the religious feelings of the people and British regard for these feelings that hampered the introduction of western education into the emirates has been refuted in this study. So, his criticism of the British for taking the feelings of the people into account also collapses.

Thus, we can conclude this critique by simply stating that it is not in the types of sources we have used but in the perspectives from which we have approached our topic that we and Anjorin differ – by a very wide margin.

P.S.

Since writing this critique of Anjorin's thesis we have noticed a paper he presented at the Social Science Seminar of ABU in June 1971, and in which he substantially overcame the shortcomings of his thesis. This was his paper, "The Imposition of the Native Authority System in Bussa: The Rebellion of 1915," which, significantly, was based on material gathered not from the CO 446 and similar series in London, but from the SNP and CSO series in Kaduna and Ibadan.

Notes

Introduction

1. United Nations Development Program. *Human Development Report Nigeria: 2008–2009*. UNDP, Abuja, 2009, p.11.
2. *Nigeria Millennium Development Goals: Report 2010*. Federal Government of Abuja, 2010 (FGN/ MDGS 2010: www.mdgs.gov.ng 2010).
3. MDG data does not square readily with a recent UNDP report which found that "of the 38,061,333 children aged 5–17 years covered in the survey, 39.4% were outside the school system. Of this figure, 13.1% engaged in economic activities and 26.3% were domestic helps. 2009. *Human Development Report: Nigeria 2008–2009. Achieving Growth with Equity*. Abuja: UNDP, p. 70.
4. Government of the Federal Republic of Nigeria, 2010. *Nigeria Millennium Development Goals: Report 2010*, p. 14.
5. The OPHI data show staggering poverty levels in the north; in the northeast, for example, 88% of the population is MPI poor, and the intensity of deprivation among the poor is 84%.
6. Paul Lubeck, *Nigeria: Mapping the Shari'a Restorationist Movement*. Working Paper. Center for Global, International and Regional Studies, University of California, Santa Cruz, 2010; see also Adesoji Abimbola, 2010, "The Boko Haram Uprising and Islamic Revivalism in Nigeria", *Africa Spectrum*, 45, 2, 95–108.
7. See the interesting blog http://www.isvg.org/follow/blog/2011/11/07/nigerian-nightmare-visualizing-terror-in-africas-most-populous-nation; and see also Jason Burke, "Boko Haram", *The Guardian* January 17, 2012 (http://www.guardian.co.uk/world/2012/jan/27/boko-haram-nigerian-sunni-militant). See Lubeck, Paul, Michael Watts and Ronnie Lipschutz. "Convergent Interests: US Energy Security and the 'Securing' of Nigerian Democracy." *International Policy Report*. Washington: The Center for International Policy, 2007.
8. In a video released on January 15, 2012, a Boko Haram leader, Abubakar Shekau, made it clear that the group's primary motivation remained redress for the government crackdown. Negotiations with Islamist groups in the north suggest that

the Islamist demand troop withdrawal, mosque reconstruction and compensation for loss of life. It is not at all clear that this is language of jihad.

9.   On Tuesday May 14, 2013, President Goodluck Jonathan declared a state of emergency in three northern states.

10. Usman, Yusufu Bala, *The Transformation of Katsina ca 1796–1903: The Overthrow of the Sarauta System and the Establishment and Evolution of the Emirate*. Ph.D dissertation Ahmadu Bello University, 1974.

11. Tahir, Ibrahim, *Scholars, Sufis, Saints and Capitalists in Kano 1904–1974: Pattern of a Bourgeois Revolution in an Islamic Society*. Ph.D dissertation, Cambridge University, 1975.

12. Gunilla Andrae and Bjorn Beckman, *Union Power in the Nigerian Textile Industry. Labour Regime and Adjustment*. Uppsala: Nordiska Afrikainstitutet, 1998/1999; Bill Freund, *Capital and Labor in the Nigeria Tin Mines*, Humanities Press, 1981; Robert Shenton, *The Development of Capitalism in Northern Nigeria*, Oxford, James Currey, 1996.

13. In 1949–50, 1958–59, 1972, and 1977–78, Smith studied the Hausa, Kagoro, and Kadara in Northern Nigeria and his three monographs – *Government in Zazzau, 1800–1950*, London, Oxford University Press, 1960; *The Affairs of Daura*, Berkeley, University of California Press, 1978; *Government in Kano, 1350–1950*, Boulder, Westview Press, 1997 – remain important, if also controversial, source-works for the scholar of northern Nigeria.

14. Polly Hill, *Rural Hausa: A Village and a Setting*. London, Cambridge University Press, 1972; and Polly Hill *Population, Prosperity and Poverty: Rural Kano, 1900 and 1970*. London, Cambridge University Press, 1977.

15. James Scott, *Seeing Like a State*. New Haven, Yale University Press, 2000.

16. Paul Lubeck, *Nigeria: Mapping the Shari'a Movement*, 2010 op. cit.

17. Michael Watts, *Silent Violence: Food Famine and Peasantry in Northern Nigeria*. Berkeley, University of California Press, 1983.

18. Mohammed Salau, *The West African Slave Plantation*, London, Palgrave, 2011. He was able to provide evidence on the extent of slave-based production, confirming what Paul Lovejoy and Jan Hogendorn in *Slow Death for Slavery: The Course of Abolition in Northern Nigeria*, Cambridge University Press, London, 1993 suspected but were unable to fully demonstrate.

19. Stephen Pierce, *Farmers and the State in Colonial Kano: Land Tenure and Legal Imagination*. Bloomington, Indiana University Press, 2005.

20. See Mustapha, A.R. *Peasant Differentiation and Politics in Rural Kano: 1900–1987*. DPhil Thesis, Oxford University, 1990; Karaye, M. *Hausa Peasants and Capitalism*. PhD Dissertation, University of Wisconsin, Madison, 1990.

21. See Paul Lubeck's brilliant book, *Islam and Urban Labour in Northern Nigeria*, Cambridge University Press, London, 1985.

22. Umar, Muhammad S. *Islam and Colonialism: Intellectual Responses of Muslims of Northern Nigeria to British Colonial Rule*. Leiden, Brill, 2006.

23. H.Tilley, *Africa as a Living Laboratory: Empire, Development, and the Problem of Scientific Knowledge, 1860–1950*. Chicago, University of Chicago Press, 2011.

24. See for example, Paul Rabinow, *French Modern: Norms and Forms of the Social Environment*. Cambridge: MIT Press, 1989; and R. Grove, *Green Imperialism: Colonial Expansion, Tropical Island Edens and the Origins of Environmentalism, 1600–1800*. Cambridge, Cambridge University Press, 1995.

25. Helen Tilley, *Africa as a Laboratory*. 2010, op cit.

26. Naniya, Tijjani Muhammad. "History of the Shari'a in Some States of Northern Nigeria to Circa 2000," *Journal of Islamic Studies* 13:1, 2002, p.31.

27. Paul Lubeck, *Nigeria: Mapping the Shari'a Restorationist Movement*, 2010, op. cit. p.44.

Chapter I

1. For a detailed discussion of British aggression against the emirates of Bida and Ilorin in 1897 and the responses of the two emirates see R.A. Adeleye, *Power and Diplomacy in Northern Nigeria, 1804–1906: The Sokoto Caliphate and Its Enemies* (London, 1971), pp. 179–88; J.E. Flint, *Sir George Goldie and the Making of Nigeria* (London, 1966), pp. 232–56; and M. Mason, "The Nupe Kingdom in the Nineteenth Century: A Political History" (Ph.D Thesis, Birmingham, 1970), pp. 370–78.

2. M.A. Al-Hajj, *The Mahdist Tradition in Northern Nigeria,* Ph.D. ABU, 1973, pp. 166-7; Murray Last *The Sokoto Caliphate*, Longmans, 1967, pp. 139–40; R.A. Adeleye, op. cit., pp. 221–2 and 252–9.

3. Strictly speaking, Abuja was not an emirate, having maintained its independence of the Sokoto Caliphate right up to the British conquest of both the Caliphate and Abuja itself, which in fact was a continuation on a new territory of the old kingdom of Zaria, whose territory was absorbed into the Caliphate. The same applies to Argungu, which was a continuation of the old kingdom of Kebbi, which lost much of its territory to the Caliphate. So also is this true of Borno. However, for the sake of convenience I have throughout this book referred to both Abuja and Argungu as emirates and to Borno sometimes as Sheikhdom but often as an emirate.

4. See section "Resistance in Kano and Sokoto, and the Surrender of Gwandu and Katsina, February–March 1903, Chapter 1, page 17–21.

5. I am using the name "Bida" instead of "Nupe" for this emirate because, in fact, it was not the only emirate to be carved out of the pre-Caliphate kingdom of Nupe. Other emirates that were carved out of that kingdom were Lapai, Agaye, Sharagi and Lafiagi. See M. Mason, op. cit., Chapter 6.

6. J.E. Flint, op. cit., p. 234; M. Mason, op. cit., pp. 122–3.

7. Concerning the rather controversial issue of whether the early relationships between the Bida emirate authorities and the British traders were those between

Muslim rulers and weaker non-Muslims who were willing to live under and submit to the authority of the Muslim rulers, it should be pointed out that Flint,
whose total sympathy is on the side of these traders, and who relied entirely on
Foreign Office records for his book, points out that with the withdrawal of the
Lokoja Consulate in 1869,

> "[a]ll that remained in the way of an official link with the Niger was the an-
> nual naval expedition, sent to overawe the opposition of the coastal middle-
> men and their allies. The British ... began to consider how to get rid of this
> crude 'protection'... Could not some substitute ... be effected in the interior,
> so that British traders could proceed unmolested, and the naval expeditions
> withdrawn? It was natural that the British should look to the power of Nupe as
> a possible substitute. Here was a state which was recognizable as a state in the
> eyes of an Englishman; it had a central authority in the person of the Emir ... a
> standing army, a treasury and a taxation system, and a body of law — all of which
> recalled to Englishmen the systems of government of the Muslim states of the
> Middle East or India..."

He goes on to point out that:

> "it was therefore decided that an attempt should be made to carry on the trade
> under the protection of Nupe, and to withdraw British naval protection. In
> June 1871, W.H. Simpson sailed from Liverpool to negotiate with the Emir of
> Nupe to secure protection. So the first step in the effective British penetration
> of the river was to make British subjects the 'protected persons' of an African
> ruler ... and the Emir then signed a letter to the Foreign Secretary in which he
> agreed to protect British traders on the Niger between Idah and Egga, and to
> open up the Benue to trade ..." See Flint, op. cit., pp. 23–25.

There can be no less ambiguous statement of the subordination of the British
traders to the Emir of Bida. Besides, Mason (op. cit., pp. 150–1) also points out
that the Emir of Bida, Masaba, did actually give the British consulate at Lokoja
military protection against Igala attacks in 1867–8.

8.   It should be pointed out that although the Company had long manifested designs
on Bida Emirate, and although in the nature of the situation existing by 1895
both between the emirate and the Company, and between the Company and the
representatives of French and German imperialisms, the Company was bound
to attack the emirate sooner or later. The timing of the 1896/97 attack was the
result, not of relations between the emirate's authorities and the Company, but
of relations between the British colonialist regime in Lagos and Ilorin Emirate,
Bida's neighbour and frequent military ally. In short, the attack on Bida was a strategic move aimed at rendering this emirate incapable of giving military assistance
to Ilorin, which the Company had already agreed to invade on behalf of the Lagos
regime and on the instruction of the Colonial Office, which threatened to remove

Ilorin from the Company's "jurisdiction" and place it under Lagos if the Company failed to mount the attack. See J.E. Flint, op. cit., pp. 232–42.

9. See footnote 1 above.

10. Adeleye, op. cit, pp. 137–9, Mason, op. cit, pp. 330–4, 34–48 and 365.

11. Flint, op. cit., p. 235; Adeleye, op. cit., p. 139; Mason, op. cit., pp. 348–51.

12. Adeleye, op. cit., p. 179.

13. Ibid.

14. Adeleye, op. cit, p. 180.

15. Ibid., p. 180–3; Flint, op. cit., pp. 240–50.

16. The picture of the Makun Muhammadu that emerges from Kologiwa's account of the events of 1897–1901, from Adeleye's and Mason's portraiture of him – on the basis of Colonial Office records and from the Makun's own letters to the British during 1900–1 – is that of an early believer in collaboration between the British and the Bida aristocracy, an idea which he tried to sell to other emirates, notably Kano, after he himself had accepted office from the British in 1901. This is not to deny that he evinced a great reluctance to supplant Emir Abubakar, especially in 1897; but his lack of overriding ambition for the office of Emir, which is what this reluctance at best means, should not be confused with patriotism, which simply cannot be reconciled with his advocacy of collaboration between the native aristocracy and the invading British. Also, although up to the final occupation of Bida in February 1901 the Bida aristocracy was divided between those who toed Emir Abubakar's patriotic line and those who toed the Makun's collaborationist line, soon after the defeat of Bida's forces the Emir's own party deserted him and joined the Makun whom the British proclaimed Emir, leaving Emir Abubakar alone to continue his resistance. He did so by moving to the still unoccupied emirates, first, Zaria, then Kano, finally joining the fleeing erstwhile Caliph, Attahiru Ahmadu, and participating at the historic battle of Bormi, which he survived, to be captured by the British and to die in captivity at Lokoja in February 1911. See Michael Mason, "The Fall of Etsu Abubakar: The Account of Ubandawaki Bida," in *Kano Studies*, Vol., No.1, New Series 1973, pp. 57–82; M. Mason, op. cit., pp. 356, 374, 378–82, 395, 1784 and 226–9; and O/AR/11/26, Kadcaptory, NAK.

17. According to the Waziri, it was because there was "no way of making a *hijra* from this land owing to the scarcity of water along the roads ... the total lack of it along some of them as well as the severity of the heat and the presence of the Christians camped along the routes," that he and other Sokoto officials submitted to the British after the Sarkin Musulmi, Attahiru Ahmadu, had embarked on the *hijra*. (From an English translation of the Waziri's *Risalah* in R.A. Adeleye, "The Dilemma of the Waziri: The Place of the *Risalat al-Wazir Ila Ahl al-Ilmwa'l-Tradabbaur* in the History of the Conquest of the Sokoto Caliphate," in *JHSN*, Vol. IV, No.2, June 1968.)

18. Flint, op. cit., p. 298; Adeleye, op. cit., p. 198.

19. In addition to the loss of 600–1,000 dead, and apart from the fact that the British looted and burnt Bida town, Bida Emirate lost her territories to the south of the

River Niger, that was what later was to form the Kabba Province of Northern Nigeria and with these territories the tribute that Bida had been exacting hitherto (Mason, op. cit., pp. 382–6; Flint, op. cit., p. 254–5).

20. Adeleye, op. cit., p. 336, fn.32; Mason, op. cit., pp. 391–2 and 398–400.
21. Fn 9, see section on "Occupation of Kontagora and Bida", Chapter 2, pp. 45.
22. See the Makun's letters to Wallace, Lugard and Adamu Jakada in Kadcaptory O/ AR 11 No.26, NAK.
23. Flint, op. cit., pp. 232-3 and 236–8; Adeleye, op. cit., pp. 142–4.
24. Adeleye, op. cit., pp. 185–6.
25. Ibid.
26. Ibid; Flint, op. cit., p. 238.
27. Flint, op. cit., p. 238.
28. Adeleye, op. cit., p. 185–6. It is interesting that Flint was silent on this loss by Ilorin.
29. Adeleye, op. cit., p. 186; Flint, op. cit., p. 238.
30. Thus, Ilorin first suffered a casualty of about 150 soldiers including one of its four Baloguns, Adamu, in January, during its attack on a British military post at Erinmope; and during the RNC attack on Ilorin town on 15 February, the defenders, who were estimated at 8,000–10,000, of whom 800 were mounted, suffered a loss of about 200 horsemen alone, the number of those who died among the infantry being presumably much higher. Adeleye, op. cit., pp. 186–7.
31. Ibid., p. 22–3.
32. Ibid., p. 187.
33. Adeleye, op. cit., p. 223 fn 21.
34. Ibid., pp. 223–5; p. M. Dwyer, "Report on the Ilorin Province for the Quarter Ended 31 March 1907," SNP7/1569/1907, NAK.
35. Adeleye, op. cit., p. 223.
36. In the meantime the British had invaded the emirates of Agaye and Lapai in June 1898, met with resistance in both and overcame that resistance. Similarly, the British, on their way to Bida in February 1901, had first invaded the Emirate of Kontagora and there too met with resistance in spite of the fact that Kontagora had witnessed the British invasion of Bida, Ilorin, Agaye and Lapai in 1897–8. Indeed the Emir of Kontagora, Ibrahim Nagwamatse, managed to escape with a very large body of followers (20,000 according to Lugard), moved north into the emirates of Katsina and Zaria, and was not to be captured by the British until thirteen months later, in March 1902. While none of these three emirates – Agaye, Lapai and Kontagora – has yet been studied in its own right, it should be pointed out that Agaye and Lapai have been fairly extensively treated in Mason's thesis on Bida (Mason, op. cit., Chapter 6) while the history of Kontagora, specifically the history of its relations with the Kingdom of Yawuri, has received some treatment in Mahdi Adamu's thesis on "A Hausa Government in Decline: Yawuri in the Nineteenth Century," MA thesis, ABU, 1968, Chapters 5 and 6. From Adamu's thesis (pp. 308–9) it emerges that the Emir of Kontagora put up a rather dogged

resistance against the British right from 1897, not only on Kontagora territory but also in Yawuri, where Sarki Abarshi was favourably disposed towards the British; the Emir of Kontagora feigning popular discontent against them among the people of the kingdom. While the Emir's capacity to inspire resistance to the British, both in his own emirate and outside, indicates that he had a good grip on the internal situation in his emirate, there was a further and perhaps better indication of such a grip. This is the fact that after the occupation of Kontagora, the Emir successfully took along with him all his officials and relatives; (E.C. Duff, *Gazetteer of the Kontagora Province*, London, 1920 p. 127) while British attempts to integrate the emirate with the Kingdom of Yawuri, out of which it had been partly formed in the second half of the nineteenth century, failed, and Ibrahim had to be brought back from exile in Yola in 1903 and restored as Emir of Kontagora. See M. Adamu, op. cit., pp. 318-32; also E.C. Duff, op. cit., p. 12.

37. Adeleye, op. cit., pp. 231–2; Sa'ad Abubakar, *The Emirate of Fombina, 1809–1903: The Attempts of a Politically Segmented People to Establish and Maintain a Centralized Form of Government*, PhD., ABU, 1970, p. 442.

38. For Yola's relation with the RNC in the closing years of the nineteenth century, see S. Abubakar, op. cit., pp. 439–41.

39. In his letter to Caliph Abdurrahman, announcing his own ouster from Yola by the British, Zubairu pledged "I will not be two faced, on your side and on the side of the Christians too. My allegiance is to you, to God and the Prophet, and after you to the Imam Mahdi. There is no surrender to the unbeliever even after the fall of the strongholds" (Sa'ad Abubakar, op. cit., p. 494). And Zubairu kept this pledge, continued his resistance against both the British and the Germans till he was killed around Gudu, allegedly by "pagans," who mistook his identity, eighteen months after the British had forced him out of his capital on 1st September 1901 (see fn 53 below).

40. For a discussion of the internal problems inherited by Lamido Zubairu and how he dealt with them see S. Abubakar, op. cit., pp. 402–38.

41. R.M. East, *Stories of Old Adamawa*, Zaria, 1934, p. 97.

42. With respect to the *ulema*, Yola should be understood to include Girei, fifteen miles to the north of it, for many of the influential *ulema* actually lived at Girei during the period under consideration.

43. According to the understanding of the famous Qadi, Ahmad Saad of Gwandu, writing soon after the occupation of Sokoto the British "did not prohibit the practice of religion and, in fact, the rites of Islam are predominant in this land of ours. Their goal is the control of worldly affairs and their ambition the conquest of territory. As for Islam, they have not prevented anyone, from Futa to this place, from practising it." M.A. Al-Hajj, op. cit., p. 161.

44. R Adeleye, op. cit., pp. 103–7 and 202; Martin Njeuma "Adamawa and Mahdism: The Career of Hayatu ibn Sa'id in Adamawa, 1878–1898" in *Journal of African History*, XII, 1 (1971), pp. 61–77; M.A. Al-Hajj, op. cit., pp. 111–37.

45. M. East, op. cit., pp. 113, 115 and 117; M. Njeuma, op. cit., pp. 65 and 74.

46. AGS, Sokoto, 8/1/1975.
47. Ibid.
48. MAM, Nassarawo Jereng, 10/3/1975.
49. MTA, Nassarawo Jereng, 5/1/1977.
50. Ibid.
51. While the extension of British-Egyptian domination occurred in the period 1863–79. See p. M. Holt, *The Mahdist State in the Sudan 1881–1898,* London, 1970 pp. 37–44; according to Isa Alkali (*Islam in Adamawa in the Nineteenth and Twentieth Centuries,* M.A. thesis, ABU., 1976, pp. 124–5), Hamman Joda left Yola in the 1870s for the Middle East where he studied first in the Sudan under a certain Sheikh Quraishi, among whose students was said to be Muhammad Ahmad, who was subsequently to found the Mahdia; then at Cairo from where he performed the pilgrimage to Mecca and Medina, finally arriving back at Yola in the 1880s. See also Sa'ad Abubakar, op. cit., pp. 368–9. There is also a tradition in Yola that on Hamman Joda's return Modibbo Na-kwashiri, with whom he had been close friends prior to his journey, travelled up to Marwa where Hamman Joda first settled after his return, to welcome him (MTA, 6/1/1977). Given that Modibbo Na-kwashiri is said to have died in c.1882 (ibid.), Hamman Joda must have returned from the East sometime before this date and could barely have witnessed the rise of the Mahdia, much less the destruction by the British, events which took place between 1881 and 1898. See p. M. Holt, op. cit, pp. 45 and 229–43.
52. Sa'ad Abubakar, *The Lamibe of Fombina: A Political History of Adamawa 1809–1901,* ABU Press, 1977, p. 352.
53. Among the places where Lamido Zubairu fought the Germans after they had driven him out of Yola were Garwa, whose German garrison he attacked with the aid of the local population, after about six months of hiding with the people of Adumri, within "German" Adamawa; and at Marwa, the local people of Marwa who massively rallied around Zubairu, suffering very heavy casualties in the hands of the Germans, Zubairu was able to "take refuge among the pagans northeast of Marwa" to quote G.N. Barclay. From there the Emir, together with some following including Lamido Ahmadu, the chief of Marwa, moved to Madagali still in "German" Adamawa. Here the Germans caught up with him and he gave battle. After his defeat he re-entered "British" Adamawa in October 1902 after having spent one year in the German sphere. He took refuge at Gudu, a non-Fulbe town north of Song, remaining there for over five months before the British zeroed in on him; this is in spite of the fact that he was all the time issuing out propaganda leaflets against the British and "doing as much as he could to stir up the Fulani to rise." It was after the British had dislodged him from Gudu and burnt down the town that he was allegedly killed by the Lala at Go, the latter not knowing his identity. (Misc. "Yola Province: Collected Histories, 1905–1931," Yolaprof J.I. NAK: G.N. Barclay "Yola Provincial Reports Nos. 11–17 for the months of September 1902 to March 1903, Yolaprof A1, NAK: S. Abubakar, op. cit.,

pp. 446–89; M.A. Al-Hajj, op. cit., pp. 154–5; Ahmadou Bassoro et Eldridge Mohammadou, *Histoire de Garoua: Cité Peule du XIX Siècle* (ONAREST, 1977) pp. 52–3; Eldridge Mohammadou (ed.) *Maroua et Pette,* Niamey, 1970, pp. 234–9.

54. J.M. Fremantle, The Gazetteer of Muri Province, London, 1920, p. 19.

55. Ibid.

56. Ibid., pp. 17–25.

57. J.M. Fremantle, op. cit, pp. 22–23; Jalingo traditions, collected by Geoffrey M. Chaskda, August 1973, cited in G.M. Chaskda, "A Wedlock of Political Ambitions: Emir Muhammadu (Hamman) Mafindi and the British Occupation and Rule in Muri," unpublished paper read at the Nineteenth Congress of the Historical Society of Nigeria, Zaria, 21 December 1973.

58. Saleh Abubakar, "Crisis and Conflict in the Middle Benue Basin: The Evolution of the Fulbe Emirate of Muri ('Hamaruwa') c.1817–1903," an unpublished B.A. dissertation, Department of History, ABU, Zaria, June 1973, pp. 41–2.

59. Flint, op. cit., pp. 175–6; *Adeleye,* op. cit., p. 147–9.

60. G.M. Chaskda, op. cit., p. 2; *Saleh Abubakar,* op. cit., p. 60.

61. G.M. Chaskda, op. cit., p. 3; *Saleh Abubakar,* op. cit., p. 65.

62. G.M. Chaskda, op. cit., p. 3; *Saleh Abubakar,* op. cit., pp. 71–2.

63. R.A. Adeleye, op. cit., pp. 128 and 146–7.

64. R.A. Adeleye, op. cit., pp. 146–7.

65. The Sarkin Musulmi is said to have warned the Emir that "when foreigners settle in Muslim land by permission it is contrary to honesty to plunder their factories and the duty of a Muslim prince is to favour their trade and not to close the road against them." Adeleye, Ibid., p. 147.

66. Ibid., p. 202.

67. A.Y. Abubakar, "The Establishment and Development of Emirate Government in Bauchi, 1805–1903," Ph.D Thesis, ABU, 1974, pp. 672–97.

68. Ibid., pp. 687–90.

69. Ibid., p. 691.

70. Ibid., pp. 690–1 and 680.

71. Ibid., p. 693.

72. Ibid., pp. 692 and 694.

73. Ibid., pp. 696 and 699.

74. Ibid., pp, 695–6.

75. Ibid, pp. 701–2.

76. Ibid, p. 700.

77. Ibid., pp. 70–4.

78. Ibid., p. 729

79. Ibid., p. 728.

80. Ibid., p. 729.

81. Ibid p. 730.

82. Ibid *p. 730*

83. Ibid., p. 730 and p. 730 fn. 104.

84. Ibid., p. 730 and p. 730 fn. 104.
85. Ibid., pp. 730–1.
86. Ibid., p. 731.
87. Ibid.
88. See section on "Non-Resistance by Muri, Bauchi, Gombe and Zaria, September 1901–April 1902", Chapter 1, pp. 8–9.
89. A.Y. Abubakar, op. cit., pp. 737–40.
90. Ibid., p. 737.
91. Ibid., p. 737.
92. Ibid., p. 738.
93. Ibid., p. 742.
94. Ibid., p. 742.
95. Ibid., p. 742.
96. Ibid., p. 742.
97. Adeleye, op. cit., p. 239 and p. 239 fn. 82.
98. See section on "The Occupation of Bauchi," Chapter 2, pp. 53–4.
99. M.A. Al-Hajj, op. cit., p. 139 fns. 1, 2, and 3.
100. D.M. Last, op. cit., p. 52.
101. Al-Hajj, op. cit., pp. 139–41.
102. Ibid., pp. 140–1.
103. Ibid., p. 141.
104. According to Lugard, on the day the British fought the Mallam in February 1901, the Mallam had a force of "some 600 foot and 100 horsemen." See Northern Nigeria Annual Reports 1900–1913, p. 65.
105. The only work to have been produced largely on Gombe, namely that of Victor N. Low (*The Nigerian Emirates: A Study in Oral History*, NUP, 1972) suffers from a number of serious defects, some of which it shares with other works produced by people with similar background and disposition, such as M.G Smith's *Government in Zazzau* and others peculiar to it. Among these faults are conceptual weakness and a discrimination against the written documents of the period covered by the book, namely the nineteenth century. Thus, the book, which is purportedly historical, heavily depends on concepts which are clearly anthropological, concepts such as "ethnicity," "agnatic descent," "authority structure," "clientage." On top of that, the book treats the three emirates studied not as parts of the same political system which they were, but essentially as "several political systems" with an underlying similitude of administrative mode (p. xi). Concerning "ethnicity," the book tells us that "it was by the primary ethnic unit to which a free man belonged that his position in emirate society was in good part decided" (p. 8) and that members of the Fulani "ethnic unit," "shared until the jihad a common language (Fulfulde or Fula), history and social customs and institutions" (p. 8), an assertion which wrongly suggests that the pre-jihad Fulbe were all collectively either Muslims or non-Muslims, rather being divided into Muslims and non-Muslims; that there were no occupational and class distinctions among them; and

that there was a boundary between them and the non-Fulbe in all these matters. He reduced the jihad to a "Fulani conquest" which presumably all Fulbe participated in or at least supported, while the non-Fulbe groups invariably opposed it. Further, according to the book, it was only after this "Fulani conquest" that "an ever-increasing portion" of the Fulbe "exchanged their nomadic pastoralism for a village or town environment" (p. 8). This way the book suggests that the Fulbe had been non-Muslim before the jihad, since nomad Fulbe are generally known to have held aloof from Islam, adopting it or at least taking it seriously only after settling down in villages and towns, and taking to other occupations either alone or together with animal husbandry. Necessarily following from this is a further implication, namely that the jihad had nothing to do with Islam – that it was indeed a "Fulani conquest," possibly motivated by the oft-alleged feeling of "racial superiority" of this "ethnic unit." These implications are little mitigated by the information furnished later on (p. 71), that "well before the outbreak of a jihad in 1804 the Fulani communities of northern Nigeria had thrown up from their ranks a number of muslim scholars, preachers, teachers and diviners." For, even if we ignore the fact that "divination" was a pre-Islamic survival rather than an Islamic practice, it is significant that in connection with the emergence of this group among the Fulbe the book is talking not about its specific area of study but about "northern Nigeria" in general. Furthermore, besides leaving only a hint that such clerics existed in the area of study specifically, in keeping with the book's thesis of a generally undifferentiated, tribal, Fulbe "ethnic unit," there is no indication that some members of this group had broken out of that tribal shell, and still less an indication that they were in conflict with Fulbe and other tribalisms. As for sources, it should be pointed out that while protesting that "written documents from this period are themselves rare … in these emirates," the book did acknowledge the existence in the National Archives in Kaduna of "several hundred letters exchanged between the eastern emirates, especially Gombe; and Sokoto." Yet, hardly any use is made of them in the book. Instead, the book has been based partly on the works of European travellers like Barth and twentieth century ethnographers, and partly on oral testimony. It might in this connection be pointed out that the title of the book does specifically state that it is a study "in" oral history; but the point is that it is difficult to justify the choice, since the choice of sources by a historian is more than a matter of fashion. The decision to base oneself on oral tradition alone is usually governed by the absence of other sources, which is not the case here, given the admitted existence of "several hundred letters." The writer might also have been trying to counter an alleged tendency in the opposite direction, namely an "overdependence on written sources." But the charge of overdependence was not correct given that the region studied is a "virgin land" so to speak, for other historians. Apart from making this charge, the writer also offers the following as his grounds for opting for oral testimony, namely that:

"manuscript and archival material whether ascribed to a participant, unengaged witness or non-observer of the scene recorded, is inferior in several ways, to the kind which living deponents can offer. Written documents inform (as well as misinform), but they do not define their terms or supply much background on the author's motivation for writing, his biographical modes of reference, or his range of access to primary sources; we may even lack assurance that he did in fact provide the text at hand. While each of these normal concerns of the scholar might be answered from external (often oral) evidence, written documents share a further still more awkward disadvantage: *they cannot explicate a given record and be cross examined on it.* Most fieldworkers in Africa have been aware of this difference in the uses of written versus oral data." (pp. 55–6; emphasis in the original).

106. While leaving the reader to react to this attempt to take historiography back to square one, I shall restrict myself to pointing out that the writer has not, on the grounds he advances in the passage quoted above, ignored the testimonies of European travellers like Barth, and of latter day ethnographers but rather used them selectively, ignoring the "hundreds of letters" whose availability he admits.

107. M.A. Al-Hajj, op. cit., p. 141; Adeleye, op. cit., p. 91, fns. 56–60.

108. Adeleye, op. cit., pp. 91–2.

109. As far as the part of the Emir of Missau in the dispute is concerned, it was, simply stated, that with the revolt of the Galadima against the Emir of Gombe, the Emir of Missau hastened to send troops to the Galadima, to aid him in warding off the forces of the Emir of Gombe which were moving against the Galadima.

110. Adeleye, op. cit., pp. 91–2.

111. Ibid., p. 92.

112. Ibid., p. 93.

113. Ibid., p. 242, fn. 94.

114. T.N.L. Morland, "Bornu Report, No. B.M/8, dated 1 May 1902; SNP. 5/1/1918, NAK.

115. In fact, the Emir was reported to have closed the gates of Gombe town in the face of the Sarkin Musulmi when the latter tried to enter the town. See Hassan Keffi, quoted in D.J.M. Muffet, *Concerning Brave Captains,* London, 1964, p. 149).

116. Temple to Lugard dated 8/8/1903, SNP. 15 No.57 NAK.

117. Ibid.

118. See section on "The Wholesale Deposition of Emirs", Chapter 2, pp. 70–72.

119. Alkali Ahmad, Sa'ad, in his very important epistle to Waziri Buhari, says "this is precisely the type of relationship between us and them at the moment; we protect ourselves against them with tongue and by participating with them in the affairs of this world, but God forbid that we should ever love them in our hearts or follow their religion". See Al-Hajj, op. cit., p. 162.

120. Admittedly the learned Qadi's suggestion, particularly his phrase "affairs of this world," is vague, especially in view of the fact that in Islamic thought the dividing line between religion and "the affairs of this world," if at all existent, is very thin indeed. However, even if we give "affairs of this world," a very wide

interpretation, as the Qadi and the *wazir* themselves seem to have done when they settled down under the British and adjusted themselves to and applied British concepts of punishment in the case of the Qadi, British views about taxes, their disbursement, and about peasant rebellions and how to handle them in the case of the *wazir*, it still remains at least highly debatable if "affairs of this world" included the military encirclement and physical destruction of the Caliph himself. Indeed, the Qadi did specifically point out that "as for the association which may imply supporting them or seeking their help in objects which are not permitted by the Shari'a, like fighting fellow-Muslims, it is unbelief according to the *fatwa* of al-Maghili."

121. See M.F. Smith, *Baba of Karo: A Woman of the Muslim Hausa,* London n.d., pp. 68–73.

122. Ibid.

123. C.W. Orr "Zaria Provincial Annual Report for 1904," Zariaprof No.2551, NAK.

124. C.W. Orr, op. cit.; also Adeleye, op. cit., pp. 244–5.

125. Adeleye, op. cit., p. 245.

126. Ibid., pp. 245–6.

127. Ibid., p. 246.

128. Ibid, pp. 246–7.

129. Ibid., p. 247.

130. Ibid., p. 247.

131. It should be pointed out that in the meantime the British did occupy the sub-emirates of Nassarawa early in 1902, Keffi in July 1902, and Lafiya in March 1903. They did also occupy the Kingdom of Abuja in August 1902 and the Emirate of Jama'a in March 1903. Of these places, there was no military resistance at Nassarawa, Lafiya and Jama'a, while there was military resistance at Abuja leading to the death of Sarki Ibrahim. At Keffi there was no military resistance at the time of initial occupation, but later in the same year, in October in fact, the Magajin Keffi, Dan Yamusa, Zaria's representative in the sub-emirate and the most powerful man there revolted, killed the British Resident, Moloney and fled. Lugard conveniently seized this opportunity to declare that all who received the *Magaji,* such as the Emir of Kano Aliyu, were the enemies of the British. The *Magaji* nonetheless managed to make it first to Kano and then to Sokoto, where he participated in the defence of the capital, from where he once again fled with Sarkin Musulmi Attahiru, fought at the Battle of Bormi and finally emigrated with Attahiru's son, Muhammadu Bello Maiwurno, and made his way to the East. See J.C. Sciortino, *Gazetteer of Nassarawa Province,* London, 1920, pp. 6–21; Muffet, op. cit, pp. 148–9; Lugard, *Annual Reports,* op. cit., p. 75.

132. Adeleye, op. cit., p. 244 fn. 96; E.A. Ayandele, *The Missionary Impact on Modern Nigeria, 1842–1914,* London, 1966, pp. 130–5.

133. From Burdon (Bida) to Lugard, dated 5 April 1902, file no. Kadcaptory 0/R11/16, NAK.

134. Ibid.

135. Ibid.
136. AMD, Kano, 18/5/1974.
137. Adeleye, op. cit., p. 261 fns. 37–a39.
138. Adeleye, op. cit., p. 263 fn. 48.
139. Muffet, op. cit., p. 68.
140. Al-Hajj, op. cit., pp. 97–8 and 150 fn. 2
141. AMD, Kano, 17/5/1974.
142. Adeleye, op. cit., p. 271 and p. 271 fn. 85.
143. Adeleye, op. cit., p. 84.
144. AMD, Kano, 18/5/1974. W.F. Gowers, *Gazetteer of Kano Province,* London, 1921, p. 14.
145. In fact the Emir was eventually detained by the Sarkin Gobir of Tsibiri, the standard-bearer of the remnant of the prejihad regime of Gobir, and handed over to the British, who first sent him to Zungeru, then to Yola and finally to Lokoja where he died in 1926. See Gowers, op. cit., p. 14; AMD, Kano 18/5/1974.
146. AMD, 18/5/1974; Gowers, op. cit., p. 14.
147. It should be pointed out that Islamic political theory did allow a caliph to resign if he felt unable to perform the functions of his office. See Abdullahi dan Fodio, *Diya al-Hukham* (Hausa translation by Haliru Binji), Zaria, p. 13. Given that an Emir, except for the subordination of his authority and his territory to those of the caliph, was within his own area of jurisdiction very much like a Caliph, I assume that he too could legally resign if he felt unequal to the tasks facing him, and indeed, as we have already seen in the case of the Emir of Bauchi Usman, there was already a precedent in the history of the Sokoto Caliphate.
148. AMD, 17/5/1974.
149. Ibid.
150. Ibid.
151. Ibid; Gowers, op. cit., p. 15.
152. One of these small groups, however, under the leadership of the Madaki Koiranga, who had earlier antagonized the Emir by advising against the visit to Sokoto, in its own turn, returned to Sokoto rather than proceed to Kano. At Sokoto it once more fought the British and then joined the caliph's *hijra* up to Bormi, where the Madaki embraced martyrdom in the hands of the British. AMD, Kano, 18/5/1974.
153. AMD, Kano, 18/5/1974.
154. Adelelye, op. cit., p. 272 fn. 85.
155. The British troops that occupied Kano left Zaria on 29 January 1903 and entered Kano territory on 1 February, attacking Bebeji, eight miles from the border. On that day, during which attack thirty of the town's defenders were killed, seven of the bodies, including that of the Sarkin Bebeji, Jibir, were subsequently burnt to ashes by the British, in order to terrify the defenders of other towns and emirates yet to be captured, cremation being forbidden by Islam. The invaders arrived at Kano city and captured it two days later on 3 February. See A.O. Anjorin,

The British Occupation and the Development of Northern Nigeria, 1897–1914, Ph.D.,
London, 1965, p. 77; Margery Perham, *Lugard: The Years of Authority 1898–1945*,
London, 1960, p. 105; Gowers, op. cit, p. 14; Adeleye, op. cit., p. 269; A.M. Fika,
*The Political and Economic Reorientation of Kano Emirate, Northern Nigeria, c.1882–
1940*, PhD. London, 1973, p. 15–2.

156. For an account of the fighting between the defenders of the city and the British
invaders see Adeleye, op. cit., pp. 269-70; Fika, op. cit., p. 154.

157. With the fall of Kano all of the smaller emirates – Katagum, Hadeija, Daura,
Gumel, Kazaure and Missau – that the British later included in the Province of
Kano – submitted more or less peacefully when the British arrived to occupy
each in the course of the rest of 1903 and 1904. However, Hadeija was to revolt and give battle to the British when the latter insisted on deposing the Emir,
Muhammadu (1885–1906) in April 1906 on account of his general incapacity to
cooperate wholeheartedly with them and his alleged sympathy with the Satiru patriots. The surrender of these emirates was almost solely the result of the fact that
Kano, to which some of them looked during the tense period of one year or so
that preceded British invasions, had been defeated. However, it would seem that
in Missau at least there existed two strong parties, one each for military resistance and for abject surrender, from December 1902 right up to the occupation
of the town. Thus, in December 1902, the British garrison at Gujba in Borno sent
an expedition to occupy Yaiyu, a town which the British insisted should have been
part of Borno but which was in Katagum.

On the approach of this expedition, whose destination the emirs in the area
could only guess, all the emirs became terrified, those of the towns of Yaiyu and
Azare as well as the Emir of Missau to the point of fleeing their towns. Thus it
was that Ahmadu, the Emir of Missau, left his town together with the whole of its
population. However, on the same day that Ahmadu left Missau, his brother, Tafida Alhaji, together with a number of other chiefs, sneaked back into the town and
locked its gates against the Emir. Alhaji then wrote to the Sarkin Musulmi, Attahiru Ahmadu, accusing the Emir of oppression, cowardice and desertion, hinting
that he himself wanted to be recognized by the Caliph as Emir, stating "Therefore
we have written to beg you to judge between us". Ahmadu, the erstwhile Emir,
after failing to force his way back into the town, and given the rapid unfolding of
events, hung around the area till the arrival of the fugitive followers of the Upper
Niger Caliph whom the French had uprooted earlier on and who had left Sokoto
since the approach of the British there. Together with them, Ahmadu once more
tried to regain his town and failing, after a siege of six months, he joined Sarkin
Musulmi Attahiru's *hijra*. On the other side, Alhaji, who in the meantime had
declared himself Emir of Missau, sent and submitted to the British. Ahmadu for
his part fought on the side of the Sarkin Musulmi at Bormi and after the battle escaped together with Maiwurno to the East. See Gowers, op. cit., pp. 21–36; H.F.
Backwell, *The Occupation of Hausaland*, London, 1969, pp. 260–1 and 299–300.

158. P. K. Tibenderana, *Administration of Sokoto, Gwandu and Argungu Emirates Under British Rule*, 1900–1946, Ph.D., Ibadan, 1974, p.

159. See M.B. Alkali, *A Hausa Community in Crisis: Kebbi in the Nineteenth Century,* unpublished M.A thesis, Department of History, ABU, 1969, pp. 240–54, 267–78 and 279–88.

160. Alkali, op. cit., pp. 299–308.

161. For an account of these earlier relations see Adeleye, op. cit., pp. 131–6; 159–163 and 188–192.

162. For the Shehu's division of the Caliphate into an eastern and a western "halves" for the purposes of supervision, see Last, op. cit., pp. 40–45; Adeleye, op. cit., pp. 34–5 and S.A. Balogun, *Gwandu Emirate in the Nineteenth Century with Special Reference to Political Relations, 1817–1903,* Ph.D., Ibadan, 1970, pp. 103–4.

163. See sub-section on "Sokoto" Chapter 1, pp. 25–32.

164. Adeleye, op. cit., p. 189 fn. 95.

165. Ibid., pp. 194–5.

166. By this time the British and the French had reached an agreement on 14 June 1898 in Paris over their border in the area, see Adeleye, op. cit., p. 190; also J.C. Anene, *The International Boundaries of Nigeria, 1885–1960,* London, 1970, pp. 275–6; and J.R.V Prescott, *The Evolution of Nigeria's International and Regional Boundaries, 1861–1971,* Vancouver, 1971, pp. 72–76.

167. Adeleye, op. cit., p. 197.

168. Adeleye, op. cit., p. 222 fn. 19.

169. This post was re-established in 1900. See Adeleye, op. cit., p. 259.

170. Tibenderana, op. cit., p. 125, fn 1.

171. These were Hidr (Haliru) b. Umar b. Ibrahim Khalil b. Abdullahi b. Fudi and Hidr (Haliru) b. Abd al-Qadir b. Hassan b. Abdullah b. Fudi, respectively.

172. Tibenderana, op. cit, p. 126 fn. 1.

173. He was about 70 years old and died in March 1903; and he was said to be so pious that he was referred to as *dan aljanna* – son of paradise. See Balogun, op. cit, p. 372 fn. 1.

174. To be sure, the British were not sincere about some of these guarantees and there was also the fact that the British and the authorities of the Caliphate interpreted certain terms, especially the term *religion* differently, broadly in the case of the authorities, narrowly in the case of the British. But the authorities of the Caliphate, especially those already inclined towards capitulation, were not yet aware of these differences. Hence the initial acceptability – eloquently expressed by Ahmad Sa'ad in his epistle to Waziri Buhari – of these guarantees to them.

175. Adeleye, op. cit., p. 257.

176. Similarly, after the British occupied the emirate of Bauchi at the installation of Muallayidi, in succession to the ousted Emir, Umaru, the new Emir, was given a guarantee by Wallace that he would continue to send tribute to Sokoto provided no slaves were included (Morland, op. cit.), and five months later Resident

Temple did indeed allow the Emir to send tribute to Sokoto. See C.L.Temple, "Monthly Report for Bauchi for September 1902," SNP 15 No.42, NAK.

177. See p. 38 fn.16.

178. It is also very significant that after surrendering to the British, it was to Ahmadu Sa'ad, the Qadi of Gwandu, that the Waziri of Sokoto turned for consolation and reassurance.

179. Tibenderana, op. cit., p. 133.

180. Adeleye, op. cit., p. 169 and p. 170 fn. 5.

181. Ibid., p. 172–3.

182. Ibid., pp. 170–2.

183. Ibid., pp. 176-7.

184. Ibid., p. 180.

185. Ibid., p. 188.

186. Ibid., p. 192.

187. Ibid., p. 189 fn. 95.

188. Ibid, p. 190.

189. Ibid., p. 196.

190. Ibid.

191. Ibid., p. 197. However, from the account of Mahdi Adamu it is clear that the Sarkin Yawuri was not party to the ouster of the Yelwa post, the Sarki in fact seeing the British as allies against the Emirate of Kontagora. See Adamu, op. cit, pp. 307–14.

192. Adeleye, op. cit., p. 197

193. Ibid., p. 205 fn. 156.

194. Ibid., p. 221.

195. Burdon to Lugard, quoted from D.J. Muffet, op. cit., p. 39; also L. Kentish-Rankin (at Kabba) to Lugard, dated 23/1/01, Kadocaptory 0/AR/ II/5, NAK.

196. Abdullahi dan Fodio, op. cit., pp. 69–70.

197. I must, however, point out that Abdurrahman's dictatorial tendency and harshness, for which there is some evidence in oral tradition, such as included in Edgar's *Labaru,* and which has been emphasized by later writers including Johnston, Hogben and Kirk-Greene, and Last, may be an exaggeration. Suggesting this exaggeration are Abdurrahman's correct attitude towards sacking of Gwaram by Bauchi's Emir (see sub section on "Bauchi", Chapter 1, pp. 9–13), and his backing down from his original decision to appoint Abubakar rather than Abdulkadir as Emir of Katagum in c.1896; that is, backing down in the face of popular dissatisfaction in Katagum against that decision. See Low, op. cit., pp. 193–4. Other pointers to the fact that his harshness has been exaggerated are the several letters of complaints addressed to him against his favourite son, Mahe (Mahir) by the chiefs of Dogon Daji and Tambawal – admittedly members of the House of Shehu. Abdurrahman investigated the complaints, punished Mahe and got him to make restitutions. See Backwell, op. cit., pp. 19–20 and 37–38.

198. Muffet, op. cit, p. 39.

199. See footnote 212 below.
200. Last, op. cit, p. 140; Muffet, op. cit, p. 128.
201. Burdon to Cargill, quoted from Muffet, op. cit., p. 149.
202. AAMBM, Sokoto, 14/3/74; M.A. Al-Hajj, op. cit., p. 163 fn. 2.
203. See sub-section on "Gwandu", Chapter 1, pp. 22–3.
204. Margery Perham, op. cit, p. 90.
205. Of course I am not ignoring the availability of the writings of people like Clapperton and Barth which had their serious limitations, as can be seen from discussions of them in, among others, Adeleye, op. cit, p. 346; Y.B. Usman, "The Transformation of Political Communities: Some Notes on the Perception of a Significant Aspect of the Sokoto Jihad", unpublished paper presented at the Sokoto Seminar, January 1975 and Y.B. Usman, "The Assessment of Primary Sources: Heinrich Barth in Katsina 1851–1854", unpublished paper presented to the 1976/77 Postgraduate Seminar, Department of History, ABU, Zaria.
206. Adeleye, op. cit., pp. 70 and 61–62.
207. Ibid., p. 99; Last, op. cit.,p. 129.
208. Abdulkadir Waziri, "The History of Fulani and Sokoto Rulers from Usman b. Fodio to Muhammad Maiturare," in Kadcaptory 1/63, NAK.
209. See, for example, Perham, op. cit., p. 91; so much a bogey had Kano become in the eyes of the British that when the city was finally captured, Lugard was moved to comment that "as the result has proved, the opposition at Kano, where no one on the British side was killed and only fourteen wounded, in spite of the fact that they had incomparably better defences and were warned and prepared for our advance, could not compare with the fighting at Yola, which was taken quite by surprise, and where we had 47 casualties." See F.D. Lugard, *Northern Nigeria Annual Reports for 1900–1913,* p. 85.
210. This is implied in Ahmadu Sa'ad's letter as well as the Shehu's *Bayan Wujub al-Hjira* and Abdullahi's *Diya al-Hukkam.*
211. See sub-section on "Kano", Chapter 1, pp. 18–22.
212. It should be pointed out that of all the social groups in the Caliphate, apart from slaves who entertained hopes of mass emancipation, traders, especially those with North African origins or connections, were the least disturbed by the prospects of British occupation, followed by the upper sections of the *ulema.* Thus, for example, it was traders that served as British spies and messengers, most prominent among such agents being Adamu Jakada. In places like Kano, Yola and Katsina, members of this group such as Abande and Auta in Kano, Salih Sarkin Turawa in Yola and Sharu Mai Kulki in Katsina, played prominent roles either in urging submission to the British in the debates that took place on the eve of the British invasion, or during the brief negotiations that in places like Yola preceeded combat after the invasion or in the appointment of another Emir after the ouster of the erstwhile one. As for the *ulema* one can point to the role of the Qadi Ahmadu Sa'ad in Gwandu, the Qadi Hamman Joda in Yola and Waziri Buhari in Sokoto (AMD, Kano, 18/4/1974; Sa'ad Abubakar, op. cit., p. 444; Usman, *The*

Transformation of Katsina, ABU Press, Zaria, 1981. p. 518). The explanation for the conduct of the traders is certainly not difficult to find, given that long before the British occupation they had become tied up, directly or indirectly, to European commercial houses either in the riverain areas of the Caliphate or in North Africa. See R.W., Shenton, "A Note on the Origins of European Commerce in Northern Nigeria," paper presented at the Postgraduate Seminar, Department of History, ABU, 1977 and Sule Bello, "A Reexamination of the Origins, Nature and Types of Relationships Between the State and the Economy of Kano Emirate by the Last Decade of the Nineteenth Century," paper presented to the Postgraduate Seminar, Department of History, ABU, 1978. An explanation for the conduct of the upper sections of the *ulema* may be less easy to find but I believe quite explicable nonetheless. Both deserve and no doubt will amply reward specific investigation.

213. Adeleye, op. cit.
214. The Qadi for example puts it like this: "verily the world is the abode of affliction and travail..."
215. Dabt al-Multaqat (trans. M.A. Al-Hajj), quoted from Al-Hajj, op. cit., p. 167.
216. For Rabeh's background and previous history as well as his encounters with Borno's forces upto the events of Gashagar, see Al-Hajj, op. cit. pp. 125–136; L. Brenner, *The Shehus of Kukawa*, London, 1973, pp. 123–8; W.K.R. Hallam, *The Life and Times of Rabih Fadl-Allah*, London, 1977, pp. 30–115.
217. My position on Rabeh's resistance to the Europeans is that it belongs more to the history of the rivalries and squabbles amongst Borno's and the Caliphate's enemies. This is because Rabeh was himself a foreigner in Borno and his rule alien to the interests of the people of the Sheikhdom. See Hallam op. cit., p. 157–91. Hence his resistance against the Europeans, however genuine, could not have been on behalf of the people of Borno.
218. W.P. Hewby "Bornu Provincial Annual Report for 1909," SNP, No.127/10, NAK.
219. Ibid.
220. Foureau, F. *D'Alger au Congo par le Tchad,* Paris 1902, pp. 595–603; Gentil, E. *La Chute de l'Empire de Rabah,* Paris, 1902, pp. 206–9.
221. Foureau, op. cit., p. 595.
222. C.O. 446/2, Henry Morley to Foreign Office, 9 February 1898.
223. For accounts on British efforts to secure the alliance of Rabeh see Hallam, op. cit., pp. 210–24; M.A. Al-Hajj and John E. Lavers, "The Travel Notes of al-Sharif Hasan b. al-Husayn," *Kano Studies*, New Series, Vol. I, No.1, 1973; R.A. Adeleye, "Rabih b. Fadlallah and the Diplomacy of European Imperial Invasion in the Central Sudan, 1893–1902," *JHSN*, Vol.V, No.3, pp. 408–9.
224. For information about the death of Cazemajou and the French occupation of Zinder, see Fika, op. cit., pp. 136–7.
225. Foureau op. cit., p. 595.
226. Ibid.
227. Ibid., p. 601.

228. Ibid.
229. Gentil, op. cit., p. 188.
230. Ibid., p. 204.
231. Ibid, p. 206.
232. Ibid., p. 208.
233. Ibid, pp. 211–220.
234. C.O. 446/15, Lugard to Colonial Office, 12 April 1901.
235. "Abubakar Garbai's Story" enclosed in Morland, op. cit.
236. Ibid.
237. Ibid.
238. Ibid.
239. Ibid.
240. Ibid.
241. Ibid.
242. Ibid.
243. Lugard to Colonial Office, op. cit.
244. C.O.446/15, Lugard to Colonial Office, Enclosure Fadl-Allah to Hewby, 31 January, 1901.
245. C.O.446/16, Telegraph, Wallace to Colonial Office, 19 August, 1901.
246. Lugard to Colonial Office, 12 April 1901, op. cit.
247. C.O. 446/17, McCarthy Murrough to Wallace, 31 October 1901.
248. This is the term that the British always employed when describing any battle in which an African people achieved a victory over a European force, British or not.
249. Abubakar Garbai's Story," op. cit.
250. Ibid.; also Lethem, G. J. "The Shuwa Arabs" (n.d) SNP 15/12, No.215, NAK.
251. Ibid.
252. Lugard to Commandant WAFF, 26 December 1901, SNP 15/1, No.29, NAK.
253. Ibid.
254. See pp. 65–68.
255. C.O. 446/11 "The Story of Fadl-Allah's Messenger to Hewby" Closed in Lugard to Colonial Office, 2 October 1900.
256. "Abubakar Garbai's Story,' op. cit.
257. Ibid.
258. On relations between Borno and these emirates see Adeleye, op. cit., pp. 69–71, 95 and 109; Y.A.Aliyu, op. cit., pp. 514–21,; S. Abubakar, "The Lamibe..." pp. 273–5, and Sa'ad Abubakar, "A Preliminary Examination of the Relations Between Bornu and Fombina Before 1901," paper presented to the Bornu Seminar, Department of History, ABU, 3/3/1973.
259. Morland, op. cit.
260. Ibid.
261. See sub-section on "Gombe", Chapter 1, pp. 13–16.
262. Morland, op. cit.
263. Ibid.

264. Ibid.
265. Ibid.
266. Ibid.
267. Ibid.
268. R.A. Adeleye, op. cit., pp. 77–113.

Chapter 2

1. For example Margery Perham contrasted "the slightness of the forces which Britain out of economy and half-heartedness ... sent out to occupy vast areas and control large populations" in the emirates with presumably massive forces used by "other colonial powers," and goes on to mention the "natural ... moderation" of the British. See Margery Perham, C.B.E., *Lugard: The Years of Authority 1898–1945,* London, 1960, p.145. Hogendorn for his part asserts, for example, that "Kano fell after a short siege in 1903. By July 1903, a short seven months after the start of the campaign, all Hausaland had submitted and full pacification was achieved." See J.S. Hogendorn, *The Origins of the Groundnut Trade in Northern Nigeria,* Ph.D., London, 1966, p.15. Perhaps, given that Hogendorn was writing a scholarly dissertation and writing it in an era when colonialism with all that it stood for has been thoroughly discredited, it should be pointed out that he still passionately believed in the necessity of the British conquest – that is, necessity for the conquered emirates themselves. Thus, he insists that "although the seven Hausa emirates (the "Bakwai") were allied in religion and race, their history before 1900 is a long toll of wars and raids, subjugations and tributes." Indeed, he asserts that "after the Fulani jihad of 1804, during which the Hausas came under the rule of their conquerors, conditions worsened steadily through the nineteenth century, and by the 1890s the situation was chaotic," (p.14). He goes on to argue that

    "in Kano during that decade, life was continually disturbed. Hausas from Maradi campaigned against the city from the North. Pagan Ningis, erstwhile prey of Moslem slave raids but now the victimizers, raided to the south and east of the capital till the end of the century, serious dissents occurring in 1895, 1897 and 1898. In the latter year, armies of the Emir of Zinder advanced to within a few miles of Kano, and ravaged the territory up to about 1900. To the north-east, the Emir of Hadeija harried Kano's flank for ten years before that date. To add to the discomfiture, Kano suffered her worst civil war in 1893–94. All the while, slave raids were being continually carried out by powerful nobles against friend and foe alike, with Moslem farmers of Kano Province almost as likely to find themselves on the slaver's block at Katsina or Kontagora as were the more backward pagan villagers to the south. In consequence, farmers were forced to live in walled towns [where presumably there were no powerful nobles to enslave them] and long-distance trade was much curtailed," (pp.14–15).

The upshot of this "chaotic situation" – for which there is no hint of an iota of British responsibility in spite of the fact that they had already subverted the emirates economy and reduced it to an appendage of Europe's economies, specifically that of Britain – was not that an internal revolution was needed to overthrow the tyrants, but that British colonialism was thereby rendered necessary. That is to say "the semi-civilized emirates ... could not have supported any venture as large as the groundnut trade before Lugard's forces brought peace," (p.14), a duty which Hogendorn believes they had to perform for the benefit of Europe. "Clearly a precondition of any significant economic progress in Northern Nigeria" such as Hogendorn chooses to believe has occurred under British colonial domination, "was an end to this bellicosity." It should also be remarked that whereas for most of the exaggerations and concoctions quoted above, Hogendorn was citing his authorities, specifically C.R. Niven, S. Hogben and various District Notebooks, for the last assertion, namely the one about Kano's rulers capturing and selling Kano's free peasants, including Muslim peasants, he cites no authority. Robert Heussler, for his part, asserts that "in the period 1900 to 1903 the job was one of pushing garrisons northward and posting political officers at the towns of major chiefs so as to cover the Protectorate with skeletal administration." So simple and innocent was Lugard's "job" in 1900–03. See R. Heussler, "British Rule in Africa" in Prosser Gifford and W. Roger Louis, *France and Britain in Africa*, New Haven, 1971, p.597. However, elsewhere, Robert Heussler admits British violence against communities inside and around the Sokoto Caliphate but admits it only to justify it. Thus, for example, he narrates that

"in 1906 Hastings was sent by Howard, the Resident Bauchi, to take over Gombe Emirate in the eastern part of the province. Finding certain pagan communities just as determined to resist the British as they had the Fulani, he subdued them by military action. Lugard's successor, who heard about it afterwards, disapproved strongly. But the men on the spot knew that the alternative, giving in to defiance, would have meant a loss of prestige in the eyes of the local Emir, not to mention forfeiting revenue and putting up with continued outlawry. See Robert Heussler, *The British in Northern Nigeria,* OUP 1968, p.31.

Similarly, he informs us that

"to the south in Bassa where the British had to work without the benefit of strong political institutions pacification was still more important. Arriving there in 1911, Woodhouse found villagers still resisting assessment and taxation. A government representative would be sent to the area from which no taxes had been received and would demand a pledge of loyalty and immediate payment. If there was resistance the place would be attacked forthwith by government troops. A typical engagement described by Woodhouse resulted in the deaths of forty villagers and the burning of their village ... But by the second decade of British presence, tribal fighting had been drastically reduced and most communities, throughout the North, were paying their taxes without protest" (ibid., pp.31-2).

2. The records on the occupation of Agaye, Lapai, Kontagora, Yola, Bauchi and Borno, as well as the records on the pursuit of the fugitive Sarkin Musulmi, have been preserved in files in the National Archives at Kaduna while those on Bida, Ilorin, Zaria, Kano, and Sokoto are to be found on the C.O.446 series of micro-film and have been variously used among others by Flint, Adeleye, Tibenderana and M.A.Al-Hajj. In the case of the ones preserved in the NAK, I refer to the relevant file numbers whereas in the case of the others I have acknowledged the book or thesis from which I am quoting.

3. R.A.Adeleye, *Power and Diplomacy in Northern Nigeria 1804–1906,* London, 1971, pp.182–3; also M. Mason, *The Nupe Kingdom in the Nineteenth Century: A Political History,* Ph.D, Birmingham, 1970, pp.370-372.

4. Ibid., p.187.

5. Ibid.

6. Ibid.

7. This account is based on Pilcher to Lugard, letter dated 29/6/1898, SNP 15, No.2, NAK.

8. This account of the fall of Kontagora and Bida is based on Makun to Lugard, dated July 1900 in Kadcaptory: 0/AR 11 No.26, NAK; Lugard to Secretary of State, dated 31/78/01 in SNP 7/2363/01, NAK and Lugard to Secretary of State, dated 21/3/1901, in SNP 7/2363/01, NAK.

9. See Michael Mason, "The Fall of Etsu Abubakar: The Account of Ubandawakin Bida," *Kano Studies,* Vol.I, No.1, 1973, pp.73–7; also see fn. 1, Chapter 1, p.391.

10. The claim is somewhat corroborated by the Ubandawaki, who was a messenger under the British at the time of the interview, and who claimed that the Emir left Bida as soon as the Makun, who was on his way to meet the British, sighted some of their troops approaching Bida, and sent and warned him of their approach. He mentions no battle before or after British entry into the town.

11. See section on "Conditions in Bida, Ilorin, Agaye, Lapai and Kontagora Emirates at the Time of British Invasion, 1895–1901" Chapter 1, pp 2–7 .

12. Makun to Lugard, op. cit.

13. Wushishi was a sub-emirate of Kontagora and the Chief at this time was Ibrahim b. Abubakar Modibbo b. Umaru Nagwamatse.

14. Makun to Lugard, op. cit.

15. The Ubandawaki claims, in his account, that the Emir escaped being taken away only after wrestling with the troops, and that though O'Neill did not succeed in abducting the Emir, the British were able to loot his house and carry away some of his womenfolk. The Ubandawaki also mentions large casualties inflicted by this party on the defenders on that day at two gates of Bida, the Gbara and the

Wuya gates; casualties of which Lugard makes no mention. *Kano Studies.*, op. cit., pp.75–6.

16. Lugard to Secretary of State, dated 2/3/1901, in SNP 7/2363/01.

17. This account is based on Morland to Wallace (n.d.), SNP 7/2363/1901, NAK.

18. This may be a reference to Sarkin Turawa, Salih, a Shuwa Arab resident of Yola who, local traditions say, was the messenger between the British and the Emir on that fateful day.

19. In fact, it would seem many people were killed in the mosque. The Imam of Yola, Liman Gana, died in the mosque on that day. More than this one cannot say because oral tradition – as preserved by men closely related to the ruling aristocracy is, both at Yola and elsewhere in the emirates, for some obscure reason, very reticent about casualties suffered by the emirates. In fact, in Yola it is often claimed by some members of this class that only one man was killed during the whole encounter between the invaders and the defenders of the town.

20. It is interesting that Margery Perham in her treatment of this episode, while making no mention of the casualties inflicted on Yola, took care to point out that the Emir who, she claims, was "strengthened by sixty deserters from Rabeh's forces with modern rifles and by two cannons given him by a French officer in 1892," did "inflict some casualties before the palace was stormed;" See Margery Perham, CBE, op. cit., p.48.

21. Hassan Keffi to Muffet, recorded in D.J.M. Muffet, *Concerning Brave Captains: A History of Lugard's Conquest of Hausaland,* London, 1966. pp.149–50.

22. Ibid.

23. Wallace to Secretary of State (n.d.) SNP 7/388/05, NAK.

24. Ibid. According to Waziri Junaidu (Sokoto, 29/4/74), it was at Gusau that the Sarkin Musulmi appointed new officials to replace all those who refused to follow him, for example, appointing a son of Waziri Buhari who had followed him, one Usumanu Gidado, alias Shehu Gajere, as his new Waziri. The latter died with him at Bormi.

25. Wallace to Secretary of State, op. cit.

26. Ibid.

27. Ibid.

28. Morland to Wallace, dated 5/6/02, SNP 15, No.30, NAK.

29. Wallace to Secretary of State, op. cit.

30. Ibid. However, Captain Sword himself gave slightly higher figures for both sides, namely 250–300 killed, on the defenders' side and "over 60 casualties," including 2 mercenaries killed, on the British side. Muffet, op. cit., p.173.

31. Morland to Wallace, op. cit.

32. Ibid.

33. Ibid.

34. Ibid.

35. Ibid.

36. Ibid.

37. Ibid.

38. Ibid.

39. Ibid.

40. Temple to Lugard, dated 8/08/1903, SNP 15, No 57, NAK.

41. Ibid.

42. Ibid.

43. In fact, the British occupation of Bauchi took place much earlier than the Sarkin Musulmi's ouster from Sokoto and pursuit to Bormi. Yet I am treating it after rather than before the events surrounding the flight of the Sarkin Musulmi. This is because the lesson that can be learnt from the fall of Bauchi, namely, that where no fighting took place, it was the emirates that went out of their way to avoid it, *logically* comes after the main burden of this chapter, namely, that the British occupation of the Caliphate was violent and destructive of life and property.

44. This account of the British occupation of Bauchi is based on T.N. Morland, *Bormi Report BM/8*, dated 1/5/02, SNP 15/02, NAK.

45. The information that this messenger was in fact the *Barayan Bauchi* is obtained from A.Y. Aliyu, *The Establishment and Development of Emirate Government in Bauchi, 1805–1903*, Ph.D., ABU, 1974, p.74.

46. In the light of the conduct of the Emir of Bauchi in the previous five years or so, the attempt of the Bauchi chiefs to save him from being deposed may seem contradictory. However, I would suggest that the behaviour of the Bauchi chiefs was perfectly explicable and consistent with the best in the traditions of the Caliphate. Thus whereas the chiefs had definite reasons to want to be rid of the Emir, yet they were correct to reason, as they seem to have done, that the deposition of the Emir was the business, not of foreign invaders but that of the Sarkin Musulmi and even that *on their own suggestion*. Thus we should assume that the chiefs tried to save the Emir first, because, although they felt overwhelmed by British might, the demonstration of whose efficacy they had seen elsewhere, they did not want to lose the initiative so much as to include even the issue of who was going to be their Emir. Secondly, they might have felt that British presence was temporary, a feeling manifested almost everywhere in the emirates and that, therefore, there would be enough time to deal with the Emir after the British might have left.

47. This account is based on H.C. Nisbet to High Commissioner, dated 31/1/03, SNP 7/2300/03.

48. It should be pointed out that these communities, collectively known as the Nyandang and who are now in the Mayo Balwa LGA of Adamawa State, now own no cattle worthy of mention, apparently having lost their herds during the period of colonialism, just as the Herero in South West Africa and the Matabele in Zambia and Zimbabwe, owners of large herds of cattle, lost them during the course of two decades or so of German and British colonialisms respectively. See Ho Chi Minh "Report on the Colonial and National Questions at the Communist International," in Bernard B. Fall (ed.), *Ho Chi Minh on Revolution: Selected Writings, 1920–66*, Praeger, 1967, pp.66–7.

49. This account is based on Acting High Commissioner to Secretary of State, dated 7/9/1903, SNP 7/2148/1903, NAK.

50. This account is based on C.L. Temple, "Bauchi Provincial Report for November 1904," SNP 15, No.62, NAK.

51. Thus in his third Annual Report, the Report for 1902, Lugard claims that during the British march from Zaria to Kano to occupy the latter

> "the mass of the people [in the villages on the way] well knowing that, contrary to all their own experience and custom in warfare, the British troops would not harm them, remained quietly in and brought ample supplies of food and water for the troops. These were duly paid for as though no war was being waged; for, indeed, we had no war against the people of Hausaland, but only against their Fulani rulers. It was, I submit, a very striking testimony to the discipline of the troops and a very satisfactory witness of the humanity which has marked the dealings of Government with the people of Northern Nigeria that here, in the midst of a country into which no British soldier had ever penetrated, the people should have shown such absolute confidence in and knowledge of our methods instead of deserting their towns and running into the bush, which is their custom on the slightest alarm." See F.D. Lugard, Northern Nigeria, Annual Reports, 1900–1913, London, p.86.

52. All the reports on Yola Province for the period October 1901–May 1903 are contained in Yolaprof No.1, NAK.

53. J.A. Burdon, "Sokoto Provincial Report for the month of April 1903," Sokprof No.23/1903, NAK.

54. J.A. Burdon, "Sokoto Provincial Report for the month of May 1905," Sokprof No.51/1904, NAK.

55. J.A. Burdon, "Sokoto Provincial Report for the months of November and December, 1905," Sokprof 85/1906, NAK.

56. Ibid.

57. Resident Zaria to Political Assistant, dated 13/2/06, SNP 7/436/1906, NAK.

58. All of the Monthly Reports for Ilorin for the Year 1900 are contained in SNP 15, no. 11, NAK.

59. Annual Reports, 1900–1913, p.9.

60. C.W. Orr, "Sokoto Provincial Report for the months of January and February 1904," Sokprof No.315/1904, NAK.

61. M.H.D. Beresford, "Police Department Annual Report for 1905," dated 5/7/06, SNP 7/2201/06, NAK.

62. E.J. Arnett, "Zaria Provincial Report for the Quarter Ended March, 1906, SNP 7/4635/1906, NAK.

63. P.M. Dwyer, "Report on the Ilorin Province for Quarter Ended 31st March 1907," SNP 7/1569/1907, NAK.

64. G.W. Webster, "Report on the Yola Province for the Quarter Ended 31st March 1908," SNP 7/21424/1908, NAK.

65. See M.F. Smith, *Baba of Karo: A Woman of the Muslim Hausa* (London, n.d.), pp.68–73.

66. See section on "Disarming the Emirs", Chapter 2, p. 71.

67. Yet Lady Lugard, the wife of the High Commissioner, found it possible to claim that

> "A territory we found in chaos has been brought to order. The slave trade has been abolished within its frontiers. Its subject races have been secured in the possession of their lives and property … There has been no great shock and no convulsion, only into the veins of a decadent civilization new blood has been introduced, which has brought with it the promise of a new era of life" (See Lady Lugard, *A Tropical Dependency,* London, 1905, p.500; a boast that Kirk-Greene quotes approvingly, see A.H.M. Kirk-Greene, *Adamawa, Past and Present,* London, 1958, p.69.)

68. E.A. Brackenbury, "Hibango District, Report on Assessment for 19120–11," Yola J.I, NAK.

69. A.H.M. Kirk-Greene, op. cit., p.60.

70. C.L. Temple, *Native Races and their Rulers,* Frank Cass, 1968, p.42. Perhaps, the most graphic and most baseless British view of precolonial justice in the Sokoto Caliphate is that of Lady Lugard, who claims that

> "for the nails to be torn out with red-hot pincers, for the limbs to be pounded one by one in a mortar while the victims were still alive, for important people who had offended to be built up alive gradually in walls till, after a period of agony, the head of the dying man was finally walled up, were among the punishments well attested to have been inflicted in the decadence of Fulani power. It is said that a considerable number of the walls of Hausa towns are known by the people to have been so built up, and are even now called by the name of the most distinguished victims whose corpses they contain. Impalement and mutilation were among the penalties for lesser offences." See Lady Lugard, op. cit., p.401.

71. A very likely reason for the infrequency of the amputation of hands might have been that rulers and judges might have realized the very serious consequences of such a punishment and had quietly decided not to invoke it except in very rare cases. See for example the case of the Emir of Kano, Abdullahi (1855–82) and the Mallam in F. Edgar, *Littafi Na Tatsuniyoyi Na Hausa,* Belfast, 1911, Vol.I, pp.273–4 and Vol.II, pp.424–7.

72. Margery Perham was present (in 1935?) when a District Officer in an unidentified emirate asked an Alkali "How do you handle cases of adultery?" and the Alkali replied that "according to the law both are to be stoned to death." Then Margery Perham added the further question "But now?" The Alkali replied that "now I sentence the man to two years imprisonment and a beating." Then the D.O. reminded the Alkali that he had "lately persuaded you to reduce it to one year and a beating," and Margery Perham added another question of her own, "Were you

stoning people to death just before the British came?"The Alkali replied "I do not remember a case, nor does my father, nor did my grandfather but it is the law." On the D.O asking "why did you put up such strong opposition to recognizing the lesser penalty?" the Alkali replied "because the other was the law." Finally the D.O. asked "then why was it not carried out?" and the Alkali replied "because it was so difficult to obtain the necessary witnesses to the act." See Margery Perham, *Native Administration in Nigeria*, London, 1962, p.93.

73. See footnote 51 above. Indeed even Lugard was forced to retract his earlier boast and to note how "enormous numbers" of "unarmed peasantry and women" joined "in the so-called pilgrimage" of Sarkin Musulmi Attahiru. See footnote on pp.97–8 of F.D. Lugard, op. cit.

74. Ahmad Sa'ad, quoted by Muhammad Bukhari in his *Risalah* trans. M.A. Al-Hajj, quoted from M.a. Al-Hajj, *The Mahdist Tradition in Northern Nigeria*, Ph.D., ABU, 1973, p.160.

75. J.A Burdon, "Sokoto Provincial Report No. 2/1903/ for April 1903," *op.cit.*

76. R. Popham Lobb to Lugard, letter dated 26/4/03, quoted from D.J.M. Muffet, *Concerning Brave Captains*, London, 1964, p.151.

77. Ibid, p.152.

78. Dr Cargill to Lugard, letter dated 24/4/03, quoted from Muffet, op. cit., *p.152.*

79. Ibid.

80. Ibid.

81. Wallace to Colonial Office, dated 4/6/03, quoted from Muffet, op. cit., p.161.

82. Cargill to Wallace (n.d.) quoted from Muffet, op. cit., p.162.

83. Ibid.

84. Captain Sword to Cargill, dated 28/4/03, quoted from Muffet, op. cit., p.164.

85. Ibid, p.165.

86. Sword to Cargill, dated 6/5/03, quoted from Muffet, op. cit. pp.165 and 166.

87. Ibid., p.168.

88. W.F. Gowers, "Yola Provincial Report No.21 for July 1903", Yolaprof Vol.II, NAK and W.F. Gowers "Yola Provincial Report No.22 for August 1903," Yolaprof Vol.III, NAK.

89. Ibid.

90. Hassan Keffi to Muffet, quoted from Muffet, op. cit., p.150.

91. Ibid.

92. Ibid.

93. Sword to Cargill, dated 28/4/03, quoted from Muffet, op. cit., p.164.

94. Temple to Lugard, dated 8/8/03, SNP 15 No.57, NAK.

95. Ibid.

96. Ibid.

97. Ibid.

98. W.J. Sokoto, 29/4/74.

99. Ibid. Besides, throughout the first decade following the imposition of British colonial domination on the emirates, thousands of people, in the guise of pilgrims, kept on emigrating from the emirates.

100. See sub-section on "Gombe", Chapter 1, pp. 13–16.

101. See section on "The Occupation of Bauchi" Chapter 2, pp. 53–5.

102. Lugard, Annual Reports, pp.73–78.

103. Among officials who died with the Sarkin Musulmi were the chief Alkali of Sokoto, the Sarkin Kwonni of Sokoto, his new Waziri, Shehu Gajere, a son of Waziri Buhari, the Madaki of Kano, Sarkin Dutse from Kano, Sarkin Karaye from Kano, Danburan of Kano, Chiroma of Kano, Sarkin Giyade of Katagum. Among those who continued on the *hijra* under Mai Wurno were the Emir of Missau Ahmadu, the Magajin Keffi and Shehu Mai Rugga, another son of Waziri Buhari of Sokoto. Among those who returned to find that they had been replaced by others was Alkali Suleiman of Kano. See Muffet, op. cit., p.200; WJ, Sokoto 19/4/74; GAM, Kano 7/6/74.

104. "Report on the Yola Province for the Quarter Ended 31 March 1908," op. cit.

105. G.N. Barclay, "Yola Provincial Report for September 1904," Yolaprof A4, NAK.

106. Misc. "Yola Province – Collected History 1905–1931," Yolaprof J1, NAK; also Yola Traditions.

107. AMD, Kano, 18/5/1974.

108. Ibid.

109. This is clear from Shehu Uthman's *Bayan Wujub al-Hijra* and Abdullahi dan Fodio's *Diya al-Hukkam*, for example.

110. Lugard states this policy concisely when he says "Native rulers are not permitted to raise and control armed forces, or to grant permission to carry arms", alleging that "the evils which result in Africa from an armed population were evident in Uganda before it fell under British control, and are very evident in Abyssinia," and that "no one with experience will deny the necessity of maintaining the strictest military discipline over armed forces or police in Africa if misuse of power is to be avoided, and they are not to become a menace and a terror to the native population and a danger in case of religious excitement – a discipline which an African ruler is incapable of appreciating or applying. For this reason native levies should never be employed in substitution for, or in aid of troops." See Frederick Lugard, *The Dual Mandate in British Tropical Africa,* Frank Cass, Fifth Edition, p.205. In the light of the fact that the British disarmed the Emirs and in every other way reduced them to a dependent appendage of British power, the claim by some writers that "British rule helped to perpetuate the power of the Emirs" loses much of its validity. (Quotation is from John Hatch, *Nigeria: A History,* London, 1971, p.153).

111. See pp.122–123 below; and Joseph P. Smaldone, *Warfare in the Sokoto Caliphate: Historical and Sociological Perspectives,* London, 1977, pp.119–22.

112. Thus, for example, when Wambai Abbas of Kano sent a messenger ahead of him announcing to the British his intention and that of his followers to surrender on

arrival at Kano, Lugard "insisted that they should all come together by a specified gate and not in driblets and that all firearms should be surrendered;" and though it "was not possible to prevent thousands of footmen from scattering to their own towns ... the whole of the horsemen estimated by Captain Lewis, who collected about 2,500 together with some 5,000 footmen, surrendered on March 6. Only 120 rifles were collected from them, but the Wambai promised to gather in many more later from the outlying towns." See *Northern Nigeria Annual Reports*, op. cit., p.2.

113. W.P. Hewby, "Muri Provincial Monthly Report for July 1902," SNP 15 No.37, NAK; Dr. Cargill, "Nassarawa Provincial Report for January 1903," SNP No.53, NAK; G.N. Barclay "Yola Provincial Report No.14 for February 1904," Yolaprof Vol.I, NAK; A.H. Festing, "Kano Provincial Report for June 1907," SNP 7 No.3095/1907, NAK.

114. For some specific examples of the collection of these weapons which included shot guns, revolvers and Snider, Martini Henry, Lebel, Winchester, Remington and percussion rifles, see W.P. Hewby "Muri Provincial Report for July 1902," SNP 15, No.37; W.F. Gowers "Yola Provincial Report No.17 for March 1903," Yolaprof A3, NAK; R. Granville "Nassarawa Provincial Report No.1 for January 1903," SNP 15 No.53. NAK; W.P. Hewby "Bornu Provincial Monthly Report for October 1903," SNP 5/No. 48A, NAK; J.A. Burdon, "Sokoto Provincial Report No.1 of 31 March 1903," Sokprof 7/1903, NAK; G.N. Barclay, "Yola Provincial Report for January 1904" Yolaprof, A4, NAK.

115. For examples of Lugard's refusal to give permission to Residents to allow Emirs to retain a few guns for ceremonial purposes, see J.A. Burdon, "Sokoto Provincial Report No.2 for April 1903" and G.N. Barclay "Yola Provincial Report for January 1904," op. cit.

116. See W.P. Hewby "Bornu Provincial Monthly Reports for February and for May 1904," op. cit.

117. This attitude is very well exemplified in two recent studies on the Republic of Cameroon viz: Willard R. Johnson, *The Cameroon Federation: Political Integration in a Fragmentary Society,* Princeton University Press, 1970 and Victor Le Vine, *The Cameroon Federal Republic,* Cornell University Press, 1963. Thus Le Vine for example, after acknowledgements etc, correctly starts his book with a sixteen-page chapter on the Republic's "Historical Background." However, this chapter does not contain a single word, to say nothing of a sentence, indicating that the people of Cameroon Republic lived, prior to their being colonized, in organized societies, much less in fairly extensive political systems of whatever quality. Indeed all he had to say there is summed up in his opening observation that Cameroon, which "is unique among African states in the remarkable variety of its historical experiences," was

"once a major portion of the infamous West African slave coast [then] it became a German protectorate; then divided, it was transformed into two League of Nations mandates. Thereafter, by further metamorphoses, it became two

United Nations trust territories. Finally, with the passing of the trusteeships, there was brief independence for one part, and then unification of both in an independent federal republic."

Even though the chapter has a section dealing with "The Pre-colonial Period," this is devoted entirely to the eminently imperialist issue of how one European nation, Germany, outmatched its competitors, including the British, to become the one that carved out the colony of Cameroon. Johnson's book, for its part, contains a chapter, the third chapter, in which the author discusses what he calls "Patterns of Identity in the Indigenous Cultures," in which one would normally expect him to indicate that Cameroon had a precolonial history – which albeit determined by its precolonial relations with Europe – yet had a certain degree of autonomy that makes it deserve to be studied in its own right; but the author, far from making such a concession, proceeded to treat Cameroon as a collection of tribes – the Bamoun, the Bamileke, the Sassa, the Beti, the Douala, the Foulbe, the Kirdi and others – of which some are dominating others. He does not even go into the history of that domination. Looking at the heading of his next chapter – "Colonialism as a Culture Carrier" one may understand why Johnson had to regard the precolonial history of the Cameroon with such contempt. He had to prove, as it were, that colonialism, far from being the destroyer of culture, was a "culture carrier."

118. Thus for example, J.C. Anene declares that "Boundary disputes in Europe are said to arise in many instances because too much history is remembered by both parties concerned." He then goes on to assert that "too much true history is certainly safer than fictitious history based on generalizations or on popular traditions of conquest, greatness and unity in the past which had ceased to have political significance long before the Europeans appeared on the African scene. It is extremely dangerous to declare glibly that the international boundaries imposed on Africa by aliens were little adapted to indigenous historical antecedents. What were these antecedents?" See J.C. Anene, *The International Boundaries of Nigeria: The Framework of an Emergent African Nation,* London, 1970, pp.4–5.

119. Y.B. Usman, "The Transformation of Political Communities: Some Notes on the Perception of a Significant Aspect of the Sokoto Jihad," in Y.B Usman (ed), *Studies in the History of the Sokoto Caliphate: The Sokoto Seminar Papers,* Third Press International, New York, 1979, p.1.

120. These emirates were Junju, Ngaure, Say, Kunari, Torudi, Mbitimkoji, Yaga, Liptako, Bida, Agaie, Lapai, Lafiagi, Shonga, Ilorin, Gwandu, Daura, Katsina, Kano, Zazzau, Fombina (or Adamawa), Bauchi, Muri (or Hammarwa), Gombe Kazaure, Katagum, Hadeija, Jama'are, Missau, Kontagora and Jema'a. To these emirates should be added a number of sub-emirates around the metropolises of Sokoto and Wurno the twin seats of the Caliphs, sub-emirates that were directly under the Caliph himself. See Y.B. Usman, op. cit., pp.1 and 24; R.A. Adeleye, op. cit., pp.23–40; S.A. Balogun, *Gwandu Emirates in the Nineteenth Century: 1817–1903,*

Ph.D, Ibadan University, 1970, pp.108–157; Murray Last, *The Sokoto Caliphate,* London, 1967, pp.40–45.

121. G.N. Barclay, dated July 1907, in Misc. "Yola Province – Collected Histories" Yolaprof J.1, NAK; Sa'ad Abubakar, *The Lamibe of Fombina: A Political History of Adamawa 1809–1901,* ABU Press, 1980, p.38. These sub-emirates included Cheboa, Tibati, Ngaundere, Bamnyo, Malabu, Rai-Bubam Song, Zummo, Gola, Holma Pakorgel, Marwa, Bogo, Kobotshi, Laro, Belel, Daware, Mayo-Farang, Sorau, Madagali, Gider, Michika, Moda, Mubi, Uba, Mindif, Binder, Ribadu, Ribemi, Kalfu, Be, Demsa (*gisiga*), Vokna Tola, Agorma, Pette, Wuro Mayo-Najarendi, Mbere and Balala.

122. A.Y. Aliyu, *The Establishment and Development of Emirate Government in Bauchi, 1805–1903,* Ph.D., ABU, 1974, pp.479–80. The nine major sub-emirates of Bauchi were Kirfi, Fali, Ganjuwa, Zungur, Jama'a, Toro, Lere, Lafiya and Darazo.

123. M.G. Smith, *Government in Zazzau: A Study of Government in the Hausa Chiefdom of Zaria in Northern Nigeria from 1800 to 1950,* OUP Third edition, Map B, gives these sub-emirates which he calls "vassal-states" as follows: Kajuru, Kadara, Kauru, Jem'a, Keffi, Kwotto, Kagarko and Doma. Jema'a, Keffi and Kwotto were later to be constituted into emirates by themselves.

124. This reconstruction of the territorial structure of Borno in this period was done with the aid of Dr. Muhammed Nur Alkali, of the Department of History, Bayero University Kano, for whose assistance I am very grateful.

125. There were eleven of these autonomous provinces and principalities namely, Damagaram, Muniyo, Yamiya (or Maine), Kazalmari, Kanem, Kusseri, Logon, Mandara, Dungas, Miriya, Kwance. Other writers might include Gumel (or Tunbi), Dikwa and Bama. However, Muhammed Nur and myself decided it would be more accurate to treat these latter three as some of the metropolitan provinces.

126. The emirates that the French occupied were Junju, Ngaure, Say, Kunari, Torodi, Mbitimkoji, Yaga and Liptako. See S.A. Balogun, op. cit., p.547.

127. The only sub-emirates that were not lost to Fombina were Song and Daware and parts of Malabu, Mayo-Farang, Zummo, Gola, Holma, Mubi (Mirnyi), Uba, Ribadu and Tola. Indeed, even districts that were directly under the Emir and his officials in the very vicinity of Yola lost territory to the Germans. These included Nyibango and Gurin which lost most of their villages to the Germans, and Yola town itself, which lost two of its farm settlements (Mayo-Pette and Lendo). In terms of size Fombina lost three quarters of its territory, retaining only about 2,500 square miles out of a total of about 40,000 square miles. See S. Abubakar, op. cit., pp.354–9; Ahmadou Bassoro et Eldridge Mohammadou, *Histoire de Garoua: Cité Peule du XIX Siècle* (ONAREST), 1977, verbatim; Eldridge Mohammadou (ed.) *L'Histoire des Peuls Ferobe du Diamare, Maroua et Pette,* Institute for the Study of Languages and Cultures of Asia and Africa (CAA) 1976, verbatim; "Yola Province-Collected Histories," op. cit.

128. Morland, Bornu Report BM/8, op. cit.

129. J.A. Burdon, quoted from M.B. Alkali, *A Hausa Community in Crisis: Kebbi in the Nineteenth Century,* M.A. thesis, ABU, 1969, p.310.

130. W.F. Gowers, "Gazetteer of Kano Province," London, 1921, pp.25–7.

131. See section on "The Abolition of the Office of the Sarkin Musulmi," Chapter 2, pp. 80–1.

132. See section on "The Occupation of Kontagora and Bida," Chapter 2, pp. 45–6 and Lugard, Annual Reports, op. cit., p.9.

133. The fourth sub-emirate to be detached from Zaria was Doma, which was merged with the new Emirate of Lafiya.

134. J.C. Sciortino, *Notes on Nassarawa Province, Nigeria,* London, 1920, verbatim.

135. G.N. Barclay, "Yola Report No.14 for February 1904," Yolaprof, Vol.I, NAK.

136. Ibid.

137. Ibid.

138. Ibid.

139. G.N. Barclay, "Yola Report No.14 for February 1904," op. cit. Indeed, Yerima Maigari, who was later to become the Lamido of Adamawa (1924–1928), was able to accomplish an even greater feat during the First World War. Thus, in the early phase of this war, he naturally supported the Germans, but as in the course of the war it became clear that the British, rather than the Germans, were going to win the war and therefore control his territory, Maigari's loyalty to the Germans began to waver, and the latter detected this. Hence they arrested him and put him under an escort of nine soldiers en route to Kontcha. However, on the way he managed to kill four of them at night and escape with their heads to Yola where he presented them to the Resident, who at first put him under house arrest but later restored him to his fief at Nassarawa (TI and MYHJH, Yola, 28/12/1970).

140. G.N. Barclay, "Yola Report for Quarter Ended March 31, 1909," Yolaprof. No.A8, NAK.

141. E.A. Brakenbury, "Hibango District, Report on Assessment, 1910–1911, op. cit.

142. On this particular border between British and German territories, the First World War actually started at Tepe on the confluence between the Rivers Benue and Faro on 6 August 1914. During this war the Emir of Adamawa, Abba, who was given to understand that he would regain his entire territories, energetically threw his weight on the British side, supplying them with intelligence, men, horses, provision and propaganda directed at chiefs, on the other side. Thus, for example, within one month of the outbreak of hostilities, he had supplied the British with 35 tons of grain, 1,300 carriers, 800 slaughter cattle, over 140 horses, 100 pairs of native boots, 800 pairs of native sandals, 800 heel ropes, 200 head ropes, 20 beds for wounded soldiers, 800 mats as well as locally made rifle slings, cartridge belts, and unspecified quantities of potash and calabashes. This was apart from the similar assistance rendered by District and Village Heads on the border. The Emir's efforts were partially rewarded when, after the war, the British put their own share of his former emirate – that is that portion of

German Cameroon mandated by the League of Nations to them directly under him. See W.S Sharpe, "Yola Provincial Report for the Quarter Ended 30 September 1914" NAK. W.S. Sharpe, "Yola Provincial Report for Quarter Ended 31 December, 1914," Yolaprof, A8, NAK. W.S. Sharpe, "Yola Provincial Annual Report 1914," Yolaprof A18, NAK. Misc. "Emir of Yola – Claim to Portion of Kameruns (Adamawa), SNP 75/1915, NAK).

143. This is not to say that relations were always hostile within this divided dynasty. Indeed as late as a few months to the outbreak of the First World War, the Emir of Adamawa, Lamido Abba, did seek, and was granted permission to pay a visit to Babbawa at Nassarawo, the latter being his first cousin, both of them being grandchildren of Modibbo Adama. See W.S. Sharpe, "Yola Provincial Report No.85 for Quarter Ended 30/6/14," Yolaprof No.17, NAK. However, such friendly exchanges between the forcibly separated relatives were the exception and hostility even between brothers, the rule in this period.

144. Resident Yola to Resident Garua, Letter, dated 8/2/09, Yolaprof A2, NAK.

145. Ibid.

146. I visited Gurin in December 1976 to see a relation and was able to cross the border to Beka.

147. Assistant Resident Boyle to Resident Yola Province, datelined Holma, dated 24/2/1907, Yolaprof A2, NAK.

148. Ibid.

149. Resident Yola to the German Resident, Garua, dated 27/8/07 Yolapof A2, NAK.

150. Strumpell to Resident Yola, datelined Moda, dated 22/7/07, Yolaprof A2, NAK.

151. G.W. Webster, "Yola Provincial Quarterly Report for June 1911" Yolaprof A10, NAK.

152. Ibid.

153. Ibid.

154. Ibid.

155. J.A. Burdon, "Sokoto Provincial Report for the Months of September and October, 1905," Sokprof 756/1903, NAK.

156. J. Cochrane "Bornu Provincial Report for May 1902," SNP 15 No.19, NAK.

157. Ibid.

158. Kadcaptory: 0/Ar 11 No.9, NAK.

159. Burdon to Lugard, dated 7/4/02, SNP 7/3/40, NAK.

160. Lugard to Sarkin Musulmi Abdurrahman, 1/3/02; Kadcaptory 0/AR 11 No.11 NAK.

161. See section on Attitudes Towards the Sarkin Musulmi's Hijra, page 67.

162. C.L. Temple "Bauchi Report for March 1902," Kadcaptory 0/AR 11 No.18.

163. Abadie to High Commissioner, 5/4/02; Kadcaptory 0/Ar 11 No.17, also Abadie to High Commissioner 16/4/02, kadcaptory 0/AR 11 No.20.

164. C.L. Temple "Monthly Report for Bauchi for September 1902," SNP 15 No.42.

165. See A.H.M. Kirk-Greene, *The Principles of Native Administration in Nigeria,* London, 1965, pp.43–45.

166. Lady Lugard, *A Tropical Dependency*, op. cit., p.453.

167. Yolaprof Vol.II, NAK.

168. Adeleye, *Power and Diplomacy,* op. cit., p.314.

169. Sokprof No.34/1903, NAK.

170. Ibid.

171. J.A. Burdon, "Sokoto Report for July and August 1905," Sokprof 756/1905, NAK.

172. J.A. Burdon, "Sokoto Report No.29 for Quarter Ended March 31, 1906," Sokprof 578/1906, NAK.

173. Lewis, "Sokoto Report No. 5 for July 1903," Sokprof 58/1903, NAK.

174. Resident Kano to High Commissioner, 15/9/07, SNP 6/170/1907.

175. Palmer to Resident Kano, 2/9/07, SNP 15 No.378, NAK.

176. Thus, for example, Waziri Junaidu attended the installation ceremonies of the Emir of Kano in 1954 and of the Emirs of Adamawa and Muri in 1955, but only as an observer. [WJ, Sokoto, 26/4/74).

177. WJ, Sokoto 26/4/1974. Also AMD, Kano, 20/5/1974.

178. WJ, Sokoto, 26/4/1974.

179. Ibid.

180. *Gaskiya ta fi Kwabo*, 11 November 1939.

181. *Gaskiya ta fi Kwabo*, 1 January 1939.

182. See Chapter 3, page 106.

183. W.J. Gowers, "Yola Report No.23 for September 1903," Yolaprof Vol.II, NAK.

184. It should be pointed out that Lugard claimed that "tolls" had been paid between the emirates (Annual Reports, p.16). However, we need not accept that claim at face value, though it would seem that the town gates were used for collecting agricultural and industrial taxes such as the *Karofi* and the *al'adu*, all of which the British "took over" and eventually "consolidated" into the Kurdin Kasa, as will be discussed later in this book. Hence, the tolls imposed by the British could not have been a continuation of any pre-existing native tolls. In fact, Lugard himself claimed that he abolished "all tolls by native Emirs on caravans (p.16)," by which he merely meant that he prohibited the collection of the *al'adu*, etc. at the gates of the various towns; but to change the methods of collecting the *al'adu* neither made the *al'adu* which was retained and collected by new methods. Yet, while questioning Lugard's claims that there were customs barriers between the various emirates of the Sokoto Caliphate, we might accept this claim as far as it applied to movement of goods between the emirates of the Caliphate on the one hand and the states that maintained their independence of the Caliphate on the other, relations between these states and the emirates being international relations, which relation between one emirate and another were not. The indication that customs were collected on goods as they crossed the boundary between the Caliphate and polities outside it but not between one emirate and another can be seen in the information that Masaba, the Emir of Nupe (1899–1873), gave W.H. Simpson in 1877, namely that "three caravans with ivory were coming from Adamawa,

through Lafia to trade. [The Emir] had given a camel, an ostrich, and a horse to Abuja, King of Zaria to permit caravans to pass through his country. Road that way was first opened year before last; 2s was at first charged per head for passing now 6d through his intercession." See W.H. Simpson, *Report of the Niger Expedition, 1871*, dated 21 November in F.O. 84/135 and quoted from Thomas Hodgkin's *Nigerian Perspectives: An Historical Anthology*, London, 1975, p.359. This information is also corroborated by Hassan and Shu'aibu in *A Chronicle of Abuja*, Zaria, 1952, p.16.

Chapter 3

1. "Ilorin Provincial Report for July 1900," op. cit.
2. Ibid.
3. "Ilorin Provincial Report for July 1902," op. cit.
4. Confidential Reports on Chiefs for 1910, Nassarawa Province, unclassified, AHAK.
5. Confidential Reports on Chiefs for 1914, Nassarawa Province, unclassified, AHAK.
6. Confidential Reports on Chiefs for 1915, Nassarawa Province, unclassified, AHAK.
7. J.C. Sciortino, "Notes on Nassarawa Province, Nigeria," London, 1920, p.10.
8. Confidential Reports on Chiefs for 1914, Nassarawa Province, op. cit.
9. According to GAM, relations of Alkali Suleiman such as the subsequent Walin Kano, Muhammadu Bashir, a nephew of Suleiman, did spend many years outside Kano, in Adamawa, and Lafia, among others, before going back to Kano sometime in the second decade of British domination to rehabilitate the family which, in the meantime had been out in the cold, as it were. But she made no mention of A.M. Gambo among these, though the British recorded him as a son of the ex-Alkali.
10. Dr Cargill, "Report on Nassarawa Province for December 1902," SNP 15, No.15, NAK.
11. Confidential Reports on Chiefs, for 1911–17, Nassarawa Province, op. cit.
12. Confidential Report on Chiefs, for 1911–17, Nassarawa Province, op. cit.
13. Teleg. Conversation: Howard and Girouard, 19/9/08, SNP 6/137/08, NAK.
14. Teleg. Conversation: Girouard and W.P. Hewby, 21/9/08, SNP 6/137/08, NAK.
15. W.F. Gowers, "Report on the Situation in Bauchi," 12/10/08, SNP 6/137/08, NAK.
16. SNP 6/123/08, NAK.
17. W.P. Hewby, "Bornu Provincial Monthly Report for October 1902," SNP 15/1 No.19, NAK.
18. Morland, "Bornu Report, BM/8," op. cit.; Captain J. Cochrane "Bornu Provincial Monthly Report for May 1902," SNP 15/1 No.19, NAK.

19. Captain J. Cochrane, "Bornu Provincial Monthly Report for June 1902," SNP 15/1 No.19, NAK.

20. Ibid.

21. Ibid.

22. Ibid.

23. Ibid.

24. Ibid.

25. Ibid.

26. Ibid.

27. Captain Cochrane "Bornu Provincial Monthly Report for August 1902," SNP 15/1 No.19, NAK.

28. Captain Cochrane, "Bornu Provincial Monthly Report for September 1902," SNP 15/1 No.19, NAK.

29. Ibid.

30. Captain Cochrane, "Bornu Provincial Monthly Report for June 1902," Lugard's comments on, op. cit.

31. W.P. Hewby, "Bornu Provincial Monthly Report for October 1902," SNP 15/1, No.19, NAK.

32. Ibid.

33. Ibid.

34. W.P. Hewby "Bornu Provincial Monthly Report for January, February and March 1903," SNP 15/1, No.48A, NAK.

35. Ibid.

36. W.P. Hewby "Bornu Provincial Monthly Report for October 1903," SNP 15/1 No.48A, NAK.

37. Ibid. Also *Maimaina Sarkin Askira*, op. cit.

38. W.P. Hewby, "Bornu Provincial Monthly Report for October 1903," op. cit.

39. W.P. Hewby, "Bornu Provincial Monthly Report for November 1902," SNP 15/1 No.19, NAK.

40. Ibid.

41. See section on 'Disarming the Emirs' in Chapter 2, page 73.

42. W.P. Hewby, "Bornu Provincial Monthly Report for November 1902," op. cit.

43. Morland, "Enclosure to Bornu Report B.M./8," op. cit.

44. W.P. Hewby, "Bornu Provincial Report for January, February and March 1903," op. cit.

45. This opinion is based on the fact that Abubakar Garbai was present at Dikwa almost throughout the years 1893–1900, and the fact that, like him, the Egyptian messengers were detained at Dikwa by Rabeh.

46. W.P. Hewby, "Bornu Provincial Report for September 1903," SNP 15/1 No.48A.

47. W.P. Hewby, "Bornu Provincial Monthly Report for October 1903," op. cit.

48. W.P. Hewby, "Bornu Provincial Report for January, February and March 1902," op. cit.

49. H.R. Palmer, "Bornu Provincial Annual Report for 1922," unclassified, AHAK.

50. Aliyu was chosen by Lugard himself, from among two candidates suggested to him by Sultan Attahiru, the other candidate being the *Dan Iya*. Lugard settled on Aliyu because "of the two men named there could be no doubt whatever as to which was better. Iya had joined Aliyu of Kano against us (see H.F. Backwell, *The Occupation of Hausaland, 1900–1904* (Frank Cass, 1969), pp.70–1) and by all accounts had been continuously hostile and did not bear a good character. Dan Sidi on the other hand had been friendly disposed…" Put in other words, Lugard chose Aliyu because, from the British point of view, he was the lesser of two evils, not having shown any overt hostility. See F.D. Lugard, Northern Nigeria: Annual Reports, 1900–1913, London, p.73.

51. M.G. Smith, *Government in Zazzau: A Study of Government in the Hausa Chiefdom of Zaria in Northern Nigeria from 1800 to 1950,* 1970 edition, p.223.

52. "Confidential Reports on Chiefs for 1911–16, Zaria Province," AHAK.

53. Ibid.

54. Ibid.

55. Misc. "Aliyu, Emir of Zaria," CSO No.06012, NAI.

56. AMD, Kano, 18/5/1974.

57. MKSA, Kano, 17/5/1974; AMD, Kano, 18/5/1974.

58. E.J. Arnett, "Confidential Report on the Emir of Kano, 1907," unclassified, AHAK.

59. Palmer to Festing, September 1907, SNP 15 No.371, NAK.

60. Palmer to Festing, 2/9/07, SNP 15, No.378, NAK.

61. A. Festing "Kano Report No.35 for 1907," SNP 15 No.378, NAK.

62. At this time the *Dan Rimi* was in charge of District Administration and liaison with the Resident. AMD, Kano, 18/5/74.

63. Festing to Sec Admin. 11/10/07, SNP 7/42/45/1907, NAK.

64. "Confidential Report on Emir of Kano for 1908," unclassified, AHAK.

65. Rex vs ex-Maaji Sadiku of Kano, SNP 7/56 3/1908, NAK.

66. AMD, Kano, 20/5/1974.

67. Ibid.

68. Ibid; also W.P. Hewby "Memo on Status of Waziri of Kano," 3/10/08, SNP 7/5141/08.

69. "Confidential Reports on Chiefs for 1911, Kano Province," unclassified, AHAK.

70. AMD, Kano, 19/5/1974.

71. See pp.20–23 above.

72. J.A. Burdon, "Sokoto Report No.3 for May 1903," Sokprof No.34/1903, NAK.

73. Ibid.

74. In Gwandu, the *Dangaladima* was the member of the ruling house next in seniority to the Emir and designated to succeed him. AUG, Sokoto, 15/3/1974.

75. J.A. Burdon, "Sokoto Provincial Report for the Month of May 1905," op. cit.

76. See Chapter 3, page 100

77. "Sokoto Provincial Report for the Month of May, 1905," op. cit.

78. H.R.P. Hillary, "Sokoto Provincial Monthly Report for March 1904," Sokprof No.101/1904, NAK.
79. "Sokoto Provincial Monthly Report for May 1904," op. cit.
80. J.A. Burdon "Sokoto Provincial Report No.29 for the Months of July and August 1905," Sokprof 756/1905, NAK.
81. J.A. Burdon "Sokoto Provincial Report for the Months of September and October 1905," Sokprof No.756/1905, NAK.
82. Ibid.
83. Ibid.
84. Ibid.
85. Ibid.
86. Ibid.
87. Ibid.
88. AUG, Sokoto, 25/4/74; also J.A. Burdon, "Sokoto Report No.29 for the Quarter Ended March 31, 1906," Sokprof 578/1906, NAK.
89. Ibid.
90. Ibid.
91. Ibid.
92. See Chapter 7, section on "The Fate of the Zakka" page 225.
93. J.A. Burdon "Sokoto Report No.29," op. cit.
94. Cargill, "Report No.28 on the Upper Benue Province," 28/10/01, Yolaprof Vol.I, NAK.
95. Yolaprof, Vol.I, NAK.
96. Ibid.
97. Ibid.
98. Ibid.
99. G.N. Barclay, "Yola Report No.14 for December 1902," op. cit.
100. Ibid.
101. W.F. Gowers, "Yola Report No. 19 for May 1903," op. cit.
102. W.F. Gowers, "Yola Report No.17 for March 1903," op. cit.
103. Yola Report No.19, op. cit.
104. Ibid., Lugard's comments on.
105. Ibid.
106. Yola Report No.19, Lugard's comments on, op. cit.
107. W.F. Gowers "Yola Report No.20 for June 1903," Yolaprof Vol.II, NAK.
108. Ibid.
109. Ibid.
110. See Chapter 2, page 88.
111. G.N. Barclay, "Yola Provincial Report No.48 for Quarter Ended 30 June 1906", Yolaprof A6 & 7, NAK.
112. Yolaprof A6 & 7, op. cit.
113. Ibid.
114. Barclay to High Commissioner, dated 12/8/1908, SNP 15/383, NAK.

115. Ibid.

116. Ibid.

117. Teleg; Barclay to Governor 3/1/09, SNP 7/1887/1909, NAK. Letter; Barclay to Governor 11/2/1909, ibid.

118. Webster to Barclay 19/11/08, SNP 7/5388/08, NAK; Brackenbury to Barclay 4/1/09; Ibid.; Webster to Barclay, 25/1/09, Ibid.

119. Ibid.

120. Barclay to Governor, 11/2/1909, op. cit.

121. Ibid. For a fuller account of Bobbo Ahmadu's relations with the British appointed District Heads generally, see chapter 4.

122. F. Dwyer, "Yola Provincial Report No.61 for the Quarter Ended 30 September 1909," Yolaprof A8, NAK.

123. Tradition in Yola. On the other Emirs, namely Muhammadu of Hadeija, and Abubakar and Muhamman Yero of Katsina, whose relations with the British we said were also disastrous, it is unfortunate that the British records concerning them have not been preserved, having been burnt by Resident Cargill in Kano. What we know on the relations with the British is to be found in Lugard's Annual Reports, and while clearly indicating the hostility is not detailed enough to permit a reconstruction of the history of these relations.

124. SNP 5 No.11, NAK.

125. Ibid.

126. Confidential Reports on Chiefs for 1911, Ilorin Province, unclassified, AHAK.

127. Ibid.

128. Barclay to Wallace, dated 27/4/1907, SNP 7/2271/1906, NAK.

129. Ibid.

130. G.N. Barclay, "Yola Report No.17 for March 1903," op. cit.

131. Ibid.

132. Barclay, "Yola Report for December 1904, Yolaprof A4, NAK.

133. Webster, "Report on the Yola Province for the March Quarter, 1908," SNP 7/21424/1908, NAK.

134. C.L. Temple, "Bauchi Report No.199 for November 1904," SNP 15 No. 62, NAK.

135. See pp. 90–92 above.

136. Sokprof No.7/1903, NAK.

137. J.A. Burdon, "Sokoto Provincial Report No.2/1903 for April 1903," op. cit.

138. Ibid.

139. Sokprof No.58/1903, NAK.

140. J.A. Burdon, "Sokoto Report No.3 for May 1903," op. cit.

141. Ibid.

142. Confidential Reports on Chiefs for 1913 for Sokoto Province," unclassified, AHAK.

143. SNP 15 No.11, NAK.

144. Ibid.

145. P.M. Dwyer, "Ilorin Provincial Report for the Month of July 1900," op. cit.

146. Ibid.

147. SNP 15 No.11, NAK.

148. Ibid.

149. Yolaprof Vol I, NAK.

150. C.L. Temple," Bauchi Report No.3 for March 1903," SNP 15 No.39, NAK.

151. Ibid.

152. Director of Public Works to Sec. Northern Admin. 12/12/1905, SNP 7/3923/1905.

153. Lewis, "Sokoto Report No.5 for July 1903," Sokprof 58/1903, NAK.

154. Sokprof 129/1903.

155. J.A. Burdon, "Sokoto Provincial Report for January and February, 1904," Sokprof 51/1904, NAK.

156. J.A. Burdon, "Sokoto Provincial Report for March and April, 1905," Sokprof 260/1905, NAK.

157. J.A. Burdon, "Sokoto Provincial Reporot No.29 for the Quarter Ended 31 March 1906," Sokprof 578/1906, NAK.

158. Ibid.

159. J.A. Fremantle "Report for Yola for 1907," Yolaprof No.7, NAK.

160. The Resident is here referring to a very serious revolt in German Adamawa around 1906. This revolt, whose aim was to evict the Germans, was led by an Arab by name Goni Wadai, and joined by almost all the town and village chiefs in that area, although the bigger sub-Emirs stood on the side of the Germans. The revolt achieved an initial victory over the Germans, but when it later marched on Garwa, it was defeated with very heavy casualties. The defeat was followed by the execution of all the rebels who escaped death on the battlefield, including Ardo Abbasi of Agorma, Ardo Buba Adama of Wubawo, Ardo Hammadu of Chebowa, Ardo Buba of Bame and Ardo Goni of Wuro Kohel; but others managed to escape and hide in British Adamawa. See Ahmadou Bassoro and Eldridge Mohammadou, *Histoire de Garoua: Cité Peule du XIXè Siècle*, ONAREST, 1977, pp.53–58).

Chapter 4

1.   AMD, Kano, 17/5/1974.

2.   WJ, Sokoto, 30/4/1974.

3.   See section on "The territorial Implications of British Conquest" Chapter 2, pp.72–4.

4.   In Borno these were known as *Bulama*, in Adamawa as *Jauro'en* (sing *Jauro = Jaumu Wuro*, i.e. owner of the town) and in Ilorin as *Mogaji* or *Ajidungari*.

5.   In Borno these messengers were known as *Chima Gana*; in Ilorin as *Ajele*, and in Adamawa both the Hausa term *Jakada* and the Kanuri term, *Chima* were used for these administrative messengers.

6. For a more detailed discussion of the nineteenth century judicial system, see Chapter 6.

7. W.C. Moore, "Rebado Reassessment Report, December 1917," Yolaprof, G. 2Y, NAK.

8. AYR and AAYR, Zaria, 10/8/1977.

9. Ibid.

10. E.A. Brackenbury, "Namtari District Report on Reassessment 1910–11," Yolaprof G 2.W, NAK.

11. WJ, Sokoto, 30/4/1974.

12. J.A. Burdon, "Sokoto Provincial Report for the Month of April 1905," Sokprof 260/1905, NAK.

13. WJ, 30/4/1974.

14. C.L. Temple, "Sokoto Provincial Report for the Quarter Ended December 31st, 1907," Sokprof 1453/1908, NAK.

15. J.A. Burdon, "Sokoto Provincial Report for the Months of November and December 1905," Sokprof 85/1906, NAK.

16. The others included the Alkalin Daji, Sarkin Galma, Sarkin Adar, Hakimin Nufawa, and Sarkin Yaki of Binji.

17. "Sokoto Provincial Report for April, 1905," op. cit.

18. Ibid.

19. Ibid.

20. E.J. Stanley, "Sokoto Provincial Report No.36 for the Half-Year Ended June 30, 1908," Sokprof 985/1908, NAK; also WGUN, Sokoto, 22/4/1974.

21. C.L. Temple, "Sokoto Report for the Quarter Ended December 31, 1907," op. cit., NAK.

22. C.L. Temple, "Kano Provincial Half Yearly Report for June 1909," SNP 7/10, No.3635, NAK.

23. Ibid.

24. Ibid.

25. C.W. Orr, "Zaria Provincial Annual Report for 1906," Zariaprof 2553, NAK.

26. H.S. Goldsmith, "Sokoto Report No. 31 for Quarter Ended September 30, 1906," Sokprof 977/1906, NAK.

27. Ibid.

28. H.S. Goldsmith, "Sokoto Report No.30 for Quarter Ended June 30, 1906," sokprof 625/1906, NAK.

29. C.L. Temple, "Annual Report for Kano for 1909," op. cit.

30. W.P. Hewby, "Bornu Provincial Monthly Report for January, February and March 1903," SNP 15/1, No.48A, NAK.

31. Ibid.

32. W.P. Hewby, "Bornu Provincial Monthly Report for May 1904," SNP 15/1, No.48A, NAK.

33. W.P. Hewby, "Bornu Provincial Monthly Report for September 1904," SNP 15/1, No.48A, NAK.

34. A.J. Burdon, "Sokoto Provincial Report for July and August 1905," Sokprof 575/1905, NAK.

35. Ibid.

36. Ibid.

37. Ibid.

38. Ibid.

39. Ibid.

40. A.J. Burdon, "Report No.29 for the Quarter Ended March 31st, 1906," Sokprof 578/1906, NAK.

41. Actually, the Resident was less than honest in talking about the removal of Satiru from the Sarkin Kebbi, since the town was in fact completely razed to the ground.

42. A.J. Burdon, op. cit.

43. Ibid.

44. Ibid.

45. A.J. Burdon, op. cit.

46. Ibid.

47. H.S. Goldsmith, "Report No.31 for Quarter Ended September 30th 1906," Sokprof 977/1906.

48. H.S. Goldsmith, "Report No.32 for the Quarter Ended December 1906," Sokprof 50/1907, NAK.

49. G. Malcom, "Sokoto Province: Annual Report for 1912," SNP 10 No.152 P/1913, NAK.

50. C.L. Temple, "Report No.34 for the Quarter Ended June 30, 1907," Sokprof 610/1907, NAK.

51. Malcom, op. cit.

52. Ibid.

53. Sokoto Province: Confidential Reports on chiefs for 1916, unclassified, AHAK.

54. Ibid.

55. Sokprof 85/1906, op. cit.

56. C.L. Temple, "Sokoto Provincial Report for Quarter Ended 31 December 1907," op. cit.

57. H.O. Howard, "Bauchi Report No.27 for January, February and March, 1906," SNP 10 No.127, NAK.

58. Ibid.

59. Ibid.

60. Ibid.

61. H.O. Howard, "Report on the Bauchi Province for the March Quarter 1908," SNP 7 No.2303/1908, NAK.

62. Ibid.

63. F.B. Gall, "Bauchi Provincial Annual Report, 1914," SNP 168P/1915, NAK.

64. For the *Kofa* system, see Last, op. cit., p.5.

65. H.O. Howard, op. cit.

66. W.F. Gowers, "Bauchi Provincial Report for the December Quarter 1908," SNP 7 No.335/09.

67. F.B. Gall, op. cit.

68. Ibid.

69. F.B. Gall, "Bauchi Provincial Report for the Half Year Ended 30th June 1915," SNP 10 No.381P/1915.

70. J.M. Fremantle, "Annual Report for Yola Province for 1907," Yolaprof A6 & A7, NAK.

71. Ibid.

72. Ibid.

73. Yola Provincial Report on Chiefs for 1912, unclassified, AHAK.

74. Misc. "Yola later Adamawa Province – Collected Histories, 1905-1931," Yolaprof J.I., NAK.

75. W.S. Sharpe, "Quarterly Report No.65 for Quarter Ending 30th June 1910," Yolaprof, A NAK.

76. G.W. Webster, "Yola Provincial Report for Quarter Ending 31st March 1911," Yolaprof No.A10, NAK.

77. C.W. Orr, "Zaria Provincial Annual Report for 1905," Zariaprof. No.2552, NAK.

78. C.W. Orr, "Zaria Provincial Annual Report for 1906, op. cit.

79. M.P. Porch, "Zaria Province – Annual Report for 1912," SNP 10 No.178P/1913, NAK.

80. J.M. Fremantle, "Zaria Provincial Annual Report for the March Quarter, 1913" SNP 10 No.369/1913, NAK.

81. Arthur Festing, "Report on the Kano Province for the months of September, October and November 1907," SNP 7/No.5112/1907.

82. "A Strictly Confidential Letter from Cargill to the Governor of Northern Nigeria, dated 1/6/08," unclassified, AHAK; H.R. Palmer, "Kano Province – Annual Report for 1915," SNP 10 No.170P/1916, NAK.

83. Ibid.

84. H.R. Palmer, op.cit., SNP 10 No.170P/1916, NAK.

85. Ibid.

86. J.A. Burdon, "Sokoto Provincial Report for March and April 1905," Sokprof 260/1905, op. cit.

87. C.L. Temple, "Sokoto Report for Quarter Ended December 31, 1907," Sokprof No.1453/1908, NAK.

88. Ibid.

89. Ibid. Incidentally Muhammadu Raji b. Umar b. Ahmad b. Modi b. Jibril was along the male line a great grandson of the illustrious Mallam Jibril b. Umar and also a great grandson of the controversial nineteenth century Mallam Modibbo Raji. The latter's daughter, Fadimatu being the mother of Ahmad, his father. (WGUN, Sokoto, 22/4/74).

90. J.A. Burdon, "Sokoto Provincial Report for the Months of March and April 1905," op. cit.

91. Ibid; also C.L. Temple, "Sokoto Provincial Annual Report for 1907," SNP 10 No.384/1910.
92. Ibid.
93. C.L. Temple, "Sokoto Provincial Annual Report for 1907," op. cit.
94. Arthur Festing, "Reoort on the Kano province for the months of September, October and November 1907," op. cit.
95. Cargill to the Governor of Northern Nigeria, op. cit.
96. Ibid.
97. Confidential Reports on Chiefs, Zaria Province 1914, unclassified, AHAK.
98. Note from Assistant Resident Gombe to Resident Bauchi, dated 25/8/08, SNP 23093/1908, NAK.
99. C.L. Temple "Kano Provincial Half-Yearly Report for June 1909," op. cit., also H.R. Palmer, "Kano Provincial Annual Report for 1905," SNP 170P/1916, NAK.
100. Confidential Reports on Chiefs, Kano Province 1911, unclassified, AHAK.
101. Confidential Reports on Chiefs, Bauchi Province, 1912, unclassified, AHAK.
102. Ibid.
103. Ibid.; also J.M. Fremantle, "Zaria Provincial Annual Report for 1913," SNP No.107P/1914, NAK; Confidential Reports on Chiefs, Nassarawa Province, 1915, unclassified, AHAK.
104. Ibid.
105. Confidential Reports on Chiefs, Adamawa Province 1911–12, unclassified, AHAK.
106. Confidential Reports on Chiefs, Muri Province, 1911-1915, unclassified, AHAK; also C.L. Temple, "Sokoto Report No. 33 for Quarter Ended March 31, 1907," Sokprof No.343/1907, NAK.
107. Confidential Reports on Chiefs, Bornu Province, 1914, unclassified, AHAK.
108. Ibid.
109. Ibid.
110. Telegram Lugard to Resident Ilorin, dated 28/8/1900, SNP 5 No.11, NAK.
111. H.R. Palmer, "Report on a Tour in Ingawa District, May 1907" in "Kano Report for June 1907," op. cit.
112. Arthur Festing, "Report on the Kano Province for the Months of September, October and November 1907," op. cit.
113. Ibid.
114. Palmer, op. cit.
115. This was Haliru who was given the title *Sarkin Rima* and posted to Wurno. (Confidential Reports on Chiefs, Sokoto Province, 1914, unclassified, AHAK).
116. Confidential Reports on Chiefs, Bornu Province, 1911–1915, unclassified, AHAK; also Confidential Reports on Chiefs, Muri Province, 1911, unclassified, AHAK.
117. Confidential Reports on Chiefs, Adamawa Province, 1912–1916, unclassified, AHAK; also J.M. Fremantle, "Historical Notes on the Yola Fulanis," dated July 1907 in Yolaprof J., NAK.

118. H.S. Goldsmith, "Sokoto Report No. 32 for Quarter Ended December 31, 1906," Sokprof 50/1907, NAK; also see Chapter 5.

119. J.A. Burdon, "Sokoto Report No.29 for the Quarter Ended 31 March 1906," op. cit.

120. Ibid.

121. P.M. Dwyer, "Report on the Ilorin Province for the Quarter Ended 31 March 1907," SNP 7 No.1569/1907, NAK.

122. For a discussion of such depositions see Chapter 7.

123. Capt Boyle, "Hibango District" in Yolaprof J.1, NAK.

124. W.F. Gowers, "Sokoto Provincial Annual Report for the Year 1909," SNP 10 No.984/1910, NAK.

125. C.L. Temple, "Kano Provincial Annual Report for 1909," SNP 7/10 No. 6415/1909, NAK.

126. A.C.G. Hastings, "Kano Provincial Annual Report for 1914," SNP 10 No.139/1915, NAK.

127. Confidential Report on Chiefs, Zaria Province, 1915, unclassified, AHAK.

128. H.O. Howard, "Report on the Bauchi Province for the March Quarter, 1908," SNP 7 No.2303/1908, NAK.

129. Ibid.

130. W.F. Gowers, "Report on Bauchi Province for the December Quarter 1908," SNP 7 No.335/09, NAK.

131. W.F. Gowers, "Sokoto Provincial Annual Report for 1910," SNP 10 No.384/1908, NAK.

132. Thus, for example, in 1925, i.e. during a period which is outside our focus, the then District Head of Madagali, Hama Yaji, got rid of his Qadi, Mallu Aminu, with whom he had been at loggerheads for several years, by simply accusing him of slave dealing, himself procuring the witnesses whom he bribed with money and cloth as well as bribing District Officer Leonard's interpreter, Allah Kyauta, with 100/-. See *Hama Yaji's Diary*, 1912–1927," Yolaprof Acc.14. Significantly, when Hama Yaji was in 1927 being tried by the Lamido's Council, prior to his deposition, one of the charges leveled against him was interference with the work of his Alkali's Native Court, a complaint which Mallu Aminu's successor must have brought against him.

133. W.F. Gowers, op. cit.

134. Ibid.

135. W.F. Gowers, "Bauchi, Hassan, Emir of Death and Choice of Successor," SNP 7/No.123/08, NAK. The two of them were later to become Emirs of Bauchi namely Yakubu II, alias Maigari, 1909-1944 and Yakubu III, 1944–1954.

136. Ibid.

137. Arthur Festing, "Report on the Kano Province for the Months of September, October and November 1907," op. cit.

138. C.L. Temple, "Sokoto Provincial Annual Report for 1907," op. cit.

139. Ibid.

140. W.F. Gowers, "Sokoto Provincial Annual Report for 1910," SNP 10 No.765/1911, NAK.

141. H.O. Howard, "Report on the Bauchi Province for the March Quarter, 1908," op. cit.

142. G. Vertue, "Sokoto Report for the December Quarter, 1911," SNP 10 No.1041/1912, NAK.

143. J.M. Fremantle, "Zaria Province – Report for the March Quarter 1913," SNP 10 No.369/1913, NAK.

144. Ibid.

145. C.O. Migeod, "Zaria Province – Report for June Quarter 1914," SNP 10 No.410P/1914, NAK.

146. Ibid.

147. Confidential Reports on Chiefs, Muri Province, 1911–1915, op. cit.

148. C.L. Temple, "Sokoto Report No.33 for Quarter Ended March 31 1907," Sokprof 343/1907.

149. Ibid.

150. Ibid.

151. E.J. Arnett, "Gazetteer of Sokoto Province," London, 1920, p.59.

152. See Chapter 7.

153. W.P. Hewby, "Bornu Provincial Annual Report for 1908," SNP 7 No.1894/1909, NAK.

154. G.W. Webster, "Yola Provincial Quarterly Report for June 1911," Yolaprof A 10, NAK; also W.S. Sharpe, "Yola Provincial Quarterly Report for March, 1910," Yolaprof A 9, NAK.

155. Confidential Annual Reports on Chiefs, Sokoto Province, 1911–15, unclassified, AHAK.

156. S.A. Balogun, "Succession Tradition in Gwandu History, 1817–1918," in JHSN, Vol.7, No.1, December 1973, pp.29–31; also WGUN, Sokoto, 22/4/1974.

157. Confidential Annual Reports on Chiefs, Sokoto and Muri Provinces, 1911–15, op. cit.

158. See section on "Grounds and Non-Grounds for Deposing District Heads", Chapter 4, page 145–8.

159. Confidential Annual Reports on Chiefs, Kano Province 1911–15, unclassified, AHAK.

160. Governor's comments on H.O. Howard's 'Report on the Bauchi Province for March Quarter, 1908," op. cit.; also G.W. Webster, "Report on the Yola Province for March Quarter 1908," SNP 7 No.2124/1908, NAK; and Hewby, "Bornu Provincial Annual Report for 1910," SNP 7 No.1107/1911, NAK.

161. W.S. Sharpe, "Report No.66 for Quarter Ended 30 September 1910," Yolaprof No.A9 NAK; also W.P. Hewby, "Bornu Provincial Monthly Report for November and December, 1903," op. cit.

162. See Chapter 7.

163. Arthur Festing, "Kano Report for June 1907," SNP 7 No. 3095/1907, NAK.

164. Ibid.

165. Arthur Festing, "Kano Report for June 1907," op. cit.

166. W.F. Gowers, "Kano Provincial Annual Repoort for 1912," SNP 10 No.134P/1913, NAK.

167. Ibid.

168. W.F. Gowers, "Kano Provincial Annual Report for 1913," SNP 10 No.98P/1914, NAK.

169. H.R. Palmer, "Kano Provincial Annual Report for 1915," SNP 10 No.170P/1916, NAK.

170. Ibid; also AMD, Kano, 17/5/1974.

171. Ibid.

172. J.M. Fremantle, "Zaria Provincial Annual Report for 1913," SNP 10 No.107P/1914, NAK.

173. Ibid.

174. Ibid.

175. C.O. Migeod, "Zaria Provincial Report No.63 for September Quarter 1914," SNP 10 No.597P/1914, NAK.

176. C.O. Migeod, "Zaria Provincial Report No.63 for September Quarter 1914," SNP 10 No.597P/1914, NAK.

177. Ibid.

178. E.J. Arnett, "Sokoto Provincial Annual Report for 1913," SNP 10, No.104P/914, NAK.

179. H.S. Goldsmith, "Zaria Provincial Report No.64 for Quarter Ended December 31, 1914, SNP 10 No.5 1P/1915, NAK.

180. Ibid.

181. H.S. Goldsmith, "Zaria Provincial Report No.64 for quarter Ended December 31, 1914" SNP 10 No.5 1P/1915, NAK.

182. W.C. Moore, "Balala District: Assessment Papers 1917," Yolaprof G2, Y, NAK.

183. Ibid.

184. W.C. Moore, op. cit.

185. Commander B.E.A. Waters, "Reassessment Reort on the Daware District of Yola Emirate, Yola Province, August and September 1917," Yolaprof G.2Y, NAK.

186. Campbell-Irons to SNP Kaduna, Letter n.d. in Yolaprof G.2X, NAK.

Chapter 5

1.   Oliver Howard, "Bauchi Report No.27 for January, February and March 1906," SNP 10 No.127, NAK.

2.   H.S. Goldsmith, "Sokoto Provincial Report No.31 for the Quarter Ended September 30, 1906," Sokprof 977/1906, NAK.

3.   See Chapter 3 page 110–114.

4. E.J. Stanley, "Sokoto Provincial Report for the Half-Year Ended June 30th 1908," Sokprof 895/1908, NAK.

5. Ibid.

6. Ibid.

7. Ibid.

8. Ibid.

9. Ibid.

10. Ibid.

11. Ibid.

12. AUG, 156/3/1974.

13. Ibid.

14. See Chapter 4, page 134.

15. For a sample of this view see P.K. Tibenderana, *Administration of Sokoto, Gwandu and Argungu Emirates Under British Rule 1900–1936,* Ph.D, Ibadan.

16. Since Haliru's death in 1915 he has been succeeded by three of his sons, Bashari (1915–18), Usumanu (1918–38) and Yahya (1938–54) and one grandson, Harunan Bashari 1954–) and no member of any other branch of the family of Abdullahi dan Fodio has acceded to the office since then.

17. Arthur Festing, "Kano Provincial Report for June 1907," SNP 7 No.3095/1907, NAK.

18. Ibid.

19. F.B. Gall, "Bauchi Provincial Report for the Half-Year Ended 30th June 1915," SNP 10 No.381P/1915, NAK.

20. Ibid.

21. Ibid.

22. Ibid.

23. Ibid.

24. Ibid.

25. Ibid.

26. Ibid.

27. Ibid.

28. Ibid.

29. Ibid.

30. See Chapter 4, page 136.

31. G. Malcolm, "Sokoto Divisional Report No.1 for the Half-Year Ended June 1909," Sokprof 78/1909, NAK.

32. Ibid.

33. Ibid.

34. Ibid.

35. R. McAllister, "Sokoto Provincial Report for September Quarter 1911," SNP 10 No.5572/1911, NAK.

36. Ibid.

37. Ibid.

38. Ibid.
39. Ibid.
40. C.L. Temple, "Bauchi Report No. 2, March 1902," SNP 15 No. 39, NAK.
41. "Confidential Reports on Chiefs, Niger Province 1909," unclassified, AHAK.
42. C.W. Orr, "Zaria Provincial Annual Report for 1906," Zariaprof 2553, NAK.
43. J.M. Fremantle, "Annual Report for Yola Province for 1907," Yolaprof A6 & B7, NAK.
44. Ibid.
45. In fact these flags were given out by Modibbo Adama, the first Emir of Adamawa and not by the Caliph. See Sa'ad Abubakar, *The Lamibe of Fombina*, ABU Press, Zaria, Nigeria, 1977.
46. G.W. Webster, "Report on the Yola Province for March Quarter 1908," SNP 7/214 24/1908, NAK.
47. Ibid.
48. Ibid.
49. Ibid.
50. Ibid.
51. Webster, op. cit.
52. Various, "Murder, District Headman and Thirteen Followers — Emir of Yola the Instigator (Asks?) for Deportation," SNP 7/1887/1909, NAK.
53. Ibid.
54. See Chapter 3, page 126.
55. See SNP 7/1887/1909, op. cit.
56. Ibid.
57. Ibid.
58. Ibid.
59. According to traditions, this man left Yola in anger soon after his circumcision ceremony during which his mates were given gifts of cattle and horses while he was given only a hen. He was never heard of until he returned with the invading British as their guide. After the British occupation of Yola, he settled to wield enormous power as the chief native agent of the British and the liaison between the Lamido and the Resident. The British testified to Bello's power of intrigue, as we shall see later on in this chapter, and in Yola he is remembered to have intrigued first with Yerima Iyabano to secure the deposition of Lamido Bobbo Ahmadu and the appointment of the former, and eighteen months later, with Yerima Abba to secure the deposition of Lamido Iya and the appointment of Abba. It was the latter that got rid of him by implicating him in a number of cases of abduction of women.
60. This title was given to the rulers of Gurin on account of the fact that Gurin was the first capital of the Emirate of Fombina. Modibbo Adama spent over twenty years there after his appointment as Emir before he moved first to Ribadu, then to Njoboli and finally to Yola which he himself founded. See Sa'ad Abubakar, op. cit.; pp. 60–63. The theory was that, even after leaving the town, the Modibbo

and his successors remained not only the Emirs of Fombina as a whole but of Gurin as well. But since they were no longer domiciled in Gurin, they appointed a caretaker administrator, a *Khalifa*, to take care of the town in their absence. This arrangement may suggest that the abandonment of Gurin as the capital was initially not meant to be permanent. At any rate the rulers of Gurin retained this title until well into the twentieth century, when it was changed first to *Wakili* and later to *Lamido*.

61. Misc., "Gurin District Assessment Papers," Yola J.I., NAK.
62. Ibid.
63. Ibid.
64. Ibid.
65. Confidential Reports on Chiefs, Yola Province, 1912, unclassified, AHAK.
66. Ibid.
67. Ibid.
68. See fn 142, Chapter 2.
69. Confidential Reports, op. cit.
70. Ibid.
71. Ibid.
72. See Sa'ad Abubakar, op. cit., p.74, and 121–22. Although there was no law that excluded this branch of the family – the descendants of the Modibbo and a rather imperious wife of his by the name Yasebo – and although almost every time the office of Emir fell vacant one or another of them was considered for the office along with others. However, none of them ever succeeded to it until 1924 when Hamman Bello Maigari was appointed Emir, though on the initiative of the people of Yola themselves – that is, rather than the British. Since then, another member of the family Ahmadu, a son of Lamido Maigari himself was Emir (1946–1953).
73. Confidential Reports on Chiefs, Yola Province, 1911, unclassified, AHAK.
74. See Chapter 2, pp. 76–7.
75. Thus the German portion was under the joint control of Yerima Maigari and his father Yerima Babbawa while Nyibango District in the material was ruled by Bunu Hammawa, Babbawa's nephew. See Yolaprof J.I., NAK.
76. Confidential Reports, op. cit.
77. Ibid.
78. Ibid.
79. G.W. Webster, "Yola Provincial Quarterly Report for March 1913," Yolaprof A5, NAK.
80. G. Malcolm, "Sokoto Provincial Annual Report for 1912," Sokprof No.152/1913, NAK.
81. Ibid.
82. Confidential Reports on Chiefs, Sokoto Province, 1914, unclassified, AHAK.
83. Ibid.
84. Confidential Reports on Chiefs, Kano Province, 1917, unclassified, AHAK.

85. E.J. Arnett, "Kano Provincial Annual Report for 1911," SNP 7 No.1114/1912, NAK; also W.P. Hewby, "Bornu Provincial Annual Report for 1912," SNP 7 No.626/1913, NAK; and C.O. Migeod, "Zaria Provincial Report No.63, for September Quarter, 1914," SNP 10 No.597/1914, NAK.

86. See Chapter 4, page 142.

87. "Kano Provincial Annual Report for 1911," op. cit.

88. Ibid.

89. Confidential Reports on Chiefs, Zaria Province, 1911, unclassified, AHAK; and Confidential Reports on Chiefs, Bornu, 1915, unclassified, AHAK.

90. Confidential Reports on Chiefs, Bornu Province 1911–1917," unclassified, AHAK.

91. Confidential Reports on Chiefs, Kano Province, 1911, unclassified, AHAK.

92. Ibid.

93. K.V. Elphinstone, "Yola Provincial Report for December 1904." Yolaprof A5, NAK.

94. J.C. Sciortino, "Bornu Provincial Report for the June Quarter, 1911," SNP 7 No.7/5776/1911, NAK.

95. H.S. Goldsmith, "Report No.30 for Quarter Ended June 30, 1906," Sokprof 625/1906, NAK.

96. Confidential Reports on Chiefs, Kano Province, 1917, unclassified, AHAK.

97. J.C. Sciortino, "Bornu Provincial Report for December Quarter 1911," SNP 5776/1911, NAK.

98. Ibid.

99. E.J. Arnett, "Kano Provincial Annual Report for 1911," op. cit.; also Annual Reports on Chiefs, Sokoto Province, 1911–1916, unclassified, AHAK.

100. See Chapter 7.

101. J.M. Fremantle, "Annual Report for Yola Province for 1907," op. cit.

102. Ibid.

103. W.S. Sharpe, "Yola Provincial Report for Quarter Ended 30 June 1912," Yolaprof A 12, NAK.

104. Ibid.

105. E.J. Arnett, "Sokoto Provincial Annual Report for 1913," Sokprof 581/1914, NAK.

106. W.P. Hewby, "Bornu Provincial Monthly Report for November 1902," SNP 15/1 No.19, NAK.

Chapter 6

1. P. M.Dwyer, "Ilorin Residents Reports for April/May 1900," SNP 15 Acc. No. 11, NAK.

2. Ibid. From these two courts, appeals could go onto Gwandu, although such appeals were rarely made. Instead, the practice was for the Qadi and Emir to send to Gwandu asking for guidance in difficult cases.
3. G.N. Barclay, "Yola Provincial Report for February 1904," Yolaprof A3, NAK.
4. See Sa'ad Abubakar, *The Lamibe of Fombina*, ABU Press, Zaria, 1980, pp. 124–5.
5. U.F.H Ruxton, "Yola Provincial Report No.4, for January 1902," SNP 10 No. 127, NAK.
6. Ibid.
7. In the case of Yola too as in the case of the other "Eastern emirates," appeals could be made to the Caliph in Sokoto just as from the "Western emirates" appeal could be made to the Emir of Gwandu. However, there is little evidence to show that such appeals were made from Yola.
8. J.A. Burdon, "Sokoto Provincial Report No.2/1903 for April, 1903," Sokprof No.23/1903, NAK.
9. AABM, Sokoto, 11/3/1974.
10. WJ, Sokoto, 28/4/1974.
11. Ibid.
12. J.A. Burdon, op. cit.
13. For examples of such appeals, see H.F. Backwell, *The Occupation of Hausaland, 1900–1904: Being a Translation of Arabic Letters Found in the House of the Wazir of Sokoto, Bohari, in 1903*, Frank Cass, London, 1969, verbatim.
14. J.A. Burdon, op. cit.
15. Backwell, op. cit.
16. He himself admitted that for the month of July 1900, his "work in [Ilorin had] been almost nil," the only cases brought to him being "paltry women palavers and nothing else." See P.M. Dwyer, "Ilorin Provincial Monthly Report for July 1900," SNP 15/Acc. No.11, NAK. Also see Chapter 6, page 194 for a discussion of Provincial Courts.
17. This Proclamation was promulgated earlier on in the same year. (CS 08/1–22, NAI).
18. P.M. Dwyer, "Ilorin Provincial Monthly Report for October, 1900," SNP/15, Acc. No. 11, NAK.
19. Letter, Dwyer to Lugard dated 24/10/1900, SNP 15, Acc. No. 11, NAK.
20. F.H., Ruxton, "Yola Provincial Report No. 5 for February 1902," Yolaprof AI, NAK.
21. Ibid.
22. Ibid.
23. Ibid.
24. G.N. Barclay, "Yola Provincial Reports for October, November and December 1902," in Yolaprof AI, NAK.
25. W.P. Hewby, "Bornu Provincial Report for October, November and December, 1902," SNP15/1 No.19, NAK.
26. Ibid.

27. J.A. Burdon, "Report No.2/1903 of April 30, 1903 on Sokoto Province," op. cit.

28. H.R.P. Hillary, "Sokoto Provincial Monthly Report for March, 1904," Sokprof No. 101/1904, NAK.

29. W.F. Gowers, "Yola Provincial Report No. 17 for March, 1903," Yolaprof No. A2, NAK.

30. G.N. Barclay, "Yola Provincial Report for February 1904," op. cit.

31. J.E.C. Blackeney, "Bauchi Report No. 199 for the Month of November 1904," SNP 10 No. 62, NAK.

32. These were at Kukawa, Magumeri, Maiduguri and an extra-territorial court for the Shuwa Arabs. See W.P. Hewby, "Bornu Provincial Monthly Report for May 1904," SNP 15/1 No. 48A, NAK.

33. These were at Dogon Daji, Gummi, Maradun, Bukwium, Isa, Kauran Namoda, Bakura, and Tambawal. See H.S. Goldsmith, "Sokoto Provincial Annual Report No. 3 for 1905," Sokprof 86/1906.

34. Ibid.; also C.L. Temple, "Sokoto Provincial Report No. 33 for the Quarter Ended 31 March 1907," Sokprof 343/1907, NAK.

35. H.S. Goldsmith, "Sokoto Provincial Annual Report No. 3" op. cit.

36. Among the new courts were those at Yabo, Gwadabawa, Kawoje, Bodinga, Bazai and Silame. See C.L. Temple, "Sokoto Provincial Annual Report for 1907," SNP 10 No. 384/1908, NAK. Also C.L. Temple, "Sokoto Provincial Report for the Quarter Ended December 31, 1907," Sokprof 1453/1908, NAK.

37. W.P. Hewby, "Bornu Provincial Annual Report for 1906," SNP 7 No. 1756/1907, NAK.

38. These were at Gwaram, Bununu, Lere, Fali, Rauta, Toro Bula, Zungur, Darazo, Kurfi and Kafin Madaki. See H.Oliver "Report on the Bauchi Province for the March Quarter 1908," SNP 7 No. 2303/1908, NAK.

39. J.A. Burdon, "Sokoto Province Annual Report for the Year 1908," SNP 10 No. 765/1911.

40. W.F. Gowers, "Sokoto Province Annual Report for 1910," SNP 10 No. 765/1911, NAK.

41. Ibid.

42. Ibid.

43. W.S. Sharpe, "Yola Provincial Annual Repot for 1909," Yolaprof A8. See also W.S. Sharpe, "Yola Provincial Annual Report for 1910," Yolaprof A9, NAK.

44. E.J. Arnett, "Kano Provincial Annual Report for 1911," SNP 7 No. 1114/1912.

45. G.W. Webster, "Yola Provincial Report for the Quarter Ended June 1911," Yolaprof A10, NAK.

46. G. Malcolm, "Sokoto Province; Annual Report for 1912," SNP 10 No. 152/1913, NAK.

47. E.J. Arnett, "Sokoto Provincial Annual Report for 1913," SNP 10 No. 104/1914, NAK.

48. W.S. Sharpe, "Yola Quarterly Report No. 74 for Quarter Ended 31st March 1912," Yolaprof A12, NAK.

49. G.W. Webster, "Yola Provincial Report for the Quarter Ended June 1911," op. cit.; also K.V. Elphinstone, "Yola Report No. 72 for the Quarter Ended 31 December 1911," Yolaprof 11, NAK.

50. These were at Zangon Katab, Katchia, Lere, Anchang, Riga Chikun, Sola, Fatika, Sabon Gari and Kaduna. See M.P. Porch, "Zaria Provincial Annual Report for 1912," SNP 10, No. 178p/1913, NAK.

51. C.O. Migeod, "Zaria Provincial Annual Report for 1915," SNP 10 No. 138p/1916, NAK.

52. These were Inamo, Brimah and Bogola. See Warrant for the Jebba Native Court signed by Dwyer 12/10/02 in SNP 15 No. Acc. No. 11, NAK.

53. Ibid.

54. Letter, Dwyer to Lugard dated 24 October 1900, op. cit.

55. Ibid.

56. The inclusion of a representative of the Hausa being at Barclay's specific insistence on the ground that "the Hausa formed a large and influential element, not only in Yola town, but throughout the country and a concession of this sort was likely to be well received by them." The idea of setting up a "mixed" court on which people were nominated on tribal grounds "brought forth strong protestation from the Alkali and other judges though the Emir refrained from making any comments." It was not until Barclay relented and dropped the matter that the Qadi and the Emir "considerably surprised" him by selecting Mallam Usman and sending him to the Resident for swearing in. It would seem that the Emir and the Qadi of Yola, whose government had, throughout its brief history, been "ethnically heterogeneous" but not as a matter of deliberate policy, first resisted the Resident's demand because they saw it as an attempt to institutionalize tribalism. However, on turning round and finding that the person qualified to be the fourth member of the court happened to satisfy the Resident's demand, they went ahead and appointed him, a procedure which further confirmed their rejection of ethnicity both as a qualification and as a disqualification for judgeship. See G.N. Barclay, "Yola Provincial Report for June, 1902," Yolaprof, AI, NAK.

57. J.A. Burdon, "Report No. 2/1903 of April 1903 on Sokoto Province," op. cit.

58. Ibid.

59. Ibid.

60. Ibid.

61. Letter, Dwyer to Lugard dated 24/10/02, op. cit.

62. J.A. Burdon, "Report No. 2/1903 for April 1903 on Sokoto Province," op. cit.

63. G.N. Barclay, "Yola Provincial Report for February 1904," op. cit.

64. J.A. Burdon, "Sokoto Provincial Report No. 29 for the Quarter Ended March 31, 1906," Sokprof 758/1906, NAK.

65. P.M. Dwyer, "Ilorin Provincial Report for July 1900," op. cit. See also G.N. Barclay, "Yola Provincial Report No. 13 for November 1902," Yolaprof A1, NAK. C.W. Orr, "Zaria Provincial Annual Report for 1905," Zariaprof No. 2552, NAK;

and J.M. Fremantle, "Zaria Provincial Annual Report for 1913," SNP 10 No. 107/1914, NAK.

66. C.W. Orr, "Zaria Annual Report for 1905," op. cit.

67. Dwyer to Lugard, dated 24/10/1900, op. cit.

68. "Zaria annual Report for 1905," op. cit. Also "Sokoto Report for September and October 1905," op. cit.

69. C.L. Temple, "Bauchi Report No. 2 for March 1902," SNP 15 No. 39, NAK.

70. H.S. Goldsmith, "Zaria Provincial Report No. 64 for the Quarter Ended December 31, 1914," SNP 10 No. 51p/1915, NAK; C.O. Migeod, "Zaria Provincial Annual Report for 1915," SNP 10 No. 138/1916, NAK; H.R. Palmer, "Kano Provincial Annual Report for 1915," SNP 10 No. 170p/1916, NAK. Also RDN, Kano, 24/5/74.

71. "Kano Provincial Annual Report for 1915," op. cit.

72. Ibid.

73. "Ilorin Provincial Report for July 1900," op. cit.

74. Ibid.

75. Dwyer to Lugard, 24/10/1900, op. cit.

76. Ibid.

77. "Sokoto Report No. 2/1903," op. cit.

78. "Sokoto Report for July and august 1905," op. cit.

79. G.N. Barclay, "Yola Report No. 10 for August 1902," Yolaprof A1, NAK and Barclay, "Yola Report for October 1904," Yolaprof 2, NAK.

80. Ibid.

81. Ibid.; also Barclay, "Report No. 45 for September and October 1905," Yolaprof A6 and 7, NAK.

82. For my treatment of the issue of slavery in our period see page 192. However, here, it is worth digressing a little and point out that the mere facts that slaves went to court to seek their freedom and that slave-owners did go to court to get settlements in disputes over the "ownership of slaves" are positive proof that the British did not abolish slavery. The tendency of the 'native' courts, without prompting from the British, to let slaves have or purchase their freedom indicates clearly that the right of slaves to manumission either had already been firmly established or was in the process of being so established by the time the British occupied the emirates. Hence, in granting slaves this right – as they did – the British were merely giving sanction to a right that was already there.

83. Oliver Howard, "Bauchi Provincial Report No. 27 for the Months of January, February and March 1906," SNP 10 No. 127, NAK.

84. G.N. Barclay, "Yola Provincial Report for Quarter Ended June 30, 1909," Yolaprof A8, NAK.

85. W.S. Sharpe, "Yola Provincial Quarterly Report for March 1910," Yolaprof A9, NAK.

86. J.A. Burdon, "Report No. 2/1903," op. cit.; also H.R.P. Hillary, "Sokoto Provincial Report for March 1904," op. cit.

87. J.A. Burdon, "Sokoto Provincial Report for September and October 1905: Lugard's Comments on;" Sokprof No. 756/1905, NAK.

88. J.A. Burdon, "Sokoto Provincial Report for July and August 1905," Sokprof 575/1905, NAK.

89. H.S. Goldsmith, "Sokoto Report No. 31 for Quarter Ended September 30, 1906," Sokprof 977/1906, NAK; also G.N. Barclay, "Yola Report for March 1904," Yolaprof A4, NAK.

90. W.F. Gowers, "Bauchi Report for the June Quarter, 1907," SNP No. 3401, NAK; G.N. Barclay, "Yola Report for the Quarter Ended June 30, 1909," Yolaprof A8; also M.P. Porch, "Zaria Provincial Annual Report for 1912," op. cit.

91. P.M. Dwyer, "Ilorin Residents' Report for July 1900," op. cit.

92. Abdullahi dan Fodio, *Diya al-Hukkam*.

93. G.N. Barclay, "Yola Report No. 20 for June 1903," Yolaprof A2, NAK; also J.A. Burdon, "Sokoto Provincial Report for the Month of April 1905," Sokprof 260/1905, NAK.

94. Abdullahi dan Fodio, op. cit.; also pp. 190–1.

95. "Ilorin Report for July 1900," op. cit.

96. Ibid.

97. Dwyer to Lugard 24 October 1900, op. cit.

98. In fact the warrants stipulated that "any member of [a] court who accepts bribes to act in a corrupt manner as to his decision of a case is liable to a fine of £50 or imprisonment for a period not exceeding two years with or without hard labour."

99. G.N. Barclay, "Yola Report for June 1902," op. cit.

100. Ibid.

101. Ibid.

102. Ibid.; Lugard's Comments.

103. G.N. Barclay, "Yola Provincial Report No. 13 for November 1902," Yolaprof A1, NAK.

104. G.N. Barclay, "Yola Report for March 1904," Yolaprof A4, NAK; also Major McClintock, "Bornu Annual Report for 1907," SNP 7 No. 1761/1908; M.P. Porch, "Zaria Annual Report for 1912," op. cit. "Zaria Provincial Annual Report for 1913," op. cit.; W.F. Gowers, "Kano Provincial Annual Report for 1913," SNP 10 No. 98p/1914, NAK; and A.C.G. Hastings, "Kano Provincial Annual Report for 1914," SNP 10 No. 139p/1915.

105. W.S. Sharpe, "Yola Report for Quarter Ended 30 September 1912," Yolaprof A13, NAK; also W.F. Gowers, "Sokoto Provincial Annual Report for 1910," SNP 10 No. 765/1911, NAK; "Zaria Provincal Annual Report for 1913," op. cit.

106. G.N. Barclay, "Yola Report No. 48 for Quarter Ended June 30, 1906," Yolaprof A5, NAK.

107. W.F. Gowers, "Annual Report on the Bauchi Province for the Year 1907," SNP 7 No. 889/1908, NAK; C.L. Temple, "Sokoto Provincial Annual Report No. 4 for 1907," Sokprof 39/1908, NAK; W.F. Gowers, "Sokoto Provincial Annual Report for 1910," SNP 10 No. 765/1911, NAK; C.L. Temple, "Sokoto Provincial Annual

Report for the Year 1909," SNP 10, No. 984/1910, NAK; M.P. Porch, "Zaria Provincial Annual Report for 1912," op. cit.; W.F. Gowers, "Kano Provincial Annual Report for 1912," SNP 10 No. 134p/1913, NAK; W.F. Gowers, "Kano Provincial Annual Report for 1913," op. cit.; G. Malcolm, "Sokoto Provincial Annual Report for 1912," SNP 10 No. 142p/1913, NAK; E.J. Arnett, "Sokoto Provincial Annual Report for 1913," SNP 10 No. 104p/1914, NAK; W. S. Sharpe, "Yola Provincial Annual Report No. 84 for the March 1914 Quarter;" W.S. Sharpe, "Yola Provincial Report No. 85 for Quarter Ended 30/6/1914," W.S. Sharpe, "Yola Provincial Report for Quarter Ended 30/9/1914," all in file No. Yolaprof No. 17, NAK; also W.S. Sharpe, "Yola Provincial Report for Quarter Ended 31 December 1914," Yolaprof No. 18, NAK; A.C.G. Hastings, "Kano Provincial Annual Report for 1914," op. cit.; C.O. Migeod, "Zaria Provincial Annual Report for 1915," op. cit.

108. C.W. Orr, "Sokoto Provincial Report for January and February 1904," Sokprof No. 5/1904, NAK.

109. Ibid.

110. J.A. Burdon, "Sokoto Provincial Report No. 29 for the Quarter Ended March 31, 1906," op. cit.

111. Emphasis mine. That Burdon had made up his mind that the men should be sentenced to death can also be seen in his reference to "open condemnation" of them. According to a former Alkalin Alkalai, Sokoto, Burdon did actually instruct the Qadi, Alkali al-Mustapha, alias, Alkali Modibbo, that the men should be sentenced to death for killing the three British officers and other men of the detachment sent against them. To this, the Alkali is said to have objected that he did not find it possible to condemn Muslims for killing non-Muslims in battle. Burdon then threatened to dismiss him. The issue was resolved in a way that both satisfied Burdon and calmed the uneasy conscience of the Qadi when someone pointed out that the men had not only killed the British officers and their mercenaries in the men's own village, Satiru; they had also killed fellow-Muslims during their attacks on a number of the villages surrounding Satiru. In the light of the latter fact, al-Mustapha gave Burdon the guarantee of a death sentence against the men, who were arraigned before him as a pure formality. (AABM, 11/3/1974).

112. See Chapter 6 on "The Role, Functions and Powers of 'Native' Courts," page 180.

113. J.A. Burdon, "Sokoto Provincial Report No. 29 for the Quarter Ended March 31, 1906," op. cit.

114. Ibid.

115. I use the word *primarily* both to emphasize the political necessity for these courts to the British and to concede that the other reason often advanced for the establishment of these courts, namely, the logistical impossibility of replacing them, and indeed other "native institutions" is also admissible.

116. Ibid.

117. Ibid.

118. Ibid.

119. Ibid.

120. J.A. Burdon, "Report No. 2/1903 for April 1903 on the Sokoto Province," op. cit.

121. J.A. Burdon, "Sokoto Provincial Report for the Months of September and October 1905," op. cit.

122. Ibid.

123. Ibid.

124. J.A. Burdon, "Report No. 2/1903," op. cit.

125. Howard, "Bauchi Report No. 27," op. cit.

126. H.S. Goldsmith, "Zaria Province – Report No. 64 for the Quarter Ended December 31, 1914," op. cit.

127. G.N. Barclay, "Yola Provincial Report No. 14 for December 1902," op. cit.

128. Ibid.

129. W.F. Gowers, "Report No. 21 for July 1903," Yolaprof A2, NAK.

130. AABM, Sokoto, 14/3/1974; WAY, Kano, 1/6/1974.

131. G.N. Barclay, "Yola Provincial Report No. 15 for January 1903," Yolaprof A1, NAK.

132. Ibid.

133. Sokoto Report No. 2/1903, op. cit.

134. "Sokoto Report No. 2/1903," op. cit.

135. J.A. Burdon, "Sokoto Provincial Report for September and October 1905," op. cit.

136. Ibid.

137. Ibid.

138. Ibid.

139. Ibid.

140. Ibid.

141. Ibid.

142. Ibid.

143. Ibid.

144. Dwyer to Lugard, Letter dated 24/10/00, op. cit.

145. Ibid.

146. Dwyer to Lugard, Letter dated 24/10/1900, op. cit.

147. Ibid.

148. C.L. Temple, "Bauchi Report No. 2 for March 1902," op. cit.

149. Ibid.

150. Ibid.

151. Ibid.

152. C.L. Temple, "Bauchi Report for June 1902," SNP 15, No. 40, NAK.

153. J.A. Burdon, "Sokoto Report No. 29 for Quarter Ended 31 March 1906," op. cit.

154. Ibid.

155. J.A. Burdon, "Sokoto Provincial Report for July and August 1905," op. cit.

156. Ibid.

157. Ibid.

158. "Sokoto Report No. 29," op. cit.

159. Ibid.

160. This was the man to whom Waziri Buhari turned for solace and reassurance after surrendering to the British, and he seems to have been the teacher of a whole generation of *ulema* including Modibbo Abubakar Bube who, in his turn, was to become very famous in Sokoto, with his students coming from all over the emirates and including Waziri Junaidu of Sokoto. Among Ahmad Sa'ad's students was also Modibbo Murtala b. Raji who was the leading Islamic educator in Adamawa from around 1905 till his death around 1915.

161. H.S. Goldsmith, "Sokoto Provincial Report No. 30 for the Quarter Ended June 30, 1906," Sokprof 625/1906, NAK.

162. Ibid.

163. H.S. Goldsmith, "Sokoto Provincial Report No. 30 for the Quarter Ended June 30, 1906," op. cit.

164. Howard, "Bauchi Report No. 27," op. cit.

165. Ibid.

166. E.G.M. Dupigny, "Report on the Zaria Province for the Quarter Ended 20 June 1907," SNP 7 No. 2729/1907, NAK.

167. Resident Kontagora to Governor, Northern Nigeria, Confidential letter, dated 1908, SNP 17/1909, NAK.

168. Assistant Resident Gombe to Resident Bauchi, dated 25 August 1908, in H.O. Howard, "Report on the Bauchi Province for March Quarter 1908," op. cit.; also W.S. Sharpe, "Yola Provincial Annual Report No. 63 for 1909, op. cit. Of these the *Tuhfat* was written by El-Qadi Abu Bakr b. Asim al Qaysi (d. 829 AH/1427 AD); the *Mukhtassar* was written by Khalil ibn Ishaq (d. 776 AH/1365 AD), while the *Risalah* was written by Abi Zayd al-Qairawani (d. 386 AH/996 AD).

169. See section on "Relations Between the British and the 'Native Courts'," Chapter 6, page 185.

170. G.N. Barclay, "Yola Provincial Report No. 9 for July 1902," Yolaprof A1, NAK. It should be added that this custom in Yola further supports my contention earlier on that although the Shari'a prescribed the amputation of the hands of thieves, there is very little indication that this injunction had been carried out in precolonial days. Besides, in the specific case being quoted here, it was the native Qadis that were being humane and the British Resident harsh, a situation which is reversed in British claims and in the secondary literature on the topic that accepts British pronouncements on the issue at face value.

171. Ibid.

172. G.N. Barclay, "Yola Provincial Report for October 1904," op. cit.

173. Ibid.

174. Ibid.

175. J.A. Burdon, "Sokoto Provincial Report for the Months of May and June, 1905," Sokprof 315/1905, NAK.

176. Lest it be wondered why the British so much desired imprisonment for theft and other offences, it should be pointed out that imprisonment helped to procure labour for the British, a fact which Barclay emphasized in his report when he pointed out that "imprisonment of a farm or domestic slave means the loss of his services to the master during the term of imprisonment as all prisoners have to be employed on municipal works alone."

177. H.R.P. Hillary, "Sokoto Provincial Report for March 1904," op. cit. According to Acting Resident Hillary, the "idea" which had "so much become a part of the customs and ideas of the country that its abolition would revolutionize the social fabric," was a payment for the loss of either part of the body or of life. The maximum payable was 1,000,000 cowries. This amount was "subdivided according to the injuries inflicted, each injury being valued at a certain price – for the loss of life, emasculation, or the loss of two members, the full *dia* must be paid. For the loss of one of two members, the full dia must be paid. For the loss of one limb (or an eye), the *nisifu dia* or ½ [was] paid. For a serious injury (*inamunalit,* something that causes all beholders to express pity or horror), the *sulusin dia* or ⅓ [was] paid. For a serious blow such that a bone [was] exposed the *ushurin dia* or ¹⁄₁₀ [was] paid. For a minor injury the *nisifin ushurin dia* or ¹⁄₂₀ [was] paid." (Hillary [enclosure] on "the Dia or Blood Money" in "Report for March 1904," op. cit.

178. "Sokoto Report for March 1904," op. cit.

179. J.A. Burdon, "Sokoto Provincial Report for July and August 1905," op. cit.

180. See Chapter 6, page 191.

181. Ibid.

182. J.A. Burdon, "Sokoto Provincial Report for September and October 1905," op. cit.

183. *Majalisa Na Kasashen Arewa: Majalisar Sarakuna, Gamuwa to Biyu 26 da 27 ga Yuli,* Government Printer, pp.19–22.

184. J.M. Fremantle, "Annual Report for Yola Province for 1907," op. cit.

185. W.F. Gowers, "Sokoto Provincial Annual Report for 1910," op. cit.; also H.S. Goldsmith, "Sokoto Provincial Report No. 31 for Quarter Ended 30 September 1906," op. cit.

186. G.N. Barclay, "Yola Provincial Report for June 1904," op. cit.

187. W.F. Gowers, "Yola Provincial Report No. 23 for September 1903," Yolaprof vol. III, NAK.

188. J.A. Burdon, "Sokoto Provincial Report No. 29 for the Quarter Ended March 31, 1906," op. cit.

189. Various, "Murder District Headman and 13 followers," – SNP 7/1887/1909, NAK; also G.N. Barclay, "Yola Provincial Report for the Quarter Ended March 31, 1909," Yolaprof A8, NAK.

190. G.N. Barclay, "Yola Provincial Report No. 10 for August 1902," op. cit. G.N. Barclay, "Yola Provincial Report for December 1904," op. cit.

191. J.A. Burdon, "Sokoto Provincial Report for July and August 1905," op. cit.; also J.A. Burdon, "Sokoto Provincial Report for the Months of September and

October 1905," op. cit.; and W.S. Sharpe, "Yola Provincial Report for the March Quarter 1910," op. cit.

192. G.N. Barclay, "Yola Provincial Report for December 1902," op. cit.

193. Ibid.

194. Ibid.

195. Ibid.

196. Ibid.

197. Ibid., Lugard's Comments.

198. "Sokoto Report No. 29", op. cit., Lugard's Comments.

199. G.N. Barclay, "Yola Provincial Report for August, 1904," Yolaprof Vol.5, NAK.

200. Ibid.

201. "Yola Report for October 1904," op. cit.

202. "Yola Provincial Annual Report for 1907," op. cit.

203. "Yola Provincial Report for the March Quarter 1910," op. cit.

204. E.J. Arnett, "Sokoto Provincial Annual Report for 1913," op. cit.

205. Ibid.

206. P.M. Dwyer, "Ilorin Report for July 1900," op. cit.

207. See Chapter 3.

208. C.L. Temple, "Bauchi Provincial Report No. 2 for March 1902," op. cit.

209. Ibid.

210. G.N. Barclay, "Yola Provincial Annual Report for 1904," op. cit. See also Confidential Reports on Chiefs, Kano Province 1919, unclassified, AHAK.

211. W.S. Sharpe, "Yola Provincial Annual Report for 1910," op. cit.

212. I am discussing the role of the Emirs in the judicial system here rather than earlier on in the chapter, because I want to emphasize the relegation of the Emirs to the background and the usurpation of their precolonial position by the Residents and the High Commissioner.

213. P.M. Dwyer to Lugard 24/10/1900, op. cit.

214. Ibid.

215. "Yola Provincial Report No. 8," op. cit., Lugard's Comments.

216. W.P. Hewby, "Bornu Provincial Monthly Report for December 1902," op. cit.

217. Resident Zaria to SNP Confidential Letter, dated 30 October 1908, SNP 116/1908, NAK.

218. Resident Kontagora to Governor Northern Nigeria, Confidential Letter dated 26 November 1908, SNP 116/1909, NAK.

219. Ibid.

220. Resident Zaria to SNP Confidential letter, dated 30 October 1908, op. cit.

221. Resident Sokoto to SNP Letter, dated 12 April, 1915, included among Annual Confidential Reports on Chiefs, Sokoto Province, unclassified, AHAK.

222. G.W. Webster, "Yola Provincial Quarterly Report for March 1913," Yolaprof A15, NAK. For the purely formal nature of the functions of the Emir's Courts see "Sokoto Provincial Annual Report for 1912," op. cit.

223. See Chapter 6 sub-section on "Provincial Courts," page 194.

224. Sokoto Provincial Report 2/1903, op. cit. See also H.E. the Governor to the Resident Bauchi Province, Confidential Letter, dated 15/1/09, SNP 17/1909, NAK.

225. Teleg. Secretary, Zungeru to Resident Zaria, dated 3 August 1908, SNP 116/1908, NAK.

226. Teleg Resident Zaria to SNP Zungeru, dated 4 August 1908, SNP 116/1908, NAK.

227. H.S. Goldsmith, "Zaria Provincial Report No. 64 for Quarter Ended December 31, 1914," op. cit.

228. Ibid.; Governor's Comments.

229. W.P. Hewby, "Bornu Provincial Annual Report for 1906," op. cit.

230. H.O. Howard, "Report on Bauchi Province for March Quarter 1908," op. cit. See also J.M. Fremantle, "Annual Report for Yola Province for 1907," op. cit.; W.S. Sharpe, "Yola Report No. 74 for Quarter Ended 31 March 1912," op. cit.; and Webster, "Yola Provincial Report for March 1913," Yolaprof A15, NAK.

231. G.W. Webster, "Yola Provincial Annual Report for 1912," Yolaprof A14, NAK,. Governor's Comments on.

232. G.W. Webster, "Yola Provincial Quarterly Report for June 1911," op. cit.; also see Chapter 5, for relations between District Head Gurin and Qadi Gurin, page 165.

233. F.H. Ruxton, "Bornu Provincial Annual Report for 1914," SNP 10 No. 169/15, NAK.

234. H.S. Goldsmith, "Sokoto Report No. 30 for the Quarter Ended June 30, 1906," op. cit.; also "Yola Provincial Annual Report for 1910," op. cit.

235. C.L. Temple, "Sokoto Provincial Report No. 33 for Quarter Ended March 31, 1907," op. cit.

236. W. F Gowers, "Annual Report on the Bauchi Province for the Year 1907", SNP 7 No. 889/1908. op. cit.; also Bornu Quarterly Report for December 1911", op. cit.

237. C.O Migeod, "Zaria Provincial Annual Report for 1915", op. cit.

238. W.S Sharpe, "Yola Provincial Annual Report No. 63 for 1909", also J. Withers Gill, "Zaria Provincial Annual Report for 1910, SNP 7 No. 950/1911, NAK.

239. G.W. Webster, "Yola Provincial Report No. 77 for Quarter Ended 31 December 1912", op. cit.

Chapter 7

1. G.N. Barclay, "Yola Provincial Report for the Month of January 1904," Yolaprof A4, NAK.

2. See, for example, the list of precolonial taxes supposedly collected by some of the Emirs in W.F. Gowers, "Yola Provincial Report No.22 for August 1903," Yolaprof A3, NAK; also Lugard to Secretary of State, dated May 18, 1903, accompanying

the "Local Revenue Proclamation of 1903," drafted by Attorney General Bernard A. Platt in SNP 7/1281/1903, NAK.

3.   See, for example, Lugard's speech at the installation of Sultan Attahiru at Sokoto on 21 March 1093, in A.H.M. Kirk-Greene (ed), *The Principles of Native Administration in Nigeria: Selected Documents 1900–1947,* OUP 1965, pp.43–44.

4.   F.H. Ruxton, "Yola Report No.5 for February 1902," Yolaprof A1, NAK.

5.   Ibid.

6.   Ibid.

7.   Ibid.

8.   G.N Barclay, "Yola Provincial Report No.8 for June 1902," Yolaprof A1, NAK.

9.   Ibid.

10.   Ibid.

11.   Ibid. Similarly, though much, another British Resident, Temple, justified the imposition of these taxes on the convenient ground that historically "all authority of native over native and all recognition of authority by natives [was] based on collection and payment of some kind of material tribute, i.e. rents, taxes or presents, and that for that reason the only way to make the authority of Emirs, District Heads and Village Heads over the native population continually effective was to ensure that "taxes [were] regularly collected; paid and accounted for." See C.L. Temple, "Kano Provincial Report for the Half-Year Ended 30 June 1909," SNP 7/10 No.3635, NAK.

12.   "Yola Provincial Report No.8," op. cit.

13.   Ibid.

14.   Ibid.

15.   Ibid.

16.   C.N. Barclay, "Yola Report No.14 for December 1902," Yolaprof Vol. I, NAK.

17.   Ibid.

18.   G.N. Barclay, "Yola Provincial Report No.16 for February 1903," Yolaprof A1, NAK.

19.   Ibid.

20.   W.F. Gowers, "Yola Provincial Report No.24 for October 1903," Yolaprof A3, NAK. In the meantime, the British had five months earlier, in May 1903, enacted a "Proclamation to Enforce a Contribution by Chiefs" otherwise cited as "Land Revenue Proclamation, 1903." It was this proclamation that Lugard claims provided a "theoretical basis" for taxation and it was its enactment that, according to him, set his "Administration" a notch or two higher on the scale of European civilization than the colonial "Administrations" of other "nations of Europe (Germany, France and Portugal) [which] have sought no theoretical basis for the extremely onerous taxes they have imposed in Africa." It also made the imposition of his taxation holier than "the imposition of the Sierra Leone hut tax upon tribes who had hardly made a submission." It is interesting that, in spite of this moral humbug and in contradistinction to some of his own Residents, Gowers for example, Lugard did not claim that this tax was imposed for "benefits conferred"

on the indigenous population by British conquest. Instead, as in his speech at the installation of Sultan Attahiru two months earlier at Sokoto, Lugard forthrightly based the imposition of this tax "on the right of conquest, a term which in [his] view include[d] the cases in which submission [had] been made without actual fighting in the face of superior force, a term which [he said] may not inaptly be termed 'potential conquest.'" See Lugard's covering letter to Secretary of State, dated 18/5/1903, op. cit.

21. "Yola Provincial Report for January 1904," op. cit.
22. G.N. Barclay, "Yola Provincial Report for October 1904 and G.N. Barclay, "Yola Provincial Report for November 1904," both in Yolaprof A5, NAK; also Lugard to Secretary of State, op. cit.
23. G.N. Barclay, "Yola Provincial Annual Report for 1904," Yolaprof A5, NAK.
24. Ibid.
25. J. Cochrane, "Bornu Provincial Monthly Report for May 1902," SNP 15/1 No.19, NAK.
26. W.P. Hewby, "Bornu Provincial Monthly Report for November 1902," SNP 15/1, No.19, NAK.
27. W.P. Hewby, "Bornu Provincial Monthly Reports for September, October, November and December 1903," SNP 15/1 No.48A, NAK.
28. Ibid.
29. Ibid.
30. Ibid.
31. Ibid.
32. Ibid.
33. W.P. Hewby, "Bornu Provincial Monthly Report for May 1904," SNP 15/1 No.48A, NAK.
34. Ibid.
35. Ibid.
36. C.N. Ubah, *Administration of Kano Emirate Under the British 1900–1930,* unpublished Ph.D thesis, Ibadan, 1973, p.526.
37. C.L. Temple, "Kano Provincial Report for the Half-Year Ended 30 June 1909," op. cit. On this point, even such a seasoned writer as Professor Ikime was taken in by the clauses of British Proclamations, which he accepted rather uncritically. Thus, he repeats the claim of the Native Revenue Proclamation, 1906, that only tribute, Kurdin Sarauta, Gaisuwa and Jangali were recognized," though he points out in a footnote that he was not quite clear which of the precolonial taxes now went to make up "tribute." See Obaro Ikime, "The British and Native Administration Finance in 'Northern Nigeria' 1900–1920," unpublished seminar paper.
38. "Kano Provincial Report for the Half-Year Ended 30 June 1909," op. cit.
39. Ibid.
40. Ibid.
41. Ibid.
42. Ibid.

43. Ibid.

44. Ibid.

45. Ibid.

46. Ibid. Governor's Comment.

47. C.N. Ubah, op. cit., pp.98–102.

48. C.L. Temple, *Native Races and their Rulers*, London, 1968, pp.103–122.

49. See R.A. Adeleye, "The Dilemma of the Wazir: The Place of the *Risalat at Wazir ila ahl al-ilm wa'l – tadabbur* in the History of the Conquest of the Sokoto Caliphate," *JHSN*, IV, No.2, 1968.

50. "Kano Provincial Report for the Half-Year Ended 30 June 1909," op. cit.

51. See Chapter 8, page 261–3.

52. J.A. Burdon, "Sokoto Report No.2/1903 for April 1903," Sokprof 23/1903, NAK.

53. Ibid.

54. Ibid.

55. Ibid.

56. H.R.P. Hillary, "Sokoto Report No.22 for January 1905," Sokprof No.401/1905; NAK.

57. On this, too, Professor Ikime has been taken in by Lugard's bogus claims. Thus, he observes that "one of the major aims of the enactment [The Land Revenue Proclamation of 1906] was to reduce corruption *and the incidence of tax on the peasantry*" See Obaro Ikime, op. cit., p.6.

58. W.F. Gowers, "Yola Report No.17 for March 1903," Yolaprof Vol.II, NAK.

59. See for example C.L. Temple, "Half-Yearly Report for Kano for June 1909," op. cit.

60. E.A. Brakenbury, "Namtari District: Report on Assessment, 1910–11," Yolaprof G2W, NAK.

61. E.J. Arnett, "Kano Province, Annual Report for 1911," SNP 7 No.1114/1912, NAK.

62. E.A. Brackenbury, "Report on the Reassessment of Namtari District, 1916," Yolaprof G2W, NAK.

63. C.L. Temple, "Kano Half-Yearly Report for June 1909," op. cit.

64. This will be dealt with in more detail in Chapters 7 and 8 on the effects of British taxation on the native economy.

65. J.A. Burdon, "Sokoto Report for April and May 1905," Sokprof 315/1905, NAK.

66. J.M. Fremantle, "Report on the Yola Province for the June Quarter 1907," SNP 7 No.3/68/1907, NAK.

67. S. Withers Gill, "Zaria Emirate: Taxation and Industrial Organization of the Hausa Towns," dated May 1909, in SNP 7 No.4252/1909, NAK.

68. Ibid.

69. Ibid.

70. W.F. Gowers, "Yola Report No.17 for March 1903," op. cit.

71. G.N. Barclay, "Yola Report for January 1904," op. cit.

72. "Sokoto Report for April and May 1905," op. cit.
73. Ibid.
74. Ibid.
75. Ibid.
76. "Sokoto Report for April and May 1905," op. cit.
77. J.A. Burdon, "Sokoto Provincial Report for November and December 1905," Sokprof No.85/1906, NAK.
78. Ibid.
79. Ibid.
80. J. Withers Gill, "Zaria Provincial Annual Report for 1910" SNP 7 No.950/1911, NAK; also J. Withers Gill, "Zaria Emirate: Taxation and Industrial Organisation of the Hausa Towns," op. cit.
81. "Zaria Provincial Annual Report for 1910," op. cit.
82. J.M. Fremantle, "Yola Provincial Annual Report for 1907," op. cit.
83. G.N. Barclay, "Yola Report for Quarter Ended June 30, 1909," Yolaprof Vol.9, NAK.
84. Ibid.
85. "Sokoto Provincial Report for November and December 1905," op. cit.
86. W.F. Gowers, "Report on the Bauchi Province for the September Quarter, 1907," SNP 7 No.4455/1907, NAK; also W.S. Sharpe "Yola Provincial Annual Report for 1910," Yolaprof Vol.1 A9, NAK. For a detailed discussion of the *zakat* on animals see among others the *Risalah* of Abu Muhammad Abd Allah b. Abi Zayd al-Qairawani.
87. H.R.P. Hillary, "Sokoto Report No.22 for January 1905," op. cit.
88. W.S. Sharpe, "Yola Provincial Annual Report for 1910," op. cit.
89. W.P. Hewby, "Bornu Provincial Monthly Report for May, 1904," op. cit.
90. W.F. Gowers, "Bauchi Provincial Report for the September Quarter 1907," Governor's Comments, SNP 7 No.4455/1907, NAK.
91. Ibid.
92. W.P. Hewby, "Bornu Provincial Monthly Report for September 1903," op. cit.
93. J.A. Burdon, "Sokoto Report for July and August, 1905," Sokprof No.575/1905, NAK.
94. Ibid.
95. H.S. Goldsmith, "Sokoto Provincial Annual Report No.3," Sokprof No.86/1907, NAK.
96. Ibid.
97. C.L. Temple, "Sokoto Provincial Report for Quarter Ended December 31, 1907," Sokprof No.1453/1908, NAK.
98. Ibid.
99. "Half-Yearly Report for Kano for June 1909," op. cit.
100. G.W. Webster, "Quarterly Report for June 1911," Yolaprof Vol.10, NAK.
101. Ibid.
102. AMD, Kano, 26/5/1974.

103. G.N. Barclay, "Yola Report No.8 June 1902," op. cit.; also F.D. Lugard, *Northern Nigeria Annual Reports, 1900–1913*, London, 19 p.16.

104. J.A. Burdon, "Sokoto Report for April 1903," op. cit.; also F.D. Lugard, op. cit.

105. "Yola Report for January 1904," op. cit.; also Barclay, "Yola Report for June 1904," Yolaprof Vol.IV, NAK.

106. "Yola Report for June 1904," op. cit. also "Yola Report for November 1904," op. cit.

107. This list was compiled from virtually all the files used in this chapter rather than from one or even a few of them.

108. W.F. Gowers, "Yola Report No.20 for June 1903," Yolaprof Vol.III, NAK.

109. J.A. Burdon, "Sokoto Report for September and October 1905," Sokprof 756/1905, NAK.

110. "Yola Report for November 1904," op. cit.

111. "Yola Report No.17 March 1903, op. cit.

112. "Sokoto Report for July and August 1905," op. cit.

113. W.F. Gowers, "Yola Report No.20 for June 1903," op. cit.; also Gowers, "Yola Report No.21 for July 1903," Yolaprof Vol.3, NAK.

114. Sokoto Report for July and August 1905," op. cit.

115. Ibid.

116. "Sokoto Annual Report No.3 for 1906," op. cit.

117. "Yola Report for January 1904," op.cit; also "Yola Report for June 1904," op. cit.

118. "Sokoto Report for April 1903," op. cit.

119. Ibid.

120. "Sokoto Report for April 1903," op. cit.

121. Ibid.

122. "Yola Report for January 1904," op. cit.

123. Ibid.

124. Ibid.

125. Ibid.

126. Ibid.

127. "Sokoto Report for July and August 1905," op. cit.; see also C.W. Orr, "Zaria Provincial Annual Report for 1905," Zaria prof No.2552, NAK.

128. Wallace to the Earl Elgin, dated 28/2/1907, SNP 7/1630/1907, NAK.

129. Ibid.

130. P.M. Dwyer, "Report on the Ilorin Province for the Quarter Ended March 31, 1907," SNP 7/1569/1907.

131. Ibid.

132. Ibid.

133. "Sokoto Report No.2 for April 1903," op. cit.

134. Ibid.

135. Ibid.

136. Ibid.

137. "Sokoto Report No.2 for April 1903," op. cit.

138. Ibid.

139. Ibid.

140. C.W. Orr, "Zaria Provincial Annual Report for 1905," op. cit.

141. "Sokoto Report No.2 for April 1903," op. cit.

142. See Shehu Uthman's *Kitab al-Farq*.

143. "Yola Report No.21 for July 1903," op. cit.

144. "Sokoto Report No.2 for April 1903," op. cit.

145. Ibid.

146. Ibid.

147. Ibid.

148. W.S. Sharpe, "Yola Report No.84 for the March 1914 Quarter," Yolaprof Vol. XVII, NAK.

149. F.H. Ruxton, "Yola Report No.5 for February 1902," Yolaprof Vol.I, NAK.

150. "Yola Report No.14 for December 1902," op. cit.

151. Ibid.

152. Ibid.

153. Ibid.

154. "Yola Report No.21 for July 1903," op. cit.

155. "Yola Report No.22 for August 1903," op. cit.

156. Ibid.

157. Ibid.

158. Ibid.

159. "Yola Report No.24 for October 1903," op. cit.

160. Ibid.

161. C.W. Orr, "Zaria Provincial Annual Report for 1904," Zariaprof No.2551, NAK.

162. Ibid.

163. Ibid.

164. C.W. Orr, "Sokoto Report for January and February 1904," Sokprof No.5/1904, NAK.

165. Ibid.

166. Ibid.

167. Ibid.

168. "Sokoto Report for July and August 1905," op. cit.

169. Ibid.

170. Ibid.

171. "Sokoto Report for July and August 1905," op. cit.

172. "Sokoto Report for July and August 1905," op. cit.

173. "Sokoto Report for September and October 1905," op. cit.

174. Ibid.

175. "Sokoto Report for November and December 1905," op. cit.

176. Ibid.

177. Ibid. Similarly, in 1907, Resident Arthur Festing in Kano reports that "as regards sanitation and other progress in Kano town, itself [i.e as opposed to the European

station] I regret I have little to report but this I look upon as a matter of time nor do I see so long as we continue to make such large calls for labour and transport that we can well expect the people to do much in other respects …" Punctuation as in the original; Arthur Festing, "Report on the Kano Province for the Months of September, October and November 1907 (Handing Over Notes), SNP 7 No.5112/1907, NAK]. This was both a revelation of the lack of importance that the British attached to the welfare of the indigenous population and an admission of the great magnitude of demand made on the labour time of that population.

178. "See Zaria Provincial Annual Report for 1910," op. cit.

179. Ibid.

180. Ibid.

181. Ibid.

182. Ibid.

183. Ibid.

184. Ibid.

185. J.M. Fremantle, "Zaria Provincial Annual Report for 1913," SNP 10 No.107P/1914, NAK.

186. Ibid.

187. Ibid.

188. Ibid. (Emphasis mine).

189. C.O. Migeod, "Zaria Provincial Report for the June Quarter 1914," SNP 10 No.410P/1914, NAK.

190. Ibid.

191. Ibid.

192. Ibid.

193. C.O. Migeod, "Zaria Provincial Report No.63 for the September Quarter, 1914," SNP 10 No.597P/1914, NAK.

194. Ibid.

195. Ibid.

196. J.A. Burdon, "Report No.29 for Quarter Ended March 31, 1906," Sokprof 578/1906, NAK.

Chapter 8

1.   G.N. Barclay, "Yola Report No. 8 June, 1902," Yolaprof Vol.I, NAK.

2.   Ibid.

3.   W.F. Gowers, "Yola Report No.17 for March 1903," Yolaprof Vol. I, NAK.

4.   "Yola Report No.8, June 1902," op. cit.

5.   Arthur Festing, "Kano Report No.35 for 1907" SNP 15/378, NAK.

6.   This fact contrasted with the claim prevalent in Western writings on the subject that "a British resident was stationed in each Emir's court, but he interfered only

to a minimal degree, unless he happened to be an enthusiast, as SOMETIMES occurred" [Emphasis mine], John Hatch, *Nigeria: A History,* London, 1971, p.153.

7. W.F. Gowers, "Yola Report No.22 for August 1903, Yolaprof Vol. III, NAK.

8. G.N. Barclay, "Yola Province, Annual Report for 1904," Yolaprof Vol. V, NAK.

9. J.A. Burdon, "Sokoto Report for November and December 1905," Sokprof No.85/1906, NAK. Also W.S. Sharpe, "Yola Report No.65 for the Quarter Ended June 20th 1910," Yolaprof Vol. IX, NAK.

10. Blackeney, "Bauchi Report No.19 for November 1904," SNP 10 No.62, NAK. It is interesting that, Margery Perham, who, perhaps more than any other writer besides Lugard himself, helped to popularize the myth of "Indirect Rule" implicitly and probably absent-mindedly admits the tremendous involvement of British officers in the assessment of the Kurdin Kasa and the Jangali when she states that

> "the assessment by the small political staff in a country so large and so little explored was a formidable piece of work. In the course of two or three years they visited and reported upon almost every town and village except those of the pagans in the hills or outlying regions. Assessment reports soon became something more than their name implied. They took on the character of general investigations which went far beyond questions of taxability into those of history and ethnology, and gave an opportunity to young officers to show their ability and their understanding of the people," See Margery Perham, *Native Administration in Nigeria*, London, 1962, p.54.

So also does Robert Heussler, another propagator of the myth of "Indirect rule" admit that

> "Assessment was much more than a census. Before anything of practical effect could be done, whether on indigenous or European lines, the British had to have not only the basic demographic, economic and linguistic facts in each area but down-to-earth grasp of how society held together ... whether or not one had an anthropological bent, the day was full of learning, gathering facts, sorting out apparent contradictions, and discovering in the course of hard knocks what could and could not be done and at what cost," See Robert Heussler, *The British in Northern Nigeria*, OUP, 1968, p.30.

On the other hand, as if to re-establish the validity of the myth of "Indirect Rule," Heussler goes on to claim that

> "in some places the Protectorate made very little real difference at first. Larymore and the Emir of Hadejia met each other in 1904 much as too brother potentates do ... greetings were exchanged. The Emir accompanied the Englishman seven miles out on his way to Kano. Larymore asked that the *mallams* pray to Allah for his safe journey. Europe then disappeared over the horizon and Hadejia relapsed again to virtually complete independence."

Nor was this "virtual independence" peculiar to Hadeija, for "in Borgu it was much the same, a tour of inspection rather than the hand of government reaching out to grip local society." Indeed, even "in some areas with permanent European staffs in residence there was a tendency to let the local Fulani manage things perhaps aided by the clerks ... Tomlinson, on tour through Sokoto Province in 1907, remarked blandly '... in a country so vast as this we do not pretend to do much in the nature of direct government but, whenever we can, we do employ native administration'" (Ibid., pp.32–33).

11. "Sokoto Report for November and December 1905," op. cit.; "Yola Report No.65 for June 1910," op. cit.

12. K.V. Elphinstone, "Yola Report for December 1904," Yolaprof Vol. V, NAK, also according to those who believed in the reality of "Indirect Rule," it was rule "through the Emirs ... The authority of the Emir and the Native Court was *quietly* but firmly supported... The very title "Resident" emphasized the self-effacement required of the British adviser..." See Hogben and Kirk-Greene, *The Emirates of Northern Nigeria*, OUP, 1966, pp.132–33. According to A.N. Cook "the Emirs, Chiefs, native councils, native courts and native police were built up as active forces in the life of the people. European influence was brought to bear on the native *through* his chiefs and not through European staff (Arthur Norton Cook, *British Enterprise in Nigeria,* Frank Cass, 1964, p.178). In fact, Cook does admit that this "self-effacement" did not hold for the "early days" of British colonial domination over the emirates, but only in the years after 1906, a date which falls far short of 1915, by which date the British, rather than the Emirs, were actively engaged in the assessment and collection of taxes.

13. "Yola Report for December 1904," op. cit.

14. In this regard Margery Perham was correct in claiming that under "Indirect Rule" "Chieftainship acted as a shock absorber. It took the impact [of popular reaction against British measures] from the new rulers, and ... distributed its effects among the components of the tribal society." See Introduction to Lord Lugard, *The Dual Mandate in British Tropical Africa*, Fifth Edition, p. xliv.

15. H.O. Howard, "Bauchi Report No.27 for January, February and March 1906," SNP 10 No.127, NAK.

16. J.E. Arnett, "Report on the Zaria Province for the Quarter Ended 31 March 1906," SNP 7/4635/1906, NAK.

17. H.S. Goldsmith, "Sokoto Report No.32 for the Quarter Ended December 1906," Sokprof No.50/1907, NAK.

18. Ibid.; also Burdon, "Sokoto Report No.29 for quarter Ended 31 March 1906," Sokprof 578/1906, NAK.

19. Ibid.

20. C.L. Temple, "Sokoto Report No.33 for the Quarter Ended 31 March 1907," Sokprof 343/1907, NAK.

21. Ibid.

22. Ibid.

23. Temple, "Sokoto Report No.34 for the Quarter Ended 30 June 1907," Sokprof No.610/1907, NAK.
24. Ibid.
25. Temple, "Sokoto Report for the Quarter Ended 31 December 1907," Sokprof 1453/1908, NAK.
26. Ibid.
27. "Sokoto Report for Quarter Ended 31 December 1907," op. cit.
28. Ibid.
29. C.L. Temple, "Kano Provincial Half Yearly Report for June 1909," SNP 7/10, No.3635, NAK.
30. Ibid.
31. Ibid.
32. Lugard, "Northern Nigeria, Annual Reports, 1900–13, p.20.
33. See for example, Barclay, "Yola Report for October 1904," Yolaprof Vol. V, NAK. Also Barclay, "Yola Report for November 1904," Yolaprof Vol. V, NAK.
34. "Sokoto Report for November and December 1905," op. cit.
35. "Sokoto Report for September and October 1905," op. cit.
36. Ibid.
37. "Sokoto Report for September and October 1905, op. cit.
38. Misc. "Tofa Patrol: Patrol in the Madawaki's District, Kano Province," SNP 7/1974/1908, NAK.
39. G. Malcolm, "Sokoto Divisional Report No.1 for half Year Ended 30 June 30 1909," Sokprof Nov.78/1909, NAK.
40. W.S. Sharpe, "Yola Report No.62 for the Quarter Ended 31 December 1909," Yolaprof Vol.VIII, NAK.
41. W.S. Sharpe, "Yola Report No.62 for the Quarter Ended 31 December 1909," op. cit.
42. G.W. Webster, "Yola Report for the Quarter Ended 31 March 1911," Yolaprof Vol. X, NAK.
43. Ibid.
44. W.S. Sharpe, "Quarterly Report No.74 for the Quarter Ended 31 March 1912, Yolaprof Vol. XII, NAK.
45. Ibid.
46. Morgan, "Killankwa Patrol November 1912," Minnaprof 673/12, NAK.
47. "Annual Reports on Chiefs, Nassarawa Province 1916," unclassified, AHAK.
48. G.W. Webster, "Yola Report No.77 for Quarter Ended 31 December 1912," Yolaprof Vol. XII, NAK.
49. Ibid.
50. Ibid.
51. Sharpe, "Yola Report for the March 1914 Quarter," Yolaprof XVII, NAK.
52. Ibid.
53. W.P. Hewby, "Bornu Provincial Monthly Report for November 1902," SNP 15/1/19, NAK.

54. H.Hewby, "Bornu Provincial Report for October 1903," SNP 15/1/48A, NAK.
55. W.P. Hewby, "Bornu Provincial Monthly Report for November and December 1903," SNP 15/1/48A, NAK.
56. Ibid.
57. Hewby, "Bornu Provincial Monthly Report for January 1904," SNP 15/1/89, NAK.
58. Ibid.
59. Hewby, "Bornu Provincial Report for September 1904," SNP 15/1 No.48A, NAK.
60. Hewby, "Bornu Provincial Report for October, November and December 1904," SNP 15/1 No.48A, NAK.
61. Hewby, "Bornu Provincial Monthly Report for January and March 1903," SNP 15/1/48A, NAK.
62. G.J. Lethem, "The Shuwa Arabs," SNP 15 No.CC0020, NAK.
63. Hewby, "Bornu Provincial Annual Report for 1906," SNP 1756/1907, NAK.
64. Hewby, "Bornu Provincial Annual Report for 1905," SNP 10/1815/1905, H.R. Palmer, "Report on the Shuwa Patrol," SNP 15 No.CC0020, NAK.
65. "The Shuwa Patrol," op. cit. Also W.B. Thompson, "Bornu Provincial Annual Report for 1913," SNP 10/No.95/1914, NAK.
66. Ibid.
67. "The Shuwa Patrol," op. cit.; Thomson, "Bornu Provincial Annual Report for 1913," op. cit.
68. "Confidential Annual Reports on Chiefs for Bornu Province," unclassified, AHAK.
69. "The Shuwa Patrol," op. cit. also Hewby, "Bornu Provincial Annual Repoort for 1912," SNP 7/626/1913, NAK.
70. "The Shuwa Patrol," op. cit.
71. Ibid.
72. See Chapter 10, section on "Ousting the Maria Theresa Dollar..." page 300–3.
73. F.H. Ruxton, "Bornu Provincial Annual Report for 1914," SNP 10 No.169p/1915, NAK.
74. "Yola Quarterly Report for Quarter Ended 31 March 1912," op. cit.
75. Barclay, "Yola Report No.48 for the Quarter Ended 30 June 1906," Yolaprof Vols.VI and VII, NAK.
76. "Bauchi Report No.19", op. cit.
77. Howard, "Bauchi Report No.27," op. cit.
78. Ibid.
79. Ibid.
80. W.S. Sharpe, "Report on the Kontagora Province for the Quarter Ended 31 December 1906," SNP 7/4637/1906, NAK.
81. Ibid.
82. Ibid.
83. H.S. Goldsmith, "Report No.30 for the Quarter Ended 30 June 1906," Sokprof No.625/1906, NAK.

84. Ibid.

85. Sharpe, "Yola Report No.62 for Quarter Ended 31 December 1909," Yolaprof vol. VIII, NAK.

86. Ibid.

87. Sharpe, "Yola Report No.62 for Quarter Ended 31st December 1909," op. cit. Also Teleg. Hewby to High commissioner dated 15th July 1907," SNP 7/2958/1907, NAK.

88. Barclay, "Yola Report No.14 for December 1902," Yolaprof Vol. I, NAK.

89. "Yola Report No.62 for Quarter Ended 31st December 1909," op. cit.

90. Ibid.

91. Sharpe, "Yola Annual Report for 1910," Yolaprof Vol. IX.

92. Ibid.

93. Webster to Lugard, dated 21/6/1911, Yolaprof Vol. IX, NAK.

94. Ibid.

95. Sharpe, "Yola Annual Report for 1911," Yolaprof Vol. X, NAK.

96. Sharpe, "Yola Quarterly Report No.34 for Quarter Ended 31 March 1902," Yolaprof Vol. XII.

Chapter 9

1. See, for example, M. Perham, *Native Administration in Northern Nigeria* (London, 1962), pp.51–3 and 64. But, whereas Margery Perham would emphasize the "inability" of the emirates to "pay their way" as it were, Robert Heussler comes very near to admitting that the emirates were not such a financial "burden" on the Imperial Government when he states that "although subventions from London increased in the first few years, it was clear that the Protectorate's development would be geared in the long run to its own wealth... Zungeru's hand was strengthened in 1903 by the imposing of caravan tolls and thereafter by taking fixed percentages of chiefs' taxes and gradually exercising more supervision over their own shares" See Robert Heussler, *The British in Northern Nigeria*, OUP, 1968, p.31.

2. W.S. Sharpe, "Yola Quarterly Report No.74 for the Quarter Ended 31 March 1912," Yolaprof Vol. XII, NAK.

3. Ibid.

4. For example, see M. Perham, op. cit., pp.51–3 and 64.

5. See Chapter 11.

6. C.L. Temple, "Kano Provincial Annual Report for 1909," SP 7/10 No.6415/1909, NAK; J. Withers Gill, "Zaria Provincial Annual Report for 1910," SNP 7 No.950/1911, NAK. G.W. Webster, "Yola Provincial Quarterly Report for June 1911," Yolaprof A10, NAK; W.P. Hewby, "Bornu Provincial Annual Report for 1912," SNP 7 No.626/1913, NAK; F.B. Gall, "Bauchi Provincial Annual Report for 1914," SNP 10 No.168P/1915, NAK; G. Malcolm, "Sokoto Provincial Annual

Report for 1912," Sokprof No.152/1913, NAK; C.L. Temple, "Kano Provincial Annual Report for 1910," SNP 7 No.951/1911, NAK.

7.   WJ, Sokoto, 26/4/1974; AJ, Maiduguri, 27/11/1973; MY, Yola 2/1/1970, AMD, Kano, 18/5/1974. According to Waziri Junaidu it was the duty of the Sultan to provide newly arrived Mallams with houses for themselves and the most important of their students as well as to maintain those houses, even to the point of sending repairers to see them after every stormy rain. He also shared out a substantial portion of his salary among such Mallams. Among Mallams who were so maintained were the Waziri's own former teachers, Modibbo Abubakar Bube, and Alfa Nuhu, an immigrant from Masina in Mali; and in Yola one of the Emirs, Maigari (1924–1928) adopted the custom of having a bugle blown around 2:30 pm every afternoon to summon all who wanted to come and eat or collect food.

8.   Ibid.

9.   "Kano Annual Report for 1909," op. cit.

10.   Ibid.

11.   It should, however, be pointed out that the repairs to these houses as well as to the houses of District Heads were undertaken with unpaid labour extracted from the peasantry, a practice which seems to have been carried over from nineteenth century emirates when the Emirs' house and those of emirate officials were maintained by communal labour. See M.B. Alkali, *A Hausa Community in Crisis: Kebbi in the Nineteenth Century,* M.A. 1969, p.214.

12.   See Chapter 6.

13.   "Kano Annual Report for 1909," op. cit.; "Zaria Provincial Annual Report for 1910," op. cit.; "Yola Provincial Quarterly Report for June 1911," op. cit.; "Bornu Provincial Annual Report for 1912," op. cit.; "Bauchi Provincial Annual Report for 1914," op. cit.; "Sokoto Provincial Annual Report for 1912" op. cit.; "Kano Provincial Annual Report for 1910," op. cit.

14.   Thus, according to Temple in Kano "the funds [were] entirely controlled by the Emir and his Council and accounted for by the Beit el-Mal officials. We are merely supervising and giving him advice." See C.L. Temple, "Kano Provincial Report for Half-Year Ended June 1909," SNP 7/10 No.3635, NAK.

15.   In fact, direct British control of the Native Treasuries continued throughout the period of British colonial domination, the custom later on being to designate a whole officer in charge of the Treasury with his desk right inside the Treasury and performing no other duties apart from controlling the Treasury. This was the "D.O. Office" (AAGG, Sokoto, 30/4/74; ABDD Kano, 28/5/74).

16.   J.C.P. Sciortino, "Bornu Provincial Report for the September Quarter 1911," SNP 7/5776/1911, NAK.

17.   H.B. Bryan, "Yola Provincial Report for the Quarter Ended 30th September 1911," Yolaprof A10, NAK.

18.   W.F. Gowers, "Kano Provincial Annual Report for 1913," SNP 98P/1914, NAK.

19.   Ibid.

20. J.M. Fremantle, "Zaria Provincial Annual Report for 1913," SNP 10, No.107P/1914, NAK.

21. Ibid.

22. F.H. Ruxton, "Bornu Provincial Annual Report for 1914," SNP 10, No.169P/1915, NAK.

23. H.R. Palmer "Kano Provincial Annual Report for 1915," SNP 10 No.170P/1916, NAK.

24. Ibid.

25. Significantly to this information the Governor retorted "I do not understand this; the Emir has not voluntarily surrendered anything. By the special terms of his letter of appointment he accepted office on the condition that he should be to all intents and purposes a salaried officer of the Crown, and he no more surrenders the Kurdin Sarauta and the Ujera than he surrenders the hoe tax or any other form of contribution by the people." See J. Withers Gill, "Zaria Provincial Annual Report for 1910," op. cit.

26. "Yola Provincial Report No. 74 for quarter Ended 31st March 1912," op. cit.

27. "Kano Provincial Annual Report for 1913," op. cit.

28. Ibid.

29. H.R. Palmer, "Kano Provincial Annual Report for 1915," SNP 10 No.170P/1916, NAK.

30. J.M. Fremantle, "Zaria Provincial Annual Report for 1913," op. cit.

31. Ibid.

32. Ibid.

33. Ibid.

34. Ibid.

35. "Kano Provincial Annual Report for 1909," op. cit.; E.J. Arnett, "Kano Provincial Annual Report for 1911" SNP 7 No.1114/1912, NAK; W.S. Sharpe, "Yola Provincial Annual Report for 1911," Yolaprof A10, NAK; McAllister, Sokoto Provincial Report for September Quarter 1911," SNP 10 No.5572/1911, NAK; G.N. Vertue, "Sokoto Provincial Report for the December Quarter 1911," SNP 10 No.1041/1912, NAK; W.P. Hewby, "Bornu Provincial Annual Report for 1912," SNP 7 No.626/1913, NAK; J.M. Fremantle, "Zaria Provincial Annual Report for 1913," op. cit.; M.P. Porch, "Zaria Provincial Annual Report for 1912," SNP 10 no.178P/1913, NAK.

36. "Kano Provincial Annual Report for 1911," op. cit.

37. Ibid.

38. J.C.P. Sciortino, "Bornu Provincial Report for the December Quarter 1911," Maiprof A40, NAK.

39. K.V. Elphinstone, "Yola Provincial Report No.72 for the Quarter Ended 31 December 1911," Yolaprof A11, NAK; W.S. Sharpe, "Yola Provincial Annual Report for 1911," op. cit.

40. See Chapter 11.

41. "Sokoto Provincial Report for the December Quarter 1911," op. cit.

42. Ibid.

43. "Kano Provincial Annual Report for 1909," op. cit.

44. McAllister, "Sokoto Provincial Report for the September Quarter, 1911," SNP 5572/1911, NAK.

45. "Kano Provincial Annual Report for 1909," op. cit.

46. Thus, once when the Resident Yola reported that the Emir, Bobbo Ahmadu tended to ignore his councillors, Lugard minuted that the Emir should indeed be encouraged in that tendency.

47. "Kano Provincial Annual Report for 1909," op. cit.

48. Ibid.

49. E.J. Arnett, "Kano Provincial Annual Report for 1911," op. cit.

50. G. Malcolm, "Sokoto Provincial Annual Report for 1912," SNP 10 No.152P/1913, NAK.

51. E.J. Arnett, "Sokoto Provincial Annual Report for 1913," SNP 10 No.104P/1914, NAK.

52. F.B. Gall, "Bauchi Provincial Annual Report for 1914," SNP 10 No.168P/1915, NAK.

53. "Kano Provincial Annual Report for 1911," op. cit.

54. "Sokoto Provincial Annual Report for 1912," op. cit.

55. "Sokoto Provincial Annual Report for 1913," op. cit.

56. Confidential Circular No.16/1915, from SNP to All the Residents of the N.P. excepting Muri, dated 30/1/1915 in File No. SNP No.39/15, NAK.

57. Reference of document not properly recorded (CY93-OY, Africana Section, University of Ibadan).

58. Ibid.

59. Ibid.

60. Ibid.

61. "Sokoto Provincial Annual Report for 1916."

62. C.O. Migeod, "Zaria Provincial Report No.64 for the September Quarter 1914," SNP 10 No.597P/1914, NAK.

63. Ibid.

64. Ibid.

65. C.O. Migeod, "Zaria Provincial Annual Report for 1915," SNP 10 No.138P/1916, NAK.

66. Ibid.

67. Ibid.

68. "Bauchi Provincial Annual Report for 1914," op. cit.

69. Letter from Lt. Governor, N.P. to Governor, Nigeria dated 15 March 1915, in File No. SNP No.39/15, NAK.

70. Circular No.16/1915, op. cit.

71. Ibid.

72. Ibid.

73. Ibid.

74. "Sokoto Provincial Annual Report for 1917," Sokprof 155/1918, NAK.

75. Ibid.

76. AAGG, Sokoto, 27/4/1974; ABDD, Kano; 28/5/1974.

77. ABDD, Kano 28/5/1974.

78. AAGG, Sokoto 17/4/1974; ABDD, Kano, 28/5/1974.

Chapter 10

1. W.S. Sharpe, "Quarterly Report No.65 for the Quarter Ended 30 June, 1910," Yolaprof Vol. IX, NAK.

2. G.N. Barclay, "Yola Report for the Quarter Ended June 30, 1909," Yolaprof Vol. IX, NAK. We shall see the influx of these companies in another section of this chapter.

3. Ibid.

4. The Maria Theresa dollar as well as cowries had been introduced into the emirates and Borno by the Niger Company and North African traders fronting for European commercial houses as early as the second half of the nineteenth century and, by the end of the century, had become the dominant currencies of the area, the dollar particularly predominating in Borno, judging by the Provincial Reports.

5. G.N. Barclay, "Yola Report No.14 for December 1902," Yolaprof Vol. I, NAK.

6. Ibid.

7. G.N. Barclay, "Yola Report No.14 for December 1902," op. cit.

8. W.F. Gowers, "Yola Report No.21 for July 1903," Yolaprof Vol. III, NAK.

9. Ibid.

10. Ibid.

11. Ibid.

12. Ibid.

13. Ibid.

14. Ibid.

15. H.R.P. Hillary, "Sokoto Report No.22 for January 1905," Sokprof 401/1905, NAK.

16. C.L. Temple, "Kano Provincial Annual Report for 1909," SNP 7/645/1909, NAK.

17. J.A. Burdon, "Sokoto Report for November and December 1905," Sokprof 85/1906, NAK.

18. C.L. Temple, "Sokoto Report No.33 for the Quarter Ended March 31, 1907," Sokprof 343/1907, NAK.

19. Ibid.

20. J.M. Fremantle, "Yola Annual Report for 1907," Yolaprof Vol.VI & VII, NAK.

21. Ibid.

22. "Kano Annual Report for 1909," op. cit.

23. Sharpe, "Yola Quarterly Report for March 1910," Yolaprof Vol. IX, NAK.

24. Ibid.

25. AIT, Sokoto, 1/5/1974.

26. For statements of this view, see V.I. Lenin, "Imperialism, the Highest Stage of Capitalism" in V.I. Lenin, *Selected Works*, Moscow, 1971, pp.169–263, and K. Nkrumah, *Neo-Colonialism: the Last State of Imperialism* London, 1971, verbatim but especially Chapter One.

27. Lord Lugard, *The Dual Mandate in British Tropical Africa*, London, 1965, pp.48-64.

28. Yolaprof Vol. I, NAK.

29. The export of ivory from Adamawa to Britain had been going on at least since the 1870s. See W.H. Simpson, "Report of the Niger Expedition, 1871" in F.O. 84/1351, quoted in Thomas Hodgkin, *Nigerian Perspectives* (London, 1975, p.359).

30. SNP 15 No.39, NAK.

31. Sokprof 260/1905, NAK.

32. Yolaprof AI, NAK.

33. See Chapter 10, section on "The Precolonial Economy of the Emirates" page 305.

34. "Yola Report for June 1902," op. cit. All other quotes are from the same reports that were used for Chapter 7 for British taxes.

35. I shall deal with the business methods of the Company in the next section of this chapter.

36. Barclay, "Yola Report for November 1904," Yolaprof Vol. V, NAK.

37. Thus, there is no basis whatever for Margery Perham's boast that the imposition of direct British taxation on the population of the emirates acted "as a binding rather than a dissolving force upon the [village] community and its constituent families." See M. Perham, *Native Administration in Northern Nigeria*, London, 1962, p. 53.

38. F.D. Lugard, *Northern Nigeria Annual Reports*, pp. 19–20 and 39.

39. Annual Reports, pp.16 and 39.

40. Pedler, F., *The Lion and the Unicorn in Africa: The United Africa Company, 1787–1931* Heinemann, 1974, pp.166 and 168; Maimaina Sarkin Askira: An Autobiography, p. AMD, Kano, 17/5/74; B. Shenton, "A Note on the Origin of European Commerce in Northern Nigeria," ABU Department of History Seminar paper, February 1977.

41. See pp. Chapter 4, section on "Grounds and Non-Grounds for Deposing District Heads" page 145–8.

42. C.L. Temple, "Kano Provincial Annual Report for 1910," SNP 7 No.951/1911, NAK and E.J. Arnett, "Kano Provincial Annual Report for 1911," SNP 7 No.114/1912, NAK. The only company that operated in the emirates outside the riverine areas during the first decade of the century was the London and Kano Company, which was established at Kano in 1905; but its presence made little impact until the arrival of the railway. See J.S. Hogendorn, *The Origins of*

the Groundnut Trade in Northern Nigeria, Ph.D., London 1966, pp.131–132, B. Shenton, op. cit.

43. Ibid. These were the Niger Company, the Tin Areas of Nigeria Ltd., the Lagos Stores and the French Company, CFAO. These were in addition to the London and Kano Company, which had been existing there since 1905.

44. The additional companies were Paterson Zochonis, Gaiser & Company; Messrs J. and M. George & the British Cotton Growing Association. See W.F. Gowers, "Kano Provincial Annual Report for 1912," SNP No.134P/1913, NAK.

45. These firms were the John Holt and Company Ltd., the Tin Areas of Nigeria Ltd; the Niger Company Ltd, and the Bank of British West Africa Ltd. See M.P. Porch, "Zaria Provincial Annual Report for 1912," SNP 10 No.178P/1913, NAK.

46. The firms established in 1912 were Pagenstecher and Company Ltd, Ollivant and Company Ltd., Lagos Stores Ltd; the CFAO Ltd, Paterson Zochonis Ltd, John Walkden and Company Ltd and the British Cotton Growing Association Ltd., Ibid.

47. The two new firms were Messers L.A. Ambrosini and G.L. Gaiser; while the nine mining companies were given as Benue (N.N.) Tin Mines Ltd., at Leren Dutse and Karre; Champion Tin Fields at Dutsin Wai and Leren Dutse; Rafin Pa Tin Company Ltd at Rafin Pa; Wassakoo Concessions Ltd, at Kudaru, Keffin Hausa Syndicate Ltd, at Rafin Baba; B.K.S.W. Syndicate Ltd at Kogin Karami; S.G. Brounger at Kudaru; Nigerian Plateau Ltd, and Yelwa Ltd. See J.M. Fremantle, "Zaria Provincial annual Report for 1913," SNP 10 No.107 P/1914, NAK.

48. The five non-European firms were Messrs Francies, J.H. Doherty, C.B. Edwardes, L.S. Thomas and Company, and Alfred Barligh. (C.O. Migeod, "Zaria Provincial Report for the June Quarter 1914," SNP 10 No.410P/1914, NAK; H.S. Goldsmith, "Zaria Provincial Report No.64 for the Quarter Ended December 31, 1914," SNP 10 No.51P/1915, NAK and C.O. Migeod, "Zaria Provincial Annual Report for 1915" SNP 10 No.138P/1916, NAK).

49. "Zaria Provincial Annual Report No.64," op. cit.

50. "Zaria Provincial Annual Report for 1915," op. cit.

51. Ibid.

52. F.B. Gall, "Bauchi Provincial Annual Report for 1914," SNP 10 No.168/1915, NAK. According to Pedder (op. cit., p.167) the Gombe station "possibly the first trading post established by the company at a distance from the river banks," was opened in 1909.

53. "Bauchi Provincial Annual Report for 1914," op. cit.

54. "Kano Provincial Annual Report for 1912," op. cit.

55. Ibid.

56. W.P. Gowers, "Kano Provincial Annual Report for 1913," SNP 10 No.98P/1914, NAK.

57. J.M. Fremantle, "Zaria Provincial Report for the March Quarter, 1913," SNP 10 No.369/13, NAK.

58. "Zaria Provincial Report No.64," op. cit.

59. Ibid.
60. "Bauchi Provincial Annual Report for 1914," op. cit.
61. "Kano Provincial Annual Report for 1911," op. cit.
62. Ibid.
63. Ibid.
64. Ibid.
65. "Kano Provincial Annual Report for 1912," op. cit.
66. Ibid.; and "Kano Provincial Annual Report for 1913," op. cit. However, in the 1913 report the Resident gave the following figures for exports in 1912, viz: groundnut 674 tons, dressed skins, 598 and undressed skins, 200 tons.
67. See Chapter 11 page 353–6.
68. "Kano Provincial Annual Report for 1913," op. cit.
69. A.C.G. Hastings, "Kano Provincial Annual Report for 1914," SNP 10 No.139P/1915, NAK.
70. Withers Gill, "Zaria Provincial Annual Report for 1910," SNP 7 No.950/1911, NAK.
71. Fremantle, "Zaria Provincial Report for September Quarter 1912," SNP 7/6607, NAK; and "Zaria Provincial Report for the Quarter Ended 1914," op. cit. Concerning the procurement of cotton for export, the Residents did specifically advise that the only way to do it, in view of the strong competition by local weavers for the available cotton, was to get the peasants to produce more and better types of cotton so as to satisfy both local and European demands. See "Zaria Provincial Annual Report for 1910," op. cit.
72. "Zaria Provincial Annual Report for 1912," op. cit.
73. "Zaria Provincial Annual Report for 1913," op. cit.
74. "Zaria Provincial Report for the June Quarter 1914," op. cit.
75. Ibid.
76. Ibid.
77. "Zaria Provincial Report No.64," op. cit. It should be pointed out that no figures for the export of Tin were included in these Reports on Zaria.
78. "Kano Provincial Annual Report for 1913," op. cit.
79. "Zaria Provincial Report No.64," op. cit.; "Kano Provincial Annual Report for 1914, op. cit.
80. Ibid.
81. C.O. Migeod, "Zaria Provincial Report No.63 for the September Quarter 1914," SNP 10 No.597P/1914, NAK.
82. C.N. Barclay, "Yola Provincial Report No.14 for December 1902," Yolaprof A1, NAK.
83. In theory, what Barclay says was true, especially with regard to the European firms combining to dictate to local traders. However, we have seen that the introduction of non-European traders later did not help matters in the far northern emirates.
84. "Yola Provincial Report No.14," op. cit.

85. "Northern Nigeria: Annual Reports, op. cit., p.19.
86. Ibid.
87. Ibid.
88. "Northern Nigeria: Annual Reports," op. cit., p.19.
89. Ibid.
90. Lugard's theory and the practice of the companies, it should be pointed out, perfectly fitted in with Lenin's observation (1916) that imperialism, among other things, involved the "division of the world among capitalist associations" and the "division of the world among the Great Powers." See V.I. Lenin, "Imperialism: The Highest Stage of Capitalism (January to June 1916), included in V.I. Lenin, *Selected Works,* Moscow, 1971, pp.169–263).
91. Perhaps it will be easier to understand the importance of the Niger Company when it came to the wages which Lugard paid his servants if it is remembered that in the period under consideration, namely 1900–1, the population of the emirates had not yet accepted the currency of British coins and paper money; and that this fact meant that trade was carried on mainly through barter, with cowries which did not always exchange hands as the main standard for fixing the relative values of commodities. Hence, Lugard's servants, who were paid in British money, had, first, to buy goods from the Company and then use those goods to barter for food, etc from the local population. That was why Lugard became largely dependent on the Company's cooperation in the matter of the wages of his regime's servants.
92. Thus, according to Lugard,

    "soon after the transfer of the administration to Her Majesty's Government I raised the question of the rates which should be charged by the Niger Company to government soldiers, for the ordinary barter goods (cheap cloth and salt & cotton), with which they purchase (six) their food in the market, and the rates at which similar goods should be sold to the government of the Protectorate when compelled to use them (in lieu of coinage as currency in the interior). I demanded that such goods should be supplied to Government or to soldiers and company (on cash payments), at reduced rates. The Company at first refused any reduction but latterly agreed to certain 'wholesale rates.' The result was not merely to maintain an unnecessary cost of all establishments to Government, but to enhance the labour rates, since the Company by paying their labourers in goods instead of coin, and selling those goods at a profit to Government, compelled Government to pay a higher rate for labour than they did themselves." See Ibid., pp.19–20.

93. "Northern Nigeria Annual Reports," p.19.
94. Lugard, op. cit., pp.19–20. It should be pointed out that Lugard did also raise what he called "the very important question of competition by small native traders," but he did so only in order to dismiss these "small native traders" who were mainly from southern Nigeria and other British colonies in West Africa, on largely

racial grounds. Thus he says he was "not of opinion that in Northern Nigeria – in Southern Nigeria the case [might] be different – the small trader from the coast will be of any great use, while he is quite certain to give much trouble in his dealings with the natives, and by his fondness for litigation. Experience has moreover, I am told, shown that, as a matter of fact, he does not travel in the interior and open up markets, but is content to remain to the full as stationary as a European. The immigrant black trader is, in fact by no means a desirable person, but every effort should be made to encourage natives of the Protectorate to become small traders and collectors of local produce." Once again, he regretted that "the Niger Company, who by their enterprise, and the experience gained by years of successful effort, have secured an unrivalled position in the Protectorate have not seen their way so far to utilize that position to the enormous good of the country and their own ultimate benefit, by encouraging local natives to become small traders, and by making advances against their stock or utilizing their agency." See Ibid., p. 20. It might also here be pointed out that this attitude of Lugard towards the Niger Company stands in sharp contradiction to the claim made on his behalf by Margery Perham that "he fought long and hard against any suggestion of exploitation in Africa by business elements or of departure from the principles of freedom of trade even where the ex-enemy Germany was concerned." See her introduction to Frederick Lugard, *The Dual Mandate in Tropical Africa*, Fifth Edition, p. xxx.

95. G.N. Barclay, "Yola Report for June 1904," op. cit.

96. W.S. Sharpe, "Yola Annual Report for 1910," Yolaprof Vol. IX, NAK.

97. K.V. Elphistone, "Report No. 92 for the Quarter Ended 31 December 1912," Yolaprof Vol. XI, NAK.

98. W.S. Sharpe, "Quarterly Report No. 74 for Quarter Ended 31 March 1912," Yolaprof vol. II, NAK.

99. W.S. Sharpe, "Yola Report No. 84 for March 1914 Quarter" Yolaprof Vol. XVII, NAK.

100. See Chapter 7. The military and administrative values of the roads, and canals are not being overlooked here.

101. C.W. Orr, "Zaria Provincial Annual Report for 1906," Zariaprof No. 2553, NAK; Memo from Ag. Political Assistant to All Residents, N.N., dated 15/8/06, Yolaprof Acc. 2, NAK; J.W. Gill, "Zaria Provincial annual Report for 1910" SNP 7 No. 950/1911, NAK; "Yola Provincial Quarterly Report for March 1912," op. cit., "Kano Provincial Annual Report for 1911," op. cit.; "Zaria Provincial Report for September Quarter, 1912," op. cit.

102. "Zaria Provincial Annual Report for 1910", op. cit.

103. H.O. Howard, "Bauchi Provincial Report for the March Quarter, 1908," SNP 7 No. 2303/1908, NAK; E.A. Brackenbury, "Balala District, Assessment Papers 1907," Yolaprof G2Y, NAK; Anon. "Taxation of Mines Labourers," SNP 7 No. 6667/1911, NAK, also see Chapter 7, on British Taxation.

104. B.C. Duff, "Bauchi Provincial Report for the December Quarter 1910," SNP 7 No.952/1911, NAK.

105. "Bauchi Provincial Report for the December Quarter 1910" op. cit.

106. "Zaria Provincial Annual Report for 1913" op. cit.; "Zaria Provincial Report for the March Quarter 1913," op. cit.; C.O. Migeod, "Zaria Provincial Annual Report for 1915," SNP 10 No.138P/1916, NAK.

107. See Chapter 7 and Chapter 11.

108. W.P. Hewby "Bornu Provincial Annual Report for 1912," SNP 7 No.626/1913, NAK. I find Hogendorn's application of the spurious theory of "vent for surplus'" to Northern Nigeria and his rather timid conclusion that there was in the emirates some surplus labour awaiting mobilization of colonialism for cash production, etc untenable, in the face of the fact that with the introduction of large scale export crop farming and mineral extraction, food production suffered a drastic setback. From all indications, there was no surplus labour waiting to be mobilized for raw material production. In fact what enabled the European companies get their demands were, first, the taxes imposed by the British which, after 1906, had to be paid in British money or products needed by the Niger Company; the Caravan Tolls that the British used to discriminate against local industry and the outright prohibition of certain industrial activity such as tin smelting. For the application of the theory of "vent for surplus" to Northern Nigeria, see H.S. Hogendorn, "The Vent for Surplus Model and African Cash Agriculture to 1914" in *Savanna*, Vol.5, No.1, June 1976, pp.15–28.

109. A good example of government intervention to curtail Tin smelting by local smelters was in Riruwai – both Riruwen Kano in Tudun Wada District of that emirate and Riruwen Bauchi. We are told that by 1910, smelters here had been "playing their trade" for over 100 years. "The ore was smelted at their furnaces, run into straw-tin and found its way through the length and breadth of the Protectorate." However, "after some difficulty, the origin of the tin was located by the Niger Company. The Ibi route was opened in 1902 and various leases granted to the Company." This "led to friction with the Liruwei tributers, who on appeal to the Resident, were told to confine their operations to places not included in the leases." Allegedly, "little hardship was fared by this prohibition until the middle of [1900] when the great influx of European miners suddenly closed the whole country to the Liruwei tributers." When they appealed to the Resident Bauchi "the position of the law was carefully explained to them and [the Resident] earnestly advised them to at once locate land of their own and apply for a mining lease." The local miners "proceeded to do but in a half-hearted manner and eventually staked out a claim, which [was] granted them rent free." This grant was made to the local smelters on "the conditions that they [were] only to use three furnaces – the seven they [had had] being far in excess of the ore yields of their [allotted] land; and that on misbehavior, i.e. persistent purchase of stolen ore their 'privileges' [would] be rescinded." To his credit the Resident called the nature of the "privileges" granted the Riruwei miners into question by himself

putting the word "privileges" in inverted commas. He also expressed his "deep regret that the effects of the mining rush [had not been] anticipated earlier, and a larger and more suitable reserve granted to the native smelters", confessing that "the land granted them" – 100 acres in size – was "of little value and [that] for all practical purposes as regards their land, their ancient industry [had] been brought to nigh upon extinction." The Resident was merely full of "hopes of an arrangement being made by which their knowledge of smelting work may be profitably availed of, in connection with neighbouring mines." That is to say, the Resident was in fact expressing the "hope" that these smelters would end up being employed by the European mining companies, possibly as "semi-skilled" labourers. At any rate all indications are that even the trifle concession made to the Riruwei miners were going to be taken away. Thus, although these concessions were made with the approval not only of the Governor but also of the Secretary of State for the Colonies, "strong opposition was shown by the [European] Mining Community" to the so-called "support afforded the Liruei men." Given colonialism's prime purpose of creating conditions for the unhampered exploitation of colonies by imperialist companies, we should assume that these European miners needed to apply only a little more pressure and these "privileges" and "support" to the local miners would be withdrawn. See "Bauchi Provincial Report for the December Quarterly 1910," op. cit. Indeed four years later in 1914 the grant of fields to the Riruwei miners was "cancelled on commutation of annuity granted to former holders." See "Bauchi Provincial Annual Report for 1914," op. cit. It is also very likely that it was because of the destruction of their mining activity that at one point the "pagans" of the Jos area contemplated attacking "the Europeans at a Mine in the South of Naraguta Division." (Ibid.).

110. J.M. Fremantle, "Yola Provincial Annual Report for 1907," Yolaprof A6 and 7, NAK; "Zaria Provincial Annual Report for 1910," op. cit.; C.O. Migeod, "Zaria Provincial Report for June Quarter, 1914," SNP 10 No.410:P/1914, NAK.

111. "Yola Provincial Annual Report for 1907," op. cit.

112. Good examples were Fufore and Dulo Markets, both in Balala District in Adamawa Emirate. Both had been very important before the advent of colonialism, but that of Fufore sharply declined and that of Dulo almost collapsed by 1917. See "Balala District Reassessment Papers 1917," op. cit. In fact this report mentioned a number of other important markets in this District which hardly exist today. These included Sofa Jaule, Gembardu, Ribadu and Dasin. On the other hand, the weaving industry showed its strength in the fact that at Dasin and the neighbouring Farang-Farang up to 1917 "practically every man and boy over ten [was] a weaver." See also "Yola Provincial Quarterly Report for Quarter Ended 31 March 1912," op. cit.; "Zaria Provincial Annual Report for 1912," op. cit.

113. Some western writers more or less readily admit this destruction of the emirates' economy. John Hatch, for example, admits that

"before European political control was imposed, African economies were dependent on the export of commodities whose prices were determined by the purchasers ... often according to powerful forces that the individual trader or agent himself could not influence ... this position was not altered by the arrival of imperial rule ... In some ways indeed it was strengthened ... [C]olonial governments, often under orders from their own masters in European capitals, could subordinate the interests of their subjects to those of the merchants, manufacturers and financiers in Europe."

He goes on to admit quite frankly that "it was no objective of colonial rule to undermine the foreign dependence of colonial economies or to replace it by independent self-propelling economies." See John Hatch, *Nigeria: A History* (London, 1971, pp.169–170).

Chapter 11

1. For example, Margery Perham claims that "in the first few years of our occupation the treatment of the slavery question was a vital part of the whole political settlement. In no part of British Africa, except perhaps, in the Sudan, did this issue seem so formidable. In the advanced parts in the north *the whole social* system was based upon slavery..." This was allegedly why "it was quite out of the question for the Government to abolish slavery; as an immediate measure it was neither possible nor desirable, as the bottom would have dropped out of society..." See Margery Perham, *Native Administration in Nigeria*, OUP 1962 Edition, pp.49–50.

2. Notable exceptions to the tendency to neglect the issue of relations of production and class struggle are K.O. Dike, *Trade and Politics in the Niger Delta, 1830–1885*, Oxford, 1956; and Y.B. Usman, *The Transformation of Katsina: c.1796–1903*, Ph.D., ABU Press, 1981.

3. For an exposition of pre-capitalist modes of production and class relations, see, for example, Karl Marx, *Pre-capitalist Economic Formations*, trans. Jack Cohen, London, 1964, verbatim.

4. It must however, be pointed out that some information concerning these aspects of slavery in the society of the Sokoto Caliphate can be gleaned from Mary Smith's *Baba of Karo*, London, 1965. So does M.G. Smith touch on these aspects in his book, *The Economy of the Hausa Communities of Zaria*, London, 1955. Polly Hill does the same in her book, *Rural Hausa: A Village and a Setting*, CUP, 1972, and her paper "From Slavery to Freedom: The Case of Farm-Slavery in Kano Emirate," presented at the Kano Seminar on the *Economic History of the Central Savanna of West Africa*, Kano, 5–10 January 1976. But all these works suffer from a lack of concise use of concepts including the central concepts 'slave' and 'slavery'. Another paper on slavery, this time in the Sudan generally, is Claude Meillassoux's "The Role of Slavery in the Economic and Social History of Sahelo-Sudanic Africa," which was translated and presented for him at the Kano Seminar by R.J. Gavin. Apart from the lack of precision in the use of concepts, this paper suffers the additional defect of not even raising the issue of the position, role, duties and rights of slaves

in the societies (mainly those of the middle Niger area) studied. Hopefully in the remainder of the book on the theory and practice of slavery in West Africa, of which the author says this paper is a first part, these issues will be raised.

5.   According to the edict supposedly "abolishing" slavery while "Children born after March 31, 1901 [were] to be free," a "domestic servant [was] to work for his master from dawn to noon on every day of the week except Thursdays and Sundays in or about the doing of such work as his master [directed] him to do;" and "any domestic slave breaking the above regulation was to be fined £5 or imprisoned for one month or both." (Quoted from Draft Rules Relating to Domestic Slavery, File No.CSO 8/6 Vol.3, NAI). Indeed in his first "Annual Report" the Report on the period, 1st January 1900 to 31st March 1901, Lugard rather ambiguously informed the Colonial Office that the "Slavery Proclamation" was "directed principally against the enslaving of any [free] person, and only affects domestic slavery in so far as it abolished the legal status, and declared all children born after April 1901 to be free. The penalties incurred by a British subject for any transaction in slaves is extended to all non-natives and freed slaves. Domestic slaves may not be removed for purposes of sale, gift or transfer. See F.D. Lugard, *Northern Nigeria Annual Reports 1900–1913*, London, p.15. The ambiguity of this passage which mainly lay in the phrase "and only affects domestic slavery in so far as it abolishes the legal status," was, to my mind, removed when, in his second Annual Report, the Report on the period 1st January 1901 to 31st December 1901 (sic), Lugard stated categorically that "it was not the intention of the government to interfere with the institution of domestic slavery *vi et armis*." See Ibid., p.32.

6.   These rights included the right to work for themselves on certain days of the week, the right not to be sold, and the right to self redemption. See Draft Rules, op. cit. All of these rights, and indeed the right of second generation slaves not to be sold, had been enjoyed in the precolonial society. See Mary Smith, op. cit., pp.16–20; also Polly Hill, "From Slavery to Freedom," op. cit.

7.   Lugard himself admitted that "throughout Africa – East and West – much injustice and oppression has been unwittingly done by our forces acting on crude information and accusations of slave raiding & co. brought by enemies of the accused to procure their destruction," Ibid., p.9.

8.   For a discussion of the reasons why the British turned against the Trans-Atlantic slave Trade see for example Eric Williams, *Capitalism and Slavery,* London, 1964, especially chapters 8, 9, 10, 11 and 12; and Eugene D. Genovese, *The Political Economy of Slavery,* Random House, 1961, Chapters 8 and 9.

9.   It should be pointed out that the emirates were not the only place in Nigeria where the British, after outlawing slavery in Britain and the Trans-Atlantic Slave Trade, came out in open support of slave masters against slaves. In fact, they did so in Calabar in the middle of the nineteenth century, a period when slaves were fighting arms in hand for their liberation from plantation slavery throughout the Delta states. See Dike, op. cit., Chapter 8.

10.   G.N. Barclay, "Yola Report No.8 for June 1902," Yolaprof A1, NAK.

11. Ibid.

12. H.O. Howard, "Bauchi Provincial Report No.27 for the Months of January, February and March 1906," SNP No.127, NAK.

13. C.L. Temple, "Sokoto Provincial Report No.33 for the Quarter Ended March 31, 1907," Sokprof 343/1907, NAK.

14. J.M. Fremantle, "Annual Report for Yola Province for 1907," Yolaprof A6 and 7, NAK.

15. G.N. Barclay, "Yola Provincial Report for the Quarter Ended March 31, 1909," Yolaprof A8, NAK.

16. E.A. Brackenbury, "Namtari District: Assessment Papers 1911," Yolaprof G2, W, NAK.

17. W.C. Moore, "Balala District: Reassessment Report December 1917," Yolaprof G.24, NAK.

18. Ibid.

19. Ibid.

20. Ibid.

21. See Chapter 7.

22. These aims included training young members of the ruling houses – who, it would seem, the British wanted to convert into private landowners – to train them in "the management of their future estates," See H.S. Goldsmith, "Sokoto Provincial Report No.30 for the Quarter Ended June 30th, 1906," Sokprof No.625/1906, NAK; as well as training young members of the ruling houses and of the literary circles as scribes, surveyors and bookkeepers so that they would come out and work in the Native Treasuries, Native Courts and the District Administrations. So also did the aims include the training of young members of occupational groups in their fathers' occupations. Hence the subjects that were taught were Reading and Writing in the Roman alphabet, simple Arithmetic, elements of Geography, Land Measurement and the use of simple instruments of survey; handicrafts, carpentry, smithery (the last three only in the so-called Kano Industrial School), and towards the end of our period, English and Arabic. Given the background of the pupils and the aims towards which they were being trained, it may not be surprising, but it is worth pointing out, nonetheless, that the first game the British taught these pupils was polo. See McAllister, "Sokoto Provincial Report for September Quarter, 1911," SNP 10 No.5572/1911; NAK; E.J. Arnett, "Sokoto Provincial Annual Report for 1917," Sokprof 555/1918, NAK; H.S. Goldsmith, "Sokoto Provincial Report No.31 for Quarter Ended 30 September 1906," Sokprof No.977/1906, NAK; H.R. Palmer "Kano Provincial Annual Report for 1915," SNP 10.170P/1916, NAK; C.O. Migeod "Zaria Provincial Annual Report for 1915," SNP 10 No.138P/1916, NAK.

23. G.N. Barclay, "Yola Provincial Report No.9 for July 1902" Yolaprof A1, NAK. Indeed in his second Annual Report (op. cit.), which was written as late as 10 October 1902, Lugard admitted that "the Government has not yet done anything to promote education except in so far as that (1) the Public Works Department,

the Printing Department, the Workshops, and the Telegraphs, all have a certain number of apprentices who are being educated in the respective trades; and (2) that the Freed Slave Home will soon, I hope constitute an Infant School, and to a smaller extent, a training establishment for older girls in laundry work, & co.," Ibid., pp.47–8.

24. Ibid.
25. G.N. Barclay, "Yola Provincial Report No.9 for July 1902," op. cit.
26. Ibid., Lugard's comments. Indeed it was not until December 1909 that the first Mission to establish a station in Adamawa Province, the Sudan United Mission, did so, at Bulla in Numan outside the Emirate. See W.S. Sharpe, "Yola Provincial Annual Report No.63 for 1903," Yolaprof A8, NAK.
27. K.V. Elphinstone, "Yola Provincial Report No.72 for the Quarter Ended 31 December 1911," Yolaprof A11, NAK.
28. These were Dahiru b. Isa b. Raji, who later became Adamawa's first Native Treasurer, then the Galadima and Senior Councillor; Muhammadu b. Mallu Babba, more popularly known as Mallu Hamman, who later became Assistant Native Trasurer, then Native Treasurer, and then Waziri and Senior councillor; and Muhammadu b. Murtal b. Raji, who later became first a Court Chief Scribe in Yola, then Native Treasurer for Shelleng Native Authority, then District Head Michika with the title Sardauna, and still later District Head Maiha with the same title. See Webster, "Yola Provincial Annual Report for 1912," Yolaprof A14, NAK; MTA; Nassarawo Jereng, 6/1/1977.
29. Ibid., also LHY to Isa Alkali, Yola, 6/7/1974.
30. The Confidential Reports on Chiefs, Adamawa Province, for 1917. The age of Dahiru, who was then the Native Treasurer, was given as 32.
31. Dahiru for one, when he returned to Yola and became the Native Treasurer, did double up as an Islamic educator, establishing a school which his students, including Liman Husseini, the present Imam of Yola, consider the best in the town. (LHY to Isa Alkali).
32. W.S. Sharpe, "Yola Provincial Annual Report for 1911," Yolaprof A11, NAK.
33. Ibid., Governor's comments.
34. W.S. Sharpe, "Yola Province Quarterly Report No.74 for the Quarter Ended 31st March 1912," Yolaprof A12, NAK.
35. W.S. Sharpe, "Yola Province Report for the quarter Ended 30th September 1912," Yolaprof A13, NAK and Webster, "Yola Provincial Annual Report for 1912," op. cit.
36. Ibid. In the meantime, the mission station established at Bulla had for one reason or another folded up; for we are told that in September 1912 "Dr. Bronnum of the SUM arrived with a view to establishing a station at Numan." G.W. Webster, "Yola Provincial Report No.80 for Quarter Ended June 30th, 1913," Yolaprof A15, NAK.
37. W.S. Sharpe, "Yola Provincial Annual Report for 1913," Yolaprof A15, NAK.

38. W.S. Sharpe, "Yola Provincial Report No.86 for the quarter Ended 30 September 1914," Yolaprof A17, NAK. In the meantime, by June 1914, Dr. Bronnum of the SUM at Numan had been joined by two other missionaries "who hold a small school daily" as well as treating "those sick people who appli[ed]." G.W. Webster, "Yola Provincial Report No.85 for Quarter Ended 30 June 1914," Yolaprof A17, NAK. By December, this small school had 18 pupils, mostly male adults who were taught reading, writing, arithmetic, "very elementary geography and astronomy" and the "principles of the Christian Religion," the last of which subjects was introduced "at the definite request of the respective town-chiefs and their elders" – W.S. Sharpe, "Yola Provincial Report No.87 for the Quarter Ended 31st December 1914," Yolaprof A17, NAK.

39. A.H.M. Kirk-Greene, *Adamawa, Past and Present*, London, 1958, p.106.

40. C.W. Orr, "Zaria Provincial Annual Report for 1905," Zariaprof No.2552, NAK.

41. Ibid.

42. C.W. Orr, "Zaria Provincial Annual Report for 1906," Zariaprof No.25523, NAK.

43. Ibid.

44. Ibid.

45. C.W. Orr, "Zaria Provincial Annual Report for 1910" SNP 7 No.950/1911, NAK.

46. Ibid.

47. Ibid.

48. Ibid.

49. J.M. Fremantle, "Zaria Provincial Report for September Quarter 1912,"Appendix "B", SNP 7/6607/1912, NAK. Original in Hausa, translation by writer.

50. J.M. Fremantle, "Zaria Provincial Annual Report for 1913"SNP 10 No.107P/1914, NAK. Hausa original not seen. Translation included in Report.

51. Ibid.

52. Ibid., and C.O. Migeod, "Zaria Provincial Report for the June Quarter 1914," SNP No.470P/1914, NAK.

53. H.S. Goldsmith, "Zaria Provincial Report No.64 for the Quarter Ended December 31st 1914," SNP 10 No.51P/1915, NAK.

54. C.O. Migeod, "Zaria Provincial Annual Report for 1915," SNP 10 No.138P/1916, NAK.

55. "Bauchi Report No.27," op. cit.

56. Ibid.

57. Ibid.

58. Ibid.

59. Ibid.

60. W.F. Gowers, "Bauchi Provincial Report for the December Quarter 1908," SNP 7 No.335/09, NAK.

61. E.J. Arnett, "Sokoto Provincial Annual Report for 1916," Sokprof: 561/1917; E.J. Arnett, "Sokoto Provincial Annual Report for 1917. Sokprof 555/1918.

62. Confidential Annual Reports on Chiefs, Bauchi Province, 1913, AHAK.

63. F.B. Gall, "Bauchi Provincial Annual Report for 1914," SNP 10 No.168p/1915, NAK.

64. By this time, the CMS had stations at Panyam, Kabwir, and Ampier, the SUM had stations at Bukuru and Forum and the SIM had a station at Miyango. Of these the CMS was said to have "made considerable progress in the simple education of the pagans in the vicinity of their stations."

65. F.B. Gall, "Bauchi Provincial Report for the Half Year Ended 30 June 1915," SNP 10 No.381P/1915, NAK.

66. E.J. Arnett, "Gazetteer for the Sokoto Province," London, 1920, p.47.

67. C.L. Temple, "Sokoto Provincial Report No.33 for the Quarter Ended 31st March 1907," Sokprof 343/1907, NAK.

68. C.L. Temple, "Sokoto Report No.34 for the Quarter Ended June 30th, 1907," Sokprof 610/1907, NAK.

69. W.F. Gowers, "Sokoto Provincial Annual Report for the Year 1909," SNP 10, No.984/1910, NAK.

70. McAllister, "Sokoto Provincial Report for the September Quarter, 1911," SNP 10 No.5572/1911, NAK.

71. G.N. Vertue, "Sokoto Provincial Report for December quarter 1911," SNP 10 No.1041/1912, NAK.

72. "Gazetteer for the Sokoto Province," op. cit., p.56.

73. Major McClintock, "Bornu Provincial Annual Report for 1907," SNP 7 No.1761/1908, NAK.

74. W.P. Hewby, "Bornu Provincial Annual Report for 1908," SNP No.1894/1909, NAK.

75. McClintock, "Bornu Provincial Annual Report for 1909," SNP 7 No.1271/10, NAK.

76. Hewby, "Bornu Provincial Annual Report for 1910," SNP 7 No.1107/1911, NAK.

77. Hewby, "Bornu Provincial Annual Report for 1912," SNP 7 No.626/1913, NAK.

78. W.B. Thomson, "Bornu Provincial Annual Report for 1913," SNP 10 No.95P/1914, NAK.

79. Ibid.

80. F.H. Ruxton, "Bornu Provincial Annual Report for 1914," SNP 10 169/1915, NAK.

81. Ibid.

82. G.J. F. Tomlinson, "Bornu Provincial Report for the Half-Year Ended June 30, 1915," SNP 10 No.471P/1915, NAK.

83. Up to now there was no mention of missionaries in Borno.

84. "Bornu Provincial Annual Report for 1907," op. cit., Governor's comments on.

85. Ibid.

86. P.K. Tibenderana "British Educational Policy in Northern Nigeria, 1906–1928: A Reassessment", Paper presented at the Social Sciences Staff Seminar, Ahmadu Bello University, Zaria, Nigeria, on 23 March 1977.

87. W.F. Gowers, "Kano Provincial Annual Report for 1913," SNP 10 No. 98P/1914, NAK.
88. Ibid.
89. In a sense, this school had been in existence ever since the beginning of British taxation which demanded the measurement of farms and houses with chains and compasses. Hence the term *Mallaman Kampus,* which came to be the local name of tax assessors in Kano.
90. "Kano Provincial Annual Report for 1913," op. cit.
91. H.R. Palmer, "Kano Provincial Annual Report for 1915," SNP 10 No.170P/1916, NAK.
92. Ibid. As yet there were no missionaries in any part of Kano Province, though there had been periodic tours of the Province by missionaries based outside it, among them Dr. Miller – "Kano Provincial Annual Report for 1915," op. cit.
93. These were Kano, Katsina, Daura, Kazaure, Gumel, Hadeija, Katagum, Missau and Jama'are emirates.
94. We have already seen the promptitude with which the British established and consolidated taxation, and District "Administration," and Native and Provincial Courts; and, of course, by the time our period opens, the West African Frontier Force, of which the Northern Nigeria Regiment was a part, had already been established and was fully operational. In essence and especially in a colonial context such as the one we are considering in this book, all these institutions are profoundly negative; and the extent to which the British neglected the education – and the health – of her "Wards" under the obnoxious "dual mandate" can still be better grasped if it is contrasted with the promptitude the British exhibited in establishing these negative institutions as well as the attention they invested in them.
95. Indeed, in a sense, the British introduced the institution of prisons, for in the precolonial days prisons as distinct houses specifically so designated were all but unknown in the emirates. To be sure, there had been a jailer, the *Yari* in each emirate; but there had been no prisons which, significantly enough, are nowadays known as *gidajen fursuna*, as *gidajen kurkuku*, the latter apparently, a Hausa corruption of the English word "incarceration", which was very often used by the British. What there had been were *gidajen yari* or "jailers' compounds", and these functioned primarily as the residences of the jailers and secondarily as prisons. It was the British that first built houses in the emirates which were not only primarily but also solely meant for jailing people. Certainly that did not make the British the first ever oppressors in the emirates; but it did make them the first open and barefaced ones. Margery Perham may well be admitting this fact when she states that "Residents were instructed to encourage the Alkalis to improve their procedure, to keep records, to standardize their punishments and *to build proper prisons.* See M. Perham, op. cit. p.56.
96. See for example, C.W. Orr "Zaria Provincial Annual Report for 1904," Zariaprof No.2551, NAK.

97. "Kano Provincial Annual Report for 1912," op. cit.; "Bornu Provincial Annual Report for 1911," op. cit.; "Bauchi Half-Year Report for June 1915," op. cit.

98. See for example W.F. Gowers, "Kano Provincial Annual Report for 1912," SNP 10 No.134P/1913, NAK; and G. Malcolm "Sokoto Provincial Annual Report for 1912," SNP 10 No.152P/1913, NAK.

99. G.N. Vertue, "Sokoto Provincial Report for the December Quarter, 1911," SNP 10 No.1041/1912, NAK.

100. C.W. Orr, "Zaria Provincial annual Report for 1904," op. cit.; C.L. Temple, "Sokoto Provincial Annual Report for 1907," SNP 10 No.384/1908, NAK; G.N. Vertue, "Sokoto Provincial Report for the December Quarter 1911," op. cit.; J. Withers Gill, "Zaria Provincial Annual Report for 1910," SNP 7 No.50/1911, NAK, "Zaria Provincial Annual Report for 1913," op. cit.; H.S. Goldsmith, "Zaria Provincial Report for the December Quarter, 1914," SNP 10 No.51P/1915, NAK; E.C. Duff, "Bauchi Provincial Report for December Quarter 1910," SNP 7 No.952/1911, NAK; H.R. Palmer, "Kano Provincial Annual Report for 1915," SNP 10 No.1708/1916, NAK.

101. "Zaria Provincial Annual Report for 1913," op. cit.

102. "Zaria Provincial Report for the December quarter 1914," op. cit.

103. Ibid.

104. W.F. Gowers, "Kano Provincial Annual Report for 1913," SNP 10 No.980/1914, NAK.

105. A.C.G. Hastings, "Kano Provincial Annual Report for 1914" SNP 10 No.139P/1915, NAK.

106. Ibid.

107. G. Malcolm, "Sokoto Provincial Annual Report for 1912," SNP 10 No.152P/1913, NAK.

108. "Sokoto Provincial Annual Report for 1913," op. cit.

109. "Bauchi Provincial Report for the December Quarter 1910," op. cit.; "Zaria Provincial Annual Report for 1913," op. cit.; "Bornu Provincial Annual Report for 1906," op. cit.; "Bornu Provincial Annual Report for 1910," op. cit.; "Bauchi Provincial Report for the Half Year Ended 30 June 1915," op. cit.

110. G.N. Barclay, "Yola Provincial Monthly Report for July 1904," Yolaprof A4, NAK.

111. "Zaria Provincial Report for the December Quarter 1914," op. cit.

112. "Bornu Provincial Annual Report for 1910," op. cit.

113. "Zaria Provincial Report for 1913," op. cit. We can now say that in 1914, the year Zaria got its first "government school, the Emirate had a total of 186 policemen and 204 prisoners as compared to 36 pupils."

114. "Bauchi Provincial Report for the Half Year Ended June 30th 1915," op. cit.

115. "Bornu Provincial Annual Report for 1912," op. cit.

116. "Zaria Provincial Annual Report for 1904," op. cit.

117. Ibid.

118. "Bornu Provincial Annual Report for 1907," op. cit.; C.L. Temple, "Sokoto Provincial Annual Report for 1907," SNP 10 No.384/1908, NAK.

119. H.S. Goldsmith, "Zaria Provincial Report No.64 for the Quarter Ended December 31st, 1914," SNP 10 No.51P/1915, NAK; F.B. Gall, "Bauchi Provincial Report for the Half Year Ended 30th June 1915," SNP 10 No.381P/1915, NAK; C.O. Migeod, "Zaria Provincial Annual Report for 1915," SNP 10 No.138P/1916, NAK.

120. C.L. Temple, "Sokoto Provincial Annual Report for 1907," op. cit.

121. W.F. Gowers, "Kano Provincial Annual Report for 1913," SNP 10 No.98P/1914, NAK; H.S. Goldsmith, "Zaria Provincial Report No.64 for the Quarter Ended December 31, 1914," SNP 10 No.51P/1915, NAK; W.B. Thomson, "Bornu Provincial report for the Half Year Ended 31 December 1915," SNP 10 No.152P/1916, NAK.

122. "Zaria Provincial Report No.64 for Quarter Ended 31 December 1914," op. cit.

123. "Bornu Provincial Report for the Half Year Ended 31 December 1915," op. cit.

124. "Yola Provincial Report for July 1902," op. cit.

125. Ibid.

126. Ibid.

127. Ibid.

128. Ibid.

129. Ibid.

130. Ibid. Lugard's comments.

131. "Bornu Provincial Annual Report for 1907," op. cit.

132. "Bornu Provincial Annual Report for 1913," op. cit.

133. H.D. Foulkes, "Bornu Provincial Annual Report for 1916," SNP 10 No.145P/1917, NAK.

134. Ibid.

135. Ibid.

136. "Sokoto Provincial Report for June 1906," op. cit.

137. H.S. Goldsmith, "Sokoto Provincial Report No.31 for the Quarter Ended September 30, 1906," Sokprof 977/1906, NAK.

138. C.L. Temple, "Sokoto Provincial Report No.33 for the Quarter Ended March 31, 1907," sokprof 343/1907, NAK.

139. Ibid.

140. Ibid.

141. C.L. Temple, "Sokoto Provincial Annual Report for 1907," SNP 10 No.384/1908, NAK.

142. Ibid.

143. W.F. Gowers, "Sokoto Provincial Annual Report for 1910," SNP 10 No.765/1911, NAK.

144. See Chapter 11, page 335.

145. C.O. Migeod, "Zaria Provincial Report for June Quarter 1914," SNP 10 No.410P/1914, NAK.

146. Ibid.

147. Ibid.

148. "Kano Provincial Annual Report for 1905," op. cit.

149. AMDK, Kano, 19/5/1974.

150. H.R. Palmer, "Kano Provincial Annual Report for 1915," SNP 10 No. 170P/1916, NAK.

151. Ibid.

152. H.R. Palmer, "Kano Provincial Annual Report for 1915," op. cit.

153. Ibid.

154. Ibid.

155. Ruxton, "Yola Provincial Report No.4 for January 1902," Yolaprof, Vol.I, NAK.

156. Ibid.

157. Barclay, "Yola Provincial Report No.19 for July 1902," Yolaprof A1, NAK.

158. Ibid.

159. Ibid.

160. See S. Abubakar "The Foundation of an Islamic Scholastic Community in Yola," Faculty of Arts and Social Sciences Seminar, ABU, Zaria, 1972); Isa A. Abba, *Islamic in Adamawa in the Nineteenth and Twentieth Centuries*, M.A. Thesis, ABU, 1976, pp.107–16.

161. W.S. Sharpe, "Yola Provincial Annual Report for 1911," Yolaprof 10, NAK.

162. S. Abubakar, op. cit, and Isa Alkali, op. cit.

163. W.S. Sharpe, "Yola Provincial Annual Report for 1914," Yolaprof A18, NAK.

164. Hewby, "Bornu Provincial Annual Report for 1912," SNP 7 No.626/1913, NAK.

165. See p.397 above.

166. A.G. Hastings, "Kano Provincial Annual Report for 1914," SNP 10 No.139P/1915, NAK.

167. M.P. Porch, "Zaria Provincial Annual Report for 1912," SNP 10 No.178P/1913, NAK.

168. Ibid.

169. "Zaria Provincial Annual Report for 1915," op. cit.

170. "Bornu Provincial Annual Report for 1912," op. cit.

171. MTA, Massarawo, Jereng, 6/1/1977.

172. M.A. Al-Hajj, *The Mahdist Tradition in Northern Nigeria*, Ph.D., ABU, 1973, p.176; LHY to Isa Alkali, 6/2/1974; AJWS, 28/4/1974.

173. M.A. Al-Hajj, op. cit., pp.93–99.

174. Ibid.

175. R.A. Adeleye, *Power and Diplomacy in Northern Nigeria, 1804–1906*, Longman, 1971, p.169; M.A. Al-Hajj...op. cit.

176. Northern History Research Scheme Interim Reports Nos I – IV, Department of History, Ahmadu Bello University, Zaria, Nigeria.

177. Ibid.

178. Ibid.

179. "Yola Provincial Report No.46 for November and December 1905," op. cit.

180. Ibid.

181. "Yola Provincial Report No.46 for November and December 1905," op. cit.

182. Ibid.

183. Ibid.

184. Ibid.

185. Feargus Dwyer, "Yola Provincial Report No. 61 for the Quarter Ended September 30th, 1909," Yolaprof A8, NAK.

186. Ibid.

187. C.O. Migeod, "Zaria Provincial Report for the June Quarter 1914," SNP 10 No.410P/1914, NAK.

188. Ibid.

189. Barclay, "Yola Provincial Annual Report for 1904," op. cit.

190. G.N. Barclay, "Yola Report for June 1904," Yolaprof Vol. IV, NAK.

191. G.N. Barclay, "Yola Report No.48 for Quarter Ended 30 June 1906," Yolaprof Vol. V, NAK.

192. Ibid.

193. Ibid.

194. Fremantle, "Yola Annual Report for 1907," op. cit.

195. C.W. Orr, "Zaria Provincial Annual Report for 1904," Zariaprof No.2552, NAK.

196. Ibid.

197. Ibid.

198. Ibid.

199. G.N. Vertue, "Sokoto Provincial Report for December Quarter 1911," SNP 10 No.1041/1912, NAK.

200. E.J. Arnett, "Sokoto Provincial Annual Report for 1913," SNP 10 No.104P/1914, NAK.

201. W.F. Gowers, "Kano Provincial Annual Report for 1913," SNP 98P/1914, NAK.

202. Ibid.; See also A.G. Hastings, "Kano Provincial Annual Report for 1914," SNP 10 No.139P/1915, NAK.

203. W.B. Thomas, "Bornu Provincial Annual Report for 1913," SNP 10 No.95P/1914, NAK.

204. Ibid.

205. Ibid.

206. F.B. Gall, "Bauchi Provincial Annual Report for 1914," SNP 10 No.168P/1915, NAK.

207. Ibid.

208. Ibid.

209. Ibid.

210. "Zaria Provincial Annual Report for 1914," op. cit.; "Kano Provincial Annual Report for 1914," op. cit.

211. H.R. Palmer, "Kano Provincial Annual Report for 1915," SNP 10 No.170P/1916, NAK.

212. See P.411 above. Also W.F. Gowers, "Yola Report for July 1904," Yolaprof A.IV, NAK.

213. H.R. Palmer, "Kano Provincial Annual Report for 1910," SNP 7 No.951/1911, NAK.

214. Barclay, "Yola Provincial Report No.9 for July 1902," Yolaprof A1, NAK.

215. W.S. Sharpe, "Yola Provincial Report No.84 for March Quarter 1914, Yolaprof No.17, NAK, and Webster, "Yola Provincial Quarterly Report for June, 1911," Yolaprof A10, NAK.

216. J. Withers Gill, "Zaria Provincial Annual Report for 1910, SNP 7 No.950/1911, NAK.

217. Ibid; and C.O. Migeod, "Zaria Provincial Annual Report for 1914," SNP 10 No.138P/1916, NAK.

218. E.J. Arnett, "Sokoto Provincial Annual Report for 1913," SNP 10 No.104P/1911, NAK.

219. Ibid.

220. Hewby, "Bornu Provincial Annual Report for 1912," SNP 7 No.626/1913, NAK.

221. F.B. Gall, "Bauchi Provincial Annual Report for 1914," SNP 10 No.168P/1915, NAK.

222. See Chapter 11, page 354.

223. "Yola Provincial Annual Report for 1910," op. cit.

224. E.A. Brackenbury, "Namtari District: Report on Assessment, 1910–1911," Yolaprof G2, W, NAK.

225. W.F. Gowers, "Kano Provincial Annual Report for 1913," SNP 10 No.98P/1914, NAK.

226. Ibid.

227. A.C.G. Hastings, "Kano Provincial Annual Report for 1914," op. cit.

228. Ibid.

229. Ibid.

230. Ibid.

231. Ruxton, "Bornu Provincial Annual Report for 1914," SNP 10 No.169P/1915, NAK.

232. Emphasis mine.

233. Lugard personally was very much in favour of this separation, part of the reason being that the British had decided to keep 80% of the proceeds of taxes collected in "independent" "pagan" chieftaincies, instead of sharing it on a 50–50 basis with these chieftaincies, as in the case of taxes collected in the emirates. See Chapter 9, page 280–81.

234. This was the case, for example, with the Kilba chiefdom of Hong, which having all but maintained its independence of Yola until the British conquest, was nonetheless included in Yola Emirate. For Hong's independence from Yola in the nineteenth century see S. Abubakar, *The Emirate of Fombina, 1809–1903*, Ph.D., ABU, 1970, pp.314–15.

235. See Chapter 6.

236. See Chapter 4.

237. See Chapter 11, page 359–65.

238. Resident Zaria to Senior District Engineer, Zaria, Letter dated 27 November 1912 – Appendix "A" in "Zaria Provincial Report for the September Quarter 1912," SNP 7 6607/1912, NAK.

239. Resident Zaria to Senior District Engineer, Zaria, Letter dated 27 November 1912, op. cit.

240. J.M. Fremantle, "Zaria Provincial Annual Report for 1913," SNP 10 No.107P/1914, NAK.

241. Ibid.

242. Ibid.

243. J.M. Fremantle, "Zaria Provincial Annual Report for 1913," op. cit.

244. Ibid.

245. Ibid.

246. Thus, in Kano for example, they lived either in Kano City or in Fagge, a pre-British settlement of Kanuri and Hausa traders outside the walls of the City. See M. Maiden "Native Reservation, Kano Township – Report on," in Kanoprof No.4292, NAK. In Zaria the native foreigners lived either in Zaria city or in Sabon Gari along with emirate "natives." See J.M. Fremantle, "Zaria Provincial Annual Report for 1913," op. cit.

247. RDN and YA, Kano, 3/6/74. The assertion by John Paden that "in 1912 non-Muslims were prohibited by the Emir [of Kano] from living inside Kano City" See John N. Paden "Communal Competition, Conflict and Violence in Kano," in R. Melson, and H. Wolpe (eds.) *Nigeria: Modernization and the Politics of Communalism,* Michigan, 1971, p.122, has no written evidence to support it while it is contradicted by oral evidence in Sabon Gari itself.

248. M. Maiden, "Native Reservation, Kano Township", op. cit.

249. Ibid.

250. Ibid.

251. W.F. Gowers, "Kano Provincial Annual Report for 1913," op. cit.

252. Ibid.

253. Ibid.

254. Ibid.

255. Ibid.

256. According to YA and RDN, it was not only the Yoruba but other elements of the "foreign native" population that continued to live in the city long after the establishment of the Sabon Gari, until the British decided they had no option but to move to the latter place, at a time that lies outside our period of study. RDN and YA, Kano, 3/6/1974.

257. A.C.G. Hastings, "Kano Provincial Annual Report for 1914," op. cit.

258. Ibid.

259. YA, Kano 3/6/1974.

260. A.C.G. Hastings, op. cit.

261. J.M. Fremantle, "Zaria Provincial Annual Report for 1913," op. cit.

262. Ibid.

263. H.S. Goldsmith, "Zaria Provincial Report No.64," op. cit.

264. Ibid.

265. Ibid.

266. Ibid.

267. Ibid.

268. C.O. Migeod, "Zaria Provincial Annual Report for 1915," op. cit.

269. H.R. Palmer, "Kano Provincial Annual Report for 1915," SNP 10 No.170P/1916, NAK.

270. Ibid.

271. Ibid.

272. Ibid.

273. RDN, Kano, 24/5/1974.

274. Ibid.

Bibliography

Official Records – Archival

The SNP Series, NAK.
> No.5/1/18
> Nos.6/170P/1906 – 6/137/1908
> Nos.7/2363/1901 – 7/75/1915
> Nos.10/127/1902 – 10/170P/1916
> Nos.15/2 – 15/383
> Nos.17/16/1908 – 17/171909 (sic)

The Kaduna Series, NAK.
> Nos.0/AF11/5 – O/AR/11/63

The Provincial Series, NAK.
> Maiprof No.A40
> Minnaprof No.673/1912
> Sokprof Nos.7/1903 – 555/1918
> Yolaprof Vols.1/1901 – 18/1914
> Also Yolaprof G2W, G2Y, J1 and Acc.14
> Zariaprof Nos.2551/1904 – 2553/1906

The CSO Series, NAI.
> Vol. 3 Nos. 8/6 and 06012.

British Official Records – Published

Kirk-Greene, A.H.M. (ed.). *Gazetteers of the Northern Provinces of Nigeria,* Vols. I–III, London, Frank Cass, 1972.

Kirk-Greene, A.H.M. (ed.). *The Principles of Native Administration in Nigeria,* London, OUP, 1965.

Lugard, Lord, n.d., *Northern Nigeria 1900–1913*, London.

Majalisa na Kasashen Arewa: *Majalisar Sarakuna, Mahawara: Gamuwea Ta Biyu,* 26 da 27 ga Yuli 1948 (Government Printer, 1948).

Gaskiya ta fi Kwabo, 1/1/1939.

Gaskiya ta fi Kwabo, 11/11/1939.

Precolonial European Sources

Barth, H., *Journal of Second Expedition into the Interior of Africa from the Bight of Benin to Soccatoo*, London, J. Murray, 1829.

Crowther, S.A., *Journal of an Expedition up the Niger and Tshadda Rivers,* London, Church Missionary House, 1855.

Denham, D. and Clapperton, H. *Narrative of Travels and Discoveries in Northern and Central Africa*, London, J. Murray, 1826.

Foureau, F., *D'Alger au Congo par le Tchad*, Paris, Masson, 1902.

Gentil, E., *La Chute de l'empire de Rabah*, Paris, Hachette, 1962.

Kingsley, M., *Travels in West Africa*, London, Macmillan, 1897.

Lander, R. and J., *The Travels of Richard and John Lander into the Interior of Africa*, London, W. Wright, 1836.

Mizon, Lt. de V., *Exploration en Afrique 1890–93*, Paris, Société Anonyme de Publications Périodiques, 1895.

Nachtigal, G., *Sahara and Sudan*, 3 Vols, Berlin, Weidmann, 1879–81.

Tilho. *Documents Scientifiques de la Mission Tilho*, 2 Vols, Paris, Imprimerie nationale, 1911.

Nineteenth Century Sokoto Sources

Abdullahi b. Fudil. *Diya al-Hukham* (Edited and translated by Alhaji Haliru Binji, Zaria, n.d).

Muhammad Bello. *Infaq al-Maysuri* (Ed. C.J. Whitting, London, 1951 and A. Gummi, Cairo, 1964).

Muhammad Bello. *Usul a-Siyasa* (translated by B.G. Martin as "A Muslim Political Tract from Northern Nigeria: Mohammad Bello's *Usul al-Siyasa*" in D.F. McCall and N.R. Bennet (eds.) *Aspects of West African Islam*, Boston University Papers on Africa, IV, 1971.

Uthman b. Fudi. *Kitab al-Farq* (Edited and translated by M. Hiskett as "Kitab al-Farq: A work on the Habe Kingdoms attributed to Uthman dan Fodio," *BSOAS XXII*, 1960.

Uthman b. Fudi. *Bayan Wujub al-Hijra* (Edited and translated by F.H. El-Masri as "*A Critical Edition of Dan Fodio's Bayan Wujub al-Hijra ala 'l-ibad,* Ph.D thesis, Ibadan, 1968.

Other Precolonial Sudanic Sources

Various—The Kano Chronicle (Edited and translated by H.R. Palmer in *Sudanese Memoirs*, London, 1928.

Various—Arabic Letters (Translated by H.F. Backwell as *The Occupation of Hausaland*, Lagos, 1927.

Published Books

Abubakar, S., *The Lamibe of Fombina: A Political History of Adamawa, 1809–1901*, Zaria, ABU, 1979.

Adeleye, R.A., *Power and Diplomacy in Northern Nigeria, 1804–1906: The Sokoto Caliphate and Its Enemies*, London, Longman, 1971.

Afigbo, A.E., *The Warrant Chiefs: Indirect Rule in South-eastern Nigeria, 1891–1929*, London, Longman, 1972.

Ahmadou Basoro et Eldridge Mohammadou. *Histoire de Garoua: Cité Peule du XIX Siècle*, Yaounde, ONAREST, 1971.

Alexander, Lt. Boyd. *From the Niger to the Nile*, London, Edward Arnold, 1907.

Anene, J.C., *The International Boundaries of Nigeria: The Framework of an Emergent African Nation*, London, Longman, 1970.

Askira, M.S., *Autobiography*, Zaria n.d.

Ayandele, E.A., *The Missionary Impact on Modern Nigeria, 1842–1914*, London, Longman, 1966.

Ayandele, E.A., *The Educated Elite in the Nigerian Society*, Ibadan, IUP, 1974.

Baba of Karo, *Autobiography*, translated and edited by Mary Smith, London, Faber, 1954.

Bello, Sir Ahmadu, *My Life*, Cambridge, CUP, 1962.

Brenner, L., *The Shehus of Kukawa: A History of the El-Kanemi Dynasty of Bornu*, London, Clarendon Press, 1973.

Burdon, J.A., *Northern Nigeria: Historical Notes on Certain Emirates and Tribes*, London, Waterlow and Sons, 1909.

Burns, Sir Alan, *History of Nigeria*, London, Allen and Unwin, 1929.

Cabral, Amilcar. *Revolution in Guinea: An African People's Struggle*, London, Stage 1, 1969.

Coleman, J.S. *Nigeria: Background to Nationalism*, Cambridge, CUP, 1959.

Cook, A.N. *The British Enterprises in Nigeria*, London, Frank Cass, 1964.

Crowder, M. *The Story of Nigeria*, London, Faber, 1966.

Crowder, M. *West Africa Under Colonial Rule*, London, Hutchinson, 1968.

Crozier, N.F.P. *Five Years Hard: Being an Account of the Fall of the Fulani Empire*, London, Jonathan Cape, 1932.

Dike, K.O. *Trade and Politics in the Niger Delta 1830–1885*, Oxford, Clarendon, 1956.

East, R.M. (ed.). *Labarun Hausawa da Makwabtansu*, Zaria, Northern Nigeria Pub., Company, 1932.

East, R.M. (ed.). *Stories of Old Adamawa*, Zaria, ABU, 1935.

Edgar, F., *Litafi na Tatsuniyoyi na Hausa*, Vols. I–III, Belfast, W. Erskine Mayne, 1911–1913.

Elderidge Mohammadou (ed.). *Maroua et Pette*, Niamey, Centre régional de documentation pour la tradition orale, 1970.

Fall, B. (ed.). *Ho Chi Minh on Revolution: Selected Writings 1920–1966*, New York, Praeger, 1967.

Fisher, A.G.B. *Slavery and Muslim Society in Africa*, Doubleday, New York, 1971.

Flint, J.E. *Sir George Goldie and the Making of Nigeria*, London, OUP, 1960.

Geary, W.M.N. *Nigeria under British Rule*, London, Frank Cass, 1965.

Genovese, Eugene D. *The Political Economy of Slavery*, New York, Random House, 1961.

Hallam, W.K.R. *The Life and Times of Rabih Fadl-Allah*, London, Heinemann, 1977.

Hassan, Alhaji and Shuaibu, N. *A Chronicle of Abuja*, Zaria, AUP, 1952.

Hastings, A.G.C. *Nigeria Days*, London, John Lane, 1925.

Hatch, J. *Nigeria: A History*, London, Secker & Warburg, 1971.

Heussler, R. *The British in Northern Nigeria*, Oxford, OUP, 1968.

Hill, P. *Rural Hausa: A Village and a Setting*, Oxford, OUP, 1972.

Hodgkin, T. *Nigerian Perspectives*, Oxford, OUP, 1960

Hogben, S.J., and Kirk-Greene, A.H.M. *The Emirates of Northern Nigeria*, Oxford, OUP, 1966.

Hogendorn, J.S. *Nigerian Groundnut Export: Origins and Early Development*, Zaria, ABU, 1978.

Holt, P.M. *The Mahdist State in the Sudan, 1881–1898*, London, OUP, 1970.

Johnson, S. *The History of the Yorubas*, Lagos, CSS Books, 1921.

Johnson, W.R. *The Cameroon Federation: Political Integration in a Fragmentary Society*, Princeton, University Press, 1963.

Johnston, H.A.S. *The Fulani Empire of Sokoto*, Oxford, OUP, 1967.

Kagara, Muhammadu Bello. *Gandoki*, Zaria, Northern Nigeria Pub. Co., 1934.

Kanya-Forstner, A.S. *The Conquest of the Western Sudan*, Cambridge, CUP, 1969.

Kirk-Greene, A.H.M. *Adamawa, Past and Present*, London, OUP, 1958.

Last, D.M. *The Sokoto Caliphate*, London, Longman, 1967.

Lenin, V.I., *Selected Works*, Moscow, Progress Publishers, 1971.

Lewis, I.M. *Islam in Tropical Africa*, Oxford, IAI, 1966.

Low, Victor. *Three Nigerian Emirates: A Study in Oral History*, Evanston, IL., Northwestern Univ. Press, 1972.

Lugard, Lady. *A Tropical Dependency*, London, Nisbet, 1905.

Lugard, Lord. *The Dual Mandate in British Tropical Africa*, London, Frank Cass, 1922.

Mani, Abdulkadir. *Zuwan Turawa Nijeriya Ta Arewa*, Zaria, Northern Nigeria Pub. Co., 1970.

Mao Tse-Tung. *Selected Works, Vols. I–IV*, Peking, Foreign Language Press, 1967.

Marx, Karl. *Pre-capitalist Economic Formations*, Translated by Jack Cohen, London, Lawrence & Wishart, 1964.

Meek, C.K. *Land Tenure and Land Administration in Nigeria*, London, HMSO, 1957.

Miller, Rev. W.R.S. *Reflections of a Pioneer*, London, CMS, 1936.

Morel, E.D. *Nigeria: Its Peoples and Its Problems*, London, Frank Cass, 1911.

Muffet, D.J.M. *Concerning Brave Captains*, London, Andre Deutsch, 1964.

Nadel, S.F. *A Black Byzantium: The Kingdom of Nupe in Nigeria*, London, IAI, 1942.

Nicolson, I.F. *The Administration of Nigeria 1900–1960: Men, Methods and Myths,* Oxford, Clarendon Press, 1969.

Nkrumah, K. *Neo-Colonialism: The Last Stage of Imperialism*, London, Thomas Nelson 1971.

Orr, C.W.J. *The Making of Northern Nigeria*, London, Macmillan, 1911.

Pedler, F. *The Lion and the Unicorn in Africa: The United African Company, 1787–1931,* London, Heinemann, 1977.

Perham, M. *Lugard: The Years of Authority 1898–1945*, London, Collins, 1960.

Perham, M. *Native Administration in Nigeria,* London, OUP, 1962.

Prescott, J.R.U. *The Evolution of Nigeria's International and Regional Boundaries, 1861–1971,* Vancouver, 1971.

Rodney, W. *How Europe Underdeveloped Africa*, Dar es Salam, Tanzania Pub. House, 1972.

Ruxton, F.H. *Maliki Law*, London, 1961.

Smaldone, J.P. *Warfare in the Sokoto Caliphate*, London, CUP, 1977.

Smith, Sir Bryan Sharwood. *"But Always as Friends": Northern Nigeria and the Cameroons, 1921–1957*, London, Allen & Unwin, 1969.

Smith, J. *Colonial Cadet in Nigeria*, Durham, Duke Univ. Press, 1968.

Smith, M.G. *Government in Zazzau: A Study of Government in the Hausa Chiefdom of Zaria in Northern Nigeria from 1800–1950,* Oxford, OUP, 1960.

Smith, M.G. *The Economy of Hausa Communities of Zaria Province*, London, HMSO, 1955.

Stalin, J.V. *Economic Problems of Socialism in the USSR*, Peking, Foreign Language Press, 1972.

Stalin, J.V. *Problems of Leninism*, Peking, Foreign Language Press, 1972.

Tamuno, T.N.T. *Police in Modern Nigeria, 1860–1965*, Ibadan, Ibadan Univ Press, 1965.

Temple, C.L. *Native Races and their Rulers*, London, Frank Cass, 1968.

Toure, A.S. *The Doctrine and Methods of the Democratic Party of Guinea,* Conakry, n.d

Toure, A.S. *The International Policy of the Democratic Party of Guinea*, Conakry, n.d.

Toure, A.S. *The Political Action of the Democratic Party of Guinea for the Emancipation of Guinean Youth*, Conakry, n.d.

Toure, A.S. *Militant Poems*, Conakry, Imprimerie Nationale Patrice Lumumba, 1976.

Trimingham, J.S. *A History of Islam in West Africa*, Oxford, OUP, 1962.

Vine, Victor le. *The Cameroon Federal Republic*, Cornell, Cornell Univ. Press, 1963.

Whitaker, C.S. *The Politics of Tradition: Continuity and Change in Northern Nigeria, 1946–1966*, Princeton, University Press, 1970.

Williams, Eric. *Capitalism and Slavery*, London, Andre Deutsche, 1964.

Published Articles

Adeleye, R.A. "The Dilemma of the Wazir: The Place of the *Risalat al-wazir ila ahl al-lm wa l'tadabbur* in the History of the Sokoto Caliphate," in *JHSN*, Vol. IV, No.2, 1962.

Adeleye, R.A. "Rabih b. Fadl-Allah and the Diplomacy of European Imperial Invasion of the Central Sudan 1893–1969" in *JHSN*, Vol. V, No.3, 1969.

Adeleye, R.A. "Rabih Fadl-Allah 1879–1893: Exploit and Impact on Political Relations in the Cental Sudan" in *JHSN*, Vol. VI, No.2, June 1970.

Afigbo, A.E. "The Establishment of Colonial rule 1900–1918" in Ajayi, J.F. and Crowder, M., *History of West Africa*, Vol. 2, Longman, 1974.

Al-Hajj, M.A. "The Thirteenth Century in Muslim Eschatology: Mahdist Expectations in the Sokoto Caliphate," in *Research Bulletin of the University of Ibadan (RBCAD)*, Ibadan, Vol. III, No.2, 1967.

Al-Hajj, M.A. "Hayat b. Sa'id: A Revolutionary Mahdist in the Western Sudan" in Yusuf Fadl Hassan (ed.), *Sudan in Africa*, Khartoum, 1971.

Al-Hajj, M.A. and Biobaku, S. "The Sudanese Mahdiyya and the Niger–Chad Region," in Lewis, I.K. (ed.), *Islam in Tropical Africa,* London, 1966.

Al-Hajj, M.A. and Lavers, J. "The Travel Notes of al Sharif Hasan b. al-Husayn," in *Kano Studies*, Vol. I, No.1, 1973.

Falogun, S.A. "Succession Tradition in Gwandu History 1817–1918," in *JHSN*, Vol. 7, No.1, December 1973.

Bivar, A.D.H. "Arabic Documents of Northern Nigeria" in *BSOAS*, Vol. XXIII, No.2, 1959.

Bivar, A.D.H. and Hiskett, M. "The Arabic Literature of Nigeria to 1804," *BSOAS*, Vol. XXV, 1962.

Crowder, M. "The 1914–1918 European War and West Africa," in Ajayi, J.F. and Crowder, M., *History of West Africa,* Vol. II, Longman, 1974.

Fage, J.D. "Slavery and the Slave Trade in the Context of West African History," in *JAH*, Vol. X, No.3, 1969.

Fieldhouse, D.K. "The Economic Exploitation of Africa: Some British and French Comparisons," in Gifford, P. and Louis, W.R. (eds.) *France and Britain in Africa: Imperial Rivalry and Colonial Rule,* London, 1971.

Flint, J.E. "Nigeria: The Colonial Experience from 1880–1914, in Lewis H. Gann and Peter Duignan (eds.) *Colonialism in Africa 1870–1960*, Vol. I, Cambridge, 1969.

Hargreaves, J.D. "The European Partition of West Africa," in Ajayi, J.F. and Crowder, M., *History of West Africa*, Vol. II, Longman, 1974.

Heussler, R. "British Rule in Africa," in Gifford, P. and Louis, W.R. (eds.) *France and Britain in Africa: Imperial Rivalry and Colonial Rule*, London, 1971.

Hiskett, M. "Material Relating to the State of Learning among the Fulani Before their Jihad," in *BSOAS*, Vol. XIX, No.3, 1957.

Hiskett, M. "Materials Relating to the Cowry Currency of the Western Sudan," in *BSOAS*, Vol. XXIX, Nos.1 and 2, 1966.

Hodgkin, T. "Mahadism, Messianism and Marxism," in Yusuf Fadl Hassan, *Sudan in Africa*, Khartoum, 1971.

Hogendorn, J.S. "The Vent for Surplus Model and African Cash Agriculture to 1914," in *Savanna*, Vol. V, No.1.

Kanya-Forstner, A.S. "Military Expansion in the Western Sudan – French and British Styles" in Gifford, P. and Louis, W.R. (eds.) *France and Britain in Africa: Imperial Rivalry and Colonial Rule*, London, 1971.

Kirk-Greene, A.H.M. "The Major Currencies in Nigerian History," in *JHSN*, Vol. II, No.1, December 1960.

Last, D.M. "Arabic Source Material and Historiography in Sokoto to 1864: An Outline," in *RBCAD*, Vol. I, Nos. 2 and 3, January and July 1965.

Last, D.M. "Aspects of Administration and Dissent in Hausaland 1800–1968," in *Africa*, Vol. XL, No.4, 1970.

Markov, W. and Sebald, P. "The Treaty Between Germany and the Sultan of Gwandu," in *JHSN*, Vol. IV, No.1, December, 1967.

Mason, M. "The Fall of Etsu Abubakar: The Account of Ubandawaki Bida," in *Kano Studies*, Vol. I, No.1, 1973.

Muffet, J.D.M. "Nigeria – Sokoto Caliphate," in Crowder, M. (ed.) *West African Resistance*, London, 1971.

Njeuma, M. Adamawa and Mahdism: The Career of Hayat ibn Said in Adamawa 1878–1898," in *JAH*, Vol. XII, No.1, 1971.

Olusanya, G.O. "The Freed Slave Homes: An Unknown Aspect of Northern Nigerian Social History," in *JHSN*, Vol. III, No.3, 1966.

Paden, J.N. "Communal Competition, Conflict and Violence in Kano," in Melson, R. and Wolpe, H. (eds.) *Nigeria: Modernisation and Politics of Communalism*, Michigan, 1971.

Rodney, W. "African Slavery and Other Forms of Oppression on the Upper Guinea Coast in the Context of the Atlantic Slave Trade," *JAH*, Vol. VII, No.3, 1966.

Smith, M.G. "A Hausa Kingdom: Maradi Under Dan Baskore 1854–75" in Forde, D. and Kaberry, P. (eds.), *West African Kingdoms in the Nineteenth Century*, Oxford, 1967.

Smith, M.G. "Pluralism in Pre-colonial African Societies" in *Pluralism in Africa*, edited by Kuper, L. and Smith, M.G., Los Angeles, 1969.

Smith, M.G. "Historical and Cultural Conditions of Political Corruption Among the Hausa," in *Comparative Studies in Society and History*, Vol. VI, No.2, January 1964.

Tamuno, T.N. "Some Aspects of Nigerian Reaction to the Imposition of British Colonial Rule," in *JHSN*, Vol. III, No.2, December 1965.

Waldman, M.R. "The Fulani Jihad: A Reassessment," *JAH*, Vol. IV, No.3, 1965.

Waldman, M.R. "A Note on the Ethnic Interpretation of the Jihad," in *Africa*, July, 1966.

Unpublished Theses and Articles

Abubakar, A.Y. *The Establishment and Development of Emirate Government in Bauchi 1805–1903*, Ph.D Thesis, ABU., 1974.

Abubakar, Sa'ad. "A Preliminary Examination of the Relations between Bornu and Fombina before 1900," paper presented at the Bornu Seminar of the History Departments of ABU, and ABC on 3/3/1973.

Abubakar, Sa'ad. "The Foundation of an Islamic Scholastic Community in Yola," Paper presented at the Faculty of Arts and Social Sciences Seminar, ABU, in 1972.

Abubakar, Saleh. *Crisis and Conflict in the Middle Benue Basin: The Evolution of the Fulbe Emirate of Muri (Hammaruwa) c.1817–1903*, B.A. Dissertation, History Department, ABU, June 1973.

Al-Hajj, M.A. *The Mahdist Tradition in Northern Nigeria*, Ph.D. Thesis, ABU, 1973.

Alkali, M.B. A Hausa Community in Crisis: Kebbi in the Nineteenth Century, M.A. Thesis, ABU., 1969.

Abba, I. Alkali. "Islam in Adamawa in the Nineteenth and Twentieth Centuries," M.A. Thesis, ABU, 1976.

Anjorin, A.O. "British Occupation and the Development of Northern Nigeria 1897–1914," Ph.D. Thesis, London, 1965.

Anjorin, A.O., "The Imposition of the Native Authority System in Bussa: the Rebellion of 1915," Paper Presented at the ABU Social Sciences Seminar, in June 1971.

Balogun, S.A. "Gwandu Emirate in the Nineteenth Century with Special Reference to Political Relations 1817–1903," Ph.D Thesis, Ibadan, 1970.

Bello, S. "A Re-examination of the Origins, Nature and Types of Relationships between the State and the Economy of Kano Emirate by the Last Decade of the Nineteenth Century," Paper Presented at the Postgraduate Seminar of the History Department, ABU, 1978.

Chaskda, G.M. "A Wedlock of Political Ambitions: Muhammadu (Hamman) Mafindi and the British Occupation and Rule in Muri," Paper Presented at the 19th Congress of the Historical Society of Nigeria at Zaria, December, 1973.

Fika, A.M. "The Political and Economic Reorientation of Kano Emirate, Northern Nigeria c.1882–1940," Ph.D Thesis, London, 1973.

Hill, P. "From Slavery to Freedom: The Case of Farm Slavery in Kano Emirate," Paper Presented at the Kano Seminar on the Economic History of the Central Savanna of West Africa, January, 1976.

Ikime, O. "The British and Native Administration Finance in Northern Nigeria 1900–1920," Paper Presented at the Congress of the Historical Society of Nigeria, Zaria, 1973.

Mason, M. "The Nupe Kingdom in the Nineteenth Century: A Political History," Ph.D. Thesis, Birmingham, 1970.

Meillassoux, C. "The Role of Slavery in the Economy and Social History of Sahel-Sudanic Africa," Translated by R.J. Gavin and presented at the Seminar on the Economic History of the Central Savanna of West Africa, January, 1976.

Njeuma, M.Z. "The Rise and Fall of Fulani Rule in Adamawa 1809–1901," Ph.D Thesis, London, 1969.

Shenton, R.W. "A Note on the Origins of European Commerce in Northern Nigeria," Paper Presented at the Post-Graduate Seminar of the Department of History, ABU, 1977.

Tibenderana, P.K. "The Administration of Sokoto, Gwandu and Argungu Emirates under British Rule 1900–1946," Ph.D. Thesis, Ibadan, 1974.

Tibenderana, P.K. "British Educational Policy in Northern Nigeria 1906–1928: A Reassessment," Paper Presented at the Social Science Staff Seminar, ABU, 23/3/77.

Tukur, M.M. "Shehu Abubakar Garbai Ibn Ibrahim El-Kanemi and the Establishment of British Rule in Bornu, 1902–1914," Paper Presented at the Bornu Seminar of ABU, and ABC History Departments on 19/5/1973.

Tukur, M.M. Some Comments and Reflections on Professor Ayandele's Most Recent Book *The Educated Elite in the Nigerian Society,* a newspaper review article.

Ubah, C.N. "The Administration of Kano Emirate Under the British 1900–1930," Ph.D Thesis, Ibadan, 1973.

Ukpabi, S.G. "The West African Frontier Force: An Instrument of Imperial Policy 1897–1914," M.A. Thesis, Birmingham, 1964.

Usman, Y.B. "The Transformation of Katsina 1796–1903: The Overthrow of the Sarauta System and the Establishment of the Emirate," Ph.D Thesis, ABU, 1974.

Usman, Y.B. "The Transformation of Political Communities: Some Notes on the Perception of a Significant Aspect of the Sokoto Jihad." Paper presented at the Sokoto Seminar in January 1975.

List of Informants

This research started originally as a study on the Emirs. The material that was gathered through interviews was very largely of a biographical type. But with the change in the emphasis of the study shifting from the Emirs to the Emirates, its basis also changed from oral tradition to written documents, specifically British records. Hence, the greater part of the material collected have not been used; except for the fact that we have made occasional references to individuals, a list of informants could be dispensed with. Yet, we have decided to include such a list both because such occasional references have been made and in order to give an indication of what oral resources are available for tapping. This has been done without prejudice to what we have said on the nature of the oral tradition in the note on sources. All the interviews were conducted in either Hausa or Fulfulde, except in two cases when it was conducted in English. However, all notes were taken in English.

Alkalin Alkalai Bello Maiwurno – AABM – was in his early fifties and in charge of the projected archives section of the Sokoto History Bureau at the time I interviewed him in March 1974. Previously, he had been a student at the Sokoto Middle School and the Kano Law School, a District Alkali, an Alkalin Alkalan Sokoto and an Inspector of Native Courts in both the Northern Nigerian and the North-Western State Governments. All his ancestors, going back to his great, great grandfather had held the post of Alkalin Alkalan Sokoto. Hence he was very knowledgeable in the judicial history of both the Sokoto Caliphate and especially the Sokoto Sultanate. I interviewed him in his office at the History Bureau on seven occasions between the 11th and the 29th of March 1974. Our discussions centred mainly on the judiciary, touching on the education and teaching activities of the Qadis, the difficult cases they confronted in the pre-colonial and colonial periods, their relations with the Caliphs in the nineteenth century and the British Residents in the twentieth century, the system of appeals, etc. However, we did also discuss the biographies of other twentieth century scholars in Sokoto, their teaching activities, their relations with the Native and Provincial Authorities, their sources of income, etc. He also brought from his house and showed me a very large number of letters in Hausa using Arabic script that were exchanged between the Alkalin Alkalai and various District Heads and District Alkalai or sent by the Alkalin Alkalai to the British Residents informing them about the settlement of cases. I found him very useful.

Alhaji Abubakar Garba Gunmi – AAGG – was in his late forties and the Treasurer of the Sokoto Local Government Authority. I was introduced to him by the Sokoto L.G.A Councillor for Finance, Alhaji Aliyu Dogon Daji. We had long discussions in his office at the Treasury on four different occasions between 26th May and 2nd June 1974. Among other things, we discussed the establishment of the Sokoto Native Treasury, its organization, the role of the Sultan and the British in running it, its sources of income, and the directions of its expenditure, dwelling for quite some time on the system of investing money abroad. We also touched on the establishment of the various departments of the L.G.A and their functions. I found him very cooperative and useful.

Alhaji Bello Dandago – ABD – was 70 years old and the District Head of Gabasawa in Kano Emirate with the title of "Sarkin Dawaki Maituta" at the time when I interviewed him in June 1974. Previously, he had been a student of the Kano Provincial School and Katsina College as well as the Northern Peoples' Congress (NPC) Chief Whip in the Federal House of Representatives. I was sent to him by Alhaji Salihi Bayero and went with Alhaji Mai Sangon Dan Rimi. Our interview took place on 3 June 1974 in the entrance hall to his house at Dandago in Kano City, in the presence of his son, Sarki and Alhaji Mai Sango. We discussed mainly the introduction of western education into the Emirate. I found him to possess a very good memory though his estimation of British efforts at introducing educa- tion was too high. He could remember his teachers at both Kano and Katsina as well as the text books used. The information I gathered from him would certainly have been very useful if the period covered by this thesis had been extended to 1920 and beyond. As it is, I have not found occasion to refer to him; nonetheless the study has benefited from insight I gained from our interview.

Alhaji Baba Dara-Dara – ABDD – was in his mid-forties and the Kano Local Government Treasurer at the time of our interview in May 1974. I was sent to him by Alhaji Salihi Bayero and I went in the company of Alhaji Mai Sangon Dan Rimi. I interviewed him alone in his office on 27 May 1974. Our discussion cen- tred on the organization of the Kano Native Treasury, its sources of revenue, and the directions of its expenditure during the colonial and post-colonial periods, with particular emphasis on the sending of money for investment abroad. I found him very cooperative and useful.

Alhaji Dan Sarai – ADS – who was born and brought up inside the Emir of Kano's palace, was 74 years old and a dogari in the Kano Local Government Treasury, in charge of taking cheques to the Madaki and the Emir to sign, at the time of our interview in May 1974. Traditionally, the Dan Sarai was the messenger who took tribute from Kano to Sokoto. I was introduced to him by the Treasurer, Alhaji Baba Dara-Dara, and I had one interview with him inside the Treasury on 27 May 1974, in the presence of Alhaji Mai Sangon Dan Rimi. Our discussion touched on pre-colonial taxes, their incidence, methods of collection, and the disburse- ment of their proceeds. We also touched on the biographies of the people who held the post of Treasurer from just before the British invasion up to the time of our interview.

Alhaji Garba Said – AGS – was over 50 and working for the Kano State Government when we met at the Sokoto Seminar in January 1975. I was introduced to him by Professor M.A. Al-Hajj and discovered he knew one of my uncles and knew of my grandfather and great grandfather. Soon I was taking down notes for him on his translations of the Fulfulde poems of the Sokoto jihadists, which he was to pres- ent at the Seminar. It was in between these translations that we discussed history with no particular end in view and without my taking down notes. He had a very good background for knowing the history of the Emirates in both the nineteenth and twentieth centuries. He was a grandson of Hayat b. Said, a scion of Sokoto who emigrated to Adamawa in the 1870s and later, with his base at Balda, tried to convert the Sokoto Caliphate into a province of the Mahdiyya, before he was dislodged by Lamido Zubairu in c.1890. Then Hayat moved on further east and joined Rabeh, whose Imam he became before they quarrelled and Rabeh killed him. Alhaji Garba's own father, Modibbo Saidu, who was still alive in 1975, re-es- tablished contacts with the Mahdi's son, Abdurrahman, in c.1916, at a time when the Modibbo was at Marwa in the Cameroons. When he later moved to Fika in Bornu Province, he was accused of sedition by the British who, in 1923, arrested and deported him to Buea in what was then the Cameroons Province of Eastern Nigeria. Alhaji Garba stayed with him there until 1949 when the Modibbo was transferred to Kano and placed under restriction. All the while, the Modibbo maintained close links with his father's and his own followers in Adamawa, on both sides of the boundary, and with his cousins and relatives in Sokoto. In addition, Alhaji Garba spoke and could read very fluently in Arabic, English, Fulfulde and Hausa. During our discussion he displayed very remarkable knowledge of the history of Sokoto, Adamawa and Kano, and the discussion, mainly in Fulfulde, was free-ranging and frank.

Alhaji Ibrahim Tambawal – AIT – was 55 years old and a school supervisor in-charge of ten primary schools under the Sokoto Local Education Authority at the time of our interview in April 1974. I was sent to him by the late Alhaji Umaru Gwandu. I interviewed him alone at the Sokoto L.E.A Headquarters on four occasions between 26th April and 1st May 1974. We discussed mainly the introduction of western education into the Sultanate of Sokoto with particular reference to the attitude of the Sultans and their officials towards that type of education. In the process, he gave me the names of the sons and grandsons of the Sultans from Attahiru II down to the present Sultan as well as of their leading officials that were sent to western schools. We also touched on the Satiru Revolt, famines in the Sokoto Province, iron-making and weaving in the province, the introduction of such modern habits as cigarette-smoking and how the companies induced people to take to these habits. I could not use much of this information due to the widening of the scope of my thesis and the shortening of the period it covers. So I have not been able to test the accuracy of much of what he told me. But as far as the period covered in this research is concerned, I found much of his information corroborated by the British records. He was a very friendly and cooperative informant.

Abubakar Ja'afar – AJ – was 73 years old and retired at the time of our interview in Maiduguri in November 1973. He had once been a school teacher and Borno's Chief Alkali. We discussed Rabeh's invasion, the imposition of British colonialist domination over Bornu, the taxes they imposed, how these compared with pre-colonial taxes, the division of the proceeds of the taxes and what the Shehu did with their share.

Alhaji Mai Sangon Dan Rimi – AMD – a son of the well known Dan Rimi Nuhu, was 75 years old and a Yaron Sarki attached to the Emir of Kano's office when I interviewed him in May 1974. I was introduced to him by Alhaji Salihi Bayero and he became my closest companion throughout my stay in Kano. He was the first informant I was introduced to and he was my main source of information, apart from accompanying me to most of the places I went to within the city. Altogether, I interviewed him on eleven different days between 17 May and 2 June 1974 at the rate of one interview a day. The first interview took place in the morning at the office of Wazirin Kano, Alhaji Shehu Gidado, which was located in the Emir's palace, and in the presence of Mallam Garba, a son of the Emir Abbas, and himself a Yaron Sarki. The other interviews took place at Alhaji Mai Sangon's house near the palace, in the afternoons, mostly between 4 and 6 pm, and usually alone, except for the presence of his grand children. Occasionally his son, a trader who lived in another part of the city, could drop and sit in. We touched on almost every topic relating to my research, which, was then conceived in biographical terms. Among other things, we discussed the circumstances surrounding the British invasion of Kano and the appointment of Abbas as Emir; the biographies of the Emirs from Aliyu to the present one and of almost all their grown up sons and some of their daughters; the names and titles of the first set of District Heads appointed in Kano and the towns to which they were posted; the leading mallams of Kano City in this century, including all the Qadis, walis and imams; the leading businessmen in Kano during this century and how they made their monies; the introduction of western education into the Emirate and the attitude of the aristocracy towards it; the introduction of British taxation; the occurrence of famines and the measures taken to deal with them. I collected quite a wealth of material from this informant though I have used only a little of it in the book, owing to the change in my topic.

Alhaji Muhammadu Sani — AMS — was about 57 years old and in charge of a Kano state government project for repossessing and preserving historical documents in Kano when I interviewed him in May 1974. Previously, he had been a Provincial judge in Kano and Adamawa. I was sent to him by Alhaji Salihi Bayero and our discussion at his office, near the former Provincial Office, on 31/5/1974 centred on the Shahuci Judicial School, of which he was among the first set of students. For some reason which I cannot quite remember, our first interview was never followed up.

Alhaji Umaru Gwandu — AUG — a direct descendant of Abdullahi dan Fodio, was about 62 and the Chairman of the committee that was overseeing the activities of the Sokoto History Bureau at the time of our interview in March and April 1974. Previously, he had been Private Secretary to the Emir of Gwandu, Sir Yahya, and a Clerk and subsequently speaker of the Northern House of Assembly. I was introduced to him by the Acting Secretary to the Bureau, Mallam Abdullahi Magaji, and I interviewed him at his own office at the Bureau on three days, viz: 15th and 16th March and 21st April 1974. We discussed the British occupation of Gwandu, the traditional and the colonial systems of selecting an Emir of Gwandu, and the judicial and Islamic educational systems as they existed in Gwandu in the twentieth century. I found him very useful and we parted on the understanding that whenever I returned to Sokoto and was ready, he would take me to both Gwandu and Birnin Kebbi and facilitate my research there. Thus, it was with profound regrets that I learnt of his death in a motor accident, when I returned to Sokoto to finalise arrangements for the Sokoto Seminar that held in January 1975. He is one of the two of my informants that I know to have died since our interview, the other being Alhaji Bello Dandago. I wish them a perfect rest.

Babban Mallami na Madabo, Alhaju – BMMA – over 60 at the time of our interview, was the head of the long established educational centre at Madabo in Kano City. I was sent to him by Alhaji Salihi Bayero and went with Alhaji Mai Sangon. I interviewed him on 29 and 30 May 1974 at the entrance to his house and in the presence of one other mallam who very much participated in our discussion but preferred to remain anonymous. Several of their students were also present. Our discussion centred on the school, viz; its origin, orientation, past heads and students, and its relations with Kano's authorities in the pre-jihad, post-jihad and colonial periods.

Goggo Ai'shatu Mama – GAM – was a daughter of Alkali Suleiman, the Alkalin Kano who followed the Caliph Attahiru Ahmadu to as far as Bormi and refused to re-turn to Kano after the famous battle. She was about 74 years old at the time of our interview at the house of the late Wali Bashir who was her first cousin. I was introduced to her by the latter's son, Alhaji Ali, Alkalin Kasuwa, to whom I was taken by Alhaji Mai Sangon Dan Rimi. I had two interviews with her, on 7 and 8 June 1974, both in the afternoons and in the presence of the Alkalin Kasuwa. We discussed the origin and history of the Genawa clan of Kano Fulani from which most of the Alkalis of Kano in the nineteenth and twentieth centuries came. So did she also give a complete list of all the Alkalis of Kano from the time of the Emir Suleiman to the present. I found her well informed about her clan and its scholastic and marital relations with other segments of the Kano aristocracy. On the few points in which she was in doubt her nephew came to her aid. On the sec-ond day of our interview another nephew of hers, Justice Abubakar Bashir Wali dropped in and he, together with Alkali Ali, gave me a list of the legal texts that Qadis in Kano used for settling cases before the enactment of the Penal Code.

Liman Husseini Yola – LHY – was over 80 years and the Imam of Yola when Isa Alkali interviewed him in 1974. Born in Ribadu, he spent his life from youth in Yola town and received his education in the hands of almost all its modibbe in the first four decades of this century, and, besides, was a living witness of all the changes that took place in Adamawa in the century.

Limamin Kano, Alhaji Dalhatu – LKAD – and Naibin Kano, Alhaji Umaru seemed to be in their 60s and 50s respectively when I interviewed them together in June 1974. The Naibi for one had once been an Alkalin Alkalan Kano. The interview took place at the house of the Liman on 9 June 1974. I was taken and introduced to them by Alkali Ali, who also stayed during the interview, which was made rather short by the undisguised displeasure of some of the Imam's students at the sight of a young man interviewing an elder, though the Imam and the Naibi, espe-cially the Imam, remained very friendly and cooperative. Relatively short though the interview was, I managed to elicit a complete list of the Imams of Kano from its incorporation into the Sokoto Caliphate up to the time of our interview. However, I could not go into their educational backgrounds and scholarships, the full range of their functions, their sources of income, etc.

Mutawallin Sokoto, Alhaji Aliyu Dogon Daji – AADD – was the Sokoto Local Government Councillor in charge of Finance when he granted me a brief interview at the Local Authority Treasury on 25 April 1974 before he handed me over to the Treasurer because he himself had to attend a Council meeting at the Sultan's palace. We discussed the Local Authority's sources of income and directions of expenditure. Though brief, the interview was useful.

Mallama Adama Birnin Kebbi – MABK – was in her mid-forties and a teacher in Magajin Rafi Primary School in Sokoto at the time of our interview. I was taken and introduced to her by Alhaji Ibrahim Tambawal who was present when I interviewed her in a classroom at the school on 1 May 1974. The informant was in the first set of students of the Women Training Centre, the first ever girls' school opened by the British in the Emirates, in Sokoto in 1939. Our interview centred on the early days of the school and we discussed the teachers, the courses available, and the first set of the Centre's students and their subsequent careers.

Mala Ahmadu Marafa – MAM – was 49 years of age and the District Alkali of Nassarawa Jereng District in Adamawa when we had the discussion. The discussion took place in my father's entrance hall in the evening in my father's presence. The informant is a grandson of Modibbo Hamman Joda, the man who was the Qadi of Yola at the time of the British occupation of the town and who continued in that office till his death in February 1908. Ahmadu's own father was a District Head posted to Verre District, but his uncle, Modibbo Mahmudu, was the Alkalin Alkalai of Adamawa from 1908 to 1938 and from 1942 to 1945. Another uncle Mallu Hamidu held the post from 1938 to 1942. As such Mala Ahmadu, who grew up in Yola with his uncles and went to the Elementary and Middle Schools there, is very conversant with Yola's politics in this century. Not only is he willing to discuss this with researchers but has done some writing, having in fact published a pamphlet in Hausa known as "*Ranar Tabbatadda Lamido*" (Lamido's Installation Day).

Madakin Kano, Shehu Ahmadu – MKSA – was over 60 and Kano's most powerful councilor when we discussed, rather briefly, in his office, on 17 May 1974 before he introduced me to Alhaji Salihi Bayero, whom he charged with sending me round to the people who could answer my questions. Apart from his age, the Madaki had a background that should enable him answer researchers' questions about the history of the Kano aristocracy. Thus, his clan, the Fulanin Yola had held the office of Madaki since the nineteenth century, while he himself was at both the Kano Provincial School and Katsina College. Besides, he had been a District Head for several years before being transferred to the city to enter the Emir's Council in the 1940s. Since 1954, he had been Kano's most powerful Councillor, being in charge of Central and District Administrations, a position which he took over from the former Chiroma Kano, Alhaji Muhammadu Sanusi, when the latter became Emir. On top of that, he had been a member of the Northern House of Assembly between 1952 and 1966, and its Deputy Speaker from 1961 to 1966.

Muhammad Tukur Aminu – MTA – is my father and is now about 69 years of age. He is a grandson of a nineteenth century mallam, Modibbo Nakashiri (H. Na-Kwashiri) and though he himself was never a qadi, his father as well as a number of his brothers have been Qadis, one of them being the Adamawa Native Authority Councillor for the Judiciary, or Wali, between 1955 and 1963. So also have dozens of his cousins. He himself was a District Scribe between 1938 and 1969, and in the course of that career was posted to Mayo Farang, Toungo, Binyeri, Maiha and finally Nassarawo Jereng, where he has lived since his retirement. As such, he is quite conversant with the history of the Islamic scholars of Adamawa, especially those coming from the families of Modibbo Raji, Modibbo Nakashiri and Modibbo Sufiyanu which have merged and taken the common name of Fulbe Hausa (Fulanis from Hausaland) since their arrival in Yola in the middle of the last century. Not only is he conversant with that history, but I have always found him willing to answer my questions about Adamawa's history in general and the history of the Fulbe Hausa in particular. As such I have spent a lot of time with him in the evenings either asking him questions or listening to him discuss with his peers. However, even in the case of those discussions which I referred to in this book, I took no notes though I noted down the dates.

Mai Unguwa Ahmadu – MUA – was 75 years old and a Ward Head in Fagge at Kano when I interviewed him in May 1974. I was sent to him by Galadima Bura, the village head of Fagge and went with Bukar, a messenger in the Galadima's office. The interview took place at the informant's office. We discussed the origin of Fagge, the occupational and ethnic composition of its population, and its administration up to 1974.

Mallam Yahya Assada – MYA – was about 50 and the headmaster of Magajin Gari I Primary School in Sokoto at the time of our interview on 1 May 1974. I was taken to him by Alhaji Ibrahim Tambawal specifically to discuss the sources of iron and other metals in the pre-colonial and colonial periods, his father and ancestors having been black or other types of smiths before the Jihad. Indeed, even presently, though he himself did not practise smithery, having taken to teaching and lived in a section of Sokoto that is predominantly inhabited by blacksmiths. Our discussion went back to before the Jihad and came right up to the present. In the course of it, he shed much light on the local iron-making industry, its technology and its organization in the pre-colonial period as well as its collapse in the colonial period. He also discussed the trade links between Sokoto and Yorubaland – as far as Badagry – in the pre-jihad period, as well as the impact of the Jiihad on that trade. He gave me not just a list of the stopping places on the way but also the organization of trading expeditions and the names of some expedition leaders (H. Madugari). In the course of the interview, he did also mention the "difficulty" that the Jihad – which his ancestors supported as armament and utensil makers – imposed on smiths (excluding black smiths who did not need to import iron). This was the fact that with the establishment of the Sokoto Caliphate, its government prohibited the export of slaves to the south on the grounds that it was unlawful to sell Muslims, both actual and potential, to non-Muslims. This ban, as far as he knows, put a stop to slave trade with Yorubaland until the 1880s when Sarkin Musulmi Umaru (1881–1890) lifted the ban, which the informant sees as a significant departure from the ideals of the Jihad. It also emerged from our discussion that as a result of this ban, "white" and "red" smiths were forced to devise means of procuring their raw materials locally. In other words – though he did not put it that way – this ban helped to push local technology forward. If for nothing else, our interview was very useful for this bit of information which one hardly finds in the existing literature on the Jihad. I find the information not only significant but also very reliable in that it was offered voluntarily, unconsciously, in the course of a discussion which was not at all centred on the Jihad.

Magaji Yola, Hama Jam – MYHJ – was about 70 and the Village Head of Yola when I interviewed him in December 1969, during the course of a research for my B.A. dissertation on the introduction of party politics into Adamawa. The interview took place in the office of Yola's District Head, in the latter's presence. Apart from his age, the Magaji was well placed to know the history of Yola, his family having held the Headship of the town since Yola was founded in the 1830s and he having himself held the office for over 30 years by the time of our interview.

Raphael Dick Nyamsi – RDN – was born a Balua at Bagante in what is now East Cameroon in 1906. He went to school successively in Lagos, Lokoja, Onitsha and Eviano Podi between 1917 and 1925 and arrived in Kano in 1928 as a clerk at the Provincial office. He had lived in Sabon Garin Kano since then, although he used to visit Bagante, to which he sent back his children for upbringing and education, once every two years. Furthermore, he was the President of the Kano branch of the National Council of Nigeria and the Cameroons (NCNC) from 1947 to 1964, the Chairman of its Northern Working Committee from 1954 to 1964, and the Chairman of the Waje Town Council from 1962 to 1966. Thus, he was very well placed to know the history of Sabon Gari and of intercommunal relations in Kano and Northern Nigeria. I was introduced to him at the Waje District Office by the District Head, Alhaji Muhammadu Habibu, the Gado da Masun Kano. I had three long sessions with him at his property, Victory Hotel, Sabon Gari, whose repair he was supervising, on two days, the 23 and 24 May 1974. We discussed the establishment of Sabon Gari, the ethnic and occupational composition of its population, its relations with the Kano Native Authority, and the 1953 Kano disturbances. I found him to have very little regard for the British Administration and a lot of regard for the Emir of Kano, Abdullahi Bayero, whom he portrayed as very friendly towards the residents of Sabon Gari who, in their own turn, preferred to take disputes to him for arbitration to taking them to the British officer known as the "Local Authority" whom, he said, was officially in sole charge of all the affairs of Sabon Gari up to the 1940s. Although the informant discussed many issues with me, he never contradicted himself even once.

Tafida Idrisu – TI – was about 60 years, District Head of Yola District and a member of the Lamido's Council when I interviewed him in his office in December 1969 in the course of my research for a B.A. dissertation on the introduction of party politics into Adamawa. His parents and grandparents were traders, but he was among the earliest students of the Yola Provincial School which was opened in 1920, and also attended Katsina College. After that he taught at the Yola Provincial School and became its headmaster before being appointed District Head Michika and subsequently a member of the Lamido's Council, a member of the Federal House of Representatives and a Senator.

Wali Aminu Yakubu – WAY – was 54 years at the time of our interview in June 1974. He was an informant with a very useful background and very good memory. He was a son of a former Alkalin Alkalan Zaria (1921–1930), and he was educated at the Zaria City Primary School, the Zaria Middle School and the Kano Law School. He later taught at the latter school for six years. This was punctuated by one year, 1943 to 1944, when he served on the Zaria Judicial Council. Then he became simultaneously a judge in the Kano Emir's Council, an Inspector of Kano District Courts and the emirate's Land Officer, all from 1954–1963. At the time when I interviewed him, he was the Personnel Manager in the Nicco Sweets Factory at Kano. I interviewed in his office in the afternoons of 1st, 2nd, 3rd and 5th June 1974, having been sent to him by Alhaji Salihi Bayero. Given his background, I found him very knowledgeable in the structure and operation of the Judicial Councils in Kano and Zaria, and the history of the Kano Law School, which we discussed in terms of the backgrounds of the staff and the first few sets of the pupils, the curriculum and text books used, the relations between the School and the Kano and other Native Authorities. Other topics we discussed were the functions of the Kano Land Office and the relations between the Native Authorities in Kano and Zaria and the Sabon Garis there. Though, due to the subsequent adjustment in the topic of my study, I have not used the material I collected from him, I gained a lot of insight into the Native Authority system from our discussions.

Wazirin Gwandu, Umaru Nassarawa – WGUN – a son of Wazirin Gwandu, Muhammadu Raji (1906–1925), was about 59 and the Northwestern State Commissioner for Works when I interviewed him. I was introduced to him by Alhaji Umaru Gwandu and I interviewed him in his office on 22 April 1974. We discussed the structure of the Emirate Council in Gwandu in the pre-British and colonial periods with a special reference to the office of Waziri. In the process, he threw a lot of light on the pre-colonial power structure in Gwandu and on its simplified system of succession to the office of emir.

Waziri Junaidu – WJ – a son of Wazirin Sokoto Muhammadu Buhari (1886–1910) and Sokoto's Senior Councillor, is the best known of all the people I interviewed, having been interviewed by virtually all those who did research on the Sokoto Caliphate or its emirates. He was 68 at the time of our main interviews at his house in Sokoto on 28 and 29 April 1974; but I also did discuss with him problems arising from my research in the National Archives, at various times during his visits to Kaduna to attend meetings of the Jamaatu Nasril Islam. So also did

I visit him on two occasions in Sokoto in 1972 and 1975 together with other members of the History Department of Kano and Zaria. Although on these two occasions, few questions were raised specifically pertaining to my topic and period, nonetheless, the discussions we had with him did help me have a feel of the texture of life among the Sokoto aristocracy in the nineteenth century, a fact which contributed to my understanding of developments in the twentieth century. As far as our two main interviews were concerned, the issues we discussed included the Islamic educational system in Sokoto in the early decades of the twentieth century. This discussion was, for convenience, organized around his own education and included a list of his teachers, the subjects and books he read with them, the sources of their incomes and of his own sustenance while he was still a student, which lasted until he was in his thirties and had started raising a family. In the process, I gained an insight into the crisis brought about among the ulema by the imposition of British colonialist domination and into the role of the Sultans in upholding Islamic education under the conditions created by colonialism. So also did we discuss his brothers, their own education and subsequent careers. Similarly, we discussed the children of the twentieth century Sultans and their careers. This was with a view to finding out the attitude of Sultans towards education in general and western education in particular, as well as to have an insight into the basis of appointments into the service of the Native Administration.

Yusufu Akitayo —YA — said he was 104 years at the time of our interview in 1974. He was supposed to have been born in c.1870, in Ibadan. Certainly he was very old, no longer moving out of his house and his hair, which formed a circle around a big central baldness, being in the process of turning from white into yellow. I interviewed him on 3 June 1974 at his house, No. 58 Yoruba Road, Sabon Gari, Kano, having been taken to him by Mr. R.D. Nyamsi, who also helped me whenever I had difficulty with YA's pidgin English. He said he came to Kano in 1913, i.e. 61 years before our interview, as a carpenter in the Nigerian Railway. Later, he transferred to the Native Authority workshop and as an Native Authority employee, helped in the building of the Wudil Bridge, the Kano Middle School and the Kano Airport. We discussed the founding of Sabon Gari, its earliest and subsequent settlers, its administration and the relations between it and the Native Authority. He confirmed what RDN had told me earlier about these issues, especially the preference of the residents of Sabon Gari to take their litigation to Abdullahi Bayero. In spite of his remarkable age, he had a wonderful memory, especially of the names of people. I found his way of looking at events and his expression very down to earth and without pretence.

Index

A

Abadie, G.F., Capt. 17, 81, 82, 430
Abba Mallam 169, 270, 271
Abdurrahman, Sarkin Musulmi 1, 14,
    18, 25–30, 80–2, 129, 135–7, 382
abolition of slavery xli, 365, 369, 386,
    457, 484
Abubakar Atiku, Sarkin Musulmi 133
Abubakar Garbai 32–8, 80, 94, 104,
    169, 198, 209, 252–3, 267, 271,
    303, 416, 433
Abuja xxxviii, 1, 70, 97–9, 248, 253,
    266, 399
Academic Staff Union of Universities
    xv, xvii, xliv
Adamawa 42, 56, 70, 72, 77, 114–8,
    128, 139, 145–6, 152, 156, 165,
    167, 172, 208, 234, 248, 264–7,
    274–5, 300, 305, 309, 313,
    331–4, 352, 356, 373, 379, 380,
    383
Adamu Jakada 18, 106, 107, 402, 414
Adamu, Mahdi 413
Adeleye, R.A. xx, 14, 27, 84, 399–406,
    408–9, 427, 431, 462, 492
Afonja 5, 394
Agaye 1, 2, 6, 12, 40–45, 399, 402, 419
agrarian dynamics xlii
agrarian question xxxix
agriculture xxvii, xix, xl, xliii, xliv,
    212–9, 304–9, 325, 372, 386–7
Agriculture, Forestry and Roads
    Proclamations 202

Ahmadu, Attahiru, Sarkin Musulmi 1,
    15, 28, 49, 50, 67–71, 82, 84, 89,
    92, 109, 123, 124, 161, 372, 382,
    384, 401, 409, 411, 424, 434, 460,
    461
Ahmadu Bello University (ABU) xiii,
    xvi, xvii, xx, xxi, xxxvi, xxxix, xl,
    396, 488, 492
ajele xxvi, 4, 163
Ajia xxvi, 5, 65, 135, 139, 169, 270, 290
al'adu 216, 217, 431
Al'adu xxvi
Aliyu Babba, Emir of Kano 130
Aliyu dan Sidi, Zaria 105–6, 162, 200
Aliyu, Muhammadu, Gwandu 106,
    109, 112, 114
Alkalan Alkalai 182
Alkali xxiii, xxvi, 85
Alkalin Gari 175, 177
Allah-Bar-Sarki 143
amalgamation 385, 394, 395
Amir al jaish xxvi
analogous districts 155
Andrae, Gunilla xxxix, 398
Anene, J.C. 412, 427
Anglo-French rivalry 3
Anglo-German agreement 380
"Anglo-Mohammedan" law xliii
Anjorin, Abel Olorunfemi xiii, xiv,
    xxxix, xl, 377–396
  Critique of Anjorin's Thesis 377–396
Anka revolt 135
Ardo xxvi
Ardo Jabbo 118, 164, 165, 166

Argungu 22, 24, 30, 39, 70, 75, 76, 80,
    109–13, 126, 168, 177–8, 181–2,
    189, 218, 219, 229, 230, 234,
    239–40, 295, 338, 346, 399
Arnett, Edward John 106–9, 199–201
Asala Shuwa 269
Ashanti 125, 382
Attahiru I xxxii

B

Babbawa, Yerima 77–8, 117, 167, 430,
    447
Badegi 44
Baghirmi 33–4
Bajibo 3, 26
Bala Usman, Yusufu xiii, xiv, xxxvi,
    xxxix, xl
Bale 364
Balogun xxvi, 4, 5, 96, 120, 125, 145,
    176, 179, 183, 190, 198
Bamnyo 6, 132
Banjeram 353
Bank of British West Africa (BBWA)
    325, 477
Barclay, G.N. 56, 62, 78, 117–9, 121,
    122, 129, 177, 180, 183–4, 188,
    192, 195–6, 207–9, 221, 300, 306,
    307–18, 321–2, 330–3, 344–5,
    352–3, 451
Barde xxvi
Barlow, Maj. 51, 52
Baro 388, 389, 391
barter 317, 320, 479
Barth, Heinrich 407, 408, 414
Bashari, Muhammadu 149
Bassa 418
Battle of Bormi 49, 401, 409
Bauchi 1, 8–17, 22, 24, 29, 30, 32, 36,
    37, 39, 41–2, 50–5, 60, 61, 66,
    69–77, 81–2, 95, 99, 100, 126,
    138, 146–9, 159, 162, 174, 177,
    182, 185, 190, 192, 197, 200, 204,
    206, 234, 242, 247, 256, 273, 284,
    287, 293–4, 301, 305, 309, 314–5,
    327, 330, 336–58, 372, 379, 384,
    387, 391

Bay'a 157
Bayero, Abdullahi 71, 108, 140, 143, 149
Bebeji 68, 134, 291, 384, 410
Beckman, Bjorn xxxvi, xxxix, 398
Beddoes, H.R. 53
Begra 32, 33
Beit el-Mal 203, 284, 286
Bell, Hesketh 322, 392–3
Bello, Muhammad, Emir of Kano
    (1883–1892) 18
Bello, Muhammad Mai Wurno 70
Bello, Muhammad, Sultan 83
Bello, Sule xxxvi, 415
Benue River 12, 40, 49, 53, 100, 114,
    119, 268, 299, 305, 321, 352, 395,
    400, 405, 429, 477
Beri-Beri 209, 348
Biafran War xxxvi
Bida 1–6, 9, 12, 16–18, 23–9, 39–47, 66,
    70, 72, 76, 80, 81, 125, 162, 218,
    232, 287, 313, 334, 379, 383, 385,
    388, 390, 399, 419
    impact of the defeat of Bida 3
Birnin Kebbi 137, 141, 142, 149, 191,
    240, 257, 338, 355
Bobbo Ahmadu 6, 72, 84, 109, 114–21,
    195, 436, 446, 474
Bobbo Ahmadu, Lamido 155, 162–9
Bobboi Yero 119, 164–6
Bokki Hampeto 47–8
Boko Haram xxxvii, xxxviii, xliv, 397
Borgu 3, 23, 26, 467
    Anglo-French rivalry 3
Bormi xxxii, xlvi, 13, 15, 41, 49–52, 69,
    70, 72, 382
    Battle of Bormi 49
Borno, Bornu xxxviii, xv, 21, 26, 32–40,
    51, 62, 73–76, 80, 92–94, 100–5,
    134–8, 144–5, 170–172, 177, 198,
    203, 206, 209–12, 221, 224–5,
    237–8, 248, 252–255, 267, 268,
    269, 270, 282, 284, 285, 287,
    299–303, 327, 338–345, 349–358,
    372, 373, 378, 380, 383, 386, 399,
    411, 475
Boyle, Capt. 265

Brakenbury, E.J. 429, 462
British Cotton Growing Association (BCGA) 313–6, 324, 391–3
Browne, Hamilton 51, 52, 261, 263
Bubon 58
Buhari 29, 30
Bulama xxvi
Burdon, J.A. 25, 50, 62–3, 6–88, 109–12, 123–8, 135, 141–2, 177, 179, 181, 182, 186, 189–192, 196, 200–4, 218–41, 256, 305, 313, 338, 372
Bussa 3, 23, 239, 396
Buzai 264

C

Cabral, Amilcar xxxix, 377
Cameroon 79, 426–7, 430
Canoe Tax 231, 232, 277, 280
Cantonment Magistrate 361
Cantonments Proclamation 363
capitalism 297, 329, 479
Caravan Tax 227–8, 230–2, 236
Caravan Tolls 90, 205, 277–80, 309–11, 324, 481
Cargill, Featherstone 50, 54, 68, 87, 107, 114, 140, 143, 212, 261–3
Carnegie, David Wynford 96–7, 119, 120, 124–5
Catholic Mission 389
Cazemajou, Marius-Gabriel 23, 26–7, 33, 415
Compagnie française de l'Afrique Occidentale (CFAO) 477
Chamba 77–8, 139, 265
Chamberlain, Joseph 381
Chayanov, Alexander xl
Chima xxvi
Chiroma xxvi
Christianity xli, xlii, 67, 100, 216, 249, 333, 335–6, 383, 395, 396
Church Missionary Society (CMS) 108, 335, 337, 355, 389
civilizing mission 374
Cochrane, J. 46, 62, 100–2, 210, 267–8, 430, 432, 433, 461
Cole, Teju xxxv

colonialism xiv, xviii, xix, xlii, 5, 30, 58, 74–5, 180, 204–5, 234, 237, 249, 297, 305–6, 326–9, 350–1, 356, 365–9, 371, 374–7, 387, 390–5
commerce 298, 306, 325, 391, 415, 476
commoner classes 247, 327
Conference of Chiefs 89
Cook, Arthur Norton 468
cotton 221, 298, 302–3, 307, 308, 313–6, 324–5, 385, 387, 391–3, 477–9
cowries 300–4, 475, 479
Crawley, Lt. 56, 58
currency xix, 91, 217, 230, 237, 271, 297–304, 312, 325, 479
customs duties 205, 230–1, 277

D

dagaci 365
Dakri 352
Damagaram 18, 32, 33, 428
Danburam xxvi
Dan Fodio, Abdullahi 410, 413, 425, 445, 453
Dan Fodio, Uthman 82
Dangaladima xxvi, 86, 87, 109–11, 149, 158, 167, 193, 352, 434
Dangville, Capt. 36, 38
Danko 58
Danzabuwa 261–2
Dar Fur 145
Daura 87, 88, 101, 108, 341, 349, 398, 411
Dawakin Tofa 140, 151–3, 263–4, 372
Dawakin Tofa revolt 232, 247, 261–4, 372
Demsa 132
deportation 111, 158, 197
depositions xxiii, 10–13, 16, 70, 72, 87, 89, 97, 99, 105, 107, 109, 113, 119, 129, 135–6, 145–8, 166, 186, 194, 197, 210, 256–7, 279, 421
dia 457
Digma xxvii
Dikko, Muhammad 95, 96
Dikko, Muhammad, Katsina 327
Dikwa 7, 32–8, 76, 80, 345, 433

Dirimari 355

disarming the Emirs 73, 433

District Heads xxiii, 136–72, 199–213, 225–9, 236, 241, 251–259, 265, 270, 277, 281–4, 289, 294, 298, 375

District Reorganization 140, 155–62, 172

dogari, dogarai 161, 172, 202–3, 229, 340, 342

dual mandate 394, 489

Dumbulum 261, 262

Dwyer, P.M. 64–5, 97, 120, 125, 176, 178, 181, 183, 190, 198, 232

E

Eaglesome, John 389–91

economy 278, 297–326

education xix, xxxvii, xli, xlii, 278, 289, 291–4, 332–51, 365, 369, 396, 486–7

Egypt 7

El-Kanemi 29, 30

El-Kanemi dynasty 32

Elphinstone, K.V. 322, 333–4, 448, 451, 468, 473, 486

emigration 143, 172, 208, 242, 274–5, 350–1

"emirate natives" 362–4

epidemics xxiv, 328, 352, 356, 365, 366, 369, 374

Ethiopia xxxvi

expeditions 8, 11, 12, 26, 27, 32–8, 58, 60, 61, 89, 265, 269, 374, 380, 381, 384

export xix, xxxvi, 231, 246, 295, 298, 304, 307, 314–7, 325–6, 393, 476, 478, 481–2

Extension of British Administrative Control 131–51

F

Fadel-Allah, Fadl-Allah or Fad-el-Allah 34–37, 104–5, 380–3

Fagge 360, 362, 495

famine xxiv, xli, xlii, 79, 243, 298, 316, 325, 328, 352–7, 365, 374

Fanon, Frantz xxxix, xli

Faro River 49, 78, 429

fees and fines 57, 73, 173, 183–4, 192, 197, 277, 279, 374

Festing, Arthur 87–8, 107–9, 142, 144, 465, 466

feudalism 329

First World War 79, 139, 166, 294, 304, 313–4, 429–30

Fito xxvii

Fombina 6, 7, 16, 34, 66, 75, 76, 132, 178, 349

food 207, 243, 266, 273, 289, 303–5, 325, 330, 353–7, 390, 422, 472, 479, 481

forced labour 206, 236–44, 298, 324, 325, 332, 344, 356, 375

"foreign natives" 361–4, 495

Foucault, Michel xlii

Foureau-Lamy expedition 32, 33

France 3, 8, 17, 23–7, 32–39, 75, 76, 80, 91, 92, 104, 105, 127, 149, 168, 228–30, 237, 240, 252, 268, 351, 354, 356, 377, 381, 383, 387, 392, 399, 418, 460

Fremantle, J.M. 106, 117–8, 128, 162, 171, 242, 279, 285, 331, 405, 437, 440–8, 452, 457, 459, 463, 466, 473, 477–8, 485, 487, 493, 495

Freund, Bill xxxix, 398

Fulani 53, 62, 78, 81, 82, 85, 101, 103, 107, 114–118, 121, 139, 144, 145, 148, 156, 159, 172, 179, 192, 196, 197, 207–9, 234, 251, 266, 274, 275, 286, 331–4, 344–5, 348, 353, 379, 380, 382, 394

G

Gaini, Jibril Mallam 13, 15, 37, 50, 440

Gaisei 88

Gaisuwa 81, 461

Galadima xxvii

Galadiman Gari 133, 142, 175, 290

Gall, F.B. 159, 160, 268

Galoo 43, 44
Games Licence 277
Game Tax 232–3
ganduroba 369
Gani, Muhammadu 97–9, 253, 266
Gashagar 32, 38, 415
Gaskiya Corporation 375, 376
Gassol 8, 148–9
Gellner, Ernest xxxix
General Tax 225, 264
Gentil, Colonel 33, 415–6
German Adamawa 114, 128, 139, 172, 208, 275, 380, 437
German mark 297–300
Germany 6, 7, 33–9, 49, 70, 75–80, 91, 92, 114–7, 128, 139–40, 149, 167, 172, 208, 228–30, 237, 252, 269–76, 299–300, 304–9, 314, 349, 380, 383, 387, 392, 404, 426–7, 460, 480
gero 243
Gill, Withers 242, 459, 4623, 471, 473, 478, 480, 490, 494
Girei 47, 175, 177–8, 180, 195, 229, 237, 334, 349, 403
Girouard, Percy, E 119, 261, 384, 387, 388, 246
Gobir 39, 64, 135, 137, 410
Gold Coast 365, 382
Goldie, George D. T. Sir. xxxiii, 3, 5, 26, 380, 381, 386
Goldsmith, H.S.W. 106, 112–4, 134, 136, 151–6, 180, 201, 202, 225, 245, 390
Gombe 1, 8, 10–16, 22, 24, 32, 36, 39, 50, 51, 69, 70, 71, 77, 95, 96, 122, 138, 139, 146, 159, 160, 177, 192, 234, 272, 273, 284, 294, 314, 337, 354, 408, 418
Gongola 51, 209, 299, 309, 353
Goni, Lawan 163, 164, 165, 167
Goodair, Mr. 272
Government Reservation Area (GRA) 359, 360, 361, 362, 363, 364
Government Residential Area 281, 359

Gowers, W.F. 84–5, 100, 115–7, 221, 245, 284–5, 301, 356, 410, 411, 424, 426, 429, 431–2, 435, 440–4, 450–67, 472, 475, 477, 487, 490, 493–5
groundnuts xlii, 298, 315–7, 305, 325, 387, 392–3, 418, 478
guinea corn 302
Gujba 21, 35–8, 51, 52, 101, 144, 170, 411
gum 298, 302, 305, 321–3
Gumel 76, 88, 349, 355, 411, 428, 489
guns and ammunition xli, 43–52, 59, 73, 103–4, 210, 426
Guraza, Malik b. Muhammad b. Abdullahi b. Fudi 158
Guriga 264–5
Gurin 49, 78–9, 119, 152, 164–6, 177–8, 229, 305, 428, 430, 446–7, 459
Gusau 50, 160
Gwandu 1, 17, 22–6, 31–2, 39, 67, 72, 76, 80, 85–7, 95–6, 109–14, 126, 127, 133, 136–7, 141, 146, 149, 156, 158, 168, 172–95, 206, 218–21, 234, 238–40, 244, 247, 253, 256, 257, 260, 263, 273, 338, 346, 354, 379
Gwaram 11, 13, 39, 82, 413, 450
Gwarang, Sultan of Baghirmi 33, 34
Gwari 21, 335, 388
Gyel 61

H

Hadd 30
Hadeija 1, 70, 88, 107, 109, 253, 263, 284, 327, 341, 347, 348, 349, 355, 357, 384, 411, 417, 467, 489
Haiti xxxvii
Haliru, Bashari (1915–18) 445
Haliru, Basharu 24, 96, 137, 156, 158, 168, 180, 191, 346–5
Haliru of Kalgo 86
Haliru of Raha 86
Hama Gabdo 167, 168
Hammaruwa 8

Hanafi, Basharu 86, 87, 110, 137, 156, 157

haraji 212, 259

Hastings, A.C.G. 418, 442, 453, 454, 478, 490–4

Hausa xxxvii, xl, 85, 97, 140, 179, 188, 209, 267, 337, 346, 348, 358, 359, 369, 380, 394, 398

Hausaland xiv, 19, 81, 380

Hawker's Licence 205, 277, 279, 311

Hayat b. Said 6, 7, 13, 379

health xxiv, xxxvii, xli, xliv, 352, 355, 365, 369

health infrastructure 355

Hegel, Georg xxxv

Heso River 49, 78

Heussler, Robert xiii, 418, 467, 471

Hewby, W.P. 12, 34–5, 94, 100–5, 134, 135, 177, 210–12, 267–71, 338, 372

hijra 28–9, 31, 49, 67–9, 72, 92, 351, 372, 382

Hillary, H.R.P. 110–12, 127–8, 193, 302, 435, 450, 452, 457, 462–3

Hill, Polly xl, 398, 483

historiography xxxv, xl, xliv, 328, 374, 408

Ho Chi Minh 377

Hogben, S.J. xiii, 413, 418, 468

Hogendorn, H.S. xiii, 398, 417, 418, 476, 481

homologous districts, units 117, 131–9, 141, 142, 153, 163, 341

Hong 494

Hong Kong 295, 385, 395

Hosere xxvii

Howard, H.O. 99, 100, 135, 138, 156, 182, 256, 273, 330, 372, 384

human poverty index xxxvii

Hunting and Wild Animals Proclamation 202

Huyum 132, 140

I

Ibadan xl, 4, 373, 391, 396

Ibi 9, 12, 34, 38, 53, 333, 383, 481

Ibo 359

Igala 400

Ikime, Obaro 461–2

Illo 23–7

ill-treatment of workers 388–91

Ilorin 1–12, 23, 25, 26, 39, 40–43, 53, 64, 65, 70, 72, 88, 95, 96, 119, 120–125, 148, 174, 176–9, 181, 183, 190, 197–8, 206, 232, 234, 253, 313, 359, 380, 385, 396

imperialism xix, 367, 374, 377, 381, 387, 393–4

India 294, 400

Indirect Rule xli, 173, 185, 198, 201, 246, 277

inequality xxxvi, xxxvii, xl

Institute for Agricultural Research (IAR) xl

inter-communal relations 328, 358–365

Islam xxxviii, xli, xlii, xliv, 6, 7, 11, 30, 31, 251, 336, 395, 398, 403, 404, 407, 410

Islamic education xlii, 328, 334, 348–51, 365, 374

ivory 476

Iyalema xxvii, 255

J

jakada, pl. jakadu xxvii, 106, 132, 134, 138, 156, 160, 161, 163, 172

Jalingo 7, 9, 405

Jama'a 60, 76, 138, 409, 428

Jama'are 11, 68, 341, 349, 354, 427, 489

Jangali xxvii, 113, 143, 145, 150, 153, 172, 205–227, 236, 247, 251–61, 269–284, 301–4, 311–2, 461, 467

Jebba 3, 45, 65, 96, 120, 124–5, 176–9, 181, 183, 324, 388

Jega 23, 110–3, 126, 145, 177, 180–182, 186, 189–94, 229–30, 234, 240, 256, 257, 298, 303, 305

jihad xxxviii, 30, 39, 87, 127, 235, 351, 352, 371, 380, 398

jizya xxvii, 23, 219

Joda, Hamman 6, 7, 179, 274, 333, 404, 414

John Holt 477
Jonathan, Goodluck 398
judicial councils 177, 198–203
judicial system 173–204
Jukun 8

K

Kabba 396, 402, 413
Kachalla Ari Afuno 73
Kaduna xl, 89, 202, 241–243, 373, 396
Kaffirawa 111
Kaigama xxvii, 133
Kameroun, Kamerouns, Kameruns 79, 274, 276, 430
Kanawa 384
Kano xxxviii, xxxix, xl, xlii, xliv, 1, 11, 14, 17–22, 24, 29–33, 39, 40, 50, 63–72, 87–9, 93, 97, 100, 106–9, 114, 117, 122, 131, 133, 136, 140–153, 168, 178–81, 185, 197, 205–19, 226, 232, 238, 241, 242, 247, 248, 253, 259–63, 278, 282–94, 298, 302–3, 309, 313–6, 327, 333–4, 337–41, 345–9, 354–7, 360–364, 371, 379, 383–4, 387, 388, 391, 392, 398, 411
Kano Survey School 339
Kanuri 28, 101, 358
Kardi 137, 156, 157
karofi xxvii, 212–17, 431
Kasar Hausa xxxvi, xl
Katagum 1, 15, 21, 39, 53, 68, 70, 88, 146, 169, 341, 349, 354, 355, 357, 411
Katsina xl, 1, 16, 17, 32, 63, 64, 69, 70, 72, 87, 88, 95, 96, 106–9, 137, 141–4, 147, 150, 159, 160, 169, 197, 206, 216, 219, 244, 253, 263, 278, 279, 284, 287, 291, 292, 315, 327, 339, 340, 341, 346, 347, 349, 357, 375, 376, 398, 417
Katsina College 375, 376
Katuka xxvii
Kaura xxvii
Kazaure 88, 341, 349, 357, 411, 427, 489
Kebbi 399

Keffi 1, 18, 76, 98, 99, 253, 383, 384
Keyes, Capt. 24, 25
Keynes, John Maynard xl
Kiari 27, 28, 32, 38
Kilba 265
Kirk-Greene, A.H.M. xiii, 413, 423, 430, 460, 468, 487
knowledge production xliii, 2, 19, 88, 134, 135, 199, 215, 222, 257–8, 310, 335, 345, 347, 393, 422, 482
Kofa xxvii, 115–6, 156–60, 260
kofofi 156–163, 172
Koko 58
Kona 8, 9, 140, 147
Kontagora 1, 2, 6, 12, 16, 17, 23–8, 40, 41, 45, 46, 53, 66, 70, 72, 80, 81, 137, 197, 199, 240, 273, 313, 336, 383, 402, 403, 413, 417, 419, 427, 456, 458, 470
Koranic schools 340, 348, 349
Kudaku 57
Kukawa 104–5, 135, 211, 268–9, 288, 415, 450
Kunkuru 61
kurdin karofi 215
Kurdin Kasa xxvii, 143–5, 150, 153, 205–7, 211–27, 232, 236, 247, 251–61, 264–7, 272–84, 298–304, 311, 312, 354, 431
Kurdin Sarauta 286, 461, 473
Kurdin Shuka 215
Kurdin Su 205, 236
Kwararafa 380
Kwatorkwashi 384

L

labour 298, 382, 391, 457, 481
labourers 126, 223, 243, 302, 312, 325, 360, 388–90, 479, 482
labour gangs 388, 389, 390
Lafiya 76, 77, 409, 428, 429
Lagos xxxv, 4, 5, 124, 202, 241, 298, 303, 306, 313, 359, 387, 388, 391, 392, 394
Lala 265
Lamdo Adar xxvii

Lamdo Kabi xxvii
Lamdo Katsina xxvii
land xl, xlii, 78
Land Revenue 151, 232, 286
Land Tax 206, 280
Lapai 1, 2, 6, 12, 40–5, 399, 402, 419, 427
Last, Murray xxxvii, 399, 406, 428
Lawal, Muhammad 11
law and order 153, 173, 175, 278
Leaba 3
League of Nations 426, 430
Lenin, Vladimir xxxix, 377, 479
leper settlement 287, 355
Liddard, Mr. 353
life expectancy xxxvii
Limamin Juma'a xxvii
Limamin Kona xxvii
Liman xxvii
linguistic barriers 188–9
Liquor Tax/Licence 27, 234–5, 279–80
Liruwei 481
Lobb, Popham 50, 424
Lokoja 2, 15, 17, 35, 40, 43, 45, 52, 72, 108, 117, 119, 126, 130, 164, 168, 197, 239, 299, 301, 312, 317, 383–9, 400, 401, 410
London and Kano Company 315, 476–7
Lovejoy, Paul 398
Lubeck, Paul xxxviii, xli, xliv, 397–9
Lugard, Frederick xxxiii, 5, 13, 16, 18, 24, 27, 27–40, 29–30, 35–7, 46, 47, 62, 64, 67, 73, 80–6, 97, 100–107, 111–17, 123, 125, 129, 135, 137, 149, 168, 170, 176, 177, 181–98, 206–11, 218–25, 231–40, 247, 251–5, 259–60, 268–9, 271, 281, 293, 300–10, 318–24, 330, 333, 345, 348, 377, 380–87, 392–6, 402, 406, 419–20, 479, 494
Lugard, Lady 423, 431
   A Tropical Dependency 423
Lugard's Proclamation 5, 13, 24, 27, 28, 80, 176, 197, 240, 256, 330, 460, 462

M

Ma'aji xxvii
Madaki xxvii
Magaji xxvii
Magaji dan Yamusa 383
Magajin Gari xxvii, 31, 133, 142, 149, 175, 290, 291
Magajin Rafi 133, 136, 137, 142, 175, 290, 346
Magira xxviii, 135
Maguzawa 242
Mahadi, Abdullahi xxxvi
Mahdi 7, 89, 112, 126–8, 185, 403
Mahdia 7, 404
Mahdist 13, 39, 50
Mahmud Modibbo Tukur Educational Endowment Fund (MTEEF) xvi
Maigari, Hamman Bello 77, 447
Maiturare, Muhammadu 90, 123, 137, 149, 258, 298, 346
Majidadi Usumanu 346
makarantun allo 340
makarantun ilimi 340
Makun xxviii
Malabu 118–9, 164–6, 177–8, 188, 229
Malcolm, G. 160, 264
Maliki, Emir of Bida 2, 3, 158
Mallam, Mallama, mallams xxviii, 48, 107, 127, 128, 175, 179, 270, 282, 333–4, 338–9, 343, 350, 467
Mallam Agali 346
Mallaman Kampus 489
Mallum xxviii
Manga, Muhammadu 11
Mao Tse Tung xxxix, 377
Mapindi, Muhammadu 8, 9
Marafa xxviii, 90, 123, 137, 258–9, 298, 346
Maria Theresa dollar 34, 297, 300–5, 475
Marwa 77, 274, 305, 404, 428, 507
Marxist tradition xxxix
Marx, Karl xxxv, xxxix
Maslaha xxviii, 15
Mava 268

Maxim 43–5, 50–52, 56, 58, 92, 209, 262
mayo xxviii
Mbilla Malabu 118, 164–6
McAllister, R. 111, 161, 172, 186, 445, 473, 474, 485, 488
McClintock, Major 35, 37, 48, 345, 383
Meillassoux, Claude 483
mercenaries 18, 23, 43–66, 91, 112, 127, 252, 394, 420, 454
Messrs Gaiser 314
Messrs Ollivant and Company 314
Messrs Pagenstecher 314, 477
Middle East 7, 351, 400
Migeod, C.O. 151, 443–4, 448, 451–9, 466, 474, 477–8, 481, 482, 485, 487, 491–4
migration 28, 31, 153, 272, 274, 328, 350, 358
military expeditions xxvii, 2, 3, 9, 13, 21–30, 35, 37, 40, 43, 46, 56, 59, 66, 73, 91, 112, 124, 126, 129, 218, 220, 244, 248, 260, 265–8, 276, 294, 302, 337–8, 372, 379–82, 384, 387, 394, 400, 402, 409, 411, 418, 425, 480
military post 3, 23, 27, 402
military resistance 12, 19
military rule xliv
Millennium Development Goals 397
Miller, Walter 108, 109, 335, 346
mining xl, 299, 312, 314, 325, 359, 393, 394, 477, 481, 482
Missau 9–16, 39, 50, 68, 70, 72, 88, 95, 96, 141, 341, 349, 354, 408, 411, 425, 427, 489
missionaries xli, 333–7, 487
Modibbo xxviii
Modibbo Na-kwashiri 404
Modibbo Raji 440
Modibbo Sufiyanu 7
Moloney, Capt. 383
Molony, Resident 98
Moor, Ralph, Sir. 245, 394
Morland, T.N.L. 37, 38, 47, 48, 49, 53, 54, 55, 93, 96, 115, 383, 384
Mubi 34

mudu xxviii
Muhammad Dikko 327
Muhammadu Abbas 106–9
Muhammadu Abbas, Kano 71, 253
Muhammadu Aliyu, Emir of Gwandu 244
Muhammadu, Emir of Hadeija (1885–1906) 411
Muhammadu Raji 440
Muri 1, 7–12, 24, 39, 53, 56, 77, 89, 100, 114, 148, 149, 313, 337, 396
muskuwari 78, 305
musta'mins 2

N

Nagwamatse 17, 346, 402, 419
Namtari 132–3, 175, 177, 331, 356
Naniya, Tijjani xliv, 399
Naraguta 242, 299, 312, 314–5, 337, 341, 482
Nassarawa 42, 60, 76, 77, 98, 99, 108, 167, 283, 287, 313, 333–40, 343, 345, 347, 358, 409, 426, 429, 432, 441, 469
Nassarawa School 108, 334–40, 345, 347
Nassarawo 78, 404, 430, 486
nationalist development xxxvii
Native Authority 161, 277–80, 287, 293, 335, 338, 341, 342, 359, 360, 364, 373, 375, 396
Native Courts xlii, 128, 153, 173–204, 287, 332, 334, 348, 372–5, 386, 396, 442, 451, 468
native foreigners 180–81, 495
Native Liquor Licences 27, 205, 234–5, 280
Native Location 363
Native Reservation 360, 364, 495
Native Revenue Proclamation 461
Native Townships 180
Native Treasury xviii, xxiii, 277–95, 325, 334, 343, 350
Ngaundere 6, 275, 305
Niger Company 300, 307
Niger Delta xxxvii, 483
Nigeria Tin Company 314

"Nigeria War Committee" 294
Niger River 40, 76, 239, 273, 299, 381, 395, 400
Nikki 381
Ningi 10, 77, 192, 330
Nkrumah, Kwame xxxix, 377
non-commissioned officers (NCOs) 12, 43–9, 56, 59, 238
non-Muslim communities xxvii, xlii, 56–60, 73, 78, 219, 222–4, 234, 272, 276, 280, 358, 384, 388, 391, 400, 406, 407, 454, 495
"non-native Africans" 359
non-resistance 8–17, 22
North Africa 313, 351, 414, 415
Northern Nigeria xiii, xiv, xxviii, xxxv–xlvi, 70, 80, 82, 88–91, 125, 143, 149, 154, 169, 206, 213, 227, 283, 298, 312, 318, 319, 368, 371, 378, 380–88, 392–99, 402, 406, 411, 414–19, 422, 424, 426, 428, 434, 440, 441, 456, 458, 464–9, 476–81, 484, 488, 489, 492
Northern Nigeria Regiment 298, 312, 387, 489
Numan 323, 334, 349, 355, 486, 487
Nupe xxvi, xxviii, 9, 23, 26, 43, 53, 88, 206, 234, 301, 322, 359, 380, 399, 400, 419, 431
Nya, Abubakar 8, 9
Nyandang 421
Nyibango 77, 78, 146, 167, 172, 229, 428, 447

O

Ogidiolu, Ajia 5
oil boom xxxvi
oil revenues xxxvi
Okonta, Ike xliv
O'Neill, Major 46, 47, 419
oral tradition 282, 371, 375, 407
Orr, C.W. 64, 110, 134, 162, 235, 239, 409, 422, 438, 440, 446, 451, 452, 454, 464, 465, 480, 487, 493
Oxford University Poverty and Human Development Initiative xxxvii

Oyo 120, 394

P

Paden, John N. 495
pagans 78, 107, 123, 139, 147, 164, 171, 209, 238, 242, 272, 315, 333, 358, 403, 404, 467, 482, 488
Palmer, H.R. 87, 88, 105–7, 150, 159, 217, 218, 271, 286, 347, 431, 433, 434, 245, 440, 441, 444, 452, 470, 473, 485, 489, 490, 492
passive resistance 26, 95, 96, 99, 107, 129, 190, 190–192, 248, 271–76
Pate, Abdulkadiri 164
Paterson Zochonis Ltd. 477
peasantry xlii, 34, 36, 145, 211, 212, 215, 276, 294, 329, 343, 391, 424, 462, 472
   commercialization xlii
Perham, Margery xiii, 129, 377, 411, 414, 417, 420, 423, 424, 467, 468, 471, 476, 480, 483, 489
Pierce, Stephen xlii, 398
Pilcher, T.D. 43, 44, 45, 419
police force xxxviii, 63, 65, 125, 130, 152, 229, 235, 238, 273, 283, 327, 333, 338, 340, 342, 364, 365, 425, 468, 490
political economy xxiii, xxxvi, xxxix, xl, xli, 90
poll-tax 209, 219–23
population 153, 314, 328, 356
population decline 328, 356–358
Portugal 460
precolonial economy 297, 305–13
precolonial judicial system 174–76
precolonial period xxxix, 74, 75, 91, 131, 156, 158, 167, 171, 178, 179, 183, 192, 199, 204, 206, 214, 216, 218, 219, 221, 223, 234, 244, 281, 282, 297, 299, 306, 348, 367, 368
prisons 232, 295, 327, 333, 338, 340, 341, 365, 489
propaganda 252, 375–7, 404, 429
proselytisation 333–6, 346
Protectorate Proclamation 24

Provincial Courts 63, 173–204, 210, 238, 321, 359, 372, 374
public works 199, 243, 278, 283, 319

Q

Qadi xxviii, 5, 7, 28, 31, 67, 165–6, 173–203, 333, 344, 345, 350
Qadiriyya xxviii, 88
Queen Victoria 3
Qur'an, Koran xliv, 22

R

Rabeh b. Fadl-Allah 6, 7, 26, 32, 33, 34, 37, 39, 75, 102, 104, 210, 380, 415, 433
railway xli, 242, 294, 324, 359, 360, 387–92, 395, 476
Red Cross 294
religion 126, 186, 190, 226, 235, 249, 335, 336, 358, 396, 403, 408, 412, 417
Renasco & Co. 101, 103
Reserve Fund 293
resistance 1, 4, 5, 8, 9, 17, 190, 271
revenue xlii, 138, 151–3, 157, 173, 175, 183, 184, 197, 202, 208, 213, 217, 218–246, 262, 277–296, 280, 281, 307, 374, 393, 394
Revenue Proclamation 256
Ribadu 49, 132, 178, 428, 446, 482
Ribat xxviii
Rodney, Walter xxxix, 377
Royal Niger Company (RNC), also the Company, or Niger Company xxiii, xxxiii, 2–6, 9, 12, 18, 22, 23, 26, 27, 33, 40, 43, 47, 104, 120, 228, 230, 236, 298, 300, 301, 305, 308–325, 352, 379–83, 385, 400–3, 476, 479–81
Ruxton, F.N. Capt. 86, 110–16, 125, 126, 207, 230, 239, 260, 261, 305

S

Sa'ad, Ahmadu 413, 414

Sabon Gari 135, 180, 334, 359, 360, 361, 362, 363, 364, 365, 366, 495
Sa'i xxviii
Salafist xxxviii
Salau, Mohammed xlii, 398
Salih Sarkin Turawa 414
Sallama xxviii
Sarakuna xxviii, 99, 133, 160–2, 168–9, 171, 182, 457
Sarakunan Gari 132
sarauta xxxix, xli, 461
Sardauna xxviii
Sarki xxviii
Sarkin Baura xxviii
Sarkin Dawaki Maituta xxviii
Sarkin Hausawa 174
Sarkin Sudan xxviii
Sarkin Yaki xxviii
Sarki Turawa xxviii
Satiru 70, 88, 89, 112, 113, 126, 127, 128, 135, 136, 145, 148, 180, 186, 191, 192, 196, 256, 260, 372, 384, 387, 454
Satiru Revolts 174, 372
Scott, James xl, 398
segregation 363
Segu 25, 26
serfdom xxiv, 133, 327, 329, 330, 332, 365
shahada xxviii, 31
Shari'a xxviii, xxxvii, xxxviii, xxxix, xlii, xliii, xliv, 30, 66, 67, 190, 192, 199, 214, 216, 250, 399, 409
Sharpe, W.S. 172, 199, 266–7, 274–6, 322, 323
Sharu Mai Kulki 414
shea nut 298, 302, 322
Shehu Abubakar Garbai 36, 37
Shehu Kiari 32, 38
Shehu Umar 33
Shekau, Abubakar 397
Shenton, Robert xxxix, 398, 415, 476–7
shuka 212–17
Shuwa Arab 34, 35, 101, 102, 211, 269–71, 372, 450
Sierra Leone 365, 460

Simpson, W.H. 400, 431–2, 476
Slave Homes 386
slave-labour xlii
slavery xxii, xiv, xli, xlii, 12, 21, 78, 79,
    81, 101, 106, 108, 115, 116, 120,
    121, 138, 145, 148, 163, 181,
    182, 192, 193, 199, 223, 240,
    306, 327–32, 353, 365, 369, 382,
    385–7, 412, 414, 417, 426, 452,
    457, 483–4
Slavery Proclamation 330, 331, 484
Smith, Abdullahi xiii, xx
Smith, Mary 66, 483, 484
Smith, M.G. xl, 379, 483
social policy 278, 327–66
Sokoto xxxii, xl, 1, 3, 6, 7, 10, 16–42,
    49, 50, 56, 62–118, 122–210, 216,
    218–41, 247–8, 256–9, 262–4,
    274, 275, 278, 282, 284, 287, 290,
    291, 293, 295, 302–306, 327, 338,
    341–2, 346, 350, 351, 354, 355,
    357, 371–80, 383, 384
Sokoto Caliphate xiv, xviii, xxiii, xxx,
    xl, xlii, 1, 6, 7, 16, 18, 24, 32, 37,
    39, 41, 42, 56, 62, 66, 67, 73–7,
    80, 90–2, 161, 205, 210, 227, 229,
    274, 275, 282, 350, 379, 399, 401,
    410, 418, 423, 425, 427, 428, 431,
    462, 483
Songhai 380
South Africa 89, 388, 389
Southern Nigeria 4, 120, 228, 366,
    385–8, 394–5, 480
spies 43, 111, 121, 145, 180, 186, 313,
    414
Stalin, J. 377
Station Magistrate 364
Strumpell, Capt. 78, 79, 430
Sudan 7, 70, 72, 122, 133, 141, 338, 339,
    350, 386
Sudan Interior Mission (SIM) 336, 488
Sudan United Mission (SUM) 334, 336,
    337, 355, 487, 488
Sufi xxxviii, xlii

Sultanate xli, 123, 136, 141–9, 151, 153,
    160, 161, 170, 177, 178, 185, 189,
    190, 338, 342, 346, 354, 355
Suntai 9

T

Tahir, Ibrahim xxxvi, xxxix, 398
talaka, talakawa xxviii, xxxvii, xli, 127,
    128, 144, 148, 262, 382
Tambari, Muhammadu 89, 137
Tambawal 136, 148, 149, 240, 273, 274,
    330, 346
Taqiyya xxviii, 16
tariff 90–2
Tariqa xxviii
taxation xxiv, xxvi, xxvii, xxix, 79, 83,
    90, 100–3, 133, 139, 152–4, 160,
    172, 205–80, 297–311, 321, 324,
    325, 331, 338, 343, 344, 356, 357,
    368, 372, 394, 400, 418, 460–2,
    473, 476, 481, 489, 494
tax revolts 174, 205, 220, 232, 247,
    261–4, 372
Temple, Charles L. 50–2, 61, 66, 69, 82,
    126, 138, 142, 148, 162, 190, 191,
    197, 213–17, 256–9, 302, 305,
    330, 346, 460, 461
territoriality 74, 134
textile xxxviii, xliv, 305, 307
Thompson, W.B. 271, 470
Tibenderana, P.K. 25, 412, 413, 419,
    445, 488
Tijaniyya xxix, 88
Tilde Expedition 60
Tilley, Helen xliii, 399
tin xxxix, 314–6, 325, 385, 391, 393,
    394, 398, 477, 478, 481
Tiv 383, 396
Toure, Sekou 377
townships 180, 360–4
trade xlii, xliv, 90, 227, 228, 230, 232,
    236, 242, 278, 280, 300–25, 332,
    383, 395, 400, 405, 417, 418, 423,
    432, 479–81
traders 2, 3, 57, 62, 63, 65, 103, 227–9,
    234, 236, 243, 280, 300, 301, 303,

308–19, 321–2, 325, 360–61, 399, 400, 414, 415, 475, 478–80, 495
trading firms xix, xxiii, xxiv, 180, 195, 230, 231, 243, 297–9, 312–19, 324–5, 364, 392–3, 475, 477–8
trans-Atlantic slave trade 330
Tsibiri 64, 65, 410
Tudun Wada 59, 363, 366, 481
Tugwell, Herbert, Bishop 16, 17, 389–90
Tukur, Mahmud Modibbo xiii, xiv, xv, xvi, xxxv, xxxvi, xxxvii, xxxix, xl, xli, xlii, xliii, xliv
Tukur, Muhammadu 149

U

Ubah, C.N. 215, 461–2
Uba Hosere 79
Uba Mayo Bani 79
Ubandawaki 401, 419
Ubandoma xxix
Uganda 391, 425
Ujera 473
ulema xxix, xli, xliii, 6, 7, 31, 39, 186, 350, 351, 376
Umar, Muhammed xlii
Umar Sanda Kairimi 32
Umar Sanda Kura 32–8, 170
Umaru b. Ali b. Bello 10, 379
Umaru b. Salmana b. Yaqub 10–15, 39, 70, 72, 81, 82, 96, 122, 149, 288, 412
USAID xl
Usumanu, Modibbo b. Raji 7
Uthman dan Fodio xxviii, 6, 13, 425

V

Vamgo Malabu 118–9, 164, 165
vernacular science xliii
Verre 77, 78, 163, 167, 264, 265, 267
Victoria Settlement 385
Village Heads 150, 152, 158, 202, 212, 213, 217, 226, 254, 255, 258, 260, 263, 266, 273, 276, 277, 281, 282, 284, 375, 429, 460

violence xviii, xix, xliv, xlv, 3, 41, 42, 53, 56–67, 80, 91, 102, 148, 184, 196, 276, 368
Vischer, Hans 108, 338, 339, 396

W

Wallace, William 35, 49, 52–5, 59, 68, 80, 81, 190, 232, 261–2, 389, 393
War Fund 294, 295
Wase 9, 12
Waters, B.E.M. 99, 444
Watts, Michael xxxv, 397, 398
Waziri xxix
Weber, Max xxxix
Webster, G.W. 79, 122, 163, 226, 275
West African Frontier Force (WAFF) 12, 18, 45, 47, 62, 64, 94, 326, 382, 489
western education xxiv, 278, 327, 328, 332–44, 347, 365, 369, 374, 396
Wilmot, Patrick xxxvi
Women's Training Centre 89
Wurio 8, 9
Wurno 133
Wushishi 4, 41, 46, 47, 273, 419

Y

Yadserem River 79
yan Sarki 158
Yaron Sarki, pl. Yaran Sarki xxix, 255
Yawuri 23, 26, 27, 402, 403, 413
Yelwa 17, 23, 27, 413, 477
Yerima xxix
Yerima Maigari 429, 447
Yero, Bobboi 72, 119, 164–6, 244
Yero, Muhammad 142, 253
Yero, Muhamman 88, 109
Yola 1, 5–9, 12, 17, 24, 29, 37–41, 47–9, 53, 56–8, 62, 65–80, 84, 88, 93, 95, 103, 109, 114–29, 132, 133, 139, 145, 155, 162, 165–98, 206–10, 212, 219, 221, 226, 229, 236–8, 264, 265, 274, 277–87, 300–307, 310, 317, 322, 327,

330–38, 344, 348–9, 352–8, 371,
383, 384, 396, 419, 446
Yoruba xxvi, 234, 303, 359, 361, 388,
394, 495

Z

zakat xxviii, 214, 224, 463
zakka xxix, 209, 214–8, 221, 222, 225–6,
250–1, 259, 279, 280–4, 302
Zamfara 124, 127–8, 133, 135, 137, 142,
147, 160, 170, 257, 258
Zamfarawa 128
Zangon Katab 59, 140, 451
Zaria xiii, xvi, 1, 8, 16, 17, 18, 22, 24,
32, 39, 46, 50–2, 59–80, 82, 97,
105, 108, 119, 134, 140, 143, 146,
147, 151, 162, 170, 178, 185, 192,
197–202, 221, 234, 235, 238, 241–
3, 247, 256, 273, 277–9, 284–87,
294, 313–17, 327, 335–55, 362–4,
376, 379, 245
Zazzau 82, 147, 253
Zinder 17, 23, 32, 33, 316, 387, 415, 417
Zubairu, Lamido 5–7, 66, 69, 70, 72, 77,
115–6, 121, 122, 126, 162, 209,
274, 383, 403, 404
Zungeru 52, 63, 72, 112, 114, 116, 127,
235, 238, 261, 293, 313, 316, 386,
388, 410, 459, 471